DAVID LLOYD GEORGE
a political life

DAVID LLOYD GEORGE
a political life

The Architect of Change
1863—1912

Bentley Brinkerhoff Gilbert

B. T. Batsford Ltd. London

First published 1987

Typeset by Progress Typesetting Ltd
and printed in Great Britain by
W. & J. Mackay Ltd
Chatham, Kent

Published by B. T. Batsford Ltd
4 Fitzhardinge Street, London W1H 0AH

British Library Cataloguing in Publication Data
Gilbert, Bentley B.
  David Lloyd George: a political life.
  The Architect of change, 1863-1912
  1. Lloyd George, David   2. Prime ministers
  — Great Britain — Biography
  I. Title
  941.083'092'4   DA566.9.L5

ISBN 0-7134-5558-6

Contents

Preface

One must provide an apology, or at least an explanation, for adding to the crush of scholarship, and sensationalism, that has appeared about the figure of David Lloyd George since his papers became available two decades ago. Most of these books are interpretive monographs, written by established academics, dealing with some aspect of the man's political life, of his part in foreign affairs or the labor movement, or his apparent penchant for coalitions. All of these works are useful, the authors have gone to the sources and read the secondary material, yet each is in a way misleading. Lloyd George never operated within the boundaries of a single political framework. He had views on every topic, but commitments to none save land reform and Welsh nationalism. Every project was dependent on another. To try to identify and describe, say, Lloyd George's labor policy is to distort both the man and his work.

But in the last ten years several full-scale biographies have appeared. To my mind, as a work of scholarship none is satisfactory. The biographer of a politician must explain the political world as his subject affected it. Hence a biography deals with the levers and handles that control the governing process rather than with the process itself. The business of the biographer is to examine the parliamentary machine as his subject saw it, to illuminate for his reader the significance for the future of his subject's decisions, and to explain how those decisions were arrived at. It is not history, but, as it has been called, it is the prism of history. The biographer must consider besides the characters not only of his subject but of his friends and opponents.

All of this means that the biographer of a politician must have in his mind not only the textbook facts but the cross-currents and the nuances of the world in which his subject moved. He needs to show what his subject read and understood about the topics which appeared in the daily newspaper, but as well the reactions among the opposition. In effect the writer needs to know more than his subject about what is happening.

This sort of intimacy cannot be gleaned from references to ordinary secondary historical accounts of the period used to supplement the Lloyd George papers. Biography, again, is more than history with one person in the foreground. One can write an entertaining anecdotal life-and-times story of a man's career using only letters fleshed out by secondary sources. Both Lloyd George and, particularly, Churchill, with his papers in print, have been subjected to this treatment. These books are pleasant to read but they will tell the historian little he does not already know.

Finally, Lloyd George has had a peculiar problem with recent biographers because of the presence of Frances Stevenson and the publication of her diary, and because of rumors of his other liaisons. Writers seem to be unable to leave the question alone. But the story of Lloyd George is worth telling not because of his many sexual encounters—in this he was hardly unique in Edwardian Britain—but rather because in spite of them he was the most important and influential British political figure of his time and probably of the twentieth century. Certainly if his subject had a personal life that intruded on his political one, as did Herbert Asquith's, the biographer must address it. But if the subject was a twenty-four hour a day politician for whom women were only a diversion, this sort of scholarly voyeurism is out of place, a waste of time. Asquith liked young women also and was far more indiscreet than Lloyd George. But Asquith's principal relaxation was bridge. One would not write his biography in terms of card games. Franklin Roosevelt collected stamps; Churchill laid bricks and painted. Of course, Lloyd George had several brushes with disaster that could have ended his career permanently, and these must be dealt with, but his story cannot, and should not, be interrupted for accounts of irrelevant and imperfectly documented love affairs.

Hence there remains a place for an account of the life of David Lloyd George as the archetypal political man who presided over the introduction of twentieth century politics in Great Britain; for whom politics was not a duty but a passion; who seized the traditions of Bright and Chamberlain and invented populist politics in Britain; who understood that, faced by an aroused electorate, the legislature was almost powerless; and who with a new Liberalism tried to revive what he saw as an expiring Liberal party. Yet his medicine may have helped to kill it.

Some conventions I have used require a word of explanation. For Welsh place names, surely a thicket an American enters at his peril, I have tried to follow the *Times Gazetteer*. In quotations from letters I have used the most easily available source. Thus if a manuscript letter has been subsequently printed, the citation will be to the publication unless the printed version does not contain the entire quotation. For newspaper clippings found in collections of papers I have cited both the title and date and the item code in the collection.

In this volume the term 'Unionist' refers to the coalition formed in 1895 of Conservatives and Liberal Unionists. Men who subsequently received titles I have identified by their status at the time, without mentioning that they later became a peer or a knight. I have also tried to refrain from lectures in footnotes pointing to where other writers have made mistakes of fact or interpretation.

I thank the editors of the *American Historical Review*, the *Historical Journal* and *Albion* for permission to print parts of articles that appeared in those magazines, and Michael Joseph Publishers for allowing me to reproduce some paragraphs of a previous book. I also thank the Guggenheim Foundation and the University of Illinois Institute for the Humanities for fellowships that allowed the freedom of several academic years for research.

I must express my gratitude to my colleague Professor James Sack, who read and criticized this manuscript, and to my graduate student Julia

Baskes who did the same; to Neville Masterman; to Professor Stephen Koss, whose death represented to me both a professional and personal loss, for much good information and advice; and to Dr Kenneth Morgan for similar help. Dr Morgan's book, *Wales in British Politics*, was a solitary beacon that helped to keep me on course in dealing with Lloyd George's early years in politics.

Finally, I dedicate this volume to my youngest son, Francis Hopkinson Gilbert, who allowed me to work by taking himself through childhood, almost alone and without complaint.

Chicago, Illinois   Bentley Brinkerhoff Gilbert
20 February 1986

Introduction: The Man

Every man composes his own biography. Some, to be sure, may systematically save, while others destroy, certain written records. But everyone, in some way, finds it necessary to explain and justify his life's activity, to account for his place in the world. The Black who blames his misfortunes on his color is making the same explanation of his position as the Cabinet minister who attributes his success to the discipline of poverty or to the stern precepts of his mother. The information on his early life that a man imparts to his contemporaries usually tells less about the infant than it tells about the adult. And the more removed a person is from his childhood, the sharper, but more distorted, become the childhood images.

The biographer must begin with the man's vision of himself, what he tells of himself in his letters, what his contemporaries report of his recollections, what he announces in his speeches as he explains, excuses, or rationalizes. Sometimes the old man puts it all together in the form of a memoir, a novel written by the aged. Sometimes, as with David Lloyd George, he sponsors biographies throughout his lifetime. Both are useful but neither is trustworthy. At the end of his life a man knows what he wants to have remembered or forgotten. In mid-career, he may not know what he has done. In the former the colors are brighter; in the other the perspective is wrong.

Saying that all public figures, indeed all men, are conscious of the shadows they will cast for posterity is not to assert that the historian is at the mercy of his subject. Politicians are required by the nature of their craft to forego anonymity and those particularly, such as Lloyd George, who take part in writing their own history, will by this act alone tell more than they intend. For some, the urge to tell about themselves is irresistible. Late in his life, shortly after his seventieth birthday when he was composing his *War Memoirs,* Lloyd George remarked to A.J. Sylvester that after the necessaries of food and shelter, which meant security, 'The next thing that mattered was advertisement.'[1] Lloyd George was usually clear, if not always candid, about the realities of his place in history. He understood the handicaps of his humble background, lack of education, and national origin. But he saw equally well, and used, the advantages, the freedom from the restraints of family position, personal modesty, and perhaps good form, that his origins gave him. But although he never sought to change his place, and in fact traded upon it, relishing the flexibility of political style it permitted, it is clear that the memories of his childhood as a fatherless village boy and the snubs and insults he received as a rustic and uneducated freshman Member of Parliament affected his political behavior throughout his life. He was a political outsider, and he knew it. Even in 1908, when he was Chancellor of the Exchequer, he spoke to Herbert Lewis 'of the unconscious and only half conscious contempt with which the Englishman regarded the Welsh people and said it would be a long fight to overcome that.'[2] One is reminded of Lord Hartington's drawling comments about Disraeli. He 'came to the House of Commons from the outside. D'ye know what I mean? I mean he was not English exactly, and he had not been at the "Varsity", and all that. And he never learned very much about the House. To the very end he kept running his head against walls—walls often of prejudice, but sometimes walls which I hope won't be overthrown for many years to come.'[3]

As Lloyd George never lost the prejudices and animosities of his childhood, conversely he never learned, nor, one may imagine even understood, the conventional anti-capitalist rhetoric of the British labor movement, even though like many Labour party politicians he advertised and exaggerated his humble origins. But on the other hand, his early poverty never made him despise self-made wealth. Businessmen who fought their way to success were his friends. He had done much the same himself. On precisely these terms he began, as soon as he left Wales, the composition of what would be his customary life-story: the small town boy who had made good. But he had done more than this; Lloyd George was a Welsh cottage lad without education or family connections, who had made good in England, who had conquered the English at their own sport and in their own arena, Westminster politics.

The effect of Wales on Lloyd George was entirely what he chose to make it. On the public platform and indeed in his private correspondence, his illustrations, his accounts of learning experiences, almost invariably proceeded from the principality: the memory of deprivation in childhood, the economic intimidation of farm tenants during the election of 1868, his first glimpse of the House of Commons in 1874, the bigotry of the Church in Wales. The tales hardly changed; he was reporting them in his seventies. They turn up in every biography that has been written of him. All this does not mean that these parables are wrong, but like the stories of the Bible, each has a meaning intended to be part of a larger picture that the author seeks to convey. And like the Bible also, they are almost impossible to confirm from independent evidence.

Lloyd George participated in the composition of five books about himself during the seventeen years of his ministerial life, beginning with J. Hugh Edwards, *From the Village Green to Downing Street* in 1908 and concluding with Harold Spender, *The Prime Minister* in 1920. They all tell the same story of the bright, fun-loving, village boy, a natural leader among his friends, early affected by a strong sense of injustice which reinforced a firm inherited religious morality, who determined as an adolescent to enter the law and who became in the courtroom and on the lecture platform the champion of the oppressed, who overthrew the Caernarvonshire political establishment by being adopted at the age of twenty-five as the Liberal party candidate, and who entered the county council and finally the House of Commons well before he was thirty. Within tolerable limits this is all true, even if it does not tell the whole story. As he rose in political rank he tended to dwell less on his years as a Welsh nationalist and more on his early poverty. With varying emphasis as his place in politics grew larger, the cottage at Llanystumdwy grew smaller. Like many uneducated men who in their lifetime become closely associated with great events, Lloyd George liked to simplify history and pinpoint the cause of important changes. Harry Truman did the same. The technique lent drama and understandability to public affairs.

But all this does not mean that the things he said about himself and the beliefs he professed to hold were false or hypocritical. A sense of injustice can be the foundation for fierce ambition. And sympathy for the underprivileged may support, and sometimes be replaced by, hatred of the privileged. There were others in the Liberal government, Asquith for instance, of undistinguished if not impoverished origins, who kept the details of their childhood as private as their bank accounts. Why did Lloyd George go to such lengths to advertise and build upon his social alienism? The answer is simply that it was useful; an inheritance that could not be disguised, he made an advantage. It gave him, he believed probably correctly, a singular insight into working class needs which made it possible for him to disregard the political judgment of party oracles such as whips and newspaper editors. It could justify his very personal form of radical politics. Almost any parliamentary initiative could be explained in terms of some Welsh social abuse.

Lloyd George was the first British politician to take advantage of what in America is the log cabin tradition. Indeed he frequently compared himself privately with Abraham Lincoln. A better comparison, in many cases almost an exact one, is with the American Senator Huey Long. Kenneth Morgan, in his excellent article 'Lloyd George and Historians,' argues against this point of view, saying that Lloyd George was not the 'Kingfish of Wales' which is perfectly true.[4] The comparison is valid, however, not so much because of Lloyd George's personality or of his eventual domination of Welsh politics. The parallelism proceeds from the position the two men achieved in national politics. Even in the United States Senate of the 1930s, which was a far less homogeneous place than the House of Commons of the 1890s, the junior Senator from Louisiana was for a time not taken seriously. Then he was looked upon as a political trickster, first as a buffoon or a rustic windbag, but later as a dangerous sectional radical. He succeeded in transforming essentially local grievances, out-of-state oil companies in Louisiana and extremes of wealth and poverty, as Lloyd George made the Anglicized land monopolizing aristocracy of Wales, into major national issues which focused politics for years.

Hence the details of Lloyd George's early life, like Abraham Lincoln's or Huey Long's, or for that matter Harold Wilson's, are important in a way that the childhood and early adolescence of, say, Sir Edward Grey, are not. He made his Welshness and his poverty part of his public personality; he used them, as he used his religion, to identify himself. He was a professional Welshman as Harry Lauder was a professional Scot. This led many of his contemporaries, not to mention subsequent biographers, to regard him as something of the quintessential Welshman. One finds endless references to his 'Celtic fire,' his adroitness, his eloquence, and so forth, as well as to his duplicity, shallowness and cruelty. Without entering into the debate about whether these are exclusively Welsh characteristics, or whether there are such things as national characteristics except in the mythology of foreigners, the biographer must question this ordinary conception of Lloyd George.

He was a Welshman to Englishmen, but to everyone else the chief impression he gave was not that he was Welsh, but that he was, perhaps to some refreshingly, not English. Edward M. House found him very American. Conversely Albert Thomas, Lloyd George's opposite number in France while he was at the Ministry of Munitions, thought him French. Even Frances Stevenson noted in her diary his hardness, his coolness and determination in action and in political calculation, his lack of personal attachments. (One of his favorite sayings was 'There are no friends at the top.') To her these were French characteristics.

He did not, in fact, like Wales very much, particularly after the death of his daughter, Mair. 'Criccieth is just like this old sea for me, always an old gray mixed up miserable place,' he told D.R. Daniel in 1908 when, nevertheless, he was building a house on the bluff above the village. In London, he continued, 'there's always some interest and endless life there, somewhere to go, something to see, you feel you are in the stream of life there. The life of the country village is deadly and uninteresting. The most unpleasant season of my life by far was my childhood and boyhood spent in Llanystumdwy. I'd never go through it again at any price.'[5]

To define Lloyd George in terms of Wales is valid only as it would be valid to describe Napoleon in terms of Corsica. Each came to manhood as an alien in a rigid and status-conscious society and each carried with him the burden of provincial mannerisms and prejudices (with perhaps Thomas Gee playing for Lloyd George the part of Paoli). But the important fact is that in the end each conquered his adopted country. They were first of all condottieri. Not being English gave Lloyd George a detachment from affairs and freed him from preconceptions and loyalties. His childhood in Wales gave him a radical political program, to be sure providing some lifelong hatreds, but an English country village might have done that. He had in fact, certainly in later life, a national rootlessness. After he established himself in England he broke all but his most formal ties with Wales, and once overthrown he had no native land. Lloyd George is not the hero of Welsh politics. Of course he went back to the banks of the Dwyfor to die, but by then he had no other home.

The marvel of Lloyd George's career, crowned as it was by the highest political success and power, lies in the essential changelessness of his personality. No one was less affected by appointment to office. No man, observed Lucy Masterman who saw him often in the half dozen years before the war, was clearer sighted about himself and his own capabilities. He was totally without vanity and indeed in many ways highly conventional in his perceptions and reactions. Asquith, for example, regarded him as a perfect 'foolometer' in that his opinion of public statements or appointments would be that of the man on the Clapham omnibus.[6] The same, of course, has been said of Queen Victoria. The humbug dimension of English political life irritated him, as it does many Americans. Lloyd

George was understandably proud of his accomplishments, but he never believed he was a great man, or should behave differently, because he held a great office.

Yet here, in a sense, one may find the key to his undoing. As he felt that other politicians took themselves too seriously, so also he had little regard for the standards of conduct that regulated British public life. Harshly realistic, and indeed selfish in his own decisions, he was accused of being without principle. Other men were the same, he would have retorted privately, except that they dilated pompously about honor and good form which he regarded as hypocrisy.

One suspects Lloyd George saw something of himself in Teddy Roosevelt whom he and Asquith had met in June, 1914 and whom he had liked, although Asquith did not. Writing about him in the *Sunday News* in 1926 he recalled:

> There was something about him which frightened the timid and the conventional and the men who in their walks never stray from the well trodden and dusty paths of party platitudes. The commonplace thought him violent, the pedantic thought him unprincipled, the correct thought him undignified, the kind of stern party men that treat the party headquarters as if they were the temple of their faith thought him simply wicked. But the common people heard him gladly, and they thronged to greet him and listen to his speeches.[7]

This surely could be Lloyd George's description of himself. (One must hasten to add that no one took more pleasure than Lloyd George in the public posture of self-righteous indignation.)

Lloyd George's worst prevarications appeared in the form of promises, the solution to a problem or the grand outline of a program that he intended to produce. Too often, at the time of the announcement of his project he had no plan whatever as to how he intended to proceed. He was essentially a manufacturer's representative marketing a commodity or a process he did not yet possess. Such tactics are not necessarily immoral. Certainly at the beginning of his career he achieved some important successes simply by creating a public demand for a product which he subsequently invented, national insurance for example. But after he became Prime Minister and failed to redeem the promises of a better Britain, the effect was devastating, not only upon himself but upon the party and the nation.

Essentially, then, Lloyd George was a salesman, the most representative figure of the twentieth-century commercial society. He knew by instinct the first rule of salesmanship: to sell oneself before selling the product. For many years it seemed he could not fail. The secret of his power, said Harold Nicolson in 1961, was charm. 'There were two things about him that charmed,' Nicolson told Kenneth Harris:

> His manner—his physical manner—was engaging. When you entered the room he would come bounding up to you, lead you in, throw his arms about as he spoke, give a great impression of friendliness, exuberance and simplicity. His voice was very attractive, very warm and

intense. He was a good listener, too, and when he was listening, or pretending to—half the time he wasn't—he used to look at you as though you were the only intelligent person he ever met.[8]

It has often been noted that when a person met Winston Churchill he came away feeling that he had encountered the greatest man in the world, but when a man met Lloyd George he departed feeling that he was himself the greatest man in the world. Lloyd George would smile and nod, exclaim approval, 'quite so,' 'why haven't I thought of that,' and so on.

As is usually the case, the initial friendliness did not last. As he was always so courteous and unassuming, so interested in their conversation, people tended to exaggerate their intimacy with him. He suffered many fools, but not gladly, and the results were often painful when he suddenly rebuffed and disavowed a friendship. Harold Spender, who served twenty-five years as a species of amanuensis and public relations agent to Lloyd George, suffered this treatment and was reminded of the rebuke of Henry V to Falstaff: 'I know thee not old man, fall to thy prayers.'[9] Similarly, Harold Nicolson, who dealt with him only at the end of the war, found him impossible to work for.

> When the effects of the flattery had worn off and one's eyes had opened he was terrible. He was dishonest and unscrupulous; you couldn't trust him. You could never be sure if what he was telling you was the truth. One thing Lloyd George could never do was create trust. The good fairies gave him everything at his christening, but a bad fairy said: 'People won't trust him.'..
> One other thing I didn't like about Lloyd George: he would never admit not knowing anything. Sometimes you would tell him something which you knew perfectly well he had never heard before. He would behave as though he had known it all along.

Nicolson was a gentleman as he admitted, and a snob, albeit a perceptive one, and Lloyd George was neither. Lloyd George distrusted the Whitehall establishment. Nicolson was at its center in the Foreign Office. It is hard to imagine two men temperamentally more unsuited to each other. Yet Nicolson also recorded the views of a more robust figure, Winston Churchill. When he complained to the War Secretary that it was difficult to be loyal to the Prime Minister, Churchill retorted: 'Nobody who wasn't with the little man in March, 1918 (he always called him the little man) has any right to criticize him. He alone displayed courage when everyone else was knocking at the knees.' (Like everything else about Lloyd George, his height is controversial. He was not much shorter than Churchill whose stoop developed very early and Richard Lloyd George says he was five feet eight inches tall, which would have been of average height for males in the early twentieth century. This seems unlikely. On the other hand Geoffrey Shakespeare, his private secretary as Prime Minister, says he was five feet six and one half inches tall.)

Still, he would not be a good man to go tiger hunting with, not for lack of pluck, of which he had plenty, but because, as several of his contemporaries observed, there was always the danger that he might take the side of the tiger.

Nicolson admitted that Lloyd George was enormously energetic, powerful and effective:

…he had the great politician's gift of knowing what was going on in other people's minds. You can't succeed in politics without this. Luck or a combination of circumstances may take you to the top, but you won't stay there very long if you don't have this particular gift. Lloyd George had it abundantly. Then there was his oratorical power, which was superb, and there was his intelligence. It was nimble. His intellectual intuition was fantastic. He lacked Asquith's intellectual power—not the same steady, driving force—Lloyd George buzzed from subject to subject like a bee. He was extraordinarily able to disengage from one problem and take up another as if he hadn't ever left it. Wasting very little time on rebriefing himself. That's awfully important in politics. And, of course, his physical strength and his health were outstanding.

Asquith and Lord Rendel came to approximately the same conclusion when discussing Lloyd George in Rendel's villa at Cannes in January, 1910. He lacked so much, yet within him there was a force that enabled him to control events. After the conversation Rendel wrote:

Of Lloyd George, Asquith said he was very good where he was good, but he never looked at a figure and could not be made to do so. He echoed my observation that since Lloyd George could, as it were, neither read nor write, he was not unwise in thus recognizing his limitations and concentrating upon his genius for speech and on his remarkable native readiness and resource.[10]

In the end, Nicolson thought Lloyd George a good man.

I've known some men in his generation who on balance I should call evil men. Not Lloyd George. I never thought of him as wicked. He had a moral purpose and his objectives were good and unselfish. But he had no moral sense, no moral discipline, no sense of moral method appropriate to bringing his moral purpose to fruition. That's what I found so hard to take.[11]

Lloyd George's intentions were good. His promises of a better world were sincere. One cannot doubt that he was perfectly serious when he said to Harold Spender, of economic security: 'You people can never understand what it is to be hungry and out of work.'[12] One may question whether this rhetoric accurately described the conditions of his childhood, but the anger implicit here was genuine. He hated exploitation and privilege. 'All down history,' he complained to Lucy Masterman in the autumn of 1909, 'nine-tenths of mankind have been grinding corn for the remaining tenth and have been paid with the husks and bidden to thank God they had the husk.'[13]

Nonetheless, to the standard view of a class-ridden society Lloyd George added a characteristically personal feeling for the citizen's rights and duties, totally removed from the proliferating socialism with which he was surrounded. He had no quarrel, as the following chapters will show, with entrepreneurial capitalism. And he kept, as well, a sense of the organic wholeness of British society that Burke would have recognized. In defending the four penny contribution for national health insurance at a time when five-sixths of the population was conscious of no national taxation whatever, and just after he had raised taxes for the well-to-do to what were regarded as intolerable levels, he observed in a statement that has previously received no attention:

> I am not of those who thinks that anybody who is earning anything ought to escape altogether from contribution. I think everyone ought to contribute his mite toward the National Revenue, but the method of raising that money is a matter which I think will be worth the while of those who are interested in the finance of a country taking a much greater concern about. I have never had any sympathy with the idea that someone has got to be exempt from taxation because he is earning a small amount. It ought to be more or less the principle which you have in a place of worship where everyone is supposed to contribute something, however trifling, because they feel they have a common interest in the common work which is going on and there ought to be some common interest in the work of the Empire, and one way of realizing that is to get every member of the community to contribute. The only principle I would lay down would be that they ought to contribute in proportion to their means.[14]

He was of course continually saying that he hated landlords, and there is no reason to question that he did—although there is no need to take too seriously statements like those to Lucy Masterman about 68 evictions on the Ellis-Nanney estate in 1868.[15] To young and pretty women he was liable to say anything. Yet in his nature there was more than a trace of the reckless romanticism of Squire Western. He loved the countryside, the land, the people on it. He had a myopic eighteenth century vision of England, before enclosures, based on Wordsworth not on fact, but no less real for that. And he shared more than rural romanticism with Fielding's squire. If British politics represents the continuing war between the bloody-minded and the soft-hearted, Lloyd George's nature, like Churchill's, was on the side of the former even though in this, as in many other things, he was out of step with his party. During the war, but well before he became Prime Minister, his allies were men like Edward Carson, Bonar Law, and F.E. Smith.

As has been said of many men, his conscience was his accomplice, not his guide. He was incapable of self-criticism. In private behavior he was willful and, as time went on, irascible. In public he was self-righteous, but always amiable. He never admitted publicly any impurity in his own motives and never trusted the generous impulses of others. Moreover he never hesitated to denounce in others weaknesses that were manifest in himself. Still he was capable, occasionally, of devastating candor.

Yet all this may be the necessary equipment for a constructive statesman. Stubbornness in adversity is also courage. The readiness to deny mistakes can be determined purpose. Ambition for office can be described as a desire to serve the nation and may reflect, indeed, the sure confidence in one's ability to do so.

If Lloyd George accepted, and cheerfully, the gratuities and favors that went with his high place, he was not seduced by them. He would accept gifts—the discount on steamship tickets, the lease of a house, or even an annuity for life—from men anxious to buy his acquaintanceship or his time. But he would not sell his vote or his influence. (He became eventually very rich in office, leaving at his death £139,855. Among Prime Ministers who took office in the first half of the twentieth century, only Baldwin left more.)[16]

I

Llanystumdwy, where Lloyd George grew up, lies at the base of the Lleyn Peninsula about two miles inland from the waters of Tremadoc Bay, midway between Pwllheli to the west and Portmadoc to the east, each about six miles away. Its neighbor is Criccieth, approximately two and one half miles eastward. While the shoreline of Lleyn is austere, grand, and bleak, a traveller inland, even the short distance to Llanystumdwy, will find the country softer, wooded, pleasant, and the village itself at the intersection of the coastline road and the River Dwyfor, quiet, isolated and beautiful.

The mantle of North Wales, now the local government region of Gwynedd, folded around the vast triangle of the Tremadoc arm of Cardigan Bay, with the linked villages between Pwellheli and Portmadoc virtually at its center, constituted for its inhabitants, in the nineteenth century, as it still does, the heart of traditional Wales.[17] In the counties of Caernarvonshire, Merioneth, West Denbigh and Cardiganshire, the ancient kingdoms of Gwynedd and Powys Fodog, the Welsh language was still common, Sunday observance and temperance agitation most pervasive, and land reform most imperative.[18] Here, not surprisingly, by the last third of the nineteenth century, Gladstonian Liberalism had found its firmest roots. And here, after 1868, first appeared those sparks of anti-Englishness, the cultural, economic and religious struggle between the almost classless Welsh majority and the tiny Anglicized squirearchy, that transformed Wales and inspired the radical revolution that brought Lloyd George and others like him into the House of Commons.[19]

Politically and economically, as well as demographically, Wales by the second half of the nineteenth century was two nations. Steel, metal-working and coal-mining drove the South forward. With English immigration its population soared. Railroads turned it toward London, while the expanding trade, flowing through Cardiff and Swansea, opened it to the world. Increasingly as the twentieth century approached, South Wales lost its Celtic singularity. Wealth was industrial; politics labor-oriented and radical, and its concerns those of the mine, mill and dock, not of nonconformity and temperance.

As the South grew, the North declined. The railways that had opened the English market to South Welsh coal and steel, brought instead into the North competition from English factories to ruin the small, indigenous North Welsh textile industry while the cheaper transportation instantly killed the drover's business. Ironically, the railways served to enhance, rather than to diminish, the separateness of the two Welsh nations. As the South looked to London, the North looked to Liverpool. While the South grew in population, the North remained static. Where economic class, working-men's grievances and world market concerns—the McKinley

19

Tariff of 1891 destroyed within a few years the South Welsh tin plate industry—became political issues in the South, the last decade in the 19th century saw the North keeping, indeed reviving, its insular Welshness, finding its causes in disestablishment and the monopoly of land.[20] English influence was represented by the growing attractiveness of a few coastal towns for tourists, but above all by the landlord and his appurtenances in the Church and village school. The cleavage in North Welsh county society between the landlord and the tenant and between the separate cultures that each represented provides the force that shaped Welsh politics to the First World War, gave the program to Welsh radicalism after 1885, and furnished David Lloyd George with the one political issue he maintained throughout his life.

The hierarchy of country life in Wales contrasted sharply with that of England. The ties of religion and dialect between the gentry and the villager, the sympathy of a common culture that surmounted economic differences and kept English rural life stable and politically conservative into the 20th century, long after the grant of household franchise, simply did not exist in Wales. Although they may have been Welsh in origin, the great families of the North, the Wynns of Wynnstay in Denbighshire and their cousins, the Wynnes of Peniarth in Merioneth and the Douglas Pennants of Caernarvon, or for that matter Hugh John Ellis-Nanney, Justice of the Peace of Criccieth and Squire of Llanystumdwy were, in fact, Englishmen.

This proximity and yet alienness of the landlord gave Welsh radicalism the peculiar character which distinguished it both from the ordinary tenant grievances of England and Scotland and from the violent nationalistic separatism of Ireland. A problem for Wales basically was that except for language and folklore, it was difficult to identify specifically what constituted Welsh civilization. Nationality it had once had, but there remained no political inheritance from it. Its political institutions were English. The distinct law of Scotland or the separate administration of Ireland did not exist for Wales. Even the social and cultural vehicles in which Welshness could manifest itself—nonconformity, popular education and the Eisteddfod—were largely of 19th century origin and, at least in the first half of that century, were hardly available as agents for political protest. (The first modern Eisteddfod was held in Corwen, Merionethshire in 1789 as a regional festival. The committee to plan for an annual national festival came into existence only in 1858 and the National Eisteddfod Association was established in 1880. Calvinistic Methodism, the first of the nonconformist sects to establish itself strongly in Wales, and even in Lloyd George's day by no means radical, arrived in the decade of the 1740s, and the Wesleyan Methodist and the Baptist movements came only at the end of the century.)[21]

Even within the principality Welshness suffered from a lack of recognition of its own worth, particularly in comparison with England. As a result, nationalism in Wales found its earliest expressions in opposition to the indigenous symbols of the English world: the Squire, whose political power was exercised through the monopoly of land with the custom of annual leases, and the Church, with its tithe and its control of village education. This is not to say that Welsh grievances were not genuine, but they were, in a literal sense, emblematic, representing an abstraction felt, but hardly defined. There is no reason to suppose that the Welsh tenant suffered more than the English tenant at the hands of his landowner, and he suffered far less than the Irish. Although leases tended to be shorter and without compensation for improvement, land pressure was less than in England and the landlord far less likely to be an absentee than in Ireland. Neither was the village church more corrupt nor the schools that it ran noticeably worse than elsewhere in Britain. The issue was Englishness. To be a Welsh patriot meant chiefly to oppose things English.

This xenophobic character of the mid-nineteenth century Welsh political revival accounts for its relative lack of success in the years before 1914. The trouble was that the genuine Welsh grievances, rural poverty, tenancies at will, the flight from the land, landlord political exploitation, and the Church leverage in education, were shared to a greater or lesser extent by other parts of the United Kingdom and so the Welsh part was unimportant. Meanwhile the rest of the Welsh program, Sunday closing of public houses and the desire for statutory recognition of Wales in various units of national administration, indeed the disestablishment of the Church, were, to most of the huge English electorate, neither good nor bad in themselves but simply irrelevant. Moreover, the Welsh were divided. Geography and economics separated the North and the South. By 1886, when questions of the tithe and Church disestablishment were sweeping the North, the South was already absorbed with industrial problems. Political leaders and Members of Parliament from the North and South cooperated, to be sure, but also competed. Attempts toward the end of the century to merge the North and South Wales Liberal Federation, in which Lloyd George participated, were unsuccessful and proposals to form a Welsh parliamentary party on the model of the Irish were scarcely taken seriously. Even in the North, nationalism by no means received unanimous support from Liberal voters who found the young, demagogic parliamentary candidate's promises to reform the Church and the land system socially dangerous and personally unpleasant.

In short, Welsh nationalistic radicalism was an exotic plant.[22] Although a Welsh party could have produced half as many Members of Parliament as the Irish Nationalists, the Welsh radicals were never able to approach half the influence of the Irishmen. Welsh nationalism resembles nothing so much as the prairie Populism that boiled up within the United States Democratic party at the same time in the 1890s, with Easterners, money lenders and railroads as the generalized enemy, and free silver as the symbolic issue.

The critical factor is that Lloyd George's background was less specifically Welsh than rural, that it was not industrial, that his enemies were landlords, not capitalists. He grew up in reduced but respectable circumstances which drove him toward personal achievement, not elevation of class. His sympathies for the poor were muted by years of collecting rents, fees, and industrial insurance premiums as a solicitor's clerk among a cunning people for whom the disguising of the signs of wealth had achieved the status of a fine art, while his own ambitious self-reliance made him suspicious, if not hostile, toward men, for instance trade union leaders, who professed too loudly and often that their only concern was for the welfare of others. He had the countryman's, not only the Welsh countryman's, distrust of officially constituted self-important authority, which first helped him toward local celebrity as the 'Poacher's Lawyer' and which may have accounted for his singularly casual attitude toward high court judges, barristers, and above all toward the established Civil Service. His Celtic peculiarities, always described by writers, reflected only the usages of rural people everywhere, for whom government power is either mistrusted or slightly irrelevant. But the more common mistake is the assumption that there was in his makeup a species of left-wing reformism associated with South Wales and that somehow he was, or should have been, an ordinary labor-oriented, social reforming, anti-capitalist, radical.[23] The Labour party and working class ideology were foreign to him. His avenues to it were closed. He was neither a member of the proletariat nor a university intellectual. He was not a 'gentleman,' as he proudly admitted. He was 'a Welsh country solicitor.'[24]

Lloyd George was born, not in Wales, but at 5 New York Place, Roberts Street, Manchester, on 17 January 1863, the first son and second child of William George and Elizabeth Lloyd. William George was a schoolmaster, a man of considerable intellectual attainment, with much charm and good looks and a restless disposition. His family was Welsh and Baptist in origin. He had been born the son of David George, a prosperous farmer of Trecoed, Jordanstown in Pembrokeshire in 1820 but he had spent much of his life in England and, according to his son, scarcely spoke Welsh. Returning from the funeral of his eldest daughter in December, 1907, Lloyd George gave Herbert Lewis, his best friend among the Welsh Members of Parliament, one of the few unromanticized accounts of his family background. Lloyd George said that he began with English, his father's knowledge of Welsh was inadequate and he could not write it. His mother spoke broad Caernarvonshire. He said that he had been told by an old man who knew his father that his father should have been a preacher and that he had a magnetic personality.[25]

Elizabeth 'Betsy' Lloyd was much more a child of the North Welsh tradition. She had been born in Llanystumdwy in 1828, the second daughter and second of three children of David and Rebecca Lloyd. Her father, David Lloyd, was a shoemaker, founding the business which would eventually pass to his third child, Richard. But more important to him, the central interest in his life, was his post as unpaid but ordained pastor of the Baptist congregation of Capel Ucha in Criccieth. During David Lloyd's incumbency, about 1835, the north Welsh Baptists were assailed by the primitive Christian doctrines of Alexander Campbell, and his followers, the Disciples of Christ. David Lloyd resisted the pristine fundamentalism of the Campbellite doctrine among his flock during his lifetime. But two years after his death in 1839, at age 39, the Criccieth Chapel adopted the Campbellite practice, among the tenets of which was the abolition of the office of pastor. Richard Lloyd, five years old when his father died, succeeded his parent in the cobbler's shop and later followed him into the lay pastorate of the Criccieth Disciples of Christ to provide the household atmosphere of unsophisticated Christian devotion and the discipline of work in which Lloyd George grew to manhood.

William George and Elizabeth Lloyd were married in Pwllheli on 16 November 1859. William had come to the town the year before to take a post as a master at a nonconformist school, while Betsy had lived there for several years working as a domestic servant and, at the time of the marriage, as a lady's companion.[26] The couple had met at functions at the Baptist chapel near William's school although neither, in fact, was a member of the congregation, and were married at St. Peter's Parish Church. (There is a family tradition that William George had been married briefly about two years before during a sojourn in Pembrokeshire, where for a few years he attempted to conduct a school of his own, which he had opened in April, 1854 in Haverfordwest. William George is hazy and misleading about it.[27] W.R.P. George concludes that if a previous marriage occurred, it must have been in Haverfordwest between 1854 and 1857, and that the winding up of the school was a result of his wife's death. The woman's name in the family legend is 'Mrs. Brown.')[28]

For a short time after their marriage, the couple lived in Llanystumdwy with Betsy's mother, Rebecca, and her brother Richard at Highgate Cottage. While there, Betsy gave birth to her first child, a girl, who evidently died before christening and was buried at Capel Ucha.[29] But even the warmth of the close-knit Lloyd family could not induce William to stay in one place for long. By 1861, he had moved with his wife, now pregnant again, and with Betsy's nephew, David Lloyd Jones, a boy of fourteen, to Newchurch, Lancashire where a second daughter arrived on 8 November 1861. She was named Mary Ellen.

The Georges were barely settled in Newchurch before William in the autumn of 1862 began to search for a new appointment. Eventually he found a rather satisfactory temporary post at a factory school in Manchester as a replacement for the headmaster who was ill. So it fell that Betsy gave birth to the couple's first son in that city on 17 January of the next year. He was christened 'David Lloyd' after his cousin, David Lloyd Jones, who by this time was clearly dying of tuberculosis.[30]

Before the new baby was four months old, William George had moved his family again, this time back to Pembrokeshire in the English-speaking southern part of Wales. Here he took a farm of thirty acres, 'Bullford' near Johnston, intending to give up teaching. The reasons for this last change may have been his health about which he was always concerned, as his frequent letters to Richard Lloyd show. He appeared to have believed, probably correctly, that he, like David Lloyd Jones, was consumptive. In any case, his life as a farmer was short. Late in May, 1864, he caught a cold which rapidly turned to pneumonia and on 7 June, William George's restlessness was finally quieted. He left a net estate of £760, two infant children and a wife expecting still another, in a community in which all were strangers.

Evidently, Betsy never considered anything except a return to Llanystumdwy. A telegram, 'Tyrd Richard' (come Richard), brought her brother. He departed immediately, walking twenty miles to the closest railway station, in those days in Caernarvon.[31] After seeing to the sale of the furniture, the evaluation of the crop of turnips in the ground, and the assignment of the lease, he took his sister and her brood back to the village on the Dwyfor that she had left as a girl. And here in the heart of tribal Wales, a vastly different world than his father would have given him, David Lloyd George grew up.

Llanystumdwy Parish in the mid-sixties was losing population, as were most of the rural areas in North Wales. (Between 1861 and 1871 the population of the parish fell from 1126 to 1087.) The census commission attributed this to the introduction of agricultural machinery.[32] At the same time the arrival in Caernarvonshire of the coastal railroad in 1867, linking Pwllheli, Criccieth and Portmadoc, gave these larger centers a new vitality. Criccieth particularly began to prosper as a resort and Pwllheli, the capital of the Lleyn peninsula, grew as a market center.[33] But despite a rapidly growing professional and commercial class in the coastline towns, the gentry still controlled the country, and the census of Pwllheli Union, which included Llanystumdwy, in 1871 noted 12 men and 72 women who were returned as 'persons of Rank or Property, not found under other occupational categories'.[34]

The decade of the sixties saw the gathering of a revolt against the landlords and the social structure they represented. The first cracks in the smooth surface of county gentry political hegemony occurred, not surprisingly, in the single member constituency of Merionethshire in the election of 1859. (The year 1859 was the watershed in the swing from Conservative to Liberal in Wales. Except for the election of 1832 itself, the Conservatives had always returned more Members of Parliament than the Liberals, usually twice as many. After that date they never approached the Liberals.) Here, in a seat that was in every sense a pocket borough for his family, W.W.E. Wynne, who had been unopposed in 1852 and 1857, nearly lost his place to nonconformist David Williams. In fact the objections to Wynne were not political but religious. He was an ardent tractarian and so alienated his almost entirely nonconformist tenantry. But the religious issue became political when the Wynnes took revenge upon their insubordinate farmholders by turning them out. The number of evictions is unclear, although testimony more than a decade later before the Select Committee on Parliamentary and Municipal Elections suggests that it was not large. But it was unprecedented and unforgotten in the country where memories are long.[35] The evictions of 1859 aroused anger not only against the landlords involved, but against every other symbol of the established Welsh political hierarchy. The Anglican clergy themselves were involved. Frequently they were landlords, farm rent being part of the stipend for the living, and like other landlords, they brought their tenants to vote in a body. Invariably they supported their patron's cause from the pulpit and helped to fix in voters' minds the identification of Toryism and the Church.[36]

The sheer injustice and crudeness of the landlord's revenge after the Merioneth election made the social cleavage in Wales a political issue among people for whom the differences between the upper and lower classes were already religious topics. The men who lost their holdings were not radicals or nationalists. By definition, they were substantial farmers.[37] They were simply Liberals and nonconformists. This injustice lighted a fire that could never be put out. In 1865, Wales returned 18 Liberals and 16 Conservatives to parliament.[38]

The final victory in Wales arrived with the Reform Act of 1867 and in the general election, 'The Great Election', the next year. The Tory delegation from Wales was reduced to eight among 30 seats. In Merioneth, W.R.M. Wynne withdrew, so David Williams was finally returned, unopposed.[39] In Denbighshire, George Osborne Morgan, son of a vicar, but a strong supporter of disestablishment, won a seat from a reactionary Whig, Col. R.M. Biddulph, whose family, with the Wynnes, had dominated the county almost without interruption since the beginning of the century. The sensation of the North, however, was in Caernarvonshire where Thomas Love Jones Parry defeated the Honourable George Douglas Pennant, son of Lord Penrhyn, the wealthiest man in North Wales, who, with his father, had held the seat, not only without interruption but without opposition, since 1841.

The new Liberals elected were hardly radical. In terms of Westminster, they were country-oriented, whiggish Gladstonians. Jones Parry was a well-to-do landowner of Madryn Castle, Pwllheli, a man of unorthodox social and moral habits whose father had sat briefly for Caernarvon District. Osborne Morgan was an Oxford educated barrister, forceful and honorable and devoted to Wales, but profoundly conservative. David Williams was a wealthy landowner of Penrhyn-deudrath. He had been High Sheriff of Merioneth and his son was at Eton. (Although Morgan went on to become Judge Advocate General and Parliamentary Secretary of the Colonies, neither Jones Parry nor Williams made any impact in Westminster. Douglas Pennant recaptured Caernarvonshire in 1874 and Williams died at the end of 1869.) But again the landowners' revenge against Liberal voting tenants, exaggerated and mythologized as it may have been in the folk memory of Welshmen, evoked a hatred for Toryism that virtually guaranteed a further movement to the left among Welsh Liberals.[40] The evictions of 1859 were repeated now on a far larger scale and included, reportedly, dismissal of workers from the quarries in Merioneth.[41]

Whether in fact folk memory or imagination, the notices to quit of 1868 became a staple of Lloyd George's rhetoric and conversation. The images, accurate or not, of honest and prosperous farmers ordered from their tenancies at a day's notice, of childhood friends suddenly withdrawn from school, of landlords convening at the county hotel haphazardly to choose one of their number to become the next Member of Parliament and issuing peremptory letters instructing tenants on the exercise of their franchise, clearly stayed with him for the rest of his life. These, he always claimed, were his first memories of politics.

1 Childhood, Youth, the Law and Politics

Davy Lloyd, as he was first called, was seventeen months old when his father died. He confessed later only to the dimmest recollection of the man. Evidently, however, he was aware enough of what had happened to help his sister pile stones against the gate of the farmhouse in Johnston, Pembrokeshire during the sale of furniture in a childish effort to prevent strangers from carrying off his mother's familiar belongings. The place of a father in his life was now filled by his uncle, Betsy George's brother, Richard Lloyd, the shoemaker.

'Uncle Lloyd' was of such importance in David's early years that he must receive some attention here. His work in the cobbler shop that he had inherited from his father supplied the family's material needs, perhaps more fully in the years before 1868 than after, but the rhythm of the life at Highgate was dictated not by commerce but by his Christian beliefs and by the demands of his lay pastorate in the Free Baptist (Disciples of Christ) Chapel at Criccieth. Although a saintly character, old fashioned in many ways, untraveled and uneducated in any formal sense, he was friendly, cheerful and approachable. He maintained an intense interest in mundane affairs, read seriously on many subjects, and was a staunch Liberal in politics. In fact his intense spiritual feeling rarely showed. He never criticized or lectured. Behavior in others which he would have deplored in himself received no admonition, whether the culprit was a member of his family, of the village or of the congregation. Yet the force of his own piety led those who knew him to hide their transgressions from him even if they did not end them. His nephew, William George, reports the anxiety of the men of Llanystumdwy to avoid coming within the view of Richard Lloyd when entering or leaving the village pub, which was nearly opposite the shoeshop.[1] This embarrassment continued even in the much larger town of Criccieth after the family moved there.[2]

Lloyd George felt as strongly as anyone the power of his uncle's exemplary character. As an adult he certainly never emulated the older man's behavior, but he sought throughout his life to please him and like the rest of the village, to keep his misdemeanors well hidden. This may not have been hard, for Richard Lloyd could never see a defect in his sister's older son and spoiled him outrageously to the exclusion of the two other children, Mary Ellen, and William. Even at the age of ninety-three, William George recorded that he found his uncle's assumptions about the perfection of his brother's conduct 'a bit trying.'[3]

Understandably Richard Lloyd's unswerving adoration of his nephew affected David's opinion of himself, enhanced his belief in his own intellectual talents, which, although exceptional, may not have been outstanding, and clearly stimulated a precocious ambition to get on. For his part Lloyd George made much of his uncle throughout the older man's life. Even though as he rose in the political world he sometimes found correspondence a chore, he communicated regularly in letters full of affection and self-congratulation, while admitting nevertheless the burden of the standard of conduct he was expected to maintain. When, at the age of fifteen, he left Highgate Cottage and moved to Portmadoc to begin a trial period as a law clerk, he relished the freedom he had acquired. Eventually he came actually to resent the supervision of the 'Esgop' (Welsh for bishop). When, finally in the middle 1880s, he and his brother employed Uncle Lloyd as a clerk, David tended rather to patronize the older man for his timidity and innocence in carrying out the sometimes abrasive duties of writ service and debt collection.[4]

Thus, although Richard Lloyd's influence as an object of veneration declined as his nephew matured, he must be accounted as David's first and most influential teacher. Even though his personal conduct was governed by a code of rigid moral precept, and the household he headed was a religious, not a political one, his own views were sensible and practical, his advice, even after his nephew entered parliament, was shrewd and frequently heeded, and his approbation was sought even when it was not deserved.[5]

Richard Lloyd himself was an insatiable reader and despite Lloyd George's later statement that he possessed only two books in English as a child, and some old copies of the *Examiner,* Highgate Cottage was well stocked with books, both in English and Welsh.[6] The habit of reading, young David Lloyd acquired early. Childhood memories of him in the village are of a small, rather quiet, serious boy always carrying an enormous bundle of books. Unlike his adult behavior, he was a systematic reader, often making notes, as did his uncle, on the back of books that interested him.[7]

Besides Uncle Lloyd, the only element in David Lloyd's early life which could be defined reasonably as an intellectual influence came from the master of the village school, David Evans. The Llanystumdwy National School was fairly new, having been established in July, 1851, under the patronage of the local landlord, O.J. Ellis-Nanney. David Lloyd entered it as a pupil at age three and one half in September, 1866. (The designation 'National School' meant specifically that the school was operated by a Church of England parish and taught the Anglican Catechism, and that it received funds from the Exchequer. By 1866 nonconformist congregations were also establishing local sectarian schools which received government aid and were distinguished by the title 'British Schools').

Evans, earnest and somewhat humorless as befitted a local schoolmaster, was devoted to his school and to his charges. His own learning was well above the average for an academic appointment in which devotion to Anglicanism was the principal qualification. His knowledge of Latin and particularly of mathematics was considerable. Most important, for both David Lloyd and William, was Evans's offer of tutorial instruction at a level above the seven forms that his appointment obliged him to provide. Indeed he cared enough for the craft of teaching to provide special help to both boys even after the rector of the Llanystumdwy parish, the Reverend David Edwards, had proposed, and suffered the refusal of, pupil-teachership for the two, the highest scholastic honor the school had available. The possibility that David Lloyd George might have become a village schoolmaster is interesting, not only for the thoughts evoked about the effects of chance in the affairs of men. (L.G. himself reflected on this in a letter to his brother of 13 October 1906, when he was President of the Board of Trade. He noted that a schoolmate who had accepted the offer of pupil-teachership was by then a canon of the Church.)[8] First of all it provides an example of the influence of David's mother, Betsy George, whom David evidently loved but who otherwise seems to have had little impact on his adult life. The appointment as a pupil-teacher would have required eventually, of course, that the candidate be in communion with the Anglican Church. This Betsy quickly rejected. She would rather see her sons breaking stones at the side of the road, she is remembered to have said, than 'have them turn their backs on the little Baptist Chapel at Penymaes.'[9]

As an illustration of the character of David Evans, the story has further significance. The offer of the pupil-teachership, the acceptance of which would have justified further individual instruction, came in 1876 when David Lloyd was 13, shortly before the occurrence of one of the most characteristic and best known of his youthful efforts at self-assertion, the revolt over the catechism. As a Church of England foundation, Mr. Evans's school required the study of the Anglican catechism over which the students, five-sixths of them nonconformist, were examined formally by the rector once a year in the presence of various notables of the parish including the patron of the school, by this time the founder's son, Hugh John Ellis-Nanney. The accounts of this escapade, which occurred in late 1876 or early 1877, vary, but William George who was himself involved, says that it amounted to a unanimous refusal by the students, organized by David Lloyd, to recite the creed. The silence only lasted a minute after which William, out of sympathy for Mr. Evans whose face, he recalls, was 'ashen and pitiful to behold,' rescued him with the words, 'I believe...' after which the boycott dissolved. But the annual examination disappeared. David Lloyd may have administered a thrashing to his younger brother for breaking the conspiracy of silence, but William George's account does not mention it. The important fact is that the entire episode was acutely humiliating to Mr. Evans who had suffered from other boycotts involving a number of students, also organized by David Lloyd, against the Ash Wednesday service in the church which the school customarily attended. But in spite of his many embarrassments, with no hope that David would ever become a schoolmaster, Mr. Evans gave his undisciplined and antagonistic pupil an extra level of education, which, Lloyd George frequently admitted later, made it possible for him to pass the preliminary examinations of the Incorporated Law Society and so eventually to leave the world in which he had been born.[10] In a singular way Lloyd George recognized his debt to his schoolmaster. His later views of his childhood, as will be seen, were harsh, narrow and bitter, but David Evans, like Uncle Lloyd, he idealized. Although he would have many unkind things to say about the Church in Wales, and of Church schools in particular, he always spoke of his own teacher in glowing terms.[11]

I

The story of David Lloyd between the summer of 1864 when he and his mother returned with Uncle Lloyd to Llanystumdwy and the summer of 1878 when he left Mr. Evans's school and entered law offices in Portmadoc is necessarily anecdotal and intermittent. Beside Lloyd George's own recollections of it—which clearly reflect more of the portrait of himself he desired to project as an adult than of what actually occurred in his early life—the sources are sparse and narrow and, except for William George, are essentially hearsay, or family or village tradition. The details of the revolt over the catechism, for instance, in which the young David appears a recusant hero in the triumph of freedom over obscurantism appeared first in a long interview that Lloyd George gave the *Review of Reviews* in 1904 and was embellished in Edwards's and DuParcq's biographies, both of which were clearly prepared with his active cooperation and, to some extent, under his supervision.[12] There was really no independent confirmation of the story until William George's book appeared in 1958 and he clearly felt then that what his brother had done was an act of effrontery to a kindly man.[13]

Again, there is Lloyd George's well known insistence on early poverty. He repeated stories about this condition even to Frances Stevenson and Harold Spender, two people with whom he remained close for many years. Publicly, he continually used stories of the hard times of his childhood to reinforce his position as the tribune of the ordinary people. Like his Welshness, these early hardships served to draw a line between himself and the rest of the political establishment. He would refer to the 'luxury of half an egg' that he received on Sunday.[14] 'I can remember it so clearly, so very clearly,' he told Harold Begbie in 1915 or 16,

> That it was always—not once or twice or occasionally but always—a struggle for my Mother at the end of the week. The last expense of every week was a coin of destiny. My mind was impressed at the time by the terrible importance every week of the last sixpence, and it is still impressed upon my memory; it is the strongest impression of my childhood.[15]

In fact, the economics of David Lloyd's early childhood, measured in terms of rural North Wales at a time when even the rather austere farming economy of the region was beginning to decline, were fairly easy. His may not have been the most comfortable family in Llanystumdwy, as one biographer has suggested it was, but before they moved to Criccieth at least, they were far from impoverished.[16] Richard Lloyd after all was a master craftsman who for a time before the arrival of Elizabeth George and her brood had employed two assistants. And as long as his own mother, Rebecca, David's grandmother, was alive, that is until 1868, accounts were punctually collected. Moreover, Betsy George received about £50 per year from her husband's estate. This sum alone was considerably more than the annual wage of the ordinary agricultural labourer of the time and about the average wage of a village schoolmistress. On the other hand, family income was much reduced in 1879 when £180 of the principal were spent on the premium and stamp duty for David's articles as a solicitor's clerk, and the principal was diminished again, in 1882, by a similar sum for William's. Characteristically Lloyd George forgot the contribution of his mother toward his education and attributed the support of his legal training entirely to Richard Lloyd.[17]

The fact is that David Lloyd's early economic circumstances fall into two distinct periods. The first from 1864 to 1879 saw a reasonably comfortable and financially easy existence in Llanystumdwy. But the second was indeed a period of respectable poverty, endured mostly in Criccieth, from 1879 until at least 1887 when William George joined his brother in the solicitor's firm of Lloyd George and George and the practice became modestly profitable. In his later life Lloyd George chose to speak of the unhappy days of Criccieth as if they were the whole of his childhood and adolescence. Even so, financial stringency was more a humiliation than a hardship, although no less real for that. It left him with a lifelong anger against inherited wealth and left him also defenseless against even the most improbable schemes of financial speculation.[18]

All in all the childhood years at Llanystumdwy seem to have been less idyllic than Lloyd George allowed earlier biographers to describe them. To be sure, there are allusions, in which William George concurs, to boyhood games along the Dwyfor, to raids for nuts and fruit into local orchards, to fights and near fights fortuitously interrupted. David Lloyd emerges as the leader and chief planner of escapades, a boy of courage and quick wit, who was recognized as such by village children and adults alike. He was secure in the bosom of a loving family. His uncle was a respected village sage. Certainly these things are true, yet there are disquieting notes. After 80 years William remembered the boycott his brother organized against an English boy attending the Llanystumdwy school which eventually drove the infant from the village. And he recalls the deliberate tormenting of a small child, much younger than David Lloyd, who himself could not have been older than 14, by attempting to shake him from a tree in which the boy had been idly amusing himself by bouncing on a branch.[19] Cruelty and ruthlessness were as much a part of Lloyd George, the man, as physical bravery and a ready tongue. By the time he finished Mr. Evans's school he had already achieved some importance in the village, took himself immensely seriously, and felt himself to be a person marked for greater celebrity than his peers. Yet at the same time, one suspects he was not entirely or even moderately happy. He was quiet, something of a bookworm. He was not adept at games. The contemporary view was of him as the 'old Methodist.'[20] He was not as 'quick' as some of his classmates, records a contemporary. There were several others with more wit, although David Lloyd surpassed them in general knowledge. He was always to the front in geography and arithmetic.[21] He tended to dream, and to keep himself slightly apart. 'He was a lonely creature', mused Lucy Masterman after walking about Criccieth with him in 1911. 'I would not have my childhood again' was Lloyd George's terse comment.[22] He was 'discontented, cramped and unhappy' as a boy, he told Frances Stevenson 35 years later, adding that he never saw 'the brighter side of life' until after he was 20.[23]

Finally there is the curious entry in the diary he had begun to keep when he entered Breeze, Jones and Casson. The occasion was the removal of the family from Llanystumdwy to Criccieth:

> Sunday 9 May 1880. Very nice day. Very hot. Sunday School. Recited chapter. Baptizing day. R. Lloyd (2) splendid. W. Williams (6) good. A very lively singing meeting. Singing some anthems and cantatas which Ann Jones brought there. Sitting in the middle of girls—in the arm of Jennie—ha! To Llanystumdwy, and slept there for the last time, perhaps forever.
>
> Monday 10 May 1880. Dull. To Portmadoc with 8:20 train. Left Llanystumdwy without one feeling of regret, remorse nor longing. Read a little on some case which Mr. Casson gave me to study, but in no mood to study.[24]

II

When Richard Lloyd brought his household to Criccieth David had been away from Highgate Cottage for nearly two years serving as articled law clerk in Portmadoc. So long as the family was in Llanystumdwy he lived and boarded for ten shillings per week at the house of a local auctioneer, David Lloyd Owen, from whom he would later rent rooms when he began to practise. Usually he returned home on weekends. The exact reasons for the move are not clear, although in general the motive was financial. The payment of the cost of David's articles in January 1879 had reduced Betsy George's capital. Moreover, Richard Lloyd's health had weakened and since the death of his mother, the business side of the shoe-making establishment had been allowed to slide. So the once prosperous shop that his father had opened was given up. David could now live at home, which would save the small allowance his mother gave him, and the new house in Criccieth, called Morvin House, was large enough to accommodate paying guests.

David Lloyd remained in Portmadoc for a month after his family arrived in Criccieth and finally returned to the new home with reluctance. 'I feel rather queer' he wrote on June 7, 'something bordering on unpleasant at first in the change, but believe it will be better ultimately that so much of what I may regard as liberty is curtailed.'[25] But even though he was to live again with his family until his marriage in 1888, the law had brought an end to the old life and had begun a new one.

The impulse for the choice of a legal career is assigned in family tradition to a Liverpool solicitor, Thomas Goffey, who had managed Elizabeth's inheritance since William George's death, who indeed had been a friend of William George's, and whose thoughts and advice were frequently sought by the family on important decisions.[26] Although neither Lloyd George nor his brother had ever met Goffey, he was held in high esteem by the family, was sent a turkey each year from Highgate, and was understood to earn £300 a year.[27] The law needed no better recommendation than this, but the first step toward the law was the accomplishment of the Preliminary Examination of the Incorporated Law Society. This required, among other things, an elementary knowledge of Latin and French. Mr. Evans could help with the first, but French, David had to learn from a

Parisian copy of Aesop's fables and a French grammar book, with the encouragement of Uncle Lloyd who undertook to learn the language himself. For the Preliminary Examination, David and Richard Lloyd journeyed to Liverpool in late October, 1877. The news of his success reached Llanystumdwy on 8 December, evoking an approving entry in David Evans's diary and absolute euphoria in David Lloyd.[28]

Finding a law firm willing to accept David Lloyd as an articled clerk for a period of five years now became a serious matter. Fortunately a friend of Richard Lloyd who shared an interest in Welsh culture was Edward Breeze, the senior partner of the Portmadoc firm of Breeze, Jones and Casson. Through his intervention young David was permitted to enter the office for a trial period of six months, beginning in July, 1878. If at the end of this time everything was satisfactory, formal articles of clerkship between David's guardian, Richard Lloyd, and the firm would be signed.

However accidental its selection, Breeze, Jones and Casson was an ideal place for the legal training of a rather unworldly, slightly bookish, highly ambitious, village boy. The firm had a large and varied practice. Mr. Breeze, at the age of 42, was a man of considerable standing, clerk of the Lord Lieutenancy of Merioneth and of two Petty Sessions divisions. Although a churchman, he was Liberal agent for Merioneth and South Caernarvonshire while at the same time maintaining an informed interest in Welsh history. A kindly and generous nature led Edward Breeze to extend to the boy from Llanystumdwy the hospitality of his house, Morfa Lodge, to which David made almost daily visits in the early months of his apprenticeship.

Breeze, Jones and Casson were solicitors for the estate of W. A. Maddocks, the founder of Portmadoc, which held ground leases on all the houses in the town. The leases stipulated that fire insurance on the premises was to be carried by an office approved by the lessor. In fact this meant that the estate handled the insurance and young clerks in the law offices collected the semiannual premiums. David Lloyd was assigned to this task immediately: there is a note in his journal of 12 November, 1878, that he received 15 shillings from Mr. Holl, the firm's cashier, who was in charge of the work.[29] David was also thrown into the general management of the Maddocks property, delivering leases and engrossing mortgages, collecting rents, seeing to rate appeals and attending court sessions. Not yet 16, he had become a part of the legal side of the real estate business, receiving a practical education in small property management that would affect his outlook for the rest of his life.[30] Withal, there is no evidence that he disapproved of the system at this time. Mr. Breeze's law firm was an honest and compassionate landlord asking reasonable rents and readily selling lease reversions to sitting tenants.

At the same time, David was supposed to be learning the law. During the autumn of 1878, he worked systematically at Williams's *Real Property* and at Hallam's *Constitutional History of England,* making notes on both and writing a detailed synopsis of Williams. He was reproved for writing untidy mortgages and resolved to do better. The picture emerges here of an earnest, slightly self-important adolescent, full of good resolutions, who, not yet even an articled clerk, had begun to think of himself as a lawyer. He studied shorthand and tried to improve his penmanship. Much of his spare time was spent at the home of Edward Breeze where he played with the children and wrote letters at the dictation of the firm's senior partner. The frequent visits to Morfa Lodge confirmed that David Lloyd George was still the slightly aloof, rather solitary, figure that he had been at Llanystumdwy. He was criticized for this attitude and the reflections upon it in his diary suggest that even at age fifteen and one-half he was preparing himself to be the jolly, accessible politician of later years with many confidants but no friends.

> J. G. Jones, clerk of the County Council Office said that I was regarded as independent and reserved. I'm not acquainted with the great majority of people in Portmadoc and therefore cannot make myself familiar with them. However, I feel I cannot continue independent and reserved towards unacquainted people if I really mean to be a success as a lawyer. We should study people as well as their conveniences; besides instead of making myself more respected, I will make myself a perfect fool and snob in the sight of the people. I would be regarded as a would-be nuisance to society and a plague in everyone's eyes. Let me try to make myself more affable towards everyone—a beggar even is not to be scorned. You cannot say what even a mouse may do in the way of a lion (save the mark). Clients are not to be gained by a 'hitherto-thou-shalt-come-and-no-further' mien and attitude. Think of it.[31]

Mr. Breeze invited the young apprentice clerk to his house for Christmas at the end of the first six months of his work, but David returned instead to Llanystumdwy. Soon after the holidays and seven days after David's sixteenth birthday, on 24 January 1879, Uncle Lloyd appeared in the office of Breeze, Jones and Casson and paid £180 for premiums and stamp duty for his nephew's articles. David now became a legally articled clerk to a junior partner, Randall Casson, and celebrated the occasion by a typically sententious entry in his diary.

> Q. Your chief ambition?
> A. To promote myself by honest endeavour to do benefit to others.
> Q. The Aim in Life.
> A. 1) to develop my manhood
>   2) to do good
>   3) to seek truth
>   4) to bring truths to benefit our fellows.
> Q. Your idea of Happiness.
> A. To perceive my own efforts succeed.[32]

As well as being the director of his legal education, Randall Casson was for a few years an important influence in David Lloyd's personal life. Casson was an Englishman who had come to Wales to provide legal services to the Anglicised gentry. He was young, vigorous, worldly, a captain in the Volunteers and generally far removed in outlook from both Welsh puritanism and Welsh political radicalism. He encouraged his young clerk to move outside the narrow confines of the lawbooks, chapel attendance and political disputation with friends in Portmadoc selected for him by

Richard Lloyd. He introduced David Lloyd to the virtues of beer, wine and cheese and during 1882-83 recruited him into the battalion of Volunteers.[33] David Lloyd seems to have enjoyed his only experience with military life but was clearly an indifferent soldier.[34]

By this time the family had moved to Criccieth, David was again living with them, and certain new facets of his nephew's character had to be kept from Richard Lloyd and from David's mother. This was sometimes difficult. David records being seen by his mother planting a chrysanthemum on Sunday. She'…appeared terribly shocked', he recorded, 'so I bolted'.[35] Almost certainly the convivial Randall Casson was behind the clear relaxation in David's attitude toward Sabbath observance and indeed he helped to push along his young clerk's rapidly changing ideas about religion in general.

The question of the strength, or even existence, of David Lloyd George's religious convictions has troubled the minds of most of his recent biographers. Some of the confusion on this matter, as on many other things, derives from the conflicting facts provided by the man himself. The most elaborate and circumstantial story he told to Frances Stevenson in 1915. When he was 11 years old, she wrote,

> he suddenly came face to face with the fact that religion as he was taught it was a mockery and sham. He says he remembers the exact moment—he was in bed—when the whole structure and fabric of religion fell before him with a crash and nothing remained. The shock to him was so great that he leapt out of bed. From then on and for years he was in mental distress on the subject of religion—he felt like a man who has suddenly been struck blind and is groping for the way but can find no support. He says the thought was horrible to him that the universe should be under no direction, with no purpose, no supreme control and at last he confided to his uncle the state of mind he was in. Strangely enough, old Richard Lloyd was not in the least shocked but seemed to understand perfectly well, but David says that the religious meetings and services were a source of unhappiness to him for years. There was a prayer meeting which was held every week on a Thursday to which D used to look forward with loathing, the same prayers, the same phrases; (D gave me a reproduction of some of the happenings at them.) The same talk, week after week.[36]

It was not until he was 18, after reading *Sartor Resartus* and Renan's *Life of Jesus* that he began to recover some peace.

He told the story differently to D. R. Daniel, saying that he was baptized at 12 and experienced his revelation of mortality the next night. To Lucy Masterman, who, like Frances Stevenson, was young, pretty, and a sympathetic listener, Lloyd George became exquisitely emotional. At age 11 he felt, 'a sudden breaking of something in his brain.' 'From that time on,' he said, 'I was in hell, I saw no way out!' He added that he told his uncle about it at age 14. He did refer to the reading of *Sartor Resartus*, from which he quoted, but Mrs. Masterman records on another occasion that he found much comfort in a sermon of Charles Spurgeon that he heard when he first visited London at age 17.[37]

These are typically stirring Lloyd George tales of his early life. He presents himself here wrestling with the devil for command of his soul. They are told with full attention to dramatic effect and with great precision and detail. But there are problems. A minor one is the question of his baptism. He was baptized by Richard Lloyd in the brook by Penymaes Chapel on 7 February 1875, three weeks after his 12th birthday. According to the stories to Frances Stevenson and Lucy Masterman, the crisis of spirit occurred when he was 11 and somehow, therefore, he allowed himself as an agnostic to be put through a ceremony which meant for the Disciples a spiritual rebirth in Christ and marked as well the official entrance into the congregation. This would have been possible, of course; he would not want to offend Uncle Lloyd by refusing. But in the stories to the two women, he never mentions baptism. To D.R. Daniel he reverses the order of events and the baptism comes first. Surely the connection of the two cataclysms could hardly have escaped his mind, particularly after he had been so clear on other details.

But the larger question, turning precisely on the early years of the articled clerkship, was the spiritual desolation he insisted he suffered after his loss of faith. In fact nothing in his journal substantiates any claims of agony of soul, or more easily checked, any detestation of religious services. Arguably, he could not have escaped attending these so long as he lived in Wales, but there was nothing requiring him to enjoy them, which his journal shows he clearly did. His private estimates of preaching and the music are entirely placid and invariably he found his uncle's sermons 'splendid'. But even when, in his professional judgement, certain parts of the service or the singing were poor, there is no suggestion that he was uncomfortable and no hint of the loathing he recalled to Frances Stevenson. 'As a boy, I admired and revered the great preachers,' he told Lord Riddell in 1918. 'I was never tired of listening to them.'[38]

Finally the elaborate ethical sentiments which David regularly confided to his journal, while fairly non-religious in tone, are perfectly consistent with Christian belief. Certainly they are not the writings of one whose framework of externally founded morality has been shattered and who is struggling for a personal system of belief. And so, while it is clear that in the years between 1878 and 1881 David Lloyd lost, along with his village innocence, most of the old religious faith in which he had been raised, he seems to have gone through none of the torment which he chose to remember later on. Contemporary evidence simply is not there. Why he should have made his loss of childhood religious faith, a traditional event in adolescence, such a dramatic occurrence, beyond his general tendency for self-dramatization, is hard to say. Possibly it was simply habit. Frequently in later years in political affairs he would invent a crucial detail to explain a tendency or decision that had been slowly evolving over months.

More important, however, is what went in the place of the old Disciples of Christ faith. Both his brother and his nephew deny in the strongest terms that he lost entirely his belief in God.[39] However, the evidence they present generally deals with the period after 1881. By this time Lloyd George had matured sufficiently to realize that whatever his personal feelings, institutional religion and its subsidiary operations such as temperance and

Church disestablishment, were powerful forces in Wales and anyone aspiring to any sort of public career had better come to terms with them.

What the evidence seems to point toward is a gradual diminution of David's unquestioning childhood religious conviction, all of which was a part of the general widening of his horizons that came with his move to Portmadoc. There was at the same time a very normal private adolescent search for principles that could constitute a personal scheme of ethics. But in the midst of all this, he continued regular church attendance and enjoyed it—indeed as he would do for most of the rest of his life. He was a connoisseur of church preaching and singing. Whether he believed in a transcendent divine force that directed men's lives, or a supreme judge who would order mercy or damnation on Doomsday, whether he ever prayed (unless someone happened to be watching), are questions which can never have proven answers. His letters to his wife, brother and uncle, all of whom retained strong sectarian religious ties, contained very little to suggest that the writer shared their belief. Even at the death of his beloved daughter, Mair Eluned, at the end of November 1907, which wounded him more than any personal tragedy in his life, Lloyd George seemed neither to have felt, nor sought, the comfort of genuine spiritual consolation.[40]

By the time he reached late adolescence, David Lloyd could not be described as a person of profound philosophic conviction on any matter. He had a few personal principles which were usually combined with contradictory prejudices. He loved the land, but hated landlords. He honestly believed that his task in life was to help the poor but his hatred of inherited wealth and influence, a passion that he carried to a point uncommon in one who manifested broad social sympathy, was more powerful. His personal code from very early in his life was puritan. He had nothing but contempt for the drunkard, the glutton, or the sluggard. But these attitudes were simply a reflection of his one basic principle, a belief in his own worth, to which was added a conviction that, if his ambition were to be satisfied, it would be as a result of his own efforts. These attitudes are neither an affirmation nor denial of religion. They are not agnostic, for there was little inquiry or reflection. He had never rejected belief. It had quietly slipped away as he had grown older. 'I know I have the religious temperament,' he told D.R. Daniel in August, 1910 as the two men roamed the fields between Llanystumdwy and Criccieth, 'but if an angel from Heaven came to demand it I could not write down what my religious convictions are.'[41] An interest in ceremonial forms remained, enjoyable and perhaps even comforting at times, but the substance withered. Lloyd George was simply a day to day philanthropic materialist whose conviction of his own destiny provided most of the ethical guidance he needed.

III

Lloyd George's active political life began with the election of 1880 when he was seventeen years old. Arguably it did not end until his death, 65 years later. Political education, on the other hand, had begun earlier. One of his first friends in Portmadoc, possibly asked to look after him by Richard Lloyd, was John Roberts, a candle maker whose shops furnished tapers for the Blaenau Ffestiniog quarries in Merionethshire. Roberts was a deacon and lay preacher in the Disciples of Christ chapel in Portmadoc, but he was also politically a radical republican. His influence on the intellectual and social development of his young friend in these critical years was as great as Randall Casson's for whose ideas, it has been suggested, Roberts's points of view constituted something of an antidote.[42] At Roberts's home David began to attend the Portmadoc debating society and there, some time evidently in the autumn of 1878, he made his first speech on public affairs, denouncing the Beaconsfield government for jingoism in the Eastern Mediterranean. In the next year he spoke several times, supporting a mild egalitarian republicanism and free trade while denouncing the aristocratic monopoly of the land.[43] His notes for these speeches reflect the thinking of his political mentor, John Roberts, but also demonstrate a more or less systematic beginning of the economic prejudices that he would hold throughout his life.

By the autumn of 1879, the Conservative government, formed in February, 1874, was in its sixth year. 1880 would surely see a general election. David Lloyd was concerned enough in August to order a thin pamphlet, 'Five Years of Tory Rule', which he found 'very damaging to the Tory Cause'.[44] A few weeks earlier, he had gone to hear his friend Mr. Breeze oppose a female speaker, 'Miss Becker' (evidently Lydia Becker, one of the founders of the Manchester Society for Woman's Suffrage) on the subject of the women's vote. Although he thought the woman spoke badly, he sympathized with her point of view to the extent of noting in his diary: 'I do not see why single women and widows managing property, should not have a voice in the adjustments, etc., of the taxes'.[45]

Despite the rising partisan interest stimulated by Gladstone's so-called Midlothian Campaign, which was in fact a series of speeches from Liverpool to Edinburgh in late November and early December, the election came as something of a surprise. Parliament had reconvened on 5 February 1880 but in the wake of encouraging by-election results Lord Beaconsfield ordered a dissolution on 8 March.

In North Wales the political balances had changed somewhat since the 'Great Election' of 1868. In Merioneth, David Williams, the victor over the Wynne family, had died after a year in the House of Commons, but in 1874 the county had remained staunchly Liberal under Samuel Holland. However in Caernarvonshire, George Douglas Pennant, the son of Lord Penrhyn, had returned to defeat Thomas Love Jones Parry in 1874. As a result in 1880 the constituency Liberals adopted Watkin Williams who had won Denbigh District for the party in 1868. A little more than a week after the dissolution David Lloyd, as well as other members of the firm of Breeze, Jones and Casson, was already devoting most of his time to the cause of Williams in south Caernarvonshire and of Holland in Merionethshire, both of whom were the responsibility of Mr. Breeze as election agent.

Tuesday, March 16, 1880
Fine. Watkin Williams here with 4:30 train. Splendid reception. He made a speech at Town Hall. Very good but nothing brilliant. A very good meeting throughout. Stephens' Commentaries a little in morning.

Wednesday, March 17
Dull. To Llandecwyn [Merionethshire] with Edwards canvassing. Know nothing of country. We would get more done than we might have done with more knowledge of country.

Thursday, March 18.
Very fine. Off with first train in morning. Canvassing all day. Very hurried. Home with last train. Out with Mary Lloyd.

Friday, March 19
Fine. With 11:30 train. Mr. Jones and self canvassing. Home with last train.

Saturday, March 20.
Very fine. Went with John Caerdyni [John Jones of Caerdyni a cousin] who was here, up to Prenteg to see someone about his vote.

Wednesday, March 24
Fine. Went to Talsarnau with a Methodist Minister. Some of the voters attended a committee at Penrhyn. Home with car. Mr. Casson, Edwards and others. Had supper. Edwards and I with Mr. Casson.

Thursday, March 25
Fine but cloudy. To Penrhyn sessions with 11:30 train. Nothing scarcely to do. Went up to Llanfrothen with Mr. Casson with the intention of canvassing but voters all in vestry.

Friday, March 26
Dull.   With my brother through morning. In Criccieth, p.m. with my sister and brother. Went to see proposed new house. To Caerdyni and Jenny came there. I went to Criccieth with John Caerdyni. Saw the girls afterwards. Was reserved with Jenny. I want to get rid of her. We are being talked about. Uncle knows it this long time!

Saturday, March 27
Fine. To Port with 8:20 train Douglas Pennant here. Almost insulting reception carrying effigy before him with red herrings in its mouth (it was two faced) and rabbit skins on its arms! To Criccieth in car with Davies, Police Station. Pennant was there. Meeting was mixed. Gwynfryn ladies there, but his reception not at all good. [Gwynfryn was the seat of the Squire of Criccieth, the local landowner Hugh John Ellis-Nanney]. Saw Jenny there—took scarcely any notice of her. Avoided her. Walked with uncle.

Monday, March 29
Fine. At Mr. Jones' request on Saturday with 8:30 train. Jenny here; avoided her. Mary Ellen and brother here in p.m. Went to cover. It costs me some trouble to get rid of that girl but in flirting with her I have everything to lose and nothing to win. This shall be regarded as proof of my pluck. If I cannot resist this, how do I expect to gain other things which require a good deal more determination. She attempted to tease me by flirting with others—bastards.

Thursday, April 1
News of first Liberal victories. Am glad. It is very likely that they will
carry everything before them now.

Wednesday, April 7
Weather fine. Polling in Merionethshire and news in p.m. that Watkin
Williams got in for Caernarvonshire. Scenes of wildest enthusiasm. Even
a butcher got hold of a donkey that was passing and shouted in its ears
that its brother had lost! Bonfires and fireballs, out till ten to twelve with
Mary Lloyd. The victory beyond the most sanguine expectations.
Figures, 3,303 Williams, 2,206 Pennant. A great blow to landlord
terrorism and quite a triumph for the ballot. [During the campaign,
Douglas Pennant had been required to vow that there would be no
evictions after the poll]. Stephens' Commentaries, few pages. News that
night Holland in for Merioneth, 800 majority. A good crowd here in the
night to celebrate return of Holland.[46]

As the diary entry suggests, these were busy weeks for David Lloyd
George. In addition to his political duties for Mr. Breeze, he was attempting
to study for the Law Society Intermediate Examination. Moreover, his
family was preparing to move to Criccieth and the surveillance of his
blooming social life by his uncle and sister had already begun to embarrass
him. Then on 1 October Edward Breeze, shooting pheasants, received a
bullet in the eye. For a time it appeared that he would recover. He returned
to the office in December and promised David that he would help to find a
firm to which William George could be articled.[47] But complications set in.
He went to London for treatment and died there on 10 March 1881. David
wept when he heard the news.[48]

Within a month after Mr. Breeze's accident, political warfare had
broken out again in Caernarvonshire. On 1 November 1880 Watkin
Williams gave up his seat to accept a judgeship and a second election
became necessary. On the same day that the vacancy was announced, David
made his first excursion into political journalism. After reading five pages
of Stephens' *Commentaries,* he composed a letter about the Marquess of
Salisbury, Foreign Secretary in the Beaconsfield Cabinet, and sent it with
some hesitation to the *North Wales Express* in Caernarvon. Contrary to his
expectations it appeared on 5 November.

The letter was a rather purple denunciation of the demoralization and
inconsistency of Her Majesty's late Principal Secretary of State for Foreign
Affairs. 'He is a relic of what has been, the ruins of a character which, if not
noble, at least seemed to be stable.' In his recent speech at Taunton, the
letter continued, Salisbury had charged the government with all the vices he
had himself practised while in office; having secretly mishandled British-
Turkish relations he now blamed the Liberals for clearing them up. After
preparing to take legal action against Irish leaders, he now attacked the
government for doing the same.

In past times, the letter concluded, the Tory party had stood forth as 'a
champion of weak nationalities in their desperate struggle for liberty—for
freedom from the yoke of inhuman despots—for very existence. By so
much was the Canning of ancient Toryism superior, nobler than the

Salisbury of modern Conservatism.' The young defender of liberty signed his letter 'Brutus'.[49]

The enthusiasm of the young Liberal publicist, already aroused by the success of his impeachment of Lord Salisbury and the coincidental announcement of the Caernarvonshire by-election, was further excited by the selection as Tory candidate of the Squire of Gwynfryn, Hugh John Ellis-Nanney, Justice of the Peace, owner of 12,000 acres in Caernarvon, Merioneth and Montgomeryshire, and patron of David's village school. Ellis-Nanney, who after living with sisters until middle age, had recently married, was a decently responsible landlord and despite the things Lloyd George would say of him in the next several decades, remained on fairly good terms with his tenants.[50] The fact that his father had been a member of Parliament for Caernarvonshire for two months in 1835, had been unseated on a petition and was never able again to win a seat, may account for this unforceful man's willingness to allow himself to be put forward, as he would again in 1885, 1890 and 1895.

The Liberal candidate was the far more formidable William Rathbone, a wealthy Liverpool merchant and social reformer, who had been MP for his native city since 1868. David was in Criccieth on Wednesday, 16 December, to meet Rathbone when he arrived for his first meeting. This time he was no longer canvassing but rather helping the disabled Mr. Breeze with candidates' arrangements. He escorted Rathbone from Criccieth to Portmadoc in the Morfa Lodge coach (Rathbone inside, David on top) and gave the considered judgement after the Portmadoc meeting that Rathbone was 'a very poor orator, but a sensible speaker.' At midnight he walked home from Portmadoc to Criccieth. 'No Stephens' Commentaries.'[51]

The day before the Criccieth meeting and three days after the two candidates published their election addresses, Brutus sent the *North Wales Express* a second letter addressed to Mr. Ellis-Nanney. The letter was a violent, indeed insulting, attack upon the innocent Conservative candidate, based on a number of rather foolish statements in his election manifesto. The letter is of interest first because the *Express* thought well enough of it to feature it in its broadsides, but more important, because the letter concluded with a presentation, for the first time, of the ordinary political line that Lloyd George would take during his early years as a Welsh nationalist: that such a gulf lay between the landowning Welsh squirearchy and the people that they did not and could not represent the nation. Indeed they were, as David termed Ellis-Nanney, in a phrase that the editor prudently deleted, 'vampires'. The Welsh people could be better served even by an Englishman.

'Race and Religion' were a potent cry, David noted significantly in his diary on 1 December when Rathbone was declared winner at Caernarvon, 3,080 to 2,051.[52] Meanwhile Brutus, in the city for the occasion, took the opportunity to visit the offices of the *North Wales Express,* whose editor encouraged him to send more contributions, an invitation upon which he would act many times in the years ahead.

After returning to Portmadoc, he took up again Stephens' *Commentaries* which had suffered in the last few weeks. Politics was hard work.

'Electioneering', he noted in his diary 'makes you neither a cool statesman nor a profound lawyer nor a more ardent religionist (!)'.[53]

IV

In later life Lloyd George maintained that he had his first thoughts of going to Westminster in 1886 after meeting the Irish Land Leaguer, Michael Davitt. This is the version in the early authorized biographies.[54] Nevertheless after the election of 1880, his public life had begun and he was taking steps to make himself known. What is clear from his journals is that ambition had taken hold. Where it would lead, he was not certain, but he felt a sense of destiny that would be realized if he were not undone by his own weakness. He wrote in his diary on 31 December 1880.

'The present year is flying to preterite eternity....' Ambition itself has had a greater sway in my thought than the means of gratification. To my lasting shame, be it said—love can fairly record me amongst its infatuated brained-skinned devotees. Stephens' Commentaries—my attention to this book might have been closer.[55]

Nine months later, on 19 September 1881, he pondered the news of the death after six months in office of the American President, James A. Garfield, a fellow member of the Disciples of Christ who had risen from humble beginnings to head what surely would have been a profoundly conservative Republican administration. Perhaps there was a parallel for his own future.

22 September 1881.
See by the Daily News of y'day that Europe echoes with the reports of his good deeds. There is not to be found one paper running him down. The feeling throughout both continents is intense— there never was anything similar. For myself, I could not feel so much for any public man. Such is the influence of a good man. Is there not a hint of success here? Can he not be emulated? It is worth trying, at any rate—the failure would not be ridiculous, because the intention would be too good to excite such commensuration.[56]

Early in November, he visited London for the first time to sit for the Intermediate Law Examination. While there he went to Westminster Palace, although unfortunately the House of Commons was in recess. 'Went to the Houses of Parliament,' he noted in his diary, '—very much disappointed with them. Grand building outside but inside they are crabbed, small and suffocating, especially the House of Commons. I will not say that I eyed the assembly in a spirit similar to that in which William the Conqueror eyed England on his visit to Edward the Confessor, the region of his future domain. Oh, vanity.'[57]

Between 1881 and 1885, Lloyd George, as he was now beginning to call himself, pursued what must be assumed to be a conscious and planned program of self-advertisement. Certainly he understood he would need local recognition after he began legal practice, but the areas of local controversy into which he chose to inject himself manifested larger goals. He never sought, as might have seemed prudent for one who hoped to invite the patronage of influential land owners and prosperous town merchants, to take positions of reasoned caution, to appear as a sound young man. Deliberately he looked for the radical fringe, which was well populated already by men whose views were bound to offend the county hierarchy upon whom a young lawyer might be presumed to depend for clients. Instinctively he appears to have been carving out for himself a political position which might help in the pursuit of public office but which could only hinder a legal career.

Lloyd George's first step was to gain membership to the Portmadoc Debating Society to which he was elected on 28 November 1881, presumably under the sponsorship of John Roberts, the candlemaker, in whose home the society frequently met. He had, of course, attended its meetings before and notes for speeches indicate that he addressed the group as well. This body and the Criccieth Debating Society, of which he later became a member and chairman, were useful platforms. His speeches were widely reported and, much to Lloyd George's satisfaction, usually approved.

Probably more important, the next year, in the summer of 1882, he took the Blue Ribbon Pledge (for abstention from alcohol) and joined the United Kingdom Alliance. He made his first address under this auspice before a temperance meeting in December, 1882 in Llanystumdwy. After some 'stammerings and stutterings' he felt he had done well and was gratified by praise from his uncle and his frequently censorious sister. After this, until 1886, he made many speeches on temperance, licensing and Sunday closing, throughout Caernarvon, Merioneth and Denbighshire, gathering thereby considerable local renown and, even more useful for the future, political acquaintanceships. At the same time, he began to preach with some regularity to Disciples of Christ congregations. His nephew W.R.P. George suggests that this activity began because with his Intermediate Law Examination behind him, Richard Lloyd had made clear that he expected his nephew to participate in the chapel services in Criccieth. Here, Lloyd George for a time was unwilling to more than read an occasional lesson. But he escaped the charge of worldliness by accompanying his friend and political mentor, John Roberts, also a lay preacher, to help conduct a mission the older man had begun in Penmachno about twenty miles northeast of Portmadoc on the Denbighshire border.[58]

This evangelical work occupied Lloyd George intermittently for several years. He took it seriously, eventually extending his range to other villages, and became widely known both for his preaching and for his interest in young women. His diary entries as late as 1885 show him giving lectures at Blaenau Ffestiniog.[59]

Probably it is not too much to say that after 1880 Lloyd George was continually campaigning, not entirely unconsciously, for the office that became his in 1890. He had been truly honest with himself, especially on his reasons for joining the temperance crusade in the summer of 1882, which paradoxically was during his service in the Volunteers at the time Randall Casson was introducing him to the pleasant English world of pub lunches. He noted in his diary:

It may give me somehow an opportunity of exercising, maybe displaying (!) my oratorical (?) powers sometime[60]

Hence, as he turned twenty, still an articled clerk, the boy from Llanystumdwy had become, at least throughout northern Wales, a public figure. His name was known, his characteristics were recognized. If he was not yet a politician, there were many who believed that at least he aspired to some sort of community leadership. During the summer of 1883 the *Caernarvon and Denbigh Herald* began to publish bits of poetry characterizing local celebrities and on 2 June Lloyd George was linked to a verse by Doctor Johnson:

When first the college rolls receive his name,
The young enthusiast quits his ease for fame,
Restless burns the fever of renown,
Caught from the strong contagion of the gown

This evoked a wry note in the subject's diary,

June 2 — tidbit of poetry...referring to my thirst for renown, etc. Perhaps (?) it will be gratified. I believe it depends entirely upon what forces of pluck and industry I can muster.[61]

The evolving political man seriously endangered the articled clerk for whom the family had made so many sacrifices. These were difficult times for Morvin House. William's articles, also to Mr. Casson, further depleted Betsy George's capital. David's continual speaking trips consumed both money and time.[62]

Except for an occasional odd job and boarders in the summer there was virtually no income and Richard Lloyd had to resort to borrowing. Even the money for the journeys to London for the Intermediate Law Society Examination in 1881 and the Final Examination in April 1884 had to be lent by William Williams, the co-pastor at the chapel, who was also a Criccieth draper and cousin of G. P. Williams, the landlord of Morvin House, who was himself from time to time also a family benefactor.[63] All of this was degrading to Lloyd George. He hated the admission of paying guests to Morvin House. He complained of leaky shoes. He was unable to afford a subscription to the local Law Library because he had spent the money intended for this purpose on a copy of Henry George's *Progress and Poverty*. Eventually a sum for this too had to be borrowed so that the young clerk could begin to cram for his final examination.

The competition between Henry George and the Law Library perfectly illustrated Lloyd George's dilemma at this time. Although his work for Randall Casson was perfectly satisfactory and his relationship with his principal had matured into a warm friendship, his formal studies languished under the pressure of other activities. Hence, through the winter of 1883-4 he struggled to make up for the lost time, studying late into the night, sleeping little and so working himself that he became sick.[64] He was still unwell and miserable as he left for London on April 19. When he arrived he felt so ill that he feared that he might not be able to take the Final Examination let alone the Honours Examination for which he was entered. However, he was encouraged by the simplicity of the early questions and sat for the Honours Examination. By the time this was complete Lloyd George was fully recovered and determined to spend several extra days in London. He visited C.H. Spurgeon's famous Metropolitan Tabernacle in South London and found him excellent, unlike other English preachers. 'A capital speaker I must say', Lloyd George recorded and, providing a small testimonial to the state of his religious beliefs by this time, observed, 'he was very inspiring—he almost galvanized my dead faith into something like a transient somnolence, if not life.'[65]

On 28 April he went to the House of Commons, this time in session, with a ticket obtained from the Caernarvonshire Member William Rathbone, and watched with delight, tempered by proper Liberal disapproval, an attack by Randolph Churchill upon Gladstone.

The report that he had passed the final examination arrived at Morvin House on 11 May and on 27 May the family heard that he had received third class honors. Early in July he was back in London to be sworn in as a solicitor and to sign the rolls at the Petty Bag Office. He was now a lawyer.

The question at hand was what to do. The middle eighties were hard times, particularly in agricultural areas. As Breeze, Jones and Casson was unable to collect many of its bills for legal services, prospects for a young and penniless solicitor, just beginning practice, were not encouraging. Consideration of these dismal facts had begun well before Lloyd George took his final examination. Eventually, for lack of a better alternative, Randall Casson and Robert Jones, the surviving partners, offered him a post as an Assistant Solicitor at one pound per week with a commission on new business brought into the office. Casson apologized for the small amount of the salary but Lloyd George, after considering the proposition for some time, took up his duties on 12 May, the day after he learned that he had passed his final examination.

The period from the spring of 1884 until at least the summer of 1885 may have been personally the most difficult months of Lloyd George's life. First of all, as an Assistant Solicitor at Breeze, Jones and Casson, the relationship with his former principal deteriorated from warm amicability to mutual and enduring hostility. The cause of this friction was probably suspicion on the part of Casson that Lloyd George was attempting to use his time with a well-known firm to build a clientele with which he could begin independent practice.[66]

Such things were not unprecedented in the legal fraternity. There were prospects that he might take charge of a branch in Criccieth or in Dolgellau, but the state of business or distrust of Lloyd George dictated otherwise. But there is evidently another side to the story. Justifiably Lloyd George was immensely proud of his new dignity as a solicitor. Now technically Casson's equal, he insisted upon forms of etiquette that Casson was unwilling to practise. Before Lloyd George had been two weeks in his new position, his brother William, who was now Casson's articled clerk, had recorded in his diary:

Skirmish between David and Mr. Casson. They are both too sensitive to live in peace together. David uneasy about the future.[67]

The unhappy situation at the law office affected William first of all, but

45

bothered the rest of the family as well. William was soon reduced to carrying messages between his brother and Casson, who could not, or would not, converse with each other. But meanwhile David's testiness was turned toward his family who were now suffering the worst of their chronically straitened fortunes. William records that in July his brother, by threatening to leave the house for good, had forced his mother to forego 25 shillings a week from a lady who wished to rent a room. This ultimatum was, in fact, withdrawn a few days later and lodgers were accepted after all, 'David having given his gracious consent', noted William.[68]

For William, the situation at the Portmadoc law office was little short of desperate. Caught between two jealous and vindictive personalities, owing loyalty to both, he endured both personal distress and interference with his legal training.[69] Most critical, he intended to take the Intermediate Law Society Examination himself in January 1885. In December, Randall Casson recognizing the situation, or taking pity, told him to leave the office altogether and go home to study. In addition, he offered financial help so that William could spend extra time in London after taking his examination.[70]

When William returned from London he discovered that his brother and Breeze, Jones and Casson had dissolved their relationship, on whose initiative is not clear, and that the new single-handed law firm of D. Lloyd George had opened an office in the back parlor of Morvin House in Criccieth at the beginning of 1885. However, this departure did not end the feud, for David began almost immediately to call upon William for help in his office. When he heard of this, Casson, naturally hot-tempered, swore to make things unpleasant for the new lawyer. The chief sufferer again was William whose conditions of service in Portmadoc became more difficult than ever. To all this, Lloyd George appears to have been entirely oblivious. His diary for the period shows absolutely no awareness of the cruel position in which he had put his brother. He nursed his own grudges against his former principal, swore vengeance against him, and pursued his career of self-advertisement. The truth was that in the early months of 1885 Lloyd George was not overloaded with legal work. But his time was occupied by temperance, missionary, and Portmadoc and Criccieth Debating Society speeches, to which he added in the spring the Liberation Society (for Church disestablishment). The law office did not need William, but Lloyd George's career did.

The new lawyer's broad acquaintanceship throughout North Wales paid an immediate and important dividend. On 3 January he received a letter from Dr. R.D. Evans of Blaenau Ffestiniog, whom Lloyd George already knew through temperance work, urging him to set up an office in the neighboring town of Ffestiniog. (Evans was the father of Thomas Carey Evans who would marry Lloyd George's second daughter, Olwen.) A Ffestiniog office opened inauspiciously on 24 January 1885—through eight hours 'not a soul called to see whether I was alive or dead'—but his base of operations provided contacts with advanced Merionethshire politicians which were of great significance for the future.[71]

Lloyd George received his first law case at the end of January, an assault charge which he had the good fortune to win because the plaintiff, who was supposed to be at work, falsified the hour of the attack.[72] After this, his work, which had been mostly debt collections, began to grow in quantity if not profitability. He made something of a specialty of defending poachers, partly because few established lawyers would take on these unremunerative cases, but also, it may be speculated, because their cause enlisted his social sympathy. These were not easy cases to try. Poaching was, and is, something of a special Welsh misdemeanor, almost a pastime, a way of showing one's contempt for legal authority, combining the elements of anti-Englishness and anti-officialdom.[73] But at the same time it aroused the prejudices of county magistrates in a way few other actions could do. Also it meant that he had to endure for a time the 'nasty, mean conduct' of Randall Casson, who customarily represented the landlords. Nevertheless at the end of his first week in county court, when Casson 'did his worst,' and Lloyd George had lost most of his cases, he felt, as he took the train to Ffestiniog, that he 'would make a tolerable advocate.'[74]

As the load of work grew during 1885, and the distractions of an impending general election diverted him, Lloyd George increased his demands upon his brother for help in his office and early in 1886 sought to have William transfer his articles to himself. 'I have more points of law to decide in a week than Breeze, Jones and Casson have in a year,' he noted in his diary in February 1886.[75] In fact, William, now studying for his examinations, was already working many hours at night for his brother and with Richard Lloyd as his assistant was handling the business side of the new law office, tasks which Lloyd George could not bring himself to address. Not surprisingly, Randall Casson refused to consider releasing William from his articles. But had he done so and allowed William to join his brother before he was fully qualified, it could well have meant the end of William's aspirations for a career as a solicitor. David remained unconcerned. As he would throughout his life, he was quite willing to allow the fire of his own ambition to consume others, not only without letting it burden his conscience, but in fact without noticing it.

In the end William kept his head, assisted his brother when he could, forfeited the innumerable advantages that David assured him would derive from the transfer, and passed his final examination with first class honors in April 1887. On 10 May he joined his brother in the firm with offices now moved to Criccieth High Street. (Eventually there was a branch in Portmadoc and offices or at least office hours at Pwllheli and Ffestiniog.) The two men made an excellent team. The firm of Lloyd George and George quickly prospered and provided the financial base, indeed for many years the sole support, of David Lloyd George's political career.

V

During the summer of 1884, while Lloyd George and Randall Casson pursued their grievances against each other in the law office at Portmadoc, the House of Commons was completing work on the Representation of the People Bill, usually known as the Third Reform Bill. In early July the House of Lords rejected the bill, making it known however that they would reconsider the matter if it were accompanied by a redistribution of seats. Accordingly, two measures, one for franchise reform and the other for redistribution, were reintroduced in the autumn session and became law in 1884 and 1885. Nowhere had the reform and redistribution acts greater impact than in Wales. In the United Kingdom as a whole the extension of household franchise to the counties added two million votes to an electorate of three million. But in Wales the electorate nearly tripled. The effects appeared not so much in the formal party balance. In 1880, after all, Wales and Monmouthshire had returned only four Conservatives as opposed to 29 Liberals. Rather they were evident in the deliberate combativeness and rebelliousness of the men who entered Parliament after the reform. The heroes of 1868, David Williams, Osborne Morgan, and Watkin Williams in the North, and Henry Richard in the South, were solid Gladstonian Liberals, who, except for their insistence on nonconformist rights, had little to distinguish them from other well-to-do members of their party and class. The ancient order of things in North Wales was not yet undone.[76] But after 1885 the character and personnel of the Welsh parliamentary delegation began to change. The new men, particularly in the North, were of more humble origin — 'cottage bred' men Lloyd George would style them — with more advanced programs. To the traditional concerns of the tithe and Sunday closing and disestablishment, they added a wide range of social and economic issues, tenant grievances, land reform and legislative recognition of the principality, all of which were promoted under the general umbrella of Welsh nationalism and always with the threat of a separate Welsh parliamentary party. (It must be noted that among the new Welsh nationalist MPs were also a number of wealthy industrialists from the South.)

It was Lloyd George's good fortune that the new era in Welsh politics evolved at precisely the time his own public life began. He did not invent the Welsh radical program, nor in fact make much of a contribution to its ideology, but in every way it suited his own personal attitudes and prejudices and the rhetoric of the countless speeches he had made since 1880. On the other hand, he carved a place for himself in Welsh radical politics entirely by his own efforts. He was not one of the Aberystwyth University College intellectuals who had studied since 1880 the success of the Irish party in the House of Commons or who saw in the national cultural revival of Hungary and Italy a pattern for Wales. Lloyd George's world was the temperance, the missionary and debating society platforms. His style until 1885 was generally that of Christian evangelicalism far more than of political reflection or disputation. Although he had worked enthusiastically for Mr. Breeze in the election of 1880, in no sense was he a member of the inner council of North Wales politics. His most influential friends were nonconformist divines such as A.J. Parry and Herber Evans, both of whom he met on a temperance circuit, whose political importance was indeed substantial, but who were hardly practising politicians.

Lloyd George's entrance into party politics came principally through three more or less intertwined organizations with which he became involved in 1885 and 1886. These were the Liberation Society, the Welsh Farmers' Union and the Anti-Tithe League. The importance of these societies for Lloyd George was that each included as a leading member Thomas Gee who by the eighties was a first rank Welsh public figure. Gee, born in 1815 of an English father, was a Denbigh publisher and ordained Methodist minister. He had used his newspaper *Baner ac Amserau Cymru* ('Banner and Times of Wales') to turn the election of 1868 into a referendum on the gentry and the Church. The Liberal victories in North Wales were testimony to the force of his agitation. Throughout the seventies his articles in the *Baner*, urging the Welsh to concentrate on their own affairs and to meditate on the differences between themselves and the English, were the most powerful literary expression of nationalism in North Wales.[77] Even so gentle a character as Richard Lloyd read the *Baner* carefully.

Of the three societies the largest was the Liberation Society. This was in no sense an exclusive Welsh organization. It had been founded in England in 1844 to promote Church disestablishment and became active in Wales only after 1862. (The Society lasted until the Second World War and occupied Lloyd George's attention well into the nineties when he served on its Executive.) For Gee the association with the Liberation Society was largely opportunistic even though he was for years the sole Welsh member of its Executive. He had, to be sure, always included the tithe as an item in his attacks on English influence and as early as 1854 allowed his goods to be seized and sold rather than pay the hated charge to the Church of England. But he had no concern for English, or indeed Irish, affairs. He was uninterested in Home Rule and for that matter cared nothing about the position of the Church outside Wales. Although of the greatest political influence in the last decades of the nineteenth century and a correspondent of nearly all important Liberal figures, he was a difficult colleague. Nevertheless Gee became Lloyd George's political mentor, supporting him during his campaign for the House of Commons and, afterwards, in his struggles with the senior members of the Liberal party. Much of Lloyd George's early political style, a narrow concentration on Welsh, rather than national, issues, his demagoguery and public demonstration rather than party accommodation and compromise, paralleled Gee's. 'I am one of his political children,' Lloyd George wrote Gee's daughter on her father's eightieth birthday in 1895.[78] 'He treated me always as a father would a child' he wrote to Margaret at the time of the old man's death.[79] And after Lloyd George became Chancellor of the Exchequer a picture of Gee hung on the wall of Number 11 Downing Street.

Lloyd George began to make speeches for the Liberation Society in March 1885 at the hectic time when he was trying to establish his law practice, as well as fighting with Randall Casson for the services of his brother, and addressing meetings nearly every night in the cause of evangelism or temperance. The advent of household franchise had convinced nonconformists everywhere that the next great reform would be disestablishment of the Church of England, while the news of the death of General Gordon in Khartoum in January had made clear Gladstone's government was doomed. An election was approaching and the Liberation Society was busy among prospective Liberal candidates.[80]

The force behind the rapid evolution of the political situation in Wales that grew from household franchise, was increased by the agricultural depression that struck all of Great Britain in the late seventies. It was especially severe in North Wales and gave to the old generalized cultural resentment against the landowner's alien ways and affiliation with the Church of England an immediate and intimate economic dimension. This was particularly expressed in a revived protest against Gee's old enemy, the tithe. Anti-tithe agitation had begun in 1883 and in the autumn of 1884. Gee gave the campaign national prominence by bringing the hero of nonconformity, Joseph Chamberlain, to Wales where he spoke in Newtown on 18 October and at Denbigh on 25 October. The day before the speech at Newtown, Lloyd George welcomed Chamberlain to Wales with an admiring article in the *North Wales Observer and Express,* which he concluded with a denunciation of the landlords in the style that would be the Lloyd George signature for many years to come.

> He is a radical and doesn't care who knows it as long as the people do.
> He is convinced that the aristocracy stands in the way of the development
> of the rights of man and he says so unflinchingly though he may be
> howled at as an ill-mannered demagogue by the whole kennelry of
> gorged aristocracy and of their fawning minions.

In a way the tithe bridged the gap between conventional Welsh nationalism and Church disestablishment, and agricultural tenants' grievances. Since the Tithe Commutation Act of 1836 the tithe had been legally an obligation of the landlord to the Church which the former collected as a rent charge. But Welsh landlords had evaded their responsibility for it by requiring entering tenants to assume the obligation themselves, in effect by contracting out. Its payment symbolized all the tribute, cultural, economic, and political, that the Welsh nonconformist had to pay to his English overlord. At the same time its forced collection, the distraint and auction of goods, showed local officialdom at its ham-fisted worst.

A specific economic, as opposed to religious, objection to the tithe was that while many landowners had lowered rents in the past years to reflect declining agricultural prices, tithe owners, most conspicuously the Ecclesiastical Commissioners and Christ Church College, Oxford had refused to do so.[81] Although protest had been building for several years, active resistance to payment and seizure of goods began only in 1886 with the disturbance at Llanarman in Denbighshire on 26 August when police had to be called in and were attacked by a crowd.[82] Thomas Gee entered the dispute immediately with the announcement over the signature of his son Howell of an organization for tithe resisters to be headed by himself and a Denbighshire farmer, John Parry, to be called the Farmers' Tithe Defence League.

The league was chiefly a money-raising and propaganda organization. It did not, Howell Gee insisted before John Bridges, a London police magistrate who was commissioned by the government to look into the matter, advocate violence.[83] Such violence as there was, attacks upon bailiffs during the distraint of goods, was confined almost entirely to Denbigh and Flintshire, although there were protests in nearly every county in Wales. Lloyd George became, or perhaps appointed himself, secretary of the South Caernarvonshire branch of the Anti-Tithe League. In this capacity he traveled energetically through the last months of 1886 and into 1887, denouncing tithe owners and landowners, intimidating Anglican clergymen, and publicizing himself.[84] Beriah Evans suggests that Lloyd George attempted to stimulate violence in Caernarvonshire. There are no reports that he was successful.[85]

The Tithe War, even though it was the most conspicuous element of the Welsh nationalist revolution of the eighties, was by no means the only focus of it. It was at bottom a convenient way of encouraging the Welsh to make trouble, of emphasizing the difference between Wales and England, and of embarrassing the English administration. Is not 'this tithe business,' Lloyd George observed cheerfully in a letter to Thomas Ellis in May 1887 when the worst violence was occurring, 'an excellent lever wherewith to raise the spirit of the people?'[86] But it was hardly a program and Gee had never intended to end his agitation there. The tithe revolt, as Gee put in a letter to John Bridges, was only a sign of English domination of Wales and agricultural distress was not the cause, but simply the occasion for trouble.[87] One contemporary commentator, R.E. Prothero, has suggested that Gee had raised the standard of the tithe revolt because the failure of agricultural agitation in the previous several years was causing the *Baner* to lose circulation. The tithe was chosen as the object of resistance because the vicars were more vulnerable than the landlords. Indeed suffering among isolated Church of England clergymen appears to have been considerable.[88] But such a neat explanation is not likely. Discontent about both the tithe and tenant conditions had begun together in the early eighties and continued to the end of the decade. Gee, indeed, had made a speech at Rhyl on 16 June 1886 proposing the establishment of a land league on the Irish model to gain for Wales land courts to enforce tenant rights. The tithe revolt began only two months later. In fact, the two causes from the beginning were virtually one and Lloyd George was involved in both.

At bottom, Welsh grievances, like Irish grievances, were cultural and economic far more than they were religious. The tithe and its larger expression, disestablishment, provided simply a convenient way of articulating a wide range of discontent. Disestablishment and disendowment of the Irish Church had not dampened nationalism in Ireland, nor indeed would it in Wales so long as the sense of separateness and economic discrimination remained. After he went to the House of Commons Lloyd George championed disestablishment as a contrivance to bring Welsh affairs to the attention of parliament but he never had more than the most formal interest in it. On the other hand, in land reform, first Welsh and later national, he found a lifelong cause. For him it was a real, as opposed to a symbolic, issue, something that would make a visible difference in the lives of his countrymen.

Farm tenant agitation, aiming at better terms for the holding of land and for the rebatement of rent, had begun with the depression of the early eighties, paralleling the anti-tithe agitation. It had in its background, however, not the old nationalist overtones of the tithe but the recent agonies of the evictions of 1868-9 and the still more recent example of the Irish Land Act of 1881. Lloyd George became involved through a law office client, J. A. Davies of Caertyddn who invited him to attend and address a meeting in Pwllheli of the Farmers' Union.[89] The date of the Farmers' Union meeting at Pwllheli is not clear but is of some importance. Almost certainly it was in 1885 because Lloyd George protested when invited that although interested in the farmers' movement, he was not a farmer and had never spoken in public before except to the Portmadoc Debating Society. He requested Mr. Davies to accompany him to the meeting because he was much too shy to attend an unfamiliar gathering alone. Even allowing for a certain amount of manufactured ingenuousness, this could hardly be the Lloyd George of 1886, the date that Mr. Davies recollected a quarter-century later, the Lloyd George who was the hammer of vicars and tithe owners. In support of the earlier year Mr. Davies points out that the case that had brought him to the Criccieth law office in the first place involved Lloyd George's first appearance in the county court at Pwllheli and the young solicitor's diary indicates that he appeared there at least as early as June, 1885 when Brynmor Jones presided for the first time.[90]

This date is worth establishing in order to uncover first of all a beginning for Lloyd George's long association with land reform and to find the sequence of events at a time of his life in which much was unclear. But it is also important for the fact that if the Pwllheli meeting occurred in June, 1885 it preceded Gee's call for a land league but promoted nevertheless another tie to the Denbigh agitator which drew Lloyd George still further from the main body of Welsh Liberalism. Finally, the most significant result of the involvement with the Farmers' Union and land reform was Lloyd George's meeting with Michael Davitt and Michael Daniel Jones of Bala, from which event, he always said later, sprang the conviction that the time had come for him to get into parliament.

The meeting with Davitt on 12 February 1886 has been chronicled by most of Lloyd George's biographers, but it needs to be put into context. Davitt, the organizer of the Irish Land League, a supporter of land nationalization, the sponsor of agrarian violence in Ireland, who had spent two terms in jail, was to say the least a controversial man in peaceful North Wales. No one of less stature than Michael Daniel Jones, a leader of Welsh agitation of the eminence of Gee, would have dared to invite him. But it should be remembered also that less than two months earlier Gladstone had announced his conversion to Home Rule. There were, to be sure, many in Wales who cared nothing for the papist Irish, but who understood that the great constitutional struggle over Ireland would preempt for years any parliamentary consideration of Welsh discontents. And there were some who believed, more importantly, that the Irish example of agrarian violence was the only means to success. Here, certainly, must be the strategic beginning of Welsh tithe and land resistance. If so, by supporting a vote of thanks for Davitt, possibly after more prudent public men had declined, Lloyd George was making clear a point of view on the tactics of Welsh struggle.

Yet to take this side was perfectly consistent with all that he had done in the past, with the character of his practice as a lawyer, with his thoughts about politics, and most of all, of his reflections on the recent General Election. The 1885 election from which Wales had expected so much, had come to a disappointing and inconclusive end in mid-December. Lloyd George had participated actively as usual. Although involved with no particular candidate, he spoke at Liberal meetings throughout Caernarvon and Merionethshire. He attended also the Conservative meetings of Edmund Swetenham, the Tory candidate for Caernarvon District, and the meetings of his old enemy Hugh Ellis-Nanney, in the new 'Eifion' or south division of Caernarvonshire, principally to heckle. He served as a Liberal poll watcher and was threatened with violence during the last days.

When the North Welsh returns were in on 4 December, he found only discontent and disillusion. Gladstone's majority in the House of Commons had disappeared and although the Liberals won all but three seats in Wales, margins were down. 'Feel weary, sleepy and utterly down today', he complained to his diary. 'Great Liberal victories in the counties. Very glad of it. Am convinced that this is all due to Chamberlain's speeches. Gladstone had no programme that would draw at all. The people do not understand what entail, etc. mean.'[91] A week before on 26 November when the extent of his party's losses in the boroughs was becoming clear he had recorded a sentence that was probably Lloyd George's nearest approach to a philosophy of political action: 'Humdrum Liberalism won't win elections.'[92] Here is the Lloyd George of the People's Budget, National Insurance or the Land Campaign, the Welsh magician with the new programs, the new angles, the ideas for changing the world. The Third Reform Bill had changed the basis of politics. It was not party leaders who counted any longer. It was the voter, and Joseph Chamberlain had shown how reckless, uncompromising innovation could inspire the electorate.

Thus, a few days after he addressed 150 people promoting a Farmers' Union in the Liberal Club at Criccieth, Lloyd George readily accepted an invitation from his old friend, R.D. Evans of Blaenau Ffestiniog, to hear Michael Davitt who was trying to organize a Land League for Wales. In addition, Evans asked Lloyd George to speak and to spend the night at his house. When Lloyd George arrived on 12 February he was unprepared and was, he said, 'gnawing his fingers,' having spent his time playing draughts instead of preparing a speech. Accordingly, when he found the hall packed, he was appalled, and when the chairman, Michael Daniel Jones, announced him as a speaker, he felt, for a time, he would have to refuse. However, with a few notes, he was able to make a resounding oration seconding the vote of thanks to Davitt.[93]

He began with a reference to the two Michaels on the platform, noting that while the Archangel Michael had been unable to dispose of Satan, two Michaels might be able to subdue the devil of aristocratic landlordism. Most of the rest of the address was a call for farmers to stop voting for their enemy who enslaved them and to reject the aristocracy who were 'squandering money earned by the sweat of the working man's brow.' All that was needed now was organization. This a land league could give them.[94] The address, although short and aimed principally at the promotion of a farmers' union, rather than at land nationalization which was Davitt's and Michael Jones's interest, made a tremendous impression, was widely reported, and appears to have satisfied Lloyd George himself. After the meeting the two Michaels and Lloyd George ate dinner at Evans's house where he was applauded by all, including Davitt who had not understood a word because Lloyd George had spoken in Welsh. Lloyd George was enchanted. 'My speech gone like wildfire through Ffestiniog,' he wrote in his diary, '—they're going to make me an M.P. Michael Jones for it. Long talk with him, Pan Jones [the Rev. Evan (Pan) Jones of Flintshire, a land reformer. Not to be confused with the Rev. Evan Jones of Caernarvon] and Mr. Davitt at the L. and N.W. Railway Hotel—scheming future of agitation—I feel I am in it now.'[95]

Afire with eagerness Lloyd George began almost immediately to canvass his chances for adoption in Caernarvon District, a single constituency made up of the six largest towns in Caernarvonshire of which Criccieth and Pwllheli were two. The sitting member was Thomas Love Jones Parry, the Caernarvon county victor of 1868, for whom the five year old Davy Lloyd had carried a banner and for whom he had again worked the previous December. But Jones Parry's margin in 1885 had been only 65 votes and his great wealth, aristocratic pretensions, and dubious allegiance to Gladstone had made him unpopular with the sober clergymen, business and professional men who dominated the district's Liberal associations.

Unfortunately, neither was Lloyd George's loyalty to Gladstone above suspicion. At the end of March Chamberlain had resigned, or had been driven, from Gladstone's cabinet after being unable to weaken the proposed terms of the coming Home Rule Bill. For Lloyd George and for many Welsh Liberals this caused a crisis. Chamberlain was the nonconformist hero, the apostle of land reform, and the only front bench English politician interested in helping Wales. Either from personal conviction, or the influence of Gee, or both, Lloyd George's faith in Chamberlain seems to have been unquestioning. (Gee's paper supported the Liberal Unionist candidate, Colonel William Cornwallis West in West Denbighshire in 1886.) But through April as he attended meetings of county Liberals discussing questions of Gladstone versus Chamberlain, while trying at the same time to interest his colleagues in his own candidacy, Lloyd George found his attacks on Home Rule largely unsupported and his personal position weak.[96] Richard Lloyd, himself a Home Rule supporter, recorded in his diary in June: 'G.P.W. [G. P. Williams, cousin of the Morvin House landlord, a Beriah Chapel deacon, and one of Lloyd George's staunchest early supporters in Criccieth] told me this morning that D.Ll.G. must be careful or he would be accused of being against the party.'[97] (As it turned out, Caernarvon District adopted Jones Parry again. He was defeated by Edmund Swetenham on 7 July, but by a margin of only 134 votes.)

The muted enthusiasm for his candidacy encountered in his rather tentative inquiries in his home constituency turned Lloyd George's interest to Merionethshire. In Merionethshire he was in some ways more widely known than in Caernarvonshire and, with a solid corps of radicals in the Ffestiniog quarrymen, in a more congenial political atmosphere. Some friends in Harlech asked permission to propose his nomination despite his professed Chamberlainite connections. He consented and so together with three other men, Morgan Lloyd, Robert Flint and Thomas Ellis, his name was submitted for adoption.

The coming man in Merionethshire was Thomas Ellis. He was four years older than Lloyd George. His father was a tenant farmer of Cynlas who had seen four relatives evicted in 1859, and he spoke Welsh. But there the similarity with Lloyd George ended. Ellis was a Calvinistic Methodist, had attended Michael D. Jones's grammar school in Bala, the University College of Aberystwyth, and New College, Oxford. He had been drawn into the political world soon after leaving Oxford in 1884 by working as secretary for John Brunner, industrialist and Member of Parliament for Northwich. His ideas of nationalism derived from the study of Mazzini. He was, to be sure, an admirer of the Chamberlain program but deplored the violence of its presentation. Similarly, he disliked the influence of chapels in politics, the 'chapel screw' as it was called, and was a staunch Home Ruler. His clothes and manners were of Oxford and London. He was polished, graceful, attractive, of sterling character, a romantic in politics, a Welsh Essene. In virtually every way he was a contrast to Lloyd George.[98]

With the backing of Michael Daniel Jones and the Ffestiniog quarrymen, Ellis was clearly a stronger candidate for the nomination than Lloyd George even though there were some who mistrusted him as another Anglicized Welshman, a lost son.[99] But Ellis had a problem of financial support. Lloyd George had evidently allowed himself to be put forward in the contingency that Ellis could not find the necessary funds. But almost immediately he had doubts.

> When alone and calculating the possible consequences and ways and means, I regretted my temerity, but have found way of getting the cash as I think—by getting friends to guarantee fund in Bank—but I would not be in nearly as good a position as regards pecuniary—oratorical or intellectual capacity to go to Parliament now as in say 5 years hence. Now I would put myself in endless pecuniary difficulties—an object of contempt in a House of snobs. Besides, I am not yet as thoroughly established in judgement as I ought to be.[100]

Lloyd George wrote this on 20 June 1886. He had met Ellis for the first time about two weeks before at a temperance meeting in Blaenau Ffestiniog, not, as he usually claimed after Ellis's death, at the meeting with Michael Davitt.[101] Lloyd George had spoken and Ellis, afterwards, had congratulated him.

The state of Lloyd George's own candidacy at this time is not clear although an election was imminent. The second reading of the Home Rule Bill had been defeated on 7 June (22 Welsh Liberals voted for it and 7 against). Gladstone had announced a dissolution and all parties were scrambling to adopt candidates. In any case Lloyd George wrote to his new friend immediately, saying that he had just had a letter from supporters of Morgan Lloyd (a Chamberlainite who had been badly defeated standing as an independent Liberal in December 1885 in Harlech) who wanted Lloyd George to propose Lloyd at Blaenau next Tuesday, but he had put them off until he knew what Ellis intended. He thought Ellis the best candidate and offered Ellis his support 'to rescue Wales from the grip of respectable dummyism.'[102] Even with the support of Michael Jones and the quarrymen, Ellis's nomination was by no means assured. Morgan Lloyd was a respected figure, who although opposed to Home Rule, had commanded the quarrymen's support against the official, non-Welsh, Liberal candidate in the previous election. (The winner in 1885, Henry Robertson, a Scot, had resigned as a Liberal in protest against Home Rule.) In the end, Ellis defeated Lloyd for the Liberal nomination, 91 to 82, and went on to win the election easily.

The election of Ellis in July, 1886 against the trend elsewhere, and the relative stability of the Liberal delegation from Wales in the face of a Liberal disaster throughout the rest of the nation, confirmed the Welsh radical revival. The swing against the Liberals in Wales was only 1.9% as opposed to 5.7% for Great Britain as a whole.[103] Although Ellis was not an insurgent in politics as Lloyd George would be—rebels are not the stuff of which whips are made—he was an honest Welsh nationalist and a son of the soil, even if educated in Oxford. Neither a landowner nor a wealthy professional man, he had defeated not only the Tories, but the very conservative Liberal establishment in North Wales. As if in response to the altered tone in Welsh politics, the North Wales Liberal Federation was founded at Rhyl on 14 December 1886 and adopted, as its initial platform, disestablishment of the Welsh church with endowments to be appropriated to Welsh matters, fair rents set by land courts, long leases, and the sale of improvements for agricultural tenants. In addition there appeared a resolution that 'for the sake of the efficiency of the imperial Parliament' the 'principle of National self-government' should be applied to Wales. This was introduced, although the meeting adjourned without ever voting on it.[104]

Lloyd George was never really a contender for the Liberal nomination in Merionethshire, even though in the first flush of enthusiasm after the encouragement from Davitt and Michael Jones, he had briefly thought he was. If Merioneth had desired a Chamberlainite it would have been Morgan Lloyd. However, many of his biographers take seriously the possibility that he might have entered the House of Commons as a Liberal Unionist, so altering the course of twentieth century politics. As a matter for philosophical speculation such a prospect is interesting. But for Lloyd George the more important aspect of the events surrounding the 1886 election was the establishment of his own views on Irish Home Rule. There is no evidence that except for the removal of the disturbing element in the House of Commons, he ever cared whether Ireland had self-government or not. He claimed later that he had always felt, as did many others, that the Welsh Liberals, by accepting the Gladstonian commitment to Irish Home Rule without protest, had put off indefinitely a consideration of their own national grievances.

As with most things Lloyd George's attitude toward Ireland was entirely pragmatic. However, a proposal in which he was uninterested might still be enlisted to help one for which he cared. If the cry for Irish rights could be made to include Welsh rights, he would support it. And so his usual answer to questions on Home Rule was Chamberlain's, that he was in favor of 'Home Rule all round.' An assembly for the principality, he always made clear, would make easier the solution of other Welsh problems, land reform and disestablishment, which were always lost in the huge British political world.

VI

After the 1886 election Lloyd George returned to Criccieth, to temperance speaking, and took up seriously land and tithe agitation—by 1887 the two counted virtually as one movement—and in May 1888 entertained the eminent Thomas Gee in Criccieth as a speaker for Gee's newly organized Welsh Land League.[105] By this time, however, he was beginning to withdraw from public participation in the land league although he kept up his friendship with Gee and helped in organization throughout the summer.[106] Six months before, in September, 1887, he had been approached about putting himself forward in the competit   n for t e Liberal nomination for Caernarvon District. He found this 'an interesting proposal', but in contrast to the feckless enthusiasm with which he had pursued the nomination for Caernarvonshire the year before, this time he soberly calculated what he would have to do. Probably, he recorded in his diary, there would not be an election for three years.

> There are two or three impressions I must be careful to make in the meantime. 1st and foremost that I am a good speaker. 2ndly that I am a sound and thorough politician. 3rdly that I can afford to attend to parliamentary duties. To succeed in the first I must avail myself of every opportunity to speak in public so as to perfect myself & attain some reputation as a speaker. To succeed in the 2nd point I must put into those speeches good sound matter well-arranged so as to catch the ear of the intelligent who always lead & gain the name of the sound as well as fluent speaker. I must also write political articles on Welsh politics so as to show my mastery of them. To attain the 3rd reputation I must (1) attend to my business well so as to build up a good practice (2) practise economy so as to accumulate some matter of wealth (3) get all my cases well advertised (4) subscribe judiciously.[107]

By December, he had begun to consult with political friends, David R. Daniel and Ellis, about strategy.[108] He had met Daniel the previous summer in Portmadoc. Daniel, a friend of Tom Ellis since boyhood, was a little suspicious of him as he was known locally as having been a staunch supporter of Morgan Lloyd.[109] In October he saw Daniel again and won his support. Daniel's description of Lloyd George in a letter to Ellis of 22 October 1887, may be worth recording. 'Lloyd George of Criccieth was here to tea with us yesterday,' he wrote. 'I met him once before. I think him a very pleasant young man, clever in his work as a solicitor and becoming fast a power among the radicals of Lleyn. Just the man to fight the beefy parsons of these parts. [The previous June, Lloyd George standing, as he recorded in his diary, upon a beer barrel, had verbally thrashed the curate of Sarn in the Lleyn for suggesting that the clergy were suffering because of widespread refusal to pay the tithe. The debate had been printed in the press and was widely discussed.][110] We had an interesting chat on the questions of the day. I understand you and he are very friendly'.[111]

Daniel was by profession a journalist and was working at this time for the United Kingdom Alliance. He had strong radical sympathies, was a fine writer, and would be a warm backer of Lloyd George the politician until 1915 when Lloyd George became a supporter of conscription.

The beginning of his campaign for the Liberal nomination in Caernarvon District opened a new phase of Lloyd George's career. In May, 1887 William George had joined the law firm and the two began to build a flourishing practice. As a result the weight of poverty that had burdened so many earlier decisions began to lift, although there were debts to Richard Lloyd to pay. In January, 1888, he founded with the help of Daniel and a few others, but doing most of the work himself, a Welsh language newspaper *Udgorn Rhyddid* ('Trumpet of Freedom') to comment on Welsh affairs. It was to be 'altogether Nationalist and Socialist, a regenerator in every respect,' he stated in a form letter soliciting supporters.[112] The short twelve-month life of this venture began on 18 January 1888. *Udgorn Rhyddid* had little impact and within a month Lloyd George was discouraged with it although he remained active in its management.[113] Meanwhile he pursued the Liberal nomination with quiet determination through letters to the press by himself and friends and by carefully choosing chapel appearances, especially before congregations where an influential Liberal happened to be deacon. His particular advantages now were the well-established acquaintanceship on the temperance circuit and his own reputation as a temperance speaker. Attacks on the liquor trade in a political world where nonconformity and temperance were practically synonymous with Liberalism were not only conventional but required. On the other hand, in his many letters to the leaders of borough Liberal associations, land reform and disestablishment, let alone Home Rule, were rarely mentioned.[114] He was, he always said, invoking the most important political figure he knew, 'a Liberal of the Ellis type.'

By July, 1888, he had succeeded in gaining the support of the Liberal associations within the three southern towns of the constituency, Criccieth, Pwllheli and Nevin. The northern towns, more English-oriented, Caernarvon, Bangor and Conway, were a problem and were dangerous because each of the former two had about three times as many electors as all the southern towns together. He needed much help, he wrote to D.R. Daniel.

> You have heard that the Caernarvonshire boroughs have taken up my candidature.... spontaneous combustion...at the meeting of the Pwllheli Liberal Association... the only dissident vote was our mutual friend D.D.D. he felt that forsooth I was too extreme and addicted to socialistic views.... Humphreys Owen was rejected with scorn....I shall be the Nationalist candidate for the boroughs. Now you have done your part in urging me onto this...are you prepared to help me in the drag after helping me into it?

Could Daniel get his friends, such as Michael Daniel Jones, to help? Would Daniel write a 'spirited letter' to a Caernarvon paper describing Lloyd George as a Welsh Nationalist of the Ellis type?[115] Daniel's letter appeared in the *Carnarvon Herald* on 10 July. In writing to thank Daniel Lloyd George was as usual most optimistic. Everything was set. Caernarvon would support him with a large majority. 'Bangor will follow the same good example.'[116]

In fact he was receiving gloomy reports from supporters questioning whether the more conservative north, particularly Bangor, would ever consent to the nomination of an advanced radical who might even be a socialist.[117] But paradoxically, there was in his favor the fact that Caernarvon District was a difficult constituency. Geography prevented the formation of a homogeneous, or even a unified, Liberal organization. The result had usually been the nomination of a well-to-do nondescript such as W. Bulkeley-Hughes, who had held the district almost without interruption from 1837 until his death in 1882, successively as a Conservative, Liberal, and Liberal-Conservative, or the unstable T.L. Jones Parry. 'No Welsh constituency,' said the *Liverpool Mercury* on 13 July 1888, 'seems to have greater difficulty in finding a suitable candidate than Caernarvon Borough and no constituency is so apathetic in the face of difficulty.' He had heard that Lloyd George, the writer continued, was a 'sound politician and able speaker and popular in South Caernarvonshire.' Whether he would commend himself in the north was more doubtful.[118] The fact was of course that Lloyd George's youthful energy and radicalism were precisely what the constituents needed. He represented the new politics of Wales which so far had not touched Caernarvon District and which had left it the only uncertain Liberal constituency in the north. Lloyd George understood this well. 'I could see for myself,' he wrote on 24 August after being adopted unanimously by the Liberal Association in the English-speaking cathedral city of Bangor, 'that I was the popular candidate despite all the machinations of my enemies. I will succeed. I am now sailing before the wind and they against it.'[119]

Nevertheless there remained the towns of Caernarvon and Conway with their ancient traditions and English influence. Into the autumn these two associations held out against him and when the Caernarvon District Liberal Association met in October a decision was postponed.[120] He received support from the Reverend Herber Evans of Caernarvon, one of the most influential nonconformist ministers in Wales, who himself had been offered the nomination and had declined. But the critical event in his quest for the nomination was his victory in the Llanfrothen, Merionethshire burial case.

The Llanfrothen action resulted from the incredible bigotry of the local rector, Richard Jones, who refused to sanction the dying request of an old quarryman, Robert Roberts, that he be buried beside his daughter in the local churchyard with services conducted in the Methodist form. The precise part of the churchyard in question was a recent gift to the parish which had been made without deed in 1864. The acceptance of the gift had been noted in the parish record, however, and a wall had been built in 1869 enclosing the new land. In 1880, parliament passed the Burials Act, usually named the Osborne Morgan Act after Gladstone's Solicitor General who had sponsored it, permitting nonconformists to be buried in parish churchyards using their own rites. To the rector the act was blasphemy although he could not avoid its requirements for the old part of the churchyard, which was in any case full. But the fact that the conveyance of 1864 had not been recorded, except by the parish itself, provided a loophole for the new part. Therefore, in 1881, after Robert Roberts's daughter had been buried under the provisions of the Burials Act, he persuaded the donor of the 1864 gift, a Mrs. Owen, to remake her grant, this time conditionally, under a trust deed with himself as trustee. The terms of the trust specified that only the Anglican service could be used in the burial and as Mrs. Owen remained technically the owner of the land, the Burials Act did not apply.

Accordingly, in the spring of 1888 when Mr. Roberts's brother, Evan Roberts, asked the rector to use the graveyard for a service to be read by a nonconformist minister, he was refused. Evan Roberts then sought advice from Lloyd George who told him to break down the gate barring the entrance to the new churchyard and conduct his burial. This Evan Roberts did on 27 April. Immediately Richard Jones brought an action for trespass against Roberts and the rest of the burial party which was heard on 16 May in Portmadoc County Court before Judge John Bishop.

The facts of the case were not in dispute. The question at issue was the ownership of the new plot. If it was part of the Llanfrothen churchyard, or, in effect, if it had been accepted as such for the twelve years required by the Statute of Limitations, the rector, under the Burials Act, had no right to exclude the Roberts burial party and there had been no trespass. If, on the other hand, there had been no gift in 1864, and since 1881 only a conditional gift, the new plot still belonged to Mrs. Owen as a private burial ground for which the rector was simply the trustee and within which she could impose whatever liturgical requirements she liked. Lloyd George, who had appeared before Judge Bishop on other occasions and found him 'dreamy, slow, & lacking in perspicacity,' asked for a jury trial.[121] The jury found the conveyance of 1864 good and that the new plot had been occupied and accepted by the parishioners as a burial ground ever since. Mrs. Owen, therefore, had no right in 1881 to set new stipulations for the use of the land that she no longer owned. After receiving the verdict, Judge Bishop reserved judgement and adjourned the case for two months. When he announced his findings on 25 July Lloyd George discovered that the judge had wrongly recorded the jury's decision and intended to award damages to the plaintiffs and costs to Mr. Roberts. In his favor, it would appear that Judge Bishop's error was the result of incompetence rather than bias in favor of the Church of England; however he refused to amend his notes even when Lloyd George produced the written verdict of the jury and announced he wished to appeal. In the appeal, heard on 14 December in London, armed with the jury's written findings and with William George's shorthand transcription of the entire hearing, Lloyd George secured a reversal and a threat by Lord Chief Justice Coleridge to bring Judge Bishop's conduct to the attention of the Lord Chancellor.

As it turned out, the Reverend Richard Jones was promoted to a better living and Judge John Bishop remained on the County Bench until 1910, three years before his death. But for Lloyd George, the Llanfrothen Burial Case was a widely reported triumph and an almost unbelievable piece of luck. He always professed to believe that it was the burial case that brought him nomination in Caernarvon District.[122] The victory over a bigoted rector and a stupid judge by a young Welsh lawyer in the name of justice for nonconformity contained all the elements of heroic folk mythology. Lloyd George was famous throughout North Wales. On 3 January 1889, two weeks after the victory was announced, at the annual meeting of the Caernarvon District Liberal Association he was adopted, amid cheering, as the constituency's Liberal candidate.[123]

VII

In the crowded year when Lloyd George moved from the position of a reckless enthusiast of Welsh populism to being the accepted, if controversial, champion of the Liberal party of Caernarvon District, while also establishing himself solidly as one of the more gifted courtroom advocates in North Wales, he married. Lloyd George's relations with women, a mutual fascination which lasted throughout his adult life, have equally fascinated most of his biographers. Yet for his political career they are extraneous. This is simply a fact of Lloyd George's character. His concentration on himself, his will to succeed, precluded any lasting attachment to women, or for that matter to male friends who were not useful to him. Even though, within the terms of North Wales, it was an advantageous match, his wife, Margaret Owen, meant nothing in his life similar, for instance, to what Margot Tennant symbolized in Asquith's or Charlotte Bruce in Campbell-Bannerman's. He had no interest in London political society in which a wife could be a help, and consistently refused invitations to London and country houses. To be sure, as long as he was in office, he enjoyed inviting political cronies to Criccieth, but there he was the center of attention. His wife was little more than a housekeeper even though in a very real sense the house in Wales was her home, not his. He demanded a great deal of his wife, but gave little of himself.

Withal, Lloyd George certainly loved his family and doted particularly on his youngest and eldest daughters. But he did not value domesticity, or rather he equated domesticity and personal convenience. The house in Criccieth, like travel, indeed like women in general, was for relaxation. He enjoyed female company, as do many public figures whose business and battles are chiefly with men, and probably preferred it to male company. But this portion of his life was separate. With women he was charming, gentle and funny, but twenty-four hours a day he was a politician. The many women who were in his life were not a part of it.

As his diary suggests, by the age of 15 he was finding the Criccieth and Portmadoc girls both a temptation and a burden. That he, slim and handsome with black hair and blue eyes, was evidently attractive to girls was pleasing. Less pleasing was the realization that he was likewise attracted to them. They demanded time and money, and of both these he had very little to give. The sermons on self-improvement that he regularly inscribed in his diary show that he understood very quickly that a preoccupation with girls would harm his reputation in the village and divert his attention from more important matters. Continually, he urged himself to give up girls altogether. 'This I know', he wrote on 17 June 1880 after a solemn reprimand from his sister, Mary Ellen, for flirting,

> that the realization of my prospects, my dreams, my longings for success are very scant indeed, unless I am determined to give up what without mistake are the germs of a 'fast life'.... What is life good for unless some success, some reputable notoriety be attained — the idea of living merely for the sake of living is almost unbearable — it is unworthy of such a superior being as man.[124]

Lloyd George's evangelical work for John Roberts in 1882, when he was 19, brought him into contact with a young lady whom his nephew believed was the first love of his life, a Miss Jones of Penmachno. This affair lasted well over a year. Miss Jones ended it, so Lloyd George understood, because someone had told her that he was a notorious flirt and was in fact having a simultaneous affair with another girl.[125] Although Lloyd George had recorded in his diary that the rival to Miss Jones of Penmachno was supposed to live in Portmadoc, in fact at about this time, the summer of 1883, he was becoming hopelessly and miserably infatuated with another Miss Jones, Miss Elizabeth Jones, of Criccieth. Dark-haired, dark-eyed Lizzie Jones drove him to despair. The loss of control over his feelings was an agony. 'In earnest, I do not know what to do with the girl', he wrote on 25 November 1883. 'I wish to God I had never meddled with her, but I am afraid it is too late now. She has acquired a wonderful mastery over my idiot heart.'

'What anguish it would have saved me if I would have known in time', he recorded a week later, on 2 December 1883 when Lizzie, who was a singer, broke an engagement without an explanation. 'Let every young man be wary in time of falling in love. It is replete with peril.'[126]

By spring 1884, it was clear that Miss Jones was about to marry someone else and though Lloyd George accepted the news philosophically, reflecting that at least he would not have to pay for voice lessons, his pain lasted for months, becoming particularly acute when she, a Baptist also, appeared at chapel.[127]

> I wish to God she would keep away altogether. I might feel it keenly, perhaps for a while, but I'd sooner get it over by not seeing her at all, than by being compelled, as I am now, to see and hear her voice twice a week.[128]

In the same month, June 1884, as he struggled to regain his emotional independence of Elizabeth Jones, he met Margaret Owen. 'A sensible girl without any fuss or affectation about her', he recorded. She was a sharp contrast to the exotic Liza Jones. In 1884, she was eighteen years old, by no means beautiful with bad teeth, already slightly plump, pleasant, humorous, but with a stubborn mind of her own.

Although he saw her again that summer and the next, indeed on one occasion escorting her part way home after a Criccieth Debating Society party and on another spending most of a boating picnic excursion in her company, he did not pursue the acquaintanceship until late in 1885. By this time he had discovered that he was by no means the sort of man that Maggie Owen's parents wished to see as their only daughter's companion, even temporarily.

Richard and Mary Owen of Mynydd Ednyfed Farm were distinctly people of substance and standing, verging on gentility. Mr. Owen tilled over 100 acres, possessed local investments, was much in demand as a land valuer, and served as a deacon in Capel Mawr, the Criccieth Calvinistic Methodist Church. Margaret had been carefully educated in an English language girls' school in Dolgellau, as was suitable for her parents' prosperity. Whether they objected to Lloyd George because of his poverty, his connection with unfashionable Free Baptists, his radical opinions, his reputation as a ladies' man, or a combination of all these is uncertain. But he was not welcome at Mynydd Ednyfed and was forced to resort to ambushing Maggie Owen on her way to and from chapel, to communicating with her through letters carried by a conspiratorial Owen serving girl, and to arranging furtive meetings on neutral ground. When one considers that the last months of 1885 and 1886 were also the period of two general elections in which he was very active, of his meeting with Michael Davitt and of his subsequent unsuccessful attempt to capture the Liberal nomination either in South Caernarvonshire or in Merionethshire, and of his greatest involvement in the tithe war and the Farmers' Union, while he was still running his law practice singlehandedly, the energy with which Lloyd George pursued his intended sweetheart is little short of astonishing. Nevertheless, his diary shows none of the agony that attended his passion for Liza Jones two years before. This time he was fully in control of himself. 'At six p.m. met Maggie Owen by appointment on the Marine Parade,' he wrote on 6 February 1886 after his courtship had been in progress perhaps for four months. 'With her until 7. I am getting to be very fond of the girl. There is a combination of good nature, humour and affection about her.'

Ten days later after a concert he 'waylaid Maggie Owen to take her home.'

> Never felt more acutely than tonight that I am really in deep love with girl. Felt sorry to have to leave her. I have I know gradually got to like her more and more. There is another thing that I have observed in connection with this, that my intercourse with Liza rather tended to demoralize my taste; my fresh acquaintance has an entirely different influence. She firmly checks all ribaldry or tendency thereto on my part.

Occasionally he was almost patronizing.

> 9 March [1886] Up to meet M. Walked in public with her without a blush.... Think I have at last made a prudent choice.
> Met M. First time I have ever used an expression of endearment towards her. Feel I am becoming very fond of her.[129]

In June he told his austere sister of his decision to propose marriage and received for once warm approval of his intentions, although Mary Ellen suggested that he wait five years before marrying. Margaret conveniently left Criccieth at the end of August, 1886, to visit relatives at Llanwnda a short distance south of Caernarvon. Lloyd George followed her on Wednesday, 25 August, and, posing as a messenger from her father, was able to speak to her and induce her to steal away from the house and meet late in the evening. She finally escaped at 9:45 p.m. and during a long drive in a carriage he had hired in Llanwnda he asked her to marry him. Admitting affection for him, she nevertheless asked time to consider.[130]

Now that he had surmounted the first hurdle he pressed his suit with vigor. 'Write me your answer to the question I gave you on Wednesday evening (or Thursday morning—I am not sure which it was!),' he demanded in a letter on August 28 three days after the proposal.

Do, there is a good girl. I want to get your own decision on the matter.
The reason I have already given you. I wish the choice you make,
whatever it be, to be really yours & not anyone elses....

He concluded promising to tell her some recent adventures and explaining
he did not include any terms of endearment as they disfigured the letter.[131]
He spent as many evenings with her as he could, much to the distress of
Richard Lloyd who, not knowing yet of his nephew's new interest, took to
walking the streets of Criccieth looking for him. Lloyd George ended this
practice by hiding his uncle's boots.[132]

For a time in the autumn affairs ran smoothly, although in October she
admitted that she did not always trust his faithfulness to her and made clear
at the same time that both she and her mother deplored his 'skeptical
vagueries.' He reassured her about his love and told her emphatically that
'even to win her' he could not pretend a religious belief he did not have.[133]
On 11 November she kissed him for the first time and in December he
ordered her to tell her mother of his proposal and of her inclination toward
him.[134] Then suddenly there was a crisis which could have broken up the
courtship, but which concluded with Lloyd George making clear that their
relationship, if it continued, would be on his terms rather than hers. At the
end of the year he accepted instruction in a breach of promise suit brought
by Miss Annie Jones, whose mother ran a fish shop in Criccieth, against
Lloyd George's cousin, John Jones of Caerdyni. This was a surprising case
for Lloyd George to take. In addition to being a relative, John Jones had
been an occasional benefactor of the Richard Lloyd menage during their
period of poverty. He was also a personal friend of Lloyd George and the
two had been partners in several adventures with women. But still worse,
Annie Jones was the sister of Liza Jones who had caused so much pain
eighteen months before, and the preparation of the case would entail visits
to the house, with the inevitable gossip. Criccieth was a small town which
was already fascinated by Lloyd George's doings. Margaret Owen quickly
heard of the new instruction. Evidently to calm her Lloyd George sent her
Annie Jones's letter outlining the case. She replied begging him to give it
up. 'I know there are relatives of mine at Criccieth,' she wrote, 'and other
people as well who will be glad to have anything more to say to my people
about you, to set them against you and that will put me in an awkward
position.'

> If she were a stranger to you and you took her case, people would wonder
> why on earth you took it against your cousin, knowing that your relations
> were against your doing so: but now they will draw a different
> conclusion— that you are on friendly terms with these people....[135]

Lloyd George's reply to this letter was a pompous attempt to put her off.
He had to hurry to Bangor, he wrote on 6 January 1887, and could not see
her. But

> as to the affair you refer to, the reasons you find are undoubtedly
> weighty and entitled to respect and consideration. I only wish you had
> told them to me last night. I feel I have now committed myself. Anyhow
> you need not fear my in any way compromising you. I have too fond a
> love for you to do that....

But we shall fully and freely discuss this unfortunate business when we meet next on Saturday. It undoubtedly requires tact and discretion—but honour must be satisfied.[136]

Highsounding as all this was, it remained unsatisfactory and in a second letter Margaret insisted that he choose between herself and the case. There were by now rumors that told of entertainment and singing occurring during the visits of the young lawyer to his client, who was also, to Margaret's fastidious sensibilities, distinctly lower class. Although he began his reply to the second letter with the salutation, used for the first time, 'My dearest Maggie,' Lloyd George delivered a counter ultimatum. He would not give up the case, which might earn him between £50 and £100, because of the gossip of some 'dried up, dessicated (*sic*) and blighted old maids' who object to a 'little harmless music' during a professional visit. As for her social position he and the Joneses were in the same chapel and one of the few doctrines of the creed in which he still believed was equality, even with the daughters of a fishmonger. This last was emphasized with the appropriate scriptural citations.

But if she insisted on a decision, the choice would be hers. Margaret had evidently suggested that he had made a blunder in his choice of a future wife. 'Well I do make mistakes,' Lloyd George concluded, 'but it does not usually take me two years to find them out.'

> And besides…my ideas as to the qualifications of a wife do not coincide with yours. You seem to think that the supreme function of a wife is to amuse her husband—to be a kind of toy or plaything to enable him to while away with enjoyment his leisure hour. My ideas are very different—if not superior— to yours. I am of the opinion that woman's function is to soothe, sympathise and not to amuse. Men's lives are a perpetual conflict. The life that I have mapped out will be so especially—as lawyer and politician. Woman's function is to pour oil on wounds —to heal bruises of spirit received in past conflict—to stimulate renewed exertion….
> As to setting you free that is a matter for your choice not mine. I have many times impressed upon you that the only bond by which I have any desire to hold is that of love. If that were lost then I would snap any other bond with my own hand….You ask me to choose—I have made my choice deliberately and solemnly. I must now ask you to make your choice. I know my slanderers—those whom you allow to poison your mind against me. Choose between them and me—there can be no other alternative.[137]

Evidently Margaret's resistance on the breach of promise suit collapsed after this challenge. There are no more direct references to the Jones girls, although relatives were reported to have asked Mrs. Owen as late as March about her prospective son-in-law and 'Nansi the herring's daughter,' and how he was able to stand courting her.[138] Lloyd George had asserted the priorities in his life and she had seemed to accept them. There remained an aftermath of hard feelings, not only on Margaret's part but also in her family. In the middle of January, perhaps to reestablish his respectability, he sent her two letters he had received from Thomas Ellis urging that Margaret read them to her mother. 'She'll pull as wry a face as if she were drinking a gallon of assafatida. Did you tell her what a scandal she has created about us throughout Lleyn peninsula?' On 26 January 1887 he ordered a ring through a Portmadoc jeweler.[139]

Margaret remained bitter and suspicious and her parents tightened the discipline on their daughter. There were nagging letters on both sides about appointments broken and embarrassing encounters. At the end of the month, with the ring ordered, but apparently not accepted, he sent her the clearest possible statement that the determining factor in his future decisions would be his own career and that he would, if pressed, sacrifice his love for her for his future. To this secondary place in his life she would have to accommodate herself. After a detailed charge about the number of engagements with him that week she had broken after he had altered his professional schedule to suit her, he wrote:

> Another thing—you well know how you lecture me about my lack of self respect. [Possibly this was an oblique reference to the Jones case.] Well, how is it you conduce this quality to me? By showing me the utmost disrespect. You stick me for half an hour in a conspicuous spot to wait for you and having made an exhibition to all passersby, you coolly send word that it is your mother's pleasure I should go home to avoid another disappointment. Now, once forever let us have an end to this long standing wrangle. It comes to this. My supreme idea is to get on. To this idea I shall sacrifice everything—except, I trust, honesty. I am prepared to thrust even love itself under the wheels of my Juggernaut, if it obstructs the way, that is if love is so much trumpery child's play as your mother deems courtship to be. I have told you over and over that I consider you to be my good angel—my guiding star. Do you not really desire my success? If you do, will you suggest some course least objectionable to you out of our difficulty? I am prepared to do anything reasonable and fair you may require of me. I cannot—earnestly—carry on as present. Believe me—and heaven may attest the truth of my statement—my love for you is sincere and strong. In this I never waver. But I must not forget that I have a purpose and however painful the sacrifice I may have to make to attain this ambition I must not flinch—otherwise success will be remote indeed....[140]

Margaret seems now to have realized she could easily lose the man she loved. Her abrasive tone changed. Her letters now began for the first time 'Dearest David' and ended: 'With Much Love, Maggie.' Lloyd George had gained his sweetheart and kept his independence. The juggernaut of his career was not going to be deflected by women.

The question remained: how could the elder Owens be convinced of their daughter's determination and when could the couple be married? A new element that made planning more flexible was William's successful accomplishment of his final examinations and his entry, in May 1887, into the law firm. But a complicating factor also appeared in the summer of 1887 in a dispute within the congregation of Capel Mawr of which Richard Owen was a deacon. The controversy turned partly on personalities and partly on the recognition and welcome to be given to English speaking Methodists who were appearing in Criccieth in increasing numbers. It involved therefore one of the most sensitive functions of Welsh nonconformity, the guardianship of the Welsh language. The result was secession of about one-half of the congregation including Mr. and Mrs. Owen and the minister, John Owen. Lloyd George's sympathies were entirely with the Owens in the dispute and he hoped briefly that they might leave the Methodists for the Independents and so become members of his church.[141] His nephew suggests that the evidence of his sympathy gained him at last permission to visit Margaret at her parents' home, although no oftener than three times a week.[142] Unfortunately, however, Richard Owen was so affected by the battle with his friends that he determined to sell his interest in Mynydd Ednyfed and move away.

This added difficulties. Lloyd George had mused in his diary in August whether a marriage as soon as possible, which he admitted to himself he wanted, was prudent. He decided, characteristically, that the following spring would be more sensible.[143] He discussed this with Maggie in mid-September, after spending the early part of the month on anti-tithe business. She agreed to wait until early spring, but suggested reasonably that if the church squabble (identified as 'the Davies affair' in the diaries) were not settled by then they should get married anyway.[144] Through the rest of September and into October as the Davies's affair dragged on the couple discussed marriage, agreeing that it should be as soon as possible—while worrying about the reaction of the parents on each side. Lloyd George, showing some hesitation, noted in his diary that he and Maggie would 'get married soon provided my uncle did not upon talking the matter over with him show good cause to the contrary.'[145] When he finally spoke to Mr. and Mrs. Owen on 1 November he found that Margaret's parents also urged waiting at least a year, until they could sell the stock on the farm to a new tenant. They said they would be able to give no financial help or housing until they had resettled, although Lloyd George insisted that he wanted nothing.[146]

The interview with the Owens had left Lloyd George furious. He suspected that Margaret's parents were raising housing and financial difficulties in order to postpone the marriage. Her parents could not seem to make up their minds what they wanted or thought, he wrote Maggie angrily on 9 November. 'We ought to know definitely whether they object and also where they propose we should go in the interval between our marriage and their leaving Mynydd Ednyfed. Unless they tell us to stay with them we must lose no time in looking out for a house and furnishings.'[147]

Perhaps the event that decided the question of further postponement of the marriage was the amicable settlement of the church dispute and the Owens' decision not to leave their farm after all. Thus it became possible for Lloyd George, who had been unable to find a house in Criccieth and had thought briefly of moving to Portmadoc, to live with his in-laws after marriage. In any case, at about the beginning of 1888, Lloyd George, with the Owens' blessing, determined to marry immediately. There were now difficulties about where the wedding should take place—Mr. Owen insisted that it should be in a Methodist chapel—and Richard Lloyd had to be told that his favorite nephew was about to marry a girl he had never met. He accepted the news without demur, as he customarily bowed to ordinances of fate, and agreed to participate in a small ceremony. Lloyd George celebrated the end of his bachelorhood with Howell Gee and a few friends in Denbigh in what was for him a debauched evening, which he did not enjoy.[148]

On 24 January 1888, the couple were married in Pencaenwydd Methodist chapel in the country a few miles from Criccieth. Richard Lloyd and the Rev. John Owen, who had himself asked Margaret to marry him the previous summer, officiated jointly. The wedding was attended by only a few friends, but when Lloyd George and his bride drove down to take the train for London their carriage was pelted with rice and Criccieth itself acknowledged the affair with decorations and fireworks.[149]

The ten-day honeymoon in London included sightseeing, a return to Spurgeon's Metropolitan Tabernacle and a visit to the Globe Theatre for a performance of *Hamlet*. When the couple returned to Criccieth on 3 February, after a near fist fight in Euston Station between Lloyd George and a cabman over a tip, a large crowd was waiting to welcome them.

Lloyd George and his wife settled in with Margaret's family with whom, after an awkward beginning, he became remarkably friendly. Mynydd Ednyfed remained his official home for the next three years. Here his first child, Richard, was born on 15 February 1889 and his first daughter, Mair Eluned (Mary Ellen), on 2 August 1890. Finally, in 1891, the Owen family at last sold their interest in the farm and built a pair of houses on the Portmadoc road in Criccieth. The growing Lloyd George family lived in one of these, next door to Margaret's parents, until 1908 when, with Mr. and Mrs. Owen both dead and with at last a substantial ministerial salary, Lloyd George built Brynawelon ('hill of breezes') on a site overlooking Criccieth. This house remained Margaret's home, if not precisely his, for the rest of their life together.

VIII

In the year between January, 1888 when he was married and January, 1889 when he was adopted as Liberal candidate for Caernarvon District, Lloyd George moved from the slightly disreputable rebellious fringe to the center of the North Welsh political world. He had in addition achieved a certain legal celebrity. The practice of Lloyd George and George was receiving a large number of, if not always well paying, instructions. He had married prudently and well and the bitter days of poverty were behind him. As he passed his twenty-sixth birthday on 17 January 1889 he could reflect that the career which meant so much to him was progressing satisfactorily.

Already in January, as soon as the contest for the Liberal nomination ended, he began a new project. The Reform Act of 1884 had made it inevitable that the structure of local government would be democratized. The ordinary citizen, who now voted for his Member of Parliament, would not long endure a system of rural local administration which left power in the hands of the non-elected, largely self-perpetuating, sometimes corrupt, oligarchies of county gentry operating through quarter sessions. Accordingly, C.T. Ritchie's Local Government Act of 1888 created 62 elected county councils for England and Wales to take over virtually all non-judicial functions of the old quarter sessions. The council elections under the new law began in 1889. Lloyd George was invited by several

Caernarvon districts to stand for the office of councillor. He refused to contest a seat himself but campaigned actively for other candidates throughout Caernarvonshire, several of whom, the Reverend Herber Evans for example, had been Lloyd George supporters for the Liberal nomination. Lloyd George had been among those that had insisted that county council elections be fought as partisan contests and he used the occasion of the election to build a personal clientele within his county's Liberal party that would bring the district behind him in the race for parliament.

The county council platform provided also the site for his first meeting with Arthur Herbert Dyke Acland, a Member of Parliament for Rotherham and a close friend of Tom Ellis, who, even though an Englishman and son of an eminent political family, owned a house at Clynnog and took an informed interest in Welsh affairs.[150] Although Acland retired from parliament because of ill-health in 1899, he would remain a collaborator and associate of Lloyd George into the days of the land campaign on the eve of World War I. He also helped to make real the friendship with Tom Ellis which Lloyd George may have used slightly too often as a political password. In any case, after the county elections on 24 January, when 30 Liberals and 14 Conservatives were chosen for the Caernarvonshire County Council, Acland and, with some pressure from Tom Ellis, Lloyd George were chosen as aldermen.[151] Throughout the principality Liberals carried every Welsh county but Brecknockshire. Thomas Gee became the first chairman of the Denbighshire County Council. But among the Conservative councillors in Caernarvon was H.J. Ellis-Nanney who defeated William George for Llanystumdwy by eight votes.

At the first meeting of the Caernarvonshire county council, Lloyd George impressed the Welsh radical program upon the assembly with a resolution passed amid cheers, 36 to seven, to petition parliament to enact leasehold enfranchisement.[152] Lloyd George would remain a Caernarvonshire Alderman, his first political office, for the rest of his life and he retained, at least until 1914, an active interest in local government, reinforcing his hold upon the constituency and giving himself local contacts that were invaluable at the time of the education revolt and the land campaign.

Meanwhile Lloyd George thought of his coming race for parliament. The Liberal party in Caernarvon District was in deplorable shape, he wrote in April to the great Francis Schnadhorst of Birmingham, architect of the caucus and secretary of the National Liberal Federation. Its defeat by Edmund Swetenham in 1886 'was due entirely to poor organization and apathy.' It suffered from lack of funds.

> Registration has not therefore been energetically attended to and one or two clubs have collapsed. The Tories on the other hand are plentifully supplied with cash. As to registration, our weaknesses have to some extent been remedied by the efforts of volunteers, but the clubs still languish....

He concluded by asking for advice on organization and fund raising.[153]

Not only in Caernarvon District was the Liberal party in Wales in disarray. Even though Wales had sustained herself, the election of 1886 had been a disappointment. And within the party Welsh MPs were disregarded—'an inferior category, a cheaper sort of Member'—the most eminent of them, Stuart Rendel, remarked. The lack of a united party in the principality and the inability of the Welsh Members of Parliament to speak with a united voice, or even to agree upon what they stood for, vitiated and wasted the remarkable Liberal loyalty of the Welsh voter. Immediately after the county council election, Lloyd George had argued in a speech at Hope Hall, Liverpool on 12 February that the almost universal Welsh sweep of the local authorities represented the authentic voice of Wales.[154] But as usual he couched his address in terms of North Wales, of farm tenant versus aristocratic land owner, terms that were becoming obsolescent in much of the South where the leader of the Cambrian Miners' Association, William Abraham, had already been elected for Rhondda in 1885.

At Hope Hall, Lloyd George had himself demonstrated the peculiar, single-issue, political parochialism that kept North and South Wales separated, but as soon as he became a parliamentary candidate he took up vigorously the cause of political unification and organization, speaking in North and South at every opportunity. This was a dangerous tactic for one not yet even in the House of Commons, young and relatively inexperienced politically. It put him into conflict with men upon whose support he depended. Further, after his election to the House of Commons, his cause, the formation of a Welsh national league with local organizations in every locality which would absorb the nebulous North and South Wales Liberal Federation, expanded to include an organized Welsh party in the House of Commons. This, in turn, aroused even more suspicion among Welsh Members of Parliament, who saw a separate Welsh party principally as a vehicle to advance the career of the young Member for Caernarvon District, who no doubt expected to become its leader. Beriah Evans, not an entirely friendly contemporary journalist, wrote later that Lloyd George hoped to 'capture' the existing Liberal party organizations and transform them into nationalist societies. Failing this he intended, in words which Evans quotes, to 'smash existing Liberal Associations and reconstruct from the ruins a systematized Nationalist machine which would control all elections, Parliamentary and Municipal, in the Principality.'[155]

Behind all this lay one durable Lloyd George project which he kept in the back of his mind during his first ten years in the House of Commons, bringing it out at appropriate moments, putting it aside when tactics required, but never dropping it entirely until after the Boer War when it was superseded. This was home rule for Wales. Only an organized Welsh party and parliamentary delegation could bring home rule, Lloyd George's reasoning went. The arguments for it were even more persuasive than for Ireland. A Welsh legislative assembly, and only a Welsh assembly, would bring the disestablishment, tenant rights, Sunday closing and restriction of pub licences, and a host of other reforms that a generation of nationalists demanded. The example of the Irish was irresistible. The Nationalist party controlled politics from parish to parliament. And Irish home rule seemed very close in 1889 and 1890. In February 1889, just as the county council elections drew to a close, the sensational charges of complicity or approval of murder against Irish Nationalist leader Charles

Stewart Parnell were blown to pieces by the admission that the critical evidence had been forged. For the next 18 months the cause of Irish self-government seemed triumphant: Gladstone received Parnell at Hawarden in December. Had there been an election, British fair play would have ensured a Home Rule majority.

However, Ireland was organized; Wales was not. Two Welsh Liberal organizations, with different policies, wasted their energy attacking each other. 'A kind of Punch and Judy exhibition', Lloyd George argued in October, 1889, was made of Welsh Liberalism and 'we become the butt of our foe's ridicule and not the object of his terror.'

> But there is another reason why an attempt should be made to organize all the available force of Liberalism in the Principality. The battle is becoming more and more intense, as the disgraceful record of Tory intimidation which occurred during the last by-elections will amply prove. Anyone who scans the objects of the Welsh National Council must foresee without much prophetic vision, that the fight for attainment of those objects will be a life-and-death struggle. What are those objects? Emancipation of the land and its tillers, the disestablishment and disendowment of the Church, local option, and an extensive measure of local government for Wales....
> And how do we propose to protect working men who have been deprived of their means of sustenance because of their adhesion to our programme? At present our Liberal organization can barely eke out a miserable half-starved sustenance. Now unless we protect the victim of our opponents' intimidating tactics from destitution, such terror will be struck into the hearts of the timid and less eager spirits that Liberalism will become an impossibility in the country. But supposing each and every working man who happens to be subjected to the persecution of a Tory employer of labour or his minions were to realize the fact that there was a league, numbering amongst its members 200,000 of the sturdiest of his countrymen, ready to rescue him from the consequences of his devotion to principle, then the worst terrors of the Primrose League might be defied with impunity. Liberalism could then become the ruling force in our country, and I cannot help harbouring an earnest conviction that thousands who now temporize in order to save themselves and their families from being turned out upon the world whose resources are distributed by monopolists, would welcome the opportunity that such a league would afford them of emancipating themselves from the grip of a tyranny which they must heartily detest.'[156]

This speech had been made at Caernarvon on 17 October 1889 in a meeting of the North Wales Liberal Federation in support of a motion, which Lloyd George had himself inspired, to establish a 'Welsh National League' with a widespread grass roots organization.[157] The proposal was defeated—an influential figure in opposition being Thomas Gee—but at the meeting in Cardiff of the South Wales Liberal Federation a few months later on 4 February 1890, he broadened the attack. Here the resolution was frankly a resolution for Home Rule in Wales and Scotland as well as Ireland. The arguments for Home Rule for Wales were at least as good as·

those Gladstone had made for Ireland, Lloyd George insisted. It received the same neglect from the English parliament; its parochial interests were equally incomprehensible to foreigners. But more, Wales had even better claims. It had a national language, which Ireland had not except in the minds of poets. It had no Ulster problem and a grant of Home Rule to 'the land of white gloves' would not mean handing the land over, as it was argued against Home Rule for Ireland, to moonlighters and assassins.

The conference had pledged itself to a program of reforms, Lloyd George concluded, disestablishment, land reform and local option, but these were all simply fringes of a far greater social question in the solution of which the Welsh nation should play a part.

> The ennobling influences of Christianity have not played upon her heart
> for a whole century in vain. They have elevated and guided her
> impulses, they have awakened the fervour of her national enthusiasm.
> That is why I feel so sanguine that were self-government conceded to
> Wales she would be a model to the nationalities of the earth of a people
> who have driven oppression to the hillsides, and initiated the glorious
> reign of freedom, justice, and truth.[158]

Lloyd George's was not conventional wisdom, even in South Wales, where radicalism was already being taken for granted. In the atavistic nationalist context of Caernarvonshire, advocating a break with England could have brought trouble. Although the Cardiff speech was widely applauded in the South, and newspapers, noting that he was a prospective Liberal candidate, optimistically anticipated his coming election, he was far in advance of general opinion in the North, particularly in the towns of Bangor and Caernarvon. Thomas Ellis's most forthright speech on Welsh Home Rule, it should be noted, was not made until six months later on 18 September 1890 and then in the sympathetic surroundings of Bala. Even there it was coolly received.[159]

All of this became a problem immediately. On 19 March 1890 the Conservative Member for Caernarvon District, Edmund Swetenham, dropped dead. This was a blow to the Conservatives— they had now to find a candidate by nomination day, 2 April—but it was also a shock to Lloyd George who had expected no election for two years. Fifty years later Margaret Lloyd George recalled how his face looked grim when she handed him the telegram saying 'Swetenham died last night.' The two had planned a day's holiday in Caernarvon which they took anyway, but the coming election spoiled it.

Lloyd George's position in a constituency so far untouched by the new Welsh politics was far from secure. He was certainly well-known, but equally he was regarded with misgiving. He was not prepared for a fight and Maggie was, as she told D.R. Daniel in 1910, 'quite against his going into the House of Commons.'[160] He was undoubtedly a nationalist, but his Liberalism was uncertain. He was young, a member of the smallest, poorest, and least respectable of the four Welsh non-conformist sects. He was eccentrically opinionated, without the scholarly polish of Tom Ellis whom he professed to follow. He had had difficulty gaining the nomination and there still were open wounds about his victory. The electorate in the six

Caernarvon boroughs was heavily middle class. Only 36% of the males were on the register and in Caernarvon town, with an electorate of 1746, nearly all were heads of families. Only 15 men were registered as service or lodger voters.[161] Lloyd George received a cool estimate of his chances from the veteran nonconformist leader, Dr. John Thomas.

> I know it will be a hard fight: and a desperate fight. I am afraid of some of our most moderate men, that they will not take a bold line and make your advanced views their excuse. I must say that I cannot go so far as you go on what is termed Home Rule for Wales; and I am afraid that the prominence given to this question may do us harm in some places; and especially in the Boroughs. Our great question in Wales is disestab-lishment.I care little for the question of Home Rule, even for Ireland compared to this question. You are quite safe with the advanced party. The danger is with the moderates, as they wish to be called, and we cannot carry Caernarvon Boroughs without them.[162]

Unfortunately, neither was he, in fact, 'quite safe with the advanced party.' The journal *Cymru Fydd* ('Wales to Be'), which had been established in 1888 primarily to give voice to intellectual Welsh nationalism and which found its hero in Tom Ellis, chose March, 1890, to print an article denouncing the 'screamers' in Welsh politics. 'They scream about land laws, tithe, education, and especially Welsh Home Rule,' the article asserted in a clear reference to Lloyd George, 'blessings to be attained by constant and steady effort not by fitful screaming.' The screamers, said *Cymru Fydd*, 'were men of superficial knowledge and shallow conviction who sought principally to draw attention to themselves.'[163] All of this was discouraging. Beriah Evans has remarked that there was more romance and surprise about Lloyd George's election in 1890 than about his becoming a cabinet minister in 1905.[164]

To be sure he had some advantages. Swetenham's election had been a fluke.[165] Traditionally the district was Liberal by about three hundred votes. And he had the support of two of the most influential political figures in North Wales, the Reverend Herber Evans, now his colleague on the county council, and above all of Thomas Gee. But perhaps his greatest asset was his opponent. The Conservatives scurried desperately to find a candidate. Several men declined the honor of contesting the difficult Boroughs. After a week they persuaded the squire of Llanystumdwy, Hugh John Ellis-Nanney, to stand for the House of Commons against the nephew of the former shoemaker of his village.

The diffident but determined Ellis-Nanney, who had been among those earlier refusing the nomination, was a perfect foil for Lloyd George. 'For the sake of Mr. Lloyd George a better man could hardly have been selected,' remarked the *Cardiff Times*.[166] Although he had been already twice defeated, Ellis-Nanney and his supporters believed that his friendly disposition and reputation for local philanthropy would make him an even stronger candidate than the amiable but non-resident Edmund Swetenham, who had lived in Rossett, Denbighshire. Therefore, overconfidence, compounded by disinclination toward public speaking, led Ellis-Nanney to neglect the platform and depend upon outside speakers. He despised his adversary and assumed his election would come from his social position and public renown.[167] He thus deliberately gave away to Lloyd George the political advantage of the underdog and made himself, at the same time, the personification of everything that the new politics of Wales deplored.[168]

Lloyd George's electoral address appeared on 24 March, before Ellis-Nanney had accepted the candidature. When compared with the character of the subsequent campaign it was a sober and non-political document promising that its author would support 'justice for Ireland,' 'religious liberty and equality in Wales,' 'measures for simplifying and cheapening the transfer of land, for the taxation of ground rents, the enfranchisement of leaseholds; and for improving the condition of the Tenant farmer and labourer,' and temperance legislation. The Liberal candidate was also interested in the closer regulation of rivers, harbors and fisheries. The delicate question of Welsh Home Rule was disposed of in the Delphic sentence: 'I believe in a liberal extension of the principle of Decentralization.'[169]

Among Welsh radicals these were conventional sentiments, although in fairness it should be said that Lloyd George remained committed to nearly all of them, and especially land reform, throughout his political career. But they did not define remotely the issues of the campaign. As he would do in many future contests Lloyd George sought to personalize his opposition. In his first election contest he fought not the Conservative party but the hapless Mr. Ellis-Nanney. As soon as the Conservatives named their candidate, Lloyd George set the tone for the race. An example of the political style from which he would rarely depart in public speeches, this address must be quoted at some length. He began by cheerfully telling the audience at the Guild Hall in Caernarvon that he would not detain them long and would see most of them again anyway. He observed that the last time he had spoken to them he was under the disadvantage of not having an opponent. Now he had one.

> But after fishing in London and all over the country, their opponents had succeeded in persuading the squire of Gwynfryn to lead them in battle. He was not going to say anything against the Conservative candidate as he was a gentleman. They were neighbours — Mr. George and Mr. Nanney — and never were seen better neighbours than they were. They met each other often on business matters, and, once the election would be over, they would be as neighbourly neighbours as ever. He was glad that his opponent was the Squire Gwynfryn, for, as his Party said, he was undoubtedly the best man they could bring forward. He was a capital representative of his Party; he was one of the aristocracy, a landlord and a moneyed gentleman. They now had, on one hand, a member of the aristocracy, and on the other hand one of the masses, one of the people themselves, bred and born amongst the people. He (Mr. George) had read the report of the previous night's Conservative meeting, from which he saw that one of the great qualifications which Mr. Nanney possessed in order to become the Tory Party's candidate was that he was a man of wealth and that the great disqualification in the speaker's case was that he was not possessed of any wealth. ('Oh' and

laughter). The Tories did not understand things; how could they and remain Tories? Macaulay once had said that a 'man of the 19th Century cannot make himself a man of the 17th.' The Tories forgot that they were not now living in the 17th century. He had once heard a man wildly declaiming against Mr. T. E. Ellis as a Parliamentary representative, but, according to that man, Mr. Ellis's disqualification consisted mainly in the fact that he had been brought up in a 'cottage' (laughter and applause). The Tories had not yet realized that the day of the cottage-bred man had at last dawned (loud applause). Time was—in the old feudal periods— when the Lords and Squires of the land could call upon the poor and humble masses to follow them into every squabble they chose to enter into. They had the right then to call upon the people to fight the battles for them, but the Tories of the present day did not realize that time had happily gone by forever, and the day of the masses had now dawned (applause).[170]

Lloyd George received a strong letter of support from Tom Ellis (who was in Egypt trying to recover his health), which arrived too late to do much good, and an almost incomprehensible one from Gladstone.[171] A.H.D. Acland, Gee, and Herbert Gladstone made speeches for him. Again and again he canvassed the six boroughs, particularly in the North, having to do himself what a better organization should have done for him.

Almost immediately his radicalism and well-known indifference to disestablishment began to cause trouble. At a meeting early in the campaign, the Reverend Evan Jones, the renowned and powerful pastor of the Calvinistic Methodist Moriah Chapel of Caernarvon, demanded a pledge from the young candidate that he withhold his support for Irish Home Rule unless he received a pledge from Gladstone for disestablishment. Lloyd George, aware that he was already under fire for his excesses on Welsh Home Rule, replied that he could not dictate to Gladstone. Although Mr. Jones was eventually silenced, he was not pacified and he stalked out of the meeting.

This was a disastrous beginning. Evan Jones was a man to fear and the Calvinistic Methodists would decide the campaign, ended the report of the *South Wales Daily News*.[172] Even though the Liberation Society wrote quickly to disavow any connection with Evan Jones, Lloyd George wrote to his wife remarking upon the article in the *South Wales Daily News*, that he feared the 'Hen Gorff' (the Calvinistic Methodists, literally 'the old body') would betray him, and that he was quite resigned to defeat.[173]

Finally, his son reports that his chances were nearly destroyed during the campaign when a widow in Caernarvon found herself pregnant and named him as the father, but that his career was saved when Liberal supporters bought her off with an annuity. This may have occurred. Certainly such accidents happened to Lloyd George later in his life, but the details of this first misadventure are sketchy and there is no corroborating evidence.[174]

Balloting occurred on 10 April, with counting the next day. After a possible attempt at fraud by the Tories and two recounts the result was declared: Lloyd George, 1963; Ellis-Nanney, 1945. In Caernarvon the winner's carriage was drawn by a crowd to Castle Square where the 'boy

MP' made a speech assuring the electors that the contest had been a battle of principle and that thanks to the efforts of the Ladies' Liberal League virtue had been triumphant.[175] On 16 April he left for London to take his seat. By a margin of 18 votes the juggernaut of Lloyd George's career had begun to move.

2 The Early Years in Parliament: The Welsh Parnell, 1890-95

His biographers often refer to Lloyd George as a 'Welsh Radical' as if this were a discrete category into which he fits and can thereby be explained. He was to be sure Welsh and within the customary usage of that most inexact term also radical. But Lloyd George's early career in parliament cannot be so easily crammed into a descriptive pigeonhole. Tom Ellis, Herbert Lewis, Frank Edwards, Sam Evans, and D.A. Thomas, for a time at least, were also Welsh radicals. All of them worked with Lloyd George, competed with him, admired his courage and deplored his extravagance of language and behavior, but he was not their man, nor they his. Sam Evans briefly, and Herbert Lewis later and for a much longer period, were his personal friends. Nevertheless, the essential fact of Lloyd George's first years in the House of Commons, indeed until the education revolt of 1903, is that he really worked alone and that his program, such as it was, was his own.

When Lloyd George entered the House of Commons, the leader of the Welsh Liberal delegation in parliament, since 1888, was Stuart Rendel, an Englishman and Churchman whose great wealth derived from William Armstrong, Ltd. In 1880, in middle age, he had turned out the Wynn dynasty in Montgomeryshire in a seat that had been contested only once since 1832. A close personal friend of Gladstone, Rendel put part of his fortune at the disposal of the Liberals and in 1890 married his daughter, Maud, to Gladstone's third son. Although he became a devoted champion of Welsh national causes, Rendel insisted that legislative recognition of the principality, disestablishment, and land reform, could be had only through the agency of the Liberal party. He believed in an organized Welsh group, but within, not outside, the Liberal party. As such he had no sympathy for heedless rebels who sought to blackmail Liberalism with threats of withholding votes, and for a time after 1886 Rendel had been suspicious even of Tom Ellis whose rural populism endangered the bridges he was attempting to build into the inner circles of conventional Gladstonianism.[1]

Thus Lloyd George's appearance at Westminster occasioned some misgivings. Rendel himself asserted later, in 1905, that he had liked the upstart young Member for Caernarvon District from the beginning, noting his 'quickness of perception and alertness in seizing a point,' but that some of the older Welsh Members, Hussey-Vivian, Osborne Morgan, and William Rathbone, wanted to 'snub and sit upon' him.[2] Even Ellis, who had written Lloyd George a warm letter of congratulation after his election urging him to get ready for a good sturdy fight on the Tithe Bill which would 'prepare Wales for the land struggle,' was privately somewhat more restrained, hoping that he could trust Lloyd George to be 'fairly sensible and active.'[3] The *Cymru Fydd* journal was more patronizing. It mocked Lloyd George's narrow victory. He had barely escaped shameful defeat and while wishing him success the journal warned that he would 'win his spurs in Parliament, not by cutting Irish capers, but by sound judgement and perseverance in well-doing.' Tom Ellis could serve as an example.[4]

Despite its Olympian tone, for Lloyd George this was good advice. He had a political weakness, one that he never outgrew, which hurt him again and again and nearly destroyed his career in 1914: the inability to march in step with the rest of his party. At bottom Lloyd George was a political insurgent, not a party man.[5] In office or out, the art of politics for him was the development of issues over the head of the House of Commons and its party machinery, the whips and the party central offices. With the extraordinary sympathy he felt he possessed for the ordinary voter, his practice was to develop issues which were subsequently forced by external pressure upon the organized political structures. Whether it embarrassed the front bench was almost irrelevant. Politics for Lloyd George was not Disraeli's secret game of getting into office. It was a public battle between two points of view over causes which might themselves be fluid and transient but which, taken together, flowed toward his personal goal, vivid but imprecise, of a better nation. So long as something was done it mattered very little which party took the credit so long as Lloyd George's participation was recognized. Personality, not principle, was what counted and the center of power was not Parliament Square but the county platform.

He had tried to conceal his independence during the contest in Caernarvon District. Sam Evans had assured audiences that half his radicalism would disappear in the enervating atmosphere of the House of Commons and Lloyd George had, of course, seriously jeopardized his election by refusing to promise Evan Jones to coerce Gladstone over Home Rule and disestablishment priorities. But he soon was forced to subordinate traditional party loyalty to the political claims of North Wales. His position after all was weak. His victory had been scarcely more than an accident. There was nothing to cheer in the defeat by 18 votes, among four thousand cast, of an inept Tory in a nonconformist stronghold, wrote an exceedingly perceptive but anonymous correspondent to the *British Weekly* on 18 August. On the contrary, it ought to be a cause for anxiety and a warning to English Gladstonians. Mr. Lloyd George's priorities were not those of North Wales. He 'came forward at first on the "Young Wales" platform. He soon found it did not take well. "Home Rule for Wales" has no hold as yet on the people. Its advocacy estranged some good Liberals....Some actively supported the Tory.' But neither, continued the correspondent, was Mr. Gladstone's preoccupation with Ireland acceptable. The average elector was tired of the Irish question. Tithe reform and disestablishment were the important issues for Wales and Mr. Gladstone's love for them was more than dubious.[6] Within the month the Welsh disestablishmentarians displayed their power. On 30 April, only three weeks after the election in Caernarvon District, at a special meeting at Rhyl, under the pressure of almost irresistible eloquence from a group of influential clergymen led by the Reverend Evan Jones, the North Wales Liberal Federation agreed unanimously to demand a written pledge from all sitting and prospective Members of Parliament that they exact from the government a promise of disestablishment as a price for the support of Home Rule in the next parliament.[7]

It is possible to overrate the general force of the Rhyl resolution. As was immediately pointed out, it had no legal importance unless passed by the various constituency associations, and the other Caernarvon MPs, Bryn Roberts and William Rathbone, were known to be against any such pledge. Indeed Evan Jones himself was by no means a universally beloved figure.[8]

But none of these qualifications had any importance for Lloyd George and he knew it. He did not have the independent financial affluence and the two to one majorities that belonged to his county colleagues. His election had been little more than a fluke. A swing of ten votes could have defeated him. He knew that Caernarvon District distrusted him as a country boy from the south of Lleyn, a Free Baptist, a poor man, and a social radical. He had the confidence neither of the chapels nor the conventional Gladstonians in the Caernarvon District. Caernarvon District, *The Times* noted a few weeks later, 'has the misdeeds of the establishment much more at heart than the misdeeds of Mr. Balfour.' 'Home Rule may be a good thing, but Welsh Disestablishment, say the Reverend Evan Jones and his friends at Rhyl is better, or at least a thing the Welsh care about more.'[9]

For Lloyd George the message was clear enough. He would have to find a pathway between, on one hand, a Welsh parliament and land reform, in effect intellectual Ellis-style radicalism, and on the other ordinary loyalty to English radicalism. Accordingly, even if by now the arid doctrines of the chapel meant little more to him than did the ceremonies of Anglicanism and even if disestablishment was largely a symbolic issue which would do virtually nothing, compared with land reform, to alter the living conditions of the ordinary Welshman, for the time being attacks upon the Church of England in its assorted manifestations must constitute his program. Lloyd George knew now where the power lay and 'mutiny,' as *The Times* had put it 'was in the air.' Lloyd George could do without Gladstone if he had to, but he could not remain a Member of Parliament without Evan Jones and his kind. Within a month, Lloyd George had undertaken to advertise the call for disestablishment to the leaders of his party.

On 29 May, the Engedi Calvinistic Methodist Church organized a large excursion to Hawarden Castle, Flintshire, to meet the leader of the party. Lloyd George, still without a maiden speech in the House of Commons, was among them. Gladstone's political sensibilities were too well developed to miss the significance of what was ostensibly a sight-seeing mission. He addressed the crowd on the dangers of rivalry and dissension and recommended patience and forbearance from Wales. In this, he concluded obscurely, 'will be the secret of our strength.' All of this, even from the Grand Old Man, was too much for the newly elected Member for Caernarvon District. After the speech, when a few of the more distinguished members of the congregation were invited into the house for a private conversation, he took the opportunity to importune his leader for a promise on Welsh disestablishment. Gladstone evaded, judged the Rhyl resolutions 'very unwise' and asserted that disestablishment of the Welsh Church, a part of the See of Canterbury with bishops in the House of Lords, would be far more difficult than the same for Scotland. The Welsh must be patient. Lloyd George would not be put off. The Welsh party insisted upon a commitment on disestablishment. Did the Liberal party, he demanded of his veteran leader, take it as seriously as Home Rule and would Gladstone give a promise to place it on the program of the next Liberal government?

Clearly Gladstone was much annoyed by these impertinences, although for a time he parried them politely. Eventually he administered a harsh snub to his young colleague, precisely one-third his age. Could Mr. Lloyd George, obviously an authority on Welsh nonconformity, tell him how many nonconformist chapels there were in Wales in 1742? The answer, 105, Lloyd George of course did not have. He was embarrassed and angered. The Squirrel Nutkin—Old Brown dialogue ended with Lloyd George being crushed for one of the few times in his life.[10]

Lloyd George remained, according to his own testimony, an admirer of the Grand Old Man as a parliamentary performer, but his loyalty to ordinary Gladstonianism, if it had ever existed, was quieted for good. He summed up his feelings to George Riddell years later: 'I did not like him much.'[11] And until he became himself a minister, and ironically was called upon in 1907 to put down a Welsh rebellion over precisely the same issue, he was a political nonconformist, going his own way whether or not the Liberals were in power. His guide for behavior was his own intuition and his sense of destiny, modified by his soundings in the political crosscurrents of North Wales.[12] Welsh grievances became in effect the first rung of the ladder by which Lloyd George would climb in the English political world.

I

Even though a group of London Welshmen, with a Cymru Fydd banner, came to meet the newly elected Member for Caernarvon District at Euston Station in London, and although he was greeted with cheers on 17 April as Stuart Rendel and A.H.D. Acland took him to the table of the House of Commons to take the oath, sign the test roll, and greet the Speaker, Lloyd George could not help being aware of his equivocal welcome at Westminster. He had an actor's sensitivity to nuances of speech and behavior. Despite the fact that he always insisted that he cared nothing about what people thought of him, his private feelings, at least in his early years in the House of Commons, were precisely the opposite. Clearly he felt very much alone. So he raged in his letters to his wife about snubs from the intellectual MPs, journalists, and the legal coterie who clustered about Tom Ellis and who poisoned the mind of their hero against Lloyd George. 'Your Dafydd will get on in spite of them,' he wrote his wife on 16 May. 'I have just met Ellis recently returned from Egypt. Poor fellow, he is far from well. Good sort Ellis. Tis a pity these fellows make a tool of him.'[13]

He was aware he had neither the polish nor a wealthy patron like Tom Ellis, the learning of Osborne Morgan, nor the fortune of D.A. Thomas, Alfred Thomas, or Stuart Rendel. Although he later became friends with several of the men whose criticism he resented most in his early months in parliament—Ellis Griffith and Vincent Evans—his first year in the House of Commons was hard and perhaps less successful than he realized. Even as late as February 1891, John Brunner could report to Tom Ellis that judging from the 'Welsh Notes' in the *Manchester Guardian,* to which Evans, and indeed eventually Lloyd George, contributed, Lloyd George was evidently 'a failure in the House and completely eclipsed by Sam Evans.' Lloyd George, Brunner thought, was attempting to overcome this weakness by dramatic oratory.[14] He was of unimpressive personal appearance, recalled L.A. Atherley-Jones thirty-five years later, and his 'early speeches were, with a thin thread of argument, incoherent declamations, so much so…that according to what a press gallery reporter told me, they required the most "dressing up" before they were fit for publication.'[15]

Brunner's may have been an unduly harsh estimate of Lloyd George's impact on the House of Commons, but his observation that Lloyd George was seeking to secure his reputation with dramatic oratory, by definition outside the precincts of Westminster Palace, was perfectly true. Lloyd George's first London speech, an invitation he accepted almost immediately after arriving in the metropolis, occurred at the annual meeting of the Liberation Society, held in the Metropolitan Tabernacle on 7 May. A disestablishment meeting, coming only a week after the Rhyl resolution, was perhaps a dangerous public forum for a young, only half-accepted, Member of Parliament who belonged to a political group whose leader was trying to improve his countrymen's relations with Gladstone. But it appeared even more unprofitable when Lloyd George, after arriving, found himself at the bottom of a substantial list of speakers. By the time he arose most of the press and part of the audience had gone and he feared that it would be unreported.[16] In fact, however, the speech went well enough and he received a gratifying response even though he concentrated on the iniquities of the Church in Wales evoking, a few days later, an angry reply from the new Bishop of St. Asaph, A.G. Edwards. The peroration dealt with a still unclear, but no less genuine, danger to disestablishment, the obviously increasing vitality and the growing numbers of communicants in the Church in Wales. Lloyd George dismissed all this as a 'sham and mongrel prosperity.'

> If this proselytizing were a genuine movement like that of
> Nonconformity at the beginning of this century—a movement which
> elevated the moral and intellectual tone of Wales, a movement which
> emanated from and appealed to the best and the highest sentiments of
> the heart, a great and sublime movement in the interests of humanity, I
> for one would say 'All Hail' to it; but as it is a movement which appeals to
> the worst, the degraded and sordid motives of our nature, I am here
> tonight to denounce it in the name of my country—to denounce it as the
> greatest curse which ever afflicted little Wales.[17]

Rendel apparently took no offense at the speech and afterwards congratulated Lloyd George upon it saying that he had heard from someone that it was very good.[18]

Lloyd George was soon deluged with invitations to speak, mostly, as in

Wales, from disestablishment and temperance groups. One invitation he accepted was from the United Kingdom Alliance for a speech at Free Trade Hall in Manchester on 4 June. The Free Trade Hall speech Lloyd George remembered forty years later as the best he ever made.[19] At a time when he was a new boy, suspecting that he was despised, and above all lonely, the tremendous response he evoked made a lasting impression upon him. As an important statement of policy, or even as a successful rescue of himself from a difficult position, the Cardiff speech of 1907, the Limehouse speech of 1909, the Bedford speech of 1913, his destruction of F.E. Smith and the Queen's Hall speech in 1914, are far more significant. But none so engraved itself in his memory as his first important public address as a Member of Parliament. The speech itself was a routine denunciation of the principle of compensation for publicans, a topic he would take up again many times, without a quotable sentence and delivered to a half-empty hall at the end of the program.[20]

But at Free Trade Hall his chapel *hwyl* set the audience afire. He confessed to his family that he was nervous when he got up but immediately won the crowd for himself by proclaiming that he too was from Manchester. 'Mr. Lloyd George had not been on his feet for five minutes,' reported the *Cambrian News*,

> before he fairly 'brought down the house' apologizing for keeping his audience so long. He was overwhelmed by cries of 'go on' and a voice from the gallery saying 'we will stop with thee all night, my boy.' Mr. George spoke with a pronounced Welsh accent, and exactly like a Welsh preacher giving the hwyl—this style of oratory proved almost too much for the Free Trade audience who were always used to dry speeches however able they may be. The people became almost unmanageable when Mr. Lloyd George sat down. The audience sprang to their feet like madmen, cheering, waving hats and handkerchiefs in a paroxysm of something very much akin to madness. The Chairman William S. Caine, MP, Liberal Unionist and Vice President of the United Kingdom Alliance having to sit down being unable to bring the people to order to terminate the meeting. The orators may be plentiful in Wales, but in Manchester, and even in England they are very scarce. It is to be regretted that Wales does not send more of these young men to represent her in parliament.[21]

Lloyd George, who in his letters rarely underestimated the dramatic effect of his speeches, was in this case quite accurate when he wrote Margaret later that evening that he had 'scored the greatest success of his life.' He reported being told by the chairman that he had made his reputation in England. Closer to home, he noted with satisfaction that Thomas Gee's daughter had been on the platform.[22] Whether or not he was appreciated by the political grandees at Westminster, he was reaching the people who counted.

A word may be appropriate on Lloyd George's speech making. By common consent, his best efforts were on the public platform, not in the House of Commons. He developed in the House, to be sure, a witty, off-hand debating style that was probably best displayed in committee. His quick tongue and talent for vivid metaphor—Randolph Churchill's 'mushroom teetotalism' in his maiden speech and his remarkable memory for inconvenient facts or remarks made by his opponents supported him here. The same genius would make him later a superb negotiator and mediator. He could turn a phrase and tell a story. He was a master of dramatic timing. But these are the talents of the stage entertainer.

However, in a set House of Commons speech, in the exposition of a bill or a budget statement, the logical presentation of facts moving from the general to the particular, the sort of thing that gave Asquith the nickname 'The Hammer', Lloyd George was at his worst. His budget presentations were uniform disasters. They so frightened and exhausted him that he broke down in the middle of the 1909 Budget speech and again during the presentation of the National Insurance Bill in 1911. So long as he lived he was at home on the public platform. Here the task was to communicate feelings, not facts. Like any good actor he associated the audience with his own emotions. His pathos, anger, and humor became the audience's. Nearly always his public speeches were attacks, the message was outrage, and the punctuation humor. Rarely, virtually never, did he explain in any detail what it was he intended to do to eliminate the particular horror he denounced. A few examples, endlessly elaborated, describing grasping landlords, worldly and hypocritical bishops, corrupt arms manufacturers, or starving children in concentration camps, would suffice.

Hence the researchers will not find much in Lloyd George's public speeches about any legislative program. He dealt with problems, not solutions. Oratory, he once told Winston Churchill, was the 'art of successful dilution.'[23] He gave more detailed advice to Harold Macmillan during the future Prime Minister's early years in parliament in the 1920s. Say

> just one thing; when you are a Minister two things, and when you are a Prime Minister winding up a debate perhaps three. Remember your own position. There will be few listeners. What you want is that somebody will go into the smoking room and say 'you know Macmillan made a very good speech.' 'What did he say?' someone will ask. It must be easy to give a ready answer—one point. Of course you wrap it up in different ways. You say it over and over again with different emphasis and different illustrations. You say it forcefully, regretfully, perhaps even threateningly; but it is a single clear point. That begins to make your reputation.[24]

This did not mean that he thought oratory unimportant or easy. The management of public feeling through the spoken word, Lloyd George felt, was the highest of all arts and he took great pains with his speeches, memorizing the most important parts and reinforcing himself with cue cards. For a big speech, Lloyd George told Herbert Lewis after he was in office, he took the day off, stayed in until about ten in the morning and then went for a walk. He thought of nothing. At about two he began to think of the speech, making notes, and at about six he was ready for a shorthand writer. He would then dictate the speech, and if it were carefully thought out he could remember it all word for word, although occasionally he wrote down heads of paragraphs. There were times, he remembered, that he forgot the whole speech except the first two lines. This appears to be a good summary of his technique of preparation except that he had remarked also on this occasion that he never gave his speeches to the press ahead of time, at most only to one reporter.[25] Unfortunately Beriah Evans reported the opposite in 1915. Lloyd George was a godsend to the 'working journalist', providing neatly typed copies of his speeches well before delivery, sometimes, it would appear, with 'cheers' already written in.[26]

Unquestionably Lloyd George's best oratory came in the years between 1890 and 1914, and perhaps before 1905, at the time when he could only persuade, not command. His sense of timing, the altered cadences, the throaty whisper followed by a roar, the swelling peroration, were all tricks learned, one suspects, by Churchill, who added a literary style and a sense of history that Lloyd George did not possess. But Churchill never moved the audiences to tears or frenzy. He riveted them to a meaning of their own heritage by explaining and exemplifying it, but he did not, as Lloyd George did, carry them with himself. Men died for him, but no one ever stood to shout from the back of a provincial tabernacle 'Thank God for Winston Leonard Spencer Churchill,' although they may have said it in their prayers. One should note however that Churchill's style was not good for campaign speeches while Lloyd George's was perfect. Throughout his political life Churchill had constituency trouble. In addition, he could not remember names. He was one of the greatest parliamentarians of his age, but he had difficulty in remaining a Member of the House of Commons.

II

The first words uttered by Lloyd George in the House of Commons to be recorded by *Hansard* were pronounced on 24 April, a week after his introduction, when he asked the Leader of the House, W.H. Smith, whether the government intended to take steps toward the enfranchisement of leaseholds.[27] He received the unpromising answer that the government had no plans at that time to deal with this ancient Welsh grievance. (It could be noted that enfranchisement of leaseholds was finally enacted at the behest of another Welsh Member, James Callaghan, in 1969.)

For the Welsh, the important issue before the House of Commons in the spring of 1890 was the Tithe (Rent Charge Recovery) Bill. This measure had been first put down in 1889 and withdrawn. It had been subsequently reintroduced on 27 March 1890 just as Lloyd George was fighting his battle for Caernarvon District. It would make the tithe a direct charge on the landlord and was the direct result of the tithe disturbances of the late eighties and of the agonies suffered by Welsh vicars in their efforts to collect what they thought was due them.

Lloyd George's attitude toward the bill was complex. On one hand, with the tithe harder to evade, the bill would increase its worth to tithe owners. As such, it was opposed in principle by Thomas Gee and some of the nonconformist radical group for which he was the spokesman and to whom Lloyd George usually looked for advice. But, on the other hand, Lloyd George and at least a few of the young Welsh nationalist MPs honestly looked forward to the day when the tithe would be appropriated, presumably with disestablishment, to the benefit of the Welsh people for educational and social ends. Therefore, keeping its payment sure and its amount undiminished was not undesirable. 'It adds twenty-five percent to the value of the tithe,' he wrote on 3 December 1890, 'and that is no mean thing by the time it is nationalized.'[28]

These calculations underlay his first parliamentary act of rebellion. On 5 June, a few days after his humiliation by Gladstone at Hawarden, he and D.A. Thomas accompanied the Conservatives into the lobby in opposition to an instruction to the standing committee considering the Tithe bill moved by Mr. F. S. Stevenson, Liberal of Northeast Suffolk. The instruction empowered the Committee to 'provide for the equitable revision of tithes in accordance with the altered condition of agriculture,' in effect for a lowering of the tithe. The instruction had official Liberal support and Rendel spoke in favor of it.[29]

Lloyd George was roundly attacked in the Welsh press for his 'Tory vote.' It was 'an error not to be lightly passed over and certainly not to be repeated,' wrote one journal, even on the grounds of conscience by a person who, 'in refusing to give the pledge which the Rev. Evan Jones had so imperiously demanded during the trying time of the Parliamentary by-election,' had shown himself 'to be a man of stout backbone.'[30] If Lloyd George desired success in the House of Commons, lectured the *Carnarvon Herald,* he would be well-advised to 'turn a deaf ear to such will-o-the-wisps as the senior member from Merthyr,' i.e. D.A. Thomas.[31] Both of these assumptions were wrong. Lloyd George was not under the influence of D.A. Thomas, nor was his risky vote against his party the product of an excessively developed moral sense, although he defended himself in these terms to Uncle Lloyd. The rebellion against the Stevenson instruction was the declaration of a calculated posture of independence. And he was sure that whatever loss he suffered in his standing in the party at Westminster—of which he had none in any case—in the long run it would be more than recovered in Wales. This was immediately confirmed in a letter sent to the press by John Parry, Gee's partner in the tithe rebellion. Later Lloyd George explained himself with careful logic in an open letter to J.E. Roberts, the chairman of the Caernarvon District Liberal Association. Pledged as he was 'to a policy of nationalizing the tithe, I strongly object to the adoption of any suggestion which will result in the frittering away of this valuable national endowment. The notion that any part of the savings would be passed along to the tenants is fanciful.'[32]

As it turned out the government, pressed for time, withdrew the Tithe Bill on 14 July, promising to introduce it yet a third time. Still this was not the end of the matter. In July Lloyd George and Thomas were in Aberdare where they had to explain their vote again and insist that Members be given liberty of judgement on second and third rate measures.[33] There were repercussions also in London where Rendel strove to bind up the wounds. He called a meeting of Welsh MPs at his house at No. 1 Carlton Gardens on 7 June to attempt to restore relations between the Welsh and Liberal leadership—a matter that was already causing comment in the papers. Although Lloyd George chatted amiably with Gladstone, the meeting accomplished nothing and itself evoked further comment. In the end, even though both Gladstone and Harcourt were reported to have approved

Lloyd George's maiden speech when it finally came on 13 June, the new Member's reputation after the first session was of a political insurgent.[34]

Lloyd George's maiden speech needs to be mentioned only briefly. It was in support of an amendment by his friend A.H.D. Acland to devote the six pence per gallon tax on spirits that had been included in the budget for compensation for suppressed pub licenses, to technical education. The £350,000 that the spirit tax would produce, which was proposed to be devoted to 'pensioning the publicans,' was not enough, he said, to have an effect on the drinking problem even in the county of Caernarvonshire, let alone the whole country. He scoffed at the motives of the Members opposite who proposed plans to reduce drinking without hurting anybody. There was, for instance, the Member for South Paddington (Lord Randolph Churchill) whose enthusiasm for temperance seemed to have disappeared. 'His, at best, was a kind of mushroom teetotalism, which grew no one knew why or where and which had disappeared, where no one exactly knows.' He understood again, that the brewers had recently interviewed the Member for West Birmingham (Joseph Chamberlain) asking for a promise that they would receive compensation. How, wondered Lloyd George, could they have doubted the Right Honorable Gentleman's concern for the trade? 'He could quite understand his Liberalism being doubted, but on this great question...he ought to be above suspicion.'[35]

These sallies against two of his former heroes, witty, penetrating, and unfair, became the model for Lloyd George's future House of Commons style, as indeed the same highly personal invective had frequently been used by the men he denounced. Although estranged from his Liberal colleagues, Chamberlain, the former messiah of advanced radicalism, was nevertheless attempting to keep intact his credentials as a reformer and it was precisely in these terms, as a secret capitalist exploiter mouthing an insincere and seedy Liberalism, that Lloyd George attacked him.

The Acland Amendment was of course defeated, but the results were vast. On 26 June the compensation clauses were dropped from the Licensing Bill then under consideration, but the Speaker ruled out of order Chancellor of Exchequer Goschen's proposal that the money already raised by the spirit duty be allowed to accumulate and be spent by subsequent legislation. Therefore, as Acland had wished, Goschen persuaded the House to devote the 'whiskey money' to technical education administered by county councils, thus putting the councils firmly into the business of education, but more important, stimulating at the same time the illegal, as it turned out, development of secondary education by local school boards. England and Wales acquired therefore two competing secondary education authorities, all of which led to the tangle that Balfour and R.L. Morant sought to unravel in the 1902 Education Act.

Toward the end of the session Lloyd George planned, with Sam Evans, a new foray during supply debate, this time attacking ceremonial expenditures, small sums proposed for the investiture of Prince Henry of Prussia with the Garter, for the equipage for the Earl of Zetland as Lord Lieutenant of Ireland, and for £180 to defray the expenses of the funeral of the Duchess of Cambridge. Denunciations of these inoffensive celebrities would hurt him within the party but that was not important. 'I cannot gain much in the House of Commons by my speech,' he wrote on 12 August, after several days of preparation. On the contrary. 'I may lose much influence—these MPs are so frightfully decorous and respectable. My audience is the country.'[36] His speech in support of an amendment reducing these expenditures was in the tradition of his maiden speech, funny, outrageous, and bitter. What had Prince Henry done for his own country, let alone Great Britain, to merit an expenditure by the House of Commons? Again, the Lord Lieutenant was not the governor of Ireland, the Chief Secretary was, as he frequently pointed out. The Lord Lieutenant was 'simply a man in buttons who wears silk stockings and has a coat of arms on his carriage.' The post was a sinecure. (The Lord Lieutenant, in fact, received £20,000 per year, twice as much as any other member of the ministry.)

By this time the supply committee was in an uproar and Lloyd George was sharply reminded by the chairman that an office placed upon the consolidated fund could not be criticized in the House. Nevertheless he pressed on, comparing the uselessness of the £3,000 proposed for the Lord Lieutenant to the importance of another £3,000 listed for the Dublin Metropolitan Police, a force 'which is as necessary to the present system of government as the Lord Lieutenant is unnecessary.' Finally he observed that the £180 toward the funeral of the Duchess of Cambridge, for a family that already received about £3,000,000 from the Exchequer, would undermine patriotism in the country. Such burdens on thrifty toil and additional oppression on the misery of the poor were a blot on civilization. 'I do not believe,' he concluded, 'that this gorgeousness and this ostentation of wealth is necessary in order to maintain the Constitution. On the contrary I think it does far more to repress, than to promote, sentiments of loyalty.'[37]

Lloyd George left the committee debate in a shambles. One member, in a fury, offered to pay the £180 himself. Moreover, the young Member for Caernarvon District had the satisfaction of seeing two of the most skilled forensic humorists at Westminster, Henry Labouchere and Timothy Healy, intervene to prolong the chaos. In the end his amendment did not, in fact, do badly. It drew 27 votes to 49 against it.[38]

On 18 August the session ended. Within the terms he had set for himself, his first four months in London had been successful. Even if his behavior had not conformed to the standard usually expected of new Members of the House of Commons, he had drawn attention to Wales and to himself with a crude vigor that would not soon be forgotten. After a shaky start, he had squared himself with his constituents in Caernarvon District, had pestered the government with questions about leases for mineral extraction on crown land or whether the mayor of Caernarvon would be appointed Constable of the Castle, and he had seen his insubordination over the tithe and ceremonial expenses come to be applauded in Welsh newspapers. (No doubt he would have been proud to know that his speech of 13 August had evoked a complaint from the Queen to the Prime Minister.) He had made himself a public figure. Whether he received approbation or abuse made no difference so long as his name was known. It was far better to be the center of controversy than to be forgotten.

III

Amid all his public activity, his domestic experience had been unhappy. He had received invitations from Welsh-connected Londoners, from D. H. Evans the draper, who seems to have offered him a directorship which he scornfully rejected, and from Sir John Puleston of Pwllheli, Tory MP for Devonport, who had supported Ellis-Nanney in 1890, and who would himself become Constable of Caernarvon Castle in August. But he soon found that he liked neither of them. The continuing theme of his correspondence during the first parliamentary session is his loneliness for Margaret. Except for a brief stay in London with her husband at the home of R.O. Davies in Acton—which allowed him to practice his Metropolitan Tabernacle speech to her—she did not come to London again until 1891. He returned to Wales only rarely.[39] In his letters he wailed about the dreariness of his life and of how he hated to leave the exciting precincts of Westminster for his gloomy room, which may have reinforced usefully his expressed intention to learn the rules and practices of the House of Commons as quickly as possible, but which also made his letters a curious combination of self-congratulation and self-pity. He lived most of the summer in a room at 6 Craven Street next to Charing Cross Station, which was convenient to the House of Commons and which had the attractiveness of the Embankment Gardens nearby, but was otherwise dark and sooty. After parliament rose he returned to his family still in, but soon to leave, Mynydd Ednyfed farm and now enlarged by the arrival of Mair Eluned on 2 August. However, even the birth of a first daughter could not keep him from politics. He was busier than ever at speeches and now not only in temperance and disestablishment rallies. Whatever were the estimates of his weight in the House of Commons, the leaders of the Liberal party no longer had any doubts about his power to influence the public outside and so in the autumn of 1890 he appeared for the first time in the company of front bench party leaders at official party meetings dealing with questions of daily importance. On 20 September at St. Helen's he shared a platform with John Morley in a denunciation of Balfour's administration in Ireland and of the arrest of John Dillon and William O'Brien (both of whom, in the event, escaped and made their way to the United States). Balfour he asserted was 'the fiendish spirit of aristocracy incarnate.' Concluding as he usually did with a reference to Wales he reminded the audience of the similar

> miserable minority in Wales, who because they are of a certain class and of a certain religion think they have the right to monopolize the resources of the soil, to monopolize the educational advantages of the country, and, more than that, to set their lords and baronets to defame and revile my country in the ears of Royalty. And why? It is because Welshmen prefer to worship at the simple altars of their fathers rather than to bow down in the House of Rimmon. That is the secret of it. And in the fight Irishmen are making against religious inequality, I would say 'heaven help them.'[40]

The effort at St. Helen's was important as his first appearance as a

Liberal party spokesman outside his own constituency and was followed by a gratifying accolade from Morley. But it was only one of ten full-scale public addresses in Wales and England that Lloyd George made between the beginning of September and the middle of November, mostly before the familiar anti-drink and anti-Church audiences, and including, as at St. Helen's, usually a reference to Ireland's struggle for freedom and the obvious parallels in Wales. However, in Bangor on 11 November, at Penrhyn Hall he returned to the topic of land reform and dealt with it now in terms that would remain little changed for the next quarter century.[41]

Although through the autumn Lloyd George had rarely made a speech on any topic without some reference to the record of Conservative misgovernment in Ireland, one may question the depth of his personal commitment to Irish Home Rule. But until the middle of November there seemed no doubt that Irish grievances would provide a Liberal electoral opportunity. Parnell's triumphant vindication on the matter of the Pigott letter, in February, 1889, appeared to have transformed Gladstone's proposal for an Irish parliament from a just but hopeless dream into a practical and valuable political asset. For eighteen months Liberalism and Home Rule seemed inevitable. The next election would see their triumph. (On 22 October 1890, in the Eccles division of Lancashire, the Liberals captured, solely on the Irish issue, a seat that had been Conservative without interruption, through various boundary changes, since 1859.) Then on 17 November 1890 all these optimistic prospects fell to pieces with the announcement in the newspapers that Captain William O'Shea, former Nationalist MP for County Clare, had been granted a divorce from his wife Katherine and that C.S. Parnell had been named corespondent. There had been no defense.

Unhappily the revelations of Parnell's long adultery with Kitty O'Shea came on the eve of the National Liberal Federation meeting in Sheffield on 20 and 21 November, which Lloyd George himself attended and addressed. There was as yet no public word on the attitude of the leader of the party, but there were many angry complaints about the Liberals' association with a party led by so disreputable a man. (J.J. Colman, the mustard maker and Liberal MP for Norwich, predicted that the party would lose at least five seats in East Anglia alone.[42] More serious, a number of prospective Liberal candidates announced that they intended to withdraw.) The rising disaffection among Liberal politicians remained private at first, but public outrage in the newspapers, particularly those directed at nonconformist readers, appeared instantly and between 17 November and 25 November, when parliament reassembled, grew steadily in volume. Opinion, private and public, voiced a uniform demand. Parnell could not remain the leader of the Irish party if the Liberals were to support Home Rule. However, Parnell refused to resign and denounced the Liberals for attempting to dictate to the Irish. The Liberals, correspondingly, were in despair. 'Anger and despondency reigned supreme on the Liberal benches,' wrote Lloyd George that evening. 'A gloom has overcast our late jubilance. The Tories, on the other, can hardly restrain their joyousness. Confound it all.'[43]

Lloyd George's thoughts on the Parnell tragedy, reflected in his letters to Wales during late November and early December, demonstrate the strict separation that he always maintained between personalities and public events. On one hand the Irish party was a problem for the Liberals. Parnell had allowed his personal life to intrude into politics. Because 'he could not restrain a single passion' he had destroyed the momentum toward Home Rule and more important had harmed the chances of an overwhelming Gladstonian victory, not to mention ruining his own career. In Lloyd George's mind this was base and unprofessional behavior. But it was 'a still worse business for some of us fellows holding doubtful seats. Parnell's fame is certain were he to resign at this moment. Not so most of us who have our spurs to win and this fellow by his idiotic misconduct ruins us all.'[44]

On the other hand, he retained a private admiration of Parnell's calm arrogance in the face of attack. Parnell walked about 'as cool and defiant as ever, puffing at his cigar,' he wrote on 3 December. His fight 'is simply sublime. It shows what a leader he is and the stuff he is made of. He is a grand fighter.'[45]

There were those among Welsh Members of Parliament who saw an opportunity for Wales in the Liberal leadership's suddenly weakened position. This would be the time to demand a priority for disestablishment. Spokesmen in Wales and Hugh Price Hughes in London thundered against Parnell and, by implication, the Irish cause which for many of them had never commanded more than a lukewarm enthusiasm in any case. Lloyd George himself had written in November to Ellis who was now seeking to regain his health in South Africa that 'for Wales I see but one way out of the difficulty and that is to fight the next election on disestablishment and practically ignore the Irish question...We are absolutely demoralized. There is no fight left in us. The House simply rushes through business. There is practically no opposition...the Welsh Party (!) met on Tuesday and elaborately resolved to do nothing.'[46] But Stuart Rendel, who himself had nearly retired from his seat in 1886 as a result of the breakdown of the party truce in Montgomeryshire over Home Rule, nevertheless continued to try to mediate between Wales and London. 'Gladstone has burnt every bridge but his own,' he is reported to have said bitterly. But 'to force Wales forward now,' he wrote on 26 December 1890 to Gee, who was himself an ardent Wales firster, would be 'as mean and contemptible as it would be injudicious and intemperate.'[47]

For Lloyd George personally, loyalties, public and private, were contradictory. His real admiration for Parnell was one thing. But he cared nothing for Home Rule unless Wales were included. However, his public position had to be precisely the reverse. He could not for a moment condone adultery before the starchy conventionalities of Caernarvon District nonconformity, but neither could he go so far as many other Welshmen and denounce Home Rule. Some of his 'best supporters' were Caernarvon Roman Catholics and he had found it necessary to remonstrate as recently as July when the local school board had attempted to resist a government grant to a Roman Catholic school.[48]

So for once, at least briefly, Lloyd George agreed with his leader. On 3 January 1891, he wrote to the newspaper *Genedl Gymreig* urging his countrymen to draw a distinction between Parnell the man and the cause of Home Rule. 'Time is quickly effacing the unfortunate impression caused by

Parnell's betrayal,' he observed, 'and the country, having had time for reflection, is beginning to realize that the misconduct of a gentleman, who happened at the time to lead the Irish nation, is not the reason for withholding privileges from his followers.'[49]

Lloyd George may have felt that the fortunes of Irish nationalism, whatever he thought of them privately, and those of Wales were somehow intertwined. Paradoxically, the fall of Parnell seems to have hurt, rather than helped, the Welsh nationalist movement by allowing the Liberal party to turn its attention to other, less arcane, matters in which the Welsh were not concerned. Possibly a contributing factor was the renewed illness of Tom Ellis at the end of 1890 and his long absence from Westminster through the spring of 1891. More important was the split in the Irish party into an anti-Parnellite and, much smaller, a pro-Parnellite faction, whose competition for attention in the House of Commons would mean, as it turned out, less, not more regard for Welsh affairs. But at the same time, the loss of Parnell's implacable authority made possible within the next few years the renewed insertion of a Tory wedge, 'killing Home Rule with kindness,' between English Liberalism and its Irish allies.

At any rate, after the winter of 1890, the steam went out of the intellectual Welsh nationalist movement. Interest in Welsh Home Rule had begun to subside in North Wales. Even in September when Ellis, at Bala, called for a recognition of Welsh 'nationality and brotherhood,' he evoked no response. In the spring of 1891 the voice of the movement, the journal *Cymru Fydd*, died. At the same time in the South nationalism was being replaced by economic issues.[50]

All this did not mean that Lloyd George, Sam Evans, D.A. Thomas, and to some extent Ellis himself, would give up diversion and obstruction, the bringing of Welsh affairs to the attention of the House of Commons, or that the fight for disestablishment was over. Indeed, 1894 and 1895 would see disestablishment for the first time actually under debate in the House of Commons. But the heroic days of the later eighties, of the romantic Welsh revival, of the Wales-to-be idealism that Ellis had represented and which had helped bring Lloyd George to the House of Commons, were over. When Welsh nationalism revived in the middle of the decade, with Ellis now a Liberal Whip, it was strictly a non-ideological political organization with which Lloyd George hoped to organize the Welsh electorate.

IV

Among the effects of the Parnell crisis was the absence, temporarily, of the Irish members from the House of Commons and accordingly a sudden expedition of parliamentary business. In a letter on 3 December 1891 Lloyd George noted that without Irish obstruction, the second reading of the Tithe Bill, which had been reintroduced on 27 November, had taken only one night instead of two.[51] But in place of the Irish, Lloyd George and Sam Evans, assisted by William Abraham and Osborne Morgan, set out themselves on a program of systematic harassment. Together they fought the bill by delay, diversion, and occasionally by sheer fantasy. No possible ramification of a clause was too remote to require amendment. Night after night the House was forced to debate the possible application of rules designed for the entire nation south of the Tweed to the peculiar usages of Wales. There were of course advantages here for the Liberal party but it might also, Lloyd George thought, teach them something in the art of obstruction.[52]

The third Tithe Bill was shorter and simpler than the second, but aimed to accomplish essentially the same things. As before Lloyd George had still no desire to destroy the bill, and less to see the tithe reduced. His goal was to draw attention to Welsh grievances, to the Welsh party, and to himself. 'Of course, we shall be defeated,' he wrote to Gee on 2 February, 'but by these discussions we manage to keep the pot boiling and the Liberal party thereby is awakening to the fact that Welsh questions are very useful—quite as useful as Irish ones—to hurl at the government.'[53]

When it was over he was satisfied. 'It was such a glorious struggle for Wales,' he wrote Ellis on 11 April, about two weeks after the Tithe Bill received the Royal Assent. 'Wales practically monopolized the attention of the House for fully three weeks. To my mind that is the great fact of the Tithe Bill opposition.' Now, he thought, was clearly the time to begin a new disestablishment campaign which would go on unless 'regrettable jealousies between N. and S.W. Lib Fed upset business.'[54] 'You have heard,' Lloyd George continued, 'of our victory in the local veto bill. Quite unexpected as all Welsh were absent except the staunch teetotalers amongst them.'[55]

The reported triumph referred to the Liquor Traffic Local Veto (Wales) Bill introduced by W. Bowen Rowland of Cardiganshire. It would have allowed a local authority to close all public houses within its area under certain circumstances. The measure, to everyone's surprise, received a second reading on 18 March (185 to 179), after the government, in an attempt to appease the United Kingdom Alliance, had allowed a free vote. Lloyd George spoke forcefully in its favor but his Caernarvonshire colleague, William Rathbone, had been seen leaving the chamber without voting. The victory in any case was entirely symbolic. The committee stage was adjourned by the Tories who chose instead to attend the Derby and the bill was withdrawn on 21 April.[56]

After his frantic activity early in the session Lloyd George spoke little in April and May. Except for an attempt to reduce the army estimate by £100 late in the session, on the excuse that troops had been used in Wales to suppress tithe disturbances, an idea evidently given him by Gee in February, he made only one other major speech during the session.[57] This came on the Elementary Education Bill, which was a major government effort to settle on a substitute for payment by results in elementary schools and more important to secure at the same time the place of Church schools in the national system by abolishing school fees in voluntary schools and board schools alike and giving each instead ten shillings per pupil from the Treasury. This frankly political step on behalf of sectarian education—the chief beneficiary from fees were the voluntary schools—had been taken lest the Liberals do something worse. As such the bill offered a splendid opening for an attack upon the Church and for an airing again of Welsh grievances in general, while embarrassing also his own party, whose leaders found it difficult to oppose a bill extending the principle of public education.[58] In a speech on 23 June and continued on 24 June, Lloyd George dwelt as usual entirely on Welsh and specifically Caernarvonshire grievances, deploring unjustly, in terms of his own experience, the quality of Church education and dwelling on the problems of nonconformists who attempted to construct schools of their own.[59]

These were cheap shots which aroused even Hugh Ellis-Nanney to compose an open letter reminding the world that Lloyd George himself had been educated in a Church school, but the cumulative effect was to give the session of 1891, even more than 1890, the stamp of Wales.[60] Welsh obstruction was not much less distressing to Liberal leadership than Irish obstruction and more visible in the recent session because of the crisis in the Irish leadership.

On the whole, the 1891 session was unremarkable even in an age when voters expected less from their elected representatives. But from the first, the Salisbury government had not been exceptionally popular. Whereas Disraeli's administration had suffered a net loss of five seats at by-elections in six years, Salisbury lost a net of twenty in the same length of time and, except for a few weeks after the temporary fillip of the Parnell scandal, the government in its last two years was obviously running out of energy. All this made it easier for Welsh insurgents to upset the routine of a House of Commons that was continually being counted out. But it raised before Lloyd George also the prospect of a renewed fight for his seat before he had fully established himself either at Westminster or in his constituency. He had received a warning of trouble to come the previous August when the government, ignoring representations from the town itself that were reinforced by questions in the House from Lloyd George, had appointed Sir John Puleston, recently adopted candidate for Caernarvon District, as Constable of Caernarvon Castle.

Puleston contrasted in every way to the diffident Ellis-Nanney and indeed, at the time of Lloyd George's adoption in 1889 he had been the man, it was generally assumed, who would replace Edmund Swetenham, whom the Conservatives were anxious to drop.[61] He was cheerful and outgoing. 'Pleasant Puleston' was a nickname. He had a house near Pwllheli. He was as much a figure at Eisteddfod as Lloyd George. 'The Eisteddfod Knight' was another nickname. Finally, he had given up a constituency with a solid one thousand majority to contest Caernarvon District. Clearly Lloyd George's was one Welsh seat the Conservatives intended to recover. The election in Caernarvon District would be a 'test election' remarked the *Cambrian News* in 1891 when Puleston was adopted. Lloyd George was one of only three or four Members of Parliament who spoke for Wales. The rest might as well represent 'Timbuctoo', and a Liberal defeat in Caernarvon District would be a blow to disestablishment.[62]

These considerations were perfectly clear to Lloyd George. His correspondence through 1891 showed increasing concern about the safety of his seat and his frequent absences from parliament after the passage of the Tithe Bill were the result of trips to North Wales for speaking and politics.

On one of these occasions at Penrhyn Hall in Bangor on 21 May 1891, in the course of an attack upon the tithe and Tory landowners, he touched upon the topic of rating of ground rents as a means of attacking the landlords' untaxed income. And he reiterated again his old demand for leasehold enfranchisement. Because these were of such exceptional importance for his future career the speech deserves to be quoted at length. 'Tories,' he began, 'are landowners, they are landlords who squander the wealth of the country. They are monopolists, men who own much but who do nothing.'

> These are the governing forces of the Tory party. The land of this country was distributed amongst its owners, the predecessors of its present holders, for the expressed purpose of enabling them to organize and maintain a military system in the country for the defence of its coasts, and even for aggressive purposes when necessary. The land was also to maintain royalty, and to bear the expense of dispensing justice and preserving law and order. Now, what has happened? The land is still in the possession of a privileged few but what has become of the burden of maintaining the army, law, order, and royalty? It has been shifted upon the shoulders of the toilers of this country.
>
> Why in this very Bangor union, where you have noblewomen and squires enjoying riches which they are at their wits' end to know how to squander and commanding such amplitude of resources that they are absolutely running to waste for want of use, I was startled to observe in the last return of pauperism that on January 1 last, one out of every twenty of the population was in receipt of parish relief.
>
> In London with all its deplorable poverty, the paupers constituted but one out of every 39 of the population.
>
> As the law stands at present a landlord may let his land for building purposes, charge a ground rent ten times the agricultural value of that land, and at the end of sixty years take possession of land, buildings, and all. And yet, although the local rates are being spent to improve his property by drainage, gas, street improvements, and in other ways, he does not contribute a penny toward that expenditure. The whole of the local expenditure, so far as the land is concerned, falls upon the poor householder who, after paying heavy rates and extortionate ground rents, has to surrender the whole fruits of his labour to his landlord, who does nothing. Now, when the Liberal Party, during the present session of Parliament, proposed that the landlord should at least bear his share of the local rates, the Tories in a body voted against it.[63]

Behind the violence of language lay the germ of a program of land reform that finally would appear in the budget of 1909. Indeed the speech itself paralleled, in some parts almost line for line, the much more famous Limehouse speech of 30 July 1909.

At Bangor, as in a host of less important addresses to follow, Lloyd George was of course looking to the next election. He needed issues. With the assignment of its payment to the landlord, the tithe issue was dead, while disestablishment, the larger expression of tithe resistance, however useful for rallying Calvinist Methodist support, was at bottom largely a symbolic issue. Its achievement would not alter at all the living and working conditions of the ordinary Welshman.

But more important, he was attempting to develop a personal political position, establishing a place for himself on social and economic land issues distinct from the all-out nationalization advocated by Michael Daniel Jones and Evan 'Pan' Jones while staying far in advance of anything supported by the official Liberal Party. These notions changed very little through his career. Rating of site values, leasehold enfranchisement, control of rent and land usage, the speeding of acquisition of land for public use by local authorities, issues that evolved very early, would remain the constant in a varied and hectic political life. Although they were born as facets of Welsh nationalism they survived to become major national issues in British politics long after the Welsh demands with which Lloyd George had associated had either subsided or had been fulfilled. Thus the Bangor speech, coming at a time when Lloyd George was chiefly occupied with attacks on the Church, is of exceptional importance as a public declaration of war on landlords that would culminate in the Budget of 1909 and the land campaign of 1913 and 1914.

V

After the 1891 session was prorogued on 5 August Lloyd George plunged again into a frenzy of speech making, interrupted occasionally by short excursions into legal practice. At the beginning of October he was at Newcastle for the annual meeting of the National Liberal Federation urging his party colleagues to include Welsh disestablishment in the program that would become theoretically the party platform in the coming election. Here he repeated his sneers, first displayed in the Metropolitan Tabernacle seventeen months before, about the now worrying Church revival in Wales.[64] Although his speech received the usual favorable newspaper notices, it was clearly Tom Ellis's earnest plea for justice for Wales, far more than Lloyd George's tirade, that won for disestablishment second place on the famous Newcastle Program, after Home Rule.[65] Gladstone's apparent acceptance of the program on 2 October and particularly of disestablishment, muddled as his statement was, constituted for the Welsh nonetheless a great victory. However, disestablishment now would have to compete with a host of other proposals of far wider national appeal.

Then, with singularly unfortunate timing, the Church of England chose the week following the convention of the National Liberal Federation to hold its Annual Church Congress at Rhyl. Lloyd George affected to regard this assembly as an insult to the dignity of Welsh nonconformity and used the occasion of a free church meeting the next month, also held at Rhyl, for an attack on Church wealth and on its pretensions to represent Wales that may have achieved a new level of sarcastic imagery. 'The priests of this church,' he said,

> arrogantly claim to be the spiritual successors of Peter, the plain gloved, honest old fisherman. Why if he could have turned up at the Church Congress held in this town the other day there is not a prelate or Prebendary or a dean amongst them who would not have shunned him. They would probably hand him over to some convenient curate to be proselytized, and he, no doubt, would warn him against the pernicious habit of attending conventicles to listen to an unordained carpenter's

son. But can you by any stretch of the imagination picture Peter coming down to attend the Church Congress in a special train, with a man in buttons dancing about him, carrying a jeweled crozier, and marching in an elaborate procession to attend the Congress? Can you portray him driving up in a brougham to the door of the House of Lords, lolling on its scarlet benches, and in his archiepiscopal twang drawling out a series of speeches in favor of county courting and imprisoning his co-religionists for refusing to pay a tribute to which they have conscientious objection? Can you imagine him dwelling in a stately mansion with a host of menials ministering to his luxuries? Can you fancy him drawing a salary large enough to keep the temple going for months—and all this with the poor rolling in misery at the very gates of his palace?

You may recall the indignation that was excited in clerical circles with my association of the so called church revival in Wales with the pewter pot. Well the surroundings of the recent Church Congress gave to my remarks some countenance. The congress ran two beer booths on its grounds. Can you fancy any Non-conformist bodies in Wales providing whiskey and bitter beer to their assemblies? I am told that a good number of Proselytes were induced to serve as samples to the English bishops of what the new process turned out. If that be so, then I am not at all surprised to hear that with such refreshment sold on the ground the recent Church Congress turned out to be a great financial success.[66]

This speech provoked A.G. Edwards, Bishop of St. Asaph, as after the Metropolitan Tabernacle address, to make a reply which evoked a counter-blast from Lloyd George, leading to a series of speeches and rebuttals which kept North Wales entertained, and Lloyd George in the public eye, for months.

But even while occupied with his continuing war with Bishop Edwards, Lloyd George had begun another extremely important project directed, as was everything he did at this time, toward securing his reelection. By December he was forming a syndicate composed chiefly of Welsh MPs with some prominent nonconformist ministers to purchase a number of Welsh newspapers. This was a far more ambitious project than had been the founding of the modest *Ugdorn Rhyddid* in 1889 (which appears to have survived for one year only). This time Lloyd George was in a position to solicit help from a number of men of real wealth, of whom two of the most important were Alfred and David Alfred Thomas. The two Thomases, who had no familial connection, were both from South Wales and, by 1891, were both MPs of some standing among the new radical generation, Alfred Thomas from Glamorganshire East since 1885 and David Alfred Thomas from Merthyr since 1888. Although Alfred Thomas was fifteen years older, at that time wealthier, had been in the House of Commons longer, and had a background of distinction in local politics as well as a strong grip on nonconformist affairs through his presidency of the Baptist Union of Wales, he was, by the early nineties, being surpassed among the coming Welsh leaders by D.A. Thomas, a far more forceful and intelligent figure, who was just beginning to emerge as South Wales's leading colliery owner and coal broker.[67] The careers of both these men would be entwined with

Lloyd George's for many years. Alfred Thomas remained a consistent supporter, both political and financial, until the end of his active parliamentary life in 1910 when he retired to appear as Lord Pontypridd in 1912. D.A. Thomas took the lead in destroying Lloyd George's attempt to convert the feeble Welsh parliamentary party into a political machine on the Irish model, but returned to Lloyd George's service in 1915, at great danger to his own health, to save the floundering British munitions program in the United States and Canada.

Lloyd George undertook at the end of the year negotiations for the formation of a syndicate to purchase *Y Genedl Gymreig* ('The Welsh Nation') now the most popular Welsh language newspaper in the North. By December 1891 plans were well advanced. On 21 December he wrote enthusiastically to Ellis asking for an article to appear in the first edition of the paper under the new management. Everything, he assured his correspondent, was going splendidly. The leading divines of all four denominations had offered help. D.A. and Alfred Thomas 'have promised to come in,' as had Ellis Griffith, Herber Evans and T. Parry. 'Rathbone will also, I think, remain with us. He had £500 in the old concern.' (Presumably the now defunct *Ugdorn Rhyddid*.) But incidentally Lloyd George was looking to Ellis for £100, Sam Evans for £200, and Herbert Lewis for £50.[68]

By spring the syndicate formed to buy the *Genedl* had become the Welsh National Press Ltd. and had acquired also the *North Wales Observer and Express,* which as the *Express* had printed in 1880 the first 'Brutus' article on Lord Salisbury's ruined character, and *Y Weryn* ('The Democracy'), a labor paper devoted to quarrymen's affairs.

The directors of the company, which announced its existence on 13 May 1892, had altered somewhat from the list of prospective supporters of the previous winter. Beside Lloyd George, Ellis, and Sam Evans, included now were William Abraham, the miners' MP from the Rhondda, David Randall, MP for Gower, Alfred Thomas, and Major Evan Rowland Jones, proprietor of the *Shipping World,* the United States Consul for South Wales, and Liberal candidate for Carmarthen District.[69] Major Jones was elected in 1892 and was for a short time a close social friend of Lloyd George. One may speculate that he and Alfred Thomas represented some of the important financial strength for what was by now a most expensive undertaking. Beriah Evans became Managing Editor.

The proprietorship of some of the most powerful newspapers in the North, added to the unwavering help of Gee's *Baner,* could not fail to make Lloyd George a little more secure in what remained none the less a difficult Liberal constituency. Beriah Evans wrote twenty-five years later that after the election Lloyd George agreed the papers were responsible for his increased majority. Similarly Sir John Puleston blamed Evans's editorial support for helping Lloyd George win.[70] This may be true, but the insignificant increase in Lloyd George's majority in June 1892 was far smaller than the general swing to the Liberals in Wales in that year. Whether his newspaper support, or his earnest propagation of the Calvinistic Methodists, or his careful attention to his constituency was the cause of this victory is impossible to say. Lloyd George did not approach what could be termed a safe majority until 1906. But there can be no doubt that the formation of the Welsh National Press Limited was a most important expression of Lloyd George's continual fascination with newspapers and newspapermen. He never doubted that it was far more important to influence voters than to court popularity among parliamentary leaders. He rated good notices in the press, and the friendship of editors and proprietors who could produce them, as vital ingredients of political success.[71]

Parliament reassembled in February 1892 for what proved to be a short and generally undistinguished session. For Lloyd George and for the Welsh insurgents, the principal interest was the Clergy Discipline (Immorality) Bill. This harmless measure, supplementing the Church Discipline Act and the Public Worship Act of 1874, was designed to facilitate discipline in the Church by making simpler the removal of immoral but non-felonious incumbents of livings. The bill was endorsed by friends of the Church on both sides of the House. Gladstone himself was a warm supporter.

Previously, in the 1891 session, Lloyd George and Sam Evans had succeeded in embarrassing the government over the bill when the Chancellor of the Exchequer, G.J. Goschen, had incautiously presented the first four clauses, dealing only with the bishops' removal of incumbents, in the hope that even so late in the session these four (the whole already had passed the House of Lords) might be put into law. Sam Evans immediately moved an amendment that it was no part of the business of the state to interfere in the affairs of the Church and that the remedy for clerical indiscipline was disestablishment. Further, he said, the government had promised that no contentious measures would be taken up. After the failure of this amendment, Lloyd George moved that the debate be postponed for three months. There was a second row and eventually Goschen allowed debate to be adjourned.[72] Except for moving postponement of debate Lloyd George had hardly contributed to the government's discomfort. He nevertheless was in high spirits after Goschen's surrender. 'I don't see why we should be bothered with a confounded ecclesiastical bill,' he wrote to his wife the next day, 'when the session is already so late and there is so much essential work to be gotten rid of.'[73]

Finally, on 4 August, Goschen unhappily withdrew the truncated measure, admitting that even so simple and uncomplicated a bill could not be passed late in the session in the face of opposition from a few members 'chiefly from Wales' who seemed to be determined to prevent it.[74] When the House reassembled early in February the disposal of the criminous clerks appeared again in the Queen's speech. Its second reading in the House of Lords appropriately coincided exactly with the debate on a resolution by Samuel Smith, MP for Flintshire, for Welsh disestablishment. Such resolutions were by now almost an annual occurrence and Lloyd George's part, an attempt to deal with the problem of the apparent growing numbers of Church communicants in Wales, was undistinguished. But the debate should be noted for its general violence, particularly in attacks upon Thomas Gee, and for the speech of Sir John Puleston, who used it to open his campaign against Lloyd George by linking him with articles in the *Genedl*, which the Member for Caernarvon District was said to control, that were disloyal to the Queen and approving of republicanism.[75] After passing the Lords a second time, the Clergy Discipline Bill received its second reading in the House of Commons on 29 April. It was introduced by the new Leader of the House, A.J. Balfour, who had succeeded at the death of W.H. Smith the previous October. Balfour had already received some of Lloyd George's verbal missiles. While Chief Secretary for Ireland he had been the incarnation 'of the fiendish spirit of aristocracy.' His well-bred detachment made him an ideal target but his subtlety and quickness of mind provided him with defenses unavailable to more pompous Tories. Yet his unfailing good humor and charm eventually won him Lloyd George's friendship and the political lives of the two men were parallel for the next thirty years.

Balfour's speech on the Clergy Discipline Bill was, as customary, detailed and precise. Lloyd George's response as the first Liberal speaker was equally characteristic of the man. He ignored all Balfour had said. On an amendment that it was not the 'function of the State to attend to matters of spiritual discipline' (which was not in any event what the bill proposed), he launched into an attack on the Church itself. Why were bishops and archbishops not included in the bill? Why could not the Church be allowed to manage its own affairs? And anyway the remedy for everything was disestablishment.[76] The feature of the debate, quoted by *The Times* in a long and caustic lead article devoted entirely to Lloyd George's 'contradictory and puerile allegations,' was the intervention by Gladstone immediately following Lloyd George.[77] The Grand Old Man, at length and with many flourishes of antique parliamentary courtesy, undertook to explain to his young colleague that he had totally misapprehended a most desirable measure in the mistaken belief that to enact it would be to retard disestablishment.[78] To be taken seriously by the G.O.M., even in a fatherly lecture to a slightly backward child, was for Lloyd George most flattering.[79] But the encounter is of more importance than this. It demonstrated first of all Gladstone's complete parliamentary guilelessness which two generations of English politicians had used to make reputations. But more important for the moment, it suggested the veteran leader's total ignorance of what was going on within the Welsh wing of his party. This innocence disappeared in the standing committee on law when the bill was referred there. Lloyd George arranged to have himself, Sam Evans, Tom Ellis and Wynford Phillips, a Welshman sitting for a Scottish constituency, put on the committee, but Gladstone, whom no one remembered ever serving before on a parliamentary committee, asked to be appointed also. In committee the little band of Welshmen began again the tactic of systematized obstruction, useless amendment, and filibustering that they had employed against the Tithe Bill. Gladstone's response from the first day was no longer patient reasonableness but anger.[80] This time, however, the committee chairman, Henry Campbell-Bannerman, suffered the outrage for four days only. On 24 May, he effectively broke the resistance of the rebels by limiting the number of times each could speak on a single amendment. As there were only four of them, the power to delay until the government had dissolved parliament, which Lloyd George reported to his wife was his tactic, disappeared. After a row they withdrew from the committee vowing to reintroduce their one hundred odd leftover amendments at the report stage.

On 2 June, then, the battle began again, this time before the entire House. Through the afternoon and into the evening the business of state waited upon the determination of a bishop's power to discipline the occasional fun-loving but non-criminal vicar. Eventually at about 10 o'clock an exasperated Attorney General, on the open invitation of the Speaker, moved closure, which passed 151 to 21, and the bill was read a third time.[81] It received the royal assent on 27 June and parliament was dissolved the next day. The government had triumphed.

Lloyd George enjoyed the whole affair. His letters home are full of the usual encomiums on his own parliamentary skill interspersed with remarks upon the lethargy and ineptitude of the rest of the House. But he was aware also that behind the customary parliamentary courtesy and restraint that he enjoyed from his opponents there was growing a genuine dislike for him and his ways, particularly within his own party. Putting Wales before Liberalism might have been a necessity for his election and was at least understandable in the Tithe Bill. But by resisting the Clergy Discipline Bill, a measure of no particular concern to Wales and one ardently desired by the leaders of his party either because of devotion to the Church or because they wished to see the parliamentary session quickly ended, he was dividing his Welsh colleagues among themselves and alienating them from the party. The only conceivable benefit was to the Unionists and himself.

The chief sufferer was Stuart Rendel who only the previous autumn had been hailed by *The Times* as the first real leader Wales had found, one whose ascendancy was so great he was able to force good manners on ruffians like Lloyd George and Sam Evans.[82] After the rebellion in the law committee and Gladstone's denunciation of obstruction, Rendel was in despair. His laboriously built house was 'tumbling down like a pack of cards' he wrote to A.C. Humphreys-Owen on 28 May.[83] He could not understand the 'madness of Wales slapping John Morley and Mr. Gladstone in the face,' he continued to the same correspondent the next day.[84] Rendel insisted nevertheless that the party must continue to support Lloyd George for the sake of the seat. However, Morley was reported to be hoping that Lloyd George would lose.[85]

In case of a misstep Lloyd George could expect no indulgence from his colleagues, let alone the opposition. He experienced a brush with danger at the end of May when the insurrection over the Clergy Discipline Bill was at its height. On 29 May he attended a Mansion House dinner with Sam Evans, who, he had noticed at a previous City dinner, tended to drink too much and 'lose his dignity.'[86] At the Mansion House Evans, 'on a sudden impulse,' refused to rise to toast the Queen. There was an immediate uproar. Lascelles Carr, ardent Churchman and, more important, editor and proprietor of the largest Welsh newspaper, the *Western Mail* of Cardiff, was barely restrained from throwing a glass of wine in Evans's face. Another man wanted to throw him out.[87] Although Lloyd George, who himself had stood without raising his glass, entirely disapproved of Evans's behavior, the ensuing charges of indifferent patriotism continued for weeks and were aimed partly at him.[88] As it turned out, the charges followed him to

Caernarvon District and provided his first experience as a target of political violence.

VI

Even with an endless stream of congratulatory telegrams, resolutions of local Liberal federations, and encouraging editorial statements from Wales, Lloyd George was under no illusions that the fight over the Clergy Discipline Bill had solved his electoral problems. Early in May, when he was still assuming that he could blockade the bill until the end of the life of the parliament, he wrote Margaret outlining his plans for the campaign he expected then to begin about the middle of July and warning her he would accept no speaking engagements outside the Boroughs.[89]

Accordingly, once the Clergy Discipline Bill received its third reading and was beyond his mischief, Lloyd George left London for North Wales. By the second week of June he was busy with meetings and canvassing, principally in the critical towns of Caernarvon, Bangor and Conway. He appointed a new election agent, R.O. Roberts, a Caernarvon solicitor, and reported, as usual, 'splendid meetings.' He was 'more hero than a candidate' and everyone was very helpful. Nevertheless, he assured Maggie, 'it will be a very stiff contest.'[90] Earlier, *The Times* had freely predicted that Puleston would win.[91]

In a number of Welsh constituencies, particularly in the North where Calvinistic Methodists were strong, Unionist candidates, usually Liberal Unionists, were attempting to use anti-Catholic sentiment as a weapon against Home Rule. There was a report from Cardiganshire of a bargain offered by Chamberlainites to trade support for disestablishment for nonconformist resistance to an Irish parliament.[92] This strategy might have been dangerous to Lloyd George. He could not neglect Home Rule entirely. He needed the sizable block of Catholics in Caernarvon. But even more, he could not offend the Calvinistic Methodists, who usually were dedicated Gladstonians but who were now, as he had painfully discovered in 1890, interested in nothing but disestablishment.[93] Fortunately, Puleston was ill-equipped to raise this issue. He had been born a Presbyterian and had converted to the Church of England. Even more troublesome, there remained in Bangor his sister, Mary Ann, and a nephew, John Puleston Jones, a well-known blind preacher and great admirer of Evan Jones, who campaigned actively against Puleston.[94] Finally, Lloyd George now had the mighty figure of Evan Jones at his side. Not only did the pastor of Moriah, 'a capital chap,' speak for him, but he accompanied the candidate on his canvass in Conway.[95] He had also, as before, the help of the two Welsh folk heroes, Thomas Gee and the Reverend Herber Evans. The latter gave up attendance at the annual assembly of the Welsh Congregational Union in Ferndale to speak in Caernarvon District.[96] As a disestablishmentarian, Lloyd George's credentials this time seemed virtually unimpeachable.

Nevertheless at the beginning of the campaign Puleston made an attempt to find a crack in Lloyd George's Welsh nationalist armor. Gladstone, he charged, had been saying that Lloyd George was insincere in his opposition to the Clergy Discipline Bill. There was much potential harm in this and Liberal supporters immediately telegraphed the G.O.M. for a statement. Gladstone's reply, dated 13 June, was oracular but sufficient. He had 'no opinion on the conduct of Mr. Lloyd George' nor had he the 'title or occasion to give any.' But he concluded by saying that were he an 'elector for Caernarvon Boroughs I should vote against Sir J. Puleston and in favour of Mr. Lloyd George.'[97]

After this sally, Puleston concentrated on attacking Lloyd George personally while Welsh Unionists elsewhere attempted to weaken the inexperienced and under-financed Liberal headquarters by intimidating other candidates, many strongly pressed themselves, so as to prevent outside speakers appearing in Lloyd George's support. William Rathbone, the beneficiary of one of the collusive electoral arrangements that continued to exist in Wales even after the third Reform Bill, was threatened with a contest if he appeared for Lloyd George in the Boroughs. As a consequence, Lloyd George, whose poll was set very early in the voting period, had much less help from other MPs than he had enjoyed in 1890.

The election degenerated into a debate over personalities: Lloyd George claiming that he was a more authentic Welshman, who had done more for constituency interest than Puleston, and Puleston arguing that Lloyd George's patriotism was suspect. Repeating the charges made in the debate over the disestablishment resolution the previous spring, Puleston reminded the electors of his opponent's insensitiveness to the feelings of the members of the Royal Family and of the dangerous republican sentiments that appeared regularly in the *Genedl*. Finally, toward the end of the contest he allowed to be circulated a story that during the session Lloyd George had declined to rise during a toast to the Queen. This tale, which could not easily be contradicted without involving Sam Evans, aroused a good deal of anger. On 23 June, emerging from Penrhyn Hall in Bangor, where windows were broken during his speech, a man shouting 'Shame' threw a fireball of paraffin at Lloyd George which set fire to Maggie's dress.[98]

Polling in Caernarvon District took place on 9 July, a Saturday, and the results were announced the following Monday. The Conservative and Liberal totals were up over 1890, as well as over 1885 and 1886. Lloyd George increased his own poll by 191 to give him a vote of 2,154 while the Unionist's total grew by only 13 to 1,958. Lloyd George's majority of 196 was sufficient, but it was the smallest to be received by any Liberal in North Wales and except for a difference of one vote, the smallest of any Liberal in the principality, where majorities of over one thousand for the Liberals were the rule. (In Pembroke and Haverfordwest District, C.F.E. Allen won by 195.) Lloyd George continued to hold one of the shakiest Liberal seats in Wales.

Overall the Liberals won 31 of 34 seats in Wales and Monmouthshire, all, except for the three, by substantial majorities. But elsewhere in the nation the results were disappointing. The Liberals won only 270 seats to 268 for the Conservatives, who were in addition reinforced by 47 Liberal-Unionists. The Conservatives and Liberal-Unionists won 47% of the total vote while the Liberals received 45.1%, virtually the same percentage they earned in 1886. In England the number of votes per elected member in fact dropped slightly compared with 1886. Gladstone himself, who carried Midlothian in 1885 by four thousand votes and was unopposed in 1886, received a majority of less than seven hundred and his spokesman on Home Rule, John Morley, was humiliated at Newcastle by seeing the other seat there captured for the first time since 1874 by a Conservative who also led the poll. The Liberal majority depended upon the Irish Nationals.

The cry 'Ireland Blocks the Way' had hurt both the cause of Home Rule and the cause of Liberalism, commented the strongly Gladstonian *British Weekly* on 14 July when the shape of the new parliament had become apparent. It had discouraged and angered those segments of the party with other priorities. Evidently, the journal continued, Gladstone did not perceive the unhappiness among his followers. Wales now had an opportunity and the Liberal triumph at Caernarvon District was the guarantee of the independence of the Welsh party.[99]

The possibility of an independent Welsh party was a real threat in a House of Commons where even with the support of the Irish Nationalists the Liberal government would be able to muster a majority of only about 40. Obviously any large abstention of Welsh MPs would put the Liberal administration in jeopardy and the defection to the opposition of scarcely more than half of them on a matter of confidence would turn the government out. On his own, Lloyd George issued a warning on this matter that bordered on effrontery. At Conway, on 22 July with polling substantially complete, speaking as he customarily did in the name of all Wales, he asserted his countrymen's essential independence of the Liberals. Even though Wales had voted overwhelmingly for the party, he said, Welshmen did not care that they had simply made it possible for one group of men to enjoy office over another.

> ...the Welsh Members want nothing for themselves, but they must get something for our little country, and I do not think that they will support a Liberal ministry—I care not how illustrious the Minister who leads it—unless it pledges itself to concede to Wales those great measures of reform upon which Wales has set its heart. Wales has lived long on promises. She has in hand a number of political I.O.U.s...and is in a splendid position, by the exigencies of the electoral results, to insist upon prompt payment.

Wales wanted 'its own progress.' 'What is Wales going to get in victory?' 'Wales is not going to be trifled with to obtain emoluments for English statesmen (tremendous cheering).'[100]

Besides its truculence, this speech was notable for the absence of any mention of the only issue with any currency in Wales at the moment, disestablishment. In a sense, the Conway speech was a repudiation of the Rhyl pledges.[101] But more than this Lloyd George was preparing the Welsh party for a declaration of independence.

Suddenly the momentum provided by the new Welsh leverage was interrupted with the news that Tom Ellis was to be appointed Deputy Whip. This was by no means a new decision by Gladstone, nor was it as some men believed an attempt to undermine Wales's proclaimed independence. Acland had proposed Ellis for the post in April when Gladstone, always optimistic, was expecting a majority of one hundred.[102] But the implications were unprecedented for the Welsh parliamentary party and were as agonizing for Ellis as for his colleagues. Ellis is reported to have consulted with Sam Evans, Herbert Lewis, recently elected for Flint District, and Lloyd George, as well as with Beriah Evans. All urged him not to take the post.[103] Ellis later denied in a letter to Ellis Griffith that Lloyd George had spoken to him on the subject and he received, to be sure, a warm letter of congratulations from his Caernarvon District colleague.[104] But Lloyd George always maintained afterwards that he had opposed Ellis's decision even though in the eyes of the press it made him now a leader of the 'forward section' of Welsh Liberals.[105] 'A man like him with the whole nation behind him,' Lloyd George told D.R. Daniel,

> being persuaded by those who had nothing behind them to accept a job far lower than the ones they were angling for...he should at all costs have refused with scorn, turned to the country, raised a storm with the majority that he had. The old man would have had to give him a seat in the Cabinet in less than three months.[106]

Lloyd George was rarely candid in his recollections of his past opinions and motives. He may indeed have opposed Ellis's acceptance of the Junior Whip appointment because he believed Ellis could have received a better post by waiting. But the historian may be fairly confident that no matter what congratulations he conveyed to Ellis, he in fact disapproved of the latter's defection to the government. It deprived the Welsh insurgents of their best liked and least controversial leader. Worse, it diluted the threats of revolution as Rendel, who warmly supported the appointment after refusing office himself, well understood.

As soon as parliament reassembled, on 8 August 1892, the Welsh party met, reelected Rendel leader, and passed unanimously a resolution calling upon Gladstone to put disestablishment second, after Home Rule, in the Queen's speech. The group also formed a committee of five, including Lloyd George, to consider a Welsh policy.[107] Three days later the Salisbury government, which had not resigned, was defeated on a motion of confidence, and on 18 August Gladstone assumed his fourth premiership. He clearly resented the Welsh impertinence, but he could not ignore it. He had indeed agreed in consultation with Harcourt to take up disestablishment, among other things, as a way of conciliating various sections of the Party 'in preparation for the coming clash with the House of Lords.'[108]

An opportunity soon arose for a gesture of conciliation. During this parliamentary recess Gladstone was to be in Snowdonia to open a hiking road built by an old friend and Liberal MP, Sir Edward William Watkin (now ironically a Liberal Unionist) and also to spend a few days at Watkin's chalet on the slope of the mountain. Evidently Ellis suggested to Herbert Gladstone that the trip might be expanded to provide at least the appearance of consideration of Welsh affairs.[109] Gladstone seems to have accepted the suggestion eagerly and allowed Ellis to arrange the trip to include excursions to Caernarvon and Portmadoc.

The great salute to Wales began in Caernarvon on 12 September. Lloyd George, just returned from his first trip abroad to a meeting of the

Interparliamentary Union in Geneva, and Ellis accompanied the Prime Minister in his carriage from the railway station to Castle Square. There, after a rousing address by Lloyd George, the G.O.M. received a petition from the Caernarvon Liberal Association praying for 'religious equality' in Wales.[110] Gladstone responded with a long speech offering the usual praise of Welsh devotion to its national institutions, to Liberalism, and to good causes in general, but including a more specific promise of action than any he had made publicly before.

> I will venture to say that I hope whatever the pressure of Irish demands may be, even one session of the Parliament will not be allowed to pass without being able to give some earnest to the people of Wales of our desire to deal with and, as far as we can, to promote and push forward the realization of their just demands (loud cheers).[111]

The next day, after dedicating the Watkin road and listening to further speeches in Welsh by Lloyd George, Bryn Roberts and Ellis, the Prime Minister, on the south slope of Snowdon, delivered a second address, this time promising in conditional terms an investigation into Welsh land and tenures.[112] This ambivalent concession rather dampened the enthusiasm aroused by his previous day's speech, which was assumed to refer to disestablishment although Gladstone had not mentioned the word. *The Times* a few days later interpreted the promise of a land investigation as a 'sop' intended to stave off for a time demands for disestablishment. Land reform was a well known interest of Tom Ellis, who, the paper noted, was now in the government.[113] The fact was, according to his wife, Gladstone had not intended to make a speech on Snowdon at all and the reference to the investigation appeared only as a bow in the direction of his new whip.[114] He had not even settled on the form of the investigation, select committee, departmental committee, or royal commission, and the eventual royal commission was not in fact appointed until May 1893 after much pressure from Rendel and Ellis.

After the Snowdon speech Lloyd George and Ellis returned with Gladstone to Watkin's chalet at Beddgelert for dinner. Mrs. Gladstone, who evidently had been taught by her husband to regard Lloyd George as little better than a common burglar, was appalled. Nevertheless, much to her amazement, the meal was quiet and civilized.[115] Gladstone, perhaps remembering his awkward conversation with the young Member from Caernarvon District at Hawarden eighteen months before, monopolized the table talk. Lloyd George himself was much impressed by this encounter with the great man and described it at length in his *War Memoirs* forty years later.[116]

VII

Between September 1892 and the middle of January 1893 when parliament met, Lloyd George was busy with a multitude of private business affairs. On 3 April 1892, his second daughter Olwen had been born and so Maggie's reasons for not coming to London again were reinforced. As a result he gave up the Verulam Buildings flat in Gray's Inn Road, which he had occupied since the beginning of 1891, and moved for a time back to the

National Liberal Club. He worked irregularly at legal business, complaining ungraciously of the demands made by William who expected him 'to do all the dirty work of the office' without sending the necessary papers.[117] As always he made speeches. But by mid-October most of his time was devoted to an improbable scheme for mining gold in the Corcovdo area of Chubut province in southern Argentina. This interlude is only of marginal importance for his political career, even though it occupied him intermittently until the end of 1896 when, between August and October, he in fact traveled to Argentina ostensibly to inspect the mining claim owned by his syndicate. But the Patagonian gold adventure is worth describing, first because Lloyd George with his customary energy threw himself into the selling of shares in the syndicate and participated rarely in the long parliamentary session which lasted from 31 January 1893 until 1 March 1894. Second, it illustrates his precarious financial position. His interest in the 'Welsh Patagonian Gold Field Syndicate,' which was chartered early in 1893, seems to have proceeded chiefly from his interest in the ten percent commission he earned from selling shares and in the fees he received for attending directors' meetings as Deputy Chairman.[118]

Until he began to draw a ministerial salary in 1905, in a day when backbench Members of Parliament were unpaid, the attraction of even relatively small sums such as he earned for writing for newspapers was very great. In 1892 he had no dependable patron such as Ellis had in John Brunner, who continued to subsidize the Member for Merioneth even after he became a Junior Whip.[119] Unquestionably Lloyd George received help from time to time from Alfred Thomas but he had no regular stipend for a growing family.

Yet there was even a deeper motivation. On one hand he hated inherited privilege and the social authority he associated with landownership. But he desired as ardently the security and ease that came with wealth. This involved him in many improbable speculations during his life, and in the Marconi scandal brought him close to ruin. He had the nature of a gambler with the courage to try his hand at an enterprise about which he knew very little. Speculation, offering the possibility of ruin against the chance of large reward, is one of the keys to his political as well as his economic behavior.

The first phase of the Patagonian gold fever lasted about two years, until the summer of 1894. During at least the earlier part of this period Lloyd George was, as usual, a whirlwind of optimistic energy, a securities salesman, visiting brokers in Paris and in Dublin, getting also quotations on mining machinery, and attending meetings of the board of directors of the syndicate headquartered at Effingham House, Arundel Street, which were also the offices of the *Shipping World* owned by Major E.R. Jones, Lloyd George's colleague in Welsh publishing and MP for Carmarthen District. For support, he drew in, among others, his brother William, his cousin William Jones of Caerdyni and R.O. Davies of Acton whom Lloyd George visited often during the autumn of 1892 until January 1893 when he took Sam Evans's chambers in the Temple. Of course there was Alfred Thomas, who was always included in any scheme requiring money. The striking thing to one reading the stream of enthusiastic letters that passed from London or Paris to Criccieth is that with the bustle of activity which he reported daily, no one, least of all Lloyd George, seems to have been concerned about whether in fact there existed any gold under the Patagonian pampas. Only at the end of 1892, after all shares had been allocated, did the syndicate send to Argentina David Richards to assess the potential value of the operation. Richards held the original mineral rights and by selling to the syndicate what finally proved to be a worthless claim, may have been the only one to profit from the venture.

Through the spring and summer of 1893, while the eyes of the political world were on Gladstone's second Home Rule Bill, work for Patagonian Gold Fields Limited proceeded at a slightly more relaxed pace. Then on 15 August Lloyd George reported disaster. After a long and gory description of a visit to the dentist, with full details about how bravely he bore the pain by thinking about her, he wrote to Maggie:

> Confidential. Patagonia is, I fear, a failure. Don't let Uncle or anybody else know a word. Hoefer [a mining expert employed by the syndicate early in the year evidently to check up on Richards] wires 'the property falls short of representations....' Will and I may be able to save ourselves to a great extent by a stiff lawyers bill but we must of course lose a lot of money. Just like our luck. [in Welsh] No word to anybody except to Will. Tell him tomorrow night.[120]

There were proposals to take deep core samples, thoughts of trying to unload syndicate shares in Buenos Aires where gold fever was high 'and it would be easy to feed that excitement and dispose of the whole thing...,' and of sending Hoefer back to do some more prospecting.[121] But on the whole affairs were at a standstill. In Wales the report from Bethesda, where many shares had been sold, announced the syndicate stock was worth nothing.[122]

Then, just before Christmas, Lloyd George reported an offer from a Dublin group to take 3200 shares at 30 shillings per share. This would keep the company going for eighteen months, Lloyd George reported happily, and he foresaw a 'boom' in company shares. Why Irishmen should be interested in paying £4,950 for worthless gold mining stock appeared neither to trouble nor interest him.[123] Nevertheless through the spring of 1894 Lloyd George's participation in syndicate affairs dwindled and by the middle of the year references to it had practically disappeared from his letters.

VIII

After all the pressure and promises of the previous autumn, the Queen's speech, 31 January 1893, made no reference to Welsh disestablishment. But it did include the promise of a measure to prevent the growth 'of new vested interests' in the established Church in both Scotland and Wales and so provided the 'earnest' that Gladstone had offered at Caernarvon. There were no Welsh protests during the debate on the address and very early in the session, on 23 February, evidently at the behest of Lloyd George and Herbert Lewis, H.H. Asquith, the Home Secretary, introduced the Established Church (Wales) Bill designed to forbid compensation for new livings created in anticipation of disestablishment.[124] The Tories, led by Sir John Gorst, whom Loyd George privately admired, attempted to filibuster the bill in the Welsh manner and the first reading was finally passed only by the imposition of closure. Lloyd George himself did not speak, but wrote a long report to the *Genedl* on 28 February 1893 describing the debate and, more interesting, commenting upon the Home Secretary as the 'hope of the rising generation of Radicals.... It is considered that on the whole he fills the same position in the Parliament of 1892 [i.e. elected in 1892] as Mr. Chamberlain did in that of 1885.'[125]

The Suspensory Bill never proceeded to a second reading and was withdrawn on 18 September. But it had been clear for many weeks that, even with the auspicious beginning during which Gladstone had been provoked to utter the fatal words 'Welsh Disestablishment,' it would not be passed in 1893. As a result, by June, there were rumbles among Welshmen in Wales and at Westminster. For once Lloyd George was not leading the rebels. Whether it was his friendship with Ellis, which was particularly warm at this time, or his preoccupation with Patagonian gold, or an instinct for political tactics, he was unwilling at the moment to embarrass the government publicly. He consistently applauded Liberal performances on Home Rule and counseled the readers of the *Genedl* to blame Chamberlain for the lack of progress on Welsh Church affairs. 'For my part,' he wrote on 20 June, 'I shall be quite satisfied if we get Disestablishment next year.'[126]

Privately, however, he was less restrained. He introduced a motion in the Welsh caucus, opposed only by Bryn Roberts, to write to Gladstone asking that disestablishment be given a priority, citing the Newcastle Resolutions of 1891 which put it in second place. Gladstone waited a week to reply. He 'never considered,' he wrote Rendel on 5 July, that the deliberations at Newcastle 'announced any plan with regard to the order of business beyond the expressed declarations which may have been contained in them.'

This exercise in wordy prevarication upset Lloyd George. 'I don't care for the reply,' he wrote his wife that day in the first reference to political business that had appeared in his letters since early spring, 'and we must press him hard. He will try to get out of it if he can. But we must not allow him to do it.'[127] At the following week's meeting of the Welsh Members, he urged them to try again.[128] This time there was more opposition, including among others Sam Evans and Rathbone. There had to be a second angry meeting on 28 July which finally resulted in a second letter, drafted by Lloyd George, reminding the G.O.M. of Wales' 'so far unswerving' loyalty and praying that there would not be 'any misunderstanding which would have the effect of imperiling that devotion...' and so on.[129]

Gladstone's reply on 7 August, when trimmed of the customary circumlocution, left a tiny morsel of hope: Wales's parliamentary leverage would not remain unnoticed.[130] Lloyd George considered this reply a refusal when he wrote his wife that night telling her that Rendel had shown him the letter confidentially. He thought he would publish it after the meeting of the Welsh Members the next day. But by that time Ellis had dissuaded him. 'Ellis told me last night that he thought the old man would give in after all,' he wrote.

He'll give us a vague promise in his next letter and something more definite still if we press him still further. Well we shall see the very text of the letter tomorrow and Ellis and I are going to keep ourselves free tomorrow evening so as to discuss it together.

The old man announced this afternoon that there would be an autumn session. I have a good mind to pair if all is well about disestablishment and run over to Buenos Aires to see our title complete— that is if the Coy will pay my way and some remuneration for the job. The sea voyage will set me up for years and I shall be doing good work as somebody must go. Alfred Thomas will join me. He is eager for it. What do you say? Don't mention it to Uncle.[131]

Besides referring to Buenos Aires as if it were a stop on the railway between Criccieth and Caernarvon, this letter reaffirms that the motive behind Lloyd George's uncharacteristic moderation in political loyalty on the matter of Gladstone's promise must be found in his trust in his friend Tom Ellis. He and Ellis were closer socially during 1892-93 than at any time before, or indeed afterwards. Lloyd George visited him at Cynlas, asked him for patronage support—could J.R. Hughes be appointed factory inspector at Caernarvon, 'you know how well he served our cause at the last election'—and attended the theater with him—*The Second Mrs. Tanqueray* was 'a horrid affair.'[132]

Lloyd George's posture as an ardent, but moderate and loyal, Liberal was almost immediately tested by a rebellion in South Wales. On 14 August the South Wales Liberal Federation at Aberdare, after electing D.A. Thomas president of the federation, carried unanimously a motion calling for the formation of an independent Welsh party unless it received assurances that disestablishment would be first priority in 1894.[133] Notwithstanding that this was a position Lloyd George had often taken himself, now, in cooperation with Ellis and Rendel — the latter had written from Skye on 26 August warning that rebellion would be to shoot off all ammunition at once — he prepared to resist it. When parliament returned to take the third reading of the Home Rule Bill, D.A. Thomas began to try to organize a group to withdraw from the party immediately, with a view to opposing the last vote on Home Rule.[134] Lloyd George quickly undermined the solidarity of the dissidents with a compromise resolution presented to the Welshmen by faithful Alfred Thomas, proposing that unless Welsh disestablishment were taken in the next session the Welsh would 'reexamine their position' within Liberalism.

The following day, 1 September, the Welsh party convened in the morning for an acrimonious meeting. For three hours the 31 Liberals debated whether to do nothing about disestablishment, alone suggested by Bryn Roberts; to revolt immediately as proposed by David Randall supported by D.A. Thomas, Major E.R. Jones, whom Lloyd George liked, and by Edward Reed, whom he despised; to form an independent party if no definite assurance were received about disestablishment in the next session—this was supported reluctantly by Lloyd George and Ellis; or to do something unspecified at some future time, which was Lloyd George's and Ellis's original proposal. None of the first three commanded more than seven votes and the last, almost meaningless, proposal was agreed to by less than a majority of the party with many abstentions.[135] 'We beat all sections all round,' wrote Lloyd George to his wife, 'the extremists and Bryn Roberts together. Ellis and I stuck together all through.' Rendel supported them but Sam Evans was absent. Also, Lloyd George reported, he was very short of money. Had his cheque from the *Manchester Guardian* come?[136] That evening at 1:05 am, 2 September, the Home Rule Bill received its third reading with a majority of 34 votes.

Perhaps because the Lloyd George papers were not available when he wrote, Kenneth Morgan may have overestimated the gravity of this rebellion. Probably it is too much to say that after this a Welsh party was unlikely or that henceforth Welshmen despaired of uniting for disestablishment.[137] What the meeting showed, in terms of Welsh national history, was that the North and South were, as usual, out of step. The South Welsh revolt in fact had been torpedoed before it was really launched by the men of the North led by Lloyd George. In a little more than two years, however, Thomas would do the same to Lloyd George's far more ambitious nationalist enterprise.

For the career of Lloyd George, on the other hand, the attempt at secession may be of some significance. It confirmed his belief that the term 'Welsh Parliamentary Party' was a name to be used in mockery.[138] It reinforced the conviction he had held since before his election that the Welsh parliamentary party was, as he had termed it in 1889, a sort of Punch and Judy show that inspired not terror but laughter, and that the only way to make Wales a force in London was to build an organization in Wales that Members of Parliament would be bound to heed. Control of elections in Wales could yield control of Westminster. Such an organization had made Parnell dictator of Ireland. It would work in the principality as well. Here lay the essence of the Revolt of the Four and the Cymru Fydd movement which grew from it.

However ridiculous the Welsh revolt had seemed, the government, nevertheless, was preparing in the autumn of 1893 a Welsh Disestablishment and Disendowment Bill. Work began in November and a draft, put together by Asquith, was complete at the end of the month. Ellis prepared a Cabinet memorandum generally approving the measure early in the year and on 8 February 1894, at Newton, he promised the North Wales Liberal Federation that within the next few weeks there 'will be a surprise to some of the bishops.'[139]

So far everything was going well. Lloyd George appointed himself steward of the nonconformist political conscience not only in Wales but in England. Early in January, in a style worthy of Evan Jones, he undertook to bring pressure from the Liberation Society on H.J. Torr, Liberal candidate in a by-election in the Horncastle division of Lincolnshire. Mr. Torr had declined to endorse disendowment as well as disestablishment. 'I consider his victory would be a disaster for Wales,' Lloyd George wrote Maggie early on New Year's Day. 'I have taken in hand the matter of either bringing him round or punishing him...I don't see why those snob churchmen should be allowed to ride on Nonconformist votes into the House of Commons to oppose Noncon principles.' He was able to induce the Liberation Society to pass a resolution against Torr which he publicized with money solicited from Charles Dilke and Henry Labouchere, two dependable non-Welsh sources of funds. He reported on 5 January that he was happy to see radical MPs were looking for ways to break the promises they had made to speak for Torr.[140]

As it turned out the Conservatives won the seat on 11 January by about the normal margin. Two days later the Prime Minister left England for Biarritz. While there he learned of the Lords' mutilation of the Employers' Liability and Parish Councils Bills. With Home Rule already rejected in the upper chamber, this represented the destruction of most of the work of a long and exhausting session. From France Gladstone telegraphed the Cabinet urging a dissolution on the issue of the House of Lords. Although his colleagues rejected this proposal, Gladstone returned to London on 10 February still tired, and unhappy with the prospect of a renewed struggle within the ministry over naval estimates. Before the end of the month he had determined to retire. He announced his intention to the Cabinet in the meeting of 23 February and made his last speech in the House of Commons, a spirited attack on the House of Lords, on 1 March. On 3 March he left the premiership.

Gladstone's departure affected the Welsh party immediately. Among the resignation honours was a peerage for Rendel who used receipt of the dignity to resign, perhaps gratefully, the leadership of the Welsh MPs. He complained to his close friend Arthur Humphreys-Owen of the lack of generosity displayed by Welsh Members like Lloyd George. In a clear reference to disestablishment he continued to Owen 'in Welsh affairs there seems to be a conscious preference for unrealities.'[141]

More seriously, Gladstone's departure removed a leader of great strength who was, if not specifically an enthusiastic friend of Wales, at least a deep believer in the principle of nationality and one who, after many delays, was at last preparing a disestablishment bill.[142] His successor, Archibald Primrose, Lord Rosebery, appeared to be, and remained throughout his life, an unknown quantity, a conundrum. Although he routinely welcomed the new Prime Minister, Lloyd George had never trusted him. 'What is the truth about Rosebery?' he wrote to Ellis when Rosebery had reluctantly accepted the Foreign Office in 1892. 'Does he mean mischief? The outlook is rather gloomy as far as foreign affairs are concerned.'[143] Now, in March 1894, Lloyd George wrote Rosebery asking him to receive the Welsh party. He got in reply a brief haughty note that could have been sent to a deputation of greengrocers. The Prime Minister had no time.[144]

The Queen's speech, already written when Gladstone retired, and indeed presented on 12 March before there had been a Cabinet, finally announced that measures would be presented for 'Dealing with the Ecclesiastical Establishments in Wales and Scotland.' This was a hopeful sign, but the Welsh sought reassurance in an interview with the new Leader of the House, William Vernon Harcourt. On 16 March six Members including the new leader of the Welsh party, George Osborne Morgan, and Lloyd George and D.A. Thomas, asked for a pledge that disestablishment would be carried through the House during the present session. Harcourt affirmed that this was the government's intention and that it would not be satisfied only with a second reading. The report of this meeting in Lloyd George's own newspaper stated that the group considered this reply satisfactory.[145]

Nevertheless it was soon clear that, promises or not, the government would be unable to retain for disestablishment the high priority that Harcourt had allowed his visitors to infer it possessed. There were others that the ministry feared more than the Welsh. These were the Irish. Gladstone's retirement had been a shock even more to the Irish than to the Welsh, not only because he had promised to reassemble Grattan's Parliament on College Green but because he was living proof that England did care about Ireland's problems and that all Englishmen were not swaggering landlords or arrogant Orangemen. However, since the defeat of Home Rule the Irish party had suffered a loss of confidence among themselves and a decline in interest in Westminster among their constituents. One result, it became apparent in the spring of 1894, was increased bickering among the majority anti-Parnellite faction which, when combined with the flagging enthusiasm in Ireland, caused a fall in political subsidies, 'indemnities' as they were called, a decline in discipline in the party, and poor attendance at Westminster. All of this reduced the government's slim majority.[146]

But more important, on 12 March, Lord Rosebery, the Prime Minister for only nine days, had remarked in the House of Lords that Home Rule would never pass until England 'as the predominant partner in the Three Kingdoms' was 'convinced of its justice and equity.'[147]

The Irish retaliated immediately. The next day, warmly supported by English and Welsh radicals, including Lloyd George, D.A. and Alfred Thomas, Herbert Lewis, and Sam Evans, they succeeded in passing an amendment to the address put down by Henry Labouchere, regretting the continued legislative power of the House of Lords.[148] Although the amendment passed by only two votes in a thin house, the government, and its new Chief Whip, Tom Ellis, were seriously embarrassed. Most troubled was John Morley who believed that the Liberals had an obligation to the Irish because they had forced the Nationalists to give up their revered leader.[149] He appears to have seen in the Irish defection, above all in the virtually unanimous support of the Labouchere amendment by the anti-Parnellites, a signal that the government had failed its duty. Moreover, in the reconstructed Cabinet after Rosebery's accession, Morley had remained at the Irish office, as he allowed the new Prime Minister to believe, only from a sense of duty. He had thus exceptional influence in the government, which was reinforced by the fact that next to Harcourt, to whom the Prime Minister scarcely spoke, he was in terms of cabinet service the senior Liberal in the House of Commons. Hence, to the demonstrated Irish leverage in the lower chamber could be added an exceptionally powerful and sympathetic spokesman in the Cabinet.

To thus restore their self-respect and to demonstrate to their countrymen that the party retained its vigor, the Irish, in the days after their surprise victory in the debate on the address, began to insist that the government take up immediately a bill that had begun the previous year as a private member's bill, the Evicted Tenants' Bill. This would have established offical arbitrators who, on appeal, could order not only the compensation, but the reinstatement of all tenants turned out of their holdings since 1879, in effect since the founding of Land League.

Within a few days it became clear that the Evicted Tenants' Bill would be taken immediately. The decision to postpone the Welsh bill was probably made at the Cabinet of 12 April—there had been no Cabinet since 14 March—although there were earlier warnings in the nonconformist press that the government would not honor its commitment to the Welsh.[150] In any case, the first reading of the Evicted Tenants' Bill was taken on 19 April although the second did not come until July. (After a long committee stage, the measure, renamed the Tenant's Arbitration (Ireland) Bill, was duly killed in the House of Lords on 14 August by a vote of 249 to 30.)

The immediate effect of the Irish intervention was apparent on the evening of 12 April after the Cabinet decision. Lloyd George, D.A. Thomas, and Frank Edwards announced to the *Times* lobby correspondent that they intended to accept no further communications from the Liberal Whip who, since the beginning of the session, ironically, was Tom Ellis. The 'interposition of the Evicted Tenants Bill,' recorded *The Times* 'Political Notes' in what was obviously nearly a direct quotation from the Member from Caernarvon District, was 'a breach of faith.' 'Mr. Lloyd George and his friends are quite willing to stretch a point in favour of the government...but in view of the backwardness of public business generally they failed to see how Sir W. Harcourt is to fulfil his pledge to send Welsh Disestablishment up to the House of Lords....'[151]

So began what would become, with the addition of Herbert Lewis, the famous Revolt of the Four, a gesture of defiance that Lloyd George would attempt to fan into a general revolution of Welsh Liberalism against the English party and which eventually would lead him to his first important political defeat. Even though he had served as a spokesman for the rebels, it is not clear that Lloyd George was the instigator of the revolt. Llewelyn Williams says flatly, and Neville Masterman agrees, that the first man to repudiate Liberal party discipline was D.A. Thomas.[152] Thomas, Lloyd George's senior in the House of Commons, a man of wealth with an impregnable seat in the South, had far more freedom of action than Lloyd George. But if this is true Lloyd George moved forward quickly. He could not allow himself, after behaving as a moderating influence in September, to be twice outflanked on the left on the same matter. Finally, and this may be more important, Lloyd George expected at the beginning that the fifteen or so of the Welsh party who had voted for his resolution on 1 September would follow. If there was to be a general movement away from the Liberals, he would have to lead it.

His explanations at the Reform Club in Caernarvon, where he went on 14 April to announce his decision to his constituency, and the press comment upon the revolt, tend to support these conclusions. He told of the deputation to Harcourt who, he said, declined to pledge that disestablishment would be taken after voter registration and the budget. There were at least six items in the government's list, disestablishment was last. There simply was not enough time in the session. The Welsh had made their threat the previous September and everyone had laughed. Now they must insist upon their demands. Are we to go to the government in a 'humiliating spirit,' he demanded in reference to the decision of the previous autumn, 'and say that we have transgressed and that we only meant to frighten after the manner of Sir Andrew Aguecheek, in one of Shakespeare's plays, who after making a challenge cowered when he found his opponent ready to stand his ground? Have we, as a nation, enough firmness to face difficulties? If not, then we are not worth fighting for. We must rely upon our strength, for the English people are not in earnest. They are inclined to regard the Welsh as mere parasites.' In closing, he repeated the imagery of the Conway speech of July, 1892. 'Hitherto the Welsh people have had nothing but promissory notes at the hands of the Government. It is high time we had cash down. I confess that I am not prepared to renew the bill except on one consideration — namely that it is to be paid on its next presentation.' He expected, he told a reporter for the *British Weekly*, that about one half the Welsh Members would be with him.[153]

Reaction to the defections in London was either angry or scornful. Even Harold Spender, possibly the most admiring of all Lloyd George's biographers, who was in 1894 a lobby correspondent for the *Manchester Guardian*, recalled the bitterness among the Liberals at the pressure from the Welsh, which further embarrassed the government, still smarting from the defeat of Home Rule.[154] The Liberal press was more harsh. 'No importance is attached to the *émeute* of Messrs. Lloyd George, F. Edwards, and D.A. Thomas,' quoted the *British Weekly* from an unnamed Liberal paper, evidently *The Chronicle*. 'Those three Taffys are in a state of chronic revolt, especially the first named. They have been overruled on several previous occasions by their clearer headed colleagues and will be overruled again.' The government knew, contended the *British Weekly* miserably, that Wales had no friends and that the rebels would have to come back into line. To be sure there would be a disestablishment bill but without the time to pass it. As it was put, the paper concluded, 'in the elegant language of the lobbies, "Taffy will have to eat the leek."'[155]

Even as the revolt began, the evidence was clear that the original aim, a revision of the government's legislative schedule, or an autumn session, would not be accomplished. The government was not prepared to waste valuable parliamentary time on a bill of no interest to the majority of voters and which in the House of Lords unquestionably would have even less popularity than Home Rule had possessed. Although Lloyd George had always maintained he cared nothing about what the House of Lords did to the bill — if the peers destroyed the bill the people would destroy the peers — the government knew better and so, of course, did Lloyd George.

More telling was the failure of any Welsh colleagues except Frank Edwards and Herbert Lewis to join Thomas and himself. Lloyd George had written to Ellis shortly after the Caernarvon meeting, (the date is uncertain), explaining that he was resigning the whip because of the refusal of the autumn session and because the bill, so far as he knew its terms, while disendowing the Church of properties acquired before 1703, promised lifetime pensions for the holders of livings. It would be better, he thought, to throw out the government than to support such a measure. Yet there was the offer of a concession. Could the government undertake not to advise the prorogation or dissolution of parliament before the bill was through? Would Ellis, finally, come out and be their leader?[156]

Whether this letter shows a belief that Lloyd George soon would be able to defeat the government, as one historian has suggested, is not clear and is unimportant.[157] But within days two things were obvious: first, that other Welsh Members greeted the revolt with the customary dithering, consternation, and dismay, and second, in Wales, as opposed to London, the revolt was wildly popular. But even with Wales behind them, the rest of the Welsh party, the 'White Feather Brigade' as he had once called them, had displayed their cowardice again and this time they were far out of step with the principality.[158] Hence the next move was obvious for Lloyd George. For him there was never a debate on the relative importance of claims from the constituency and the caucus. He must organize Wales. An independent organization in the principality would bring an independent Welsh party to Westminster made of sterner stuff than the present fainthearted incumbents.[159] Thus what became in the next few weeks the beginning of the Cymru Fydd movement appeared ironically in the days immediately after the introduction by Asquith on 26 April of the long awaited Established Church (Wales) Bill of 1894.

For Lloyd George, a bill at this late date was not an important event. Nonetheless he prepared carefully, with the help of William George, for his speech on 30 April and awarded himself afterwards the usual good marks for his performance.[160]

He attacked the principle of lifetime compensation for incumbents, but most of his speech was devoted to the chronically worrying but irrelevant topic of the relative size of Church and chapel congregations.[161] However, still warmed by the fire of his oratory he began to think about the next step. 'I am continuing in receipt of congratulations from all parts,' he reported to Maggie on 3 May. 'I am also receiving daily resolutions from different parts of Wales in support of my actions. The feeling is evidently growing and some of the details of the govt bill will assist us greatly in converting the country. Our aim now is independent party at the next election.'[162]

The Revolt of the Four, with Herbert Lewis, who joined on 5 May, vowing to Ellis that he would 'never again fight a constituency as an official Liberal,' moved now from Westminster to Wales.[163] The aim was unashamedly a fourth party on the Irish model. Lloyd George's message was always the same and could have been taken as a text from Parnell's blunt announcement of a policy of obstruction at the beginning of his fund raising trip to the United States: 'Experience has shown that England will not pay any attention to Irish affairs until the position has become unbearable for herself.'[164] The Celtic nationalities of the United Kingdom, said Lloyd George, suffered from neglect, or positive opposition, while anything England wanted of parliament was instantly attended to. Yet one of the Celtic nationalities, after years of oppression, had suddenly forced its will at Westminster so that even English measures were forestalled. How had this been done? By the organization of the national spirit. Behind the Members of Parliament was an organization for manifesting the national will that dominated the party at Westminster and determined its policy.[165] His would be a 'Young Wales' party with 'national motives' he told the *Westminster Gazette* on 16 May.

> You will find it an accomplished fact after the next election. The idea of nationality is a vigorous and growing one, and as a compact band, we shall get our wants proudly attended to by the Liberal party, in addition to being able to 'squeeze' the Tories when in office.
>
> Disestablishment was the first item on the Young Wales program. That question is the battleground on which our very existence as a nation has been challenged. It must therefore be decided first. Then Land Reform must come—a most pressing subject. Finally Local Veto and Home Rule for Wales. All Liberal measures, you will see, and to none of which the Liberal party is, in the abstract, hostile.[166]

He discussed with shrewd candor the political dilemma of Welsh Liberalism as he had seen it in the recent Montgomeryshire by-election, where A.C. Humphreys-Owen had barely succeeded in holding Rendel's seat aided by considerable intervention from Lloyd George. The Welsh people were suspicious of the Liberal government, Lloyd George thought, of its division and weakness. A Welsh farmer who voted his honest Liberal conviction could gain nothing and would get for himself trouble with his landlord. The government could not help him and the landlord could hurt him. He blamed no tenant in that position, Lloyd George concluded, for voting Tory.[167]

Through May Lloyd George with Thomas, Edwards, and Lewis toured Wales speaking to wildly enthusiastic meetings. At Rhyl on 19 May they secured, with only one dissent, a resolution of support from the North Wales Liberal Federation. At Caernarvon, Conway, and Denbigh, denunciation of government insincerity, and proclamations that Wales must chart her own future, received genuinely enthusiastic support.[168]

While in Denbigh on 22 May, he saw Thomas Gee. 'Gee is with us heart and soul!' he reported to his wife the next day. 'He is not in favour of giving in whether we get assurances or not. Go on with the formation of an independent party—that is his and my idea.'[169] Gee's part in urging Lloyd George forward was clearly of great importance in the next eighteen months. 'Cymru Fydd,' for which one may, by 1894, read a unified Welsh national political machine to sponsor and control the party in parliament, was for the old editor the realization of a lifelong ambition. But his uncompromising North Wales parochialism may have in the long run caused the movement to fail. Caring little more for sensibilities in South Wales than he did for those in England and without political finesse, he was bound to wound men of larger minds or wider interest. Ellis for instance, despised Gee as an intractable, narrow-minded, nonconformist philistine.[170] One may speculate that the disaster that overtook the Cymru Fydd movement was due as much to D.A. Thomas's fear that its accomplishment would represent the domination of Wales by Gee's extravagances and by chapel screw (i.e. coercion) politics as it was to his personal resentment of Lloyd George.

IX

The intent of the previous paragraphs has been to show that the Revolt of the Four must be regarded as the real beginning of the Cymru Fydd revival, a project which occupied Lloyd George for the next year and a half. Whether or not the original rejection of the whip on 12 April had been anything more than anger at cavalier treatment by a government clearly more afraid of the Irish than of the Welsh, the undeniable popularity of the revolt in Wales, combined with the pusillanimous behavior of his colleagues, made it clear to Lloyd George within weeks that Welsh organization was the next step. There was no break between the Revolt of the Four and the organization of Wales, the 'Young Wales' or 'Cymru Fydd' movement that followed. The campaign for broadening popular support in Wales for the insignificant parliamentary revolt had begun well before the Four resumed the whip at the end of May. Nor was the return to the Liberals the result of Rosebery's public promise of a disestablishment bill in 1895 or of the virtual censure of the Four by their colleagues, which together are usually taken to signify the defeat and the end of the revolt. In fact these last two events had no effect upon the rebels. Rosebery at Birmingham simply repeated Harcourt's pledge of 16 March for the following year and gave it in singularly ungracious and insulting terms. 'Some young men and daring natives of the principality,' he said at Birmingham Town Hall, 'have taken it into their heads to convert the government majority into a minority in order to obtain disestablishment.' After the inevitable cries of 'shame', Rosebery announced he did not call this behavior shame but 'strategy'. However, he continued, if the recalcitrants chose not to believe the promises that had been made to them many times, and which he now made again, that disestablishment would be carried through the House of Commons before the government met the country—he could make no promises about the Lords—if they did not believe in the government's honor and honesty, then 'the sooner they carry their threats into effect, the better I shall be pleased.' He refused, he said, to be a 'minister on suffrance.'[171] This was not a commitment, but a challenge, and the Four treated it as such. No matter what the Prime Minister said, the government would be unable to fulfill their pledges, the *Times* lobby correspondent was told the next day. Therefore the situation was 'unchanged.'[172]

The next day, 25 May, Friday, the Welsh party met to attempt to force some semblance of obedience upon its erring members. The meeting was in response to a demand for a resolution of condemnation passed by an informal gathering of about a dozen Welsh MPs the previous Tuesday, 22 May, while Lloyd George had been visiting Gee in Wales. This censuring group was led by Major E.R. Jones and W. Pritchard Morgan, the troublesome maverick Liberal who was D.A. Thomas's colleague in Merthyr Tydfil. Lloyd George, whose letters to his wife by now referred to the rest of the Welsh party as 'cowards' and 'rascals,' was able to take advantage of Major Jones's absence on Friday morning, as a result of a hangover, to induce his friend, the pliant Alfred Thomas, to move not the resolution of censure which Jones had written, but simply a feeble promise of 'consistent' support for the government.[173] Even this motion Lloyd

George attempted to amend with a statement noting 'with satisfaction' Rosebery's speech at Birmingham while adding that 'under existing conditions the Government cannot hope to perform its pledge.' Rosebery's declaration at Birmingham, he argued in the meeting, was made only after protest and was in any case 'utterly ineffective.' Moreover the Welsh party was treated with contempt by both the Prime Minister and Harcourt. The amendment was of course defeated, but the Four abstained on the main motion so a technical unity was restored.[174] Privately to his wife, and indeed publicly to the lobby correspondent of *The Times*, Lloyd George maintained that the attempt to discipline himself and his friends was a great joke. Yet they now silently consented to receive communications on voting from Ellis, who in many ways was the chief sufferer from the affair. In any case, as the measure before the House during most of the short life of the revolt had been the budget, for which they consistently voted, the refusal of the whip had had little effect on their parliamentary behavior.

But all of this now was a minor consideration. The center of attention was Wales and the resistance of any tendency toward moderation for the apparent government inclination toward compromise. Almost immediately an emergency arose at the Baptist Union Convention at Hope Chapel in Cross Keys, Monmouthshire on 29 May. Here at a meeting attended almost solely by ministers and deacons of one of the most influential of Welsh churches, Lloyd George received word that a resolution was to be introduced urging the Four to return to the fold now that Rosebery had placed disestablishment second in the Liberal program. Lloyd George, who had received only a private invitation, hurriedly made plans to attend with the intention of obtaining instead a resolution supporting an independent party.[175] His speech before the dignified audience contained a bitter attack on Rosebery and showed how little had been changed by the events of the last few days. Rosebery, he said, had no sympathy for Welsh aspirations nor for Welshmen. 'The Premier...had stated at Edinburgh that he was a believer in a State Church and did not see why they should not run a State Church as they ran a State Army. The only reason that he [Rosebery] had for conceding the Welsh demand was one of political expediency.'

As for Welshmen 'Lord Rosebery referred to them [specifically he had referred only to the Four] as "natives of the Principality" as if he were referring to a tribe of Wahabees in Central Africa. I have been reading how Stanley and his followers gave the natives empty jam pots in exchange. The policy pursued towards the "natives of the Principality" is one of empty jam pots (laughter). Others have the jam; we have the pots.'[176] His resolution was carried, with only one vote opposed.

The next weekend, after telling Maggie to reassure Richard Lloyd over the mixed press reactions to this continued defiance—Uncle Lloyd was not to worry 'at every shot fired by an idiot like Beriah Evans. Gee is like a rock today'—he was off to South Wales.[177] He was in Cardiff from 2 to 7 June staying at Bronwydd, the home of Alfred Thomas, and occupied, except for a speech, with the single project of converting to the cause of a Welsh national party the *South Wales Daily News* whose editor, John Duncan, previously had reprimanded the paper's London correspondent, Vincent Evans, for his column's bias in favor of the Four.[178] (After a rocky beginning,

Vincent Evans was now a strong and consistent follower of Lloyd George. His obituary in *The Times* referred to him as Lloyd George's 'first press agent.'[179] It cannot be said too often that in this period of his career Lloyd George regarded support from only two institutions, the chapels and the Welsh press, as worth having. The two indeed overlapped. Many preachers were also journalists. For the official Liberals, even in Wales, he cared very little and indeed within a month had told the Caernarvon District's executive that again he could not afford his election expenses and so offered to retire as Liberal candidate. And again he was overwhelmed with protests and assured that something could be done. He knew, and the constituency Liberal Association understood, that his attraction for voters was founded on empathetic genius that superseded the ordinary channels of party organization. They needed him more than he needed them.)

In Cardiff, with Alfred Thomas's money and local connections behind him, he won the *South Wales Daily News*. 'They have as you know been fiercely opposed to us,' he wrote Maggie on 4 June. 'Of course I couldn't expect them to confess that they have been wrong but I tried to induce them to drop the past and go in on general grounds for the formation of a Welsh National Party. I have succeeded with Alfred's help. They intended boycotting our meeting tonight but after my talk it has been arranged to send up the chief reporter and the editor up again to the meeting tonight. Now what do you think of that for a triumph?'[180] This elation was shortlived. By 1895 the *South Wales Daily News* had been captured by the forces opposing Lloyd George's program and he was trying to found a newspaper to support his movement.

Meanwhile at Westminster, disestablishment was off for the session. Lest the government think that the independent Welsh party was dead, Herbert Lewis and Frank Edwards, the Whips of the Four, wrote Ellis on 1 June demanding, in view of reports in the press, to know whether the government intended to take the bill in the present session, in the autumn, or in 1895.[181] The renewed pressure for an autumn session further deteriorated relations between Ellis and his former friends. 'It was all very well for Lloyd George,' Ellis wrote to Lewis in September, 'to put forward such a suggestion for an autumn session when he was in the House last session for something like sixty divisions out of two hundred and forty and when he spent the end of July and the beginning of August like a nobleman on the shores of Lake Thun in Switzerland.'[182]

Ellis's position was both difficult and unhappy. In March, with the passage of Edward Marjoribanks into the House of Lords, he had succeeded as Chief Whip. As the founder of advanced Welsh nationalism he bore in England a special responsibility for his countrymen's behavior in the House of Commons, but to the Welsh Members of Parliament his elevation meant either that he must accomplish the program he had advocated or be branded a traitor. He was irritated as a Welshman by Lloyd George's growing pressure and by attacks upon himself in the nonconformist press. As party Whip he had to bear the pain of his humiliating failure to prevent the carrying of an amendment to the address and of the studied insults from well-born English Liberals.[183]

The Disestablishment Bill was withdrawn on 18 July. As Ellis had noted,

Lloyd George was by this time preparing a vacation. In the last week of July three-quarters of the strength of the independent Welsh party, Lloyd George, Lewis and Edwards, deserted the House of Commons, the latter two with their wives, for a two-week holiday in Switzerland. Margaret avoided a flat refusal to join them until the last minute, when she announced she would stay in Criccieth. On this occasion, the excuse was more than simple unsociability. She was pregnant with her fourth child, who would be William, born on 4 December.

Beyond this interlude, Lloyd George spent his summer shuttling between London and Wales. In London he usually stayed now with Herbert Lewis and his wife in 9 Palace Mansions, Addison Road, where the two prepared to organize the principality. Already he and Lewis had begun to intervene in the selection of parliamentary candidates. W.T. Stead, despite the fact that his *Review of Reviews* had dismissed the Disestablishment Bill as unimportant, was asked to allow his name to be put forward for Montgomery District. He declined this with thanks but promised support.[184] But in North Caernarvonshire, where William Rathbone used the excuse of the retirement of Gladstone and the elevation of Rendel to announce his withdrawal from politics, Lloyd George and Ellis were able to force the nomination of William Jones, a friend and contemporary of Ellis, over the official Liberal candidate D.P. Williams.[185]

At the same time there were small problems which as the months passed forecast difficulties to come. In response to a note from Herbert Lewis that enthusiasm seemed less in the South than in the North, Lloyd George replied that it was simply a matter of getting good leaders and suggested Wynford Phillips (until recently MP for Mid-Lanark) or Llewelyn Williams, the young correspondent for the *South Wales Daily News*. 'Don't worry about D.A. Thomas,' he added significantly. 'Never you mind what he says.'[186]

This seems to have been the first intimation that relations between the North and the South were again growing strained. Hitherto Thomas had been the most active, more active even than Lloyd George, in the movement toward an independent Welsh party. The rift suggested here would grow wider and harden in the months ahead.

Almost immediately after his return from Switzerland he took the first step toward the formal organization of what would eventually become the 'Cymru Fydd League.' There is much dispute among historians about what precisely Cymru Fydd ('Wales to Be' or 'Wales of the Future') meant before 1894. An organization calling itself Cymru Fydd had been founded by Welshmen in London in 1886 and in following years similar clubs had sprung up in other Welsh centers in England, particularly in Liverpool.[187] But these organizations were social and cultural enclaves of expatriates who wished to preserve their Welsh heritage in an alien environment. Until the 1890s there appears to have been no Cymru Fydd club in Wales.

However, at the same time in Wales, during the campaign leading to the 1886 general election, appeared a political organization, more precisely a political movement or a point of view, which was normally associated with Tom Ellis, called 'Young Wales.' Young Wales was in no sense a political party. Rather it was a public expression of Ellis's romantic idealism, of his admiration of Mazzini which had developed during his university days at Aberystwyth, and of his desire to distinguish his political goals of land reform and Welsh nationalism from the chapel-centered interest in disestablishment and local veto that was the program of the older, post 1868, generation of Welsh Members of Parliament. Young Wales, thus, was not so much an organization as a conception, a political adjective. Lloyd George used the phrase to describe his own beliefs in 1890 and had begun referring to the Revolt of the Four in these terms.

These rather unspecific appellations received a more solid meaning in January, 1888, with the appearance of the political and literary journal, *Cymru Fydd,* already mentioned, under the editorship of T.J. Hughes. The name, having apparently nothing to do with the Cymru Fydd organization, although presumably designed to appeal to its members, was chosen by the Reverend Ellis Edwards. It was intended to claim for the journal the forward looking and youthful image that informed Ellis's 'Young Wales' movement and to contrast it with the narrow-minded, almost gloomy, traditionalism that generally characterized nationalist thought. Cymru Fydd was to be contrasted with Cymru Fu, 'Wales of the Past.'[188]

As a political journal, *Cymru Fydd* had a short life. It received new editors and became a more literary and scholarly periodical in 1889, even though it continued to comment upon politics, as it had done rather unfavorably upon Lloyd George's election. But it died in 1891. Nevertheless the phrase 'Cymru Fydd' continued to be used more or less interchangeably with 'Young Wales,' to describe land and social reforming Welsh nationalism. More significantly, Cymru Fydd societies, usually filled with advanced Liberal university intellectuals, began to appear in Welsh towns in the early nineties.

The Cymru Fydd League that officially was founded at Llandrindod Wells on 22 and 23 August 1894 had nothing in common with all that had gone before except the name. The new group was to be a centralized organization with branches in every Welsh community. The constitution, written at this time, specified to be sure that as its first object the league should 'confederate existing Cymru Fydd Societies' and should establish other branches.[189] But the stated aims of the league were entirely political and administrative, not ideological or cultural. The league was to 'secure legislation' for Wales, to 'promote a movement' for a 'national system of self-government,' to organize Welsh elections, parliamentary and local, and 'to conserve the national individuality' of Wales. Last of all the league was to promote also Welsh art, literature, and language. Alfred Thomas was named chairman of the conference and among the several honorary secretaries was W. Llewelyn Williams. The first convention was set for January, 1895.

Llandrindod Wells lies within easy reach of the South, but the most influential southern politician of all, D.A. Thomas, did not attend the constitutional meeting. According to Llewelyn Williams, Thomas's wife was present and Williams insists that at this time there existed no animosity between Thomas and the nationalist leaders of the North.[190] Nevertheless, in view of Lloyd George's remark to Herbert Lewis in June, there was evidently some chilliness and Thomas's absence suggested problems.

Alfred Thomas, amiable and wealthy as he was, provided no substitute.

The last months of 1894 saw a period of frantic organizing activity, with easy success for Cymru Fydd in the North and growing difficulties in the South. Lloyd George's goal, in his mind since 1889 when he became a parliamentary candidate, was the establishment of a single political organization in Wales. For this plan, Cymru Fydd was not the end, but the vehicle. The first step was the founding of local societies in every village and town under the umbrella of the national league, which could claim then, as the North and South Wales Liberal Federations had never been able to claim, that it represented the Welsh people. The second step would be to induce the Liberal Federations, North and South, to merge with the Cymru Fydd League. They had no real being in any case and were useful principally as platforms for such men as Lloyd George. Real political power in Wales rested entirely with the various constituency Liberal Association executives which were themselves usually a reflection of the mercantile, professional, and chapel composition of the given area. They had never paid attention to the resolutions of the two national groups, as Lloyd George had learned to his pain in 1890.

The last step, finally, would be the conversion of the Cymru Fydd League into a single Welsh national federation. The new organization would contain a policy-making central committee with branches in every locality. At the grassroots level it could influence voters and, most important, capture the constituency associations and so determine the selection of parliamentary candidates. Thus it would provide what Wales had never had, a homogeneous, above all disciplined, group of thirty-odd Liberal Members of Parliament who would speak with one voice at Westminster, ideally Lloyd George's, and who could be depended upon either to blackmail, or cooperate with, English Liberals as circumstances dictated.[191]

The little band of Welsh nationalists who, under Lloyd George's direction, pushed forward these ambitious plans in the autumn of 1894 included, beside Herbert Lewis and Frank Edwards, Winford Phillips, a Churchman of an old Pembroke landowning family, William Jones, who was elected for North Caernarvonshire in July 1895, the independent minister, Josiah Towyn Jones, Llewelyn Williams, J. Hugh Edwards, and Beriah Gwyneff Evans, all young radical journalists whose literary and political lives would be bound up with Lloyd George's for years to come. In January 1895 Beriah Evans was appointed secretary and general organizer of Cymru Fydd at £200 a year. Many of the more visible leaders of the movement were from the South, yet it was in the South, despite evident popular enthusiasm at meetings held there, that ominous signs of trouble began to appear. Frank Edwards, one of the original Four—a 'sticker' Lloyd George had described him on 23 April when he joined Thomas and himself in the revolt—began to drift away. He was too much 'under the influence of D.A.T.,' observed Lloyd George on 31 October to Herbert Lewis, noting Edwards's repeated absences. He needed 'bracing.' Nevertheless meetings in the South were going splendidly. Cymru Fydd would have a membership of ten to fifteen thousand 'before the winter is out. I think we'll capture the North Wales Federation through Gee. The position of the South will then be quite untenable.'[192]

D.A. Thomas was clearly by this time an enemy and was working quietly to separate southern leaders from Cymru Fydd, even though there was as yet no public breach between himself and the rest of the movement. But his influence on Alfred Thomas was always a problem. The latter was important because of his wealth, but he was somewhat untrustworthy because he was easily led. Lloyd George always made it a point to stay with Alfred Thomas when in Cardiff. 'I prefer being here,' instead of with the younger and more congenial Llewelyn Williams, he wrote to Maggie on 5 October, 'I think I can do good in keeping A.T. straight. He has already promised to give well toward the movement. He spoke very well last night.'[193]

Only a few days before, Lloyd George had intervened in a newspaper dispute between the Welsh parliamentary leader G. Osborne Morgan, and Harcourt, and had managed, as he was often able to do, to embarrass both men and also, above all, D.A. Thomas. Late in September 1894, after the prorogation, Morgan had visited Harcourt, as he had done in the spring, to obtain assurances that disestablishment would be brought forward again in the coming session. Harcourt, whose short temper was legendary and for whom most Welsh members were by now more irritating than the opposition, evidently concluded the interview by informing Morgan 'I wish you and your bill were in hell' and that Morgan was in addition one of the 'biggest bores in the House of Commons.' Lloyd George was not present at the interview, but heard about it immediately. Even though he himself had often expressed the same opinion of Sir Osborne's oratory, he now lost no time in leaking to the press the attack upon disestablishment and Welsh honor, announcing that it was 'an insult to Wales.'[194] The result was a newspaper uproar. Harcourt immediately got in touch with Morgan who replied publicly denying he had suffered any rudeness.[195] Lloyd George reiterated his assertions saying that his 'informant' stuck to his story, whereupon the informant, D.A. Thomas, was forced to identify himself and agreed that the words were spoken, but that it had not been a 'studied insult.' All of which was finally reluctantly confirmed by Morgan.[196]

Until the first of the year the divisions in sentiment between North and South were visible only to insiders, even though no less real for that. What appeared in the North to be an earnest effort by young and idealistic politicians and journalists to organize the nation so as to gain some reward for Wales's doglike Liberal fidelity was viewed by D.A. Thomas and some of his followers in the South as a cynical attempt by self-seeking rural extremists, either led or symbolized by Lloyd George, to use honest nationalism as a means for establishing an Irish-style political machine. This problem would come up again and again in the next few years concerning disestablishment, education, and local government. Wales simply was not one nation; the North and South were not identical parts of one whole. The South was far more populous, wealthy and underrepresented. (In 1895 Wales and Monmouthshire possessed 308,582 electors of whom 219,336 lived south of Montgomery and Merionethshire. The South returned 22 Members of Parliament for an average of 9,969 electors per Member. The North had 89,246 electors and returned 12 Members of Parliament for an average of 7,437 per member.) The North, socially far more homogeneous, was attempting to seize the leadership in a project about which very many Welshmen, let alone the thousands of Englishmen in the factories and docks of the South, were still unsure.

The first public reference to the now hardening division between North and South appeared in January 1895, in the initial issue of a new magazine devoted to Cymru Fydd, *Young Wales,* edited by J. Hugh Edwards, a recent graduate of Aberystwyth and an ardent Welsh nationalist. Noting the preparations for a national conference in Aberystwyth, expected at that time in February, the journal remarked: 'It is useless to disguise there exists in certain quarters a feeling of uneasiness in the possibility of the South Wales Liberal Federation holding aloof from the National Convention....It is common knowledge that the President and some of the older members of the South Wales Federation have no warm feeling of attachment towards the Cymru Fydd movement.' However, *Young Wales* continued, both sides had agreed to a conference at Llandrindod Wells in August and D.A. Thomas's statement that the Cymru Fydd movement would be 'the death warrant' of both the North and South Wales Liberal federations was groundless.[197]

Possibly more offensive to D.A. Thomas was the admiring profile, in the same issue of *Young Wales,* of the Member for Caernarvon District as a leading Welshman who was, with Ellis, the best known and 'most popular man in Wales' and who would soon inherit the mantle of the great Thomas Gee. Indeed Gee himself, continued the journal, had recently 'thanked Heaven for such a representative as Mr. Lloyd George....the incident irresistibly recalled the ancient scene where the veteran leader, having led the people through the wilderness, surrenders his leadership to his young successor when on the threshhold of the promised land.'[198] As these sentimental outpourings were printed, on 3 January 1895 leaders of the North and South met at the Principality Club at Cardiff to make an attempt at compromise. The meeting was closed to the press and what occurred is not entirely clear. One historian, citing the *South Wales Daily News* and the *Baner,* states that the southern leaders insisted that the proposed centralized constitution be modified to a federal structure of four regions with a weak council, and with Glamorgan and Monmouthshire, constituting three-fifths of the population of Wales, forming one of the regions.[199] Yet the report in the *Western Mail,* whose publisher Lascelles Carr had made his paper the organ of Church and Conservatism in South Wales, suggested a love feast. A motion to unify all Welsh political organizations was seconded with a long speech by D.A. Thomas and passed unanimously. The account concluded with an interview with Lloyd George, who, although evidently not present, commented that the resolution for approval of the single organization, 'if carried, was a great step forward.'[200] Llewelyn Williams who was present at the meeting insisted, a quarter century later, that Thomas indeed had agreed to the amalgamation of the two organizations.[201] Confirming this, the *British Weekly,* which had followed events in Wales with growing concern and which had remarked approvingly on a plea by Ellis at Conway, on the same day as the meeting, for Welsh leaders to stop feuding, announced that the problem had been solved.

> Those, who like Mr. Ellis, have been alarmed by the recent manifestation of the spirit of disunion have been much relieved by the decision which

was arrived at in the conference between representatives of the South Wales Liberal Federation and the Cymru Fydd league last week in Cardiff. Accommodation was decided upon and the prevailing tone of the meeting was one of harmony and desire for unity. There is now every reason to believe that the bickering between the supporters of the two organizations, which has caused so much ill feeling during the last few months will now be forgotten, and that the church party will no longer be able to gaze with rapture and delight upon the unedifying spectacle of Welshmen quarreling bitterly with one another on a mere question of organization.[202]

All of this, including Lloyd George's cryptic statement, only deepens the mystery of the next few months, when between January and April 1895 the loosely knit fabric of Welsh unity again became unraveled. Yet for the moment everything seemed most auspicious. Publicly the feud was smoothed over. Lloyd George had remained, purposely no doubt, at a distance from the proceedings and indeed there is no evidence of any participation by him at the Principality Club meeting. Probably the purpose of the meeting was to give Welsh politics a semblance of order during the coming convention of the National Liberal Federation scheduled for 17 and 18 January at Park Hall in Cardiff.

Before this meeting Lloyd George and Lewis had tried to induce Rosebery, who would speak on the second day, to give some notice of Home Rule all around, and Lloyd George on the first day made a brilliant speech on the claims of Ireland.[203] 'It was the best speech — fifteen minutes — I have ever heard him make, a perfect radical gem,' wrote Llewelyn Williams.[204] But on the whole the National Liberal Federation was dedicated to disestablishment. Rosebery, with a resolution welcoming him seconded, significantly, by D.A. Thomas, spoke almost entirely about the Welsh Church.[205] His speech was an ideal example of the disengaged, but clear-headed attitude Rosebery always manifested towards politics. Wales wanted a disestablishment bill. Therefore it would have one. Despite 'heartburnings' in Scotland, Welsh disestablishment was 'first on the list. (Cheers)'. But, he added, there was not a chance of its passing the House of Lords. It would be rejected by the same majority by which 'it would be passed if left to the Welsh (shame).' The Welsh, he was saying in effect, were insisting that as a reward for their loyalty to Liberalism the government waste a parliamentary year upon them. He was now agreeing to the charade, but making it clear that he fully understood what he was doing. The same candor about his own motives that made Rosebery reluctant to take the premiership in the first place, undid him after he assumed that office.[206]

The disestablishment movement, one of the most hopeless political initiatives since Chartism, was now reaching a climax. For Lloyd George, politically committed to it as he was forced to be, it was a harmless diversion. He knew as well as anybody the impossibility of its approval in the upper chamber, where the antagonism toward it was even stronger perhaps than toward Home Rule.[207] However, A.G. Edwards, Bishop of St. Asaph, remarked in his memoirs that had the Disestablishment Bill been placed before the House of Lords linked with Irish Home Rule, the peers might have been reluctant to reject both and would have allowed disestablishment to pass. He states, without providing a source, that Lloyd George had advised this course.[208] But like the tithe, disestablishment was a fine rallying cry. As the only issue that the North Wales nonconformists cared about it gave Welsh politicians, including Lloyd George, plenty of congenial opportunities for attacking the Church without having to explain what, if anything, disestablishment would do for Wales. Indeed, one may postulate that for many of them disestablishment unpassed was better than disestablishment on the statute book. Rosebery probably understood this. If a bill passed through the House of Commons would satisfy the Welsh, they should have it. On the other hand the House of Lords would save the Church. Theoretically, when it was all over, both Liberal nonconformists and Liberal establishmentarians would be happy. In a year when the House of Lords had frustrated every other government proposal it could provide a service to the Liberals.[209]

But to Cymru Fydd disestablishment was a genuine impediment. It demanded energy and time. For the young men of Ellis's persuasion, who sought Home Rule, land and social reform, it was irrelevant. It forced Welsh Members into a single-issue political straitjacket. Most dangerous of all, after all the oratory about principles had ended, the terms of the 1895 Disestablishment Bill involved Lloyd George in a series of parliamentary struggles during the committee stage that destroyed the unstable North-South truce negotiated at the Principality Club and ended for good any hope of Welsh political unity.

The Second Disestablishment Bill, 'The Established Church (Wales) Bill,' so long promised and anticipated, was introduced by H.H. Asquith on 25 February 1895. The second reading began on 21 March. The bill was virtually identical to the one introduced the previous year. The Welsh Church would no longer be a part of the See of Canterbury. Its bishops would not sit in the House of Lords nor its clergy attend convocation. This was easy enough. The disendowment provisions were more controversial. The Church would lose all endowments acquired before 1703, which meant about five-sixths of its endowment revenue. These properties were to belong to a three-member commission appointed by the government which would have the responsibility of maintaining cathedrals and parsonages. The proceeds from the tithe were likewise to be handled by the commissioners but to be allocated to county councils for public purposes, so far as possible within the county where the tithe originated. Glebe land and burial grounds would go to parish councils. Although the total sum to be disendowed was £280,000 per year, with the reduced value of the tithe because of low agricultural prices and the cost of collection, the amount to be devoted to public purposes after diverting £7,000 for the expenses of the commission would in fact be about £150,000.[210]

The allocation of Church income was to be the source of much disagreement between North and South Wales. Even before the bill had been introduced, immediately after the Principality Club meeting, on 12 January, Thomas had written to Asquith pointing out that the tithe, fixed in 1836, represented a population distribution that no longer obtained in Wales and that the differences in population between the North and the

South at the end of the century would make its management by county councils highly inequitable. (Glamorgan and Monmouthshire alone possessed in 1890 about one million of the 1,750,000 population of Wales.) It should be distributed, thought Thomas, from a central fund according to population. Although he was taken with the idea, Asquith was persuaded by Ellis from changing the bill.[211]

Thomas's intervention may have provided the motive for a mysterious, but altogether characteristic counter move by Lloyd George to try to arrange a compromise disestablishment bill with the Church forces. What happened, and what the shape of the agreed bill would have been, are unclear, but the most important figure involved was evidently Joseph Chamberlain, whose interest in avoiding a squabble over the Welsh Church was as great as Lloyd George's. Chamberlain was in touch with A.G. Edwards, and according to St. Asaph also in communication with Gladstone whom he interviewed at Cannes in January, 1895. He attempted to impress Church leaders on one hand that they should prepare to permit disestablishment if not disendowment, and to elicit from Gladstone, on the other, a statement urging Liberals not to destroy entirely the Welsh Church.[212] There also existed a plan put together early in January by a number of Churchmen associated with the cathedral school at Bangor for disestablishment without disendowment: Wales to continue as part of the Anglican community under her own Archbishop.[213] On 21 February, just before the bill's introduction, Chamberlain had told St. Asaph that Lloyd George 'was in favour of making concessions.'[214] However, also in February, Chamberlain wrote to his friend John Edwards, a Churchman and editor of the *Aberystwyth Observer,* saying that 'disestablishment must come' while admitting that the Church must have 'just treatment' about its funds.[215]

There is no evidence that the Bangor plan was to be the basis of Lloyd George's proposals, nor is there much beyond Edwards's recollections written many years later, that he had heard that the Member for Caernarvon District was seeking compromise. But a behind-the-scenes agreement to solve an intractable public problem, particularly if it involved a political issue in which he had no interest, was a normal tactic for Lloyd George. A compromise on the Disestablishment Bill would have avoided several problems and even without disendowment, disestablishment would have been a triumph for Lloyd George and, by implication, for Cymru Fydd. Moreover, he attempted to find a compromise on approximately this basis when disestablishment came up again in 1906.[216] As Bishop Edwards subsequently noted, the lines of the Bangor scheme were those upon which the Welsh Church was finally disestablished a quarter century later.

But for now the Bangor proposals were dead, killed by a premature disclosure and by the resulting outrage, first from the Church, which assumed that with the existence of the House of Lords there was no need for compromise, and second from the nonconformists who saw no gain from disestablishment if the Church kept its wealth.[217]

Lloyd George made a major effort to take the leadership on disestablishment in his second reading address on 26 March. He prepared for the speech for weeks, sending for books from home and urging Maggie to investigate the level of sacrifice within the congregations of certain more impoverished chapels. But, after flattening Arthur Griffith-Boscawen, secretary of the Church Parliamentary Committee and born in Wrexham, Denbighshire, for an inadequate knowledge of Wales, his message, as always, was not the poverty of nonconformists but the wealth of the Church. Finally he returned to the endless dispute about the relative membership of Church and chapel.[218]

He sent Maggie the routine letter of self praise—'they now listen to me with deference'—but it was not one of his better efforts. More and more it was becoming clear that his easiest parliamentary setting was not formal debate, where his lack of education and polish hindered orderly exposition and where the emotional appeal of the public platform was inappropriate, but in committee or in intervention in supply and adjournment debates where his weapons were a quick wit and tongue. 'His opening sentences answering Boscawen,' thought Llewelyn Williams, in the press gallery for the *South Wales Daily News*, 'were exceedingly happy, but he did not do anything like justice to the excellent material he had. He seemed to be afraid he would weary the House and his references to historical arguments were not clear and concise.'[219] The Disestablishment Bill received its second reading on 1 April by a very satisfactory 304 to 260. Joseph Chamberlain was one of two Liberal-Unionists recorded in the affirmative.

D.A. Thomas did not give up his attempts to modify the Disestablishment Bill after his rebuff in January but continued to advance the claims of justice for South Wales. In doing so he destroyed his fragile accommodation with Lloyd George and set the two on course for a collision that came finally at Newport in January, 1896. On 18 March, before the second reading, he wrote an open letter to Gladstone pointing out that while the ancient endowments of the Church which would remain with the new Church commission were worth only £47,000, the various properties attached to parochial benefices which would go to the county council were worth £247,000 (a considerable exaggeration of the value of the tithe which must have included also glebe lands to be vested in parish councils. Bishop Edwards stated that the net worth of the tithe was £147,948 per year, this after the cost of collection which he estimated at about 20%).[220] This was 'national property,' said Thomas, of which the more populous and poorer parishes of Wales were to be deprived in a departure from the precedent set in Irish disestablishment. Would Gladstone publish some comment upon the present bill?[221] Gladstone declined to be drawn into the Welsh squabble, saying that he was out of parliament and any comment of his upon debatable points of legislation would do more harm than good.[222] Gladstone's sensible neutrality was not enough to avert the rising quarrel. Three days after the publication of Thomas's letter Lloyd George replied.

In a *Manchester Guardian* column devoted to Welsh affairs, written anonymously by several of the younger Welsh Members of Parliament and ordinarily used chiefly to compliment each other, Lloyd George launched into his first public attack on Thomas. 'Mr. D.A. Thomas, MP, has failed to draw Mr. Gladstone on the allocation of tithe,' he wrote on 9 April

> and he will have to fight his battle single-handed unless he obtains the support of Mr. Chamberlain or some other prominent Unionist...I presume Mr. Thomas means to submit his proposal to the judgement of

the forthcoming national convention of Welsh Liberals at Aberystwyth. In any case this will be expected of him and it is to be hoped that Mr. Thomas will decide to abide by the opinion there expressed. He will probably find that he will have an overwhelming majority against him. The Welsh Members will doubtless consider it best to place on the paper as few amendments as possible to the Welsh bill when it comes to be discussed in committee, but the number and character of these will be to a great extent determined by what takes place at Aberystwyth.[223]

The Aberystwyth meeting, thus announced, represented the second part of Lloyd George's plan to consolidate Welsh political organization. Theoretically the North and South Liberal Federations and the local independent Cymru Fydd clubs would all merge with appropriate celebration into the National Federation of Wales to Be (or Cymru Fydd) under the constitution drafted at Llandrindod Wells the previous August. Thomas had signified unclearly at the Principality Club that such an amalgamation could occur. But now the difference over the Disestablishment Bill, which Lloyd George attempted to assign to motives of personal spite but which represented a real and not a symbolic cleavage of North and South Wales, had pulled the two sides apart. The breakdown of the truce clearly worried the sponsors of the Aberystwyth meeting, although they affected to believe it the work of only a relatively few highly placed malcontents who did not represent opinion even within their own constituencies. (Early in April the Glamorgan County Council had passed a resolution opposing national allocation of the tithe.)

It would be hard to overestimate the importance of the Aberystwyth convention and the weight of its authority as the voice of Wales, asserted the 'Welsh Notes' column in the *Manchester Guardian* on 17 April, the day the convention was to begin. It was 'a new departure for Liberalism' in Wales and decisions on the Disestablishment Bill 'will carry due weight.' However

> the real business before the convention will be the reorganization of Welsh Liberalism on more truly representative and national lines. It is unfortunate that a section of the party has seen fit to hold aloof from the gathering. The North Wales Liberal Federation has voluntarily sacrificed itself in the interest of the new central organization proposed by the Cymru Fyddites, but I believe that the South Wales Federation, or at least a remnant of it, still preserves an independent, though precarious, existence. Mr. D.A. Thomas MP, and those who act with him will probably find it convenient for some time to disown the new organization and to disregard its opinion upon such matters as the allocation of the tithe. As a result the new organization that comes from Aberystwyth will have to assume a militant and aggressive attitude toward the rebels.[224]

In the last weeks before the conference Lloyd George was industriously maneuvering to undermine Thomas in South Wales. 'I am very busy,' he wrote his wife on 8 April, 'engaged with Beriah Evans—whom I got up to London to arrange a counterplot to D.A. Thomas's little plan in connection with Cymru Fydd. Can't write you much in consequence. Herbert Lewis and Alfred Thomas are also with us. I think we'll upset

D.A. in spite of his little tricks.'[225] Lloyd George's plan evidently was to stimulate enthusiasm by newspaper propaganda and so to excite a stampede of rank and file Liberals from South Wales toward Aberystwyth. Therefore in the next days the battle was fought in the public press. On 10 April Beriah Evans announced that there had been 500 applications for tickets for the Aberystwyth meeting from South Wales Liberals. On the same day the South Wales Liberal Federation executive, in effect D.A. Thomas, stated that not one member of the executive, except perhaps Alfred Thomas, would attend.[226] The next day the executive met to say that the South Wales Liberal Federation would not proceed to Aberystwyth and Evans duly retorted that this contravened its promises.[227]

The Aberystwyth meeting was supposed to begin on the afternoon of 17 April. That day the *South Wales Weekly News* carried a letter signed by 'A Nationalist,' who was universally understood to be D.A. Thomas. After a long attack on Beriah Evans (for whom one could read Lloyd George) it asserted that the only people interested in Aberystwyth were those who failed to be elected to the South Wales Federation's executive committee and that 'the death Knell of Cymru Fydd has been rung.'[228] The manifest ill-nature of the letter caused more than usual anger. Even Llewelyn Williams, later the recorder of Thomas's political life, described Thomas in his diary that day as 'A most mischievious character in Welsh politics, his policy is fearless selfishness.'[229]

Amid the growing unpleasantness the Aberystwyth conference, which was supposed to provide Wales with a single political voice, convened at 3 o'clock. At that hour no one was present in the college assembly hall except Thomas Gee, who was to preside, and two newspaper reporters.[230] At 3:15 p.m. Lloyd George and Beriah Evans turned up. Eventually about thirty people appeared. The first session was technically a meeting of the North Wales Liberal Federation to consider the draft National Federation Constitution. The approval of the constitution signified the merger of the northern group into the new organization. That evening attendance was better. A large number of town people appeared to help consume the buffet.[231]

The next day's session was more meaningful and better attended. The *Western Mail* estimated that 150-200 people were there. Alfred Thomas was chosen president of the new federation and Beriah Evans, secretary. The conference considered a number of resolutions, including votes for women, that were to constitute a program. Among the last was a proposal by Lloyd George for 'an elective Welsh National Assembly to administer ecclesiastical funds' whose decisions, according to an amendment, would be final. In effect it would not be controlled by the Welsh commissioners as envisioned in the Disestablishment Bill. Finally Lloyd George closed proceedings with an appeal for Welsh unity, reminding the meeting, in a statement that brought guffaws in Cardiff, that he was himself a South Welshman representing a northern constituency.[232]

In all of this parliamentary sleight of hand there was little room for opposition, but even without D.A. Thomas, there was a powerful and dangerous dissenting voice in Lloyd George's colleague in the southern division of Caernarvonshire, J. Bryn Roberts. Roberts, an important figure in Lloyd George's life in the next few years, was a highly principled Gladstonian who would clash with the Welsh radicals many times in the months to come, less from sympathy with D.A. Thomas than from the conviction that Lloyd George intended to use a centralized organization as a means of extending his own political control in Wales. Although a devoted Calvinistic Methodist, who had been one of the numerous successful opponents of Hugh Ellis-Nanney, he was neither a Welsh Home Ruler nor even a disestablishmentarian and so had suffered since 1892 the jovian wrath of the Reverend Evan Jones. (He had been the only Welsh Liberal to vote against the Home Rule All Round Bill introduced by Henry Dalziel in late March.)[233]

Roberts distrusted Lloyd George's principles as much as he disliked his opportunist program, which seemed designed to make the Member for Caernarvon District into a Welsh Parnell. As a northerner he was not affected by D.A. Thomas's decision that members from South Wales should stay away from Aberystwyth and so at the meeting he took a position that D.A. Thomas would have held, even though on most issues of Welsh nationalism he differed from Thomas as much as from Lloyd George. At Aberystwyth he denied that the mushrooming Cymru Fydd represented anything more than the work of a few 'hasty young men' and questioned the motives of the conference leadership.[234]

Roberts however was a lonely voice calling essentially for a return to Gladstonian Liberalism and party solidarity. The real enemy of Cymru Fydd, D.A. Thomas, the man who had spent the previous weeks, in the words of the Young Wales, 'hissing his wrath and hurling invective upon men, who to say the least, are conscientious and sincere in the efforts to the national cause' was present only in spirit.[235]

Even with Thomas Gee's announcement from the podium that the South Wales Liberal Federation had 'ceased to exist' the new organization seemed to have even less substance than the ones it had ostensibly replaced. The question of course was: had anything in fact happened? The writer of 'Welsh Notes' was clearly disappointed. The Welsh National Federation, the column stated on 23 April, had 'been duly constituted,' but it was not clear who would accept its authority and it was a pity that more effort had not been made to bring the South along. 'Mr. Gee's dictum from the chair that the South Wales Federation no longer existed is perhaps more likely to stimulate that body to prolong its life than to give it what many would consider a desirable quietus.'

Although the conference had discussed disestablishment thoroughly, and unanimously condemned Thomas's resolution to allocate the tithe nationally, Lloyd George's proposal to entrust all ecclesiastical funds to a Welsh national assembly, with the three Commissioners remaining purely a judicial body, was more controversial than it had seemed at Aberystwyth. There may be some 'quiet sympathy' among Liberals all over the country for the resistance of South Wales and many 'who are suspicious of the designs of Cymru Fydd.'[236]

This was good and temperate advice which Lloyd George might have done well to heed. There were indeed many, not only Thomas and Bryn Roberts, who doubted that Wales could, or should, be politically organized, least of all under him. The Young Wales program, of which the goal was Home Rule and land reform, had brought little response even when articulated by the saintly Tom Ellis at Bala.[237] When accompanied by the well-founded suspicion that the national federation was simply a stepping stone to an independent political party with Lloyd George at its head, the antagonisms were compounded.

But for the moment all this was lost on the Member for Caernarvon District. As he would be throughout his career, he was stimulated by the very enthusiasm he raised so successfully in the meeting. He found it hard to believe that the conversions made in public tabernacle failed to survive outside its walls. And so he pressed forward with assurance, manifest even in his private letters, that everything was going well and that he had made great progress at Aberystwyth. His own oratory and enthusiasm could not fail. 'I am off now to a place called Pontlottyn,' he wrote from Thomas's home in Cardiff the weekend after Aberystwyth, 'to address a Cymru Fyd [sic] meeting in order to keep the ball rolling. We must smash up the remnants of the South Wales Federation and we shall do it.'[238] Through the summer and autumn of 1895 the fight to organize Wales under the National Federation continued, interrupted only by Lloyd George's return to London to deal with the committee stage of the Disestablishment Bill and to Caernarvonshire in July to fight his third election. The most visible opponent during these months remained Bryn Roberts whose dislike of Lloyd George grew beyond reason as time passed. As a member of the old North Wales Liberal Federation he could not be barred from meetings and as a senior figure in the Welsh parliamentary delegation, with a clever mind and a good sense of parliamentary tactics, he could not be silenced. In June, as the struggle between Lloyd George and D.A. Thomas over the disposal of the tithe reached a climax at Westminster, Roberts nearly succeeded in inducing the Welsh National Federation to dissolve itself. At a meeting on 2 June he moved a resolution that the proceedings at Aberystwyth were irregular and that there should be no tampering with the party organization until after the next election. When this was defeated he proposed that the National Federation of Cymru Fydd should appoint a delegate to confer with the South Wales Federation. 'This looked so plausible,' Lloyd George wrote to his wife the next day,

> that Gee was for a moment taken in. It really meant the continued existence of the North Wales Federation. Luckily Bryn was beaten on it. Then Herbert Lewis moved a resolution in favour of replying to the invitation of the South Wales people to enter into a conference with them by stating that we had already amalgamated with Cymru Fydd. This was carried by 15 to 7. We licked them on several other points. When Bryn's resolution was beaten poor Gee lost control over himself and flinging up his arms with a voice half choked with emotion shouted 'hurrah-hurrah'. The poor old man was very excited. He was beside himself with joy at the triumph of Cymru Fydd.[239]

The meeting projected on 2 June did, in fact, take place on 22 June at the Gwalin Hotel in Llandrindod Wells, which appears to have been regarded as neutral territory between North and South. The gathering included fourteen leaders among whom Lloyd George, D.A. and Alfred Thomas, Gee, and Beriah Evans were the most important. For over three hours the group struggled toward an agreement on the form of a national organization. The lines of dispute were the same as in the Principality Club meeting: should there be a single national executive, or a council made up of representatives of four district federations. Eventually it was agreed to accept a proposal by W.H. Brown for a national executive to be made up of delegates from parliamentary divisions allocated according to population. In effect the South had won. Although the groups succeeded in drafting a statement for the press saying that there should be 'one National Council for the purpose of focusing the national sentiment' and was able to appoint a committee to consider details, Lloyd George had no further interest in the plan. Cymru Fydd would go on as before.[240] There were further meetings between the two groups in July, but he did not attend.[241]

Even before this vestigial compromise had been announced, the conditions that prompted it were changed. On 21 June the Rosebery government was defeated in supply committee on an adverse vote on the Army's stock of cordite. The Cabinet resigned the next day. Because Bryn Roberts subsequently charged that the Liberal administration's haste to quit office over a defeat by seven votes on a minor matter in a thin house was caused by despondency over Lloyd George's loyalty to Liberalism, the events of the previous six weeks when the Disestablishment Bill was in committee need some examination.

The Disestablishment Bill as introduced provided for three appointed commissioners to handle Church temporalities, who would apportion the tithe as nearly as possible to the counties from which it arose. The actual spending of each county's share would be handled by the county councils. The issue between Thomas and Lloyd George turned about the management of the tithe, not specifically its administration but its allocation. Thomas, as has been seen, wished to insure that the populous counties of the South received a proportionate share of the wealth of which the Church was to be mulcted. To this end he had made his proposal in January for a national allocation. Like Lloyd George he was interested in funding some sort of a Welsh national body that would have money to spend and so would provide an embryonic national government for the principality. But this was secondary to proportionate allocation. For Lloyd George, the priorities were reversed. His proposal, which he moved as an amendment to Clause 3 of the Disestablishment Bill on 20 May, was that the tithe be given to a national council made up of representatives of the county councils. This, he argued, was clearly provided for in Section 81 of the Local Government Act (which allowed county councils to work jointly for common purposes). The commissioners would of course supervise the joint committee's work.[242] Lloyd George avoided during the discussion of his amendment the fact that the proposed national council would not have provided a proportionate allocation of the tithe. A body of delegates from the county councils would in fact have been evenly divided between South and North. Nor did he point out subsequently that his amendment had failed to win the approval of the Welsh parliamentary delegation when he had first presented it to them and that only at a second meeting, on 9 May, with only 11 of 32 members present, was he able to get formal approval for his proposal. Bryn Roberts immediately reported to Asquith that Lloyd George's aim was Welsh Home Rule, a matter upon which the Welsh MPs were by no means united, and that the government should reject his amendment.[243] Accordingly Asquith resisted his young colleague's amendment while the Tories, seeing a possibility of dividing the Welsh from the main body of Liberalism, moved to support it. Suddenly there appeared the likelihood that the government would be defeated if the Welsh rebels pushed Lloyd George's amendment to a division. Asquith finally agreed to take the question of a creation of a Welsh council under the Local Government Act on the ninth clause and Lloyd George asked leave to withdraw his amendment. The Conservatives now refused to allow the amendment to be withdrawn and demanded a vote. The result was that Lloyd George was forced to vote, ignominiously, against his own proposal. Even so the amendment lost by only ten votes.[244]

Through the next several weeks Lloyd George organized public pressure for his amendment with the support in Wales of Thomas Gee, who adamantly opposed redistribution of the tithe, and with help in England from the Liberation Society of which he suddenly recalled he was a member. He did not hesitate to use disestablishment to arouse the Welsh sense of grievance against the national Liberal party. Mr. Asquith, he told a meeting in Blaencwm on 6 June, had said 'he would rather wreck the Bill than accept an amendment which even the Tories said was a national one. The Home Secretary had said 'he could not trust the county councils of Wales and Monmouthshire to administer their own affairs (shame).'[245] At the same time, Lloyd George worked privately, as usual, to obtain from Asquith some agreement to a Welsh national council. He evidently got what he believed to be a promise of amendments to Clause 9 which was scheduled to be taken up on Monday, 24 June and, based upon the report of Cabinet approval, he announced this assent to a Liberation Society meeting on 17 June. But subsequently Asquith heard from Bryn Roberts and others that the national council commanded nothing like a consensus among the Welsh delegation. Already sick of a hopeless bill, the Home Secretary withdrew his promise and announced this on Thursday 20 June. (Asquith referred to his management of the Disestablishment Bill as a 'thankless task.' It was not safe, he said, to leave the front bench for more than fifteen minutes. Many papers commented on the 'odium' of the Disestablishment Bill, the bad attendance in the House, the few ministers in their seats and the dislike, even by English radicals, at being led through the lobby by Lloyd George who, it was assumed, was taking his orders from Thomas Gee.)[246] Yet the Home Secretary may have met a number of Welsh MPs although not probably Lloyd George, the next day, Friday, and was reported to have arranged a compromise.[247] All of this may well account for Asquith's subsequent studied unclearness on whether he had in fact accepted Lloyd George's amendment.[248]

But all of this was behind the scenes. The public blows to the government's prestige and self-confidence had already been delivered by D.A. Thomas who was working, virtually alone, to ensure that South Wales got its share of whatever wealth the Church was to be deprived of. On 18

June he moved an amendment to Clause 6 specifying that all property received by the commissioners, endowment as well as the tithe, should be transferred to an elected or appointed 'Welsh council.'[249] The opposition immediately woke up. Griffith-Boscawen, suddenly full of sympathy for disestablishment, reminded the House that in Glamorgan, with a population of 700,000, the value of the tithe was £16,000 per year, whereas in Anglesey, only 35,000 people would enjoy the proceeds of a tithe of £12,000.[250] The Tories surged to support Welsh nationalism; the Liberals took flight, and only one Gladstonian, Alfred Illingworth, not a Welshman, supported Thomas's motion. Thomas himself had the lonely distinction of serving as a teller opposed to his own whip, Tom Ellis. Nonetheless the motion was defeated by only 13 votes. Lloyd George himself did not vote.[251] Thomas returned to the attack two days later with a motion to drop Clause 6 altogether. This would have removed entirely the requirement that the tithe be allocated to the county from which it arose. Again the Tories sprang to help. John Gorst announced he had been about to move the same amendment, but refrained, thinking it more suitable for a Welshman to do it. James Bryce, in charge at the moment, floundered badly saying he did not understand the amendment, and received no help from his colleagues except from Osborne Morgan who succeeded only in confusing him further.[252] The next day the government was defeated over cordite.

The House had not reached the ninth clause and so Lloyd George's amendment was never considered. He announced nevertheless that the government had accepted the Welsh Council. However, Asquith told Ellis categorically in November that the government had not accepted that amendment.[253] But even if the government had not accepted Lloyd George's amendment, it did not follow that he brought the Liberal administration down. Probably the mortal blow for Rosebery's Cabinet was the announcement in *The Times* on 19 June that Gladstone, possibly influenced by the Bishop of St. Asaph, had cancelled his pair with Charles Villiers. The world knew that the Grand Old Man was distressed about the disendowment provisions of the bill and the Unionist press chose to regard this action as a withdrawal of support from the entire project, by implication a disavowal also of the Liberal administration. Whether or not this was true, the announcement clearly unnerved the government. Ellis evidently kept the letter private, even from the rest of the ministers, for some time. Harcourt recorded that his first intelligence of it came in the newspaper announcement and his reaction clearly was one of panic.[254]

The conclusion of recent research is that the Liberal departure came when it did because of discouragement over by-election defeats in May and June. Gladstone's defection was the last straw.[255] There is the report that the Cabinet, meeting on Friday night, wondered briefly, in a moment of fright, whether Gladstone might not appear in the House and attack disestablish-ment.[256] But beyond this the Welsh Church seems not to have been a factor. The cordite vote itself had been a surprise. A number of Tories hid them-selves on the terrace of the House of Commons and had suddenly appeared after Ellis had allowed a number of Liberals to leave. Neither Lloyd George nor D.A. Thomas nor any other Welsh radical was present at the critical vote on 21 June. Ellis himself believed he had an agreement with A. Akers-

Douglas against dirty tricks of precisely this sort.[257] The first reaction of the Cabinet was to order Ellis to replace the debate on Clause 9 of the Disestablishment Bill, scheduled for Monday, with a debate on Army supply and to ensure attendance.[258] Resignation came, nevertheless, on Saturday morning. If disestablishment was a factor there is no evidence of it.

But in a larger sense, the Welsh rebellion, and it was no less than that, was part of the political climate in which the government floundered. The rebels allowed themselves to become in reality the agents of Tory mischief. The Unionist opposition, secure in the knowledge that the House of Lords would never allow disestablishment to become law, could cheerfully support the most irresponsible Welsh proposals, embarrassing the ministry among Liberal Churchmen, wasting the government's time, and eroding party discipline. In the long run there could be no winner but the Tories. The government would get no credit for sincerity and the Welsh would get no bill. Instead each group would earn for itself the dislike of Liberals throughout the rest of the United Kingdom and indeed, as it became clear, within Wales.

Lloyd George's part in the Liberals' fall was not great in the terms in which he would later be charged. It is far too much to say the Liberals resigned rather than face his amendment on 24 June. Lloyd George was as happy to embarrass a Liberal as a Conservative government, but on the other hand his goals were the political unification of Wales and Home Rule, not disestablishment. He had repeatedly insisted that to bring down Liberalism would put off disestablishment for a generation and disestablishment of the Church, even if it were nothing but a symbol of Welshness, was the issue of the moment. Within the political world he had defined for himself, he could not ignore it without abdicating his leadership, particularly with D.A. Thomas challenging him. A victory for disestablishment, even only in the House of Commons, would be a victory for Lloyd George. Moreover his political style required continual attack. As he had learned with the tithe agitation, the British political system was extremely sensitive to any charge of interference in the freedom of the individual. Hence disestablishment was a fine weapon and he had no motive for bringing the government down. On the other hand, as will be seen, neither had he regrets when disestablishment disappeared as a political issue.

On Saturday morning, 22 June, when the government resigned, Lloyd George was at Llandrindod Wells with D.A. Thomas. Sixteen days later, Lord Salisbury, Prime Minister now for a third time, dissolved the House of Commons and ordered polling to begin on 13 July. Lloyd George understood well the menace of overconfidence when approaching an electoral contest, but his nervousness before the Caernarvon District poll in 1895 was more than a pose. There was, he knew, soreness among the Gladstonians in the constituency over the Revolt of the Four. As always, he was without money and he had indeed dismayed his constituency association early in the spring by informing them peremptorily that they would have to find funds for a third time for his election expenses or he would withdraw.[259] Nationally, of course, the Liberal party was in disarray with no record of achievement. Still worse, Wales itself was divided. Many of its most powerful politicians opposed him. Stuart Rendel, the only man who commanded the loyalty of both North and South, had retired and the senior Member of Parliament in Caernarvonshire, Bryn Roberts, whose home was in Bangor, hated him. Roberts, who was himself unopposed, had been asked early in July to speak for Lloyd George in his home city. He replied curtly on 13 July that he would decline to give any support unless Lloyd George ceased to behave as a 'Welsh Parnell.'[260]

Lloyd George's election address reflected the national confusion. In common with all Welsh Liberals he made a bow toward disestablishment, but was one of only five to speak of Home Rule for Wales. However, he had a few advantages. As in 1890, the Conservatives came to his aid by selecting as their candidate H.J. Ellis-Nanney, now standing for the fourth time.[261] Also helpful was the fact that in place of the distinctly frosty William Rathbone, the new Member for the North or Arfon division of Caernarvonshire was the sympathetic and eloquent William Jones whose adoption Lloyd George and Sam Evans had secured the previous summer during the Revolt of the Four.[262] As usual Gee and Ellis would speak for him. Hence in the first few days reports were cautiously hopeful.[263]

But after 13 July, when the first returns from other parts of the country began to come in, Lloyd George grew less optimistic. He had not seen the results of his own canvass, he wrote Maggie on 14 July, the day after the snub from Bryn Roberts, so he could not say how he was doing, but 'Williams of the Chronicle says I shall be out by 30 and he is prepared to bet on it.'[264] Two days later he was lecturing the canvassers in the ever troublesome Bangor, warning them of 'possible disaster' unless they worked harder.[265]

But in spite of the gloom, Ellis-Nanney as an opponent gave him the opportunity to return to the congenial and successful themes of 1890, the Anglicized landlords and the wealth of the Church. He needed to explain nothing. His behavior the previous year could be thrust aside. 'I decline to regard any government, whether Liberal or Tory, as if its decrees were the edicts of providence,' he declared when questioned.[266] This ended the discussion about Lloyd George. Ellis-Nanney on the other hand provided a wide range of subjects for spirited abuse. He was 'a downright Tory. There is no mistake about him.'

> He is one of the good old Church and Constitution sort. One prefers fighting a man of that kind.... The Tory candidate belonged to that favoured class of men who think that things as they are, are exactly as they ought to be.... He is a squire, and so the constitution guarantees him a heavy rent roll. That puts the present world all right. The Church, as by law established, secures for him spiritual consolation and counsel at somebody else's expense, and that puts the next world all right for him, so why should there be any change?

And so on.[267] The only matter of substance to appear in Lloyd George's election and speeches, and indeed the only interest he manifested in conventional social reform until he became a minister, was a demand for old age pensions. Mr. Chamberlain, he said at the Guild Hall in Caernarvon on 5 July, had announced that pensions would cost the enormous sum of

137

£5,000,000. How would it be raised? Mr. Chamberlain would raise the money from the working class. The honest way to raise pension money, said Lloyd George in a wildly impractical burst of Welsh nationalism, would be to take it from the tithe or from the landlords and landlords' profit. Ground rents, a long standing grievance, should be taxed.[268]

Lloyd George would return to the subject of pensions again at Hollywell five days later and indeed he had referred to pensions briefly in the 1892 election just after the Aberdare Commission had been appointed. But it can hardly be said that he was a consistent or active supporter of the well organized agitation for a non-contributory, tax financed, old age pension which began to grow in British reform circles in the middle nineties. To Lloyd George pensions were a useful stick not much different from disestablishment with which to belabor the Unionists and particularly Joseph Chamberlain. The fact that the Tories could not bring themselves to pass the tax supported pension, in spite of the obvious wealth available, demonstrated their lack of concern for the plight of the aging poor, exactly as the existence of the established Church in Wales demonstrated their incomplete sympathy with the spirit of religious freedom. But these were tactical diversions.

Ground rents, on the other hand, encompassed the core of all his grievances against the landlords. Vast unimproved holdings, deer parks, waste, woods, representing millions of pounds of wealth, paid no tax. Income taxes were eight pence in the pound. This wealth, as he had said of Ellis-Nanney's holdings many times, protected the Conservatives, untouched and untouchable. Here was a theme that Lloyd George had turned to again and again and it finally became the core of the legislative program initiated in the 1909 budget and carried forward in the land campaign.

The poll in Caernarvon District was declared on 20 July. Lloyd George received 2,265 votes and Ellis-Nanney 2,071. His majority thus was 194, two below what it had been in 1892. This was not a bad showing in a year when the Liberals lost 6 seats in Wales, over 100 nationally, and when the party's share of the vote in the principality dropped from 63% to 57%. Almost immediately after his own victory was announced, he received what he described with some relish to Maggie as a 'hysterical telegram' from Osborne Morgan, the leader of the Welsh party and one of the several older Liberals who found Lloyd George a nuisance, in which Morgan pled for assistance in East Denbighshire. 'At the commencement of the struggle,' Lloyd George wrote, 'he gave me a nasty jab in the ribs, which had he any strength at all, would have finished me. Now I am having my revenge in rushing to the rescue of the man who tried to drown me.'[269]

As it turned out Morgan more than doubled his majority, but by 29 July, the end of the polling period, the Conservatives and their Liberal Unionist allies had won 411 seats to the Liberals' 177. Parliament was summoned for 12 August. In those days of seven year parliaments a government with a majority over all other parties of 252 could expect a substantial period of freedom from electoral alarms and its opponents had to look forward to an equal time of virtual impotence. For the Welsh sectarians, not to mention the Irish Nationalists, the election of 1895 marked the end of an era.

Disestablishment, although Lloyd George would deny it publicly, for the time being was dead.

He saw all this with perfect clarity. The time had come to reexamine the Welsh program. The recent election was nothing less than a disaster, he declared in a thoughtful speech at Pwllheli on 10 August, later amplified in an article in *Young Wales* in October. As the two together represent as much reflection as Lloyd George ever recorded about British politics in the abstract, they are worth a brief examination. It was idle, he thought, to dangle a long list of reforms before an electorate when every honest politician knew that there was not a chance of carrying them into effect for many years. Moreover, he reminded his constituents, England was tired of Wales. This had been evident even in the last parliament. Celtic opinion was often in advance of English opinion and many of the issues that had helped swing the pendulum against Liberalism in England were those 'adapted to the needs and demands of Celtic nationalities.' Yet on the other hand, the Welsh, — and, Lloyd George might have added, he himself — too frequently penalized the Liberals for being too timid, forgetting that the party had also to listen to the English voter.

As a conclusion, in both the article and the speech, Lloyd George counseled a return to that single part of the Welsh program that had a real, as opposed to a symbolic, meaning for the principality, Home Rule All Round, federal Home Rule. Only thus could Wales be isolated from the vagaries of English politics. Only in this way, with a full federal structure including a parliament for England as well, could the tortured question of the representation of the three kingdoms and Wales in an imperial parliament be settled, and only if the burden of local issues were removed from Westminster could parliament deal effectively with imperial problems. He admitted there would be no action for at least fifteen years. There would also be opposition in the House of Lords, but this did not count for much when the electorate was united.[270] *The Young Wales* article was sent by the magazine's editor, J. Hugh Edwards, to several leading Liberals from whom came the predictable noncommittal replies. However, Lord Rosebery wrote to admit tepidly that perhaps there was something in the idea and that such measures as disestablishment might require 'devolution or otherwise.' Lloyd George triumphantly published the Rosebery letter in *Young Wales* in November.[271] At the same time he was abused by the *British Weekly* for abandoning disestablishment. He defended his change of position in a long and, for him, candid letter summarizing his arguments. He had not dropped disestablishment for good. Citing the Irish, who wanted both Home Rule and land reform and were being given the latter, Wales could do the same. English public opinion was less opposed to Welsh, than Irish, Home Rule.[272]

In all of this Lloyd George was returning to a political posture he had assumed in 1890, before his election, before the collision with Evan Jones. Home Rule was no more improbable than disestablishment for the next fifteen years, and if achieved would bring all else within reach. But the first step, now more important than ever, was the political unification of Wales. The disastrous election had not diminished, but had rather increased, the importance of Cymru Fydd. The cleavages in Wales were deeper and more complex than ever and, as Lloyd George had feared at the beginning of the year, had hardened with the disputes over disestablishment. Now a new struggle began with a charge by Bryn Roberts.

Immediately after the election, Roberts wrote to Gee's *Baner* announcing to the world that Lloyd George had asked him to speak in Caernarvon and that he had declined. 'He allied himself with Tories and Parnellites,' recounted Roberts,

> to overthrow the Liberal government. I and many others believe that his work, and the similar behaviour of Mr. D.A. Thomas, were the principal means of upsetting the ministry. They would not have resigned on a matter so trivial as the cartridges had they not been disheartened by seeing that they had lost control over their followers while their majority was already so small.[273]

This letter was the beginning of a small public struggle that would poison the last stage of the fight to unify Wales. While probably not really dangerous to Lloyd George politically, the letter constituted a rare advertisement of the malaise within the Welsh parliamentary party. It was one thing for eminent Welsh pastors such as Evan Jones to hurl admonitory thunderbolts at misbehaving young MPs. It was quite another for the Members themselves to draw knives publicly against each other.

Lloyd George understood this as well as anyone. Since the election, no matter what Evan Jones and his kind thought, disestablishment belonged to the past. The sooner the chapels learned this the better. What counted now, more than ever in opposition, was rebel unity and organization. He did not want to fight. Accordingly he remained silent.

Part of this forbearance, not a conspicuous quality with Lloyd George, was certainly his desire to keep Welsh bitterness under cover in the hopes that the squabble would subside. Also he was away through most of the last part of August in York preparing an election petition for Samuel Storey, Liberal Member for Sunderland. At the same time he was trying to sell his client the proposition of establishing a newspaper in South Wales, apparently with Llewelyn Williams as editor, to drive out of business the now despised *South Wales Daily News*.[274] Then at the beginning of September, after attending at Llandrindod what was to be the final strategy meeting for the great Cymru Fydd offensive into South Wales, he left London for Scotland with Mr. and Mrs. Alfred Thomas Davies, Herbert Lewis's law partner. Several matters concerned with this trip had more importance for Lloyd George's career than ordinarily proceeds from a modest autumn excursion.

First of all Lloyd George and Davies barely escaped drowning when a sailboat nearly capsized on Oban Bay. Davies in his recollections may have exaggerated their fright—neither could swim—but the shock was enough for Lloyd George to recall the event to his secretary thirty years later.[275] Moreover, Davies, who taught his guest to play golf on this trip, remained close to Lloyd George for some years and served as the key that finally turned the lock closing the tortured question of Welsh education, when he was appointed Permanent Secretary, in 1907, of the newly-created Welsh Department of the Board of Education. He thus provided the epilogue to one of the major stories of Lloyd George's early career, the revolt against the Education Act of 1902. (This Alfred Thomas Davies was not the Alfred Davies, MP for Carmarthen District, 1900-1906, who was also the founder of Davies Turner Freight Forwarding, nor R.O. Davies of Acton, the man with whom Lloyd George had stayed during his early days in London.[276] On Lloyd George's golf, Asquith noted nearly two decades later that while his colleague's drives and approach shots were reasonably good, his putting was execrable. Golf requires both energy and patience. In sports Lloyd George had only the former.)

The trip provides also a glimpse of Lloyd George's domestic financial circumstances at the end of five years in the House of Commons. He had changed his residence again, moving permanently to Herbert Lewis's flat in Palace Mansions in Addison Road. Lewis's wife had died suddenly in June and so he was now on his way, in great distress, to South Africa, leaving the flat vacant. Lloyd George hoped to rent the premises to someone else while Lewis was gone, in order to pay for the trip to Scotland.[277]

Finally, a trip to Scotland, when the Cymru Fydd movement was crying for his attention, when personal attacks on him by Bryn Roberts had already begun, and when his most trusted and indeed most efficient political friend, Herbert Lewis, was away, was an act either of an innocent or a fool. Lloyd George was neither, yet he cheerfully wrote Maggie on 2 September that he would give Cymru Fydd some of his time two days hence and then travel north. He would go to Llandrindod to 'attend the National Council on Thursday. I should like to get that machine going before I start for Scotland.'[278]

If there was a flaw in Lloyd George's political wisdom it was a tendency to misread the immediate impact, the shock effect, of his speeches on both public and parliamentary platforms. This does not mean that he always overestimated their success, although he had a tendency to do this in formal parliamentary addresses in his early years. On the other hand, he sometimes underestimated the enormous power of his platform oration.

But the fact is that Lloyd George's public orations were an art of complete abstraction, where the medium carried no message, where communication was entirely heart to heart, not mind to mind. He could move an audience on any topic, by the most vapid posturing on temperance as in Manchester in 1891, or by the Rosebery and the 'natives of the principality' and jampots address at Cross Keys in 1894. The audience would weep when he shed tears, and laugh when he joked. What he could not depend upon it to do was to act when he left the hall. It took Lloyd George some years to realize the practical difference between raising a mob and leading a revolution. In some senses he never learned it, and forty years later was still deluding himself that the rapturous audiences who came to hear him in the spring of 1935 really wanted a new deal for Britain with, no doubt, himself as Prime Minister.

Of course, before long, he acquired the subsidiary arts of political maneuver: investigation, agitation, promotion, negotiation, squaring of interests, the enlistment of support within the party, or at least dealing with the opposition there. He skillfully made use of party machinery during the great campaigns of 1909-14 even if he had little support among party members.

But in 1895 there was no party behind him; he was, indeed, trying to construct one. He had little help except from the faithful Herbert Lewis, William Jones, Ellis and Towyn Jones, who helped on the platform, Beriah Evans, Llewelyn Williams and J. Hugh Edwards who made noises in the press, while Gee thundered editorials and Alfred Thomas nervously produced money. Crowds came to hear him and cheered. But the cheers were for Lloyd George, not Cymru Fydd, and clearly he did not know the difference or, in a peculiar way, he thought there was no difference. He would soon learn that Cymru Fydd was in serious trouble, that out of his sight nothing happened, yet he expected evidently to prevail. It was a decade before he learned to separate himself from his issues. By 1909 certainly he had done this. He was able to develop in the New Liberalism a maneuverable tactical program, clever, innovative and successful, to clear the Conservative logjam dropped in the Liberal path by Tory social reform, tariff reform, and House of Lords obstruction. But even after this came the land campaign, the great unifying thread of his political life and the only issue in all its myriad forms except perhaps Home Rule for Wales that had any hold on his emotions. With this in 1914, as with Cymru Fydd in 1894 and 1895, his marvelous sensory antennae failed. He began to confuse as in 1895 his singular ability to raise emotion with the power to compel action. He became the victim of his own oratory and, one feels, he fused in his mind his speeches and the movement itself so that the two became one. He, who could do so much with a speech, understood least of all the extent and limitations of its power.

And so, in September, he happily departed for Scotland secure that a speech at Llandrindod had galvanized Cymru Fydd. When he returned he found that Cymru Fydd lay exactly as he had left it. He found also that the assault upon his behavior in the last parliament had been revived in the well-known Calvinistic Methodist journal *Y Goleuad,* whose editor, E.W. Evans, was a close friend of Bryn Roberts.[279]

Ignoring *Y Goleuad* for the moment, Lloyd George threw himself into trying to bring life into the Cymru Fydd organization. Things must begin to move immediately, he wrote Gee on 9 October, and all programs must be coordinated. Demands for reform of the Church, land, temperance, and education 'ought to be concentrated in one great agitation for national self government.' What had become of the county conventions previously resolved upon? He would take care of one in Caernarvonshire. Could Gee (now eighty years old) handle Denbighshire? The conventions might arrange for the formation of branches in each district. 'It would help to keep the pot boiling.'

> For heaven's sake, let something be done this Winter. Isn't that your idea? Beriah is too apt to exhaust himself in scribbling and getting about. We need something to show for all this controversy.[280]

The reference to Beriah Evans touched upon a problem that preceded the controversy with Roberts and even indeed the Revolt of the Four and Cymru Fydd itself. As such it deserves a short explanation. His complaints to Gee about Evans's unsatisfactory work could by themselves be discounted. A tendency to blame others for his own mistakes was a characteristic of Lloyd George, although not of him alone. However, in the case of Evans, Lloyd George's doubts about the journalist's capacity seem to have been well-founded and it may not be too much to say that Evans should bear some of the responsibility for the unhappy conclusions in January 1896.

Since the autumn of 1893 personal relations between Evans and Lloyd George had deteriorated. As has been noted, Evans was appointed general editor of the Welsh National Press Company in the spring of 1892. Evidently he was less than a success in this post for in November, 1893, he wrote a long letter complaining of money and personal troubles and saying that he would have resigned long ago if he were single.[281] The troubles, whatever they were, continued nevertheless. For the full year 1893, the Welsh National Press lost £800 and by early 1894 the directors were determined that Evans should be discharged.[282] As a result Evans's appointment at the beginning of 1895 as the paid organizer for Cymru Fydd has an element of apparent jobbery.

In any case it was a disastrous choice. Through the last months of 1895, Lloyd George's letters, always excepting those written to his wife, displayed an increasing anger. By December, after an unsuccessful meeting arranged for Herbert Lewis, Lloyd George determined to get rid of his incompetent assistant. 'I fear you have been a victim of Beriahism,' he wrote Lewis on 11 December. 'The arrangements for the meeting must have been abominably defective....He really must go and Towyn Jones appointed as substitute. Beriah can resign on the plea of ill health.'[283] Evans had raised no money. The organization could not pay agents and hence it did not grow. Lloyd George himself, and Gee, would have to find some funds.[284]

Meanwhile, the attacks in *Y Goleuad* continued through October and on to 27 November. Lloyd George forbore to reply until early November. He had other concerns, but a compelling reason by now for his silence appears to have been the absence in South Africa of Tom Ellis. Ellis had, in his last years, become an admirer, almost a disciple of Cecil Rhodes. He had left England in the company of Ellis Griffith and Herbert Lewis immediately after the election. Lloyd George awaited his return.

Lloyd George wrote him for help immediately. After apologizing for bothering him so soon, he launched an attack upon *Y Goleuad*. The paper, he said, was 'pillorying' him as a 'traitor to Liberalism,' for conspiring with the Tories, for pressure upon the government in connection with Clause 9. He had driven the government from office; he was a traitor to his party; worst of all, these lies were inspired and fed by anonymous Members of Parliament with whom he was ostensibly on terms of friendship. As Ellis was a party to negotiations on Lloyd George's amendment, would Ellis make a public statement answering the following question: had not Asquith accepted a joint committee of county councils in place of the commissioners? Did he not take steps to ascertain the opinion of all Welsh MPs and did they not approve? And therefore, was there any truth to the assertion that the government resigned rather than face Lloyd George's amendment?[285]

Ellis obligingly published a widely printed statement the next day, which Lloyd George triumphantly read at a Cymru Fydd meeting at Shrewsbury.[286]

Ellis asserted that the government had in fact accepted a watered-down version of Lloyd George's amendment, although Asquith was aware that many Welsh did not support the amendment. On the critical point of the government's resignation—in connection with which Ellis himself was under sharp criticism for careless whipping on the cordite vote—there were, he said, many causes but among them probably was D.A. Thomas's amendment, which had been defeated by only seven votes.[287]

A rebuttal by the impeccable Ellis caused a minor sensation and it put guilt, if any, where the historian must conclude it properly belongs, upon D.A. Thomas. It also deflected the attack from Lloyd George himself onto others who were either less controversial or his enemies.[288] Lloyd George 'has had his revenge,' declared the *Manchester Guardian*'s 'Welsh Notes' on 12 November in an admirable summary of the real dangers, but also the strengths of the position of the Member for Caernarvon District in the fall of 1895. *Y Goleuad's* attack was 'maladroit.' But nevertheless a larger group than Mr. Lloyd George believed distrusted the 'Independent Welsh Party idea and Home Rule for Wales and fear that Cymru Fydd means an independent Welsh party.' However *Y Goleuad* did not take this line, which would have provided a real service, but chose instead to attack Mr. Lloyd George for his conduct in the last parliament. Many, including the writer, who did not like Lloyd George, thought his behavior in the House of Commons fully justified. It was 'a matter of opinion whether he finally put the government in jeopardy.' The article concluded: '...it is not on such points as these that some of us are disposed to criticize Mr. Lloyd George. He has done work in the House of Commons which needed to be done and which demanded a good deal of courage and resolution.'[289]

Lloyd George had indeed defeated publicly *Y Goleuad*, and privately, as he knew, Bryn Roberts. So great was Ellis's prestige in Wales, if not in Westminster, and so spotless his character, that an affirmation by him could not easily be impeached. The impact on *Y Goleuad* may be guessed from the terse letter of 9 November from E.W. Evans, the editor, to Roberts who was himself under attack in the London press for starting the quarrel. Facts that Roberts had supplied had now been effectively denied, said Evans. He hoped Roberts could 'supply an effective reply.'[290] Evidently receiving no satisfactory answer from Roberts, Evans wrote to Asquith on 23 November asking for a statement. Asquith subsequently wrote to Ellis saying that Ellis's public statement had 'whitewashed' Lloyd George and that it was 'not strictly accurate' to say that the government had accepted the Welsh amendments to Clause 9. On the other hand in 1909, in a memorandum discussing the differences between that year's Disestablishment Bill and the earlier one, Asquith seemed to have admitted the changes.[291]

In summary, the balance of the evidence would appear to be that if Lloyd George had in some way harmed his party's government, he was nevertheless not guilty within the terms charged by Bryn Roberts. The burden of the attack on Lloyd George had been that he had 'conspired' with the Tories to use Welsh disestablishment to wreck the Liberal government. This was not true, even though Lloyd George would say later that Tory support for a National Council for Wales committed them to Home Rule.[292] The Tories had supported Lloyd George for perfectly good tactical reasons of their own. Commentators then and since have never been able to remember that Welsh disestablishment was a dummy, a sham, at best an honorable statement of good intentions. It never would have passed the House of Lords. What the Tories feared most of all was a compromise, an agreed bill. The way to avoid this was to load Church disestablishment with the other kinds of Welsh nationalist baggage. The more cargo they put on the ship the quicker it would sink.

But in Lloyd George's triumph also lay a warning. If Lloyd George was not guilty as charged, he was nevertheless vulnerable from other directions. Home Rule, the *Manchester Guardian* was saying, even in the guise of Cymru Fydd, was not politically alive. Most Welsh demanded English acknowledgement of their nationality, as the depth of concern for disestablishment showed, but they did not want nationhood. Sunday closing, local veto, disestablishment, the use of the Welsh language in courtrooms, did not mean a Welsh parliament, or even a Welsh party. It is hard to believe that Lloyd George did not understand this; he had been warned of it many times since the first encounter with Evan Jones, and his letters to Gee, Lewis, and others display a rising concern. But buoyed up by continuing personal triumphs he drove forward blindly unaware of what was to come. 'I met Pitt, the parliamentary representative of *The Times*,' he wrote Maggie on 16 November,

> who came up to me to congratulate me on shifting the quarrel onto Tom Ellis, Bryn, and Thomas. Cleverest thing I have ever done in a long time, so he said. Thomas' attack on Ellis in the papers is a very bitter one & will do us all the good in the world as it will force Ellis' friends into our Cymru Fydd camp.[293]

Federal Home Rule, he told the *Merthyr Times* a few days later on 23 November, would be easier to pass than Irish Home Rule. Many problems would be simpler, the question of representation at Westminster would solve itself.[294] 'The Rhondda is coming over to us bodily,' he wrote on 20 November. 'Last night's demonstration was simply immense,' he continued the next day '—that is the word. Nothing like it in the Rhondda—not in the memory of the oldest inhabitant....hundreds of D.A. Thomas' old colliers amongst them.'[295]

The Rhondda valley was the key to plans to win South Wales. Altogether there were over 125,000 miners in the South, who constituted the largest ethnic Welsh economic group in the principality. They were far more likely to listen to his message, Lloyd George knew well, than were the inhabitants of the increasingly Anglicized coastal cities who, Lloyd George reported scornfully to Maggie on 19 November, were 'sunk in morbid football.'[296]

The Cymru Fydd tactic was to submerge the South Wales Liberal Federation in a wave of demands for unity from the mining district. By early November Lloyd George appears to have given up the attempts to establish Cymru Fydd branches and was attempting instead to promote the formation of shadow committees whose roster of officials carried the names of local dignitaries. The specific new goal, which emerged from a letter to Herbert Lewis, was to establish a rival to the South Wales Liberal Federation, to be called 'Rhondda Liberal Association', which could then pass resolutions 'to support the aim of the Cymru Fydd movement.'[297] The need to work through front organizations derived from the intense conservatism of the miners' leaders, of whom the most important was William Abraham (usually known by his bardic name 'Mabon'), the MP for the Rhondda division of Glamorganshire since 1885, the founder of the Cambrian Miners' Federation, and the first president, in 1889, of the South Wales Miners' Federation. Abraham was a man for whom fellowship, brotherhood, and loyalty were absolute virtues, but whose world began and ended with the coal pits. He had neither concern for the wider purposes of Welsh nationalism nor for the nationalists themselves. Lloyd George's letters show that he took pains to avoid offending Mabon, whom he rather despised, while at the same time trying to win resolutions of support from the colliers, who were devoted to him.[298] All in all, Lloyd George's early experience of the narrow vision and parochial interests of trade union leaders was not happy.

The end of all this activity came suddenly and, so far as Lloyd George appears to have understood it, without warning. His correspondence with Lewis suggests he expected a meeting, for which he and Lewis were planning resolutions and strategy and which of course would be carefully packed, but not so soon.[299] Yet it was unreasonable to assume that the frantic organizing activity of November and December had remained unobserved by D.A. Thomas or that the powerful and determined Southern leader would take no retaliatory action. Early in the second week of January, evidently without much consultation, Thomas called a meeting of the South Wales Liberal Federation to be held at Newport, Monmouthshire, for 16 January. Lloyd George was at the moment in London and, although taken by surprise, was full of confidence. 'I am going to South Wales over Wednesday for the Federation meeting…,' he wrote Maggie on Saturday, 11 January, 'I am not going to let them have it all their own way in the South.'[300] 'We have decided to swamp the Rhondda with letters for the meeting of delegates which is coming up there tomorrow,' he reported the next day. 'A good deal will depend upon it. I wrote two letters yesterday on the point. If we carry Rhondda it will mean turning the scale at Newport on Thursday. Send me per return shaving brush.'[301] The next day, Monday, still in London writing letters to the Rhondda from the National Liberal Club, he noted that Beriah Evans had secured his election as a delegate to the Newport meeting. But on Tuesday he was still in a ferment about the Rhondda as he wrote his nightly letter. However, before he posted it great news arrived: 'Rhondda carried last night,' he scribbled on the envelope, 'starting Newport now.' On Wednesday riding in the train on the way to Newport he exulted, 'The Cymru Fyddites scored a "grand victory"' on the previous day in Rhondda. 'All the delegates are to vote for us tomorrow at Newport. That cripples Mabon's mischievousness.'[302]

Lloyd George believed that he had packed D.A. Thomas's meeting in favor of Cymru Fydd. But when he arrived at Newport he found that Thomas had drawn him into a trap. The evidence is fragmentary and one sided, but clearly Thomas arranged the attendance at his meeting carefully. About fifty Englishmen from Newport, *Young Wales* reported, were grouped around the platform.[303] Certain areas known to be sympathetic to

Lloyd George, East Carmarthen and West Monmouthshire, had been refused tickets. Pembroke and Cardigan received notices too late to elect delegates.[304]

Lloyd George was able to gain the platform and made a rousing speech, but was shouted down for the first time in his life when he attempted to support the critical motion for the union of the South Wales Liberal Federation and Cymru Fydd.[305]

The Newport meeting was the end of an era in Welsh politics and delimits also a phase in Lloyd George's career. The cause of Welsh party unity was dead. Welsh nationalism, whatever the poet and bard sang of it, did not exist as a political possibility. The differences between North and South were too great and even if the two sections could from time to time agree upon parallel political programs such as disestablishment, the details of their execution, as in the disposal of the tithe, remained an intractable problem.

For Lloyd George himself, Newport ends a chapter in his political life. For a few days he expected to continue Cymru Fydd agitation and wrote bravely of a great Cymru Fydd reception in Neath, then of an alternative meeting to be held in Swansea, while discussing a return to the original plan of the establishment of Cymru Fydd branches in South Wales and of renewed propaganda. But the game was over.[306] Within a few months the very name 'Cymru Fydd' became 'a term of derision.... it is now the fashion to boycott this expressive phrase as being the war cry of disaffection,' noted *Young Wales* in August, 'and to sneer at the movement which made it its appellation.'[307]

By the time this was printed Lloyd George was on his way to Argentina with Herbert Lewis and Henry Dalziel, in the last episode of the strange quest for Patagonian gold. By this time also his political orientation had begun to change. He did not, to be sure, drop Welsh causes altogether, particularly when they affected his constituency, and he made some effort in the spring of 1896 to induce the small group of advanced Liberals in the House, the so-called Radical Committee, to take up officially Home Rule All Round. He would continue to take an active part in the deliberations of the Welsh MPs. The fight with Bryn Roberts and D.A. Thomas went on.

And yet the change was real and permanent. It was not that the issues in which Lloyd George interested himself altered but that their Welsh dimension grew smaller. He would struggle with landlordism again and would spend two years attacking Church schools, but in the company of Englishmen as well as Welshmen. Wales was a base of operation to which he could always retreat, but the battlefield henceforth was in London. As the ties to Wales diminished he became ever more isolated in the House of Commons, so that when the South African War broke out and he undertook his dangerous crusade against imperialism he was without important allies. Whatever his politics in the future were to be, he would not become the Welsh Parnell. After 1895, Harold Spender asserts in his discussion of the Cymru Fydd episode, the Welsh MPs were as disgusted with Lloyd George as he was with them. 'Wales,' Spender concludes, 'practically gave him to England.'[308]

3 The Free Lancer:
The South African War, 1895-1902

There are periods in even the most tumultuous and eventful career when it is hard for the biographer to see that his subject has accomplished anything, when having begun to withdraw from his old life, he seems unable to build a new one. Between the early months of 1896 and the autumn of 1899 Lloyd George appeared, for perhaps the only time in his political life, to be without purpose or project. This is neither to suggest that he was idle, nor that he lost interest either in Welsh or parliamentary affairs, but simply that he was unclear about his political goals. Since 1885 his aims had been professional and political advancement. Until 1890 he sought to establish himself as a solicitor and make his way into the House of Commons. Every activity, the missionary and temperance lectures, the anti-tithe work, his outrageous behavior in the county court, the cultivation of Tom Ellis and Thomas Gee and of innumerable newspapermen, chapel preachers, and deacons—one could perhaps add his prudent marriage—all aimed to present him as an ardent but trustworthy friend of the cottage-bred man and as a potential leader of the Welsh parliamentary revival. Since 1890 he had fought to make Wales mean something in London, in the House of Commons and within the Liberal party. This involved uncovering a Welsh point of view in every political issue. It meant attempting also to force the Welsh Members of Parliament to put their Welshness above Liberalism. When this failed he had returned to Wales to attempt to build a political organization that Welsh MPs would be required to heed. That too had failed.

In a way Lloyd George began a new parliamentary career in 1896. Although more than suspect among the Welsh he did not withdraw entirely, to be sure, from Welsh affairs. For a time he talked of continuing Cymru Fydd agitation. He worked hard during the spring of 1896 to elicit some commitment from the Welsh party to Home Rule All Round, in which eventually he failed, although he was able to persuade his colleagues to approve the summons to a meeting at Cardiff that in 1898 achieved, on paper, Welsh unification in a substitute organization, 'The Welsh National Liberal Council.' He intervened vigorously in the House of Commons to draw attention to the report of the Royal Commission on Land in Wales and Monmouthshire, finally appointed eight months after Gladstone had promised it on the slopes of Snowdon in 1892, and to the reports of the evictions of men who had testified before it. He denounced his old enemy Lord Penrhyn for oppressing the workers in his slate quarries.

Nevertheless his focus was perceptibly changing away from Wales, not only in his political but in his personal life, and toward larger national interests. He pressed Maggie to leave Criccieth altogether, saying in an unusually terse and bitter letter of 8 May 1897, that they spent more than they earned and that either she must come to London or he would give up parliament and become a 'country attorney' again. Her complaints about bad air, soot, and noise, could be accommodated by a house in Acton or even Brighton.

Evidently finances were not entirely a ruse to bring his wife to London, for he began to look at possibilities for starting a business in London and appears to have investigated importing coffee and tea.[1] He did establish, in any case, a London law office with Arthur Rhys Roberts at 13 Walbrook near Cannon Street Station. Yet at about the same time, Alfred T. Davies recalls returning to the Addison Road flat with Lloyd George and finding the usual pile of mail below the front door. Among the letters was one from 'a well-known Oxford Street draper with a Welsh name' (probably D.H. Evans whom Lloyd George had known, and detested, since his arrival in London) saying that the firm was being turned into a limited company and offering Lloyd George a seat on the board at £300 per year. Davies urged his friend to take up the offer. 'What do they take me for, a guinea pig?' was the retort. 'No, it has not come to that yet.'[2]

His London law practice prospered modestly. After a year there were rumors in newspapers, always denied, that he was seeking to be called to the Bar and that he would give up Brynawelon and move permanently to London.[3] Finally, late in 1899, he took a house at 179 Trinity Road in Wandsworth near the Common.

Generally his correspondence with Maggie, and her complaints upon the subject, confirm that he spent less time in Criccieth than he had before 1896. He allowed himself to be appointed to the Select Committee on the Aged Deserving Poor, the so-called 'Chaplin Committee' which Chamberlain caused to be appointed in March 1899 to look into the tortured question of old age pensions. Pensions now became Lloyd George's favorite stick with which to belabor the Unionists for any expenditure however small or innocent. Particularly pensions became his weapon against Joseph Chamberlain, who for the next ten years was his example of the false and corrupt radicalism which the Unionists sought to use as a blind for their political reaction. Meanwhile, with Gladstone in retirement and the Liberal leadership in disarray, he courted popularity in England by picking fights with the Irish.

This was certainly not a new impulse for Lloyd George. He had always been, and would remain, impatient of Irish demands for special treatment, particularly if it were at the expense of some project in which he himself was interested. The difference now lay in the broader scope of his interest. By the end of the 1896 session the papers were saying he had given up Wales. This was not entirely true. Rather his old Welsh programs, disestablishmentarianism, board school education, temperance, old age pensions, and above all land reform, leasehold enfranchisement and site value rating, were now enlarged and applied to the whole nation. Taken together this rather small group of issues would compose Lloyd George radicalism, if such are the right words, for the remainder of his career. Even national health insurance began essentially as an expansion, based upon contributions, of the old age pension program to widows, orphans, and invalids.

It may not be too much to say, therefore, that the transitional years 1896-99 saw the beginning of the climb that took Lloyd George to ministerial and prime ministerial power. Well before the outbreak of the South African War, leaders on both sides of the House and the admiring following that had begun to develop in the national press, had marked him out for a place in the next Liberal government.[4]

Of course the disarray in the Liberal leadership made more valuable any younger talent capable of undertaking the duties of opposition. The leader of the House of Commons, William Harcourt, was disliked and distrusted by Lord Rosebery and even before the new government had been in power six months, the incomparable Tom Ellis suffered a blow to his prestige as a result of events in South Africa.

On 3 January 1896, Britain learned that Dr. Leander Jameson had led a body of Royal South Africa Company police in a raid into the Transvaal to take part in a revolution that was supposed to be carried out by English gold miners there. Jameson had been quickly overpowered and forced to surrender by the Boers and the resulting scandal caused by the attempts to foment rebellion in a presumably friendly nation immediately implicated the Prime Minister of the Cape Colony, Cecil Rhodes. Ellis was known to be an admirer, almost a student, of the man behind the raid and indeed in the weeks that followed Jameson's surrender he received telegrams asking him to use his political influence to help the captured raiders.[5] But because of his connections with Rhodes, Ellis was suspected, as was Rosebery, of trying to transfer the guilt for the unhappy event in the Transvaal away from Rhodes and toward the Colonial Office in London and its head, Joseph Chamberlain. The Chief Whip was therefore hindered by the suspicion of personal interest in his attacks upon the Treasury bench, which his sensitive nature could not ignore, and so, burdened by failing health, he was far less effective in the House of Commons in 1896. Lloyd George, of course, was delighted to see the government embarrassed and needed no encouragement to attack Chamberlain, but, above all, he had no connection with Cecil Rhodes. The decline of Ellis multiplied his opportunities.[6]

I

Lloyd George's rehabilitation began with an incredible gift from the Unionist leadership early in the 1896 session in the form of the Agricultural Land Rating Bill. This exemplary Tory measure to offer rate relief to cultivated land dealt with matters upon which Lloyd George had been concerned since he began his legal education at Breeze, Jones and Casson nearly two decades before, and by offering new privileges to a class he felt was weighed down with privilege already it engaged his emotions as disestablishment never came close to doing. For one who believed the ideal parliamentary tactic to be implacable and unswerving assault, it provided a perfect target.

The bill itself, introduced on 20 April, was a modest package providing for a reduction of fifty per cent in the rates on land under cultivation, the local authorities to be compensated by the Treasury. Its intent, even though Lloyd George did not see it that way, was reasonable enough: that of making farming a profitable endeavor. Rents had fallen nearly by half since the seventies, but the wages of agricultural labourers had increased by one third while acreage under cultivation had fallen by a similar amount. At the same time imports of wheat had about doubled.

For the story of Lloyd George's political life, the derating bill represents more than simply a vehicle by which he polished his rather tarnished reputation as a responsible Liberal. The bill also gave him his first opportunity in the House of Commons to enunciate his beliefs about the nature of property and wealth, which were the nearest he ever came to a social philosophy. These remained fairly constant throughout most of his life. His first speech on the bill during the second reading debate on 30 April was marked by an outrageous attack upon the Unionist administration. Lloyd George asserted, among other things, that the minister in charge, Henry Chaplin, would profit himself by derating in the amount of £700 per year and that the capital value of the estates of the members of the ministry as a whole would be increased by £2,250,000.[3] This typical invective produced the inevitable shouts, cheers, and denials. However, at the beginning of his speech, before the denunciation of cabinet jobbery, he explained soberly his convictions on the nature of wealth. He stressed the distinctions between land and personality. The latter he defined, rather loosely, as all other wealth, which, most important, was the 'creation of the industry of its owner.' Land, on the other hand, increased in value because of the trade and industry of the towns. The two million or so of Treasury money that would be given to the local authorities to make up the losses resulting from derating was simply robbery of the productive segment of the community for the benefit of the unproductive. Moreover, even if the reduction in rates aided the tenant farmer, the eventual effect would be to enable him to pay higher rents and hence would make land still more valuable. To this end, Lloyd George, during the debates on the bill, and in meetings later in the year, began to formulate the wholesale scheme of reform of landlord/tenant relations which appeared eventually in his land campaign a decade and a half later. There should be a valuation of land separate from improvements, by professional valuers, with land courts to set rents. Reduced rents, he argued, would by themselves cause reduced rates.[8]

In the spring of 1896 the sensation of parliament was the continual and ingenious obstruction of the government on a short and relatively simple bill so that it remained before the House of Commons from 20 April until 1 July. Day after day Lloyd George was in his place on the second bench below the gangway proposing amendments, raising objections, suggesting possible misinterpretations of the most straight-forward wording. On 14 May, in committee, he moved an amendment standing in the name of D.A. Thomas that the entire bill be put off to allow time for uniform valuation of rural property that would separate land and buildings. The Poor Law surveyors, he argued, creatures of the landlords themselves, could not be trusted, and in any case site and improvements ought to be assessed separately. Although he wrote to Maggie that night that when he jumped up to move Thomas's amendment he had no notion of what it was about, the law and custom of real property was a thicket in which he was thoroughly at home. He was immediately interrupted by Thomas Lough (Lloyd George mistakenly identified the man as Sir John Dorington), who told him that site and improvements already were valued separately. Only in urban districts, Lloyd George corrected him.[9] This minor triumph, duly celebrated in his letter that night to Maggie, emboldened him to embark upon a long lecture to the House on the techniques of valuing, appeals to assessment committees and to quarter sessions. There were no legal precedents, he argued. Litigation could involve the High Court and the House of Lords.[10]

Through all of this ran the constant theme that rate rebates to the occupier would result simply in higher rents to the landowner and from this the conviction would grow—indeed the germ of the idea had already appeared—that the privileges inherent in landownership justified controls not required for other forms of property. Hence rate rebates should bring rent arbitration tribunals which, he had noted many times, Ireland already possessed.

A week later Lloyd George committed his most dramatic if not his most important act of insubordination in the House of Commons. On 22 May, at 3.40 a.m., the chairman of the committee, James Lowther, noting the slow progress on the bill, refused to allow further debate upon Clause 4, which was before the committee, and allowed the question to be put. Lloyd George, Herbert Lewis, and Ellis's patron, Sir John Brunner, as well as three Irish MPs, all anti-Parnellites, and including the faction's leader, John Dillon, remained in their seats refusing to divide.

The chairman of the committee had no power to discipline the members. Thus the Speaker had to be called so that the House of Commons could reconvene. Speaker Gully asked each recalcitrant whether he would leave. Lloyd George replied that he remained 'as a protest.' Lewis denounced the rating bill as 'legalized robbery.' The next step in the assertion of the Speaker's authority was, as it had been since 1641, the 'naming' of the Members, identifying them by name rather than by constituency, so inviting the House to take disciplinary action. Besides Lloyd George and Lewis, Dillon and one other anti-Parnellite, Dr. Charles Tanner, were named. Balfour moved that they be suspended. This entailed another division for which two other Irishmen, Daniel MacAleese and Lloyd George's old mentor, Michael Davitt, refused to leave. Amid now general uproar, these two also had to be removed by the Sergeant at Arms. When the committee began work again another Irish Member, James O'Connor, refused to divide and likewise was removed by the Sergeant at Arms.[11]

The suspension of 21 May of course did Lloyd George no harm in Wales. He received innumerable telegrams of support from members of all political persuasions. He and Lewis were 'Welsh martyrs' according to the *North Wales Observer* and he was cheered when he returned to the House on 1 June.[12] He spent his free time campaigning for J.E. Barlow in Somerset, Frome, for the expenses of which Ellis gave him twelve guineas, which he told Maggie he would use for a vacation in Boulogne with Herbert Lewis.

(But he went to Putney for golf instead.) However, the tantrum in the House of Commons was of more significance than as a typical Lloyd George display of bad parliamentary manners. First of all he had disgraced himself again with his party's leader, William Harcourt, who divided with the Tories in supporting the motion to suspend Lloyd George and the others. And after the four were gone, obviously moved and upset, he made an almost incoherent speech proposing that the House adjourn. This did not last, to be sure. Harcourt's generous nature belied his hot temper. He asked Lloyd George to speak on the third reading of the Rate Bill on 1 July and referred to him in the warmest terms during his own speech. But many Liberal colleagues continued to resent the Member for Caernarvon District's ill behavior after six years in the House of Commons, particularly in association with the Irish whose tactics he seemed to be copying.

The participation in the incident by the Irish produced much newspaper comment, which focused attention upon the fact that the two wings of the Irish party differed over basic party strategy, a matter more fundamental than the reverence to be accorded the memory of Parnell. The anti-Parnellites had attempted since 1891 to continue the working agreement with English Liberals as the only possible avenue to Home Rule. The Parnellites on the other hand, although since the election of 1892 numbering fewer than a dozen members in a total Nationalist delegation of about eighty, insisted that nonconformist bigotry within the Liberal pary had killed Parnell as surely as if he had been hacked to pieces. Their leader, John Redmond, announced that he would work with either party, or neither, as circumstances dictated, and since the return of the Salisbury government he had cooperated with the new Irish secretary, Gerald Balfour, in planning a number of projects for the improvement of Irish industry and agriculture. In contrast, John Dillon and the anti-Parnellites had hitherto refused any contact with the Unionists.[13]

The Conservative leadership saw an opportunity in the bitter feuding between the Irish factions and exploited it in a variety of administrative and legislative concessions, from the expansion of land purchase funds to consultation with the Irish on civil service and judicial patronage. In the next ten years, with innumerable favors that were almost impossible for the Irish to refuse, the Unionist administration came close to superseding the Liberal commitment to Home Rule. As it happened, the first of these measures which began the near rupture of the alliance that Gladstone had forged was before the House at the same time as the Agricultural Rating Bill.

The Conservative approach to the Irish, condemned by Dillon as 'killing Home Rule with kindness', was almost certainly a factor in the Salisbury government's decision to take up as the major legislative project for 1896 a measure for the reconstruction of British state school administration and for the enhancement of state support to sectarian education. This would include, of course, Catholic education. The Education Bill of 1896, which never received a third reading, is usually dismissed as an example of Unionist ineptitude in the management of domestic affairs or as an episode in the decline of the once promising career of its manager, Sir John Gorst. In fact the bill had wider significance. It marks the opening of the breach between British nonconformity and the Irish anti-Parnellite forces led by John Dillon. On the fifth and last day of the second reading Dillon announced that with 'a great deal of pain' the anti-Parnellite forces would abandon their allies among the nonconformists and vote on behalf of the two million Irish Catholics in England for the Education Bill.[14] Dillon's statement caused an explosion of anger among nonconformists.[15] Thundered Hugh Price Hughes in the *Methodist Times*, 'When Mister Dillon, the leader of the principal section of the Irish party, sat down after giving his official support to the second reading of the Education Bill, Gladstonian Home Rule gave its last sigh and died.'[16] The Irish had 'severed the last links that bound them to the Liberal Party,' announced the *British Weekly*.[17] Dillon became the man 'who killed Home Rule' and although the anti-Parnellites numbered 70 Members of Parliament, as opposed to 11 Parnellites under John Redmond, when the two factions were united in January 1900 it was under Redmond, not Dillon.

For Lloyd George Dillon's support in the protest against the Agricultural Rating Bill illustrated the distinctly ambivalent relationship he maintained with a man whose temperament he distrusted but whose political courage he knew was the equal of his own.[18] Dillon's action was immediately attacked by Redmond in a bitter letter to his paper, the *Irish Independent*, in which he accused the anti-Parnellite leader of sacrificing Irish interests for English goodwill. Dillon, Redmond said, by his support of the Education Bill had offended English nonconformity for which Parnell had been destroyed. Now the anti-Parnellites had abandoned Home Rule. By helping to filibuster the Rating Bill he simply was 'wrecking' the Irish Land Bill (another part of Unionist policy for Irish accommodation) 'in order to rehabilitate himself in the opinion of those same gentlemen at the expense of Ireland.'[19]

Dillon's support of Lloyd George on the Rating Bill did little to revive attachment for the Irish cause among the Welsh radicals, who continued furiously to oppose the Education Bill. Lloyd George himself took little part in the resistance to the latter bill, speaking just twice, on 15 and 16 June, in the weeks before the Cabinet resolved to drop the now unrecognizable proposals. However, when the measure was resurrected on far more modest terms in 1897, he used the occasion for a vicious attack on Dillon. The new bill, renamed the Voluntary Schools Bill, made no attempt at administrative reform and dealt only with state aid to sectarian schools. Dillon proposed an amendment by which poorer schools would receive increased funds at the expense of the wealthier. Lloyd George leaped up immediately to denounce him. The Irish he said were accustomed to demanding extra money for themselves at the expense of Great Britain. Now they assumed all schools but their own were rich. The Methodists (who ran a substantial number of voluntary schools) kept up their own schools without help from the Treasury. Now therefore 'the honourable Member of Mayo proposes not merely robbing another area but robbing another creed.'[20]

After walking out on a Home Rule amendment to the address in early February 1898, Lloyd George returned to this line opposing, on 17 February, another amendment put down by Dillon asking for a Roman Catholic university for Ireland. It would be the first time that he had voted against an Irish proposal that the Irish themselves supported, he said, but the Irish had had no difficulty the year before in voting to force denominational education upon Wales, which was repudiated by a majority there.[21] In April, in a deliberate provocation, he moved a resolution that free and public non-sectarian education facilities be established within the reach of every child in England and Wales. This time the Irish refused to take the bait and abstained from voting, although the proposal drew a bitter speech from Vesey Knox of Londonderry.[22] Later in the session he fought the Local Government (Ireland) Bill which would end the antique grand jury system of local administration in Ireland and give it elective county councils on the English model, thus breaking the power of the county aristocracy, while extending also agricultural derating to Ireland. Even though he had held his first political office within a system precisely like that he sought now to deny Ireland, Lloyd George argued that the Irish Local Government Bill was the result of a corrupt bargain with the Unionists, a trade of support of £350,000 in rate relief for Irish landlords in return for the transfer of local patronage to the Catholics.[23] (These charges were not without substance. In an almost unprecedented display of independence against the Unionist administration, the House of Lords, led by a solid bloc of Irish landlords, had been persuaded to destroy the Land Bill of 1896, the first attempt at local government reform, which Redmond and Gerald Balfour had framed.) For over a year, indeed from his first attack on Dillon's amendment to the address, Lloyd George and the Irish were scarcely on speaking terms.

In an otherwise dull parliamentary year the break between the radicals and the Irish was important news. In a leading article about two months after the death of Gladstone, the *British Weekly* commented that the sentiment for Home Rule was now dead among the Liberals. The Irish had better be content with the recently passed Local Government Bill, commented the paper. Any attempt to revive Home Rule would lose more radical and nonconformist votes than the Irish contributed.[24] For Lloyd George, the anti-Irish posture did him no harm in Wales, even though as he had observed in his attack on Dillon's amendment to the address there was a Catholic population in Caernarvon, and it was bound to help his popularity in England. At the end of the 1898 session Lloyd George quoted triumphantly to Maggie a notice from the *Newcastle Leader*: "Mr. Lloyd George has distanced all his competitors. He delivered some of the more daring speeches of the session, and his attacks on the financial clauses of the Irish Local Government Bill were admirably sustained. The Member for Caernarvon has strenuously repudiated the idea that the Liberal Party is bound to support any Irish legislation which may appear to be good to the Nationalists. He earned himself some enemies but he laid the foundation of a big parliamentary reputation." Go da ynte. [pretty good, isn't it?] The North Wales Observer ought to print those things.'[25] It would have been far better, he told Herbert Lewis at Thomas Gee's funeral on 3 October 1898, for the Welsh to have told Mr. Gladstone that they declined to support him on Home Rule and to have followed Chamberlain in Home Rule All Round.[26]

Ireland's greatest mistake, Lloyd George thought, was Redmond's amendment to the address on 11 February 1898, moved a few days before

Dillon's amendment for a Catholic university.[27] It asked for 'national self-government' for Ireland, an 'independent Parliament and executive' to deal with 'all affairs distinctly Irish.' In fact it was little different in content from the one for which Lloyd George had cheerfully voted in 1894 against a government of his own party, and Redmond made clear in his speech that it was really a symbolic gesture to celebrate the centenary of the rising of 1798.

But what certainly angered the radicals, who walked out during the speech, was Redmond's assertion that the Liberal party's substitution of disestablishment, local veto, and electoral reform for Home Rule 'was a huge blunder.'[28] Of these, it could be noted, the last was more important as a project of interest to the English as well as the Welsh. Redmond asserted it was a direct attack on Ireland. The island's representation, he stated, would be reduced from one hundred to eighty. (Moreover the seats lost would be almost exclusively Nationalist. Ireland had twenty constituencies with fewer than five thousand electors and in 1898 all of these but one, North Fermanagh, were held by Nationalists.) Redmond's amendment, for which only the Nationalists voted, after an attempt to withdraw it, was lost 65 to 233. It was a thinly disguised challenge to the Liberals to remember the commitment of the Grand Old Man.[29]

Early in November, before the Newbridge Labour and Liberal Association, Lloyd George delivered what amounted to a Welsh declaration of independence from the Irish connection. The Irish, he said, 'had managed to alienate the sympathies of a large mass of the electors throughout the country, men who were as eager, as earnest, in favour of conceding Home Rule as any Irishmen among them.... All these people had been dampened in their ardour and killed in their enthusiasm, and that was to a large extent attributable to the series of follies perpetrated by the Irish leaders.' Among these he mentioned sectarian education which the Irish themselves seemed to put above Home Rule, but the supreme folly was 'the preposterous resolution moved by Mr. Redmond...insisting upon an independent parliament for Ireland...Mr. Redmond's resolution had made it impossible for them to continue the alliance....' The rest of the speech was devoted to a long, but hazy explanation of how Welsh devolution was not to be compared with the Irish demand. The Welsh simply 'wanted to manage their little local affairs,' education, disestablishment, and land reform, 'but were not going to be cut from their interest in the Empire. Welsh blood was in the very fabric; it was the cement that held the Empire together. (loud cheers).'[30]

Within a year the South African War had begun and Lloyd George would again find the Irish, particularly Dillon, at his side in opposition to Unionist policy. He would, in the future, express admiration for Redmond as a speech maker and parliamentarian. Of Parnell, he had rather stood in awe. Nor should it be forgotten that in January 1895, before the National Liberal Federation at Cardiff when Rosebery was about to concede to the principle of disestablishment, he had diverted attention from the matter at hand to press the claims of Ireland; and he and Ellis had helped to put down D.A. Thomas's rebellion over Home Rule the previous August. Yet one of the abiding lessons of the 1890s for Lloyd George was that the Irish were a political exasperation. Their importunities would burden him both as a Welsh nationalist and as a Cabinet member. Always 'Ireland blocked the way,' first for Welsh disestablishment and Welsh nationalism and later as he rose to high office for other more pressing national concerns. Among the many careers in early twentieth-century British politics that were diverted or ruined by Ireland, none was hurt more by her claims than that of David Lloyd George.

II

As the 1896 session drew to a close extended comments in newspapers on the new, rehabilitated Lloyd George suggest how far he had gone, at least in the public view, toward reforming his bad old ways of behavior. 'He started this session a little suspect with the majority of Liberals,' commented the *Westminster Gazette* on 2 July, just after the third reading of the Agricultural Rating Bill, 'but it is generally recognized now that, primarily on the Rating Bill, but also on the Education Bill, no words of praise could be too strong for what Mr. Lloyd George has done.'[31]

Unionist papers agreed. 'Mr. Lloyd George is far and away the most nimble, bold and hard-working young Radical in the House at the present time,' said the *Daily Mail* at the end of the session. 'He has dropped Wales and now goes for harrassing the Government all round. He speaks on all manner of questions without the aid of notes, and it is very uncommon for the Speaker to rule him out of order.'[32] He suffered for far too long in his career, thought *The Observer*, from 'enthusiastic countrymen who hailed him as "the Welsh Parnell." In endeavouring to live up to this mark, Mr. Lloyd George succeeded in obscuring what the House has this session recognized as sterling qualities in debate.' He resembled Healy more than Parnell, the paper concluded.[33]

All this was most satisfactory and was particularly so when newspaper enthusiasm was reinforced by hints from senior party men of both sides that he should begin to think of himself as a potential member of the next Liberal ministry. Still, it would be a mistake to regard Lloyd George's appointment to the Board of Trade nine years later as now ordained. The same genius in his character that provided his matchless wit, his courage and his humanity, had given him also a wayward sympathy and recklessness that brought him, again and again, close to ruin. His life is the story of near disasters and revivals, of clinging too long to hopeless campaigns and solitary crusades from which, nevertheless, until the last one, he always somehow was able to return in triumph. Within four years he seemed to have blasted himself anew, as he had done with Cymru Fydd, in his opposition to the South African War. Yet before the war was over the government in the Education Bill of 1902 would provide him, as it had done in the Rating Bill, with an avenue of escape allowing him to wear again the mantle of the dissenting hero that had proved so comfortable in the struggle against voluntary school legislation in 1896 and 1897.

Hence there is no straight line of inevitability about Lloyd George's career, as one might find in, for instance, Asquith's who was after all only four years Lloyd George's senior in the House of Commons, but who became Home Secretary in 1892 and who, by that time, was already identified as a future Prime Minister. The most one could say about Lloyd George in the late nineties was that he at last made himself respectable by English standards. But although he relished encomiums that came his way, all duly recorded in letters to Maggie, he clearly did not find his new dignity comfortable for long. Many British politicians have jeopardized their careers for various reasons of principle. The biographer of Lloyd George is driven to wonder whether his subject, despite intense ambition, did not at times get himself in trouble for pleasure.

The 1896 session was prorogued on 14 August. Several months earlier Lloyd George's letters began to reveal a revival of interest in the presumably defunct Patagonian gold syndicate. On 31 July, while parliament was still sitting, he notified Maggie that he and Herbert Lewis had secured passage on the RMS *Clyde* to sail to Buenos Aires.[34] On 21 August, with Lewis, and also with Henry Dalziel, Liberal for Kirkcaldy, he sailed from Southampton.

The reasons for this ambitious journey remain clouded and on the whole the interlude does not deserve much attention. To be sure, Lloyd George had from time to time mentioned unauthorized mining by outsiders on the Patagonian property, but claim jumping on land that contained no gold, then or now, would seem to be a dubious crime. Moreover, once in Argentina he never went near the Chubut province where the claim was located. He did transact some business in Buenos Aires, lodging the necessary protest to protect his claim, only to discover that the claim had been forfeited through failure to work it. Evidently no one had known of this customary requirement before. It was lucky, he told Maggie in a letter, that he had come. Even though the syndicate no longer had any rights in Chubut, they might, he explained, be able to make things so difficult for the anonymous jumpers that they would be willing to deal. All of this took little time and there were many other diversions. He visited some Welsh colonists, had his teeth worked on, and traveled to Cordoba province, northwest of Buenos Aires and a thousand miles from Chubut, for sightseeing.[35] On the whole the two month trip seems to have been both enjoyable and profitless.

The presence of Henry Dalziel requires some discussion. His reasons for going on the trip, like the man himself, are mysterious. He had come from Scotland in the early nineties as a newspaperman and after a short time in the House of Commons press gallery had won, with the strong support of the then Chief Whip, Edward Marjoribanks, the Liberal nomination for his home borough of Kirkcaldy. He entered the House of Commons after a by-election in March 1892. He was by this time, privately, one of the proprietors of *Reynolds News* and the Liberal Whip hoped to use his knowledge of the press world in the foundation of a Liberal newspaper.[36] As an MP, he took his place as an advanced Liberal and Scottish Home Ruler and soon associated himself with the Welsh nationalists. Although Lord Beaverbrook's assertion that he threatened Lloyd George's place as a leader of the radicals is much overstated, he struck out quickly on his own, moving a home rule for Scotland resolution in 1894 which was supported by Herbert Lewis.[37] The next year he moved an amendment in supply committee for Home Rule All Round. Lloyd George spoke for the latter proposal which, predictably, was opposed by the Parnellites on the ground that in any measure of this sort Ireland must come first.[38]

Dalziel and Lloyd George would be associated through the whole of the latter's parliamentary career. Dalziel became editor and business manager of the radical *Reynolds News* in 1907 and sole proprietor in 1914. In 1917 he acquired the *Pall Mall Gazette*. Most important for Lloyd George, he was a senior and wealthy coalition Member of Parliament, who on Sunday, 3 December 1916 allowed the then Secretary of State for War access to the columns of his newspaper at a critical moment in the struggle with Asquith. Finally, in the autumn of 1918 he managed Lloyd George's purchase— perhaps contributing some of the money—of the *Daily Chronicle*. Not surprisingly his name frequently appeared in honors lists under the Liberals. He received a knighthood in 1908, Privy Council membership in 1912, and a barony in 1921.

Dalziel supported the Member for Caernarvon District faithfully, and enjoyed much Liberal preferment, but he never became a newspaper confidant in the way of George Riddell and C.P. Scott. Through the nineties Lloyd George appears to have disliked him for his drinking, bad speeches, and womanizing, not to mention his seasickness on the voyage to Argentina. Lloyd George suggested in letters to his wife that he hoped Dalziel would put some money in the Patagonian gold syndicate, and perhaps he paid for the trip. The correspondence between the two has disappeared.

The trip to Argentina for Lloyd George was reasonably uneventful and after his return his connection with the Patagonian gold venture dwindled and finally died, leaving him again with the embarrassment of chronic poverty that perhaps more than any other factor soured his relations with Maggie. Nonetheless the two month South American idyll, innocent and pointless as it was, had removed him from affairs in Britain so that he was unable to take action to defend himself in an exploding scandal that began in early October 1896 and which could have seriously harmed, or ended, his political career. The irony of the case lies in the fact that, like the even more dangerous Marconi affair 15 years later, Lloyd George was probably innocent, at least as charged.

The facts of the matter are simple enough. Early in October 1896, after Lloyd George had been gone about a month, word came to William George in Criccieth that it was becoming generally known both in Wales and London that a Mrs. Catherine Edwards of Cemmaes, Montgomeryshire, had confessed to her husband Dr. David Edwards that she had committed adultery with Lloyd George and had become pregnant. She bore a baby on 19 August 1896. William at once wrote to the ship upon which Lloyd George would arrive in Southampton telling his brother that there were serious matters the two should discuss immediately and that William would meet him either in Southampton or London.[39] Lloyd George however came straight to Criccieth from Southampton and began to defend himself.

From the beginning, and throughout the affair, his posture was entirely to protect himself against damaging rumors. He was evidently confident that he could prove in court that in this case at any rate, he was not guilty. His first opponent was Dr. Edwards to whom he wrote as soon as he heard the story demanding, as he reported to Herbert Lewis, that Edwards either issue a statement that Lloyd George was not involved or take legal action so that his wife's accused lover could clear himself in court.[40] He followed this with a series of letters, evidently under false names, designed to entrap those men he felt were circulating stories about him into committing the rumors to paper so that, as he told Herbert Lewis, he could 'make an example of one of them for the benefit of the whole brood....'[41]

On 12 November he learned to his horror that Kitty Edwards's admission of adultery with Lloyd George had been put in writing and that copies of this document somehow were circulating in Cardiganshire. The confession, dated 10 August 1896 and subsequently read in court stated

> I, Catherine Edwards, do solemnly confess that I have on 4th February 1896, committed adultery with Lloyd George, MP, and that the said Lloyd George is the father of the child, and that I have on a previous occasion committed adultery with the above Lloyd George.[42]

In much agitation Lloyd George wrote to W. Bowen Rowlands, Liberal MP until 1895 for Cardiganshire, a high Churchman and not a particularly close friend, asking help. His letter, of which for once he kept a faint letterpress copy, suggests his state of mind.

> I have just heard that a prominent Conservative in your district showed you secretly a statement purporting to be a signed confession by Mrs. Dr. Edwards of Cemmaes imputing to me the paternity of her child. This report has been rumoured about and you know how difficult it is to arrest it unless I can secure proof that it has been reduced into writing and then published.

Could Rowlands tell him the names of the men circulating the statement and the circumstances under which Rowlands saw it? He had set men 'scouring the country' weeks ago and had learned only that day of the story of the confession.[43]

Lloyd George and his brother had attempted to keep the story of the Edwards case from the family. This was not difficult. The unworldly Uncle Lloyd remained innocent until after the disposal of the case by divorce court in 1897. But Maggie could not be so easily deceived. By the end of November Lloyd George was complaining of 'the nastiness' of her letters and at the end of the month she confronted him with the charge. From Aberystwyth he was forced to write the explanatory letter customary under such circumstances: that it was all a pack of lies and he had considered telling her many times but did not want to cause her pain, etc.[44] Evidently after he returned to Wales he convinced his wife of his innocence for she supported him faithfully in the following months.

Meanwhile he continued to search for someone to sue. On 18 December, he wrote Gee to thank him for a comforting note and poured out his frustrations on the 'vile slander' which 'nobody believes.' 'Dr. Edwards,' he told Gee, 'has believed it least of all and both he and his lawyers have afforded me every assistance in tracking down the lie.' The trouble was that there could be no action unless the story was reduced to writing and he could find no one who believed it to write it down. If Gee could find even a scrap of paper he should let Lloyd George know.[45]

On 29 December, he wrote to Martin Woosnam, Dr. Edwards's solicitor, indicating that his rage now was turning toward Mrs. Edwards. Had he any scrap of paper upon which to base an action for libel? 'I wish I could get hold of one of those scoundrels who have been circulating the lie. Do you know whether Mrs. E. has any separate property? To proceed against a pauper is simply to publish a scandal upon oneself at ones own expense—and as this woman is motivated by spite there is nothing she would enjoy better.'[46]

Taken together the letters to Rowlands, Gee, and Woosnam show first, that by December Dr. Edwards no longer believed that Lloyd George was the father of the child born on 19 August and second, that whatever the document Mrs. Edwards had given her husband, Lloyd George was now sure he could prove his innocence in court. All of this reinforced what had been his position from the beginning: that he cared little about the Edwards problem itself, but he cared a great deal about the rumors surrounding it.

A key factor in his change in attitude may have been the knowledge that the child born on 19 August was a full term baby as Dr. Edwards, who would have known, freely admitted. (The baby was born in a temperance hotel in Penygroes near Caernarvon.) A baby conceived in early February would have been nearly three months premature. Also with a date established for the supposed adultery, he could prove his whereabouts. Here he was fairly secure. Although he was supposed to have spent the whole of the night of 4 and 5 February with Mrs. Edwards, on the morning of 5 February he was in Cardiff addressing the Welsh Sunday School Union's Nonconformist Choir festival on the superiorities of Welsh vocal music, Sunday schools, and Welsh traditions.[47] It does not follow, of course, that he could not have journeyed to Cardiff in the early morning, but Cemmaes is isolated, on a branch railroad, off the main line from Shrewsbury to Aberystwyth. North-south transportation in mid-Wales was not easy. He would have had to change trains at Machynlleth, Newtown, and Merthyr Tydfil.

In addition, he apparently was not alone during the critical period. Immediately after the Cymru Fydd debacle in Newport on 16 January 1896, Lloyd George had gone off to Sunderland, Durham, to press an electoral petition brought by Samuel Storey, Liberal MP for Sunderland since 1881, who had been defeated in 1895 by 47 votes. Through the last week of January, 1896 he was heavily engaged in preparations for the hearing which finally took place on 27, 28, and 29 January. On Thursday, 30 January, he wrote to Maggie, 'beaten today by a prejudiced judge,' adding that the decision had been attacked in the *Newcastle Leader* and that Storey wanted him to stay until the weekend. On 31 January he was still there.[48] He had however another interest. Beside the substantial legal fee he would receive, Lloyd George's concern for the Storey case proceeded from his hope that he could persuade his client, a man of means, to purchase, or found, a newspaper that would counter the pernicious anti-Cymru Fydd editorial policy of the *South Wales Daily News*. Hence, when he left Sunderland, probably on Saturday 1 February, it seems clear that he took Storey with him, for his first letter to Maggie after departing from the North has him in Swansea, with Storey, negotiating over the purchase of the

Cambrian Daily Leader.[49] Finally, as there is no letter for five days between the 1st and 6th of February, and because he rarely let a day go by when he was away without writing to Maggie no matter what he was doing, it is apparent that the two men spent the weekend at Criccieth on the journey south. Richard Lloyd's diary confirms Lloyd George's presence in Criccieth until the morning of 4 February.[50]

If one accepts the theory that Lloyd George knew he had an ironclad alibi with which to confront any accusations of misbehavior on the night of 4-5 February, and that his concern was always with the public damage that might be done him even by unprovable charges, his subsequent reluctance in the summer and autumn of 1897 to appear in divorce court paradoxically becomes easier to explain.

Dr. Edwards brought suit for divorce of his wife on 23 March 1897 citing as corespondent not Lloyd George but the station master of Cemmaes, an Edward Wilson. This dramatic new turn, and Mrs. Edwards's earlier suit stating that her husband was the father of the child and charging him with cruelty, do not concern Lloyd George except to show that throughout the affair much of Mrs. Edwards's behavior defies explanation.

On 19 July, Bargrave Deane, QC, assisted by Ellis Griffith, appeared before the President of the Probate, Divorce and Admiralty Division of the High Court, Sir Francis Jeune, seeking to amend Dr. Edwards's petition 'to proceed without making a certain gentleman other than the corespondent named a corespondent.'[51] This mystifying request Jeune was reluctant to grant, even though Deane began his statement by saying that his client had made every effort to corroborate Mrs. Edwards's confession and could not. There simply was no case against the man unnamed. He had in October received letters from the man unnamed and more recently an affidavit denying any wrongdoing. Jeune reserved judgement.

Lloyd George had evidently been busy since the previous December and although clearly in communication with Edwards's lawyers he was not satisfied with the revised petition.

'You remember that miserable Cemmaes business?' he wrote his brother.

> The husband is now proceeding against a person unknown—the question came up on some interlocutory summons today. You know the woman now says that the 'confession' was a lie extracted by her husband with a carving knife with which he menaced her. Now, the judge today thought I ought to have a chance of denying the thing on my own. He said my letters were most proper ones and that I had taken the right course; but, he said, I might wish to be joined in order to deny the charge on my oath. Jeune insisted so G tells me upon my being given the opportunity if I wished, of being joined. I suspect some infernal treachery on G's part—that the thing has been made semi-public by his contrivance. But you will see the papers tomorrow and be able to advise me.[52]

As this letter suggests in its first sentence, Lloyd George was not keeping William abreast of the Edwards case. His confidant, 'G', was probably Ellis Griffith whom Lloyd George did not particularly like and obviously did not trust, but who was, nonetheless, a Welsh Liberal barrister of some seniority whom Lloyd George had known for years and who had entered parliament for Anglesey in 1895. His contacts with Lloyd George were evidently important.

William replied by telegrams saying that if the judge wanted him to appear he should 'go in and win,' but then, perhaps understanding that his brother had no wish to appear, followed this with a letter saying that there was no need to appear, that Lloyd George had already made vigorous denials and that he could now file an affidavit saying that although the charge was painful he remained in the hands of the court.[53]

Lloyd George agreed with his brother's more recent advice. 'The President,' he replied 'was simply anxious to furnish me with an opportunity for denying the charge on oath. That I can do by affidavit. There is not the slightest necessity for worrying the old boy about it. It will not come out now. If G had written out a sufficiently strong affidavit in the first instance there would have been no trouble. He is a treacherous hound.'[54]

The new affidavit, presumably also written by Griffith, was laid before Jeune in time for a second hearing on 17 August. Jeune now had two affidavits and at least one letter from a man he had never seen. Nevertheless he was still unwilling to excuse Lloyd George, referred to always as 'A.B.', if there was any reason, however remote, for him to appear. The 17 August hearing degenerated into a long technical dispute between Deane and Jeune on the limits of judicial discretion in cases such as this one. Eventually the President ruled, with clear reluctance, that Edwards did not have to produce the man named in the only piece of written evidence against his wife, Mrs. Edwards's confession. But what was clear was that while Edwards was determined to divorce his wife, he was determined to do so without implicating Lloyd George.

Lloyd George's name came out at last in the trial on 18 November with the introduction of the confession. But Deane hastily added that both he and the petitioner were convinced that Mrs. Edwards's accusation was designed to shield the true culprit, a practice 'not unknown in divorce court.' As the hapless Mr. Wilson, the station master, was well represented and fully prepared to defend himself, he too was dropped from the petition, so the farce ended with a decree nisi in favor of Dr. Edwards for the divorce of his wife for adultery with persons unknown. Deane repeated that there was not a shred of evidence against Lloyd George and President Jeune agreed that although he was obviously innocent, had he wished to appear in the case as a corespondent in order to prove his innocence, the petitioner would not have been allowed to proceed without him.[55]

Clearly Lloyd George had every opportunity to give his side of the story under oath. Obviously, despite his continued assertions afterwards that he had no opportunity to defend himself, he did not wish to appear in the Edwards case. The question is, what were his motives? If one assumes that he could prove his innocence of any wrongdoing on the night of February 4, either because he had Storey with him or because he had not visited Cemmaes at all, or for some other reason, why did he not appear? (Edwards's testimony always insisted that although Lloyd George had indeed stayed at his house on February 4 he was convinced that no adultery had occurred. This was never explained.) The most obvious answer would seem to be that although he retained a hearty dislike for Mrs. Edwards, for him the real villains of the scandal were neither of the principals but the politicians who were circulating stories about him. He had said many times that he wanted to bring some of these rascals to justice. Appearing as a witness in the Edwards trial then would earn no glory, would reveal his defense, and would drive his libelers to cover so depriving him of his sensational court room victory. It should be noted that while he was clearly trying to invite an actionable libel, and always denounced rumors about himself as damnable lies, he never revealed in any of his correspondence what the truth was. William, who clearly knew some of the facts, if not all, always wrote in terms that show he believed that if his brother took the stand he would be exonerated. He had urged Lloyd George about three weeks before the trial not to offer himself as a witness, but to hold himself in readiness if called upon while considering 'whether or not you should initiate proceedings of your own.'[56]

However, there may have been another reason, though this is purely speculation, for his remaining unheard in the Edwards case. Lloyd George had an ironclad alibi, one of those already adduced or some other one, to account for his actions on the night of 4 February. But Kitty Edwards's confession had stated that she had committed adultery with Lloyd George on previous occasions. Her solicitor, A.J. Hughes, hinted to Lloyd George's solicitor, his partner A.R. Roberts, on 11 November 1897, just before the trial that he possessed evidence that Lloyd George had visited the Edwards house on 15 January 1896.[57] This is clearly impossible. On that date, Lloyd George was in Newport preparing for the South Wales Liberal Federation meeting, which occurred the next day. If the child was indeed full-term, its conception would have taken place toward the end of November 1895 when Lloyd George was criss-crossing Wales for Cymru Fydd. There were any number of opportunities for him to look in at Cemmaes for a moment's comfort. He had done this from time to time at least as long before as March 1894 when he was in Montgomeryshire campaigning for A.C. Humphreys-Owen, who carried the county seat after Stuart Rendel went to the House of Lords in Gladstone's retirement honors. So he could have been the father of the child after all. If this were true, or even if he only feared it might be true, it would have been very dangerous for him to take the stand to answer probing and unfriendly questions on other visits there, not to be sure from Bargrave Deane who evidently was desperately anxious to keep him out of court, but from Mrs. Edwards's attorney, Frederic Inderwick, a senior and eminent QC who had been practising divorce and probate law long before Lloyd George entered Breeze, Jones and Casson. Here lurked disaster.

These speculations are perhaps reinforced by his behavior after the case. Even though he was excused from any misconduct on the night of 4 February and affected always to portray himself in his public pronouncements as a martyr to the asininity of the English law of libel, he was careful to specify that the charge upon which he wished to testify was his whereabouts on the night of 4 February. As that charge had been withdrawn he could not appear, although he would have appeared if the charge had been made.[58] Of Jeune's offer to reinstate the 4 February accusation should Lloyd George wish to appear, he said nothing. His public story was that he intended to be in court but that the trial was over before he arrived. Always he denounced Kitty Edwards, while adding that the slander was deliberately circulated by his political enemies and that as he was unable to prove damages he could not reply in court.[59]

But there was a strange aftermath to the Edwards divorce case. On 16 June 1899, this time before President Jeune and a jury, Dr. T. P. Beddoes, Mrs. Edwards's physician, intervened, as a member of the public, charging that Dr. Edwards was the father of his wife's child and seeking to have the 1897 decree nisi rescinded. This time Lloyd George had briefed Bryn Roberts who was present. Beddoes's case was hopeless from the beginning. Bargrave Deane announced that he had letters written by Kitty Edwards to her husband which showed clearly that in the autumn of 1896 she had believed herself guilty of adultery.

For Lloyd George this could have been calamitous. First, the confession was read again, giving it new publicity. When Bryn Roberts asked for permission to examine Mrs. Edwards and to present letters which proved his client's innocence, he was refused on the ground that Lloyd George was no longer a party to the case. However, after getting nowhere with Jeune, Beddoes's attorney appeared three days later before Justice Gorell Barnes asking that the decree be set aside so that the Queen's Proctor could intervene. Here lay an avenue of even greater danger for Lloyd George. The business of the Queen's Proctor was to bring to the court's attention possible cases of collusion in divorce. Presumably Lloyd George would have been subjected to unfriendly cross-examination by Bargrave Deane. The parellels with Sir Charles Dilke's involvement in the Crawford divorce case ten years before are irresistible; the wife's confession given under duress, Judge Charles Butts's dismissal of it and Dilke's failure to testify, virtually at the invitation of the judge. However on that occasion the Queen's Proctor had appeared, paradoxically at Dilke's invitation, and Dilke found himself involved in the trial for practical purposes as a defendant but without the advantages of a defendant. Mrs. Crawford had been able, as presumably Mrs. Edwards desired, to blacken her lover's name without giving him the opportunity to reply.[60] As it turned out the danger passed, perhaps without Lloyd George having been aware of it. Barnes declined the motion, noting that the Queen's Proctor had already had two years to take action and had not done so.

Does this episode mean anything in terms of Lloyd George's career? Politically it did not hurt him. His hold on his constituency never wavered, nor, apparently, did his standing at Westminster. But neither did the affair teach him any lessons about dallying with other men's wives. Even while the Edwards case was before the court he was flirting, perhaps innocently, perhaps not, with Mrs. Timothy Davies, the wife of a prosperous Fulham draper, and he was soon receiving the usual angry letters from Maggie who would neither leave Criccieth to care for him nor countenance his interests with any other woman. However, in the Davies affair he handled his wife's charges not by denials but by counter-attacking. When she threatened to expose his relationship with Mrs. Davies—Mr. Davies, even though the two had been married only four years, did not seem to care—he immediately dared her to do so.[61] And ten years later, when two newspapers only hinted at involvements with women, he began legal action forthwith. In the first case, simply a remark in the *Bystander* in July 1908, that the new Chancellor of the Exchequer might be subject to sexual temptation, Lloyd George threatened legal action and received £300 in an out-of-court settlement. In the second, more serious case, in January 1909, when the *People* in a series of articles about scandals in high places stated that a Cabinet minister who, although unnamed was unmistakably Lloyd George, had been saved from a citation as corespondent in a divorce case only by a payment of money to the aggrieved husband, he insisted upon a court hearing. This time he appeared with Maggie and took the stand full of righteous indignation even though Edward Carson, representing the newspaper, had privately assured Rufus Isaacs for Lloyd George, that the proprietors regretted the libel, had been unaware of it before it appeared, and would pay substantial damages.[62] As the *People* offered no defense whatever there is no way of knowing what evidence, if any, they possessed. Their quick collapse suggests they did not have much. One is left to wonder whether an enterprising newspaperman had not, in fact, picked up a belated echo of Edwards vs. Edwards.

The Edwards case, first, is part of a bundle of occurrences of the last half of the nineties which mark Lloyd George's evolution from the trumpet of Young Wales to the founder and chief of Liberal-radical dissent. While he still spoke much about Wales at Westminster he loved it less and less as the nineties waned, indulging more than ever during the parliamentary holidays in his passion for travel abroad.

Second, in terms of his longer career, the Edwards case illustrates the dangerous place Lloyd George had constructed for himself in British public life. More than most politicians he was vulnerable to rumor or attack. By making innuendo and invective a way of political life, he had won for himself enemies who hated not only what he stood for but his person. He set out to create controversy; so also he invited it. The ordinary social immunities that hedged Asquith or the Duke of Devonshire, did not protect him. He never seemed to have understood the peculiar weakness of his public position. His letters during the Edwards case and during the far more dangerous Marconi affair reveal nothing but surprise and innocent outrage that anyone would suspect him of anything. Yet neither, despite his contempt for men who jeopardized their careers through personal indulgence, did he alter his behavior.

III

The disaster at Newport on 16 January 1896 marked the end of Lloyd George's campaign to establish an Irish-style political machine in Wales, but it did not destroy his hope of organizing Wales in some way. Until the outbreak of the South African War he continued, perhaps with waning energy and attention, his campaign for Welsh political unification, Home Rule All Round, and Irish-model land courts empowered to fix rents and value improvements. These activities provide the conclusion of the Welsh phase of his political life. In the end he succeeded in establishing, on paper, an all-Wales political organization and perhaps more important he drove D.A. Thomas from the loosely defined inner circles of the Welsh parliamentary caucus, killing also the South Wales Liberal Federation. Nevertheless for Lloyd George's future these parochial victories were of small importance, even though as always he rejoiced over them in letters to Maggie. He was in this sense small minded. He rarely forgave an enemy, especially within his own party, until he had bested him. Yet after he had won Lloyd George could be extraordinarily generous.

But, although doing little to forward Lloyd George's career, the struggles to provide a Welsh sense of political identity in the House of Commons and in Wales are illuminating historically. They provide a glimpse, from the Welsh point of view, of the chaos among the opposition benches at Westminster in a period when political life in London was dominated by events foreign and imperial, and by the Diamond Jubilee, to all of which Lloyd George gave only passing attention.

Part of the general agitation for Cymru Fydd in the autumn of 1895 was the revival of the slogan of Home Rule All Round. Lloyd George had published his argument in the October issue of *Young Wales* as a special article entitled 'National Self-Government for Wales.' He sent a copy of this document to Lord Rosebery and received from the party leader a tepid but generally approving reply agreeing that finding time for measures of only local application was certainly a problem in the imperial parliament and that therefore some devolution of power was a legitimate topic for discussion. Lloyd George triumphantly published this letter in the November issue of *Young Wales* and told its editor, J. Hugh Edwards, that he believed he had won the support of the Liberal leadership for his federal proposals. He intended, as he explained to Maggie early in the session, to change the policy of the Liberal party. Home Rule All Round would move 'at once to the very front of the programme.' Dilke and Labouchere were supporting him.[63]

He raised the question in the so-called 'Radical Committee' on 18 February, a week after the 1896 session convened, and was told to bring it up later.[64] On 10 March he tried again and discovered his colleagues were more interested in discussing a proposal to separate the National Liberal Federation from the Liberal Central Office. Finally at a large meeting of 56 on 24 March, among whom there were many, Albert Spicer and Bryn Roberts for instance, who hardly counted as radicals, he was allowed to speak. He read a resolution supporting Home Rule All Round but declared he was not prepared to move it unless 'the sense of the meeting' was favorable. The meeting, it became immediately clear, was at once almost unanimously in support of United Kingdom federalism and almost as unanimously opposed to voting on such an 'abstract expression of opinion.' It would be 'inexpedient.' After two hours and many speeches the group adjourned *sine die*.[65] Although Lloyd George reported to his wife, as usual, that the meeting had gone well with much support for his project, that the chairman (Albert Spicer) had rebuked Bryn Roberts for talking too much and, untruthfully, that the group had adjourned to consider the plan at a future date, this was a final defeat.[66] Dillon's declaration of support for the Education Bill on 12 May enabled Lloyd George to assemble a group of

19, styling itself the 'Radical Manifesto Committee', mostly Welsh but including Dalziel. This body issued a call for the abolition of the House of Lords and for 'a comprehensive system of devolution or Home Rule all round to enable the imperial Parliament to adequately perform its work,' but in fact United Kingdom federalism had died. Lloyd George would mention it again frequently and he published the resolution passed on 19 May in *Young Wales* the following January. Finally it turned up in the famous coalition proposals of August and October 1910. But the project which he had taken up at some political danger to himself as a candidate for the Liberal nomination for Caernarvon District had now disappeared from his political program.[67]

What had happened? Home Rule All Round fell, as it were, into one of the many cracks that beset the post-Gladstone Liberal party. Lloyd George may not have understood this. He assumed that English radicals who supported Irish Home Rule would accept a more comprehensive installment of the same proposal. He had boasted to Maggie on 6 March that he had commitments of support from 35 MPs.[68] He exulted at the Lichfield by-election on 21 February when a Liberal landowner supporting Home Rule All Round had defeated a Liberal Unionist.[69] In fact, however, many English radicals, Sir Charles Dilke in the lead, opposed the federal proposals.[70] For many, Home Rule of any kind was simply an obstacle to other reforms. To others, to those who honored the memory of Gladstone, Morley, or C.P. Scott of the *Manchester Guardian*, Ireland must come first. Finally, the Irish themselves fiercely resisted Home Rule for anyone else. This Lloyd George had understood. He had worked to find some arrangement with Dillon and Healy.[71] He believed he had reached an agreement and altered his manifesto to meet the Irish objections. Nevertheless Dillon issued a statement immediately after the May 19 meeting denouncing the right of a 'reconstituted' Radical Committee to pledge the rest of the radical contingent to anything.[72]

However, Home Rule All Round fell foul of even deeper antagonisms among the Liberals of which Lloyd George, still in the spring of 1896 looking at parliament through Welsh spectacles, may not even have been aware. He seems to have been spurred to take up the federal cause by the collapse of Liberalism in the general election and by the belief that somehow Rosebery would support him. He and the former Prime Minister would construct a new Liberal program. But he, like so many others, did not understand Rosebery. What may have been Rosebery's motives in giving the slightest encouragement to Lloyd George cannot be known. He announced that he was no longer the Liberal leader in a public letter to the press on 8 October, 1895 at about the time he received an advance copy of the *Young Wales* article. And even after Lloyd George's failure before the Radical Committee, on 15 July, Rosebery invited him to dinner in the company of a number of party eminences, Lord Ripon and Lord Herschel, the former Chancellor, and Sir Henry Campbell-Bannerman among others, for what was apparently an extended discussion of Home Rule All Round.[73] However, if Rosebery was unwilling to lead the party, neither was he willing to fade away. Somehow he thought of himself as a national leader above the humdrum of party affairs. Certainly he opposed Irish Home

Rule, but he would flirt with United Kingdom federalism as a grand conception, as later during the South African War he made murky public pronouncements on the need for national efficiency, insisting he was speaking to the nation not the party. Yet always he drifted away into the mist of arcane contemplation when reformers appeared to ask for his leadership in the promotion of specific measures.[74]

Second, Lloyd George brought forward his proposal at a time when the Liberal party, in the wake of devastating defeat, had fallen into disarray. The leadership and the backbench distrusted and fought each other. The leadership wanted most of all to be let alone. The rank and file on the other hand looked for some text upon which to found a new Liberal doctrine. For some, loyal to the memory of Gladstone, this meant peace, retrenchment and reform. But for the radicals the scripture was the Newcastle program for which, with good reason, they doubted their leaders' affection. The Radical Committee meeting of 10 March, which had declined to hear Lloyd George's resolution on Home Rule All Round, had been concerned specifically that day with the discovery of a formula for defending the sacred statement approved at Newcastle against the tinkering fingers of the Liberal Central Office. Further, although there were probably few English or Scottish radicals who would have risked their political lives to support Irish Home Rule after Dillon's treason on the Education Bill of 1896, there were also few who wished to begin revision of the Newcastle document, which carried Irish Home Rule as its first commandment, at the behest of one whom many still considered a Welsh pirate. Thus, virtually the same group of men who had cast 102 votes for Dalziel's Home Rule All Round amendment at the end of March in 1895, refused just a year later to have anything to do with Lloyd George's proposal.

After the collapse of United Kingdom federation, Lloyd George busied himself with the Agricultural Rating Bill and appears from his correspondence scarcely to have noted the death of his mother on 19 June 1896. In the autumn came his sojourn in Argentina. After his return he suffered the shock of the Edwards case. At the end of a self-pitying letter to Gee on this matter in mid-December he brought up his new project. 'There is apathy abroad,' he wrote, 'on political questions which makes it exceedingly difficult if not impossible to organize at present. Would it not be well to wait until the Education Bill is out and then get a convention at Swansea?'[75] Since the previous spring, while still occupied with federalism, he had been urging his listless Welsh colleagues to organize themselves.[76] A measure of his lack of success may have been the small number of Welsh Members who turned up at the Radical Committee meetings. Now he was turning to Wales again.

The result of the letter was a conference of Liberals from Flint and Denbighshire, evidently sponsored by Gee, on 5 and 6 January, 1897 at which, after beating off a motion to revive the North Wales Liberal Federation, Lloyd George carried a resolution calling upon the Welsh Liberal delegation in parliament to summon a representative meeting in Wales to consider again the matter of organization.[77]

At the end of March 1897 the Welsh members met, evidently in some consternation, to consider the Flintshire and Denbighshire proposal that they call a conference to plan the political rationalization of Wales. Eventually Albert Spicer, a Londoner and eminent Congregational layman, who since 1892 had represented Monmouth District and had generally supported Lloyd George in the fight for Home Rule All Round, proposed that the MPs themselves formulate a plan. Out of this came a committee of Spicer, Lloyd George, Alfred Thomas, Ellis and Brynmor Jones.[78]

The proposals that came from this committee's deliberations were also, as Lloyd George admitted, technically Spicer's work, even though always in his letters he allowed Maggie to believe that everyone knew they were really his own. Indeed probably he knew they represented as much as the Welsh MPs would approve. Nevertheless, as he told the Caernarvon Borough's Liberal Association in September in proposing the plan's adoption, he wished they did more. They did not 'go half so far as…Cymru Fydd.'[79] In fact all that Spicer proposed was the creation of a large all-Welsh council to be made up of delegates from the various parliamentary constituency associations. The council itself could do nothing except call national meetings 'from time to time as the occasion demands…to consider questions affecting Liberalism.' All local matters, organization, registration, and most crucial of all for Lloyd George, the selection of candidates, which in most of Wales meant for practical purposes the selection of the Member of Parliament, were specifically left to the constituency associations.[80]

Nevertheless these toothless proposals, of which the best that could be said, as Lloyd George admitted to the Caernarvon Liberals, was that they were better than nothing, evoked a furious protest from D.A. Thomas and Bryn Roberts. After two angry meetings during which the plan was carried through a characteristically ill-attended caucus eleven to one, Thomas resigned from the Welsh party and thereafter operated as an independent in the House of Commons until he gave up his seat in 1910.[81] However, he did not end his opposition in Wales, using his still considerable influence to prevent the approval of a national organization among various constituency associations.

The active opposition of D.A. Thomas and Bryn Roberts, the political indifference that swept over Wales after the Liberal defeat of 1895, and perhaps most important of all, the suspicion among many of the older Liberal associations that the real goals of the Welsh unifiers were not disestablishment but land reform and interference in local politics, meant that the resolutions at Westminster would not be quickly translated into action in Wales. Thus by mid-October 1897, only 12 of the 32 constituencies in Wales and Monmouthshire had elected delegates to an organizational meeting scheduled for the end of that month in Cardiff.[82] Lloyd George wrote to Gee lamenting the slow action but saying that they could proceed with the meeting if ten more constituencies approved. In November, the Liberal association of the south or Eifion division of Caernarvonshire repudiated the recommendation of its sitting Member, Bryn Roberts, and elected delegates. By early December only Montgomeryshire held out. The sitting Member here, A.C. Humphreys-Owen, disliked Lloyd George nearly as much as did Roberts, although Lloyd George, in addressing the constituency association on 3 December, ignored him to attack D.A. Thomas. Lloyd George denied that his proposals sidetracked disestablishment and made fun of Thomas's assertion that Welsh Members were now of such personal distinction that an organization for their control was unnecessary. All of this was inapplicable, he said, as the Member for Merthyr was by 'his own choice outside the Welsh party.'[83] Montgomery, he concluded, should do as Eifion had done and join the movement for Welsh unity.

Whether or not Montgomeryshire accepted this advice, the often postponed Welsh national convention finally met in Cory Memorial Hall, Cardiff on 4 February, 1898 with Albert Spicer presiding. About three hundred men attended. After a long discussion the southern delegations forced the amendment of Spicer's original plan to require representation on the central body in proportion to the number of electors in each constituency, one for each 3,000 voters. This would produce a Council of between 110 and 120 from among whom an executive of thirty, styled the 'General Purposes Committee,' would be chosen. The organization was to be called: 'Cyngor Rhyddfrydol Cenedlaethol Cymreig' or The Welsh National Liberal Council. The only assigned function of this machinery was the summons of national conventions on appropriate occasions.[84] In May Lloyd George was duly elected one of two members of the new council for Caernarvon District and attended its first meeting in the public hall in Llandrindod in early August, as he did the next year when the South Wales Liberal Federation, now scarcely alive, offered to cooperate.[85]

If the Welsh National Liberal Council was not the Irish-style political machine that he had sought in Cymru Fydd, it was nonetheless a convenient platform from which Lloyd George could make speeches in the name of Wales. As his ties with the principality became weaker in the years to come such an institution was not unimportant. Hence as its president, he kept it in existence so long as he was active in politics. He used it effectively during the education struggle in 1903 and 1904 and in putting down discontent with the Campbell-Bannerman government for its failure to act on disestablishment in 1907. Perhaps more significant, others appear to have taken it seriously. In October 1920, when its president was Prime Minister, the council suffered a revolt of Asquithians who established their own organization, the 'Welsh Liberal Federation' with Henry Gladstone, third son of the G.O.M. and husband of Stuart Rendel's daughter, as president and with, not surprisingly, Bryn Roberts as vice president. After Asquith retired in 1925 both the council and the federation disappeared into the 'Welsh Liberal Association' with Lloyd George again as president and with its headquarters at the address of the old National Council, 82 Queen Street, Cardiff.[86]

One feature of the meeting in Cardiff had been a motion by Tom Ellis expressing the regret of the Welsh Members of Parliament at the loss of Sir George Osborne Morgan, the Welsh party leader, who had died on 25 August 1897. Accordingly within a week of his public triumph at Cardiff, Lloyd George was closeted in the nervous privacy of a meeting of Welsh MPs seeking to choose a new leader. In the English press, with his new reputation earned from opposition to the Agricultural Rating Bill and the Voluntary Schools Bill and with Ellis rapidly declining in health and soon to die, Lloyd George was incontestably the most conspicuous Welsh member. Viewed from a distance he was presumably the natural choice. But he had in 1898, as he would have all his life, difficulty in organizing a party. He could rouse the multitude, but not inspire disciples. As a result, although he was nominated for leadership by Reginald McKenna, Brynmor Jones was also nominated by Ellis Griffith and Alfred Thomas by Brynmor Jones. That fewer than a score of Welsh MPs could find three potential leaders among themselves demonstrates the level of harmony within the party. Lloyd George immediately announced he would not stand against Thomas, and Jones withdrew, so the 'worthy old pantaloon,' as Humphreys-Owen described Alfred Thomas, was elected unanimously.[87] After the meeting Lloyd George growled to Herbert Lewis that he could have won it, but the 'jealousy' of some South Wales men would have split the party as the Irish were split. He would rather 'dig potatoes' than preside over such a group. Besides, he said, Alfred Thomas 'was a nice man' and, it could be added, invariably amenable to suggestions from Lloyd George.[88]

The fact is that Lloyd George probably could have won the leadership of the small group of Welsh nationalists who came regularly to party meetings. Spicer, Herbert Lewis, Alfred Thomas himself, McKenna, William Jones and probably Brynmor Jones would have supported him. So would have Tom Ellis who in these last months of his life had moved again close to Lloyd George. But it would have been a diminished inheritance. In the country districts after 1895 Liberal party organizations were declining in vigor and activity, while in the South, Labour, galvanized by the six months coal stoppage that began on 26 February 1896, began seizing political control in mining districts. In Glamorgan Gower, where the Liberals had doubled the Conservative vote even in the disastrous election of 1895, J. Aeron Thomas only narrowly defeated the Labour candidate John Hodge in 1900, while in Merthyr, Keir Hardie easily defeated Pritchard Morgan in the same election. Meanwhile working men, sometimes to be sure under Liberal banners, were invading local authority councils.[89] All of this meant, even where the Liberals theoretically were still in power, that the new national issues of labor rights, employment, and welfare, were taking hold. The old Welsh causes, Sunday closing and disestablishment, were losing their currency.

As Lloyd George certainly knew by 1898, Welsh radicalism also had reached the end of the road. The struggles within his own group demonstrated that constitutional change and land reform never claimed the interest of the majority of his colleagues and probably never would. He had to broaden his political base. Thus, when Tom Ellis died on 5 April, 1899 and the new Liberal Whip, Herbert Gladstone, offered to appoint a Junior Whip from Wales, evidently proposing Herbert Lewis, Lloyd George moved on 18 May that the party reject the idea and form an independent party. The customary dithering began and the meeting adjourned without voting, announcing that it would meet again after the Whitsun recess.[90] But it never did, and probably he did not care.

IV

Among the important occurrences that Lloyd George missed while in Argentina was the beginning, in the autumn of 1896, of a labor dispute at the huge Penrhyn slate quarries in Bethesda, Caernarvonshire a few miles south of Bangor.[91] By the time Lloyd George had recovered from the initial shock of Kitty Edwards's confession, D.R. Daniel, who acted as secretary to the now workless quarrymen, had enlisted Tom Ellis in the cause. Ellis was a favorite of London newspapermen and was able to induce H.W. Massingham, editor of the Liberal *Daily Chronicle,* to come to Wales. Massingham then threw his paper's support into a campaign to raise funds for the Penrhyn workers. By early January Lloyd George also was touring Wales supporting Home Rule All Round but making few speeches in which he did not pause to denounce Lord Penrhyn, his ancestry, his wealth or his personal habits. After parliament convened, he, Ellis, Brynmor Jones, and William Jones, in whose constituency the quarries lay, raised the matter on an amendment to the address and on a motion to adjourn.[92] Meanwhile they arranged for a Welsh choir recital in London at Dr. Clifford's enormous chapel in Westbourne Park, to evoke sympathy and money.[93]

For most people the issue in dispute was not trade unionism but the suffering of the quarrymen at the hands of Lord Penrhyn. For Lloyd George particularly the lockout was a stunning example of the abuse of landownership. Even when he invited John Burns—elected in 1892 for Battersea as a Labourite but calling himself since 1895 a Gladstonian Liberal—to Criccieth to appear with him he confined himself to the single question of land monopoly.[94] Burns arrived and on 7 May, at the Caernarvon Pavilion, with 8,000 seats filled by quarrymen and with William Jones as well as Burns on the platform, Lloyd George made perhaps his most important speech of the Penrhyn episode. There was, he admitted, the 'principle of labour' involved in the dispute but there was also 'a principle of far greater importance…namely the right of the people to the land, to the mountains, and to the resources of the earth (cheers).' The tyranny, he reiterated, adhered to the land itself. It gave Lord Penrhyn the right to take £200,000 from the wages of quarrymen or to lock up, if he wished, the resources of the earth. As with all Lloyd George's speeches, the remedy for this crying evil was unspecific except for the promise that the House of Commons would debate the matter of crown lands in private hands within the next two weeks.[95] Nevertheless this problem, certainly not new to him, would remain untouched until the tax on mining and quarrying royalties appeared in the 1909 Budget.

In the summer of 1897 Lord Penrhyn patched up, temporarily, his dispute with his quarrymen, accepting the limited right of the quarrymen to present grievances but without a recognition of the men as a body corporate. This compromise arrived less because of Lloyd George's activity than as a consequence of the embarrassment the lockout caused Penrhyn in the public press and in society. Probably the climax of the anti-Penrhyn campaign was an interview, arranged by Ellis through Francis Knollys, between the Prince of Wales and the intransigent baron. Knollys reported to Ellis at the end of July, 1897 that the meeting was 'unsatisfactory' and that Penrhyn had refused to permit Board of Trade arbitration.[96] Nevertheless, the next month Penrhyn conceded the limited right of representation and promised to prevent subcontracting which had led to sweating of wages. The men, their relief funds almost gone, returned to work. But with Penrhyn and the men sullen and angry this armistice could hardly be called a settlement.

In December, Lloyd George wrote to Gee, who had of course furiously supported the strikers, promising 'to keep an eye on the quarrymen,' but he said he had written particularly because he was appalled to learn that Gee was thinking of giving up the *Baner*.[97] Gee was by this time 82 years old, and, as Lloyd George remarked in his letter, working far too hard. But he still declaimed throughout North Wales at every opportunity the primitive radicalism that the Member for Caernarvon District had first absorbed from him during the tithe rebellion.

Nine months later, on 28 September, 1898, Gee died. His loss seems to have affected Lloyd George more deeply than that of any other person in his career except for the death of his daughter Mair in 1907, more even than his mother or Tom Ellis. 'He treated me always as a father would his child—affectionately,' he wrote Maggie the next day. 'I must attend the funeral at all costs, business or no business.'[98] Nevertheless Gee's departure broke another tie with Wales.

Symptomatic of Lloyd George's growing interest in non-Welsh affairs was his appointment in May, 1899 to the Select Committee on the Aged, Deserving, Poor, usually styled the 'Chaplin Committee,' after its chairman, the President of the Local Government Board, Henry Chaplin. However, the sponsor of the committee, the man to whom it owed its existence, was Joseph Chamberlain. Since 1890, Chamberlain had sought, with more persistence and honesty than Lloyd George ever credited him, to interest British politicians in the establishment of some form of old age pension plan to be paid for by contributions from the beneficiaries. But at every turn he found himself opposed by the powerful parliamentary influence of the British friendly society movement. As a result, although two official investigative bodies, the Aberdare Commission reporting in 1895 and a Treasury committee under Lord Rothschild reporting in 1898, had examined contributory schemes, they were unable to recommend any of them.

By the beginning of 1899 demands for action were appearing on all sides and were seriously discomforting the government. Just before the opening of parliament, Chamberlain, Balfour and Salisbury corresponded nervously on whether a pension plan might not be moved as an amendment to the address, and a few weeks later about one hundred Unionist MPs petitioned the government to make good its promises on pensions.[99] Finally in March, to turn aside a bill put down by Lionel Holland, Unionist for Bow and Bromley, Chamberlain announced the appointment of yet a third committee to investigate the tortured pensions question. The committee however would be permitted this time to examine tax supported pensions, unlike the Rothschild Committee which had been confined by its terms of reference to contributory schemes.[100]

The importance of Lloyd George's brief service on the Chaplin

Committee is not that it shows a sudden preoccupation with social reform. He had after all advocated pensions many times before. They were, in effect, a weapon with which to attack the rich, not to defend the poor. Rather his first experience on a committee that had at least theoretical power to formulate a pension plan showed him to be, as he would remain for the rest of his life, a thoroughly prudent, not to say careful, steward of public funds, by no means so far in advance of his colleagues on the committee as he boasted to Maggie that he was.[101] To him a universal, tax supported old-age pension was an admirable slogan for embarrassing Tory landlords and clergymen and above all for abusing Joseph Chamberlain. But as a way of spending public funds, he felt in 1899, as he would feel in 1908, that tax supported pensions, if perhaps politically useful, were economically wasteful. Lloyd George did not change his early social radical ideology after he took office, as is too often suggested.[102] Except in the area of land reform, he never had an ideology. There was nothing the matter with taxes levied on certain groups whom he felt were non-producers or with public money spent for political profit. But the egalitarian doctrine of socialism repelled him as it would have any other Welsh country lawyer.

Thus, despite bragging to Maggie that he had added millions of pounds to the cost of pensions by his liberalizing amendments to the draft report, his proposals for change to the report were in fact by no means generous. Neither he nor his radical colleagues on the committee, Lionel Holland and Michael Davitt, sought to alter the essentially poor law orientation of the recommendation.[103]

More revealing was the proposal that Lloyd George himself submitted to the committee. This suggested a plan for a 5s pension to be offered to all citizens at age 65 who had not more than £26 per year in income, provided that the applicant had never been convicted of an indictable offense and had not received parish relief for more than a given period, which Lloyd George left unspecified. He added, however, a number of unusual provisions by which an individual unfit for pensions because of conviction of a crime or the receipt of parochial relief could rehabilitate himself. Such a person would be eligible if he had been a member of a friendly society or a trade union for twenty years or if he had obtained for himself a friendly society or post office annuity of at least 2s 6d per week and of at least ten years duration, or if he had been making payments for the purchase of a house for at least ten years. In effect, despite a lapse early in life, if one had returned to a status of middle class respectability and thrift, but earned no more than 10s per week, he would be rewarded with a pension.

In Lloyd George's plan the administration of pensions would be in the hands not of the parish guardians, but of the county councils who would determine eligibility. The cost of the pensions was to be borne by the local authority with grants in aid from the Exchequer which would be calculated, however, on the basis of population not on the amount given in pensions. This would encourage the councils, Lloyd George explained, to give pensions more freely than if they received only a fixed amount based upon what they themselves spent. However, if the county council wished to give more than 5s it could do so from its own resources. At no point would the pension administration touch the hated poor law, but, characteristically for

Lloyd George, his plan, while including the conventional restrictions on crime and pauperism, was nevertheless weighted heavily in the direction, not of the absence of sin, but of the positive virtues of good citizenship and providence. 'If proof of destitution is demanded as a condition precedent to receiving a pension,'—wrote Lloyd George in a marginal note on his proposal, 'there is no essential difference in character between pensions and outdoor relief.'[104]

Writing to his wife after the committee reported Lloyd George remarked cheerfully that the Chancellor of the Exchequer was already furious with Henry Chaplin. This ideal specimen of the Tory squire, with a generosity as broad as his lands in Lincolnshire, had readily approved the widening of pension terms, accepting also the stipulation from Lloyd George's memorandum, which he introduced as an amendment, that the Treasury subvention be calculated according to population. 'Never mind, it all goes to the poor who really need it,' Lloyd George wrote, but added character-istically: 'it has the additional advantage of putting these bandits who are in power in a nice fix. They can neither carry out these recommendations nor drop them—not without discredit.'[105]

Although the carefully hedged report of the Chaplin Committee recommending a 5s pension, jointly supported from rates and taxes, paid by the guardians only to the most deserving poor, was received with much enthusiasm by pension advocates outside parliament, the government, as Lloyd George clearly understood, had no intention of taking up the proposal. (In the autumn, Lionel Holland resigned as a Unionist MP over the pensions question and in 1906 contested Chamberlain's home constituency of Edgbaston as a Liberal.) Nonetheless a departmental committee set to work to determine the cost of the Chaplin scheme, but before it completed its report the South African War broke out and in November 1900 Chaplin was replaced at the Local Government Board by Walter Long, an opponent of pensions. The new circumstances made further postponement inevitable and so provided Lloyd George in the early years of the new century with many opportunities to demonstrate, in the name of poverty-stricken aged citizens, Unionist faithlessness and hypo-crisy. As he entered his second decade in parliament the pension question came frequently to serve the Member for Caernarvon District as the tithe and disestablishment had served him in his first decade. It could turn the smallest action of ministerial expediency into a national moral issue with Joseph Chamberlain, now at the peak of his career, taking the place once held by Anglican bishops and Tory landlords.

At the end of the 1899 parliament, Lloyd George could reflect that since the last election his reputation in England, whatever it was in Wales, had begun to improve. He had wound up the session with a flourish, leading the Welsh MPs in an attack on the Tithe Rent Charge Bill, a paltry measure, worth in all £87,000, to relieve vicars of the liability to the rate charges which accrued to them as a result of attaching the value of the tithe to their living. His intervention on this measure in June was acclaimed by the *Liverpool Mercury* as a 'classic,' the finest of his career and 'much more impressive than Asquith's.'[106] To be judged superior to Asquith in a rarefied technical field of this sort was an important accolade.

Yet within little more than six months, he had thrown himself again into the center of a controversy so violent that it promised to threaten his career. In denouncing the South African War, and the spasm of intolerant patriotism that accompanied it, he opened himself to the charge of insufficient national loyalty, not only from the Unionists but from many members of his own party. He appeared to be destroying what had been, in the last few years, a new found respectability. His political prospects, so recently widened, would disappear. He was irresponsible, unsound, disreputable. From time to time he was certainly in genuine physical danger. The pro-Boer campaign has been portrayed as an act of supreme folly, or of idiot courage, or both.

Lloyd George threatened not only his political future but his Welsh base. After all, North Wales cared as much for the Queen's honor as the rest of the nation.[107] What then was he trying to do? In his stand during the war he displayed, unquestionably, great courage, but he was in no way unique, although by and large he worked alone. There were others involved, some more important than he, such as Leonard Courtney, a Liberal Unionist, who destroyed a far more solid career of twenty-five years in the space of six months. No constituency would adopt him. John Morley, defeated in 1895 and newly back in parliament, deep in the reconstruction of the life of Gladstone, emerged to denounce the war as he felt his dead leader would have done. Labour Members and the Irish were uniformly against the war as were, in varying degrees, about forty-five other Liberals.[108] Others, Wilfred Lawson, John Clifford, and W.T. Stead, were attacked also during public meetings.[109] Whatever Lloyd George was up to, he did not lead, as is sometimes suggested, the crusade. (William George states that his brother 'practically led the opposition to the war, both inside and outside of parliament.')

Historians conventionally look for systematic explanations to impose upon people and events. A man must be either pro- or anti-empire preference or Home Rule, he must be either an imperialist or a Little Englander, a pacifist or a militarist.[110] Lloyd George fitted no mold. He was neither an anti-imperialist nor an imperialist with a difference. Painting the map red to him was as irrelevant as preventing Ireland from turning green. His objections to the South African War, as his speeches make amply clear, were two: that it was unnecessary, the work of a corrupt government which represented everything he detested, and that it clogged the political machine at home by diverting parliamentary time and money from matters of real importance.

Hence opposition to the Boer War was entirely within the pattern he had already set for his political life, the denunciation of established wealth and power which had begun even before his entrance into parliament. This was the line of his career in the first quarter century of his political life and the war was simply one aspect of it, in no way unusual or mysterious. As he fought for the poor by attacking the rich, for disestablishment by denouncing the Church, for land reform by dilating upon grasping and idle landlords, so he condemned the war by exposing the makers of it, personified in Joseph Chamberlain.

The war simply merged into his framework of preoccupations and became another iniquity of the Unionists. Invariably he connected the conflict with events at home. He never lost an opportunity to remind audiences that the gift to the landlords embodied in the Agricultural Rating Act, conveniently coming up for renewal in 1901, was passed by the very government now spending blood and treasure for the benefit of South African millionaires which at the same time opposed old age pensions as being too expensive.

This is not to say that he saw no moral issue in the war, only that it was less evident in his speeches, and indeed in his private pronouncements, than his charges of official corruption, dishonesty, and tenderness for vested interests. Righteous anger, indeed, was part of Lloyd George's stock in trade, like his humble background. When it became an issue, at the end of 1900, he participated vigorously in the attack on the army policy of destruction of Boer farms and the consequent relocation of dependents in camps under military supervision, which, certainly until their transfer to the Colonial Office, were abominably managed. But here, as elsewhere, the burden of his outrage was not so much that the concentration camps were evil things in themselves, but that the evil was a Unionist responsibility. He defended the Boers in his speeches, and scoffed at government statements that the British mining community, whose ostensible persecution by the Transvaal government constituted the official cause of the war, was in fact either innocent or injured. But he never suggested that the Boers should win. Rather he argued always that the government, in order to secure the fortunes of gold mining magnates, had spurned compromise and aimed in fact at annexing Boer territory. It is hard to see that he was a friend of the Boers because of a belief in the rights of small nationalities or that except in occasional rhetoric he identified the Boers with the Welsh, as is asserted in the DuParcq biography and has been studiously repeated ever since.[111] Indeed it is difficult to prove from the positions taken during his career—from his most equivocal stands on Irish Home Rule to his treatment of Poland in 1919 at Paris—that he had strong views, intellectual or ethical, on the principle of nationality anywhere except for Wales.[112]

Still Lloyd George believed, certainly he affirmed in later years, that his opposition to the South African War constituted a turning point in his life, and he was proud of it. This no doubt accounts for the fact that nearly an entire volume of the DuParcq biography, of which William George was a paid co-author, is devoted to it.[113] Thus, as in so many other cases, historians find themselves retelling stories that Lloyd George has left for them. The opposition to the South African War has become part of the official history. This is the way he wanted it to be.

Nonetheless, even if he was not quite the solitary warrior that he chose later to make himself, if he was by no means at the radical fringe of the anti-war movement, Lloyd George's opposition to the war could easily have had grave consequences for his career as it certainly did for many others.

Probably the most important and least recognized aspect of Lloyd George's opposition was that he became for the first time, in newspaper terms, a national figure. He was now 'news,' not quite in the same sense that Asquith, Fowler and Grey were news, but his speeches on general topics were now worth half a column in *The Times*. He did not receive the automatic coverage of a frontbench man, but nevertheless this was a profound change. Even though for the past decade he had regularly deluged Maggie with torrents of self-congratulation about his parliamentary efforts: 'the best I have ever made, applause on all sides,' while quoting remarks from provincial Liberal newspapers that he was likely to be in the next Cabinet, Lloyd George remained until 1901 or 1902 a distinctly regional figure. His name could be expected to turn up in reports on agricultural, ecclesiastical, and educational questions. He always took care of his constituency at question time on issues of appropriations and patronage. But his thoughts on major national issues were hardly solicited. Quite clearly he was aware of this and regularly fired off critical or approving letters to *The Times* drawing attention to the fact that his name had been mentioned, however obscurely, in a public address by a frontbench politician.[114] While he had been regarded as the coming man for several years, it was during the South African War that he arrived.

On balance, the war advanced his career, not only because of the public notice it brought him but because when it was all over he was seen to have been on the right side. The reaction against colonial adventure, against jingoism, against military amateurism abroad and against personal ostentation among the wealthy, combined with physical deterioration among the poor at home, changed the orientation of British politics. The attitudes that led to the slogans of national efficiency and to the great Liberal victory of 1906 carried Lloyd George along. Similarly the revelations resulting from the war about Britain and British civilization opened political careers to a generation of young radical philanthropists with backgrounds in settlement house work, journalism, and the civil service who became the foot soldiers, the thinkers and the scribes of the New Liberalism. With the Boer War Lloyd George exchanged his mutinous Welsh battalions for an integrated force of largely English, nonconformist, frequently pacifist, social reformist, radicals whom he led with spectacular success until it was shattered by the outbreak of the First World War.

Altogether there is much to be said for his daring even in the perspective that the risks may have been less than he chose to pretend they were. At the time he showed, it must be repeated, great courage. He set himself at odds with the most senior leaders of his party who only within the last few years had begun to regard him as something less than a parliamentary buccaneer. The men who would be the arbiters of his career supported the war, while those against it seemed mostly to be political anachronisms like John Morley and Bryn Roberts or eccentric misfits such as Keir Hardie and the Irish. At least as menacing was the fact that W. Robertson Nicoll, editor of the prodigiously influential *British Weekly*, which for a decade had given Welsh nonconformity its most powerful voice in England, was an uncompromising imperialist. But then, on the other hand, the Olympian figure of Calvinistic Methodism in Caernarvon District, the redoubtable Evan Jones, denounced the South African War, as he denounced all wars, from his pulpit in Moriah Chapel and in his newspaper *Traethodydd*. As luck would have it Evan Jones, in 1898 and 1899, also was moderator of the Calvinistic Methodist General Assembly.

Still, he risked a great deal and he knew it. It was not with much more than his customary exaggeration that he told Lucy Masterman years later: 'On the Day of Judgement when I shall have to answer for my sins—and God knows I have enough to answer for—I shall say only one thing "Sir, I was a pro-Boer," and he will let me in.'[115]

V

The fighting began on 12 October 1899 after a Boer advance into Natal following the expiration of Kruger's ultimatum, which had demanded an end to British military reinforcement in South Africa. Since the beginning of September, Lloyd George had been travelling in Canada with his friends Llewelyn Williams and W.J. Rees, at the invitation of Lord Strathcona, the Canadian High Commissioner in London since 1896, who apparently hoped to use Lloyd George for the promotion of Welsh emigration to Western Canada. He traveled to the Canadian Pacific terminus at Vancouver, marvelling at the scenery, while writing home angry letters about the behavior of the government, with comments upon the ominous news from the Transvaal.[116] Evidently, after learning that the government, on 8 September, had ordered ten thousand men to be moved from India to South Africa, Lloyd George sent his first public statement, a stirring message dated 18 September, which was read at a protest meeting in the Guildhall at Caernarvon on 6 October at which John Morley spoke. 'The prospect in the Transvaal oppresses me with a deep sense of horror', he wrote. 'If I have the courage I shall protest with all the vehemence at my command against the outrage which is perpetrated in the name of human freedom.'[117]

The pro-Boer position had been made public already on 15 September when John Morley and Leonard Courtney had denounced the coming war in uncompromising ethical terms that Lloyd George rarely used.[118] Morley's speech immediately divided the Welsh Liberals so that William George wrote to his brother, still in Canada, warning of political trouble in his constituency. The press community, he said, was upset. Courtney had called Milner a 'lost mind.' Morley's position, which would be the line taken by the most conscientious opponents of the war among Gladstonian Liberals and Labour, was that the conflict, no matter what advantages it brought to Britain in new colonies and gold mines, nevertheless was wrong. William reported he was now at 'loggerheads' with the *Genedl Gymreig* over the 'Morley policy.' He had written to the directors of the Welsh Press Limited about the newspaper's resistance and he had heard that they had passed a resolution in support of Morley. 'I think Beriah Evans is at the root of the evil there now,' William concluded, 'in a childish wish to be independent of the *Herald Cymraeg.'[119]*

Lloyd George's early public position on the war, which he would hold until the winter of 1900-1, was that the war, whatever it did to the Trasvaal, would harm Britain more, delaying reform and corrupting further the nation's political life. But privately he took some pleasure in the dilemma of the government when war seemed inevitable. 'I believe their downfall is assured. If they go on, the war will be so costly in blood and treasure as to sicken the nation. If they withdraw they will be laughed out of power.'[120]

On 12 October, when war broke out, Lloyd George was at sea. He arrived in London only on 16 October, the day before parliament convened, without, it could be noted, his moustache which he had shaved off in Canada. For the moment, he telegraphed to William, he intended to remain silent and declined to associate himself with the extreme radicals who would vote against the extension of war credits. The success of the Boer advance into Natal, he said, created a 'new situation.' 'At the present, am rather inclined to agree with the "Chronicle" than with lobby [sic. Labby, Henry Labouchere] over that. Boers had invaded our territories and until they are driven back, Government entitled to money to equip forces to defend our possessions.' This did not, however, mitigate the crime of the war, he concluded.[121]

Even though he wanted to remain quiet during the short parliamentary session from 17 to 27 October, at the end, unable to restrain himself, he bitterly attacked Chamberlain for causing the war. He denounced the Colonial Secretary for misrepresenting the causes of the conflict, for either dishonesty or culpable ignorance, and for displaying a hypocritical tenderness for the supposed civil rights of the Uitlanders while ignoring far worse grievances among citizens at home. He used the occasion also to remind the government that, as it had only recently used its majority to present a gift of £3,000,000 of taxpayers' money to the nation's landlords, some of the wealthiest of whom were among its own members, there was no cause for impeaching the Transvaal government for selfishness or corruption.[122]

Through its early months Lloyd George's reaction to the war could be described as one of private bitterness and public outrage. In his letters he sympathized with the Boers for their determination and courage, but he never forgot the equal suffering and bravery of the British troops which was harder to bear because their manliness was wasted in a bad cause. Always his anger focused upon the government in London. The leadership in South Africa he usually admired, and was willing to excuse even civil administrators such as Alfred Milner, the High Commissioner. 'What a mess in the Transvaal,' he wrote to J.H. Lewis on 31 October on the battle of Lombards Kop, '20,000 prisoners. This is the price of our stupidity.'[123]

To Maggie two days later: 'I wish this war were over. I cannot without the greatest difficulty get my mind to anything else. Bad headaches trouble me the last 2 or 3 days. Can't get my mind on the Cardiff meetings at all. Can't get hold of a single idea. Must do something as I dare not disappoint them this time. It would be the fourth this year.'[124]

Yet whatever was his inner turmoil, his attacks on the government during the rest of the 1899 session only infrequently mentioned the war. The speech at Cardiff for which he felt unprepared dealt with the old topic of disestablishment and the growing threat of sectarian schools for Wales under a Church dominated parliament.[125] His only important utterance in Wales about the war came in Carmarthen at a meeting in support of the candidature of his friend Alfred Davies for Carmarthen District, a seat then held by a Liberal Unionist. Even here Lloyd George spoke mostly of Davies's firm commitment to disestablishment and of his opposition to sectarian education. His remarks upon the war were on the whole pretty mild but exemplified the stand that he generally would take in the first year and a half of the conflict. The war 'had been forced upon us,' the nation must 'put it through,' although he hoped it would stop. Nevertheless it held up progress. 'There was not a Lyddite shell which burst upon the South African hills that did not carry away an Old Age Pension. Oh, it killed two hundred Boers—fathers of families, sons of mothers who wept for them. Are you satisfied to give up your old age pension for that?' And above all, who were those who wanted the war? The vested interests in England. There was, to be sure, corruption in the Transvaal but there was more in England where the House of Lords earned £200 million from rate relief every year. The Uitlanders for whom the nation presumably fought were German Jews. The Boers on the other hand were like the old Welsh Covenanters. They might be right or wrong but they were better than the people England was defending.[126]

This speech and his attack on Chamberlain in the House of Commons on 27 October, became the ordinary Lloyd George line. He recognized that the war in its early months was popular and he never suggested that the Boers, whatever he thought of their courage and military skills, ought to prevail. 'We cannot, of course, go cap in hand to Kruger' he told a reporter of the *Morning Herald* on 29 January 1900, 'and say "we have sinned against heaven and thee" but there are many ways of stopping the war. We have only to give word to McKinley and the thing would be done. [American President William McKinley was under pressure from the Irish and German minorities in the United States to denounce Britain's involvement in South Africa, but remembering Great Britain's friendship during the recent Spanish American War, he had refused to do so.] But the Liberal party, whatever happens, must stand clear of the whole business. The government has made their bed; let them lie on it.'[127]

He assumed that in the long run the war would weaken the Unionist government, as indeed it did. His political position therefore throughout the conflict, even after the general election and the revelations about the concentration camps for Boer dependents, was to put the Liberals in a position to profit from opposing it and to avoid sharing any blame. As time passed after the war, this became his recollection of its overall political consequences: the Boers had not lost, after all they had their land back and more. Joseph Chamberlain—it was Joe's war—had lost and the winner was the Liberal party, above all its leader, Henry Campbell-Bannerman. Campbell-Bannerman had created the Union of South Africa in an expression of the magnanimity that was the core of all Liberal principles. Around the Union constitution Lloyd George constructed one of his most durable historical myths: that Campbell-Bannerman, with only himself and Burns supporting him, had convinced a reluctant Cabinet on 8 February 1906 to heal the wounds of South Africa, to scrap the Unionist settlement and grant dominion status. Virtue and Liberalism, with Lloyd George behind them, had triumphed over Unionist greed and vindictiveness.[128]

There is no need at this time to entertain the important topic of Britain's South African policy after 1906. But it is necessary to make clear that in his opposition to the South African War Lloyd George aimed at political profit for Liberalism in the long run. After the war he was at pains that the world should know he had been right.

This practical attitude was not far from that held by the new Liberal leader, Henry Campbell-Bannerman, who had been chosen leader of the party in the House of Commons on 6 February 1899. Nonetheless his stand brought Lloyd George into conflict with many other senior members of the party, who although denouncing the government's handling of the South African adventure felt themselves required by conscience, doctrine or patriotism to support the conflict in principle. Among the Liberal anti-Boers the most important for Lloyd George was Lord Rosebery who continued, as he had since his retirement from party leadership in the autumn of 1896, to refuse to exercise any official position within the party while refusing equally to refrain from using his brilliant talents to interfere with policy making and leadership decisions. He was like an aging music hall comedian who would not perform, but would not leave the stage. Lloyd George admired, but distrusted him. Rosebery had, of course, flirted briefly with Lloyd George, professing an interest in Home Rule All Round. During the war Rosebery pursued the same curiously uncertain path, speaking out forcefully in support of the war, seeming to offer himself as leader of the imperialist wing of the party, thus accentuating the divisions between Campbell-Bannerman and his followers, yet hesitating always to take the final step. What Rosebery intended cannot be known. Perhaps he did not know himself. Time and again in speeches of impenetrable ambiguity he denounced opponents of the war, asserted that old-fashioned Liberalism, Little Englandism and Home Rule, were dead, and murmured indistinctly about the formation of a new Liberalism which would be founded upon a federal relationship among the components of the Empire and would provide social reform at home to improve the efficiency of the British civilization.

The fact was that in the years between the outbreak of the Boer War and the general election of October 1900, perhaps until the spring of 1901, many Liberals, apparently Lloyd George himself, believed their party was breaking up.[129] Campbell-Bannerman would resign as leader and a new coalition would emerge without the baggage of Gladstonianism, including principally Home Rule, dedicated to social reform at home and imperialism abroad.

But of all those hastening to produce a coffin in which to inter the corpse of Liberalism, Rosebery was the most prominent. He began soon after the war started, on 27 October 1899, with a peculiar ironic welcome to the conflict, saying that it would serve as a laboratory or a proving range for the mettle of British subjects. From this he moved soon after the general election to a full blown program of Darwinian racial imperialism, 'a larger patriotism', arguing that the war was in a sense a contest of races in which the British must not allow themselves to be bested. 'An empire such as ours requires as its first condition an imperial race,' he said in his Rectoral Address at Glasgow on 16 November 1900, 'a race vigorous and industrious and intrepid. Health of mind and body exalt a nation in the competition of the universe. The survival of the fittest is an absolute truth in the modern world.'[130]

What Rosebery meant by all this, what, if anything, he expected to result from his three year war on Sir Henry Campbell-Bannerman during which he drew away from official Liberalism many of the most talented of his party's leaders without whom the government of 1905 could hardly have been formed, whether indeed the Liberal imperialist excursion was anything more than Alfred Harmsworth's first experiment in prime minister making, must remain unclear. Rosebery's biographers provide no illumination and dwell mostly on their subject's opposition to Home Rule.[131] For Lloyd George, Rosebery's motives, whatever they were, are of importance. Next to Chamberlain, he remained through the war the public figure Lloyd George mentioned most frequently in his speeches. Even though no crime was too monstrous for Chamberlain to be guilty of it, this was only the ordinary fare of political banter. Chamberlain was merely the convenient symbol of the government of landlords and ecclesiastics. Lloyd George always admired him and frequently compared the career of the Member for West Birmingham with his own.[132] With Rosebery he was more circumspect although equally devastating. His references were always in tones of mock respect, although one frequently cannot be quite sure. 'There is much to be said,' he remarked sarcastically in a speech to the Palmerston Club of Oxford at a 'wine' at Balliol College on 29 January 1900, 'for Lord Rosebery's theory that the war may be a blessing in disguise.' Lord Rosebery had said that Europe was unanimously opposed to Britain on the war, but he had forgotten to except the Turks, who were sympathetic. Lord Rosebery and Chamberlain were rivals as the stage managers of the new imperialism. Lord Rosebery might regret the war but he denounced only the South African farmers, fighting for their homes, and called their government a corrupt oligarchy.[133]

The Palmerston Club speech received wide public notice and, coming as it did after a period of repeated British defeats, represented an unpopular point of view. Disillusionment with the war had not yet set in. The popular hysteria that greeted the relief of Mafeking, reported in London on 18 May, more nearly manifested the public mood. Moreover Rosebery was a popular figure. He was the most visible and decorative of the Liberal leaders. He had consented to be the first chairman of the London County Council. He was after all a former Prime Minister and his speeches mingled unclearly but unmistakably strength of race with struggle for empire, in effect social reform and jingoism. In a word he appeared to be, amid the disarray of Liberalism, the man of the future.

Lloyd George understood his dangerous position perfectly well. He surmised that once the news from South Africa turned good there would be a general election and he knew he was still vulnerable in Caernarvon District. In the middle of January 1900 the *North Wales Observer* surveyed the local political situation with, for it, unusual candor. If an election were held today, said the paper, the Unionists would win, not because they were strong but because the Liberals 'were not in a position to benefit from Conservative weakness.'

> What is true of the Liberal Party as a whole is true, only more so, of the Liberal Party Caernarvon Boroughs. Its leaders are openly at variance on the Transvaal issue. Nothing is being done, or attempted, to keep the Party up to its fighting strength.

There has been no public meeting for a long time past. If he will pardon our saying so, even Mr. Lloyd George might have rendered his Party more efficient service by holding a series of meetings in his own constituency since his return from Canada than by addressing London Welshmen or Flint Liberals.
Caernarvon Liberalism is robust but it needs care and is not getting it.[134]

In London in his first speech on the war in the new session of the House of Commons, Lloyd George behaved himself. He spoke forcefully during the debate on the address, in support of a cautious official Liberal amendment regretting the government's lack of knowledge, foresight and judgement in the conduct of South African affairs since 1895. The amendment had been framed to allow all Liberals whatever their views to unite against the ministry. Lloyd George vigorously attacked the Colonial Secretary for dishonesty, both about his own actions and conditions in the Transvaal. It was, W.V. Harcourt thought, one of his best efforts, worthy of Grattan.[135]

But thereafter Lloyd George moved away from the mass of Liberals in the House of Commons, both pro- and anti-war. Through March he voted consistently against service estimates in Supply Committee, succeeding in adjourning the House on the army vote, and finally, joined only by a handful of Irish members and Wilfred Lawson, he divided against the second reading of the Finance Bill on 19 March.[136]

Inevitably word of his new independent line traveled back to Wales; here he met the opposition head on. The first public protest came, predictably, from the Bangor Liberal Association whose executive announced a meeting to discuss the reported unpatriotic views of their Member of Parliament. Lloyd George immediately let it be known that he would attend and that he would not withdraw his attacks on the war. 'They can kick me out the next time if they will' he wrote his brother early in March, 'I have no doubt myself that they will.'

> But I won't recant a single syllable, no, not even moderate my reasons a shade. I know the Caernarvon Boroughs will rue this folly when they are represented by some gilded popinjay.... serving people is a vain task. Well, no, that is not true. I must be mindful of the advice grand old Gee gave me once [in Welsh] 'Never get soured.' He had as much reason for doing so as most men. No man ever experienced more ingratitude than he did.[137]

'I am going to Bangor,' he wrote a few days later on 22 March.

> I mean to insist upon it. I hear talk of the leading Liberals strongly opposed to a meeting at this juncture and they entreat me not to go. But I will not listen. Here are my reasons:
> (a) there may be a general election soon
> (b) you may rely upon Chamberlain planning dissolution at the height of the war.

Lloyd George went on to explain that the meetings were necessary if he were to justify his unpopular point of view.[138]

Despite this fighting talk he took care to moderate his position. On 6 April and 10 April 1900 the Unionist *Western Mail's* 'London Letter' carried extended discussions of Lloyd George's views on imperialism in which he was carefully disassociated from the Little Englanders and was declared in everything except South Africa to be on the side of Lord Rosebery. At the same time the Caernarvon District Liberal Association was clearly warned to support him if they wished to keep him as a sitting member.[139] As the days passed the Bangor meeting, set for 11 April, attracted much attention in the press. There were rumors that there would be violence. Lloyd George had been attacked earlier, in Glasgow on 6 March when after successfully quieting a rowdy meeting a window in his carriage was broken as he left the hall.[140] The trustees of Penrhyn Hall became nervous and demanded from Henry Lewis, chairman of the Bangor Liberal Executive, a guarantee against damage.

On 11 April, the meeting itself went well enough. William George's recollections of hostility in his book may be somewhat exaggerated. The newspaper account makes clear that inside the hall Lloyd George had at least a moderately sympathetic reception. He was able to deliver a one hour speech of the standard fare, the rights of small nations, opposition to the rumored annexation of the Transvaal and Orange Free State, the corruption of the British government, and above all the iniquity of Joseph Chamberlain. The resolution, expressing complete confidence in the Member for Caernarvon District, passed almost unanimously after an attempt by Henry Lewis to weaken it was easily beaten down.[141]

If he was in control within Penrhyn Hall, the streets surrounding the building were in an uproar. During his speech, according to the newspaper, a mob hurled stones through the windows, there was 'a continuous chorus of song, patriotic and other...' accompanied by a cornet. All this was evidently something more than a spontaneous demonstration.

After the meeting, accompanied by a strong police escort, Lloyd George emerged to be faced by a boiling crowd shouting 'God Save the Queen.' One loyal subject, evading the police, struck Lloyd George heavily on the head with a stick. Fortunately the blow was partly deflected by his top hat, but he was nevertheless momentarily stunned. The police hustled him into a nearby High Street cafe and then took up guard at the front door, allowing the besieged pro-Boer eventually to escape from the rear.[142] Lloyd George was much affected by the events of 11 April. He had come to expect popularity in his own constituency at least and in Glasgow the crowd's anger was directed at others, genuine pacifists, while he had calmed the crowd. 'The mob was seized with drunken madness' he wrote Herbert Lewis a few days after the Bangor meeting, 'and the police were helpless. I mean to try another meeting at Caernarvon next Thursday week. One must not allow this sort of ruffianism even a temporary triumph. Could you come there? They won't molest you. They let Bryn off this last affair never even booing him. All their hatred just now is concentrated on my wretched head.'[143]

Despite this gloominess the annual meeting of the Caernarvon District Liberal Association on 24 April went off successfully and Lloyd George was reelected to represent the constituency on the Welsh Liberal Council. In his speech to the association Lloyd George brought up the question that would henceforth preoccupy most of his attention in speeches on the war until the spring of 1901, the matter of the annexation of the Boer Republics. Since the capture of the capital of the Orange Free State, Bloemfontein, on 13 March the question of the disposition of the two little nations had been a public topic. Although the government had not announced any plans, it was clear by mid-March that there would be no negotiated settlement with the Boer states and that their territories would be taken under the Union Jack once their troops left the field. (Annexation of the Orange Free State, to be called henceforth the Orange River Colony, was finally announced on 29 May.) Lloyd George never went as far as the more radical pro-Boers, such as Leonard Courtney or Henry Labouchere, in demanding that the little republics be given complete independence. At Caernarvon he reminded his audience of Gladstone's settlement of 1884, essentially authority for all internal affairs, and warned that annexations would further alienate already hostile world opinion. He explained his failure to vote supplies by saying that he could support a war for equal rights or to clear Natal of invaders (as indeed he had done in 1899) but he would not support a war of aggression.[144]

On 18 May news reached London that Mafeking, under siege since 13 October, had been relieved. Despite the town's negligible strategic value, on the border of Transvaal and Bechuanaland, the raising of the siege sent all England and Wales into hysterical celebration. North Wales appears to have been no less affected than the rest of the nation. J. Hugh Edwards reports that the mayor and corporation of Pwllheli attended the festivities in their robes of office while Nevin sent a congratulatory message to the Queen. There were stories that effigies of the local Member of Parliament were publicly burned.[145]

The Mafeking frenzy, inauspicious for anyone with muted enthusiasm for the war, was followed in the next three weeks by a succession of victories. On 31 May Johannesburg was captured and on 5 June, Pretoria, the Transvaal capital. Finally, with Kruger now in flight, the Boers, retreating to the east along the railway to Delagoa Bay, fought their last substantial coordinated engagement on 11 and 12 June. By 13 June they had disappeared. The South African War seemed to be over.

This cessation of organized fighting in the Transvaal meant renewed political maneuver in Great Britain. Chamberlain, as Lloyd George and many others had anticipated, began to press the Cabinet for a dissolution. Part of his haste proceeded from the confusion within the Liberal party, which seemed to be without a leader or policy, but part also derived from his knowledge of the well known British generosity of spirit which, when combined with an equally marked tendency toward fecklessness, would soon manifest itself in a national debate about the terms of peace. The jingoism of the Mafeking celebration could fade as quickly as it had erupted and the policy of annexation, pronounced by Lord Salisbury at the end of May, could reunite Liberals. Even those who had supported the war, notably Asquith, sought for a formula which would reassert British ascendancy without extinguishing Boer independence.[146]

VI

For Lloyd George the last months of the parliamentary session of 1900 were a time of consolidation of his position on the war. He gave up the denunciation of the fruitless negotiations that had preceded the conflict. They were pointless after the war began and worse, unprofitable while the Boers were winning. Now he settled upon what remained his line until the peace: that the war, even if begun for the creditable reasons of the protection of English rights, had become a matter of naked aggression and despoliation, with Chamberlain as the chief barbarian.

Briefly the rapid, shifting political current took him close again to the anti-war pacifists and the Irish, with whom he joined in the spring of 1900 in opposing the estimates. (There may have been method in this. He would need Irish help in the election he was convinced was approaching. He duly received the public support of John Dillon who urged all Irishmen in Caernarvon District to vote for Lloyd George as a 'strong supporter of nationalist causes.')[147] At the same time he considered briefly the idea of seeking adoption in radical Merioneth, a seat held by O.M. Edwards since the death of Tom Ellis, whose admiration for Cecil Rhodes would have been an embarrassment had he lived to see the war.[148] Edwards, a former editor of *Cymru Fydd* and an expert in education, found the House of Commons, in which he never made a speech, uncongenial and announced his retirement within a year. There was a sharp fight within the constituency association during the adoption of his successor, A. Osmond Williams, a wealthy landowner and Churchman, in the solid Liberal seat. At some point a group of dissidents evidently approached Lloyd George. (In 1909 with Lloyd George in the Cabinet, Williams became Lord Lieutenant of Merionethshire, Constable of Harlech and a baronet. The next year, not surprisingly, he retired and the seat went to a humbler nonconformist and future Coalition Liberal, H. Hayden Jones.)

In early June Lloyd George made one of his last public appearances in support of the general pacifist position on the war at a meeting in the public hall in Liskeard, Cornwall, in Liberal Unionist Leonard Courtney's constituency. The speech was under the auspices of the South African Conciliation Committee, which Courtney had founded immediately after the war broke out. Courtney, who had held the seat for a quarter of a century, had recently been rejected for readoption by his constituency association. At Liskeard with A.T. Quiller-Couch, whose *Oxford Book of English Verse* had just appeared, and who was, like Courtney, a Cornishman, with Emily Hobhouse, daughter of a Cornish Archdeacon, and Eleanor Robinson, Lloyd George received another dangerous lesson in physical violence. Pandemonium raged from the beginning of the meeting. Miss Hobhouse was unable to speak, drowned out by foot stomping, the singing of 'Soldiers of the Queen,' and 'Rule Britannia' and occasionally the 'Doxology' and 'Trelawney'.

When Lloyd George arose to make an attempt to speak, forty to fifty young patriots stormed the platform. Lloyd George courageously stood his ground and engaged the youths in a shouting match. But when the interrupters realized the speaker was unwilling to withdraw they began to pile a barricade of chairs on the stage. Meanwhile a soldier in uniform was paraded about the hall on the shoulders of the mob. Lloyd George retaliated by pulling away the pile of chairs, which enraged the crowd who now attacked him personally by bumping and shoving and finally by throwing chairs in all directions. Eventually Lloyd George and the party left the hall.[149]

After the meeting, Lloyd George dismissed the event, except to exaggerate the number of attackers. 'I have just returned from the Liskeard meeting—a very stormy one,' he wrote his brother on 6 July. 'Stormed platform—wouldn't listen to anybody. Simply 100 to 150 hobbledehoys. The bulk of the meeting was with us. Assured it will do good. Courtney was very pleased.'[150] He had unquestionably, as he would show many times again, exemplary physical bravery. He had resisted the intimidation of an enraged and probably drunken mob and had retired only when it became clear that there was no chance of making a speech. Yet the Liskeard experience had an effect. Thereafter Lloyd George took precautions to protect his meetings. During the election campaign in North Wales the platform was usually guarded by stalwart Irishmen. More important he now separated himself altogether from the doctrinal pacifist group who opposed the war on moral grounds. Indeed after Liskeard he appears to have given up speaking about the war entirely on public platforms until after the election and began again to concentrate again on temperance. He could not, to be sure, avoid the war during the electoral campaign in Caernarvon District, but he was careful to separate the soldiers, notably Herbert Kitchener who was emerging in the summer as Britain's most energetic commander and who would succeed Roberts as Commander in Chief in October, from the politicians, above all Chamberlain. After Liskeard the duel between these two men achieved a ferocity and brilliance seldom seen in the House of Commons.

But also he began carefully to modify his position on the war and moved into step with the center of his party, or rather he began to develop a position on the war that the center eventually could take. From the summer of 1900 on, Lloyd George provided a method for the opposition to attack the government without attacking the war. In December 1900, after the Khaki election, he gave his last speech on behalf of the South African Conciliation Committee at Liverpool and was well received. Thereafter he appeared most regularly at official Liberal gatherings or occasionally on the temperance or disestablishment platforms, reaching out to both sides of troubled Liberalism, attempting to find areas of agreement between them. The burden of his strategy always was to carry the attack against the government, to separate, for party purposes, the army in South Africa which could be applauded or sympathized with according to one's taste, from the Unionist ministry in Whitehall. The opposition, he argued, must force the battle upon the government benches.

Arguably the new strategy began on 25 July, on a motion in supply committee by Wilfred Lawson, to reduce the salary of the Colonial Secretary by £100. Lawson was an old temperance reformer who had spoken for Lloyd George in Caernarvon District on the occasion of his first election and was an extreme pro-Boer. His amendment was supported by a number of other pacifists of the Stop The War Committee, Labouchere,

Robert Reid, and by Leonard Courtney and eventually by Lloyd George. The amendment was worded as a general attack on the war, that government policy was that of 'the free booter, the filibusterer, the burglar and the Boxer.' Lloyd George was not associated with the sponsors to the amendment and spoke only late in the debate after the Colonial Secretary, although he had of course been voting consistently against service estimates throughout the spring. Chamberlain made a speech of injured innocence, saying in effect that he was aware he was profoundly mistrusted, but could not understand why. This provoked Lloyd George's intervention. He jeered at Chamberlain's affectation of hurt feelings. The Colonial Secretary knew perfectly well why people distrusted him. His present speech was directed not at South Africa but was purely for the hustings.

> It was an electioneering performance. I venture to say that there is no worse eyeglass than the ballot box; and it was through that eyeglass that the Right Honourable Gentleman has been looking....

Although newspapers had been printing rumors of a coming surprise election for weeks, and Lloyd George had been anticipating one privately since April, this public statement was a surprise not least of all to the leader of the party, Sir Henry Campbell-Bannerman.[151] The peroration of Lloyd George's speech presaged Campbell-Bannerman's attack on methods of barbarism almost a year later and accurately predicted the tactics of blockhouse sweeps and concentration camps. Lloyd George admitted some justification for the war while denouncing the government that made it. 'We went into the war for equal rights,' he said, 'we are prosecuting it for annexation.' There could be something to be said for an unselfish war, but

> when you enter upon a war purely and simply for plunder, I know nothing which is more degrading to the country or more hideous in effects on the mind and character of the people engaged in it... you entered into these two Republics for philanthropic purposes and remained to commit burglary.... Our critics say you are not going to war for equal rights and to establish fair play, but to get hold of the gold fields; and you have justified that criticism of our enemies.... But worst of all, a change has been affected in the character of the war. Up to a certain point it was conducted with considerable chivalry and, so far as war can be so conducted, with apparent good temper on both sides. A war of annexation, however, against a proud people must be a war of extermination and that is unfortunately what it seems we are committing ourselves to—burning homesteads and turning women and children out of their homes.

In effect, the war, which officially was expected to end, would instead become more terrible.

This was the policy of Spain in Cuba, he concluded. The Colonial Secretary was in a

> great hurry to go to the country before the facts are known.... The Rt. Honourable Gentleman may not be a statesman but he is an expert electioneer and in his desire to go to the country before the country

realizes what the war means he is the one man who pronounces the deepest condemnation upon his own proceedings.[152]

The debate ended with the Liberals in confusion. Soon after Lloyd George spoke Campbell-Bannerman rose to say that as he could not agree with the extreme views of the mover of the amendment he could not support it, but equally to vote against it would suggest a confidence in the Colonial Secretary that he certainly did not possess. Therefore he would abstain. Grey leaped up to say that he and his friends would oppose the amendment and vote with the Unionists. As a result the Liberals split into three almost equal groups. Forty Liberals voted against the amendment, 31 supported it while 35 followed Campbell-Bannerman in walking out.

The Lawson amendment is often taken as the winter of Liberal fortunes in the controversy over the South African War. That evening R.B. Haldane wrote a long letter to Rosebery inviting him now to step forward and assume the leadership that so surely would be his.[153] There was speculation on both sides of the House that Campbell-Bannerman would resign and reports that he had told a small group of leaders that he could not continue to lead a party so divided.[154] But the realities were not so horrifying. Campbell-Bannerman had made clear in his speech that it was the connection of Lawson and Courtney with the pacifist committees, already proscribed by the Liberals, that made him refrain from voting for the Lawson amendment and he had resolutely refused Herbert Gladstone's suggestion that he vote against it. He had no intention of resigning and two weeks later, with parliament still in session, he left imperturbably for Marienbad.

But second, it is important to remember that the struggle between the Liberal imperialists and the pro-Boers was really about the leadership and future of the party, only symbolically about South Africa. Lloyd George's tactic, whether he realized it at the time or not, was to force the 'limps' into a position of party disloyalty by voting with the Unionists. If for the moment he embarrassed his chief, in the long run his unrelenting assault upon Chamberlain would rally Liberals around him and the Liberal imperialists would find, as indeed they did, that instead of isolating Campbell-Bannerman, they were themselves isolated. Whether Lloyd George himself preferred C.-B. or Rosebery remains a mystery. He rarely mentioned the former in this period either publicly or privately while he spoke of Rosebery constantly. He was certainly impatient with Gladstonian Liberalism, and had been so for many years, and he cautiously admired Rosebery's apparent willingness to entertain new ideas such as Home Rule All Round. But whoever was leader, he clearly wanted to hold the Liberal party together, not to divide it as the 'limps' seemed to desire. Thus in the months after the election, while referring approvingly to Rosebery's policies in public speeches, he emerged also as the chief behind-the-scenes antagonist of Robert Perks, the Liberal imperialists' parliamentary strategist, who by the spring of 1901 was referring to his opposition as 'the Lloyd George people.'[155]

In the few days remaining in the session Lloyd George led the attack on Chamberlain. His assaults were wild, unsubstantiated, often unfair, but effective. On the last day of the first session of 1900, 8 August, he struck

Chamberlain twice, first over Chamberlain's connivance in allowing the newspapers to report that letters siezed after the occupation of Bloemfontein showed that a number of English Liberals had been in correspondence with President Steyn of the Orange Free State, thus implying, without revealing the contents of the letters, treasonable sympathies. The government would withhold unfavorable war news, charged Lloyd George, but when it found something it believed discreditable to its opponents, it would announce possession of such information immediately, without, however, defining precisely what the information was. 'Was this the course of a gentleman?' sneered Lloyd George. 'I venture to say that no other Member on that side of the House would have done such a thing.'[156] (The letters were at last published on 23 August and proved to be innocuous, generally urging the moderate President Steyn to press concessions on Kruger. They provided an overture to the theme of the coming electoral campaign—that the Liberals were either latent or active traitors—but otherwise were soon forgotten.)

However, the second charge against Chamberlain, arising from the report of a committee that had been enquiring into War Office contracts, became a regular source of contention and oratorical violence. This was that a family firm of the Chamberlains, Kynoch's, of which Joe's brother Arthur was chairman, had made excessive profits in War Office contracts for cordite. This charge he did not allow to die; rather he expanded it during the election campaign when it became his customary response to the attack that the Liberals were insufficiently patriotic. In the speech on 8 August, admitting he was proceeding by innuendo as the Colonial Secretary had done with the Bloemfontein letters, he attempted to connect Kynoch's evident prosperity and its high dividends with Joe's war. Those who sought to purify the Transvaal administration, he suggested, should begin with clean hands. (Recent research indicates that Kynoch and Nobel possessed indeed an intimate and perhaps collusive relationship with the War Office but that these conditions were more the result of the Army's antique contracting procedures than of Chamberlain's presence at the Colonial Office. And in fact they antedated the formation of the Salisbury government.[157] There were indeed letters in newspapers affirming this situation at the time.)[158]

These charges against Chamberlain, first made as election propaganda, evolved into a bitter feud angering and wounding both Chamberlain and his family as few political issues were able to do.[159] The pain was worse because Chamberlain knew, and was certain Lloyd George knew, that the charges were unfounded, as would become clear in December during his reply to Lloyd George's amendment to the address. (Chamberlain's younger brother, Arthur, the chairman of Kynoch's, was in fact a Gladstonian Liberal and Home Ruler, Joe's political rival in the Midlands, and after 1903 a strong free trader.) The responsibility for the Kynoch's debate appears to lie with Harold Spender who had noted in the white paper on War Office contracts the constant references to Kynoch's and had told Lloyd George about this while the two were on top of a bus riding from Wandsworth to Westminster. He was able to organize newspaper support, which provided reporters who conducted research for Lloyd George in Somerset House.[160]

Even though this sustained assault on Chamberlain exemplifies again Lloyd George's political daring—the prospect of crossing swords with Joe often made men ill—there was much personal hazard in the sustained denunciation of a popular and powerful figure who was in these years at the pinnacle of his career. How great this was became clear on 18 December 1901 when Lloyd George was nearly killed during a riot in Birmingham. Although much has been written about this episode in terms of the war, it occurred well after attacks on pro-Boers had ceased and Chamberlain always regarded it, as indeed Lloyd George suggested in a speech five years later, as far more the product of outrage against the enemy of a local hero than an expression of jingoism.[161]

But neither was the matter closed more than a dozen years later in a far greater political crisis in Lloyd George's life, when he became marginally involved in speculation in the Marconi Wireless Company, at a time when the British company was negotiating a contract with the government of which he was Chancellor of the Exchequer. He found then that the Kynoch's debate had been neither forgotten nor forgiven. As he himself had shown no mercy as a backbencher when leading a charge against a member of the government, now he could expect none. His own phrases against Chamberlain, 'Caesar's wife,' 'grounds for uneasiness,' 'above suspicion' were quoted against him again and again.[162]

VII

Parliament was prorogued on 8 August 1900, the day Lloyd George first attacked Chamberlain on the Kynoch connection, and the dissolution, as expected, was finally announced on 25 September. Everyone understood that the election, long urged in the Cabinet by Chamberlain, was less the result of any strength in the government, which even the Colonial Secretary admitted was unpopular, than of the apparent disintegration of the opposition. This time it would be every Liberal for himself, a 'soldier's battle' as Winston Churchill described it later.[163]

For Lloyd George this condition was nothing new. His place in the affection of his constituency was his own, not transferable, and was only slightly dependent upon what went on in the rest of the nation. As usual he alternated between confidence and fear about his chances. In the last days of the session he busied himself attending to local vote-getting projects for North Wales: £5,000 for the Caernarvonshire Council to lend to a local firm for the building of a light railway in Nevin; £20,000 from the Board of Trade toward a breakwater in Pwllheli; thousands more for a waterworks at Caernarvon.[164] In these years, and indeed until the war, Lloyd George was an active constituency man. He was attentive to local patronage, always taking care that notices of his activity appeared in the newspapers. Even though his interest in Wales generally had begun to decline, he maintained solidly the contacts and loyalties that he possessed in the six towns of Caernarvon District. 'Coming between Lloyd George and his countrymen is like coming between a tree and its bark,' noted T.P. O'Connor in a newspaper column on 20 August in a survey of electoral prospects of various MPs. Lloyd George gleefully quoted this remark to Maggie.[165]

He felt safe enough to remain in London for three weeks after the House of Commons separated, negotiating for the purchase of a newspaper to support pro-Boer opinion in London.[166] He had a friendship with David Edwards, who had worked on the *North Wales Observer* in Caernarvon for a half dozen years in the late eighties and was now with the *Daily News* in London. Together the two sought to find money to purchase the *Echo*, an old and well-established evening paper which centered on nonconformist and radical causes. Unfortunately, a well-to-do and eccentric reformer, F.W. Lawrence, was also bidding for the paper and in 1901 obtained a controlling interest, subsequently installing himself as editor. (Within five years the newspaper was bankrupt.) This was no doubt a disappointment but by August Lloyd George already had learned, presumably from Edwards, that a far more influential paper, the *Daily News*, might be for sale. 'That' he wrote to Maggie on 31 August, 'would be a tremendous deal.'[167]

By early September, Lloyd George was in Wales busily mending political fences on the temperance and disestablishment circuit, and saying as little as possible about the war. His opponent this time was Henry Platt, a Bangor banker who was a colonel in the militia and customarily used his military title. He was by no means a negligible opponent, having been High Sheriff of Caernarvonshire, as well as of Anglesey, and Mayor of Bangor. Moreover, he had contested North Caernarvonshire against Rathbone in 1885 and 1886 and had been one of the men considered by the Caernarvon District Unionists to replace Edmund Swetenham, before the latter's convenient death caused the by-election that brought Lloyd George to the House of Commons.[168] He was, in effect, not the 'ghost' that Lloyd George termed him in a letter to Lewis on 20 September. (Curiously he appeared on Asquith's list of men to be ennobled if the House of Lords rejected the Parliament Bill.)

In this letter Lloyd George was reasonably hopeful. He had had some good meetings, he said, although difficulties lay ahead. 'Men who had speculated heavily in South Africa threaten my life—I mean politically. However I believe I will lick them.'[169] However as his canvass progressed he grew nervous. 'Between ourselves,' he wrote to Lewis on 26 September, the day after the dissolution, 'I am not by any means safe yet. There are 15 important defections in Pwllheli alone.'[170]

For Lloyd George the 1900 election marked the first time he was unable to make his opponent and the Church and landlordism the issue in the contest. On this occasion, as he well understood, he would have to defend himself. Hence the early weeks of the campaign found him virtually ignoring the war. He bombarded newspapers with the simplest of all appeals to North Wales, self-interest. 'What has Mr. Lloyd George done for his constituents?' asked a column in the *North Wales Observer* on 28 September. There followed a list of occasions on which the influential Member for Caernarvon District had caused the government in London to spend English taxpayers' money on Welsh local improvements. The new Caernarvon waterworks would cost £20,000 but as the Local Government Board was supplying £18,000 it would cost the city's rate payers only £2,000, and so on.[171] In another article it was pointed out that the local Member had really spent much more time worrying about domestic social questions in the recent session than about the Boers. 'Judging from the manner in which Mr. Lloyd George's action in relation to the war in South Africa is spoken of,' announced an article in the breathless tones that always foreshadow the answer to a question that no one has asked, 'one might imagine that this has been the one topic to which he devoted most attention in the House of Commons. An examination of the facts show that this is not so.' Appended was a list of eight topics from agriculture to Welsh harbors which altogether Lloyd George had discussed a total of 186 times.[172]

These were rather awkward attempts to camouflage pro-Boerism. In his speeches he was more forthright. Generally Lloyd George disposed of the war at the beginning of his address by saying that the war could have been prevented and that its effect had been the smothering of social reform in Britain. From this it was an easy transition to the denunciation of the government's inattention to the needs of the people, usually accompanied by remarks upon the commercial interests of the Chamberlain family. On 15 September, speaking at Nevin, where it was reported he had been burned in effigy during the Mafeking celebrations, Lloyd George admitted that he might be mistaken about the war, 'but it is an honest mistake' and at Caernarvon during his adoption meeting, he proposed responsible government within the British empire for the Transvaal, thus accepting the principle of annexation.[173] Lloyd George's moderating position was subsequently noted and denounced by the radical pacifist wing of the pro-Boers.[174]

Early in October he returned again to the question of land reform, explaining to his audience the concept of the taxation of the unearned increment. He did not say that he was in favor of it, only that it deserved study. At this meeting also, only four days before the poll, Lloyd George announced the only stunt of the campaign, a proposal that he and Colonel Platt meet on the same platform.[175] Theoretically this was to allow Lloyd George to answer charges that he had insulted the Queen's officers and soldiers as Platt had asserted in an election broadside. The proposal was quickly squashed by Platt's agent, H. Lloyd Carter, who said that the denunciation of Lloyd George for insulting the Queen's army had not been in question until now and that it was too late to change his candidate's plans.[176]

The polling in Caernarvon District was set for 6 October, relatively early in the election period. The results were Lloyd George 2,412, Platt, 2,116. The news was greeted with a tumultuous celebration. The ecstasy of the population, the continual shouts of 'Lloyd George forever' were reported by Harold Spender to the *Manchester Guardian* on 8 October, and they remained stamped so clearly in his mind that they reappeared two decades later in his biography when his subject was Prime Minister.[177] After a short rest the victor went off to Mongomeryshire to help A.C. Humphreys-Owen, who had been a secret competitor for the seat in Caernarvon District in 1890 and who disliked Lloyd George intensely.[178]

Invariably, historians have noted that this was his largest majority so far and that the turnout was larger than ever before. This is not surprising in view of the fact that the population of Caernarvon District increased by about three thousand in the ten years 1891-1901 and that the electorate similarly went up by about five hundred. Lloyd George had received 52% of the total vote in 1892 and 1895. In 1900 he received 53%. In comparison, for Wales as a whole, the Liberals got 56.8% in 1895 and 58.5% in 1900. Herbert Lewis, as earnest a pro-Boer as Lloyd George, doubled his majority in Flint District, and Bryn Roberts, equally staunch, was unopposed in South Caernarvonshire next door. The election was hardly the revulsion against imperialism that Lloyd George argued it had been in his speech from the balcony of the Caernarvon Town Hall. Only 6 of 25 sitting Welsh Liberals at the dissolution could be counted as pro-Boers on the basis of past speeches and votes.[179] All, to be sure, were returned, except O.M. Edwards who did not stand. But so too, after all, were Ellis Griffith in Anglesey and Lloyd Morgan in Carmarthenshire West, both imperialists who also ran unopposed. But then Alfred Spicer, a Liberal imperialist who had voted against C.B., was defeated by a Unionist. The conclusion for Lloyd George must be that he had never been in much danger in Caernarvon District, and that the war affected his electoral fortunes very little, as indeed was probably the case throughout Wales. His majority was infinitesimal in Welsh Liberal terms, but it was absolutely solid. In fact, the attack in Bangor, Lloyd George thought later, probably helped it.[180] Only the passage of time would increase it and virtually no catastrophe, outside Wales at least, could have diminished it.

Nationally the Liberals suffered more than in Wales; the Conservatives won back a few seats lost in the uninterrupted series of by-election disasters they had suffered since 1895. The pro-Boers in the House of Commons were reduced, by non-reselection, resignation, electoral defeat, from 42 to 30.[181] The imperialists had hoped that the election would bring Rosebery forward as a leader and many observers felt it had done so. J.A. Spender, presumably speaking for Asquith who had generally kept himself clear of the anti-Campbell-Bannerman conspiracies, announced in the *Contemporary Review* in November that the election had weakened the party but strengthened Rosebery. The former Prime Minister had now the duty either to step forward or to announce his retirement.[182] On 13 November Asquith wrote to Campbell-Bannerman urging him to invite Rosebery back into Liberalism. Two days later, at Dundee, Campbell-Bannerman extended a clear but guarded invitation. He would open the door, C.B. wrote his Chief Whip Herbert Gladstone, but not ring the dinner bell.[183] A few days later he told Leicester Harmsworth he would be willing to serve under Rosebery with conditions.[184]

Lloyd George's part in all this political maneuvering combined that of guidon and censor. Although in no sense privy to party secrets, he had a view of Liberal tactics which demanded unrelenting struggle against Chamberlain, with no concessions intended as peace offerings to the imperialists. But he sought also to avoid the extremes of the radical pacifists so as to make the Roseberyites' return to the party as painless as possible. He was always careful to separate the soldiers, who were brave, from the politicians who were corrupt, the suffering caused by the war from the war itself, and the essential humanity of British civilization from the debauchery of English political life attendant upon imperialist jingoism. So he drove forward, displaying always unremitting truculence against the Unionists, exemplified by Chamberlain, but never allowing himself to be pushed into out and out pacifism by the extremist pro-Boers. Equally he never hesitated to depart from his party's leadership when he saw it compromising in order to achieve a superficial unity. Thus on 10 December 1900 with the Whips' support he moved an amendment to the address in the new parliament declaring that ministers 'ought to have no interest, direct or indirect, in any firm or company competing for contracts with the crown....' (These words were quoted back to him repeatedly during the Marconi affair.) He followed this with a scathing attack upon Chamberlain, broadening the charges first made on 8 August to include equity interest acquired by the Colonial Secretary's trustee, the Birmingham Trust Company, in other firms. This foray caused Chamberlain eventually to make before the House of Commons what was clearly a humiliating public account of his wealth. In its leader on that day's debate, *The Times* referred sharply to the 'cowardliness' of the Liberal front bench which obviously 'was willing to wound but afraid to strike,' and who left the 'dirty work' to Lloyd George, 'a free lance.'[185] This amendment received considerable support among the Liberal imperialists anxious to prove their doctrinal purity.

In the winter of 1900-01 the intensity of the conflict in South Africa grew rapidly. On 21 December, Herbert Kitchener, now Commander in Chief, announced to his officers the policy not only of burning Boer farms and livestock, which had been occurring for months, but also of interning civilian inhabitants in concentration camps managed by the army. However, in early February, as the veldt was becoming dotted with columns of terrified Boer civilians fleeing the British, he followed this with a proposal to the most moderate of the Boer commanders, Louis Botha, that the two men meet to discuss peace terms.

Between these two events, in early January, Lloyd George staged an astonishing coup, angering the Liberal imperialists and bringing profound satisfaction to Campbell-Bannerman, by securing control of the *Daily News* for the moderate pro-Boers, placing himself on the board, dismissing the old editor, E.T. Cook, and after a short interval, installing in his place R.C. Lehmann, who began assembling around him a talented staff of younger pro-Boer radicals who would provide in the next decade the intellectual framework for Liberal social reform. There was some fear among the Liberal leadership that the new management of the paper might use its power to destroy the uneasy truce that had been building at the end of the previous year. Lloyd George, however, was willing to behave. The paper's 'tone, I believe, will be moderate,' wrote Campbell-Bannerman to Bryce on 18 January, noting also however, that its capture had caused 'a pretty flutter in Imp. Lib. quarters.'

> I saw J.M. [John Morley, who evidently was first invited to become editor] just before the public announcement was made, as I was passing through London. He was not in it but was consulted, and he told me that Lehmann and Lloyd George were inclined to declare a new departure and carry fire and sword into the Imp. Country. But J.M. told them that the note for the present time was 'unity of party,' that there should be no slanging at friends, but gentle argument and persuasion, seasoned with lively attacks on the government. They admitted and promised. Let us hope the result will prove right.[186]

For a time at least the *Daily News* gave Lloyd George much prestige among all Liberals. He had now to be courted and consulted. He, in turn, tried to conform so long as the Liberal center remained steadfast. On 15 February 1901, he put down an amendment to the address of the new parliament proposing that the government should make clear to the Boers that 'subject to the overlordship of the British crown...they would receive...full local autonomy' in their lands 'at the cessation of hostilities.'[187] This sounded moderate enough, but the qualification of immediate autonomy was bound, as no doubt it was intended, to cause trouble. Both Chamberlain and Salisbury had made clear that self-government for the defeated Boers could come, if at all, only after an extended period of good behavior. The Liberal imperialists would be forced to make a choice. Some welcomed this challenge and hoped to repeat the coup of the previous summer, dividing the party three ways. 'We propose not to abstain,' wrote Robert Perks to Rosebery on 15 February, 'but to speak and vote against Lloyd George.'[188] However, Campbell-Bannerman saw potential damage and wrote on the same day to Herbert Gladstone protesting the 'impolicy of the amendment.' 'Can you,' he asked his Whip, 'communicate with Lloyd George and discourage his idea of moving? He is very anxious to help.'[189] Gladstone prevailed and *The Times* stated the next day that Lloyd George would not move his amendment. Campbell-Bannerman was well satisfied. He understood better than anyone that as the pro-Boer wing of the party gained strength, he did also. 'The amendment given in by Lloyd George was drawn by Courtney,' he wrote to Lord Ripon after learning of its withdrawal.

> As a proposition I cordially agree with it; but after much colloquy and some pressure, he has promised not to move it. Harcourt, Morley, Labby and nearly all our sound men were against the amendment; my main objection being that it was not in the interests of peace and good feeling that such a reasonable amendment should be deliberately rejected....I am convinced that, so to speak, the center of gravity is palpably shifted forward. I have no complaint to make of the way I have been met even by the extremest of men — Lloyd George, H.J. Wilson, C.P. Scott, Channing, Pirie etc.[190]

In the end Lloyd George behaved. On 18 February when his amendment would have been called he contented himself with a conventionally violent speech, loudly applauded by the Irish, denouncing army brutality in the treatment of civilians and calling one officer a disgrace to his uniform. It would have been far better, commented the next speaker, the new Member for Oldham, Winston Churchill, who was making his maiden speech, if Lloyd George had moved his moderate amendment and forgotten his ferocious address. One would have to conclude that the moderation was that of his friends, but the violence was his own. Both speeches were praised extravagantly by the *Daily News*.

Through most of the spring of 1901 Lloyd George maintained a careful central position on the war. He repeatedly praised the Kitchener-Botha negotiations and blamed Chamberlain for wrecking them. He condemned the rising national expenditure and the postponement of social questions.

On the whole he said little about the war except to deplore its continuance. Clearly the public mood was changing. Everywhere his receptions were enthusiastic, even in the Midlands. For example, at Agricultural Hall in Wolverhampton on 23 April, 'the audience rose enmasse and received him with ringing cheers' which changed to laughter when he remarked upon the trepidation he felt coming into the Birmingham sphere of influence, 'Rob Roy's country.'[191] Many speeches now dealt with the old topics of temperance and disestablishment and in May, in the fourth issue of the *New Liberal Review,* he was allowed to review his plan for legislative devolution.[192]

This era of good feeling abruptly came to an end on 24 May when Milner arrived in England for a rest, only to find himself to be instead the focus of ceremonies of royal proportions and to be loaded with honors. His presence in London, and the celebrations staged on his behalf, revived antagonism among the Liberals, the more so as some imperialists, Asquith, a friend of Milner, and Grey seemed also to regard him as a hero. Moreover, the ship that brought Milner carried in addition Emily Hobhouse, the friend of Leonard Courtney, who had gone to South Africa with the Rowntrees in December 1900 to investigate conditions among the Boer civilians in the concentration camps. After her return she toured London, visiting any politician who would see her, telling the tragic tale of mismanagement, neglect, sickness and appalling infant mortality. Among those she interviewed were Lloyd George, who urged her to publish her findings as soon as possible.[193] In the second week of June, she met Campbell-Bannerman. The Liberal party leader's biographers agree that it was the information, the terrible revelations, brought by Emily Hobhouse, not any consideration of politics, that induced him, only a few days later on 14 June in a speech at the Holborn Restaurant, to denounce the concentration camps and by implication the entire conduct of the war as 'methods of barbarism.'[194] To prove that he had suffered no momentary lapse into indignation, Campbell-Bannerman repeated the phrase three days later when Lloyd George moved an adjournment of the House to discuss the treatment of Boer noncombatants. Fifty Liberals, led by Asquith, abstained on Lloyd George's motion.[195] Lloyd George, in an interview with the *Liverpool Daily Post,* emphasized that his motion for adjournment had been submitted after careful consideration with influential members of the party. He did not intend to attack his imperialist colleagues. He was, personally, friendly with Asquith.[196]

To the Roseberyites, Campbell-Bannerman's unusual violence of language, and Lloyd George's resolution following it, were a cause for consternation and panic. Asquith, Grey, and Haldane, recorded Beatrice Webb, herself no admirer of Campbell-Bannerman, had been 'working at the bar, enjoying themselves in London "society" and letting things slide.'

> Suddenly they woke up to find the Liberal Party in the House of Commons under the leadership of Lloyd George declaring itself definitely against the war, accusing Milner and the Army of gross inhumanity, and asserting the right of the Boers to some kind of independence. Campbell-Bannerman had been captured.[197]

This was not far from the truth although the dimensions of the victory appeared larger than they were. Lloyd George had not 'captured' the party leader although many people, including perhaps himself, thought so. Asquith wrote to Perks, on 19 July, 1901: 'The banquet of last Friday, [i.e. 14 June at the Holborn restaurant], incidents and consequences seem to me to suggest that it is time for those of us who are not willing that the official and propagandist machinery of the party should be captured by Lloyd George, to bestir ourselves.'[198] In fact Campbell-Bannerman, prompted by a horrible example of injustice, simply had been driven to express feelings he had long kept to himself in terms similar to those that Lloyd George had used for many months. His opposition to the war was not new. The result nonetheless was the consolidation of imperialist forces. Asquith now joined openly and he and Grey sought to pull together their followers by the organization of a series of dinners, while continuing also their futile attempts to overcome the invincible indecision of Rosebery, whom they hoped would be at least the prophet, if not the messiah, of Liberalism in the future. They had either to conquer the party or to be driven from it. 'We are fighting for our lives,' R.B. Haldane told Beatrice Webb as he attempted to enlist her husband, Sydney, as a member of the Rosebery cause.[199] In the end Sydney agreed and published the manifesto of the group in the September issue of the *Nineteenth Century*.[200]

By the summer of 1901 the division of political opinion on the war, except for the radical pro-Boers, who demanded immediate independence for the South Africa republics, had settled down to the question of whether the Boers should be offered a negotiated settlement with the promise of self-government soon after the war or whether they should be pursued until they surrendered unconditionally. On these two positions the lines hardened. On 19 June, two days after the debate on his motion for adjournment, Lloyd George spoke in London at Queen's Hall to a meeting which was to be addressed by a member of the Cape Colony parliament, J.W. Sauer, who had come to Great Britain early in the spring with Francis X. Merriman to plead the cause of Boer nationhood. In his speech Lloyd George attempted to stay within the limits he had drawn for himself, proposing a resolution calling upon the government to make such an offer to the Boers as 'brave and freedom loving people could honourably accept,' in effect, essentially the resolution he had put down and withdrawn as an amendment to the Address in February.[201] At Queen's Hall he was immediately interrupted by a resolution from the floor by H.A.B. Dixon of Battersea demanding total and immediate independence for the Boers.

The Queen's Hall meeting saw a considerable disturbance outside the building as well as a number of interruptions from the gallery inside, although these appear to have been directed principally at John Dillon who, speaking after Lloyd George, compared British behavior in South Africa to the cruelty of Spain in Cuba. Nevertheless, as Lloyd George told the *Review of Reviews* three years later, he was unable any longer to hire halls in London.[202] This may have reflected surviving jingoism in London, but as Lloyd George was neither the chairman of the meeting, who was Labouchere, nor the principal speaker, who was Sauer, more likely the boycott was a part of the general detestation for the Member from Caernarvon Distict that grew among London's well-to-do and which lasted well into 1902. He was cheered, to be sure, in popular tabernacles, but in the middle class circles into which he was taken by his recreation, legal work, and children's education, he was an outcast. 'Nothing I could ever go through again would be as bad as that,' he told Lucy Masterman late in 1910. 'My business was all going to wrack and ruin. I dared not venture on any golf course, I should have been stoned, and it was a pretty bad business making up your mind to attack Chamberlain. He once nearly came at me across the House. Oh, it was a bad time.' He became so poor, Harold Spender wrote, that toward the end of the war he was preparing to leave his house in Wandsworth and move into a worker's flat. To make money, Maggie let the Criccieth house on the Portmadoc Road and moved in with her parents, next door. At the same time he refused, with scorn, an £800 per year directorship offered him by a wealthy London department store owner.[203] Twelve year old Richard Lloyd George, at school at Dulwich College, suffered verbal and physical attacks as well. After some hesitation, he told his mother who removed him to a school in Portmadoc.[204]

As the session of 1901 drew to an end, the political writers of London were according Lloyd George the regard of an emerging but mysterious political power, visibly potent, yet so far incomprehensible. Was he a consolidating or dividing force in Liberalism? Did he want to unite the party, or lead a rebellion? He 'has risen at a bound to the actual leadership of a very considerable party in the House' concluded the *Newcastle Daily Leader*, which, it must be admitted, frequently applauded Lloyd George. 'He is the stuff of which revolutions are made.... when this war is over all eyes will turn to Mr. Lloyd George in inquiry as to what his future is to be.'[205]

The issue in the struggle for the soul of Liberalism lay in the matter of definition or doctrine. Who were the orthodox church and who were the dissenters? Had Campbell-Bannerman been captured in fact by Lloyd George as his increasingly pro-Boer speeches seemed to show or had alternatively the Member for Caernarvon District taken his troops into the leader's camp? In reality nothing had happened, argued the *Sheffield Independent*, also a Liberal paper, shortly after Lloyd George's adjournment motion on 17 June. Lloyd George was the leader of one 'cult' within the party; Asquith was the leader of the other. But, the paper concluded, the 'Liberal "Upper Ten" do not like him partly because of his pro-Boer sympathies, partly because he is so divisive and partly because he has too many friends with pens in their hands.'[206]

This distinctly unfriendly and somewhat unfair appreciation of Lloyd George, which also designated him as one of the half dozen shortest men in the House of Commons, contained nevertheless much truth. Campbell-Bannerman had called a reconciliation meeting at the Reform Club on 9 July where he had demanded, and received, a vote of confidence from his followers amid many protestations of loyalty and denials of conspiracy or cabal. Three days later Campbell-Bannerman was at Pontyprydd, in Alfred Thomas's constituency, speaking to a packed meeting which received him with cheers after choruses of 'For He's A Jolly Good Fellow.' Yet when Lloyd George rose to move a vote of thanks and to present a fulsome address from the Caernarvon Boroughs Liberal Association he received a mixed reception of cheers and boos. His speech, concluding with the assertion that C.B. possessed 'the one great and essential qualification in a Liberal leader, of being a Liberal himself', pointed in two directions.[207] The *Sheffield Independent* was entirely correct in its estimate of the distrust of Lloyd George. It could be granted that Campbell-Bannerman was indeed a Liberal of a old fashioned sort, but what was Lloyd George? The *British Weekly*, normally sympathetic to Lloyd George although strongly imperialist, referred to Lloyd George in the summer of 1901 as a 'private', non-party, Member of Parliament, while asserting that he would probably be invited to join the next Liberal government.[208]

Lloyd George was probably more loyal to Campbell-Bannerman than to any Liberal leader he served throughout his career even if the newspapers doubted it. Clearly he questioned the older man's political judgement from time to time, but he took part in none of the conspiracies against him and liked him, which could not be described as his attitude toward other old Gladstonians who eventually appeared in the 1905 Liberal government.

Nevertheless, his connections with the press, which the *Sheffield Independent* had noted, certainly caused problems. Above all there was the difficulty with the party about the management of the *Daily News*. Lloyd George, David Edwards, and Harold Spender, who was still working for the *Manchester Guardian*, had been negotiating for the purchase of the *News* since August, 1900. Chiefly this involved attempting to raise money. Spender recounts sitting in Gatti's with Lloyd George composing letters to two wealthy Liberals, Frank Thomasson and George Cadbury, the former a Bolton cotton mill owner and the latter the Quaker cocoa magnate from Bournville. By mid-December, the promoters had promises from these two of £20,000 or £25,000 each, although the total price including good will was over £100,000.[209] Cadbury, queried again, refused, in a distinctly peremptory letter on 18 December, to do more, although he suggested some names.[210] Consequently there was a scramble in the last weeks of December to obtain smaller sums from other men, mostly Liberal politicians, either as loans or as equity participation. A problem, Spender notes, was that there were many cranks among pro-Boers, stargazers, vegetarians, lovers of animals, and members of unusual religious sects. They would always stipulate that any paper they supported should take on their own cause, and while giving little money, would promise their prayers for its success.[211] John Morley lent money. R.C. Lehmann, barrister-politician-journalist-writer, contributed £10,000. Lloyd George, although he gained a seat on the board of five of which Cadbury became chairman, almost certainly contributed nothing. Nonetheless, by the end of 1900, the money had been raised. On 9 January, E.T. Cook, the paper's imperialist editor, was ejected without warning and on Morley's recommendation, Lehmann became editor, with David Edwards as manager. Although his tenure was only seven months, Lehmann collected at the paper a first rate staff, a number of whom would become the nucleus of the newspaper chorus for the New Liberalism in the next decade: H.W. Massingham, Harold Spender, G.K. Chesterton and his friend C.F.G. Masterman.

The paper had problems in management from the beginning, in

addition to the difficulties attendant upon Cadbury's stipulation that it publish no racing information and take no ads for alcoholic beverages. Lloyd George evidently had hoped that his friend Edwards would become editor. Cadbury, with the greatest financial resources, desired a stronger line on South Africa than Lloyd George wished to take but at the same time through the year of 1901 became increasingly sympathetic to Rosebery's promises of social reform and national efficiency at home. Still the paper lost advertising and circulation because of its unpopular stands in both domestic and imperial affairs and as a result Cadbury's well-filled purse became increasingly important.[212] At last on 18 July, just three days after the unflattering portrait of Lloyd George in the *Sheffield Independent,* Lehmann was replaced as editor by David Edwards who remained manager. Certainly this seemed to many to be Lloyd George's final capture of the newspaper. The two men were close friends at this time. However, Edwards was an even more ardent pro-Boer than Lloyd George but without the latter's reluctant admiration for Rosebery. He refused to enlist the paper under the banner of Liberal unity pressed upon him both by Herbert Gladstone from within the party and by George Cadbury from the directors.

As autumn waned the press, imperialist and otherwise, overwhelmed the public with predictions that Rosebery, at last, intended to drop his mysterious diffidence and step forward to claim the leadership of a new and vigorous Liberal party. Early in November, it was announced that on 16 December he would speak at Chesterfield. This address, the world was given to understand, would be of exceptional importance. With six weeks to wait, the political nation possessed more than adequate time to feed its speculations. The speech itself, when it came, was a combination of stirring eloquence and impenetrable metaphor, providing something for everyone, justice and firmness for the Boers in South Africa, reform, national efficiency, and racial revival at home, with the slate wiped clean of the smudgy marks of Liberal programs of the past. Imperialists and pro-Boers alike applauded. Cadbury was impressed. 'I think the "Daily News" is making a great mistake in not accepting the conciliatory line laid down by Lord Rosebery,' he wrote to Lloyd George on 19 December. 'If you see Spender or Edwards, you might say that I am very much disappointed in their attitude toward Rosebery, and I think that Edwards will have a bad time of it when the directors meet unless they change this attitude.'[213]

Lloyd George, as has been seen, always treated Rosebery with cautious respect, or disrespectful admiration. He compared him to Chamberlain, while recognizing him, as he certainly might have done with Chamberlain, as an asset to the Liberal party. Before the Chesterfield speech he and Herbert Lewis had conspired to induce Rosebery to include a word about devolution, which he was always convinced Rosebery saw as the real alternative to Home Rule.[214] And after the speech, in common with many others, he applauded its sentiments both on the platform and in writing, but equally he was unwilling, or probably unable, to press Edwards and the *Daily News* to overthrow Gladstonian Liberalism in the name of party unity. As a result, in the aftermath of Chesterfield, Cadbury bought the sole proprietorship of the *Daily News* and installed, in January 1902, T.P. Ritzema, proprietor of the *Blackburn Daily Telegraph*, as manager, depriving

Edwards of that post. The next month Ritzema replaced Edwards as editor with the great A.G. Gardner who had been his editor in Blackburn. Lloyd George was now removed from any direct influence on *Daily News* affairs although the paper continued to employ men, Massingham, Masterman, and Spender, with whom he was intimate. But for the moment he was angry and disappointed and in February he announced that he intended to retire from the board.[215] The bitterness lasted well into the spring of 1902. 'After the concert Edwards, Griffith and I went to the Cafe Monico and had a good old talk there,' he wrote to Maggie on 8 March 1902 about a week after Gardner's appointment.

> Edwards thinks they are ruining the D. News. They have dismissed the
> foreign correspondents. Edwards had been told that Spender is not now
> on the staff but is simply an outside contributor. Serve him right if it is
> true. He growled and grumbled quite plenty altho' he had obtained a
> better position than any he had ever previously reached. He is too
> greedy. D.E. says Ritzema is bound to fail. All these changes for the worse
> in the character of the paper are a great personal triumph for Edwards.
> He thinks that gradually Ritzema will get rid of all the first class men and
> rely entirely on third raters.[216]

A month later Spender was still retailing unfavorable gossip about the *Daily News*. Herbert Paul had been forced to resign and Spender felt he might be next.[217]

The Rosebery Chesterfield speech was viewed as a major national event even in a year which had also seen the death of Queen Victoria.[218] It provided, albeit only briefly, one of those rare political beacons in relation to which every active politician had to relate his course, towards it, away or parallel. No one could ignore it. It was the climax of the Liberal feud and to some it seemed for a few weeks either to foreshadow the breakup of the party or, at the very least, the departure of Campbell-Bannerman. But even as he spoke at Chesterfield the ground was crumbling under Rosebery's feet and soon he was left suspended, as it were, in the air, where he remained for the rest of his political life.

As Lloyd George had come to learn, and as Campbell-Bannerman had never doubted, active Liberals in the constituencies did not share the divisions and perturbations so apparent at Westminster. Campbell-Bannerman had mentioned this in June at the Pontyprydd Liberal Club, remarking that he had received many questions in his constituency during and since the election, about the fighting among the Liberals in parliament, which the voters at home were unable to understand.[219] The warmth of his greeting in South Wales was further testimony. After his return from Marienbad in mid-September, Campbell-Bannerman had begun an extended public speaking tour during which he was rewarded with cheering popular support. Sir Henry has 'enormously strengthened his hold on the public during the last two years and especially the past six months,' Lloyd George told an amazed interviewer from the *Pall Mall Gazette* on 3 January 1902, little more than two weeks after the Chesterfield speech while the furor was at its height. The journalist recorded that he 'glanced at the window with a mute appeal for breath' reflecting that 'this was recklessness with a vengeance.' 'You may look as surprised as you like' continued Lloyd George, 'but I have done a lot of platform work and I have been surprised at the success Sir Henry has achieved during this latter campaign of his up and down the country. Since Gladstone we have had no names on our side like Chamberlain, Balfour and Salisbury—I am thinking of Chamberlain in particular—which can thrill an audience into a cheer whenever they are invoked. But Sir Henry, I think, is beginning to strike the Liberal imagination; and though he has never been a fighting man, he has courage of a dogged sort, and when I say he has obtained a triumphant series of meetings I am not using exaggerated language.'[220]

This was not hyperbole. Within the next two weeks Campbell-Bannerman was repeatedly cheered and the name of Rosebery booed at the organizational meeting of the London Liberal Federation in St. James Hall on 13 January. The same demonstrations were repeated a month later at Leicester at the National Liberal Federation where Campbell-Bannerman challenged Rosebery to declare whether he was in or out of the party. Lloyd George believed that Campbell-Bannerman operated from a position of strength. Rosebery should be urged to return to the party and given a post of responsibility (Campbell-Bannerman had visited his rival in Berkeley Square on 23 December and offered him the leadership of the House of Lords) but it should be made clear that he would return to a party headed by Sir Henry and on Sir Henry's terms.[221] Campbell-Bannerman had already won and ought to know it. He should compromise no further.

These assumptions of strength account for Lloyd George's remarkable outburst on 21 January 1902 during the debate on the official Liberal amendment to the address to the throne. This amendment, moved by Sir Fredrick Cawley, who had some reputation as a pro-Boer although he had four sons in uniform, was a weak compromise designed to attract all wings of the party. In calling for an 'early termination to the war and the establishment of a durable peace,' it was not much different from Lloyd George's amendment of the previous year which Campbell-Bannerman had vetoed. However, added to it was the statement that the Liberals were 'prepared to support all measures for the effective prosecution of the war in South Africa.' The result was a blaze of anger among the Irish and a motion by John Dillon to amend the amendment to read that the methods of 'carrying on the war are barbarous and have aroused the indignation of the whole civilized world.'[222]

Lloyd George was disgusted by the limpness of the Cawley amendment and by the timidity of the Liberal front bench that it illustrated. To the delight of the Unionists he rose the next day to say he would support Dillon's amendment and, while speaking approvingly of Rosebery's Chesterfield address, he heaped scorn on Campbell-Bannerman. 'My Right Hon. Friend has been captured...and treated...as the Boers treat their prisoners, he has been stripped of all his principles and left on the veldt to find his way back the best way he can. I hope it will be a lesson to him on a question of character, compromise is impossible.' Liberals should not be asked to support what they regarded as a criminal enterprise in order to induce Liberal imperialists to vote for a proposition which they do not believe to be true. Rather, he concluded, they should say to the government: 'This war is your business. We can have nothing whatever to do with it.'[223] Dillon's amendment of course was defeated but the Liberal imperialists abstained on the Cawley amendment anyway.

Lloyd George was in earnest. He was not trying to show that he and Campbell-Bannerman were independent of each other in order to make the older man's position easier.[224] He genuinely lamented his leader's unnecessary caution, a sentiment that remained with him for months and which briefly reconciled him to the Irish.[225] Equally some of his old friends were angry at him. He received a furious letter from H.J. Wilson (not to be confused with J. Havelock Wilson, also a pro-Boer) who had stood beside him in many pro-Boer battles. 'I was shocked and pained at your language more than I should just now like to describe,' he said. Lloyd George should express public regret for his behavior.[226] This letter was one of the very few that Lloyd George saved from this period of his life. There may have been other similar letters.

The press outrage, of course, was enormous. Some papers gloried in Campbell-Bannerman's embarrassment.[227] Others speculated wildly, professing not to understand what had happened. The *Liverpool Daily Post*, noting that Lloyd George had been designated in the past as Campbell-Bannerman's 'evil genius' was mystified, while the *British Weekly* blamed Dillon and the detestable Irish for Lloyd George's insulting behavior toward his leader.[228] The *New Liberal Review* of course was ecstatic. 'The Celtic movement has much to answer for,' wrote 'an M.P.' who declared that he himself had been ready to vote for the Cawley amendment until Lloyd George's 'pettish onslaught' on Campbell-Bannerman.[229] C.B. himself felt that Lloyd George's outburst had had the opposite effect and had driven some of the pro-Boer wing—he cited Morley and Channing—to vote for the amendment. 'I see nothing to regret in the whole thing,' he told Lord Ripon. 'The centre is enlarged and strengthened.'[230] Moreover he seems to have borne no animus against Lloyd George. Probably the truth is that the two sides nearly balanced. Lloyd George's violence made it possible for some pro-Boers, and a few imperialists, Fowler for example, to support the amendment. At the same time, he had weakened the Liberal center enough to allow the imperialists, who had insisted upon the statement on the war in the first place, to walk out. Their group however was dwindling. Campbell-Bannerman attracted 123 votes and the *Daily Chronicle* named only nine imperialists as abstaining, including Asquith, Grey, Haldane, and Perks.[231]

Lloyd George worried about his estrangement from his friends, the more so because he felt, as he usually did, that the attacks upon him were unjustified. Self-pity was a mood that came to him easily. On this occasion it lasted for some time. On Sunday evening, 16 February, as the National Liberal Federation was assembling in Leicester, the faithful Herbert Lewis recorded in his diary an impression of Lloyd George's state of mind which perhaps solves also the overworked question of Lloyd George's opinions on empire. He had spent the afternoon, Lewis wrote, 'with (for the time being) the most unpopular man in England. He feels his position very keenly.... We thought the outlook for the future rather gloomy. Chamberlain is the man of the hour. How often his star has waxed and waned.'

'How greatly this man is misunderstood,' Lewis concluded.

> Because of his extreme position...with South Africa, it is supposed that he is a friend of every country but his own. As a matter of fact the most extreme Imperialist is not more impressed than he is with the need of maintaining an invincible navy.... He believes Great Britain to be infinitely better than any Continental power; we have given the Boer much better treatment than any other European nation would have accorded them...and that our land is a greater power on the side of freedom than any other Country in the world.[232]

The previous evening Lloyd George had spoken in Chelsea to the Metropolitan Radical Club where he had attempted, it appears, to extend an olive branch to the Liberal center and to separate himself a little from Rosebery. The chosen speech was a reply to an address by Rosebery in Liverpool the previous evening in which the former Prime Minister attempted to clarify and sharpen the woolly proposals of Chesterfield.[233] Significantly, Rosebery's Liverpool speech, which in retrospect seems to deserve far more attention than the taffy-like ruminations two months earlier, held out the prospect of federal devolution, in terms as unmistakable as Rosebery was capable of. The 'clean slate', Rosebery had said, meant 'a slate clean of Home Rule for Ireland until some scheme of imperial federation should allow a local and subordinate Irish legislature as part of that scheme.' This may have been meant as an invitation to Chamberlain and the Liberal Unionists. But if it was intended to be an enticement to Lloyd George it was rejected. At the Metropolitan Liberal Association the next night, Lloyd George regretted Rosebery's statement, declared a loyalty that he could not have felt to the Gladstonian program, and said that the Liberals now must fight for Home Rule harder than ever.[234] The next day, as Herbert Lewis noted, his friend was in a black mood.

Rosebery's Liverpool speech, offering promises and compromises to those he sought to attract, was also, and was intended to be, a clear challenge to Campbell-Bannerman for the leadership of the party. On 19 February at Leicester, as has been seen, C.B. challenged Rosebery to say whether or not he was a party Liberal. Rosebery responded immediately in a famous letter to *The Times*, saying that he was outside the Liberal tabernacle but not, he thought, 'in solitude.'[235] Lloyd George found this significant. It meant the 'absolute severance of Lord Rosebery from the Liberal Party,' he told a *Carnarvon Herald* reporter. In a sense he was right. A few days later, on 24 February, Grey, Haldane, Fowler and Perks, with Asquith somewhat reluctantly in train, and with a few others, met Rosebery in Berkeley Square and convinced him to agree to the formation of a new organization— whether in or out of the Liberal party was not clear—the Liberal League. After warning the small group that some careers might be in danger because there was little to separate him from the Liberal Unionists, Rosebery accepted the presidency of the new organization.[236]

Even though proclaiming publicly his loyalty to Gladstonianism, in his bitterness over the state of the Liberal leadership Lloyd George seems to have been interested enough to allow himself to be courted by the new group. Evidence is sparse and contradictory. On one hand he continued his solitary alignment with the Irish which outraged not only the more conventional Liberals but his radical Welsh supporters as well. In mid-March the announcement in the House of Commons that on 7 March, DeLaRay had scattered a British supply column near Tweebosch in the Transvaal, capturing many men including the commander Baron Methuen, caused unseemly jubilation within the Irish party. Lloyd George had not joined in this, although he expressed much satisfaction in his letters.[237] But many Unionists were, or affected to be, deeply offended. As a consequence, with tempers still high, there was a violent debate on 20 March, during which Chamberlain came close to the assertion that Campbell-Bannerman was guilty of treason, and replied to an interjection from Dillon by saying that the Irish leader 'was a good judge of traitors.' After the Speaker refused to intervene, Dillon shouted that the Colonial Secretary was 'a damned liar.' Dillon was now suspended, with Lloyd George, alone among the Liberals, joining the Irish to vote against the suspension. Lloyd George had contributed to the uproar with a long and stinging speech which compared the corruption caused by the war to the Panama Canal scandal and asserted 'that the men who profit by it sit on the government bench.'[238]

Yet during the crowded winter of 1901-2 there is evidence that the Welsh pro-Boer began some excursions in the opposite direction. Two days after the Chesterfield speech on 18 December 1901 he had gone to Birmingham to fulfill a commitment made during the summer for an address prepared to show that there was virtually no difference between Lord Rosebery's sentiments on the war and those of the rest of the Liberal party.[239] In the event he was unable to deliver his address and instead was nearly killed by a hostile mob. Nevertheless he was able to use much of it in the Vestry Hall in Bristol three weeks later and, more important, to publish it again in the January 1902 issue of the *New Liberal Review.*[240]

In the article, after showing again that Rosebery's proposed generous terms of peace for the Boers, large payments for reconstruction and full self-government soon, were unlike Chamberlain's, but were precisely in line with Sir Henry Campbell-Bannerman's proposals, Lloyd George concluded with a virtual statement of fealty:

> Apart and above the value of Lord Rosebery's practical suggestions for
> a settlement stand his acknowledgement of the cardinal fact of the
> situation which up to that moment it had seemed treason to do anything
> but ignore.... The great need of Britain is a statesman who has the
> courage, first of all to find the truth about South Africa, then to believe
> the truth, in the next place to tell the truth, and finally to act upon the
> truth. The immediate future will prove whether the empire has at last
> discovered such a statesman.[241]

The weeks that followed saw him denouncing his own party leadership for compromises and weaknesses even though in Chelsea on 15 February he condemned Rosebery's Liverpool address. Nevertheless Rosebery clearly believed that the Liberal League might win Lloyd George to itself. Some years later, evidently in 1908, Lloyd George recounted to Lucy Masterman how Robert Perks, secretary of the League, had come to him saying that

Rosebery had great admiration for his talents and would include him in the next government, but not if he continued 'on those lines.' It was a great temptation, Lloyd George admitted to Mrs. Masterman, 'but he brushed it aside.'[242] Lloyd George's recollections of his past motives and deeds, particularly when recalled for the benefit of good-looking younger women, can scarcely be assessed hard evidence, but through the rest of the year, as the fight over Balfour's Education Bill replaced the war as the great public issue, the courtship continued. Rosebery invited Lloyd George to appear with him and consulted him on speeches. What kept them apart was that Lloyd George knew where he wanted to go and Rosebery did not.

VIII

The story of Lloyd George's life during the South African War cannot conclude without a description of the events of the night of 18 December 1901 when, as already mentioned, he attempted, and failed, to deliver a speech in the Town Hall in Birmingham. Historically the address, had it been delivered, would have been a part of his mysterious liaison with Rosebery. As it turned out the reception in Birmingham was first of all one of the major engagements in the continuing war with Joseph Chamberlain with whom Lloyd George was already being linked in the press. Lloyd George for many journalists was like the Chamberlain of the late seventies and early eighties, commented the strongly imperialist *Daily Mail* on 3 October 1901.

> There is, indeed, a very remarkable similarity between the Lloyd George of today and the 'Joe' Chamberlain of twenty years ago. The man of now, like the man of then, has an indomitable unquestioning self confidence, an irresistible pushfulness. Sprung from no exalted parentage, he has forged his way to prosperity by the same dogged tenacity, the relentless business that made Nettlefolds one of the best known names in the commercial world.
>
> Like his prototype of two decades age, Lloyd George began his parliamentary career careless of his personal appearance, with side whiskers. With the advent of fame—or notoriety—side whiskers vanished, the hair was cut and groomed, and the bandbox smartness replaced the careless neglige.
>
> Look at him in debate, leaning forward, eager, keen, alert, hand to ear, ready to spring on his prey and rend him to pieces—the reflection of what his great adversary once was. His very manner of rising is reminiscent—the sudden leap to his feet, the momentary pause to shake out his coat tail and stretch his shirt cuffs; it was done just so almost in that very place years ago.
>
> The moment he opens his mouth to speak the similarity is so striking as to make the listener start involuntarily. Listen! The same clear, low pitched, cruel voice; the same keen, incisive phrases; the same mordant bitterness; the same caustic sneers; the same sardonic humour; the same personal enmity. He is the very reincarnation of the present Colonial Secretary in his younger days —a spectre of his dead self arisen to haunt him. A little more excited, you say, a trifle more violent in gesture, more

impassioned in delivery; yes, more than Chamberlain now is, but recall the turbulent outbursts of his earlier days, the fire and impetuosity of his vigourous youth, before he learned the secret that cold, bitter vitriol bites deeper than the glittering knife.

His faults are the faults of inexperience, of strength untried and untrained; but strength, force of character, individuality are there without a doubt.... Today the little Welsh lawyer is a man to be reckoned with in the councils of the nation; tomorrow he will be a controlling voice on one side or the other.... His views may not now be acceptable to the people of the country, but here time is on his side. He is the type that moulds public opinion.[243]

What Chamberlain thought of this, if he read it, whether he saw himself in the young warrior David whose barbed missiles daily pelted him in the House of Commons, makes an interesting speculation. One can hardly believe he welcomed the invasion of his own land by the insolent challenger, however he may have admired his daring.

But second, for Lloyd George himself the Birmingham riot was an undisguised blessing. To be attacked by a mob is to be taken seriously. It was evidence that he had hurt Chamberlain. On 18 December, Lloyd George showed the personal courage that no one doubted he possessed. Yet in offering himself for martyrdom and by having his challenge accepted he raised himself to the level of the mighty Colonial Secretary. Had he been ignored in Birmingham he would have been defeated. The Liberal Unionist newspapers ensured this would not happen.

Well before 18 December, the Birmingham press was reporting, in fact inviting, protests against Lloyd George's coming appearance. They suggested that the patriotic men of Birmingham would never allow the slanderer of Joseph Chamberlain to appear.[244]

Lloyd George could hardly have missed the press uproar—he was reported to have refused several suggestions that the meeting be cancelled— but he took precautions. He ascribed his first narrow escape to a timely warning from a telegraph operator in Birmingham named Morgan. This man, he told Lucy Masterman with customary drama, sent him a telegram in Welsh saying that a mob intended to meet the London express, kidnap him from the New Street Station 'and make an end of me.' Therefore he took a slower earlier train. If he had come by the express, he said 'I should never have turned up again.'[245]

There was indeed a massive crowd at New Street Station to meet the 3.12 train from London, but Lloyd George had arrived before three o'clock, was met by Mrs. William Evans, wife of a leader of the local Welsh community, and whisked off to the Evans house in Hagley Road. After dinner, at about 6.30, having refused another appeal from the Chief Constable, Lloyd George drove with Evans to the Town Hall where the largest crowd since the coronation was assembled in Victoria Square. There were 350 policemen. Somehow he managed to enter unnoticed by a side door. When the doors were opened at 6.45 the mob, now numbering possibly thirty thousand or, as Lloyd George told Herbert Lewis later, fifty thousand, stormed the building, and many who were not ticket holders, or who possessed forged tickets, managed to get inside.[246] Henceforth there was pandemonium inside the building, shouts, songs, the throwing of furniture and other manifestations of loyalty to the crown and Joseph Chamberlain. 'We'll throw Lloyd George in the fountain. And he won't come to Brum anymore.'[247]

Lloyd George proposed to speak at seven o'clock. He had been waiting in a small room off the platform, remaining outwardly calm and cheerful, oblivious to the hubbub in the hall beyond. When at last the platform party appeared the tumult increased, only to heighten again when Lloyd George rose to speak. He was allowed to say only a few words. Suddenly, as if at a signal, the crowd charged the platform, meanwhile pelting the speaker with stones, bottles, sticks, and, according to DuParcq, bricks wrapped in barbed wire. A number of policemen guarding the hall were quickly disabled.[248]

The question now was not whether Lloyd George would be able to make his speech, but whether he would leave the Town Hall alive. The mob outside was attempting to batter down the door, nearly every window was broken. Within the building the police were losing control of the crowd and had never controlled it in the streets.

The Chief Constable hustled the protesting Lloyd George from the platform and told him that the only way he could escape the hall without serious injury would be to disguise himself in a police uniform. Lloyd George was reluctant. There was an argument while the roaring both in the front of the hall and out of doors increased. Eventually he was persuaded and soon a little column of twelve policemen, with Lloyd George in the middle, wearing a coat and helmet, emerged from the building and pushed its way through the crowd which was chiefly concerned at the moment with battering down the main door of the hall.[249] The ruse was successful and soon Lloyd George was back at Hagley Road where a police guard watched the Evans house for the rest of the night. From here he telephoned Harold Spender in London to report that he was alive. The next day he returned to London taking care to avoid another mob in New Street Station that sought to make good the missed opportunity of the previous night. He arrived back in London at about midday on 19 December and wrote his brother a smug letter implying that he had outwitted a conspiracy against him.[250]

This became his usual recollection of the event. Publicly and privately, even though the details of the story varied (sometimes he said he disembarked at a suburban station before New Street) he always insisted that Chamberlain (who was in Birmingham at the time) had planned to have him murdered and had failed.[251] He told Frances Stevenson in 1935 that when the Member for West Birmingham heard of his escape he said 'someone blundered badly over his job.'[252]

Lloyd George's glee at having outwitted Chamberlain led him, as time passed, to invent more details about his Birmingham adventure. In 1905 he told Herbert Lewis that before leaving London, expecting a siege, he had filled his pockets with cigars, which he passed out to the police when he arrived. 'For a time no one could find a match. Finally one was found and everyone was beginning to enjoy themselves when the crowd battered in the door with a heavy beam.'[253] The picture evoked here of a howling mob bursting in unannounced on a group of jolly cigar smoking policemen confirms more than Lloyd George's undisputed talent for imaginative recollection. It supports also the assertion already made, that he came to understand that the Birmingham epic was a triumph for him, an important step forward politically, and an event worth embellishing and dramatizing, like his early poverty. This aspect of the affair soon completely obscured the immediate significance of the speech, Lloyd George's personal welcome of Rosebery's Chesterfield principles. He took it more and more seriously, talked about it, expanded on it, and refused to allow others to make fun of it.[254]

There is a second question about Birmingham that must be addressed: was there preparation? Was the riot planned? Is it not likely that Lloyd George, who clearly anticipated trouble, in fact welcomed the size of the disturbance? Chamberlain's biographers agree that he took some pleasure in what he saw as Lloyd George's discomfiture and in the fact that the Birmingham Liberal Association had to pay for the damage to the Town Hall.[255] He regarded himself as even for the Kynoch embarrassment. This is not to say that he was involved in planning an attack on Lloyd George, even if he grimly approved of it. Yet the events outside the hall show signs of some organization. Newspapers, Liberal Unionist rather than Conservative, had long predicted trouble. They rejoiced in the opportunity for the city to show its patriotism. The *Birmingham Daily Mail* printed a photograph of the man the mobs were to look for. During the demonstration in the hall there were speeches outside, and after Lloyd George left the platform a Mr. J.G. Pentland sent Chamberlain at Highbury a telegram suggesting that a mission had been accomplished.

> Lloyd George, the traitor, was not allowed to say a word. Two hundred thousand citizens and others passed a unanimous vote of confidence in the Government and admiration for your unique and fearless services for King and country.

Other patriotic resolutions were also passed and communicated to Highbury.[256]

Afterwards there was a good deal of anger in the press against the police. The mob had lingered well after Lloyd George escaped and was finally dispersed at about 10 o'clock by a fierce baton charge during which many were hurt and one man, Harold Ernest Curtin, was killed. As Unionist editors reflected that the ugly behavior of the mob was likely to influence moderate opinion, the unfortunate Mr. Curtin began to receive more attention than Lloyd George. 'Indignation rises every day,' thundered *The Times* in an article that scarcely mentioned Lloyd George, 'with regard to the actions of the police in charging the crowd outside the Town-Hall on Wednesday night.'[257] There had indeed been assertions in the Birmingham papers that Irishmen had been imported to defend Lloyd George and that this would surely start a riot. Publicly this was always denied of course, but Lloyd George confided to Herbert Lewis on 2 January 1902 that the Chief Constable (whose name was Rafter) was himself Irish and in fact had imported some Irish police who were strong pro-Boers, hence the violence of the charge.[258]

All in all, if the Liberal Unionist leadership in Birmingham, or more likely simply a small group of Chamberlain supporters, conspired to exact a price for what they considered an affront to their city, they made a mistake. The attack on Lloyd George may have amused Chamberlain, but he was too astute a politician not to realize that the political profit went to Lloyd George. Perhaps the correct assessment of the importance of the event appeared in an anonymous letter to *The Times* on 21 December.

> Sir: The muscular patriots at Mr. Lloyd-George's meeting last night can hardly have realized what pro-Boer work they were in reality doing and what risks they ran.
> Suppose one of the Birmingham stones had taken effect on the person of the politician himself. Why his broken skull would have done more for the enemies of England than will ever be done by his eccentric brain.[259]

A martyr would have been a valuable asset for the pro-Boers. Lloyd George, who had no aspirations whatever toward immolation, was nevertheless happy to put on whatever halo went with near-martyrdom. The attention he won from the misbehavior of the Birmingham mob did him far more good than any speech he might have made.

Although in the spring of 1902 as the fighting in South Africa subsided, to end finally on 31 May, he was still estranged from his party, he had none the less made himself a national figure. He was no longer a Cambrian guerilla, but rather a power center of his own, as he would prove in the coming struggle on the Education Bill.[260] There were proposals, for instance an open letter from Keir Hardie to the *Labour Leader* in February 1903, that he cut himself off from the Liberals and take charge of a radical alliance that would include Labour, and part of the left leaning Liberal League.[261] And on the other side Leaguers continued to ask for his support in increasingly hopeless intrigues to make Rosebery Prime Minister.

He had emerged from the wilderness in which he had been left after the destruction of Welsh nationalism, and although no one knew yet where he belonged in the heterogeneous collection of pressures, interests and personalities that was the Liberal party at the turn of the century, he was nevertheless one force, to be sure among many others, that had to be given consideration. For years there had been speculation that he would be included in the next Liberal cabinet. His skill in debate, combined with his dubious Liberalism, made a guarantee of his loyalty important. But now he could claim a place on his own. After many false announcements, he had arrived.

4 Education Reform and Tariff Reform, 1902

With the presentation of the famous Education Bill of 1902, on 24 March 1902, Arthur Balfour, leader of the House of Commons and soon to be Prime Minister, came to the rescue of the distracted Liberal party as Lord Salisbury had provided it a gift in the Agricultural Rate Relief Act of 1896. Historically, the Education Bill's effect was to weld nonconformity into a single massive political group dedicated to the Liberal interest. It destroyed the Unionist advantage accruing from the Khaki Election, when the war had divided nonconformists as it had divided the nation. In the words of the most recent historian of nonconformists: 'It was the 1902 Education Act, which Balfour presented gratuitously to his opponents, that transformed—seemingly overnight—the nonconformist commitment to Liberalism from a vague sentiment into active political alliance.'[1] This point must be made cautiously because by the end of the year, as the bill cleared the House of Commons, newspapers were saying that all Liberal wounds were healed. This was not true. Discontent with Campbell-Bannerman's leadership remained, and would continue up to the eve of his premiership, while the Irish support of Balfour's bill made the Home Rule commitment even more controversial. Thus, if on one hand the education fight gave back to the Liberals a numerous and wealthy constituency which to some extent had been seduced away by jingoism, on the other it did little to solidify the position of the Gladstonians and of Sir Henry Campbell-Bannerman. Moreover nonconformist alliance burdened the party by adding to the Liberal baggage a portfolio of nonconformist issues which would seriously embarrass the party after it came to power in December 1905. Although it gained many potential voters, as the election of 1906 would show, the Liberals were as divided as ever about their leadership, and by putting themselves under the obligation to push ahead on free church programs—education reform, licensing reform and disestablishment—the party ensured a series of collisions with the House of Lords.

On the other hand, as the organized political consciousness of nonconformity developed in the years after the Education Act of 1902, Lloyd George's national political influence grew with it. Especially after the death of Parnell's nemesis Hugh Price Hughes in December 1902, Lloyd George emerged as the political spokesman for the English nonconformist constituency. He became also an intimate of the powerful nonconformist editors. He took the vice presidency of the Liberation Society. He was endowed, without having to build it, with a following in England possessing influence, money and votes.

Finally, the Education Bill washed away for nearly a decade the vestiges of genuine interest among all but the most dedicated Liberals for Irish Home Rule. This last factor presents a side of education reform that has received little attention. The 1902 bill proposed to give rate aid to English and Welsh denominational schools, Catholic as well as Anglican. As such it was a part of the consistent Unionist program that had emerged after the election of 1895 of killing Home Rule with kindness. This had been manifest in the Education Bills of 1896 and 1897, in the Local Government (Ireland) Act of 1898, and was continued in Balfour's Licensing Act of 1904 as well as in the less visible but perhaps more important steps of opening the higher reaches of Irish local government to the patronage of the Nationalist party. The seduction of the Irish, the revival of the old division between the Nationalists and the nonconformist radicals, particularly angered Lloyd George. His cooperation with Dillon that had appeared during the war ended and he allowed himself again to be courted by the Roseberyites. Except for the most old fashioned Gladstonians, the stern pledge to make Ireland a nation once again became instead an inaudible mumble about devolution 'step by step.'

I

In 1901 English and Welsh public education remained essentially where the Voluntary Schools Act of 1897 had left it. There were 5,600,000 children under twelve years of age in school. Of these, 2,600,000 attended 5,700 board schools and 3,000,000 attended 14,000 voluntary schools.[2] More important, in about 8,000 parishes the Anglican voluntary school was the only school available and about one million nonconformist children were compelled to attend these. Lloyd George, a generation before, had been one of them.

However the immediate cause of the bill of 1902 was not the chronic stringency of the voluntary elementary schools, but a court decision holding illegal the relatively limited activities of some urban boards in offering secondary education. On 26 July, 1899, a Local Government Board auditor, T.B. Cockerton, on a complaint from the Camden School of Art, found that the London School Board had no right under the law to offer tuition in drawing to children beyond the age of twelve, nor indeed could it offer any education beyond the elementary level. There were the inevitable reviews, finally in the Court of Appeal, which held on 1 May, 1901 that Cockerton's original judgement was correct. All secondary education by school boards, throughout England and Wales, was *ultra vires*.

The government's first response was to introduce a measure, the so-called 'Cockerton Bill,' to put all secondary education under the umbrella of the county councils. When this failed, principally because of a revolt among the Unionists, the government compromised with a one-clause bill simply postponing the effect of the Cockerton judgement for a year. Meanwhile it began to prepare a massive reconstruction of all English and Welsh state education.

The turmoil in British secondary education coincided with an upheaval in the affairs of the Board of Education itself, which, as if to symbolize the precarious nature of British state education, had evolved into a permanent ministry only in 1899. The Vice President of the Board of Education, in effect the head of the English and Welsh state system, was Sir John Gorst, a talented parliamentarian and a sincere social reformer, one of the 'Fourth Party' of the 1880s who regarded himself as the last apostle of Tory Democracy, but who was also a man so embittered by the clear failure of his political career that he had become almost impossible to work with. Among others, he was scarcely on speaking terms with his Permanent Secretary, Sir George Kekewich, who had entered education more than three decades before, was an advanced Liberal in politics, and who saw his duty, and the board's, chiefly as an agent of the National Union of Teachers. Neither had much intercourse with the President of the Board, the Duke of Devonshire, also Lord President of Council, who rarely turned up. In this unstable structure, power lay with Gorst's private secretary, Robert Laurie Morant.

Morant would become one of the giant figures in the civil service in an age that found its measure in such men as Fisher, Bradbury, Anderson, and Chalmers, and would be involved in Lloyd George's career until the former's early death in 1920. Morant's basic proposal involved the abolition of elected school boards and the concentration of all former board schools, as well as all secondary education, under the control of county councils. It made no sense, he argued, to retain two democratically elected, rate collecting, bodies, the boards and the councils. The latter had not existed when the boards were established in 1870.

But the school boards were the preserve of the nonconformists and the National Union of Teachers. For the dissenting chapels the nondenominational Bible instruction offered by the board schools under the Cowper-Temple clause of the original Education Act of 1870 was perfectly satisfactory, while the NUT saw the expansion of state education, untouched by religious discrimination, as the only avenue to expanded membership. However on the opposite side of the House, most Unionists found the reform of state secondary education boring and potentially expensive. These prejudices had frustrated Gorst's Cockerton Bill earlier in the year. However necessary secondary education reform might be, as it stood it had no friends. For most of the Conservative party, including Prime Minister Salisbury, concern for education meant concern for the voluntary Church of England schools. But implicit in the debates on the dramatic increase in Treasury subsidies to Church education that had occurred in the nineties was the understanding on both sides of the House that no matter what grants Tory generosity might provide to voluntary schools, the grants would be reduced by the first Liberal government to come to power. There were too many nonconformists who wished simply to see the Church schools die. If denominational education was to be saved it would have to be established permanently as a charge on the rates. The House of Lords could be trusted to see that it was not taken off. Viewed historically, indeed as was understood at the time, the session of 1902 offered the last chance to save Church education.[3] The price of secondary school reform would be the nationalization of denominational education.

These facts were common knowledge at the Board of Education. By autumn Morant had been in touch with Bishop Talbot and, more important, with Herbert, Cardinal Vaughan, Archbishop of Westminster since 1892 and spokesman for Great Britain's two million Roman Catholics. Early in November 1901 Morant wrote to the Cabinet stressing 'the importance of the religious question. The only way to get up steam in the teeth of School Board opposition for school reform will be to include some scheme for aiding denominational schools.'[4]

For Lloyd George the denominational schools were the core of the dispute. Secondary education did not enter into it. Reformers like Morant hoped to see British education become administratively respectable and academically sound. But a bill to achieve these ends had to be passed by a House of Commons dominated by a Unionist party in which many members cared nothing about educational reform except as it would preserve Church schools as missionary centers of the Establishment. Yet aid to voluntary schools might, as Chamberlain had written on 7 November 1901, 'lose Birmingham and Birmingham influence, whatever that might be worth to the Unionist Party.'[5] In rebuttal the Conservative Whip's office reported early in the New Year that 'it would be hazardous to ignore the feeling of the great bulk of the party, in favour of rate aid to Voluntary Schools, for the sake of removing the scruples of a few Radical Unionists in the Midlands.'[6] Nonetheless, as one of the 'few Radical Unionists' was Joseph Chamberlain, Balfour had to listen.

As a consequence, with potential opposition on both sides of the House, the Education Bill that A.J. Balfour described to the Commons on 24 March contained a substantial compromise. The bill proposed to create 328 new education authorities in England and Wales which would be either the county and county borough councils or non-county boroughs and urban districts above a certain size. These new bodies would exercise their powers through committees made up of members of the council with a minority co-opted from the outside. They would receive complete responsibility for all education above the elementary level. However, in the case of elementary education, the four-square simplicity of the measure was diluted by the provision that local education committees would take over the functions of school boards or denominational schools only at the council's option. Thus, the 14,000 denominational schools and the 2,568 board schools remained outside the compulsory portions of the bill, to be taken in, presumably, only if the voters of the locality desired it.[7] Still, the bill provided that under certain circumstances a local education authority could build a state school in any of the 8,000 parishes which were currently served only by a denominational school. In this way it attacked the core of the nonconformist grievance and reversed the prohibition contained in the Forster Act of 1870 on the building of a second school.[8]

As *The Times* put it the next day, Balfour had 'skated discreetly and warily over the religious question.'[9] Moreover the bill specifically excluded London with the most powerful school board in the nation, so avoiding a major area of contention. In general Balfour made a conciliatory declaration, hoping his measure would 'stay religious strife' and conveying the philosophic balance and personal grace that constituted his charm. It was also, to some extent, a dishonest explanation of the yet unseen bill. Balfour had dwelt at length on the inefficiency of British education, on the lack of system, on the better programs available in Germany and the United States. He had emphasized the absolute power of the local authority councils and had noted also, possibly with an eye toward Lloyd George, that the measure would scarcely touch Wales where secondary education had been carried on, since Rendel and Ellis's Welsh Intermediate Education Act of 1889, by an *ad hoc* county government board under the general supervision of the Charity Commissioners. Most important, he had not defined, indeed he had scarcely mentioned, the proposed status of the voluntary schools should they be taken into the new arrangements. Certainly in Wales, where most county councils had permanent nonconformist majorities, it would have been quite possible to infer from his exposition that voluntary schools were to be turned into virtual state schools.

Lloyd George's letter to Maggie, written while the speech was in progress, reveals his misunderstanding.

> Balfour is developing almost revolutionary Education Bill. Sweeps away School Boards. Creates the county council the education authority for the county & puts the Board Schools & the Voluntary Schools under it. Llanystumdwy School will now be under the county council & a very great improvement it is. Up to the present I rather like the Bill. It is quite as much as one would expect from a Tory Government—in fact, more than anyone could anticipate.

Then as the speech progressed, he changed his mind.

> Whole thing destroyed by making the whole Bill optional—it is left entirely to the discretion of each county council! What a miserably weak thing this Government is.[10]

The rest of the House was equally at sea. Campbell-Bannerman, responding to Balfour, rambled uncertainly. T.P. O'Connor welcomed the bill for the Irish. His constituents in the Scotland Division of Liverpool, for the most part poor dockers, had for years paid a school board rate from their irregular earnings and yet contributed also toward the support of a Catholic school for their children. The two million Catholics in Great Britain, he said, would see this bill as a measure of justice.[11] Lloyd George left the House early; he was not present to vote. Evidently he did not hear the only critical speech of the evening by a relatively junior Member, Alfred Hutton, a nonconformist Liberal Leaguer who spoke just before the division.

The tone of cautious friendliness was not confined to the House of Commons. The *British Weekly*, which had strenuously opposed the 'Cockerton Bill' a year before, offered, if not applause, at least a limited acceptance. After admitting that the bill might have to be attacked eventually, it criticized, as most commentators would be doing, the option clause. Even many nonconformist communities, it asserted, would take no action unless forced to. Stockport, for example, had no school rate. Nevertheless, the measure afforded nonconformists a good deal, particularly in the direction of breaking the denominational monopoly in single-school areas. Balfour, the paper concluded, had genuinely tried to conciliate both sides.[12]

II

Lloyd George's convictions about the Education Bill, like his attitudes toward many political questions, are not easy to delineate and frequently manifested themselves at different levels of motivation. At bottom he quite approved the extension of popular education. It was part of the creed of national efficiency, which was a factor in his attraction to Rosebery. He was an intense patriot, as Herbert Lewis knew. He deplored what he had seen as Britain's botched and amateurish attempts to compete economically with Germany and America. Every English activity was hindered by inadequate education, from soldiering to farming. 'The best manure you can give the land is brains, after all,' he said at Lincoln on 10 December 1902 in a speech dedicated to the theme of national efficiency.[13]

In addition he had never believed in totally secular education. For years he had warned the more radical nonconformists, who from Henry Richard on hoped to exalt the power of free church Sunday schools by taking the Bible out of state education. His only condition was that any sectarian institution should be under public control.[14]

The 'purely secular' position of the free church radicals, making concession impossible, would cause endless trouble for Lloyd George in the months ahead during his tangled negotiations with the Bishop of St. Asaph. However, the well-known assertion made on St. David's Eve, 28 February, 1903 to a Young Wales Society meeting in the Liverpool Reform Club, that he owed nothing to university or secondary schools but 'whatever I do owe it is to the Little Bethels,' was not a testimonial, as is often suggested, to his own national school education. He was defending rather the central institution of rural North Wales nonconformist civilization, the chapel, and identifying himself, quite comfortably, as the product of that world. In fact he was replying to his introducer, Dr. John Morris, President of the Liverpool Cymru Fydd and mayor of Birkenhead, who had suggested that Wales was hopelessly old fashioned and out of touch with the rest of the nation. Wales, Dr. Morris said, echoing indeed sentiments Lloyd George himself frequently expressed, needed 'a little less singing of hymns, a little less attention to meetings of the Little Bethel every night of the week, and more of grappling with the problems of life.'[15] Lloyd George, whatever he recalled privately of his boyhood anguish during tedious sermons and endless prayers, usually acknowledged his debt to them publicly. His own tuition in David Evans's Church school in Llanystumdwy, Lloyd George knew, could have been much worse, although he rarely referred to it except to recall for reporters the various ways in which he had embarrassed his kindly schoolmaster.

If privately he knew educational reform was desirable, the bill was nevertheless the work of a Unionist government and was designed to perpetuate independent denominational schools. Further, it offered a splendid opportunity to denounce Chamberlain who, from Lloyd George's point of view, had sold his nonconformist background to satisfy friends of the Church of England schools and to buy off the Irish as previously he had pawned his convictions on social reform to pay for the war in South Africa. These were political opportunities not to be missed.

Then, after the bill was printed, it became clear, as it had not been in Balfour's speech, that Church schools were to receive exceptionally favorable treatment. The 'absolute authority' over all education that Balfour had insisted would belong to the elected county councils would in fact be exercised by a board of managers upon which the Church element was in a two-thirds majority. In addition the right to build new schools was worthless. Most of the 8,000 single voluntary school parishes were in impoverished and rural areas of small population. Nonconformist parents would not and could not incur the odium of petitioning for an unneeded school that would add to the rates. On the other hand the Church, relieved of the burden of school operation, could use the money saved to build more sectarian schools.[16]

Anyway the institutionalization of Church privilege provided a sufficient motive to attack the bill, whatever benefits it might confer. Lloyd George could begin again the familiar business of denouncing vicars and reviling bishops. For him the bill represented simply a reopening of the tithe and disestablishment campaigns. It was a means of dividing the Welsh from the English. And with it came, in the resistance to the bill after the passage, opportunities for political organization for the promotion of nationhood. Whether or not he saw this immediately, he understood it by the end of the year as the bill became law. 'The Education Act of 1902 has presented Wales with its greatest political opportunity,' he wrote in the announcement of this plan of campaign on 17 January, 1903. 'It is exceptionally equipped by training, convictions, and habits of thought, to take full advantage of this opportunity.' Then he went on, as usual, to contrast Welsh national sentiment with that of Ireland and England.

Wales presents the spectacle of a well ordered and highly disciplined community, where intense political and religious convictions produce no excesses which repel the most sensitive friend of good order. A patriotism at once as ardent and broad as that which inspires any nation in the world. A patriotism which has not fallen into the fatal error of confounding depth of greed with breadth of outlook, or in the equally fatal error of imagining that war and politics are the only fields where a man can exhibit his love of native land. A patriotism which for generations was almost purely literary before it became religious, which was religious fully a century and educational at least a generation before it annexed politics, and which, in adding new interests and activities to the national life, never forsook the old. If in this great struggle we are now entering upon Wales acts with a firm courage and dignified restraint—and I feel confident of its strength to do so—it will emerge from the conflict with a national position surpassing the dreams of the line of prophets who foretold great things for 'Gwalia Wen' ere they passed to their rest under the shadow of its hills.[17]

Rhetoric aside, the bill was simply another bit of ammunition in the battle to organize Wales. Lloyd George knew this when he saw its text and was soon receiving expert advice from his brother on details that conferred special advantages to Church schools.[18] He was not coerced into opposition by the example of English nonconformist outrage. Indeed he questioned whether the English leaders were an effective force. He despised the tactic of passive resistance to the payment of school rates and fought against it in Wales. He had no intention of allowing better organized, politically more astute, Welsh nonconformity to be used as a stalking horse for English disestablishment.[19] 'The whole fight against the Bill,' he wrote to one of the most violent of the English resisters, Robertson Nicoll, editor of the *British Weekly*, whom he had not yet met, 'seems to me, to use an educational phrase, to lack coordination. There ought to be more complete understanding between those who conduct the compaign in the country and the Members who fight the Bill in the Commons...The House of Commons is not yet convinced that Nonconformists in any part of the country except Wales mean business.'[20] Indeed in the year after the bill passed, when English passive resistance was at its height, he was privately trying to arrive at a compromise with the Welsh Church leaders. In summary, he thought of the Education Bill in political, not religious, terms.

The first political effect of the Education Bill, one that grew ever more apparent in the next few years as the power of English nonconformity solidified within the Liberal party, was the reopening of the breach with the Irish. And a corollary of the mounting disenchantment with Home Rule was the prolongation of Lord Rosebery's attempts, under the urging of Robert Perks, to recruit Lloyd George for the Liberal League. Many of the most loyal, if not the most visible, Liberal imperialists were fierce nonconformists who shared Rosebery's dislike of the Irish. Consequently, even though Balfour's bill was an important step toward educational efficiency, Rosebery found it expedient to oppose it.[21] For Lloyd George, the Irish support of the Education Bill, a measure designed to emplace in public education forever the Church of their landlords, written by the man who had been their cruelest modern oppressor, was incomprehensible, the more so because the bill did not extend to Ireland and the Catholic hierarchy in England had long since sold itself to the Unionists.[22]

This was his line in his first parliamentary address on the bill, which came on 8 May, the third day of the second reading debate, only a little more than two weeks after the birth in Criccieth on 22 April of his third daughter, Megan. He denounced in his customary terms the privileges extended to the Church, an exclusive patronage of 60,000 teachers, 'pandering to priestcraft' as he had described it in Wales a few weeks before. But he reserved his peroration for the Irish, with whom he had been allied less than two months before. Those who support the bill, he said, are the foes of the Irish and of Home Rule.

> Now this is what I put to my honourable friends. It is rather hard.
> In 1886 we threw over our most cherished leaders in this country –
> Spurgeon and Bright, Dr. Allen, Dr. Dale and even the Rt. Honourable
> Gentleman the Member for West Birmingham [Chamberlain] – we
> threw them over for one reason only; because we felt what was due to
> Ireland and it is rather hard, I think – if they will forgive me for
> speaking candidly – to be put in the plight of being beaten down for the
> cause of Ireland, and that Irishmen, of all peoples, should help our
> foes and theirs to make our defeat more intolerable. Let them

remember this. Who are the people who will benefit by the Bill? The people who benefit by it are the people who coerced Ireland, and supplied every measure for throwing the leaders of the Irish people into prison, and for keeping Ireland down with soldiers and police.

The Welsh people, he concluded, when they resist the bill will remember that the Irish were partly responsible for it. Even Cardinal Vaughan

> did his very best to help to return the Hon. Members opposite....I do appeal to the Hon. Members for Ireland sincerely, for the sake of their own country—I am not merely a Nonconformist; I believe in the sacred cause, as they do, of small nationalities of which they have been the guardian in this House—I appeal to them not to join in oppressing Nonconformists, who have been their friends, with the enemies of their faith and race.[23]

He returned to this theme on 5 June at an anti-Education Bill rally at Queen's Hall sponsored by the Liberal League where he shared the platform with Rosebery, Asquith, Fowler and Perks, who had persuaded Rosebery to invite him. The education measure was, he said, 'originated by Cardinal Vaughan and passed on by church convocation.' It was 'a Bill for that section of the clergy that is taking Protestant pay for teaching Catholic doctrine.'[24] Considering that peace with the Boers had been concluded only twelve days earlier, that slightly a year before Lloyd George had mounted the platform in the same Queen's Hall to address an angry pro-Boer meeting and that in that spring Lloyd George had himself denounced Rosebery for giving up Home Rule, the dimension of his move across the party spectrum, away from the Irish and toward the Liberal imperialists, is little short of astounding. The presence of Lloyd George on the platform with the imperialists did not mean that the party split was healed. The intrigues against Campbell-Bannerman would continue; C.B. himself was notably absent from the Queen's Hall meeting, although he sent a telegram of support. Further he had systematically excluded, over the protests of Asquith, all leaguers from the Liberal committee in charge of opposition to the bill.[25]

Whether Lloyd George ever became truly an anti-Home Ruler is unclear. Evidently the rumor that he might be concerned him enough to cause him to produce an announcement on 12 May, during a speech at an anti-Education Bill rally at Criccieth, that although the bill would take England back toward Roman Catholicism, his faith in Home Rule would not be altered by Irish support of the measure.[26] However, this declaration of faith may have been directed toward the Irish community in Caernarvon who certainly differed from him on denominational education. Nevertheless he went out of his way, only two weeks later, to tell a reporter after a speech by Rosebery at the National Liberal Club that he would back Rosebery should the former Prime Minister become again leader of the party.[27] For his part Rosebery lost no opportunity to flatter the Member for Caernarvon District, publicly commenting on his 'readiness of resource,' in his fight against the bill and inviting him to Berkeley Square to consult about the speech he would make in the House of Lords.[28]

The first phase of the opposition to the Education Bill ended on 9 July when on vote in committee, the House deleted Clause 5 which had made the assumption of the voluntary schools and the extinction of the school boards optional for the local authorities. This amendment, introduced by Henry Hobhouse, a Liberal Unionist Churchman and education expert, was probably inevitable from the beginning, and no doubt the change was intended by Balfour and Morant.[29] To have retained the option would simply have been to remove the battle over rate aid to voluntary schools from parliament, where the struggle at least would be limited in terms of duration and ferocity, and to have sent it to 328 local education authorities, making each a cockpit for the violent display of religious prejudice.

Yet there was more than the usual sleight of hand about the parliamentary maneuver on 9 July. Two days before, on 7 July, Joseph Chamberlain, the man who in the first place had forced the option clause, was seriously injured in an accident when the horse drawing his hansom cab slipped on the wooden paving blocks of Whitehall. On 9 July he lay in Charing Cross Hospital out of touch with the world. Furthermore, when the amendment was introduced, Balfour promised, in order perhaps to avoid a technical violation of his agreement with the Colonial Secretary, that the whips would be withdrawn. Every Member of Parliament could vote as his conscience and his constituents directed him. But at the same time the Leader of the House, who would become Prime Minister three days later, announced that a new grant in aid of 17s 6d per child, which the government proposed to make available, would be given only to councils that took over the school board. Thus the debate itself was, as the *British Weekly* described it, a bit of 'foolery'. 'The clause attributed to Mr. Chamberlain was clearly done away with in essence, before it was ever debated.'[30] The deletion of Clause 5 was approved by 271 votes to 102. Many nonconformists, it was noted, voted for the amendment and T.J. Macnamara, spokesman for the National Union of Teachers, supported it while Austen Chamberlain registered a protest for his father by voting against it.

During the debate on the Hobhouse amendment, Lloyd George gave his first warning in the House of the 'strife and lawlessness,' that would ensue.[31] Ten days later he wrote the letter to Robertson Nicoll asserting that English nonconformity seemed disorganized and helpless. This letter may have stimulated the fierce front page editorial in the next issue of the *British Weekly* entitled, as if in answer to Lloyd George, 'Nonconformity on Its Trial.' The worst thing about the new education proposals, said Nicoll, was their permanence. The 1870 act had never been destined to last. But the new settlement, rate aided denominational education, would be guaranteed forever by the House of Lords and the Irish. There might now have to be resistance.[32]

Besides being an uncanny prediction of the future of English education, the *British Weekly* leader may be regarded as the nonconformist declaration of war on the Education Bill. Through the rest of 1902 nonconformist agitation took the form chiefly of rallies to whip up the vote at by-elections and to denounce the principle of 'Rome on the rates.' The two leaders were John Clifford, minister of Praed Street and Westbourne Park Baptist

Church since 1858—with whom Lloyd George had already worked in Pro-Boer activities and in the provision of help for the Penrhyn strikers—and W. Robertson Nicoll of the *British Weekly*, who after 1902 was the most important nonconformist editor in the country. Lloyd George evidently met Nicoll at this time and would find his public support of increasing importance in the future.

Lloyd George contributed little to the hysterical zealotry that surrounded the nonconformist rate resistance throughout England in the months after the deletion of Clause 5. However, he appeared occasionally at rallies in Wales. Meanwhile, he maintained his Liberal League connections with an important address in R.W. Perks's constituency on 10 December immediately after the passage of the bill through the House of Commons.

The Lincoln speech illustrates the distance Lloyd George maintained from the evangelical calls to martyrdom that were now beginning to be heard and conversely how much he had absorbed of the creed of national efficiency.

At Lincoln he made, of course, the usual jeers at bishops, at the vicar's and squire's feudal control of the village school, and at the Church of England catechism. But there was absolutely no suggestion to the nonconformists of Lincolnshire that they should resist payment of rates in order to pull down Balfour's educational reform. Rather he spent the bulk of his talk in a denunciation of English educational inadequacy and in demands for more reform. He compared English parsimony in education to the generosity of Switzerland, the United States, and indeed to the secondary system in Wales. Lack of education kept the poor in their place. 'The rich man can afford to be ignorant; the poor man cannot.' Still worse, poor education retarded Britain's industrial efficiency and left its people poor citizens. In a long declamation he propounded a rough creed of education and citizenship. 'We say the government is a bad one,' he declared.

> Heaven knows it is. But it is yours. It is yours; you have sent them there. The people made them, and I hope the people are proud of their creation. The people can unmake them. And so they will. If you made bad governments they generally come from bad citizenship. It is the people who are to blame. Don't let us flatter ourselves. It is the people who are to blame for bad government in a democratic country. Let us advocate our sovereign. The people are the sovereign power. There are terrific problems in front of us. One can see them moving in the not very dim or distant future. A little distress will bring them to the front. A little of the storms of poverty, and the agitation which will come from it will sweep away the mists, and we shall be face to face with these terrible problems. The hoar frost is thick upon the ground. We see these great meetings of the unemployed, and what they demand. I don't know what the problems may be; the future will decide this country. But one thing I know, I had rather trust them to settlement by an educated, thoughtful people than I would to men who have got three years' catechism from the parsons.

Education was the essential ingredient of equality. With Christian faith, non-sectarian and unadorned, it could break the barriers of wealth and class. He concluded with a testimonial to the vitality of educated American democracy.

> I had rather have the religion which, in America, brings the millionaire's son, side by side, to learn in the same school with the carpenter's son. Why? I will tell you why. Because the millionaire's son never knows what may happen to the artisan's boy at his side. He knows that the artisan's boy can climb up to secondary school and to the university. And it is but a step for a capable man from there to the White House. There was once a rail splitter who was President of the United States. No; this snobbery is out of date. Teach religion in the schools, give the children the Bible. Let Him speak to them in His own words, so simple that a child can understand them—not confused and perplexed by these theologies that priests have for years and years defined, until no man of ordinary intelligence can comprehend them. No; let all this din and clamour of priests and the schools subside. Let the children hear for themselves the voice of the best friend they ever had, and the most dangerous foe the priest could ever encounter.[33]

III

Lloyd George had begun his Lincoln speech with the remark that someone in the House of Commons, discovering he was speaking at the invitation of Robert Perks, had declared that Liberal unity had arrived at last. Lloyd George did not suggest that he agreed. He admitted to the assembly only that the Education Bill had released the energy of the Liberal party, which the Boer War had paralyzed. Lloyd George was being generous. The battle over the Education Bill enhanced enormously his own reputation and brought, of course, to the Liberals the unanimous support of Britain's nonconformists. But it had done nothing to strengthen the position of the older, Gladstonian, Liberal leadership. Even friendly papers such as the *British Weekly* criticized the 'listlessness' and 'submissiveness' of the Liberal front bench and remarked upon the many evenings that it remained empty.[34] Morley, the apostle of liberty of the intellect, rarely intervened in debate. James Bryce, the designated spokesman for the opposition, seemed worn out. Campbell-Bannerman, distracted by his wife's ill health, was often absent. The Irish were being allowed to strengthen their relations with the Unionists in support of the bill. The paper hoped that when Lloyd George became a member of the next government, it would not be in a Cabinet of such men as now led the party.[35]

All of this only made more apparent Lloyd George's achievement. In his opposition to the Education Bill, for practical purposes he led the party. He had, to be sure, operated in this fashion from time to time in the past, in the assault on Chamberlain during the war. But then his position was controversial; he was simply performing necessary dirty work that the more fastidious members of his party did not care to undertake themselves. Now, just a few months later, he was the hero of the hour and this time not of a group of slightly suspect radical insurgents, but of the Liberal party itself. He was leading the revival of below-the-gangway Liberalism, wrote H.W.

'Ll-yd G-rge and the Dragon!' The first drawing of Lloyd George in *Punch*, 12 December 1900. The dragon is Joseph Chamberlain.

LLOYD GEORGE AND HIS DRAGON.

Punch cartoon satirising the protests of Welsh nonconformists against delays in attacking the Established Church in Wales, 16 October 1907.

'The Cabinet Cherubs (after Reynolds)', *Punch*, 22 April 1908. From top right, clockwise: Lloyd George, Runciman, Harcourt, McKenna, Churchill.

Lloyd George, *c.* 1909.   Postcard celebrating Lloyd George's 1909 budget. ▶

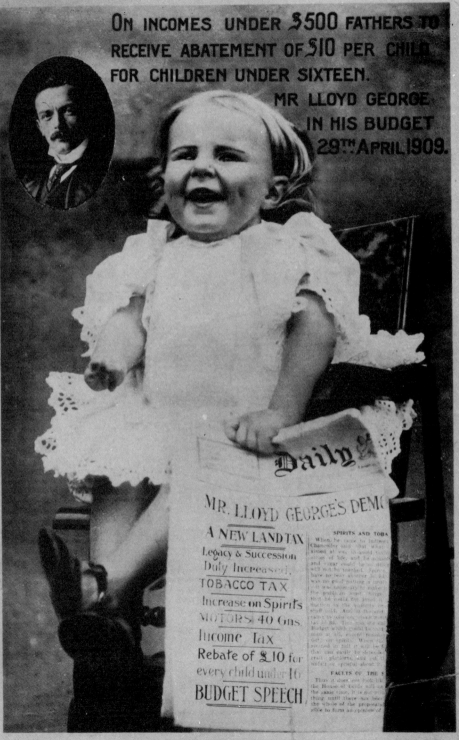

ON INCOMES UNDER $500 FATHERS TO RECEIVE ABATEMENT OF $10 PER CHILD FOR CHILDREN UNDER SIXTEEN.

MR LLOYD GEORGE IN HIS BUDGET 29TH APRIL 1909.

Daily

MR. LLOYD GEORGE'S DEMO

A NEW LAND TAX

Legacy & Succession Duty Increased.

TOBACCO TAX

Increase on Spirits

MOTORS 40 Gns.

Income Tax

Rebate of £10 for every child under 16

BUDGET SPEECH

11226 1   "ISN'T WE PLEASED DADDY?"   ROTARY PHOTO, E.C.

'Peaceful Persuasion. An appreciation of the success with which the Chancellor of the Exchequer invariably deals with deputations'. Cartoon, *c*. 1909-11.

'The Coming Olympic Struggle. Active Training for the Passive Resistance Event.' *Punch*, 3 July 1912. Mistresses and maids combined to resist the 'stamp-licking' proposals of the Insurance Bill.

'Mr Lloyd George and his Guardians' (left, C.F.G. Masterman; right, Rufus Isaacs). Max Beerbohm. *(Columbus Museum of Art, Ohio, Museum Purchase, Howald Fund)*

Massingham in the *Speaker,* a small radical Liberal weekly under the editorship of J.L. Hammond, which in 1907 would become the hugely influential *Nation.* Parliament was interesting in a way it had not been since the days of Gladstone. Although his parliamentary orations were not first class, he was the best committee debater since Gladstone. But most of all, Lloyd George had revived Liberal fighting spirit. As many others had already done, Massingham predicted he would be a member of the next Liberal government.[36]

Such testimonials were routine for Lloyd George in the autumn of 1902. The *British Weekly* compared him to Chamberlain attacking Home Rule. Balfour in his third reading speech on 3 December complimented him as an 'eminent parliamentarian' for his 'distinguished part' in the opposition to the bill, adding however, that the Member for Caernarvon District had said many things that might better have been left unsaid.[37] Altogether it provides a measure of his achievements. Day after day through the parliamentary year of 1902, until the recess of 8 August, and after 16 October when parliament reassembled, he was in his place below the gangway hindering in every possible way the process of legislation. He could not, of course, do more than slow the progress of the bill, but his strategy involved more than sheer obstruction. Early in the committee stage, less than two weeks after the repeal of the option clause, during the debate on Clause 7, he came close to compromise on what was for him personally the most objectionable consequence of the Education Bill: the fact that it subsidized and perpetuated denominational control and the teaching of Anglican dogma in 8,000 single school parishes where the majority of students in many cases, certainly in Wales, were nonconformist.

Clause 7 dealt with the administrative structure for elementary school administration. For denominational schools (always referred to as 'not provided,' i.e. schools not owned by the local educational authority) four of the six members of the school management committee would be appointed in the way stipulated in the original charter of the school, which usually meant selection by the local vicar, who often put himself on the board. Hence, effective day-to-day control of any given institution, although now it would be supported by rate payers and attended by children who might be nonconformist, would remain, as before, in the hands of Church of England clergy and their appointees. More important, Balfour had made clear from the beginning that he intended that the former voluntary, 'not provided,' schools should keep their Anglican character. The faculty would be Churchmen, the catechism would be taught, nonconformist children could not become pupil-teachers. There were to be no compromises. That Balfour, whose philosophic skepticism about all systematic theology was well-known, should refuse any concessions asked by dissenters in the name of equity, or even in the name of harmony, demonstrated the fragility of the coalition which supported his measure. With men like Morant at his elbow, he understood better than most of his attackers the desperate need for the reconstruction of English education, and he could take comfort in the fact that some of the genuine experts in education among the Liberals, R.B. Haldane and T.J. Macnamara, generally supported his measure, or at least refrained from attacking it. And he could not ignore the unhappy history of previous Unionist attempts at education reform in 1896 and 1901. But he presided over a government which was growing increasingly unpopular. In the Commons his bill was supported by an uneasy alliance of landowners, many of whom thought of education reform chiefly in terms of higher rates and who pressed continually for promises of higher Treasury grants for the new education authorities; of Church-minded Members of Parliament, backed by Convocation, for whom the dilution of the catechism was blasphemy; by Liberal Unionists whose leader, after the Hobhouse amendment, predicted nothing but doom if the bill was passed and who wanted to see only the continuance of Cowper-Temple bible reading; and by Irishmen for whom Cowper-Temple was the distilled essence of evil.[38]

Thus there was no chance that Balfour should give way on 22 July when he was presented suddenly with an unlikely meeting of minds between one of his most talented High Church supporters, his cousin Lord Hugh Cecil, and Lloyd George, the incarnation of militant nonconformity. The occasion was an amendment to Clause 7 by Reginald McKenna, whose reputation, like Lloyd George's, was greatly enhanced by his opposition to the Education Bill, proposing that non-provided schools should be considered as provided (i.e. board) schools if there were no other educational institutions within three miles. From this the debate drifted off to a discussion of the well worn matter of the plight of nonconformist children in the 8,000 single school parishes. Lloyd George was immediately on his feet reminding the House of the Diocese of Bangor with 9,500 children in voluntary schools of whom 75% were nonconformists. Lord Hugh Cecil easily admitted that nonconformists had a genuine grievance but suggested that the best remedy would be the construction of new schools as permitted by the bill. 'The further remedy,' he challenged Lloyd George, 'would be to allow different religious teachers to enter the schools and teach their different beliefs. But the Hon. Member would never accept that.' Lloyd George retorted immediately that he would.

At this point Dillon and T.P. O'Connor intervened to give general support to the right of entry of religious instructors from all sects but only at the price of ending nondenominational teaching. Balfour's coalition was beginning to crumble. He quickly admitted that he also understood the nonconformist complaints, but was unable to do anything about it. To make his point he quoted Samuel Johnson:

> How small a part of all that human hearts endure
> That part which laws or kings can cause or cure

He concluded by asking Lord Hugh Cecil, feigning disbelief, whether he really intended to vote for an amendment that would destroy the Anglican character of 8,000 schools.[39]

Balfour's consistent refusal to grant any concessions, even at this early stage of the bill's passage, evidently determined Lloyd George's parliamentary behavior for the rest of the session. Perhaps the bill would be withdrawn if the fragile alliance supporting it could be cracked, but it would not be changed. It was no use trying to make the measure tolerable to nonconformists. Amendments were now tactical. He would, as the *British*

Weekly noted in its comment on the 22 July debate, 'exhaust all parliamentary resources, so that he may say he had done so when the real fight comes.'[40]

Parliament recessed on 8 August and Lloyd George immediately left England with Frank Edwards, but without Maggie, for Zermatt in Switzerland. However, he was back in London on 3 September briefly to appear with William Abraham and D.R. Daniel before the Trades Union Congress on behalf of the Penrhyn quarrymen, who in November 1900 had renewed their strike for recognition. This meeting, at Holborn Town Hall, marked Lloyd George's first formal contact with the powerful labor organization that would play so large a part in his future political life. This time he received a tremendous welcome interspersed with a few ironic cries of 'Good Old Birmingham.' He gave a short grave report on the pathetic condition of the strikers, ending with a plea for money, not resolutions of support. Subsequently, the conference passed a resolution expressing its 'contempt' for Lord Penrhyn and promising money sometime in the future.[41] The next day he was off to Criccieth for the Eisteddfod.

By this time the sheer unpopularity of the government and its Education Bill was being reflected in electoral returns. In a long letter, written on 8 September, which the *British Weekly* featured, Lloyd George described the political climate and provided a forecast of the resistance strategy which would become manifest after the bill's passage. He urged the *British Weekly* to use all its influence to bring nonconformists to vote in the coming municipal elections. Petitions against the bill, said Lloyd George, were discredited. The same names always appeared. Protests were for enthusiasts. Only votes counted with the present government. Parliament had taken note of Bury, North Leeds, and Sevenoaks.[42] 'We are apt to talk,' he continued,

> as if the passage of the Bill through Parliament were a certainty. The Education Bill may yet founder on the parliamentary high sea.
> All the same it may become law, and to be quite candid, reckoning up the chances, they are slightly in favour of its safe passage.

Defeat on a major item, he explained, would mean resignation and dissolution. Many Tories were in unsafe seats and would not want to risk an election. Accordingly, the opposition must prepare a reception for this 'gigantic and unparalleled fraud' that was making its way through parliament. The bodies to carry out the bill would be chosen in the municipal elections of 1902 and 1903 and in the county council elections of March 1904. Caernarvonshire, he noted proudly, had already said it would not put the bill into effect. Other counties should follow this example. He concluded:

> Our purpose should be not merely to render the Bill, if carried, a nullity, but to use it as a weapon to tear down the present educational system.
> The State priests have chosen to raise the whole issue. Let free Churchmen hold them to it everywhere and all along the line until education is as free of clerical control in England and Wales as it is in our colonies.[43]

By the end of the month, the news that Birmingham Liberal Unionists, led by some of Chamberlain's major supporters, had carried a strong resolution against the bill, demanding the abolition of religious tests for teachers, and that a majority of non-provided school managers be appointed by the local authority, convinced some optimistic Liberals that they might yet defeat educational reform.[44] However, after trying unsuccessfully to press Morant for concessions on the bill, Chamberlain was able to quiet the Birmingham revolt at a special meeting of the Liberal Unionist executive on 9 October where he questioned whether, under existing circumstances, he could remain their leader. This was a real threat. With Home Rule diminishing as an issue between the parties, the personality of the Member for West Birmingham remained the strongest cement holding the Liberal Unionists together. This evoked in November a brilliant parody from Lloyd George in the House of Commons during the debate on the use of closure to shorten discussion of the amendments to the bill. Lloyd George's argument, as it had been since the bill's introduction, was that the government had no mandate from the 1900 election to take up education. The country had never been consulted and if it had been it would have rejected education reform. What would have been the slogans? 'Vote for Collins and the catechism,' 'Vote for the Colonial Secretary and the True Religion', how would Birmingham have regarded it?

> Even now the fate, not merely of the Ministry but of the Empire depends on the Bill. The Colonial Secretary has told his constituents, 'If you do not get this Bill through, well, I will have to go, and there is an end to the British Empire.' Of course the Rt. Hon. Gentleman's constituents all believe that he is the very linchpin of the British Empire. But what did they do? They passed a series of five resolutions—I do not know that any of them has yet been embodied in the Bill; at any rate there was severe condemnation of this Bill. There was no mandate even from Birmingham for this Bill.[45]

Nevertheless, the divisions among the bill's supporters were apparent. On 13 October Lloyd George sought in a letter to *The Times* to pry the cracks a little wider. The pretext was a letter from Herbert, Cardinal Vaughan to the Irish Nationalist *Freeman's Journal* contending that nonconformists in parliament were the immoral enemies of denominational teaching and urging the Irish Nationalists, who were nervously pondering the political dangers inherent in their continued support of the Unionists, to stand firm.[46] This was not new. The candid and impulsive Archbishop of Westminster had been writing public letters since July suggesting that the radicals intended to use the Education Bill to capture and destroy denominational schools. But the letter of 12 October was frankly hostile and partisan. After telling the Irish Nationalists that they should neither abstain from voting nor vote against the Education Bill, Cardinal Vaughan concluded with a testimonial of Unionist loyalty that confirmed everything Lloyd George had been saying about him in the past months. 'We are convinced that we are not likely ever to get a more satisfactory settlement in the education problem, and we see in this triumph of the Government over Nonconformist opposition as strong a guarantee as we can ever expect to get for the liberty to educate Catholic children in the Catholic religion in their own Catholic schools.'[47]

All this was a misapprehension, replied Lloyd George. Nonconformists wished only to secure popular control of schools. This could be obtained in one way, by allowing parents and local authorities, as well as whoever was designated in the school's charter, equal representation on the Board of Managers. In Catholic or Anglican areas this procedure indeed would give majority control to those who desired dogmatic instruction. As an alternative, with full control of the managers in the hands of the local education authority, the nonconformists would agree to the right of entry by all ministers of all denominations to teach children of the various faiths.

These proposals, Lloyd George knew well, were unsatisfactory both to Balfour, although clearly not to all Anglicans, and to the Catholics. The latter did not oppose the right of entry, as their support of Lord Hugh Cecil's proposal showed (and indeed they had introduced an amendment similar to McKenna's on 30 July) but they feared popular control which, in all but a few areas, would have destroyed Catholic schools.

However, Lloyd George's letter concluded with a warning both to the Prime Minister and to the Catholics, in which he repeated his plea made in his first speech on the bill:

> I would appeal to Irishmen whether they have not found less racial and religious bigotry among Nonconformists than amongst the classes who are promoting the Education Bill. Welsh Nonconformists have since 1886 returned steadily to Parliament a larger proportion of members who support the claims of Ireland than Irishmen themselves sent there to demand them. It is also true that the demands of Ireland for self government were supported in the last four general elections by a much larger proportion of English Nonconformists than of English Catholics. I would not, therefore, have Irishmen believe that nonconformists, at any rate, would treat ruthlessly and harshly the conscientious convictions of Irish Catholics who dwell amongst them in England and Wales.

But he ended with an ultimatum directed toward the Prime Minister saying that if he continued to resist all change, as he had been warned by the Irish, he will 'have raised up an agitation which makes it increasingly difficult for Nonconformist members to repeat the Liberal proposals made by them, in the interests of concord, three months ago'.[48]

With Parliament still in recess, this letter, dated 11 October, was a public declaration of the war that had been brewing since July. The nonconformists were no longer interested in concessions. Although the euphoria of the Birmingham Liberal Unionist meeting still lingered among some members of the opposition, Lloyd George was treating the bill as an act already on the statute books. He announced his strategy of resistance in an interview with the *British Weekly* in the second week of November. Asked his opinion of the rate resistance pledges that were being collected at scores of protest meetings held each day throughout the country, he scoffed as he always did at the useless waste of enthusiasm. 'I would prefer,' he said

> the Bill, if passed, to be made unworkable by the refusal of County and

Town Councils to put it into operation.... I have just had a conversation with one of the highest legal authorities in the Kingdom and his opinion is no Council can be compelled. The Council can be threatened, and called revolters, and perhaps can be dissolved, but they cannot be compelled. And if the County and Town councils do not put the law into operation, no one will have an opportunity of refusing to pay rates because the rate will not be demanded.[49]

The date of this conversation was not recorded but it could have been no later than 11 November. On that day Lloyd George had pushed through the reluctant Welsh Members of Parliament the agreement that their chairman, Alfred Thomas, should introduce an amendment to the Education Bill to designate the county and borough councils the local Education Authorities for Wales, in effect making Welsh education administration conform to England's. It appeared to be an unexceptionable housekeeping change and was readily accepted by Balfour the next day.[50]

However, the appointment of the county councils as local authorities for all Welsh secondary and elementary education meant the extinction of the existing county governing bodies which had, since the act of 1889, conducted most satisfactorily Welsh secondary and technical education. These bodies were not without friends, notably two of Lloyd George's most active critics, A.C. Humphreys-Owen who still held Rendel's former seat in Montgomeryshire and, almost inevitably, Bryn Roberts of South Caernarvonshire. In addition Humphreys-Owen was chairman of the Welsh Control Board which supervised the work of the county governing bodies. These men bitterly opposed the proposed amendment in the Welsh Members caucus and were able to raise public resentment in Wales itself.[51] Nevertheless, as Herbert Lewis recorded in admiration, 'Lloyd George swept everything before him in the peremptory fashion, and carried them [the Welsh MPs] in favour of the English plan.'[52] Thus by 1902, as the Welsh phase of his career was closing, Lloyd George, paradoxically, was gaining secure control of the Welsh parliamentary delegation for which he had connived and schemed so long. Soon there would be no opposition at all. D.A. Thomas, although he remained in the House of Commons until 1910, took little part in its affairs and devoted himself to making money. Humphreys-Owen, frail and elderly, died in December 1905 and Bryn Roberts, under circumstances which will be noted, accepted a county judgeship soon after the Liberals came to power.

Yet the Thomas amendment was more than a demonstration of Lloyd George's ruthless political ascendancy over his Welsh colleagues whom, in most cases, he despised. The county councils, as Lloyd George had just made clear to the *British Weekly*, were democratically elected, mostly nonconformist, and could not, he insisted, be coerced into carrying out the terms of the bill. As the campaign for disestablishment had already demonstrated, they were Lloyd George's favorite instrument both for the mobilization of public sentiment and for political administration. Best of all, they always provided, through joint committees, the opportunity for the sort of unified executive action throughout the principality that he hoped to make the spearhead of Welsh Home Rule.[53] Hence, the Thomas amendment, which Balfour unthinkingly accepted, gave Lloyd George the weapon he needed for the prolonged extraparliamentary struggle against the Education Act, upon which he had already decided.

The final act in the new tactics of resistance came two weeks later on 25 November at the report stage with the amendment Lord Hugh Cecil had promised in July and which Lloyd George, at that time, had said he would support. Cecil's amendment would have allowed parents to withdraw children from religious instruction in all schools while permitting religious instruction other than that provided by the school managers, should a 'reasonable' number of parents ask for it.[54] The amendment would have meant the 'right of entry' for both provided and non-provided schools and would have nearly removed the distinction between them. It contained also, it should be noted, most of the essentials of the agreement later worked out by Bishop Edwards and Lloyd George in spring of 1903 and which indeed appeared again in the bill that Edwards introduced into the House of Lords in 1908. But by this time, in the last stages of Balfour's measure, Lloyd George's interest in compromise had long since evaporated. In his speech he attacked the Prime Minister for failure to give leadership and guidance on his bill. However, the indiscriminate right of entry would be disastrous, he continued, contradicting everything he had said for the past six months and most of what he would urge for the next two years. It would result in

> hundreds of little theological Fashodas all over the country, one theological sect saying, 'That boy belongs to us,' and another saying 'He belongs to us.' At one time the child would belong to one sect and in a week or a fortnight there would be a successful Jameson Raid, or there would be some local Major Marchand, who would have the child taken away. It is not a question of superior dogmas, it is a question of superior buns. The noble Lord Hugh Cecil talks as if all the children were thirsting for Church dogma, but they are simply ravenously hungry for buns, and it is a question of blankets with the parents.[55]

In the end Lloyd George voted against Cecil's amendment while Balfour unhappily abstained.[56]

Except for Balfour's generous accolade on his performance on the bill during the wind up of the third reading debate, much of the extraordinary press attention Lloyd George received in the last days of the 1902 parliament was designed to contrast his partisan industry with the limpness displayed by the Liberal leadership, usually excepting Asquith. Even Rendel mentioned him favourably, after which the former leader was sharply rebuffed by Humphreys-Owen: 'It does not do to flourish Lloyd George too much in people's faces.'[57] But perhaps the most significant comment came from *The Times*, which, although it now printed regularly shortened versions of his speeches, still tried to ignore Lloyd George in its news columns. When it spoke of him at all in leaders, it was generally to denounce him as a trouble maker. At the end of the year in its Review of Welsh Affairs, without saying that it agreed, the paper noted that Lloyd George's friends were already speaking of him as the next Liberal Home Secretary. He had, thought the paper, demonstrated something more than simply hard work and cleverness. He also displayed political consistency. In addition he had made a new position for himself in British politics: 'Mr. Lloyd-George, ardent Welshman as he is, has won his place as the spokesman, not of Welsh causes but of militant English Non-conformity; and he seems likely to become another Henry Richard rather than a second Tom Ellis'.[58]

To compare Lloyd George to the conservative, well-to-do Richard rather than to the cottage-bred Tom Ellis, with whom Lloyd George had frequently identified himself, must have seemed incongruous. Richard's election, to be sure, had been a triumph in the great election of 1868 that inaugurated the Welsh revival and he had led the Welsh party until his death in 1888, when Rendel succeeded him. But he had been a conventional Gladstonian, intensely religious, anti-Cowper-Temple, and pro-Home Rule.

This was not Lloyd George, but in a sense *The Times* was right. In his later years Richard had become a power in the Liberation Society and a popular spokesman for English nonconformity and reform in general in a way that Ellis never could have done. Even when serving as Liberal Chief Whip he remained a Welshman. Lloyd George on the other hand, although he disliked professional chapel politicians as much as Ellis, had found friends among English nonconformists. The Cadburys and Rowntrees, Robertson Nicoll, and John Clifford, all had the power of wealth or public influence which he understood and valued. Where Welsh nonconformity with its fixation on Welsh Church disestablishment had become a drag and a bore, English nonconformity after 1902 was to be until the war his constituency. Its causes—licensing, expansion of local government activity, and humanitarian reform in general—became his platform.

IV

The House of Commons gave the Education Bill its third reading on 3 December 1902. The bill received the royal assent on 20 December. Lloyd George announced the Welsh education revolt less than a month later with an 'Address to the People of Wales' which was evidently completed on 17 January 1903, although its publication was part of a strategy meeting held in Cory Hall, Cardiff by the Welsh National Liberal Council on 20 and 21 January.[59] This document, already noted as evidence of Lloyd George's continued interest in Welsh unification, bears close study. In it lay all the elements of his strategy against the bill since its introduction, as well as the Welsh 'plan of campaign'. He had discarded civil disobedience from the first. A refusal by county councils to touch the act, he insisted, would harm Welsh education and would alienate many people who deplored the act's injustice but who were equally opposed to illegal action. The *Manchester Guardian*, a publication to which he paid much attention, had made precisely this point in a strong leading article on 19 September. Lloyd George enlarged upon this with a series of practical recommendations about the county councils' administration of secondary education, stressing always the importance of united action throughout the principality.

At the elementary level, instead of advising lawbreaking, he dilated upon the council's statutory duty to insure efficiency within the non-provided schools. As the act specified that the councils were responsible for wear and tear in the Church schools they assumed, it followed, that they were not responsible for the condition of those schools before the act came into effect. Accordingly they had the right to satisfy themselves that Church schools were in decent condition when council support began. Therefore, the denomination must be required to put the school into usable shape and a searching inspection would have to be made. Lloyd George knew, as did everyone in Wales, that hundreds of the small, impoverished, Church of England schools in rural areas were in desperate need of repair and had been certified as efficient in the past only because of the good-natured connivance of Board of Education inspectors. There were many avenues of noncompliance provided by the terms of the act itself.

These were the tactics of resistance, but Lloyd George also offered a plan for settlement. Councils should give no rate aid to denominational schools unless, first, the managers consented to 'full and complete public control of funds voted toward the support of those schools.' (This, of course, included the appointment of staff.) And second

> to forego the imposition of all religious or political tests upon the appoint-
> ment of their teachers. If any of the schools within the area declined to
> accept these conditions, money paid by the Treasury in respect of those
> schools might be transmitted to their managers, provided all the
> conditions as to efficiency, repair, etc. imposed by law are complied with,
> but no assistance should be given them out of the rates.

But there followed an offer of concessions, ambiguous and unclear. Typically for Lloyd George it was a proposal to negotiate rather than an outline of terms.

> If, on the other hand, the managers of any denominational schools
> within the area exhibited any disposition to meet the educational
> authorities on these two vital points, for my part I would advocate the
> extension to such managers of ample facilities for teaching the children
> of their own denomination the doctrines of the Church to which the
> parents belong. That is, I would in every county proffer to Churchmen
> the Colonial compromise. I believe it will be found that many moderate
> and tolerant Churchmen will deem this concession fairly meets their
> views.[60]

In these murky sentences lay the essential point of contention, so far as Lloyd George was concerned, about dogmatic education. On one hand he wanted popular control of the spending of education rates. This meant council authority in the appointment of teachers, which, he always said, would mean Church authority anyway in Anglican localities. But given this he was willing to concede broad rights for the teaching of any church doctrine, established or free, in any area where a substantial number of parents demanded it.[61] But what he could not admit publicly was that he intended to grant the right of entry not only to nonconformist pastors in the famous 8,000 parishes but also to Anglicans whose children attended board schools which currently offered only Cowper-Temple bible reading. Here he was far ahead of any of his supporters. Among the Welsh rebels there were many more violent than Lloyd George, Alfred Thomas for example, who would fight any compromise on denominational education in state schools, and there were others who opposed religious teaching root and branch, asserting that the Scripture belonged only in Sunday schools, with which Wales was well provided.

The proceedings at the Cardiff meeting were watched closely in London by Robert Morant, who was now at last in charge of the Board of Education. Balfour had lost no time, once he became Prime Minister, in reorganizing the education department. Within a month John Gorst, taking with him a political pension of £1,200, was succeeded as Vice President of the Board of Education by Sir William Anson. More important, George Kekewich was discharged as Permanent Secretary to be replaced by Morant. Because Kekewich would have retired in any case on 1 April 1903 he remained technically on leave in order to save his pension. (Hence Morant served eight months as acting Permanent Secretary.) In Morant, Lloyd George was faced by an opponent who was in fact the author of the Education Act and whose determined and unscrupulous cunning were the equal of his own. Morant, at bottom, was as eager as Lloyd George for compromise, but he so distrusted the Member for Caernarvon District that he declined to take the risk of approaching him directly.[62] As it often does chance intervened. Lloyd George, as he reported to his brother, found himself sitting next to A.G. Edwards, the Bishop of St. Asaph in the train from Chester to London on 4 February. He was, wrote Lloyd George, most friendly, willing to accept the reciprocal right of entry between voluntary schools and board schools, and asserted that in any case voluntary schools would be a thing of the past in ten years' time. Most important, he was going to see Morant.

Edwards told the Permanent Secretary on 8 February that Lloyd George was most conciliatory and provided Lloyd George with the equally satisfactory news that Morant believed that the effect of the plan of campaign would be complete deadlock. On 9 February he wrote to Lloyd George asking him to visit the Bishop's Palace.[63]

The results were more substantive discussions at a meeting at Llandrindod Wells on 27 February attended by representatives of all but two of the Welsh county councils, but with observers from the Church schools. Lloyd George was present, although St. Asaph appears to have been represented by Lord Kenyon. The press was excluded. Here the essence of the Welsh school controversy came into the open for the first time. There were two basic issues. One was the matter of control, the appointment of teachers in voluntary, not-provided, schools. If the teachers were to be appointed by a non-representative board of managers the controlling voice would be that of the vicar. 'Why should the clergyman appoint a teacher who is a civil servant?' Lloyd George had once asked. 'With equal fitness he might appoint the exciseman. Really the parson has more in common with the exciseman than with the schoolmaster for they both deal with spirits in bondage.'[64] Yet the issue involved more than simple control of patronage. For the Church the nature of the teaching faculty would determine the religious atmosphere of the school. To give up the right of teacher appointment would mean giving up in effect control of the schools and would abolish the chief distinction between the provided and non-provided schools. To this the lower Anglican clergy, even more the Roman Catholics, would never agree, no matter what concessions were urged by the Bishop of St. Asaph.

But second, there was the matter of denominational teaching. Here, equally, Lloyd George was out of step with the dour free churchmen who were the bulk of nonconformity in Wales. He wished to abolish the single denominational monopoly of voluntary schools by the Anglican Church, but at the same time he hoped to relax also the rigorously nondenominational character of state schools. His code word for this was always the 'colonial plan,' in effect the right of entry for all denominations. But he never specified which schools would be involved nor at what time denominational teaching would take place, whether during school hours or at the beginning or end of the day. At Llandrindod Wells, Lloyd George was able to avoid a direct question from Lord Kenyon, president of North Wales University College and Deputy Chancellor of the University of Wales, when he was asked: would the right of entry apply to all schools or only to non-provided schools? Lloyd George simply closed the meeting with a resolution that 'friendly arrangements between the education authorities and the church were desirable.'[65]

The Llandrindod Wells meeting had been convened to formulate proposals for a round of negotiations between representatives of the Church and of the counties, to work out a set of proposals that each side could accept or reject. Accordingly it was followed by a much larger assembly which came together at the Westminster Palace Hotel on 24 March, 1903. From this conference came the so-called 'Concordat' between Lloyd George and the Bishop of St. Asaph to which there would be many references in following years and upon which the two men would try again and again in the future to build a compromise. The Westminster Palace Conference was important, yet it demonstrated also the essential fact of the Welsh revolt that in the end prevented any agreed settlement between the established and the free church and by doing so, paradoxically, kept Balfour's measure intact even after the Liberals came to power: that while the leaders and spokesmen on each side were quite willing to negotiate and compromise, behind the generals on each side was a large phalanx of potentially mutinous troops determined to resist any conclusion other than complete victory.

Although 23 men were present at the Westminster Palace Hotel—besides Lloyd George, Herbert Lewis, Frank Edwards, and Howell Gee and Lord Mostyn and Francis Mostyn, Roman Catholic Bishop of Menavia and Vicar Apostolic of Wales—representing the Church were only Bishop Edwards and Lord Kenyon. The other three bishops of the Welsh Church under pressure from the powerful John Owen of St. David's ominously were absent. For the student of Lloyd George's life the meeting of 24 March has other significance. Although it was supposed to be strictly private, a stenographer took notes and so there is available the first verbatim textual example of the negotiating technique that Lloyd George would make famous in later years.[66] He would pretend to misunderstand questions, assert that he was speaking only for himself or assume the power to commit the county councils as circumstances warranted, contradict stands he had taken publicly when as he put it, he 'had his war paint on.'[67] Generally the conference, which lasted over six hours, was a series of dialogues between Lloyd George and everyone else. Two matters only were at issue: the right of entry of denominational teachers into all schools and the composition of the board of managers in denominational schools. On the former point, the Llandrindod meeting had agreed to concede the right to clergymen to enter state schools two days a week to teach Anglican dogma to willing children. On these occasions the school day would be shortened so that during the presence of the vicar technically the school was not in session. Surprisingly, after his bitter complaints about the thousands of innocent nonconformist children exposed to the contagious disease of Anglicanism in single school areas, Lloyd George insisted that nonconformist clergymen had really no interest in the reciprocal right of entering Church schools.[68] The reason for this apparently was that the balancing concession he wished to have from the Church was not the right of entry for nonconformist clergymen, but the acceptance in denominational schools of popular control, which, above all, meant the appointment of teachers. Instead of appointing four of the six members of the boards of managers, the Church should appoint only two. Two would be named by the council and two by the minor local authority, usually the parish council as nominees of the parents. The experiment would last three years.[69] This then became the 'concordat,' popular control of Church schools in return for the right of entry outside school hours. There would be, in effect, for a period of three years, no difference between provided and non-provided schools. All would accept outside clergymen at certain times, all would offer full, but non-sectarian, religious instruction at other times and all teachers would be appointed by the local education authority.

Obviously the 'concordat' was in no sense a contract. Rather it was a series of proposals that St. Asaph and Lloyd George would attempt to sell to their separate constituencies. The laity and lower clergy of the diocese of St. Asaph lost no time in discarding their Bishop's agreement with Lloyd George. Three weeks after the Westminster Palace meeting, on 14 April, the diocesan conference stated its terms of compromise. In fact it accepted the use of the London Syllabus (for Cowper-Temple bible reading) and the right of entry, but insisted that the appointment of teachers be handled by a joint board of twelve, equally divided between the diocese and the education authority.

Although this reverse could hardly have been unexpected—the *Church Times* had been denouncing the Lloyd George-St. Asaph negotiations for weeks on the basis that there was no reason for the Church to bargain for rights that it already possessed by statute—this unsatisfactory response worried Lloyd George. Publicly and for a time privately he was optimistic.[70] However, after the refusal of the Church to cooperate he wrote a nervous note to Herbert Lewis on the prospects of a rejection by county council representatives. 'The committee meets at the West Pal Hotel at 11:00 on Thursday (23 April) to consider the Bishop's—or rather the clergy's terms. They are quite impossible. I'll send you a copy. I wish you could be present....The next step is very important. Don't you think so?'[71]

On 23 April the county council representatives met and, rather surprisingly, accepted the instructional proposals of the clergy, but rejected the specifications for a joint board for the appointment of teachers, to the extent that the head teacher could not be chosen this way. In effect as the letter to the *Church Times* explained later, they rejected the 'church atmosphere' which the head teacher would set.[72]

Both the *British Weekly* and the *Church Times* expressed relief that the concordat had failed and Robertson Nicoll, who showed frequent irritation at Wales's lack of interest in the English rate resistance struggle, hoped now that compromise had been 'definitely rejected' Wales would come into line with England.[73] In the interval between the Westminster Palace meeting and the rejection of the concordat, Lloyd George had held a series of conversations with Perks and Nicoll in which he attempted, and failed, to win English nonconformist support for his plan.[74]

For his part, Lloyd George had now to explain to his followers that he had been negotiating behind their backs and to build again enthusiasm for a fight. This was not, to be sure, the end of attempts to find a compromise. Neither the Church leadership nor the government desired a public confrontation with Welsh rebels. Morant, for all his determination and industry, had within him a marked streak of caution which manifested itself on this occasion and on others—when indeed he was working for Lloyd George—in outbursts of almost hysterical despair. In addition his ministerial superiors, Anson and Lord Londonderry, the latter since August 1902 the President of the Board of Education, as well as the Cabinet itself, were almost totally distracted by the uncertainties attending the London Education Bill which was at that time before the House of Commons. The metropolis had been deliberately left out of the 1902 act, hence the measure had been supported by the powerful National Union of Teachers. But the 1903 bill proposed to abolish the London School Board, the one truly professional body in English educational administration, which was also a stronghold of the NUT. Thus the union, and its spokesman in the House of Commons, T.J. Macnamara, fiercely resisted the second measure and the Unionists, having won 51 out of 59 metropolitan London seats in 1900, feared the NUT as a dangerous opponent. The bitterness of the struggle over London education opened wounds that made Morant's life a nightmare during the next eight years and contributed to his translation to the national health insurance administration in 1911, while Macnamara became a radical hero. In these circumstances, with some members of the Cabinet uncertain about whether to push ahead with London at all, Morant followed the easier path of putting off the contest with the Welsh rebels by simply postponing the date upon which the Education Act came into force in the counties of the principality, from the spring to the autumn of 1903 and finally to the spring of 1904.

Meanwhile hints about the concordat negotiations appeared regularly in the sectarian press. Lloyd George vigorously defended himself. At Swansea in the third week of May he justified the conversations with the St. Asaph representatives as time well spent. At least they now knew who their friends were. Speaking to representatives of the county councils he assured them that no words of the act stipulated that rate money had to be given to voluntary schools. The act specified only that it was the duty of the local education authorities to keep them efficient. How could this be done without control?[75] He followed this immediately with an article in the *Pilot* entitled 'Educational Compromises', which stands as something of a minor masterpiece in the literature of candid revelation of half-truth. There was no dispute during the negotiations about religious education, Lloyd George insisted. Two-thirds of Welsh children were in board schools anyway. County council representatives agreed that they should have religious instruction either from the London School Board Syllabus or in their parental faith. All this St. Asaph accepted without change. The breakdown came when the parish clergy discovered they would have to give up 'the power and patronage' that went with control of the voluntary schools, the use of the teacher almost as a lay curate. The Welsh county councils could not accept terms which gave away control of the appointment of the teacher whose salary the council would pay and which would include religious tests. There was no alternative now but to 'fight it out.'[76]

It must be emphasized that Bishop Edwards's concern lay with the large majority of Welsh children, Anglican or otherwise, who received no religious instruction.[77] Both he and Lloyd George appear sincerely to have wanted to bring regular and indeed sectarian religious education back into all Welsh schools. But Lloyd George equally was anxious to break up the Church monopoly of dogmatic education in single school areas by the introduction of Cowper-Temple religious instruction. However, neither could control the followers each claimed to represent. The parish clergy of St. Asaph, let alone those in the other three Welsh dioceses, had none of Bishop Edwards's missionary spirit and were fully content to rest upon the privileges accorded them by the act. And Lloyd George, as he was beginning to discover, gravely underestimated the nonconformist hostility not only to doctrinal instruction, but to any religious instruction in state schools.

On 3 June the campaign of resistance to the Education Act was officially restarted with a second monster meeting at Park Hall, Cardiff, at which a series of resolutions were passed by acclamation urging councils to withhold rate aid from schools 'not under public control' and asking the population at large to refuse rates to those unnamed councils which refused to cooperate in resistance. Vigilance committees were to be established throughout Wales to monitor the behavior of untrustworthy county councilmen. In the evening at an overflow meeting Lloyd George assured questioners that this was not lawbreaking. No man, for example the Prime Minister, who condemned magistrates for exercising their undoubted right to refuse to renew public house licenses, was entitled to make judgements about lawbreaking.[78]

The allusion to councils which had refused to cooperate with the rest, referred to Brecknock and Radnorshire where the councils had 'sectarian', meaning Unionist, as opposed to 'progressive', meaning Liberal, majorities. The latter was the constituency of Frank Edwards, himself an Anglican and cousin of the Bishop of St. Asaph. Neither was particularly large and each had a substantial English population, but their disobedience marred the seamless unity that was necessary to symbolize Welsh resistance.

The second, more violent, phase of Welsh resistance began, therefore, not with the noisy demonstration of the second Cardiff conference, but with the triennial county council elections held nine months later in March, 1904 which brought the two recalcitrant councils into line. While both the government and the Welsh rebels waited for this event, the Unionists suffered a devastating blow with the resignation from the government of Joseph Chamberlain on 16 September 1903, which was followed, after three weeks, by the departure of the Duke of Devonshire from the Cabinet. The secession of these two popular and powerful figures, accompanied also by a host of minor changes in the ministry, was the product of the tremendous upheaval in Unionist politics that had followed Chamberlain's announcement on 15 May of his conversion to the doctrine of tariff protection. The political effect was further to divide an already weakened Unionist government while giving the Liberals the issue of free trade upon which, for once, all of them could agree. Lloyd George, of course, accepted with special pleasure the opportunity to attack Chamberlain under the banner of virtuous, unalloyed Liberalism. Accordingly, without neglecting entirely the education revolt—there was a giant Albert Hall meeting on 11 July organized by the Metropolitan Free Church Federation—he devoted much time and energy to the denunciation of import duties and the corrupt and selfish motives of the man who made them political questions. Meanwhile, he used his return to the mainstream of official Liberalism to mend friendships within the English party. He attacked Chamberlain on his second appearance before the Palmerston Club in Oxford in June and induced the Oxford Union in November to adopt by a majority of 29 votes a resolution against protection. Early in November he spoke for Bryce in Aberdeen and Campbell-Bannerman in Stirling and at the end of the month the party's leader came to Wales to speak in Newport, while in January 1904, Grey, still recruiting for the Liberal League, visited Caernarvon. The rest of the time he crisscrossed the country introducing newly adopted Liberal candidates and speaking at by-elections which the Unionists now were losing regularly. On 6 February 1904 at St. Albans, in a by-election caused by the resignation of Conservative Vicary Gibbs in order to stand again as a tariff reformer, he was assaulted by a mob as he left the hall to catch a train. The mob, evidently far more concerned with Lloyd George than with the Liberal candidate J. Banford-Slack, seemed possessed more by the jingoistic demons of the South African War than by the sober concerns of fiscal policy. There were shouts of 'Traitor', 'Pro-Boer', 'lynch him,' 'kill him.' The police were able to get Lloyd George into a cab although not before he was struck on the head by a club. Even then the mob nearly overturned the cab before the driver escaped.[79]

While the split in Unionism occasioned by the tariff reform controversy immensely weakened Balfour's political authority, paradoxically it caused Lloyd George in the winter of 1903/4 much embarrassment and probably so eroded his position as chief tactician of the Welsh revolt that, after the spring of 1904, he had no option but stonewall resistance to the requirements of the Education Act. The facts were that the departure of Chamberlain from the Cabinet, if it removed the most powerful ministerial opponent of the education scheme, had also the opposite effect of producing within the Unionist party a block of Liberal Unionist free traders who began to think about recrossing the House to the Liberals, particularly as that party's commitment to Home Rule seemed to have subsided. But nonconformist influence and the education struggle presented an obstacle. Hence, a number of these men, of whom the Duke of Devonshire was the most prominent, sought to ease their transition by finding a settlement of the sectarian school question.[80]

The possibility of a Liberal-free trade Unionist arrangement was a threat to Balfour, but hardly less a danger to Lloyd George was the possibility of independent negotiations on the Education Act. Perks warned him on 23 December that English nonconformity would never stand for the admission of Anglican clergymen into state schools.[81] Nonetheless these negotiations interested the Liberal leadership enough to cause Campbell-Bannerman to send Asquith to see Perks and Bryce to see Clifford. Both were discouraged.[82] It was possible to compromise on Home Rule, but education was out of the question. On 1 January, Churchill wrote to Lord Hugh Cecil, like Churchill a Unionist Free Trader, but also, unlike Churchill, a strong Churchman. 'I lunched yesterday privately with Lloyd George,' wrote Churchill and

> had a very interesting and not altogether unsatisfactory conversation with him. He told me that the Duke [in politics at the turn of the century the 'Duke' was of Devonshire] had, he understood, opened negotiations with Spencer [Charles, son of Earl Spencer and Liberal MP] for a compromise on education, the principle of this compromise he described to me as 'facilities for inside control' and he informed me that he had knocked it on the head as there was no use pretending he could carry his people where he could not. It is undoubtedly true that either you or he could blow up any arrangement which might be come to between the Leaders; but if you and he could reach any sort of understanding, all the educational dynamite would be safely damped. He is very anxious to meet you and have a talk and I would suggest that you and he should dine with me privately on the first night of this Session February 2nd in some quiet place.
>
> I do not pretend to understand the passions of the Education controversy, and it seemed to me, talking to Lloyd George yesterday, that some of the differences were astonishingly small and petty. For instance LG says that his people will die rather than give 'facilities for inside control', that is to say they will not give right of entry into public elementary schools (so I take it) to any religious body except the religion of Sir Henry Fowler and Mr. Perks according to act of Parliament, or what I call 'the highest common factor' religion—'neutral tint'—during school hours when compulsory attendance is required. They are perfectly prepared to give facilities out of school hours to any religious denomination, and they are prepared to shorten school accordingly. In fact, a treaty has been concluded between Lloyd George and the Bishop of St. Asaph for Wales as follows:—school hours begin at nine o'clock four days a week with half an hour of neutral tint religion; but on two days a week, they begin at nine-thirty and on these days the school would be opened at nine o'clock to denominational teachers for the instruction of those children whose parents desire them to attend.[83]

Churchill's explanation of Lloyd George's dilemma constituted a fair summary of the educational impasse in Wales at the close of the year. Lloyd George was struggling to end, before he lost control of it, an insurrection that he had himself helped to raise. And more trouble would follow. Within days of Churchill's letter, Bishop Edwards published in the *Nineteenth Century* an article entitled 'Educational Concordats' which listed the compromises arrived at in the Westminster Palace Hotel conference and concluded with the assertion, not mentioned by Lloyd George, that 'as an experiment' it had been agreed that 'teachers may, if willing, give unrestricted religious teaching in provided as well as non-provided schools.'[84]

Although the stenographic transcript of the Westminster Palace Hotel conference would have shown that Lloyd George had agreed to no such thing, it would also have shown that he did consent to the entrance of Church of England clergymen into council schools before teaching hours on certain days each week. Hence, Lloyd George, much occupied with speaking on free trade in London, immediately contradicted the article in a speech to the Caernarvon Borough Liberal Association on 5 January. But this was promptly refuted by Stanley L. Weyman, a novelist, and member of the St. Asaph diocesan educational committee, who declared Lloyd George 'had not opposed' the right of clergy to enter provided schools during hours of instruction. As a result Lloyd George was forced into another explanation which he made in an interview to the *Carnarvon Herald* on 26 January. He gave his usual answer to the charges that under the act of 1902 any religious instruction other than bible reading was illegal during school hours. But, he concluded, 'under no conditions would I be a party to a permanent settlement which enabled any sect to utilize the services of compulsory attendance to force a child to attend school while sectarian teaching was being given. This is what "facilities during school hours" means.'[85] However, he followed this with an article by Alderman Thomas John Hughes, Lloyd George's supporter in Glamorganshire, in the *Nineteenth Century* which contained the only public admission of what in fact he had done. Toward the end of the piece, after having emphasized many times that the Welsh county councils were never willing to give unrestricted facilities during school hours, Alderman Hughes stated 'I am...authorized by Mr. Lloyd George to state positively that the utmost the representatives of the Councils offered was facilities for unrestricted instruction on certain days outside school hours....'[86]

As was customary with Lloyd George the public sound and fury concealed conciliatory, indeed amicable, private arrangements. On 16 December 1903 Lloyd George and Bishop Edwards had appeared together at the Guild Hall in Caernarvon to appeal for funds for new buildings at the University College of North Wales in Bangor. Here Lloyd George joked merrily about participating in the typical Church business of raising money. Whether it was at this time or later, within the next month the two men agreed that the amendment was the only solution to the education question. Possibly this was promoted by a warning from Perks at the end of December that English political nonconformity would never stand for the remodeling of Balfour's measure along the lines being considered by the

Duke of Devonshire and Unionist high church free traders.[87] In any case on 24 January 1904 Edwards visited Morant's office again to propose an amendment to the Education Act allowing the right of entry and sectarian teaching in provided schools. Morant admitted that he was himself working on a bill along these lines but was worried that it might be opposed by the Liberal front bench. Edwards understood nevertheless that the Permanent Secretary had agreed to the proposal that the Bishop should introduce such a measure in the House of Lords.[88] All of this was occurring, of course, in the midst of the public dispute about what had, or had not, been agreed to at the Westminster Palace Hotel conference. In late March, probably as a result of the Hughes article in the *Nineteenth Century*, Lloyd George met a convention of English nonconformist leaders, including Perks, Clifford, and Albert Spicer as well as a number of others. Here he was soundly rebuffed again in the attempt to gain support even for a limited right of entry. Such a surrender, Perks reported to Rosebery, 'would take the heart out of the dissenters.' The others, he concluded, 'all agreed with me.'[89] Lloyd George continued to flirt, cautiously, with the Roseberyites. In January about a week after Grey's flattering appearance in Caernarvon, Lloyd George visited Fallodon to discuss politics with Grey, who still pursued the dream of a Rosebery premiership with Asquith as Leader of the House of Commons. Lloyd George agreed to the former proposition but not to the latter, protesting his loyalty to Campbell-Bannerman.[90]

Despite the unpromising reaction from the English nonconformist leaders, which Lloyd George who saw him regularly had surely conveyed, Bishop Edwards introduced his measure, the Education (Transferred Schools) Bill in the House of Lords on 9 May 1904. Essentially the bill would have ended the distinction between provided and non-provided schools in any area that chose to apply it. A local education authority, and any denominational school committee, could contract to set aside all provisions of the act dealing with teacher appointment, religious instruction, rent, leasing and repairs.[91] This was a simple and drastic cutting of the education knot. Except for curricular matters, decisions upon teacher appointment, dogmatic instruction, perhaps even the rate support of voluntary schools, would become a subject for private negotiation. While it would have destroyed much of the supervisory authority of his office, Bishop Edwards's bill was provisionally accepted by Lord Londonderry, the President of the Board of Education. The House of Lords gave it its first reading without a division. Lloyd George was cautious. Publicly he continued to insist that Welsh councils would never agree to sectarian teaching within school hours, 'inside facilities,' although he approved of local option.[92] Privately, as usual, he expressed a different opinion. He was already tired of the education struggle and rarely mentioned it in his correspondence. 'St. Asaph bill going well,' he wrote to his brother. 'I want Education out of the way to fight the publicans. You cannot fight on two fronts successfully.'[93] The 'publicans' referred to the government bill enacted that year to provide compensation to public house owners should local magistrates fail to renew licenses. Temperance reform was a cause that had engaged Lloyd George long before denominational education appeared and was one in which he suspected the country, certainly after the

South African War, might be willing to sanction further legislation. A crusade against drunkenness had a natural ethical dimension that was difficult to introduce into the battle against denominational education.

However, even with the cautious interest in his bill displayed by the President of the Board of Education and despite Edwards's plea in the Lords in his second reading speech for religious instruction in state schools, St. Asaph's bill died at the end of the 1904 session. He was, although evidently he was not aware of it, acting against clear Cabinet policy. There were 'grave reasons,' he was told, against any 'proposal of a conciliatory or concessive nature.' It would hinder the Church's battle and 'it would be absolutely disastrous to discuss any proposal which would admit the possibility of separate treatment from the Roman Catholics, who would consider they had been betrayed.'[94]

More influential in this regard than even the Roman Catholics, and against all compromise, was the Right Reverend John Owen, Bishop since 1897 of the oldest and wealthiest Welsh diocese, St. David's. Owen had become friendly with Morant and supplied him with information on Welsh affairs. He was determined, he wrote to the Permanent Secretary on 20 April 1903, after the Westminster Palace Hotel conference 'to nip in the bud...the St. Asaph terms.'[95] Owen, who had deliberately refrained from attending the Westminster Palace Hotel conference, was furious at St. Asaph's negotiations with Lloyd George. In the future he would emerge as a major opponent, albeit behind the scenes, of compromise on Welsh education. As legislation seemed to be impossible, Edwards, apparently on his own initiative, turned again to compromises that he could effect within the framework of existing law. On 8 September, amid much speculation in the press, Lloyd George stayed with him at the episcopal palace while presiding at the Eisteddfod at Rhyl.[96] Out of this visit, or from discussions a week later at the Athenaeum, evolved a new proposal for the transfer by lease, with a substantial economic rent, of Church schools to the Local Education Authority.[97] The Church schools would in effect become provided schools and the costs of reconstruction and repair, which were genuinely beyond the resources of many voluntary school managers, would have been borne by the county councils. However, one room at each building would be excluded from the lease and reserved for dogmatic instruction at fixed times during the school day. There would be, on the other hand, no facilities for denominational instruction in the board schools. An alternative to this plan offered a scheme whereby in return for a nominal rent, the councils would permit the right of entry by Church of England clergymen into provided schools. Edwards suggested that he take this proposal to Robert Morant. However, by this time the political climate had radically changed.

V

For a year, since the passage of the act in December 1902, the Board of Education took no action against the Welsh educational rebels except to move back repeatedly the appointed day for the application of the act to counties within the principality. The Cardiff resolutions of June 1903, stipulating that Welsh county councils should take no steps to put the act into force, to levy no rate for the support of voluntary schools, to submit no plans to the Education Department and to inspect and find fault with every Church school building had evoked no response from London. By the end of the year Balfour's administration, distracted by Chamberlain's rebellion, and laughed at even by its own supporters, seemed on the verge of collapse. Lloyd George, declared T.P. O'Connor in the *Sunday Sun* on 10 January 1904, has 'driven a County Council through an Act of Parliament.'[98]

There was one discordant note in the grand chorus of Welsh defiance, the two counties of Brecknock and Radnorshire. Here Lloyd George's writ did not run. In defiance of the Cardiff resolutions their sectarian majorities had made rate payments to voluntary schools and were preparing plans to bring the schools into the system. Lloyd George's prestige, therefore, his right to speak as the undisputed chieftain of Wales, depended upon the outcome of the triennial county elections scheduled for the first week of March. He did little speaking in Wales during the campaign, but he saw to it that every progressive candidate for a council seat signed a pledge not to support rate aid for Church schools unless the council possessed control over teacher appointments. Of the two counties the most doubtful was Radnorshire. Here the proportion of Anglicans was higher, and the percentage of Welsh speakers lower, than in any county in Wales.[99] On the eve of the election he told an audience in Bradford that he expected to win only in Brecknock.[100]

Thus the news, by the end of the second week of March, that not only had the progressives dramatically increased their majorities in most Welsh counties but that they now controlled the two recalcitrant councils by two to one, brought a flood of congratulations to Lloyd George in the House of Commons. For many, both friend and foe, the battle was over and Lloyd George had won. The *South Wales Daily News* proclaimed the 'knell of the Government's educational policy in Wales' and Lloyd George himself declared that the threat of *mandamus*—the only weapon provided by statute to compel a council to act—was now at an end.[101] An otherwise most unfriendly article in the *Independent Review* admitted that Lloyd George had defeated Balfour.[102]

One symbol of Lloyd George's growing celebrity was an invitation from Lord Tweedmouth to his house in Park Lane on 11 March 1904 to have dinner with King Edward VII. 'It is an open secret,' wrote the *Daily Illustrated Mirror*, a society paper, 'that Mr. Lloyd George's personality has for some time had a particular attraction for the King and the prominent and sensational role which this well known M.P. has taken on the political stage has made His Majesty very desirous of dinner with him.' The meeting, nonetheless, may have been less than a success. Harold Spender quotes, presumably on Lloyd George's report, the entire conversation between the two men:

King: Do you play bridge?
Lloyd George: No.
King: That is a pity for it's a very good game.[103]

Lloyd George celebrated his triumph in the county council elections by moving an amendment to the Education Act on 14 March to call the government's attention to the new unity in Wales. On the whole he was most conciliatory, blaming Welsh intransigence not on the Board of Education but on the Welsh bishops—always carefully excepting St. Asaph—who had misled the government into thinking Wales would accept the act. Now they knew it would not, and so he proposed, with an eye toward the coming St. Asaph bill, that it was time to amend the Education Act.[104]

One must assume that at this time he believed he had won. He had proven with votes that Wales was behind him. He was calling upon the government to respond, with good grace, to the decision of the people and indeed he evoked a sympathetic response from Lord Hugh Cecil. Even the staunchly Unionist *Western Mail* described his address as moderate and 'without his usual pyrotechnics.'[105]

The Cabinet had no intention of meeting Lloyd George in compromise and indeed accepted on 15 March, the day after his speech, a bill drafted by the Prime Minister himself designed specifically to save the voluntary schools at the expense, if necessary, of all the rest of Welsh elementary education. Balfour judged correctly that the Liberal leadership also were uninterested in compromise on education, even though Morant, who with Anson evidently met Lloyd George briefly on 16 March, still feared a fight. They were anxious for a settlement, reported Lloyd George to his brother.[106] Nonetheless on 26 April the so-called Education (Local Authorities Default) Bill was introduced in the House of Commons. A similar bill drafted by Morant with Londonderry's name on it, had been before the Cabinet since November.[107] But clearly the will behind what Lloyd George came to call 'Welsh coercion' was Balfour's. Ten Welsh county councils, he told the Cabinet in November 1903, had passed resolutions to refuse rate aid to voluntary schools. 'Mr. Balfour thinks,' he told the King with unusual acidity, 'that if it shall prove necessary, a short measure might be prepared putting them straight.'[108] After the March elections it was no use waiting longer.

Essentially the Default Bill permitted the Board of Education, in areas where local education authorities declined to support non-provided schools, to pay the sum owed by the defaulting council directly to the Church schools from the Treasury grant, while the portion of the grant which otherwise would have gone to former board schools became a charge against the local council and would be withheld from their Exchequer subvention. In effect the Board of Education superseded the local education authority in the support of denominational education and did it with money that the council might have spent on its own schools. The bill provided at once a fine and a bribe.

The Default Bill could not be introduced until after the Easter recess. Hence the first public response to the Welsh elections came with the dispatch of A.T. Lawrence, K.C., subsequently Lord Chief Justice, to Carmarthen to conduct an enquiry into the Carmarthenshire County Council's treatment of the 48 Church schools under its jurisdiction. The council's behavior was blatantly illegal—of the sort that Lloyd George deplored—in that it refused to recognize the Church schools in any way. It would not approve the appointment of teachers, sanction curricula, or discuss reorganization, replying always to letters that it did not wish to interfere in the management of voluntary education. Lawrence's findings resulted in *mandamus* proceedings against the council.[109] Lloyd George was not involved in the Carmarthen action but he always assumed that the government intended the public to believe that the Default Bill was the result of Carmarthenshire, not the result of the Welsh elections. During the introduction of the Default Bill Anson certainly went out of his way to convey this impression.[110] On the other hand, Bishop Owen's daughter reports that the initiative for the Carmarthenshire investigation came from her father. The Clerk of the Carmarthen Council was keeping the Bishop of St. David's informed on council strategy, which secrets he passed on to London. Owen at the same time was trying to stop a movement among the Churchmen to withhold their rates.[111]

Lloyd George's own speeches on the Default Bill were a curious amalgam of defiance and disappointment. Clearly he had hoped that after his triumph in the county council elections the government would ignore Wales for the rest of its brief tenure. He criticized the Carmarthenshire Council's behavior. The government was using it as a red herring. There was no need for the bill. There had been no complaints, he insisted, from the Church schools in Carmarthenshire during the second reading debate. The government, he said, was paying off in the crudest manner one of its many constituencies, all of which continually clamoured for danegeld. The 'Brewers Endowment Bill' (the Licensing Bill) was one example, the 'Coercion of Wales Bill' was simply another. 'One day the Goths came from Burton-on-Trent,' he explained.

> The next day they came from Lambeth, and they threatened to sack the city. Something had to be given them. The Education Act satisfied them for a year or two, but the hordes came back. Then came the Brewers Endowment Bill and, said the clergy, we cannot have this. Our consciences will not allow it. 'Oh' replied the Prime Minister, 'I'll square that' and the Right Honourable Gentleman put it right with the present Bill. It was like compounding a spree on Saturday night by putting a threepenny bit in the plate on Sunday.

He concluded with a startling charge, all but naming Bishop Owen. The bill, he said, was being pressed upon the Prime Minister by Church gossip. Only quacks prescribed on gossip and 'the Prime Minister had prescribed only on Episcopal gossip from one of the Welsh Bishops who had intrigued and bullied, and pulled wires and of course the government could not resist for they were afraid of toppling over at the slightest opposition.'[112]

Despite these hard words Lloyd George affected unconcern with the new Coercion of Wales Bill. The great weakness of Wales before had been its divisions, he told an interviewer for the *North Wales Observer.* Now these were gone and the Board of Education 'will have to fight the whole of the principality at once when it stops postponing the appointed day, as it soon will.' If the default powers were applied to Wales, the nonconformists would empty three-quarters of the Church schools in rural Wales and insist upon the construction of a new council school in each district.[113]

The process of passing the Default Bill brought quickly to a head the simmering crisis between Wales and the government. The bill, although in some ways highly technical, contained only a single clause making it easy to limit debate which, as it was bound to be contentious and had been introduced relatively late in the session, was clearly going to be necessary.[114] The collision arrived on 5 August when after two divisions and four hours of debate Balfour moved closure of the rest of the clause, in effect the entire bill. The result was a spectacular uproar with shouts of 'Dishonesty'. Lloyd George announced he would refuse to vote on the matter. Hence there was a second uproar and Lloyd George, William Abraham, and William Jones as well as 15 others were named, although altogether 50 or 60 Members remained in their seats. When Deputy Speaker Lowther, who suffered much abuse and was clearly embarrassed, was on the point of ordering their removal Asquith, after a hurried consultation with Lloyd George, led the entire Liberal party out of the chamber vowing that his supporters would take no further part in the debates.[115]

In the next few days, as the unopposed Default Bill moved briskly through its remaining stages, the newspapers and politicians' letters marvelled at the new Lloyd George. He had been described for years, of course, as a coming man, a certain member of the next Liberal Cabinet. During 1902 he was acknowledged on both sides of the House to be the most effective opponent of Balfour's Education Bill. Now, however, he was resisting not simply the Unionists in the House of Commons, but the King's government and more astonishing, he was drawing the entire Liberal party with him. They had all walked out of the House together, quite possibly at his command, over a minor measure of concern only to little Wales.[116] He had gone beyond political respectability to demagogic authority. For many he was now more than just an important political figure. He was a dangerous man. He had had a parliamentary statute passed against him, a bill of attainder as it were. The phrase 'Welsh Parnell' began again to appear.

On 9 August the Welsh Members of Parliament met to hear what their leader planned to do next. In what was supposed to be a highly confidential speech Lloyd George explained that they would of course take no further part in debate and that there would be a conference early in October, probably at Cardiff, to concert resistance. Displaying his usual casual use of figures there were for example in Caernarvonshire, he said, about 150 schools, about 60 Church and 80 council schools which together received £40,000 in Treasury grants while the council schools got a further £35,000 from the rates. If Morant, he continued, imposed a default he would be dealing not only with one school but with all schools under the education authority. 'If we ask him,' Lloyd George declared, 'to maintain all 150 schools in the county what will he do?'

> Our plan is as simple as it is effective. Let Mr. Morant schedule Caernarvonshire as a proclaimed area and declare its Council in default. The first thing we will do will be to get the managers of the seventy or eighty council schools to resign. The Education Committee of the Council will resign en bloc. The whole administration of Education in Caernarvonshire will rest with Mr. Morant and eighty of the schools will be without managers.

Where, Lloyd George concluded, would Morant get the money to supplement the Treasury grants. 'He cannot call upon the rates. The government must take all of the schools or none.'[117]

This report by a 'well informed correspondent' inaugurated a series of *Times* research studies on 'The Welsh Revolt' that continued through August and September, surveying the Welsh political situation county by county. The principality had never before received such attention. Similarly, in October 1904, the paper accorded Lloyd George front bench status by promoting him from a half to a full column for most of his speeches in England.

On the day after the MPs' meeting Herbert Lewis reflected in his diary on his friend's new preeminence,

> Wales is a one man show at the present time and yet is it not right that it should be so. People clamour for a leader and in a time of national crisis they respond to effective leadership. LlG has made mistakes and will make more but he knows his own mind and goes ahead strenuously.
> There were many doubts as to the wisdom of his Cardiff policy on the Education Act, but at the last CC election he triumphed all along the line.

Newspaper reports continually marvelled at the discipline of Wales and reminded their readers optimistically that Englishmen would be less likely to be so obedient, but Lewis concluded that he doubted whether many nonconformist parents would withdraw their children from school if asked to do so.[118]

Although it was by this time hardly unknown, Lloyd George gave the official public version of his plan of campaign to the *Review of Reviews* in a long interview with its editor, W.T. Stead, to which he added the provision that independent schools would be established to educate the children withdrawn from schools in proscribed areas.[119]

By September the papers were full of the Welsh revolt and of Lloyd George. Each day he provided new announcements, denunciations of Robert Morant, and reports of meetings. On 14 September Lloyd George was in Shrewsbury obtaining approval of his plans from the Welsh county councils. On the 16th he was back in London before the National Council of Free Churches, whose passive resistance campaign he had so frequently deplored, pleading for money to support the Welsh independent schools. The *Daily News* reported he was promised £100,000.[120]

Yet notwithstanding the exuberant rhetoric, one cannot avoid a sense that Lloyd George feared a fight. He was leading the Welsh nation into a confrontation with the state. He was telling his followers to refuse to obey the enactment of a lawful parliament of which he was himself a sworn member. On the day following the secret meeting of Welsh Members of Parliament, *The Times* devoted a long and thoughtful leading article, which was widely quoted, to the 'new Lloyd George.' The paper recognized the new position of the Member for Caernarvon District and accorded him a respect it had never shown before. With only a hint of its former condescension it called upon Lloyd George to consider whether he was not too old to conduct affairs by means of head to head confrontation.

Five or six years ago in his callow Parliamentary youth, these schemes might have been regarded as the promising methods of self-advertisement by a young politician who must at any cost attract notice. But that time is long gone by. Mr. Lloyd-George should no longer adopt the tactics worthy only of his own distant past and of Mr. Winston Churchill's present. He has become a serious politician and a serious claimant for high office...he is to be, they say, President of the Board of Trade....

What would he do then?—the newspapers asked. Regret his past actions? Disavow his evil example? Will he remember

that he condescended to become the cheerleader of rebellion; that, knowing better all the time, he consented to purchase a little notoriety and a little temporary influence with the more fanatical of his countrymen by pandering to their political passions and by consciously helping them forward on a course that tends to bring into contempt and to destroy all respect for Parliament.[121]

Whether Lloyd George read and pondered this advice cannot be known but whatever were his public declarations he was at bottom a prudent, not a reckless, man. Above all he was an ambitious man. He was anxious to emerge from the education revolt with credit. He looked forward to Cabinet office in a new government that could not be long delayed.[122] If only the government would show some flexibility he could quickly bring the revolt to an end. Later the situation might be beyond his control. There were many in the Welsh rebellion more radical than he, in Merioneth and Carmarthenshire. Probably a majority wished to see all religious teaching expelled from publicly supported schools. On 4 September, for example, the Trades Union Congress, which the year before had devoted itself sensibly to fraternal concerns such as the Penrhyn quarrymen, had voted overwhelmingly after an address by Sir John Gorst, for a resolution calling for entirely secular schools.[123]

Whether it was prudence or self doubt, he accepted quickly a proposal by Bishop Edwards on 15 September that the two try to see Morant and arrange a compromise on the basis of the revised concordat.[124] St. Asaph saw Morant the next day, had a long conversation, and a meeting was arranged for 19 September. Bishop Edwards and, it would appear, Morant himself were both near despair about the trend of events in Wales. Lloyd George 'has now roused a mob he cannot quell,' wrote Morant to Balfour the next day telling him what he had learned from St. Asaph's visit and enclosing a precis from the *Western Mail* of Lloyd George's interview with the *Review of Reviews*. Lloyd George, Edwards had reported, was afraid of what would happen to him if the 'letter of the law plan' failed. The interview on 19 September was to be kept very confidential, although Anson, of whom Morant had a low opinion, said that he must be present. But particularly Morant needed to know how long the Unionists would remain in office. This was the key to Board of Education strategy (as it was, of course, to Lloyd George's plan). If Balfour felt the government would not be in power beyond 'next June' it would be best not to fight or take any 'line of action which would bring about deep exacerbations of feeling which would leave chaotic' the educational system in Wales with much damage to the Welsh Church. This was most important, Morant reiterated several times in a long letter. He concluded on a note of deep self pity: 'I have, myself, very little previous experience in Welsh ways, but even those who have tell me that they could not have believed misrepresentation could have been carried quite so far as it has, and thus brought about so complete a wreckage of what might have been a great educational development in the principality.'[125]

After the interview on 19 September Morant immediately reported that he had committed the Board to nothing although he had pledged to keep the meeting absolutely secret. But he was even more discouraged. Lloyd George clearly had frightened him about the chaos in Wales that would follow any attempt to invoke the Default Act. Moreover, Morant reminded Balfour, there was the 'new feature' of Lloyd George's appearance before the Free Church Council on 16 September and the reported promise of £100,000, all of which could make the independent schools a reality. And yet all this added a new difficulty because Lloyd George was willing to grant facilities for sectarian teaching in board schools outside school hours while Clifford was against denominational teaching anywhere at any time. Morant was in misery. He repeated the plea from his previous letter: that the government decide whether it would fight or compromise. He personally advised a 'concordat' not on account of any fears of his own but because, as he put it, Londonderry and Anson 'quail frequently and need much moral support.' 'They are shaking in their shoes,' wrote Lloyd George to William.[126] Balfour's reply to these letters amounted to a rejection of compromise although not only because he was more courageous. Rather he was more ruthless. He cared nothing for the welfare of the Welsh Church, no more than for the welfare of the Welsh board schools. He made no promise about when his government would resign but he looked forward, as had *The Times* leader, to the anger of an aroused public and to the difficulties of the new government if one of its members 'had spent the autumn in urging his countrymen to break the law.' He suggested Morant come to Whittingehame.[127]

Morant replied on 25 September saying that he was happy to fight but that Londonderry and Anson were cowardly. He agreed all four of them should meet but only after the Welsh Cardiff Convention on 6 October. In addition, he joined his unmanly departmental superiors in urging Balfour again, a week later, to put off the administration of the Default Act until the Welsh Church had a chance to compromise.[128]

The public and visible climax of the drama of the Welsh revolt arrived on 6 October with a great 'National Convention of Wales' at Park Hall in Cardiff. As an exercise in public opinion formation, the second Cardiff meeting was an indisputable success. With 14 Members of Parliament and assorted clergymen including Evan Jones on the platform and 700 men in the audience representing 28 education authorities in Wales, the conference clearly symbolized, as it was intended to do, the unanimity of the Welsh people to resist the Education Act. Lloyd George was received with the customary rapture and a series of resolutions threatening the closure of all schools and resignation of all school and council officials in any area where the government attempted to apply the Default Act were shouted through without dissent. In his speech Lloyd George taunted the government for its fear of proceeding against Wales, dilated upon the inefficiency of the voluntary schools, and, in a reference to Morant's early service in Bangkok, joked that the working of the act was governed by the court of Siam.[129] To all who saw it, it was an impressive demonstration. In six months, commented the *Manchester Guardian*, the Balfour government had created a new Welsh nationalist and separatist movement.[130]

Yet there were disturbing elements. Despite the claim in the newspapers that all education authorities were represented, two of them, the Boroughs of Wrexham and Carmarthentown, refused to rebel.[131] Nor were all Welsh MPs there. D.A. Thomas and Bryn Roberts and four others were reported to be 'in America.'[132] Moreover it was known that less than a week before the Cardiff meeting, on 1 October, Lloyd George had met the Merioneth Education Committee to quell a revolt, not to be sure against the policy of resistance, but against his own leadership.[133] Then three days before the Park Hall Convention he had received a deputation of teachers from both voluntary and board schools at Bronwydd, Alfred Thomas's Cardiff residence, who demanded to know what would be the consequences for them if a county were declared in default. How would they live? If they resigned could they expect to be rehired? Would council schools appoint former voluntary school teachers? Lloyd George handled these awkward questions skillfully and indeed courageously. The general answer was that the government could not last longer than eighteen months and that there was enough money already in hand to support independent schools until then. He did not think that many authorities could be declared in default, but if some were voluntary school teachers would certainly be called upon to strike. However he made clear that he would have nothing to do with the proposal, which in fact was being circulated, that as voluntary schools hired only Church members, council schools should hire only nonconformists.[134]

The teachers went away from Bronwydd apparently satisfied, but fear of harm to the profession persisted and already involved the concern of the National Union of Teachers. Since August T.J. Macnamara, spokesman for the teachers through his magazine the *Schoolmaster*, had been questioning the wisdom of the school closing strategy in increasingly trenchant terms. Nonetheless, Lloyd George and Herbert Lewis were pleased with the demonstration of unity achieved at Cardiff. Lewis thought that surely the government would now draw back. 'Notwithstanding your jokes about Siam, I think Morant means well,' Lewis wrote to Lloyd George after the Park Hall meeting. 'He is sensible enough, and if those behind him and above him are not utterly devoid of sense they will not put him and themselves in an intolerable position by putting the Act into operation. No Government can afford to enter a path of coercion just before a general election.' The real problem, Lewis concluded, was that too many Welsh wanted to fight.[135]

The government was less impressed by the Cardiff demonstration than Lewis and Lloyd George believed. As the problems in Merioneth and elsewhere indicated, wrote Londonderry and Anson to the Cabinet on the day after the Park Hall meeting, there had been a 'considerable element of make believe' in the Welsh National Convention. Moreover, voluntary school managers, after a year of harrassment, were now beginning to plead with the Board of Education to apply the Default Act.[136] Most important, Balfour had decided that resistance to the law would harm the Liberals politically, just as Lewis expected the coercion would harm the Unionists.

Lloyd George usually personified his enemy in the Welsh revolt as Robert Morant, however his most implacable foe in the government was the Prime Minister himself. Balfour had waited until the Park Hall meeting to move and immediately afterward announced the war to the Cabinet in what was, for a man customarily of detached and sunny disposition, a fierce uncompromising memorandum. He simply informed his dithering colleagues that the conflict was already in progress and he therefore proposed to dictate the government's strategy. It would be prudent, he thought, to strike at two counties at once, and to have first a full, but private, investigation of conditions. Above all, the government should make sure that when the Default Act was invoked, Church authorities did not come forward with a compromise. With this in mind, Balfour ordered that no action against defaulting authorities should be taken until after the Welsh bishops met on 25 October.[137] Balfour had good reason for fearing that his bargaining position might be undermined by some pusillanimous prelates. St. Asaph's desire for accommodation of course was widely known. In addition the Bishop of Bangor, with the poorest diocese in Wales, was reported to be 'not averse' to conciliation.[138] Finally, unbelievably, on 15 October John Owen, Bishop of St. David's, wrote Morant pleading for a truce. Bishop Owen reported that he had talked that day to Tom John of Tonypandy in the Rhondda, the President-elect of the National Union of Teachers, who was proposing that until a permanent amendment of the act could be accomplished the government should increase grants to the councils enough to permit Church schools to be run with little or no rate aid. In return denominational schools would permit Bible study for those who desired it during school hours and would appoint assistant teachers and pupil teachers without religious tests. St. David concluded that the National Union of Teachers was about to propose a settlement along these lines.[139] This was virtual surrender. Whether or not the Park Hall Conference had frightened the government, it clearly had caused some fluttering in episcopal palaces. St. David explained the origins of his letter two weeks later at his diocesan convention. John, fearing hardship among the teachers, had come to see him with three other officials of the NUT on 15 October proposing compromise. Specifically he suggested that the NUT sponsor a meeting between the councils and the Bishops similar to the Westminster Palace Hotel conference eighteen months before. St. David said that he had given John cautious encouragement although he agreed with the Bishop of St. Asaph that little could be done without legislation. But the critical thing was to prevent the Welsh schools from falling to pieces before the law was amended. Accordingly, he reported, he asked Lewis Lewis, Bishop of Llandaff, the senior Bishop of Wales, to call a meeting to consider the NUT proposals. The result might have been a reopening of the negotiations of the spring of 1903 with, however, all four bishops in attendance.[140] John's invitations to a conference, sponsored by the NUT, were duly sent on 24 October to the bishops and to Lloyd George in his capacity as President of the Welsh County Councils Association. John offered no plan, he suggested simply that the two sides meet to discuss a compromise as they had done in the spring of 1903.

Disastrously, even before Tom John had written his letters, the possibility of a conciliatory meeting disappeared and with it the chance of an agreed settlement. On 22 October, Bishop Owen recounted, he saw in the *Manchester Guardian* a resolution by the 'Campaign Committee' chaired by Alderman T.J. Hughes of the Welsh National Liberal Council, which had met the day before in Cardiff. It had shocked and angered him. The committee had noted a petition of Swansea teachers asking that the bishops and council representatives confer and evidently determined to nip any suggestion of compromise off at the roots. The committee had adopted unanimously a resolution stating that its members regarded 'it as very inopportune to consider any suggested conference with the clerical body on the subject of the Education Act; it reaffirmed the determination of the Welsh people to obtain full control of the schools maintained by public money...; and it repudiated the suggestion that any facilities for denominational teaching shall be given during teaching hours.'[141]

Lloyd George was not present at this meeting. He was away in Hereford denouncing tariff reform, which now occupied most of his attention. Nevertheless Hughes's resolution ended any further possibility of mediation by John and the NUT. There was no longer any reason for a meeting, Bishop Owen explained to his diocesan conference. The bishops were invited instead to accept or reject a set of conditions laid before them. He recalled that he had declined, as had the other bishops, to attend the Llandrindod conference in February 1903 for the same reason.[142]

Lloyd George had replied immediately to John's letter saying cheerfully that the Welsh councils would be glad to meet the bishops as they had done at the Westminster Palace Conference eighteen months earlier. But the chance for compromise had passed. Llandaff wrote at the same time from Lambeth Palace regretting that he and his brothers did not feel that a conference 'had any reasonable hope of being productive.'[143] Owen reported later to his diocese that all four bishops had agreed upon this.[144] A few weeks later he confided contentedly to his diary: 'The NUT (very private) are going to make George and co. climb down. So am very cheery.'[145]

Given the fact that St. David's original proposal was little different from the concordat Bishop Edwards and Lloyd George had worked out in August and that it did not include the pernicious right of entry of Anglican clergymen into board schools but conversely did allow Cowper-Temple instruction in denominational schools, there is every chance it would have been accepted by Lloyd George no matter what resolution had been passed by the 'campaign committee' of the Welsh National Liberal Council. It may be therefore that Balfour's inference of cowardice among the Welsh diocesans, and the concern for the outcome of their meeting expressed in his notes to the Cabinet, had a real basis in fact. He was still determined not to compromise, no matter what the damage to Welsh education or the Welsh Church.

The withdrawal of the four bishops marked the end of maneuvering in the Welsh rebellion. Positions on both sides now were fixed. This cannot have been the outcome Lloyd George hoped to see. He had expected that the government, trying to hold onto office with dwindling majorities long enough to complete a secret diplomatic rapprochement with France and to redistribute enough parliamentary seats at home to cushion the impact of its inevitable fall from power, would admit at least a stalemate in Welsh affairs. Instead Balfour defiantly insisted upon a fight. The weakness in the government's position had been the Welsh Church, which would itself be in the firing line. Had the bishops surrendered Balfour would have lost his army. Again and again in his political career Lloyd George would combine the postures of extravagant public intransigence and private accommodation. The education revolt was not the first example of this, nor by any means was it the last. But in Wales in the autumn of 1904, when the bishops were ready, as they had not been in the spring of 1903, to negotiate a compromise, and when he himself was under heavy pressure from competing political interests, resistance from school teachers, and a clear decline in voter enthusiasm after the triumphs of the spring, he found his negotiating flexibility cut away by his own supporters. As Morant had sensed, Lloyd George had released forces he could not control.

The autumn of 1904 is not a period upon which Lloyd George's authorized biographers have chosen to dwell. Each, even Frank Owen in the 1950s, says in almost identical terms that Lloyd George's violence and threats so terrified the Board of Education that it made no attempt to apply the Default Act.[146] The purpose of this rather detailed examination of activities after the passage of the Default Act has been to show that quite the opposite was in fact the case. Lloyd George was eager to compromise, possibly because he feared failure—at the end of October, elections for the Cardiff Corporation Council went against him—but more likely because he wished to appear a sound and responsible man worthy of inclusion in the next Liberal government. Hence, after October, he began to withdraw from the Welsh revolt, almost imperceptibly but steadily. After the sudden illness and death in January 1905 of the aged Bishop of Llandaff, he may have believed briefly, as did others, that some reconciliation was yet possible. T.J. Macnamara in Staffordshire mentioned that there were rumours of reconciliation on the lines of the St. Asaph concordat and Lloyd George repeated this at the Cambridge Union ten days later.[147] Nevertheless, with Balfour in office there was not, and never had been, a possibility of compromise even though the Board of Education did not move so quickly after the bishops' meeting as the Prime Minister's peremptory memorandum had suggested it should. At the end of October, Cabinet meetings suddenly were preempted by the Dogger Bank crisis which exploded in the early hours of 22 October when the Russian Baltic fleet, on its way to the Far East, believing it was being attacked by Japanese torpedo boats, opened fire on the Hull trawler fleet. Good luck and the quality of Russian naval gunnery kept the number of fishermen killed below a dozen, but the result was a first class diplomatic incident which occupied the Cabinet for a month. By the time the Default Act was applied in the spring of 1905 Lloyd George was far away. His interests were largely English and his concerns were for his own political future.

VI

He had, of course, poured scorn on the bishops' unwillingness to negotiate after their rejection of the NUT invitation. He could not believe, he said at Tredegar the night after the Lambeth meeting, that they would refuse the proposals of the teachers. They were worse than Lord Penrhyn, (who a year earlier, in November 1903, had finally defeated his quarrymen). The Church would have full responsibility now for the suffering that must follow.[148] There was in fact a good deal of suffering in Welsh education during the fourteen months between October 1904 and the resignation of the Balfour administration in December 1905. Since March 1904 no Welsh council had paid a Church school anything but the money due it from Treasury grants. Some, for example Carmarthenshire and later Merioneth, had declined to touch the Church schools at all, refusing to approve syllabi, curriculum changes, or the appointment of teachers. But generally they were content, in order not to break the law, to give the schools what came from London while stipulating that the former voluntary schools carry out elaborate and expensive improvements before rate aid could be considered. The Church schools, on the other hand, unable to get aid from county authorities to pay for the modifications the counties required, were caught in a vice. Without county help they could not improve their physical plants but without improving their physical plants they could not demand county help. As a consequence by early November all Welsh bishops were writing desperate letters to English newspapers appealing for funds.[149] Lloyd George himself airily left England before Christmas with Frank Edwards and Herbert Lewis to visit Italy and to cruise the Mediterranean on the S.Y. *Zingara*, Lord Rendel's yacht. He visited Naples, Genoa, Monte Carlo, and Cannes. He would need to be rested when he returned, remarked the *Church Times* acidly. There was rising resentment in Welsh county councils.[150]

The stand taken by the bishops in October evoked something of a revival of enthusiasm among Churchmen in Wales and brought, in addition, much support from England. St. Asaph provided a slogan: 'We Mean to Keep Our Schools.' Lloyd George was accused of 'methods of barbarism.' Money flowed in. Even Bangor, the poorest diocese, was reported to have raised £10,000 within a few weeks. In Conway, one of the Caernarvon District boroughs, an energetic local vicar was able to rally his congregation to elect four Churchmen and no nonconformists in the municipal elections.[151]

After his return in the middle of January, Lloyd George did not speak on the education struggle until the next month. He then appeared in Barry where the council, threatened with the Default Act for reducing salaries of teachers in the local Roman Catholic school, had recently reversed itself.[152] Then a week later, not in Wales, but in Whitefields Tabernacle in London he announced that 'the most contemptible Government that ever governed a nation against its will' would probably first apply the Default Act in Tom Ellis's Merioneth.[153] As it turned out another month passed before the Board of Education finally informed the Merioneth Council on 1 April 1905 that the Default Act would be invoked against it for failure to make payments to a few Church schools during the period from September 1903 to November 1904. The amount due the schools turned out to be £364.[154]

Even now the Board of Education moved deliberately. On 17 April Anson admitted that he had indeed made payments directly to three Church schools and that others were making claims. But he insisted that he had not, so far, withheld the amounts from the county council grants.[155] In May however Merioneth received only £88 from the Board of Education. The result was the only real parliamentary discussion of the Welsh education revolt, which occurred on 13 May following a motion to adjourn put down by Osmond Williams, MP for Merioneth. The debate itself was unenthusiastic and centered chiefly upon whether the Church school buildings involved, now five in number, were or were not at the level of repair that was recognized under Section 7 of the act. Lloyd George wound up for the opposition with a long recitation of the compromises Wales had offered. Even with a slim House the government majority, 90, was larger than it had been recently.[156]

A second application of the act came almost immediately after the first with a resolution by the Montgomeryshire County Council in June to withhold salaries of voluntary school teachers until the council was satisfied about the repair of the Church school buildings. This time Anson moved swiftly, announcing on 25 July that he was reimbursing school managers for sums spent on teachers' salaries.[157] With the application of the act the Liberal members of the Montgomeryshire Education Authority resigned, but on this council Unionists were numerous enough to conduct business. Although the *Church Times* reported that salaries were again being paid in August, Montgomeryshire as well as Merioneth and, again, Barry remained under the Default Act until the Unionists left office in December.[158]

The question remains, what of the county wide stoppages and mass resignations that Lloyd George had threatened? The smallest action by the government was supposed to bring Welsh education to a standstill. The fact is that no such thing happened. There appears to have been considerable pressure in chapel vestries upon parents to withdraw children from schools—Carrog was mentioned as a flagrant example—but evidently not all of it was successful. An independent school was opened in Merioneth soon after the Default Act was invoked and a second was announced in August.[159] Lack of money was obviously a problem. The £100,000 promised according to the *Daily News* by the National Free Church Council in England that had so frightened Morant in the autumn of 1904, did not materialize. In so far as Lloyd George made any contribution toward the management of the revolt in the last nine months of the Balfour government, it was in his appearances at appeals for funds to support independent schools. Chapels were urged to contribute one shilling per member. Lord Rendel gave £500 and much to Lloyd George's embarrassment, the NUT offered to pay the salaries of Merioneth teachers, but the council refused.[160] In fact he was hardly in evidence. He made a bitter attack upon Anson and Morant during the education supply debate in August, but his speech dealt in general terms with such things as the low calibre of men serving the Board of Education and said almost nothing about the Welsh revolt.[161]

Unquestionably by the early spring of 1905 Lloyd George was desperately anxious for a settlement of the revolt, almost any kind of settlement that would avoid the appearance of defeat. He had bluffed and had seen his bluff called. The revolt had lost its usefulness for him and his support, particularly in England, was rapidly eroding. The nonconformist press gave it less and less space and some papers were openly hostile. The education revolt, wrote a very prominent nonconformist editor, Arthur Porritt of the *Christian World*, was in fact 'a gigantic imposture' except for Merioneth. It existed only in newspapers, he concluded, to provide publicity for Lloyd George.[162]

In Wales there were defeats and defections among county councils and borough councils. The cast-iron unity of March 1904 had disappeared. Carmarthenshire, reportedly under the influence of D.A. Thomas, with help from its MP Lloyd Morgan, and Bishop Owen, ended its resistance.[163] And there was competition for public attention from the 'Diwygiad,' the remarkable Celtic religious revival which began in November 1904 at Loughor and possessed the nation until the end of 1905. It was the work of an unlettered young miner, Evan Roberts, who preached a messianic puritanism that sent Wales into a religious frenzy, driving up declining free church, particularly Baptist, attendance, and making temperance and local option again live political issues. Lloyd George privately approved of the movement, as he did of any activity that reminded his countrymen of their Welshness, and briefly courted Evan Roberts himself, but the revival unquestionably distracted attention from politics both in Wales and England. English sectarian newspapers, as well as the daily press, gave far more space to the Diwygiad than to educational resistance and this changed focus was reflected in their readers. There remains among the few papers that Lloyd George kept of this period a letter from Evan R. Davies, town clerk of Pwllheli and one of Lloyd George's chief lieutenants in North Wales, that arrived shortly after he returned from the Mediterranean in January 1905. Davies reported that the prospects for a successful education meeting in Pwllheli on 17 January had been 'dispelled' because of a 'remarkable outbreak in connection with the Diwygiad.' Perhaps, proposed Davies, Lloyd George would care to preach a revival himself at the town hall.[164] This unpromising suggestion does not appear to have been accepted, but he spoke about Roberts's work instead of politics on 17 January.

Finally, there remained the problem to which Churchill had alluded the year before, involving the accommodation among the Liberals of those Unionists unhappy with tariff reform. There still existed a substantial body of Unionist free traders, mostly loyal Churchmen, whose convictions on import duties had destroyed their position in their own party, but who saw nothing attractive in the strife-torn Liberals who seemed to be dominated by uncouth Bible-thumping nonconformist divines.[165] There were also Liberals who were in trouble with their constituents because of inadequate enthusiasm for passive resistance and who looked forward to a compromise which would end the educational strife.[166] Liberal and Unionist alike, these people assumed that Lloyd George held the key to their political survival. But most of all Lloyd George was anxious for a settlement because he, and the political world, knew that the Balfour government's end was near. Surely there would be an election within a matter of months. Informed opinion had speculated that the Prime Minister would dissolve parliament

259

at the end of the 1904 session, as Morant had anticipated. This he had not done for a variety of reasons, one of which, Lloyd George observed, were the endless petitions he received from Unionist MPs 'who prayed to be delivered from meeting their constituents.'[167] It was, he knew, time and past time to begin thinking of the educational settlement the coming Liberal ministry would make. There could be no satisfactory and lasting accommodation in English and Welsh education if it were designed to conform solely to the sectarian prejudices of free church bigots and county council hardliners. He foresaw clearly a situation where the coming ministry would find itself unable to legislate because any measure moderate enough to win approval from the House of Lords and to survive the next Unionist government would fail to satisfy outraged nonconformist leadership already swollen by the sense of its importance to the Liberals. His own followers must be taught a few of the realities of politics.

He attempted to do this on Friday, 24 February 1905, on the eve of the National Free Church Congress set to meet at Free Trade Hall, Manchester, and which he was scheduled to address. In an interview with Arthur Porritt of the *Christian World* Lloyd George spoke with unusual frankness about the future settlement. 'I have no doubt,' said the Member for Caernarvon District, 'that the Education Settlement, when it comes, will not realize all the hopes of the ardent Nonconformists.'

> We shall not get all we want. We shall have to make concessions; and we shall be wise to do so. We have an opportunity now for making an education settlement such as may not appear again for many years. We shall not get up the enthusiasm again on the education question for a long time, and we must make a settlement which will abide. It is no use trying to carry any measure of reform of the recent Acts which will only last as long as a Liberal government is in power. We must try to effect a settlement which the Tories when they are in power again will have no excuse for upsetting. And if we are to do that we must concede something —must sacrifice some of our ideals.

Porritt asked for details of the concessions that would be necessary. Lloyd George replied that, for instance, a return to elected school boards was unlikely—'I don't think the country really demands that'—although there would be popular control with a majority of elected council members on the boards of managers. There would be in addition the abolition of religious tests for teachers. 'We must insist upon that.'

> But if we get that—and its corollary, the elimination of sectarian teaching, we might have to grant facilities. I feel sure we shall have to concede the right of entry for denominational teaching.

'You mean facilities outside school hours?' asked Porritt.

> That is what we shall have to fight for. But we may have to concede the right of entry in school hours. In Wales we should not dread that. We have the schools. Nonconformists predominate and county councils are Nonconformist in sympathy. It would be no hardship in Wales to concede the right of entry in school hours. But in England it would be a very

different thing—especially in rural districts. It would mean, in thousands of parishes, that the Anglican clergyman would give the denominational teaching under the right of entry clause and all the pressure of the Church and the pressure of territorial influences would be brought to bear on the parents to let their children receive the denominational teaching of the vicar or rector. That would be a worse state of things than the sectarian teaching of the voluntary schools with the conscience clause in operation. We shall have to fight against the right of entry in school hours, but we may have to submit to it. I know it would cause very bitter disappointment among Nonconformists, but it may come. We can't have the settlement all our own way, if it is to abide, and we may have to concede this as a compromise. Of course the removal of sectarian tests for teachers will free the teachers from all responsibility for this teaching and the clergymen and Free Church ministers would have to give the sectarian teaching. As I say we shall have to fight hard for having sect-arian teaching outside school hours, but it is just as well for Noncon-formists to realize that we may have to concede the right of entry in school hours.

There was some discussion of the position of the Roman Catholic schools. Lloyd George insisted that they, having aligned themselves with the Church of England, should receive no special favors. This would mean that the Nationalist party would oppose most of the concessions he had mentioned. Thus a clear Liberal majority without dependence on the Irish was critical in the next parliament. 'We shall need that for an educational settlement,' he concluded. 'And the sooner that is realized the better. It will avoid the dangers of overconfidence, which is the great danger that Liberals and especially Nonconformists, are running.'[168]

Lloyd George's frankness caused an explosion of anger in the nonconformist world. The Free Church Council, meeting on Monday, 6 March in Manchester, was reported to have debated Lloyd George's apostasy for three hours and finally agreed to add to its resolutions on education the statement moved the next day by Lloyd George's friend John Clifford, that the Council 'declared that it would never consent to any proposal to introduce into state-paid schools during official school hours the services and sectarian dogmas of any denomination.'[169] The President, Robert Horton, added to his prepared address to the Congress on Tuesday the assertion that 'the miseries of Ireland...were not due to ancient oppression of a stronger race; they were not due to a vicious land system—they were due to the clerical education of Irish children. A population brought up by priests was incapable of liberty.'[170] When Scott Lidgett, soon to be named the next year's President of the Council, made an appeal for funds to support the Welsh revolt, the *British Weekly* noted uncomfortably that 'many people were seen leaving the hall.' Perhaps, the paper thought, they had been wearied by the long meeting, but there was no response from the Council to Lidgett's request for funds.[171]

After the first day's session, the Reverend Thomas Law, Secretary of the Council and one of its chief political figures, sent a desperate telegram to Lloyd George: 'Will you empower me to state from our platform that you repudiate statement made in *Christian World* last week conceding right of entry during school hours you must be with us tomorrow if not you will ruin your reputation and mine.'[172] Lloyd George promptly sent the required telegram saying that he was 'strongly opposed to the right of entry' and that 'the *Christian World* must have misunderstood him.' Law read it that day amid general cheering. But, pleading the press of parliamentary business, he did not appear.[173]

When Porritt heard that Lloyd George had repudiated his statements of the previous week, even though the editor had sent him proofs of the interview, he went immediately to the House of Commons and demanded to see his former hero. Lloyd George, he wrote in his memoirs, refused to come to the lobby and sent a younger Liberal out instead. Porritt told this stranger that the *Christian World* would publish the next day either an affidavit attesting the truth of the 2 March article or a 'polite evasion.' The young man disappeared and returned to say that Porritt should publish the evasion. Porritt decided never to 'risk' interviewing Lloyd George again.[174]

In fact the statement that appeared on 9 March was somewhat less a retraction than a reiteration. 'Mr. Lloyd George' Porritt wrote the next day, 'asked me to make it quite clear that he was not advocating the right of entry either inside or outside of school hours...in discussing the matter with him ten days ago the question was not what he advocates or what he opposes but the line of the probable settlement which the next Government may be able to make—not what the Free Churchmen want but what they may have to concede.'[175]

Lloyd George again had undergone a narrow brush with disaster. If he had not known before, he learned now the consequences of telling the truth too plainly or too soon. One cannot say that he never repeated this mistake. Within two years he found himself in trouble again, with the same constituency, over disestablishment. His ordinary political style of public invective and private conciliation indeed invited such problems. He could inspire a mob, but he could not direct it. Not for the last time he had nearly lost control, by honesty, of the passion he had raised.

However, on the larger scene of Edwardian educational politics, what he had attempted to explain to the nonconformist world was absolutely correct and provides the best demonstration, so far in his career, of the brilliance of his political sensitivity. His prediction of the future behavior of the Unionists was perfectly correct. The Liberal education measure of the next year, although far less than the nonconformists wanted, foundered in the House of Lords over exactly the issues upon which Lloyd George had said the free churches would have to compromise: the right of entry, the failure of the timid Liberal government to treat equally Anglicans and Catholics, and the appointment of teachers. It is not too much to say that the gigantic disaster of the Education Bill of 1906 had its roots in the hardening nonconformist opinion at Free Trade Hall in Manchester in March 1905.

During the long Whitsun recess in 1905, from 8 to 20 June, Lloyd George made a flurry of speeches in Wales before Welsh county conventions organized to build enthusiasm for the education revolt. But except for these and a few others in October his participation in the revolt for practical purposes had ended. Shortly after parliament rose on 11

August, never again to reassemble with A.J. Balfour as Prime Minister, he disappeared with Morley to cruise again on Lord Rendel's yacht.[176] It was noted that when the North Wales Calvinistic Methodist Association met in Caernarvon, in early September during his absence, the revolt was not even mentioned.[177] Lloyd George was, on the other hand, in demand as a speaker in England, speaking for Alfred Mond at Chester, Dalziel in Kirkcaldy, and in support of Asquith's candidature for the rectorship of Glasgow University. Although usually in these addresses there was a reference of some sort to gallant little Wales, the attack concentrated on standard Liberal issues, free trade, Chinese labor in South Africa, government flabbiness in foreign affairs and indecision in domestic ones. Yet he departed somewhat from the ordinary opposition bench rhetoric in his criticism of Balfour personally. The Prime Minister never received the stinging personal references he reserved for Chamberlain. Rather he was charged with lack of attention to the House of Commons. He was unworldly and uninformed, statements with which Balfour himself no doubt would have cheerfully agreed. But Lloyd George also asserted again and again that Balfour was the government, that everyone else, as the drapers termed them, were 'remnants.' Lloyd George seems to have glimpsed early what has become a visible paradox of the British constitutional system since the Second World War, that the latent force of the office of Prime Minister appears most clearly not when the government is strong but when it is weak. With few exceptions, the Prime Minister's power to discipline his colleagues in the ministry and to exact obedience from the backbench varies inversely to the popularity of government policies.

On 4 December, A.J. Balfour suddenly resigned. Sir Henry Campbell-Bannerman's government was announced on 10 December and an election called for January 1906. Within weeks the new President of the Board of Education, Augustine Birrell, had told a deputation from Montgomeryshire that he intended to withdraw the Default Act. And shortly afterwards, with an almost audible sigh of relief, Lloyd George opened his election campaign with speeches in Caernarvon and Bangor claiming victory for free education, but urging voters to be generous with Church property. These speeches were commended for their moderation by the *Church Times.*[178]

This was not the end of sectarian educational strife in Wales. Although he continued to claim that the battle was won, Lloyd George had indeed lost control of the radical nonconformists sitting on some county authorities. The Liberal government of which he was a part, was forced to proceed in court against certain councils, notably Barry and Swansea, both of which cases it won. A.T. Davies reports that one of his first duties as Permanent Secretary of the newly established Welsh Department of the Board of Education in 1907 was to apply the terms of the Default Act against Merioneth, a county completely out of Lloyd George's control since early 1905. The final appeals were decided by the House of Lords in 1911.[179] But most of the steam went out of Welsh resistance after the failure of the Education Bill of 1906, which confirmed that Balfour's scheme was permanent. The decline of resistance may be measured by the fact that a substantial amount of money collected to support emergency schools remained unspent. Davies states that as he wrote, on 14 December 1943, £4,137-17s-6d was held for the revolt by a Bangor bank on behalf of three anonymous trustees.[180]

What had been accomplished? The revolt was more than the newspaper stunt Porritt termed it. A number of children had had their education haphazardly interrupted, not however for extended periods of time. Possibly the greatest cost fell upon teachers at voluntary schools who could not be sure for over two years whether they would be regularly paid. And school managers lived with the chronic anger and frustration of dealing with hostile education authorities who would not answer letters, provide supplies, or make the routine decisions the non-provided schools needed in order to operate legally.[181]

Yet in the end, Balfour's act was not amended, the voluntary schools remained intact, indeed with slightly increased enrollments, and the councils discovered that the Liberal government intended to enforce the law.[182] In sum, the nonconformists were beaten and the struggle left a legacy of bitterness that was immediately reflected, much to Lloyd George and the Liberal government's discomfort, in renewed demands for Welsh Church disestablishment. Accordingly, the much reduced Welsh sector of Lloyd George's political activity between 1906 and 1914 was largely occupied by attempts to explain to his countrymen why the government they had helped to put into office could not seem to get on with its duties.

On the other hand, the revolt did not harm Lloyd George's career. The daring and impudence of his challenge to the Default Act in the late summer and autumn of 1904 frightened some people and angered others. But it impressed everyone. Moreover in the county elections of 1904 he had visibly accomplished what Owen Glendower had not. For the moment he had united Wales. Some of this unity dissolved in 1905, but that was less apparent. Further, in the education revolt he finally succeeded in building in Wales a functioning political machine that operated efficiently until well after he left the Premiership. The goals he had set for Cymru Fydd, partly at least, had been achieved. For the next 16 years he was a member of the government and was able to get for Wales the regional administrative structures he had so long demanded and the patronage that went with them. The Welsh Department of the Board of Education in 1907 and the Welsh Insurance Commission in 1912, with Alderman Hughes as its chairman, were staffed by men who had served in the ranks of the education rebellion. Through the Welsh National Liberal Council the selection of MPs in many, although by no means all, constituencies came under his control. In Carmarthen District, for example, his old patron Alfred Davies, who had not shown much enthusiasm for the revolt, was thrust aside, causing some hard feelings, in favor of Lloyd George's faithful disciple, W. Llewelyn Williams. He could confer knighthoods. He had a large voice in the appointment of county court judges. Within months after the 1906 election, Bryn Roberts, after twenty years in the House of Commons disappeared to the Glamorgan County bench. He was replaced in South Caernarvonshire by a young Caernarvon solicitor and Lloyd George supporter, Ellis W. Davies. In the years that followed Lloyd George's monopoly of Welsh political appointments became a topic for bitter comment.[183]

The conclusion must be that although for Wales the education revolt was certainly a failure, for Lloyd George it must be regarded as a step forward in his career. It completed the transfer of the focus of his activities from Wales to England. Yet it gave him at the same time a smoothly functioning party organization in the principality while also establishing him as the tribune of English nonconformity, a position he kept at least until the First World War.

There is one mysterious element in the long and fruitless wrangle between Wales and the government which should be noted. Behind all the public and private maneuvering there was a still more private set of negotiations in progress that, had they been successful, would have traded peace in Wales for the establishment of a semi-independent Welsh council to administer education in Lloyd George's domain. Evidently the formal initiative came from the Glamorgan County Council, which means that it came from Alderman T.J. Hughes. In the summer of 1903, at the time the revolt was only getting under way, the Glamorgan Council asked the Board of Education to consider a scheme for a joint board of Welsh local education authorities which would have unspecified supervisory duties. The Board of Education announced in late July that it would consider such a plan but stipulated that the proposed Welsh board could not possess formal financial powers.[184]

Lloyd George certainly was aware of these negotiations although there is no evidence of what his part was. Nonetheless for a time both sides clearly expected a compromise on the basis of educational autonomy for Wales. After it was all over Lloyd George acknowledged publicly in an interview with the *Carnarvon Herald* that Balfour had behaved 'handsomely' in the matter of the Welsh education council and three years later during the preparation of the Liberal education bill he told a meeting at Colwyn Bay that Wales could have had a council under Balfour's bill but that one county authority (unnamed but perhaps Carmarthen) objected and so the measure fell through.[186] Finally, the Cabinet letters at Windsor show that on 21 June, Londonderry brought before his colleagues a plan for a Welsh branch of the Board of Education to be established in the principality. The matter was referred to a Cabinet committee.[187]

Probably it was his eagerness to get the revolt behind him, using the concession of a national council as an excuse, that led Lloyd George to announce that arrangements were complete and that the council was about to be established. This kind of optimistic prevarication, the transformation of a wish into a fact, was characteristic of him and continually would cause problems in the future. In any case the September 1904 issue of the *Independent Review*, a radical anti-Chamberlain, social reform journal that had come into existence in October 1903, carried an article by Lloyd George, which presumably he had begun fairly soon after he talked to Balfour. Most of the article concerned the need for legislative devolution to relieve the burdens of the Westminster parliament, a question he had discussed in the same terms many times before. But, as an example of how Home Rule could be accomplished a step at a time, he announced the existence of a new 'Welsh National Council.'

> Without controversy or advertisement, a national council has been set up after prolonged negotiation between the Board of Education and the representatives of the Welsh county councils. The function of this council will be the superintending and the inspecting of higher, secondary and primary education in the country, and the making of provision for training teachers for public schools. This council is to be elected more or less on a population basis by the County Councils, a cooptive element of experts to be added to the selected members.[188]

This announcement, varying somewhat from the Cabinet plan, fuzzy on detail, but unequivocal, was widely reprinted and turned out to have no substance. Negotiations were not complete. Morant was bitterly opposed to such a council. More to the point, Lloyd George's usual adversary in South Wales, D.A. Thomas, who had opposed from the beginning everything about the Welsh no rate policy, saw now in the national council simply another attempt by Lloyd George to extend his influence into the South.[189] Nonetheless, evidently with Evan R. Davies of Pwllheli in charge, negotiations continued until the fall of the Unionist government.[190] Morant saw the joint committee as bait with which to extract concessions from Lloyd George, and by leaking news of a possible agreement, he attempted to stir up opposition from Lloyd George's Welsh antagonists. In the last week of the Balfour government, Morant responded to a question from Earl Cawdor, First Lord of the Admiralty and himself from Wales, that the Earl 'need have no misgivings on the matter. There is not the faintest likelihood of our sanctioning the schemes; but it is probably tactically wise to refrain from definitely stating this as we hope to entangle Lloyd George and his friends into an admission of hopeless disagreement among themselves.'[191]

The significance of this murky episode for Lloyd George is to be found in the light it throws on the nature of the battle he waged. The embarrassment of his premature announcement could have been considerable, had he been the sort to be embarrassed, although he would do the same again and again. But it shows also that Morant was no more inclined to fight fairly than was Lloyd George himself.[192] Finally it fixed more firmly than ever his settled purpose to get a centralized Welsh education council. By March 1906 he had put before the Cabinet a clause that he intended to incorporate in the massive education bill then in preparation, which would have created such a council.[193] He did not intend to allow Wales to believe that it had fought for nothing.

VII

The great political event of the last years of Balfour's government was unquestionably Chamberlain's announcement on 15 May 1903 of his conversion to a policy of import duties. The division among the Unionists caused by his stunning proposal and his subsequent campaign to secure its adoption as party policy is too frequently presented only as a problem for A.J. Balfour, weakening his already unpopular government while bringing a new unity to the Liberals for whom free trade was holy scripture. For once they had something upon which they not only agreed but also felt strongly about. The story ordinarily ends when the Unionists were defeated in

January 1906 or after Chamberlain suffered his stroke in July of the same year. This is far too simple.

Chamberlain aimed at nothing less than a revolution in Conservatism, bringing the party of the crown, the land, and the Church, into the world of iron, steel, coal and of an aroused working class. To be sure, tariffs would bind the British Empire and help the landowner, but they would also revive British industry and pay for social reform. He was bringing the unauthorized program of two decades earlier up to date. As he had done in 1885, dazzling the young Lloyd George, he was trying to build a new platform for a dispirited coalition that had not only lost the will to fight but had nothing to fight for. This was the old Radical Joe of Birmingham applying his prescription of 'high rates and a healthy city' to the nation.

The convulsions within the Tory party that began during Balfour's administration did not end with its resignation. Rather they continued until the war, carried on by a growing faction of business-oriented, frequently middle class, often reckless younger men, who disliked the older, gentlemanly, 'whiggish' leadership of their own party nearly as much as they hated the Liberals. *The Times* described the election of 1906 as a 'protest against dilettantism in politics,' a vice it detected in both parties.[194] One eventual casualty in this revolution was, of course, A.J. Balfour himself. The result was the emergence, after the 1906 election, of a new irresponsible demagogic Toryism, perfectly prepared to compete with the New Liberalism in promises of social reform in order to gain the favor of the new politically active English working class, provided the costs were borne by import duties. Tariff reform and social reform would arrive together and, the New Toryism argued, more quickly and cheaply under their party than under the Liberals, preoccupied as they were by profitless legislative excursions pressed by the Celtic fringe and by tinkering with the Constitution.

One may account it an example of Lloyd George's genius that he saw quickly in Chamberlain's program, the product of a political talent equal to his own, an infinitely larger purpose than binding together the empire. It should be understood by Liberals, he insisted, to be more than a challenge to the ancient principles of Cobden and Bright. Even though he joined other Liberal leaders in wandering the country denouncing protection in relatively orthodox Liberal terms—England, the workshop of the world, the dominance of the merchant navy, the cheap loaf or the dear loaf, and so on—he knew, as he told a number of his friends, that mere opposition was not enough.[195] The potential appeal of tariff reform was too wide; its support too dynamic. He talked to Churchill of this at the lunch on 31 December 1903: 'Lloyd George spoke to me at length about a positive programme,' wrote Churchill in his long letter of 1 January 1904, already quoted, to Lord Hugh Cecil.

> He said unless we have something to promise as against Mr.
> Chamberlain's promises where are we with the working men? He wants
> to promise three things which are arranged to deal with three different
> classes, namely, fixity of tenure to tenant farmers subject to payments of
> rents and good husbandry: taxation of site values to reduce rates in the

towns: and of course something in the nature of Shackleton's Trade Disputes Bill for the Trade Unionists. Of course with regard to brewers, he would write 'no compensation out of public funds.' I was very careful not to commit myself on any of these points and I chaffed him as being as big a plunderer as Joe. But entre nous I cannot pretend to have been shocked. All together it was a very pleasant and instructive talk and after all Lloyd George represents three things: — Wales, English Radicalism and Nonconformists, and they are not three things which politicians can overlook.[196]

None of the points in Lloyd George's program which he had outlined to Churchill was new except for the Trade Disputes Bill, one of many put down to reverse the findings in the Taff Vale case. Nor did they add up to social reform in the sense that it would come to be understood; measures for the relief of children or the aged, or the casualties of economic life. Pensions were conspicuously absent. The program to blunt the appeal of tariff reform was in essence land reform with which he had been associated throughout his political life.

There is however a problem here. He had revived land reform already in a major speech in England, not in Wales, at the Palace Theatre in Newcastle on 4 April 1903, a little more than a month before Chamberlain's sensational address in the Birmingham Town Hall. It is difficult to say, therefore, that the revival of land reform was a response to Chamberlain. On the other hand, it is quite clear that once import duties became a matter of public debate, Lloyd George seized the issue as a demonstration that his own positive response was more necessary than ever. In effect, the land campaign, upon which he spent a substantial portion of his political capital in the last two years before the war, began at Newcastle a decade earlier.

At Newcastle he said nothing that he had not dealt with many times before in more detail, as earlier on 21 May 1891 at Penrhyn Hall in Bangor for instance and in the House of Commons again and again during the debates on the Agricultural Rating Bill. Of course the specifics of leasehold enfranchisement, valuation and site value rating, had been his bread and butter since his days at Breeze, Jones and Casson. He seldom concealed, in any address, his hatred of the landlords and their clients in the Church. These were for him automatic personal responses. But at Newcastle he proposed a Liberal program for the elimination of privilege, although not, it must be reiterated, for the elimination of wealth. He always distinguished between the idle landlord as the parasitic consumer of goods and the businessman who risked funds to produce them. He was, in effect, moving toward what became the New Liberalism. (Lloyd George himself evidently attached some importance to the Newcastle speech. It is the one address from his pre-ministerial career included in the collection of his speeches which constitute the fourth volume of Herbert DuParcq's 'authorized' biography.)

At Newcastle Lloyd George announced he was speaking for the Liberal party, the party of ideals, which were fixed, and not subject to the whims of the electorate. 'We have arrived at one of the most important stages in the history of the Liberal party,' he began.

I believe the future of this country depends largely upon the foresight, conviction, courage and devotion to principle of the Liberal party during the coming years. There is, in my judgement, too great a disposition of late years to play up to the whims and caprices of what is known as the man in the street. The man in the street clamours for war, and we all say war is the right thing. The man in the street says we must have a big Army, and we say 'right,' we must have a formidible army...But the man in the street has a relapse; he gets tired, not so much of pomp, but of the burden of war; and we all become peaceable. The man in the street then says this is not an increase in the Army you want, but a small one; and we all say the Army is too big. There is too much disposition to tune our lyre to the sounds that come from the street, instead of standing to the sound principles of Liberalism.

Britain's problems, he continued, were trusts, not the trade combines of the United States which were

creations of yesterday, the mere action of trade and industry and they occasionally collapse. Those that are still in existence the American people, with that promptitude and energy which characterize them, are preparing to deal with. But in this country the trusts I am alluding to are part of the social fabric. They have been in existence for generations and centuries. They had their commencement in the days of William the Conqueror.

Trusts were the great aggregations of established power. In his speech Lloyd George named, of course, the Church, the licensed trade, and the governing class, but most of the speech was devoted to the greatest trust of all, the land.

The land is a trust. A great financier starts his work—and I recollect it as a law student as one of the first lessons of the law of real property—by saying there is no absolute property in land.

But that was the assumption of the feudal system. In the feudal system the property owner had obligations. The modern feudal landlord recognized no obligations.

The land in London is worth about £500,000,000. It is worth more than all the municipal debt throughout the kingdom—the money which has been sunk in great municipal enterprises, in water works, sanitation, lighting, tramways and roads...Who created that wealth? It is not the landlords. London was a swamp and the landlords did not even create that. All the wealth has been created by the industry, energy and enterprise of the people who dwell in London. Every year the value of the land is improving in London by the capital sum of £10,000,000. The improved value is due to the energy of the people, not to the great landlords in whose coffers this enormous sum of money pours. Whilst the landlords are going to their race courses, the property is increasing by this enormous sum. Out of this sum of money what do they contribute to the public expenditure? If these great communities had not expended money upon sanitation and lighting and roads this value would never have been created. The communities could not have existed at all without great public expenditure that has enabled the landlord to get this value for the land. It would hardly be believed by anyone outside this country that the landlords have not contributed a penny towards that great local expenditure.

He went on as he usually did to offer examples of grasping landlords: Derby, Sefton and Salisbury, for instance, who together drew £345,000 in rents from Liverpool without contributing a penny to municipal revenues.

The monopoly of land affected everything. He had learned on the Old Age Pensions Committee that most workmen would not live long enough, to age 65, to benefit from a pension.

Why? The explanation is to be found in the terrible habitations to which the large proportion of our unskilled workmen in the large towns are driven at the end of their day's work. Here is another fact. I have told you that seven per cent of the people live in destitution, and one third live on or about the poverty line. They have not the moral or the physical stamina necessary to sustain continuous labour. How can you expect them to with homes such as these? The first thing to do in lifting up the people is to provide decent habitations. Before you can do that you must grapple with the land question in the towns — the first of these great trusts. It is all land.

There was another reason why land must be dealt with. That was

because the resources of local taxation are almost exhausted. There are instances of rates going up to 8s, 9s, and even 10s, and there is yet much that the municipalities ought to do, but cannot. It is essential that they should get new resources. What better resources can you get than this wealth created by the community, and how better can it be used than for the benefit of the community?
I would like to say something about rural land, but I am not going to dwell on that.... There is something wrong in that system. It is largely a town problem. You are driving all these labourers into town owing to this land system. These men depress wages. You take them away from their healthy environments where they have as much sun and air as providence can spare for English soil. You drive them into the town to unhealthy environments. You weaken the martial resources of this country by taking them from the country where you develop a robust and strong manhood. All these questions will demand serious consideration in your cities in the future. But that is not the whole story of the land. There is a question of mining royalties.

Here he told the story of the Penrhyn dynasty whom he identified as 'a family of slaveowners from Jamaica' who had enclosed by act of parliament a large tract of common land in North Wales at the end of the eighteenth century.

Some day they discover that this unpromising waste has a great treasure underneath it — coal, or iron, or copper, or it may be slate. What happens? Some gentleman comes round and says, 'I should like to open up that land.' The lord of the manor, 'Yes, if you pay ten times as much as it is worth.' He commences to sink, and very often sink something else — he sinks his money. If he fails, the lord of the manor compels him to pay for the damage to the surface, three times as much as the surface is worth. That is a good start, but is only a start. Supposing he succeeds and finds coal there, the lord of the manor with that three times the value of the surface in his pocket, adds a charge of 5d, 6d, or 1s a ton for all the coal raised, a third or a fourth of the wages of the miner.

He continued with the denunciation of Lord Penrhyn's treatment of his quarrymen, of the hardships of their families, and of their sufferings during the strike, which was now in its last phase, concluding with the stirring assertion 'Were I a Penrhyn quarryman',

I would rather, on the bleakest moorland road in Britain, be a stonebreaker than yield to these demands.

There were brief references to the education struggle and to the scandal of public house licences and in conclusion an attack on one-class government. This was the last trust, the gentlemen of leisure who had nothing else to do but govern others, conspired through heavy expenses, with the way parliament met, with the very hours at which it met, to keep the government in their own hands. The great weapon for the purpose was the House of Lords.[197]

The Newcastle speech is striking testimony that Lloyd George, even at the height of the education revolt, was fully aware of the issues that more theoretical reformers were putting together at precisely this time in the campaign for national efficiency. He frequently referred to Arnold White whose *Efficiency and Empire*, published in 1901, became a textbook for imperialist social reformers. Obviously he had heard of Seebohm Rowntree's finding that 30% of the population in the city of York was living at or below the poverty level.[198] But this was hardly news. Thirteen years earlier Charles Booth had discovered that the same dismal statistics applied to East London. Also, very likely through Churchill who just at this time was beginning the biography of his father, he came to know Sir John E. Gorst, Randolph Churchill's former colleague in the Fourth Party, who was spending the last three years of his parliamentary career as the most important political advocate of the cause of children's health. In the company of many others, Gorst admired German welfare institutions.[199]

More to the point, the spring of 1903 had seen the explosion of national anxiety over the appalling physical condition of recruits volunteering for military service in South Africa. Three out of five were unacceptable at the recruitment level and only one in five was fit to become an effective soldier. These figures, although not unknown before, first received wide publicity in an anonymous article, written by Major General Sir John Frederick Maurice, in the *Contemporary Review* in January 1902.[200] General Maurice amplified his charges in a second article, this time under his own name, in the same journal a year later.[201] Maurice's article caused the issuance, just before Lloyd George spoke at Newcastle, of a command paper by the Inspector General of Recruiting which confirmed his assertions.[202] Hence

Lloyd George's statement to the Newcastle Liberals that the land trust, by driving men into towns, conspired to 'weaken the martial resources of this country by taking men from the country where you develop a robust and strong manhood,' put him exactly in the mainstream of rising concern about national physical deterioration. Although he, no more than the rest of the general political world, could have anticipated Chamberlain's devastating proclamation at Birmingham Town Hall, already he had begun to construct a platform which, enlarged and strengthened in later years, provided a base for defence against a renewed, violent and intransigent Toryism.

Indications of what tariff reform meant, of how comprehensive and far reaching its ramifications would be, came within days after Chamberlain's speech. On 22 May, on the second reading of a private member's bill to provide old age pensions—introduced by J.F. Remnant, Unionist MP for Holborn and, significantly, a tariff reformer—Lloyd George made what became his most famous attack upon Joseph Chamberlain. His professed aim was to show that tariff reform was simply another phase of imperialism, in effect a continuation of the Boer War. In seeking to pull the empire together by raising the price of food in Great Britain, the Colonial Secretary was demonstrating again that his professed attachment to the cause of social betterment was only a cheap trick to gain votes. But behind this Lloyd George may already have realized that fiscal reform was a grander conception and a greater danger to classical Liberalism than was yet apparent. The South African War had demonstrated not only the need to give attention to the condition of the people at home, but paradoxically, that the resources of traditional public finance in what was always proclaimed to be the wealthiest nation in the world were perilously narrow. Borrowing for the war, even for South African reconstruction after it, had disrupted the market for government stocks. What did Chamberlain propose to do with the money import duties would provide?

Lloyd George began therefore by contradicting the government assertion that there was no money available for old age pensions. There would have been plenty but for the £250 million squandered in South Africa, from which Chamberlain had recently returned. However, the government evidently did not wish to spend its money that way. Pensions, he reminded the House, were a great electioneering cry. He recalled ten years before how the Colonial Secretary then in opposition demanded pensions before the Royal Commission on the Aged Poor had reported. The poor would not wait, he had said. But now he was too busy thinking up schemes for taxing bread and new materials 'and had no time for such things as old age pensions.' At this point Chamberlain appeared dramatically from behind the Speaker's chair rather, as several reporters remembered it, as if he had been Mephistopheles summoned by Faust. Lloyd George acknowledged his presence. It was good to see him seated on the Treasury Bench, in the dock as it were.

> He was very glad to see the Colonial Secretary present. In the debate of which he was speaking the right hon. Gentleman said 'What about the Bill now.'... Well the right hon. Gentleman himself had an old age

pension scheme. In fact he was a man of many schemes, and this was one of them. He was like the man who is fond of quack medicines. He was full of one of them for a time and then dropped it for a fresh one. He went through the country recommending it—travelling for it—and a very good living he made out of it, but the profits were not distributed among the deserving poor.... The right hon. Gentleman pocketed the votes of the working classes, and forgot all about old age pensions. He was not going to use strong language about the transaction. The statement of the facts was itself sufficient. Since the right hon. Gentleman made that speech, a great many things had happened. The right hon. Gentleman had seen the beauties of the illimitable veldt, and had forgotten all about temperance, finance, education, and old age pensions. These insignificant things were not to be put in the same category as the illimitable veldt.... In 1894, the right hon. Gentleman said that the deserving poor were impatient for this reform. Had the poor become less impatient? Or was it that they were less poor or less deserving? Why had the right hon. Gentleman altered his opinion on the question? 'What' says the right hon. Gentleman, 'deserving poor, are you clamouring for your pensions still? Turn your thoughts from these wordly insignificant affairs and contemplate the illimitable veldt...' It was monstrous. He did not care what the present occupation of the right hon. Gentleman might be. The right hon. Gentleman might have given his engagements to millionaires of Johannesburg; but the right hon. Gentleman had given earlier engagements to the deserving poor of the United Kingdom, and by those engagements he was bound. It was a cruel thing to fill the poor with false hopes, and having reaped the political advantages from them, dashed the hopes that had been raised to the ground.[203]

Chamberlain was usually immune to attacks upon him, although he was occasionally vulnerable to Lloyd George as in the Kynoch debate, but this time he was seriously wounded. However, under a threat from C.T. Ritchie, one of the leading free traders in the Cabinet and the Chancellor of the Exchequer, who had promised to rise in his place and denounce the Colonial Secretary should he speak, Balfour had extracted from Chamberlain a vow of silence.[204] But promise or not, he would not suffer this. He began by saying that he had come into the House 'accidentally' because he had 'other serious work to do.' But he was glad to have heard the extremely amusing speech just delivered. He denied immediately any interest in party advantage that might accrue from pensions. His own scheme of a decade earlier was 'a dead question.' He insisted that he was speaking without preparation so he had not the figures before him but he believed Sir Edward Hamilton's committee, which had examined the cost of the old age pension plan recommended by the Chaplin Committee, had found that it would cost £10 million.

Well, before any government can consider a scheme of that kind it must know where it is going to get the funds. I do not think that old age pensions is a dead question; and I think it may not be impossible to find the funds, but that, no doubt, will involve a review of the fiscal system which I have indicated as necessary and desirable at an early date.[205]

There it was. Tariffs and pensions were connected; Chamberlain had abandoned the illimitable veldt and leaped squarely into the center of reform politics. Balfour was furious that Chamberlain had spoken, but the sensation was immediate. Chamberlain repeated this hint, slightly more solidly, six days later in a debate on adjournment initiated by Dilke and Lloyd George, much to the anger of the Liberal leadership who wished to see the obvious split in the Cabinet develop further. Asked by Lloyd George whether the price of pensions was taxes on the working man's bread, Chamberlain emphasized that tariff reform could mean not only pensions, but higher wages for the working man.[206] Protection was becoming a broad-based program designed to appeal to everyone. After resigning from the government in early October Chamberlain began to gather around him a group of experts: civil servants, politicians, industrialists, professional economists and educators, which when announced in December, was proclaimed to be a 'Tariff Commission' assigned to investigate all aspects of the fiscal question. To the consternation of the radicals, one of those accepting appointment to the Tariff Commission was Charles Booth, the so-called 'father of old-age pensions.' Booth was a wealthy Liverpool shipowner and a nominal Tory in politics. However, since the late 1880s he had devoted himself to the investigation of the condition of the poor, inventing in the process statistical sociology, and since 1892 he had put his money and his enormous prestige behind the drive for non-contributory, tax supported, old age pensions. By capturing him the tariff reformers validated their right to join the company of friends of the common man.[207] Booth's secession may have prompted Lloyd George's statement to Churchill ten days later that the tariff proposal was a powerful force which had to be met with a positive program, not simply with taunts and jibes. But already he had spent the autumn speech-making period since adjournment, broadcasting the principles of land reform as an alternative to tariffs. Particularly in Scotland, at Aberdeen on 13 November and the next week, on 19 November at Falkirk, he insisted that land reform was necessary in any program to combat protection. Free trade, he admitted at Falkirk, had hurt agriculture. The amount of land under cultivation was half of what it had been in 1851. It had drained the land of its best people who went to the towns for higher wages. The need was to get people back to the land and to arrange the system so that the producers, the farmer and the laborer, could cooperate. The laborer needed higher wages and better housing but the farmer had to pay 25s to the landlord before he could pay his farm worker 15s. Land reform with education and temperance reform would stop the deterioration of the British race. Here, he told the Young Scots Society, was the Liberal program.[208]

Lloyd George's initiative was immediately comprehended by H.W. Massingham, who was emerging as the most powerful journalistic voice and the conscience of radical Liberalism. Writing in the *Contemporary Review* for January 1904, Massingham reiterated precisely Lloyd George's evaluation of the threat of tariff reform. 'The consequences of Mr. Chamberlain's action must be faced....' Free trade was not any longer, where Gladstone had put it half a century before, 'high and dry on the beach' safe from the tides of party controversy. Today 'no mere negative policy will in the end prevail as an answer to the protectionist revival.' Above all, the decline of agriculture was 'the one solid feature of the national economy which gives force to the revival of protectionism.' Massingham denied, citing foreign examples such as Denmark, that abolition of tariffs had been responsible for the decline of agriculture. But the palpable result was the emigration of country people to the cities and the cancer of urban poverty which Charles Booth had exposed.

A substantial portion of the article was devoted to a summary of Lloyd George's speeches in Scotland, which Massingham announced should be the program of the new radical faction, the ideas of which must inform Liberalism if the party was to survive. He concluded in the vein of Lloyd George's Newcastle speech, with a call for site value taxation, a proposal of Booth as well as of Lloyd George, and for Treasury money for MPs' salaries and election expenses to break the grip of unearned wealth upon the House of Commons.[209]

Lloyd George provided an immediate antiphony in a speech before an audience of two hundred at the Trocadero Restaurant, at a dinner in his honor given by the New Reform Club a week later on 7 January 1904. Besides politicians the audience included Massingham and A.G. Gardiner of the *Daily News.* Following his customary attack on protection, he reiterated Massingham's warning of the previous week: the struggle with Chamberlain was not going well.

> There were not the slightest doubts that the country was face to face with one of the most serious dangers that had confronted it during living memory, and he doubted if the country realized it. Mr. Chamberlain had started on a campaign that was full of the greatest peril, not only to the country, but to humanity, and it needed all the determination of the friends of freedom and progress to fight the ex-Colonial Secretary and his allies in the coming contests.
>
> What were the proposals? Here they had a wholesale, searching and insidious appeal to human selfishness (hear, hear and applause). The publican was appealed to; the priest was appealed to; in fact, a wholesale appeal was made to the cupidity and greed of every class throughout the country. Mr. Chamberlain proposed to reorganize society on the principle of universal loot (laughter). That was the matter that they had to face; that was the subject with which they had to deal....
>
> The situation was thus, it would be seen, extremely grave. What were the Liberals doing to cope with it adequately? They must not forget that they had to deal with one of the most astute electioneers that the country had ever seen. Whilst even his best friends could not say with truth that Mr. Chamberlain was a statesman, his greatest foe could not deny that he was a great electioneer.
>
> Again, he asked, what were the Liberals doing? The men were splendid, but he could not help thinking that the battle at the moment was too much of a pillow fight; there was a great show of effort of striking, but there was not much damage done. If they were to succeed, they must take the gloves off.... Whilst they were content to prove by statistics that they were fat kine, Mr. Chamberlain was capturing the lean kine in droves (laughter).

Referring again to Mr. Chamberlain, he said that parts of his premises were sound; he had said that things were not right in this country. In that he was correct. As long as there were people in this country who had not their fair share of things, he was right. But Mr. Chamberlain went with something to offer the people, and there were tens of thousands who would say: 'At least he has something to give us.' A large number would take him on those terms. It was for them as Liberals to look at that. It was impossible to feed the hungry on the statistics of our national prosperity. It was their duty as Liberals to propose something better. He for himself would say boldly: 'Public interest first; private interest afterwards' (applause).[210]

Here then, in the autumn and winter of 1903-4, are the origins of the social reforming activism that Lloyd George and Winston Churchill thrust upon the Asquith government in the summer of 1908 when, faced by revived protectionist and aggressive Toryism, Liberal momentum, apparently so irresistible two years before, seemed to have died. The Newcastle and Trocadero speeches are the direct progenitors of Swansea, Limehouse, Bedford, and Swindon. Chamberlain's bid for the working man's vote had to be met. There was nothing in tariff reform, Lloyd George understood, for complaisant self-congratulation of the sort indulged in by the Liberal leadership as they surveyed increasingly satisfactory by-election results. Campbell-Bannerman's letter of thanks to Lloyd George for his speech at Stirling on 17 November exemplified the dangerous Liberal misapprehensions.

> All our people speak hopefully of this fight. Of course JC's strength lies in the small manufacturer type of man, who had some nasty little business for which a nice little duty would be very useful — they abound in, and control, Chambers of Commerce and they have all the keenness and unscrupulousness that pecuniary interest gives them.[211]

Of course for Lloyd George nothing in the positive program was new. The core of it, rural reform, land and resource taxation, had been his stock-in-trade for years, frequently explained in more detail, although usually in terms of Wales. Now he simply applied them to the rest of the nation. Old age pensions represented a private battle between himself and Chamberlain but were by no means his personal property. Neither, of course, were education and temperance reform. Nevertheless here appeared the Liberal domestic legislative program of 1906 and 1912, complete except for national insurance, which in any case originated simply as an extension of pensions and grew indeed because of the certainty that the Unionists would undertake it themselves if they came to power. Lloyd George's personal project, the only one to which he had anything but a political commitment, was the reform of the system of British landholding. This came last, and, in the event, too late.

The Times, which had not yet accorded Lloyd George the honor of the automatic full publication of his speeches, nonetheless printed a fair summary of the New Reform Club address and accompanied it with a leader that showed genuine understanding of its importance for British politics. Unclear though Lloyd George had been as always, he was, thought the paper, clearly discontented with the Liberal program and intended to take his party into the dangerous area of competitive social democracy.

> He wants to outbid Mr. Chamberlain by an appeal to an unnamed constituency which is presumably not to include any of those corrupt classes to whose rapacity, cupidity and avarice, the principles of Mr. Chamberlain are supposed to be addressed. It is all rather vague...but we dimly gather that the only Liberal policy worthy of Mr. Lloyd George's support is one that will make a clear sweep of everything now existing, and effect a thorough redistribution of the world's goods.[212]

This was inferring a bit too much from Lloyd George's always exuberant rhetoric. He did not wish to invoke a class struggle. He had no inclinations toward economic equality, as his own ill-founded financial adventures surely proved. Indeed his domestic behavior, manner of life, and economic outlook, were, and would remain, those of the prosperous, provincial small town, self-made, businessman-solicitor that he would have been had he never entered parliament. He was essentially the figure for whom Chamberlain's appeal was the strongest. So he understood Chamberlain's power. The unauthorized program had delighted him in 1885. He was now bringing forward his own version of it. 'Humdrum Liberalism,' he had recorded in his diary in November 1885 as the extent of the Gladstonian losses in the election just ending were becoming clear, 'won't win elections.' He still believed it.

Moreover, there was in the country a new constituency, the working class voter. The Liberal world had been shaken the previous July when the party's seat at Barnard Castle, Durham, which had been a genuine nomination borough of the ancient Pease dynasty since the reign of William IV, was captured by Arthur Henderson of the Labour Representation Committee, with the Liberals coming in third. This particular disaster was caused, to be sure, by some incredible stupidity on the part of the local Liberal Association. Nonetheless the Liberals never again held the seat.

Lloyd George's attitude toward labor has been the subject of much discussion. The preceding paragraphs have been intended to show that the origins of Liberal social reform have nothing to do with the Labour party as such and that the competition, as Lloyd George saw it, came from the right, from the demagogic Unionism of Chamberlain, while the content of his program derived from his own Welsh background. He did not fear the Labour party in the House of Commons, but he never underestimated the importance of the working class voter in the country. He knew instinctively that household franchise would bring, sooner or later, the horizontal division of politics. In this to be sure he was not alone. But the working man had to be made to understand that his natural home was Liberalism. He had believed this from the beginning of his political life. 'I cannot understand why there should be any case for a separate Labour Party at all...' he had told the quarrymen at Bethesda in October 1892, a few months after James Keir Hardie, the first Independent Labour MP, had been elected in West Ham, '...they [labor] have only to express their views clearly, and to take the simple course of joining Liberal Associations and then select candidates who fairly represent their views. The demand for a Labour Party will then be unnecessary.'[213]

More than a decade later his views had not changed. At Newcastle he had repeated his usual statement, that he was never able to see the distinction between the two parties. But at Bacup in Lancashire on 5 November 1904, a few days after the Ebbw Vale miner Tom Richards had won W.V. Harcourt's old seat in West Monmouthshire as Lib-Lab, he repeated his assertion that a Labour party was 'not necessary' if 'the Liberal Party did its duty.' However he added that a real Labour party in the House of Commons would be 'a disaster.'[214] A class-based party, notwithstanding the things he always said about the Tories, had no place in parliament.

His relations with individual Labour Members of Parliament were amiable enough. As has been seen, he found John Burns entertaining and Keir Hardie a nuisance, in common with many others. He tolerated William Abraham's incorrigible singlemindedness and lack of imagination as he tolerated the Welsh rain, because he had to. Clearly neither Lloyd George nor the leaders of the Liberal party took the Labour faction seriously as a political party in the House of Commons. Herbert Gladstone, the Chief Whip, in secret negotiations between January and August 1903 with the secretary of the Labour Representation Committee, James Ramsay MacDonald, designated 31 seats in which working men would face no Liberal opponent. The fact that these favors were given freely without reciprocal concession suggests the nonchalance with which the party chieftains regarded the prospect of a Labour delegation. They were, to be sure, gravely concerned about the working man's vote, not that it would be lost to the Labour Representation Committee but to the Unionists, if not in the coming election, then in the next.[215] This was certainly the view of H.W. Massingham, who knew of the MacDonald-Gladstone talks and warmly supported them.[216] The Liberals were desperately anxious to stem the inroads into the industrial Midlands and Lancashire, made particularly by the Liberal Unionists who had shown a disconcerting ability to retain the seats taken away in 1886.

'"Joe" is going to win, and at the first time of asking I believe...' wrote James Wanklyn, Liberal Unionist MP for Central Bradford, a typical urban industrial seat, solidly Liberal for generations, which he had won in 1895. His rather silly letter, a 1904 New Year's greeting to Lloyd George congratulating him and his 'new stable companion, Winston C.' on the trouble they were making for the Liberals, nevertheless exemplified the euphoria that was boiling among Chamberlain's supporters.[217] Wanklyn represented precisely the sort of constituency the Liberals needed to win if the resurgent Unionist populism was to be contained. (As it turned out, Wanklyn retired and the Liberals regained Central Bradford in January 1906.)

Wanklyn's quaint description of Winston Churchill and Lloyd George: 'a perfect matched pair, you two...you will upset the Radical shay to a certainty between you,' may not have offered the keenest political insight, but demonstrated nonetheless an understanding of what was already becoming widely apparent, that a new senior-junior political partnership was in the process of formation. Lloyd George had indeed eaten lunch with Churchill the day before and discussed his plans, both for the Welsh revolt and the Liberal program. Churchill was at that time preparing to leave his father's party. On 7 April 1904, in a gesture of unparalleled insult, when Churchill began to speak, Balfour walked out of the House of Commons followed after a moment by all the Unionists except the free traders. He was defended only by his father's friend, Sir John Gorst. Finally on 31 May, after some dramatic hesitation at the bar of the House, he turned to the right rather than to the left and took a seat on the Liberal side on the second bench below the gangway, next to Lloyd George.

Lloyd George may have done more than offer moral support. Very early in 1904, both Churchill and his cousin Ivor Guest, also a defecting free trade Unionist who was about to be discarded by Plymouth, were secretly approached about the Liberal nomination in Cardiff District, whose sitting member, a Lloyd George enemy, Sir Edward Reed, was displaying suspicious inclinations toward protection. The selection of an English aristocrat in industrial, working class Cardiff was not so incongruous in those days as it appears. Cardiff was the second largest constituency in the United Kingdom with 27,000 electors and so required a wealthy man as a candidate. More pertinently, as a major seaport and coal outlet, it was invincibly free trade and so a man who had jeopardized his career for that principle would have an appeal whatever was his social background.

The first tentative approaches had been made without the knowledge of D.A. Thomas, who upon reading of them announced in the newspapers that while he could support Churchill he would have nothing to do with Guest. Churchill, who was already negotiating with the Liberal Association of Northwest Manchester responded regretting Thomas's opposition. In return he received from the Member for Merthyr an emphatic reiteration of his position fortified with the announcement that as he had had second thoughts he would not support Churchill either.[218] Nevertheless Guest was adopted on 27 May, four days before Churchill took his seat with the opposition. Lloyd George introduced Guest to his new constituents at Park Hall, noting at the beginning that he and Alfred Thomas had just come from a meeting in South Glamorgan in support of the Labour candidate (William Brace). He assured the audience that Guest, Churchill, and all the other newcomers to the Liberal party secretly had always disliked the Education Bill and had voted for it only under pressure from the party whips. On the other delicate topic, Irish Home Rule, he announced that even John Morley admitted that the bills of 1886 and 1893 would not be introduced again, that the only solution to the Home Rule problem was devolution all round, and that all new Liberal recruits agreed.

Before closing he used the occasion to send D.A. Thomas a typical barbed compliment commending him for his devotion to free trade and suggesting that he devote himself to that rather than to political wrecking.[219] In the next few days Thomas fired back a pair of letters to the *South Wales Daily News* attacking Lloyd George for not telling the truth and the Cardiff District Liberal Association General Purposes Committee for secrecy. Sir Edward Reed to be sure was 'an India rubber politician.' Now however Cardiff had a 'plastic politician,' putty in the hands of Lloyd George.[220] Thomas had his revenge in the January 1910 election, leaving his impregnable fortress Merthyr to elbow Guest aside and contest the far more

279

evenly balanced Cardiff District himself. Guest was consoled with a peerage and the Privy Council.

The connections with Churchill became more frequent and important after the Member for Oldham's migration to the Liberal benches. In his short parliamentary career Churchill had shown, so far, little interest in domestic political issues other than Army reform and indeed would remain generally apart from the mainstream of radical Liberalism until his stunning debut with the famous 'untrodden field' article in the *Nation* in the spring of 1908. However Lloyd George quickly began to draw Churchill toward his own peculiar brand of reform and so to lay the foundations for the partnership that would flourish between 1908 and 1911. Already in the fall of 1904 Churchill displayed the signs of Lloyd George's instruction. The two appeared together for the first time on a platform at a free trade rally in Caernarvon Pavilion on 18 October. Bryn Roberts was present and also, inevitably, Evan Jones. After referring to Lloyd George in the customary flattering terms as 'the best fighting general in the Liberal army,' Churchill ran through the litany of the Lloyd George program: education, temperance, rating reform and the reversal of the Taff Vale decision. As was appropriate in Wales he said almost nothing about Irish Home Rule. It was a 'great question' for the Liberals, but one should not pin himself down to details and Wales's claims were as good as Ireland's.

Lloyd George, following Churchill, made the point clearer. Even though the meeting was supposed to be devoted to free trade, he used it to drive home again the fact that the new radical program had little room for Irish Home Rule. He was most explicit. To be sure, he agreed, it was an important question 'but there was no hope of reintroducing such a Home Rule bill as that of 1886 or 1892 (hear hear). The question must be faced as a matter of business. There must be an effective Parliament for the whole country and they would not have Home Rule for any one section of it without granting it to all.'[221]

The significance of this first appearance of the two men together can be estimated only in the light of subsequent events in Churchill's career. Lloyd George, of course, never missed an opportunity to bring national figures to his district. Grey had spoken there earlier in the year, regarding it as a journey to the 'remote edge' of the 'Celtic Fringe.'[222] But Grey was an established politician who had ousted the Percys from their pocket borough in Berwick and had not even faced opposition in 1900. Churchill, on the other hand, was a newcomer without a solid political base and one who seemed to delight in making himself controversial. Associating himself with Lloyd George and his unconventional Liberalism was not without risk, whether he knew it or not. This proved eventually to be the case. Irish opposition, whether because of lukewarm support for Home Rule or of outright support for repeal of the Education Act, or, as he thought himself, distaste for radicalism in general, cost him his seat in Northwest Manchester in 1908 even though Lloyd George spent two days there speaking for him.[223] He would have been more secure in Cardiff. Lloyd George himself, when out of Wales, was more circumspect. By the spring of 1905, his standard speech attacking Chamberlain and tariffs, and putting forward the Liberal program of education, licensing, tax and land reform, included also the affirmation that although he was bitterly disappointed with the Irish, he was still a friend of self government for the other island.[224]

As has been seen, after parliament adjourned in 1905, Lloyd George enjoyed his usual autumn vacation on Rendel's yacht, this time with John Morley. Following this he spent some time in Wales and made a trip to Haverfordwest where he visited the little cottage in which his father had died. 'Very nice place with a real touch of style about it,' he wrote his brother.

> Most untidily kept. Mr. John told me that its present appearance gave no idea of what it looked like. [in Welsh] The family gave us a great welcome. I saw the gate Mary and I took stones to. Not the old gate. That has been taken down and part of it put up elsewhere. Dick took photos. It all rather saddened me.[225]

Then he plunged into the ritual speech making, the last he would make as a back bench Member for 17 years. He dwelt upon the customary reforms with a new addition, attacks upon the House of Lords. These usually appeared as one of the multitude of reasons for land reform. The next Liberal government must have some power, he told the Scottish Liberal Association at Kirkcaldy on 27 October. It 'must no longer plough the sands; they must plough good soil and plough the furrow to the very end. If necessary they must root out the stumps that prevented the ploughing (cheers).'[226] He continued this theme at Glasgow a few days later in support of Asquith for the Rectorship of Glasgow University. The peers were landowners and the present land system was a greater burden then the national debt. The new tenant of a house was entitled to make structural alterations.[227]

By the time of the Glasgow speech, Lloyd George was quite ill. His throat had bothered him for years and would continue to do so for the next decade. Early in the autumn of 1905 he had had his tonsils removed. This did not help. In the middle of October he suffered a severe throat hemorrage which frightened him badly. According to his brother his life was saved only by prompt action in calling the doctor by Mrs. Timothy Davies, wife of the Liberal candidate for Fulham and one of Lloyd George's reputed mistresses. His doctor, according to his brother, ordered a long rest although allowing the speeches at Kirkcaldy and Glasgow. He had already written William asking whether his brother would pay for an extended holiday, lasting perhaps two months. William agreed to bear the expense but explained that he also was tired and would go along. After some instruction from Lloyd George on the proper clothing and accessories for a British tourist on an ocean voyage—thick flannels, thick socks, a thick overcoat, a trilby hat and £50 'for contingents'— William arrived in London on 11 November and the next day the two men sailed from Southampton accompanied there by Mrs. Davies. They sailed to Genoa and travelled from there to Florence and Rapallo. In Rapallo they met an Englishman who warned them that the London newspapers considered the resignation of the Balfour government imminent. William, who felt he had been away from the law firm long enough, determined now to return, arranging to send a coded message to his brother should he find that the political situation in England made David's return expedient. On 1 December he left Italy, was in London the next morning, and concluded immediately that the Liberals would be forming a ministry within the next few days. He sent the agreed telegram and Lloyd George, who had hoped to spend more weeks in the sun, was back in London by the evening of 3 December.[228] Balfour resigned on 4 December.

Campbell-Bannerman received the King's commission to form a government the next day, Tuesday, 5 December, and on Wednesday evening his secretary wrote to Lloyd George asking him to visit Campbell-Bannerman at any convenient time on Friday, 8 December. Lloyd George did not receive the letter until the next day, Thursday. Although other aspiring office holders were filling the mailbox at 29 Belgrave Square with detailed itineraries so that they could be summoned at any hour, Lloyd George, through innocence or assurance, had failed to provide the new Prime Minister with his new address at 3 Routh Road, Wandsworth. The all-important invitation had gone to the House of Commons.

This timing is of some interest because in September, Asquith and Haldane had gone to see Grey who was fishing at Relugas in Scotland. There the three had agreed to take no office under Campbell-Bannerman as Prime Minister unless he consented to go to the Lords and allow Asquith to lead the House of Commons as Chancellor of the Exchequer. This final spasm of Liberal League activity meant that Campbell-Bannerman had no assurance that he would be able to form a government. Haldane was no doubt replaceable but he was literally searching the British Empire for a Foreign Secretary in case Grey refused to take the post. There was widespread doubt in newspapers of both parties whether he would be able to put together a ministry.[229]

Lloyd George's early invitation provides clear evidence that Campbell-Bannerman intended to begin Cabinet building on the fringes with leading radicals. Lloyd George evidently was his first choice, as Lloyd George himself believed. He was quickly followed by John Burns and Sidney Buxton, the other two certified advanced Liberals included in the Cabinet. Many others were appointed in junior posts. On the other hand there is some evidence that Campbell-Bannerman may have seen Lloyd George in terms of Wales rather than as a radical. A conversation between J.A. Pease and Herbert Gladstone, the new Home Secretary, tends to support the notion that the appeasement of faction rather than the inclusion of individuals was critical in the new Prime Minister's mind. Discussing appointments generally, Gladstone remarked in connection with Lloyd George that the Welsh would be well pleased by the naming of Lloyd George and Herbert Lewis, who had become a junior whip.[230] Certainly the junior whips were neatly balanced in this way: Lewis for Wales, Pease himself, a representative of an old advanced Liberal dynasty, Freeman Freeman-Thomas, Rosebery's secretary, and Cecil Norton of the Anglo-Irish gentry. Probably for the same reason Alfred Thomas was offered a junior post, even before Lloyd George was interviewed.[231]

Even though he had been receiving, and transmitting regularly to Maggie, predictions of his certain inclusion in the next Liberal Cabinet, the precise circumstances of Lloyd George's appointment as President of the

Board of Trade are, as with some other critical junctures of his life, not perfectly clear, partly because Lloyd George himself could not resist embroidering commonplace facts. His telegram to his brother on Friday, 8 December is straightforward enough: the Board of Trade with a seat in the Cabinet. 'They want me there as that is the department most directly associated with the Free Trade fight to defend Free Trade in the House and in the country against Joe's attacks.' He added that he had demanded, and got, pledges on educational self-government for Wales.[232] But notwithstanding Lloyd George's belief in his eloquence as a spokesman for free trade, only ten days before Campbell-Bannerman had tentatively put him at the Local Government Board.[233] The *Manchester Guardian* predicted the same as late as 8 December, with John Burns as First Commissioner of Works.[234] Perhaps because the Local Government Board came to be needed for Burns, Lewis Harcourt argued in a private note to C.B. that the Member for Caernarvon District would accept the Board of Trade as it would keep him in touch with Wales. He reported that Lloyd George believed that Tom Ellis had injured himself by losing touch with Wales in the Whip's office. Harcourt's admission that he was nervous at the idea of Burns at the Local Government Board, with unemployment growing and winter coming on, tends to strengthen the theory that Lloyd George was moved from the office to make way for Burns.[235]

There was a general rumor, which newspapers had circulated for at least two years, that Lloyd George wanted, and would get, the Home Office with a £5,000 salary and control of the Welsh disestablishment bill. Harcourt believed also that he wanted a Secretary of State's portfolio. This clearly was not mentioned, although J. Hugh Edwards states that Lloyd George was offered, and refused, the Post Office at £2,500. No doubt Lloyd George himself was the source of the story.[236]

There is other evidence that at the beginning Lloyd George was disappointed with his assignment. D.R. Daniel, who knew him well although he did not see him often, recorded that he was sure Lloyd George was disappointed and had asked him about it at the time. Lloyd George replied that he did not want the Board of Trade because labor questions were within its jurisdiction and its former president had refused to settle the Penrhyn strike.[237]

Nonetheless Lloyd George was full of enthusiasm soon again. As he reported to William, his official appointment at Buckingham Palace on Monday afternoon, 11 December 'passed off admirably. I take possession of my office tomorrow. King very gracious...I was cheered by the crowd as I walked in.' Through the next few days he positively bubbled.

December 12th 1905: Behold me for the first time in my office—a room large enough to contain the whole of Number 3 Routh Road. I have had a talk with Sir Francis Hopwood, my Chief of Staff, as to the general work of the department and we went into it very thoroughly. I am sure the work will be congenial to me. I have under me in all 1,000 men. Tomorrow I interview the heads of various departments of which there are ten. Herbert Lewis not yet settled but I hope it will be all right. The first Cabinet Meeting will be held on Tuesday at noon. We had a

preliminary chat last night in which I tell you I took my part. They
christened me the baby of the Cabinet I being the youngest.
December 13th, 1905: I am gradually getting into my work and liking it.
I believe I can make a really good job of this Department. I am surprised
you did not get my letter yesterday morning as I put on it an extra 1/2d
stamp for the last post. I could not have written it for the early post as the
Welsh M.P.s meeting was long. Dick wrote me one of the best letters I
have ever received from him. He ought to write oftener to get his hand
well in. Gwilym I hear from Dick, receives all the news with sublime
equanimity regarding it as of quite secondary importance to the football
affairs of Criccieth.! Most characteristic.
December 14th 1905: Attended my first Cabinet today. Very interesting.
Education first. Today we had to decide questions arising over Portmadoc Railway and Criccieth Foreshore. Reply immediately. What is the
position. It is within my power absolutely to stop the enterprise or let it
proceed. Pont Aberglaslyn is the difficulty. Shall await with interest news
of today's meeting at Caernarvon. Nath being the nominal agent.
Telegrams and letters still pouring in. Tomorrow morning I hold a Levee
of all my Chiefs. Been busy over Educational position in Wales.
Macnamara has refused a post under Birrell in the Board of Education.
Delighted he has. Would not have trusted him there.[238]

Macnamara had indeed declined the post of Parliamentary Secretary to
the Board of Education because, as he told the Webbs, he could not afford
to leave the *Schoolmaster* for £1,200.[239] However, a year later he accepted
quickly enough the same post at the Local Government Board under John
Burns for £1,500 and soon was translated to the Admiralty at £2,000. Lloyd
George eventually put aside his distrust of the National Union of Teachers
official and the careers of the two men would be involved for many years.

Lloyd George now, about a month short of his forty-third birthday, was a
King's minister. He would so remain for the next 17 years, the longest
continuous tenure of office in British history since the Reform Act. Ten
years before, defeated in his attempts to organize Wales, with his party
divided, and himself in some disgrace, chances for political success seemed,
after a rather auspicious beginning, more than problematical. Now, with
the aid of Tory clumsiness and his own energy and daring in the
tremendous campaigns against the South African War and the Education
Bill, he had succeeded. If he had not stopped the war against the Boers, the
nation had at least come to share his view that it was a mistake and so he had
become a hero. He had not broken the Education Act, but in the fight
against it he had organized Wales. Now he was about to begin a new career.
He, who had always been a wrecker, had now to become a builder.

5 In Office: The Education Bill and the Board of Trade, 1906-8

When Lloyd George took possession there, the Board of Trade was one of the minor offices of the government, on a level with the Local Government Board, or the Board of Agriculture and Fisheries. Although he was usually in the Cabinet, its political head received £3,000 less than the grander secretaries of state, a margin Lloyd George quickly set about trying to reduce. Moreover, its duties were the entirely Millsian ones of inspection and supervision. It had, unlike even the Board of Education, little money to give away. It looked after and regulated harbors, railways, shipping and seamen, and the registration of public companies. It supervised bankrupt-cies and collected labor and business statistics. It did not count as a 'strong department'. In the previous administration, the Board of Trade under Gerald Balfour was described by Llewelyn Williams as a 'nest of humming birds.'

Three years earlier, when Andrew Bonar Law had been appointed its Parliamentary Secretary, Lloyd George had remarked to J. Hugh Edwards that the Board of Trade offered great opportunities if one were strong enough to cut through the bales of red tape that blocked action there.[1] It had, Lloyd George understood, much latent power. So far as the late Victorian and Edwardian state undertook to impose its will in the process of the production of goods and services, to regulate industry on behalf of the consumer or to protect the working man against his employer's selfishness or neglect, its agent was the Board of Trade. If it chose to examine the myriad of wealth-making activities that made turn-of-the-century Britain rich and powerful, its eyes were the Board of Trade. There may be more than coincidence in the fact that a significant number of Britain's leading political figures of the twentieth century, Winston Churchill, Bonar Law, Stanley Baldwin, or, indeed, Joseph Chamberlain, began their ministerial careers at the Board of Trade (one could add Harold Wilson). British administrative history affirms again and again that a strong minister can make even a weak department important.

Despite his initial hope for something better, Lloyd George was perfectly aware of the attractions of his new office. It would keep him in touch with Wales. The Caernarvon Boroughs' concerns, railways, harbors, port facilities, all were within his jurisdiction. Matters that as a simple provincial Member of Parliament he had been forced to discuss with arrogant civil servants were now within his absolute patronage. A year later, at the end of 1906, upon the resignation of the unfortunate James Bryce, when he was offered the Irish Secretaryship he refused immediately, even though it

285

would have made him a secretary of state. He was by now very proud of his work at the Board of Trade. Ireland, he told Herbert Lewis, would kill him in six months. Moreover it would cut him off from Wales.[2] He added, in the patronizing tone of one whose reputation was now made, that he did not think Augustine Birrell, also being considered for the post, a good administrator.

The fact is that Lloyd George's 28 months at the Board of Trade represent the beginning of the most constructive period of his life. He had already established himself as an exceedingly dangerous parliamentary guerrilla, a destroyer of other men's projects, a skillful commander of surprise raids and ambushes, but essentially a terrorist. Now he had to be a defender. At the Board of Trade, the Exchequer, and, after the war began, at the Ministry of Munitions, he demonstrated talents which no one, perhaps he also, suspected that he possessed. He showed industry and patience, not in searching out embarrassing secrets about the private interests of parliamentary opponents, but in working out the details of complicated and frequently unglamorous bills. In the House of Commons he was amiable and willing to compromise. He was courteous and approachable. Lloyd George was the one Member of Parliament, noted a senior civil servant, whose style did not change after he was promoted to the front bench.[3] He was not, and never would be, a determined master of fact and figure, a genius of lucid and logical exposition as was, for instance, Reginald McKenna who also moved ahead rapidly in these years, becoming the President of the Board of Education at the beginning of 1907. (McKenna had entered the House of Commons in 1895 as Liberal MP for North Monmouthshire. He was a dependable Welsh radical although the public perception of him was of a white and baldheaded Man Friday for Charles Dilke. Campbell-Bannerman made him a financial secretary to the Treasury upon taking office.) Lloyd George would not read anything, his first Permanent Secretary, Francis Hopwood, confided to the central clearing house for political gossip, the Secretary of the Privy Council, Almeric Fitzroy. Rather he would call upon Hopwood to put the salient points before him. These he quickly grasped.[4] This learning technique, leaping from point to point, earned him the private nickname among civil servants of 'the goat'. This sobriquet was public property within six years.[5]

What Hopwood did not say was that Lloyd George solicited information from many sources besides his own staff. Beriah Evans asserts that at the Board of Trade he began to acquire his well-known distrust of permanent officials.[6] He frequently said that the weakness of the Balfour government was the fault of the civil service. One could also add that at the Board of Trade, for the first time, he came into contact with substantial businessmen whom, conversely, he came to like. Most important, he began to develop now his peculiar style of privately negotiated acts of parliament which would become the practice for the rest of his ministerial career. He sought opinions from all interests likely to be affected by a measure and from groups who would perhaps be opposed to it. Points of friction could be smoothed, details compromised and determined opponents bought off. All this occurred before the bill reached the House of Commons, or, more frequently, during the committee stage. This process of extramural negotiation became a Lloyd George trade mark. It reached its maturity in the passage of the National Insurance Act of 1911.

For Lloyd George a bill in parliament was not a bundle of prohibitions or imperatives, rather it was a set of goals, the most important of which might not indeed be apparent. Hence a given measure could alter its shape and become almost unrecognizable as it was molded by pressure and shocks along the parliamentary path. New items might be added or troublesome parts be excised to be dealt with by separate legislation. Nothing was fixed except the end itself. There were no unshakable principles and without principle compromise was easy.

The point, of course, was to remove any struggle from the cockpit of the House of Commons and so to give any bill the greased pathway of an agreed measure. This is not to say that Lloyd George was always successful in these tactics, which of course are commonplace today. But discovering his genius for private conciliation, for negotiated, sometimes patched up and ill-considered, compromise, always concluded with a dramatic announcement of happy agreement amid general applause, he adopted this technique as his ordinary political modus operandi. He found it worked with the Merchant Shipping Bill and the Port of London Bill. The shipowners were astounded at being consulted. Soon he applied it to the settlement of strikes. As time went on form and substance became strangers to each other. Too many loose ends dangled. He made promises he could not keep and found himself denying commitments he had made, often extracting himself by even more impossible promises. Some historians have asserted that his secret goal always was party coalition. Rather it was extraparliamentary conciliation. If formal coalition was a means, as it was in 1910, it was not the end.

But as a result, he rarely had to concede points publicly in the House of Commons. Any aggrieved constituency, useful to his parliamentary opposition, already had been squared. Debate usually did not center on matters of principle or consequence, rather on licking stamps, or the rudeness of the leaders of the British Medical Association. Lloyd George came to regard the House of Commons as a ratifying or legalizing assembly for decisions taken elsewhere. 'Gentlemen, at the present moment we are making law,' he would warn a secret but disorderly meeting of industrial insurance executives on 19 October, 1911 during a critical phase of negotiations on national health insurance.[7] Eventually the members of the House of Commons, not only among the opposition but also Liberals, would revolt. However the revolt, which could have destroyed Lloyd George's career, exploded on the eve of the First World War and was obscured, like so much else in 1914, by the death of the Edwardian world.

I

Balfour's resignation on 4 December 1905, so long expected, arrived rather suddenly. The government simply expired. 'They died with their drawn salaries in their hands,' sneered Lloyd George. More important, the Prime Minister, hoping to exploit with his surprise the divisions among the Liberals, did not dissolve the House of Commons. As a result the first important business of the Campbell-Bannerman administration was the ordering of a general election to be held in the last three weeks of January 1906.

Nationally the campaign turned almost entirely upon the record of the previous administration, the divisions over tariff reform, the Education Act, the introduction of Chinese contract labor into the goldmines in the Transvaal, the House of Lords decision in 1901 to award damages to the Taff Vale railway as the result of a strike by the Amalgamated Society of Railway Servants. There was some, but not much, discussion of old age pensions. For Lloyd George the prospect of an easy return was a new experience. He had never received a margin as large as 7% of the total vote in a land where two to one Liberal majorities were common, and two years before he had admitted that a pressing invitation to contest East Manchester against Balfour appealed to him. (Balfour had held the district since its creation by comfortable but not decisive majorities.)[8] However, this time the Unionists had clearly conceded Caernarvon District. Lloyd George's opponent was R.A. Naylor, a Warrington lumber merchant, who was, so far as anyone knew, a Liberal Unionist. In addition to unpolished oratory, Naylor had neither connection nor claim in Wales, knew no Welsh and evidently nothing of Caernarvon District. Adopted in the summer of 1903 he had made fumbling attempts to cultivate the constituency, on one occasion treating Criccieth children, including Lloyd George's own, to a circus. Lloyd George promptly expressed his thanks in the newspapers.[9] Finally, he appeared to have no sense of politics, said the *Manchester Guardian*, and 'speaks about Free Trade and protection in a rambling fashion that excites more amusement than anything else.'[10] In addition to everything else, his meetings were continually broken up, to Lloyd George's displeasure, by angry Liberals.

This oaf certainly constituted no political threat, but the 1906 election has nevertheless some importance for Lloyd George. He used his opening speech of the campaign in the Guildhall, Caernarvon on 21 December, 1905 to bind the wounds of the educational revolt. The government had no intention of robbing the Church, he said. All that nonconformists wanted was religious equality, especially in the appointment of teachers. He appealed to all fair-minded Churchmen and reminded his audience that he was himself a National School boy who retained the deepest respect for his old master. In one of his infrequent references to Mr. Evans he recounted how delicately the old master had always glossed over the offensive parts of the catechism. Lloyd George, no more than Evans, wanted an irreligious education.[11] He never mentioned R.A. Naylor.

This address, the first in his district as a Rt. Honourable, exemplifies fairly well the level of Lloyd George's fifth election campaign. Of course he always took care to explain that as a member of the government he could not speak so openly or harshly as he had before. In fact, the old personal invective was unnecessary and perhaps undesirable. Naylor suffered none of the scorn and irony Lloyd George had heaped upon Puleston and Ellis-Nanney. Instead of attacking the Church he sought to conciliate Churchmen. His speeches dealt entirely with national issues such as tariffs and ecclesiastical reform. Although he touched on old age pensions he promised neither social reform nor Home Rule and other Liberal leaders dealt with the latter in distinctly lukewarm terms. (Asquith for instance on 19 December deplored the 'demon of separatism' and insisted that with elective councils Ireland already had self-government.)[12]

He did not need to ask party leaders from outside to come to Wales for him—indeed after the first week he spent most of his time supporting other men—although he brought Evan Roberts, the evangelist, to appear with him at Conway on 28 December.[13] The foreordained conclusion of this unequal contest came on 20 January 1906 when Lloyd George defeated Naylor by 1,224 votes, more than four times his largest previous margin. The vote was 3,221 for Lloyd George to 1,997 for R.A. Naylor. He would contest Caernarvon District nine more times, but never again, despite the varying fortunes of the Liberal party nationally, was he ever in any danger.

Lloyd George's triumph reflected the victory of Liberalism throughout the country. The Conservative-Liberal Unionist coalition had won 402 seats in 1900 but it had suffered an unprecedented net loss of 21 seats during its tenure, most of these coming after 1903. With some vacant seats there were 369 Conservatives and Liberal Unionists in the House of Commons at the time of the dissolution. Of these only 156 remained after the election. Balfour himself was defeated in Manchester East, although he found a seat in February for the City of London. The Liberals elected 399 members, giving them a technical majority of 128 over all parties, and as they usually could depend upon the support of the Irish and the 29 new Members of Parliament supported by the Labour Representation Committee, they possessed the largest working majority of any government since 1832. For the only time in history, Wales and Monmouthshire returned not a single Conservative for any one of the principality's 34 seats.

The sensation of the election was the return of 29 Labour Representation Committee members. It did not appear to arouse comment that many of them, for example five from Lancashire alone, had faced no Liberal opposition under the terms of the still highly secret MacDonald-Gladstone agreement. Nevertheless, the fifty LRC candidates had received nearly 300,000 votes, a figure greater than the Liberal plurality over the Unionists. Further, when the new parliament assembled on 13 February, the LRC group, calling themselves the Labour Party, took their seats on the opposition benches. Here they were joined in the next few years by 24 other working men who had been elected as Liberals. Among the Labour MPs and those Liberals elected with trade union support, five had come from Wales, including John Williams from Glamorgan, Gower and Keir Hardie from the Rhondda (where neither had Liberal opposition). There were in addition William Brace in South Glamorgan and Tom Richards in West Monmouthshire who were beneficiaries of the MacDonald-Gladstone agreement. Taking into account the potential support for unopposed candidates, Labour Representation candidates, and the Liberal-Labour men who would migrate to the party later, Labour collected over 45,000 votes in Wales, nearly a quarter of the anti-Unionist total. Although none of these men, with the exception of Keir Hardie, could be described as a socialist and some, notably the venerable William Abraham, were scarcely radicals, if that term is meant to connote an interest in new ideas, their presence could not be ignored. At Cardiff, on 11 October 1906 before the

Welsh National Liberal Council, Lloyd George reiterated his usual theme that there was really no difference between the two groups. Labour would of course support temperance and land reform. But this time also he added a note of defiance. Does the labor agitation affect British Liberalism?

Frankly I don't believe there is the slightest cause for alarm. Liberalism will never be ousted from its supremacy in the realm of political progress until it thoroughly deserves to be deposed for its neglect or betrayal of the principles it professes. As long as the Liberals go on as they have done this Session, showing they are not afraid of their professions when they are reduced to practice, then their trust will never be transferred to a new party. The working man is no fool. He knows that a great party like ours can, with his help, do things for him which he could not hope to accomplish for himself without its aid. It brings to his assistance the potent influences drawn from the great middle classes of this country, which would be frightened into positive hostility by a purely class organization to which they did not belong.

Does anyone believe that within a generation, to put it at the very lowest, we are likely to see in power a party forcibly pledged to nationalize land, railways, mines, quarries, factories, workshops, warehouses, shops, and all and every agency for the production and distribution of wealth? I say again, within a generation. He who entertains such hopes must be indeed a sanguine and a simpleminded socialist....

But I have one word for the Liberals. I can tell them what will make the ILP movement a great and sweeping force in this country—a force that will sweep away Liberals amongst other things. If at the end of an average term of office it were found that a Liberal Parliament had done nothing to cope seriously with the social condition of the people, to remove the national degradation of slums and widespread poverty and destitution in a land glittering with wealth; and that they had shrunk from attacking boldly the main causes of this wretchedness, notably the drink and the vicious land system; that they had not arrested the waste of our national resources in armaments, nor provided an honourable sustenance for deserving old age; that they allowed the House of Lords to extract all the virtue out of their Bills, so that the Liberal statute book remained simply a bundle of sapless faggots fit only for the fire; then would a real cry arise in this land for a new party, and many of us here in this room would join in that cry. But if a Liberal Government tackle the landlords, and the brewers, and the peers, as they have faced the parsons, to try to deliver the nation from the pernicious control of this confederacy of monopolists, then the Independent Labour party will call in vain upon the working men of Britain to desert Liberalism that is so gallantly fighting to rid the land of the wrongs that have oppressed those who labour in it.[14]

This analysis of the strength of Liberalism, not so much as it existed but as he hoped to see it, and of the inherent weakness of a class-based parliamentary party, represents the most that Lloyd George would say about the advent of political labor in the years before the war. On the whole there is little evidence that he thought about it a great deal. The new political group provided only an additional argument for the necessity of the Lloyd George program. He gave an abbreviated version of the same speech in Birmingham at Temperance Hall on 22 October to the Young Liberal Federation, of which he was President. After regretting Chamberlain's 'illness' (on 11 July, Chamberlain had suffered a stroke) Lloyd George returned to his analysis of the political situation. There was an 'impatience' with the old political parties, he felt. The days of the swing of the pendulum were over. Although scarcely mentioning Labour he made clear that 'he did not believe in a new party,' but nevertheless everything depended upon what the Liberals did in the next three years. The adoption of a new Liberal program, presumably Lloyd George's, was vital.[15]

Generally in the next few years Lloyd George's eyes were on the Unionists, particularly on the tariff reformers, who he feared would barter social reform for protection and take with them the gratitude of the working class that should belong to the Liberals. He, no more than the opposition, was much concerned with the socialist goal of the nationalization of the means of production.

The new parliament met for business on 19 February 1906. Lloyd George spoke for the first time as a front bench member, answering questions for the Board of Trade, on 21 February. On 26 February he made his first speech during the debate on the address. 'Very Successful. Pleased all sides and got a general cheer,' he reported to his brother.[16] That evening he gave a public address in Birmingham Town Hall before an overwhelming and enthusiastic crowd, even though he devoted himself to attacking tariff reform. On this occasion he noted that the last time he had been in the hall he had received a different sort of welcome. The notable feature of this second address was the beginning of the systematic interruption of Lloyd George's speeches by women. Two were ejected and police coverage outside the hall, as on the previous occasion, was heavy.

As Lloyd George became increasingly a target for women's suffrage agitators in the next eight years, a brief discussion of the problem as it afflicted Edwardian England may be appropriate here. When the Liberals came to power there were in fact two women's suffrage groups. The older was the National Union of Women's Suffrage Societies, which traced its origins back to the London National Society for Women's Suffrage founded under the auspices of John Stuart Mill in 1867. Its leading spokeswoman was Millicent Garrett Fawcett. More recently, in 1903, Emmeline Pankhurst had founded a new organization, the Women's Social and Political Union, which was dedicated not to propaganda and lobbying but to public violence to draw attention to the plight of unenfranchised women. Originally it had sought to affiliate with the Labour Representation Committee. (By the turn of the century women could in fact vote in all local authority elections and sit on local authority councils.)

The Pankhurst group, known as the 'Suffragettes' to distinguish them from the 'Suffragists' of the Fawcett factions, had begun to disturb Liberal political meetings during the electoral campaign in the previous December. In the next few months, leading Liberal politicians, above all Asquith, but increasingly Lloyd George and Winston Churchill, suffered sustained interruptions of their public meetings. The fact that Lloyd George never lost an opportunity to avow his sympathy for the principle of women's suffrage appears to have made him a particular target both for shouting and for calumny in the press. In late June 1906, he published in *The Times* an open letter to Mrs. Emmeline Pethick-Lawrence of the Suffragettes acknowledging a telegram she had sent him as a result of the imprisonment of one of her workers. He said his attention had been called to a statement in the Marylebone police court 'by a Mrs. Pankhurst' that he was responsible for the molestation of Asquith a few days earlier. Mrs. Pankhurst asserted that Lloyd George had told women at a meeting of his: 'Why don't you leave your friends and go for your enemies in the Cabinet and the greatest of all, Mr. Asquith.' He had said no such thing, reiterated Lloyd George, yet despite this distortion and falsehood he remained in sympathy with the movement.[17]

II

Among all the burdens incumbent upon the new Liberal government none was more obstinate or pressing than the revision of the Education Act of 1902. No Liberal candidate had neglected to mention it; Lloyd George's entire strategy in the Welsh revolt had been based upon the assumption of early amendment; and finally, among the Liberal and Labour MPs who assembled in the House of Commons, were 177 free churchmen of various denominations, more than double the representation of the previous parliament.[18] The nonconformists, who alone outnumbered the opposition Unionists, constituted statistical evidence of the need to act. Of course, perhaps no more than half of this number could be depended upon to vote according to their nominal religious affiliations, but on the other hand there were unknown thousands of nonconformist voters in the country whose ardor had made the difference in many individual electoral contests and whose support in the future depended upon the government's performance. The Campbell-Bannerman government was, as its sorry performance would show in the next three years, more the hostage than the master of its swollen and unhealthy majority. It seemed to be at the mercy of single-issue eccentrics and special interest cranks who forced it to waste valuable parliamentary time attempting to enact huge and complicated quasi-constitutional measures that would at best benefit only a minority of the King's subjects, while the rest, the majority, if not opposed, remained uninterested. Here was a positive invitation to House of Lords' interference.

The first draft of what would become the Education Bill of 1906 was framed within the Board of Education by R.L. Morant and the new President of the Board, Augustine Birrell, an amiable, witty, easygoing Baptist minister's son who had not seen the inside of a chapel since his days at Cambridge. Except for a Cabinet committee which began meeting in February there was no outside consultation; in effect the bill was Morant's production.[19] Even the Archbishop of Canterbury did not see an outline of the proposed measure until a little more than two weeks before the bill was introduced, when he was given a copy on 20 March by Lord Crewe.[20] In fact even at that date the draft was largely the product of the man who considered the 1902 act his greatest legislative achievement, Robert Morant.

Basically the bill abolished the distinction between provided (former board) and non-provided (former Church) schools. All public education, henceforth, was to be conducted in schools under public authority. The managers of the Church schools were required to make arrangements for the transfer of their operations to local education authorities. Those Church schools that the local authority chose to accept were to be called henceforth 'transferred' schools. Technically the transferred school buildings would be rented and the rental contract could allow the denomination to use the building for its own purposes on weekends. However, education—the appointment of teachers for whom there would be no religious tests, and the control of curriculum—was to be entirely in the hands of the local education authority. All schools could offer, if they wished, non-sectarian, Cowper-Temple, bible reading.

Thus far the measure had at least the virtues of symmetry and simplicity, if not equity, but in the Cabinet, in the last few days before its introduction, the bill began to suffer the strains of political compromise. Morant's original proposal had stipulated that all schools should offer sectarian teaching two days per week, conducted and paid for by the denomination.[21] In the Cabinet on 21 March this provision was narrowed to apply only to the 'transferred' (the former 'non-provided' or Church) schools. This slim concession to the Church of England was styled in the bill as 'ordinary facilities.'[22] However, the Roman Catholics, who, unhappily but steadily, had supported Balfour's bill and who publicly threatened a boycott of the new schools, received in Clause 4 a far more generous gift, which perhaps more than any single item ensured the failure of the Education Bill.[23] Clause 4 provided that the education authority of any borough or urban district of more than 5,000 population could offer, if it chose, and if four-fifths of the parents requested it, denominational instruction every day of the week. Such instruction would be given by regular teachers and at public expense. At the same time the school could dispense with Cowper-Temple instruction. This anomaly was entitled 'extended facilities.' Although Clause 4 extended facilities were also available to Church of England transferred schools, the requirement of an urban area of 5,000 population excluded about three quarters of all Church schools while including a similar proportion of Catholic schools with about 90% of all Catholic children.[24]

The final disfigurement of the measure appeared in Clause 37 with the provision for the establishment of Lloyd George's 'Welsh Central Committee.' Lloyd George had presented his draft clause to a reluctant Cabinet only on 20 March. He admitted, later, when challenged on the point by F.E. Smith, that the Cabinet had not liked it and were anxious not to overload what was clearly an already ungainly bill.[25] The clause really explained very little except to say that a Welsh central committee would be established by Order in Council, made up of people appointed by Welsh county councils, which would have powers delegated to it by the Board of Education and would distribute in Wales the monies voted by parliament.

The Central Committee clause, like much subsequent Lloyd George legislation, was really an outline, a statement of intentions, the details of which would be filled in as necessary or prudent. The committee was simply a somewhat grander descendant of the Welsh council he had tried to extract from Balfour and Morant in 1904 and 1905. Lloyd George had consulted the Permanent Secretary of the Board of Education in February and had received from the man who three months earlier had assured Earl Cawdor that there was no chance of the approval of such a scheme, a solemn affirmation of support. Morant wrote on 28 February that he 'had long been as anxious as you to bring about...effective and complete educational autonomy.'[26]

Even if his proposal was the vaguest possible, Lloyd George always took care to build up public support for it before pressing it upon his colleagues. Consistency was an English characteristic with which, fortunately, he was unencumbered. He did not confuse it with principle but the fact of its presence among men with whom he had to deal made it possible for him to use it to his advantage. He would seek public approval of an ideal, a worthy reform, and then remind others of their announced support when the details, sometimes less palatable, emerged. 'I got a strong impression,' wrote J.A. Spender in 1927, 'that it was extremely imprudent to begin going anywhere with him unless you were prepared to go the whole way; otherwise you would assuredly find your retreat cut off.'[27] (Spender remarked also that Lloyd George had a great attraction for academic and intellectual men who saw in him qualities they did not themselves possess.)[28]

Lloyd George introduced the topic of a Welsh council publicly at a Cymmrodorion banquet in St. Andrew's Hall, Cardiff on 3 March, where amid the customary rejoicing over Welsh patriotism he asked for support for a central education committee for Wales.[29] More important, three weeks later, on 23 March, he convened a meeting at Cardiff Town Hall for which he induced the attendance not only of his friend Bishop Edwards of St. Asaph but also of Llandaff and the implacable John Owen of St. David's. There were also nonconformists and the Roman Catholic Bishop Kenyon. Again the principle of a central Welsh education authority received unanimous approval, but again also without much indication of how it would look. His argument on this occasion was that he needed support in Wales in order to convince other members of the Cabinet.[30] There is much evidence that in securing the easy and unthinking approval of this project from his political opponents, Lloyd George was less than entirely candid about what he had in mind. There exists among his papers a manuscript draft (not in Lloyd George's hand) of a message, probably a telegram, sent to a Liberal meeting in Colwyn Bay to discuss the Education Bill. The message called upon the group in plain terms to approve a 'National Council of Education' for Wales to supervise, as it says, 'teacher training and other subjects,' but no more.[31] He said much the same to the gathering of prelates on 23 March in Cardiff. When challenged in the House of Lords in November by Lord Rendel, during the discussion of the Education Bill, to explain why he now opposed the Welsh council after approving it in March, Bishop Owen replied simply that he had been misled. Lloyd George had read only part of the draft resolution upon which the group had voted, which stipulated that the council would 'have the power to supply or aid in the supply of education of all kinds in Wales.' He had understood, said Bishop Owen, who was neither a political innocent nor a fool, that they were talking about teacher training colleges. He knew now that he was wrong.[32] What Bishop Owen did not know was that the proposal he believed he was helping to prepare had gone to the Cabinet three days before he had heard of it.

Although Clause 4, extended facilities, was surely the issue which mobilized the opposition to the Education Bill—a special concession to Catholics that was effectively denied to Anglicans—Lloyd George's Welsh committee caused as much debate. Balfour immediately identified its origin as the 'inventive ingenuity' of the President of the Board of Trade.[33] Meanwhile Lloyd George made much of the approval he had obtained for his scheme. The 'Cardiff Council' which had 'passed' it had been dominated by Tories, Bishops, and Members of Parliament who were impatient with the 'stupid' and 'barren' party leadership, he asserted during his second reading debate. This brought a hot retort from Balfour which resulted in an undignified wrangle, basically over the 1902 Act.[34]

But Lloyd George's arsenal of ingenious surprises was not yet exhausted. On 17 July during the committee stage he renewed the uproar by moving an amendment to give the Welsh council its own spokesman in parliament. In effect he was creating a new ministry. Balfour again was on his feet. There had been no suggestion of this before. The bill was under closure. Constitutional changes could not be effected by an Order in Council. Lloyd George was giving Wales 'educational Home Rule.' The whole thing was 'an insult to the House.' Lloyd George may have been a little taken aback by his opponent's fury. He could only reply by reminding Balfour that his Education Bill also had been closured. The result again was a shouting match.[35] Nevertheless he wrote to his brother the next day with his usual cockiness. 'Had a great field day yesterday. Balfour angry beyond control when he saw what my concessions were. They took the wind completely out of his sails and that drove him to hysteria.'[36]

However Lloyd George, probably innocently, had committed a serious breach of parliamentary etiquette. He knew the written rules of procedure of the House of Commons as well as anyone, but the underlying principles of constitutional usage he would not, or could not, learn. His strength was in dealing with men, not methods, his thoughts were fixed on the goal ahead, Welsh autonomy, not the means to get there. If a thing were not clearly prohibited he would try it.

This time he had outraged the sensibilities of men more important to him than the leader of the weakened Opposition. King Edward VII saw his prerogative in danger. On 18 July the Prime Minister received a letter from the monarch's secretary, Francis Knollys, the first of a series of royal complaints about Lloyd George's behavior.[37] Lloyd George's reply to an unusually angry letter from the imperturbable Prime Minister was the essence of contrition. He apologized for having 'transgressed constitutional authority,' it was all the result of ignorance and inexperience. He did not intend to create a new ministry. The spokesman would be someone already in the government. He had consulted Asquith before moving his amendment because he could not find the Prime Minister.[38] (Campbell-Bannerman was frequently absent from Westminster Palace in the summer of 1906 to attend his wife, who died on 30 August.) Lloyd George followed this letter with a second written in even more humble terms for transmittal to the King. He apologized anew, in every possible way, and promised to amend Clause 37 again on report to make it clear that the Council of Wales would be under the control of the Treasury and to omit all references to a parliamentary spokesman. Knollys replied with a terse note saying that the King was satisfied and would not pursue the matter.[39]

In general Lloyd George's scheme for a Welsh central office for education must be accounted less than a political success. It was a personal project, a vindication of the Welsh revolt, and one upon which he spent a good deal of time even in the crowded first year of office when he was also busy with more important departmental legislation. No doubt he hoped also that it would win some popularity among nonconformists for the increasingly unsatisfactory Education Bill. One may imagine that it was in these terms, with the added attraction that three of the four Welsh bishops had approved it, that he commended it to the Cabinet.

The fact is that even though conventional Liberal history has always designated the House of Lords' rejection of the Education Bill as an appalling example of the upper chamber's disregard for expressed public opinion, the bill that the peers received was a warped and misshapen monster that commanded the affection of no church, established or Roman Catholic, nor indeed chapel.[40] Lloyd George had always argued that a workable modification of the 1902 Act would involve compromise. He had attempted to educate the British nonconformist community in his unpopular interview with the *Christian World* in March 1905 and he had tried to work out private agreements with Bishop Edwards many times before that. If the Liberal educational settlement were to last, it should be fair. He had no real religion, but he had a basic sense of equity. He hated privilege and prescriptive right. The justice to which he had appealed in refusing to admit that he believed in one Holy Catholic and Apostolic Church on prize day in David Evans's National School in Wales held equally that children in English country villages should be able to recite the same creed if they wished.

There was however a second practical, not ideological, reason for compromise, the presence of the House of Lords' veto. The Unionists depended on the Lords to save denominational education. To excite their Lordships' interest had been the reason for attaching elementary schools to Balfour's measure in the first place. As Lloyd George had stressed in his conversation with Porritt, if the nonconformists insisted upon a bill that was satisfactory to no one but themselves they would get, in effect, no bill at all. This was the meaning of his unusual outburst at Liverpool on 24 May when he declared that although he had always regarded the upper chamber as a menace to progress, he had only now, as a responsible minister, come to know what in fact this meant. 'It sat as a skeleton at the Cabinet table. The government was always obliged to take the views of the peers into its calculations—as if they really mattered a scrap.'[41]

The upshot was that the nonconformists indeed made it impossible for the government to shape a bill that the upper house would approve. Lloyd

George had heard rumblings in Wales soon after parliament assembled, well before the bill was published, and he had attempted, as has been seen, to allay them with his meeting at Cardiff. On 8 April, a worried Herbert Lewis, who had not seen the measure, not printed until 12 April, wrote Lloyd George that there were three things 'our people will not have at any price: (1) the right of entry in provided schools (2) denominational facilities in any school during school hours (3) denominational instruction by staff teachers. These are very important.' There were, he thought, already enough concessions to Conservatives on other matters.[42]

When the bill was introduced on 9 April the outcry began in earnest. A delegation from the Welsh National Liberal Council, led by the ubiquitous Alderman T.J. Hughes, visited Birrell to protest Clause 4 on that day. Denominational teaching by the regular staff, every day of the week, without Cowper-Temple bible reading, and paid for out of public funds, was simply out of the question. The Catholics in effect were to be allowed to keep their schools. As Balfour pointed out many times during the passage of the measure, this was simply a recognition of popular control for which Lloyd George had argued so eloquently in 1902 and the same privileges should be extended to the Anglicans. There was however more to the objection to denominational instruction by staff teachers than simple chapel bigotry. It was on this point that the fate of the bill finally would depend. As the regularly assigned instructors were to teach the catechism, many politicians, including Lloyd George himself, felt that it would follow that most of faculty in schools with extended facilities would have to be members of the denomination. Hence, even in the absence of formal rules, religious tests would be imposed. Almost certainly the peers would never pass the bill without this provision. Already there was complaint. On the 9th Herbert Lewis wrote Lloyd George: 'I heard a man express what I think is the general feeling when he said, speaking of the safeguards for denominationalism which are talked of, "if we are to be asked to do the dirty work of the Tory party in the House of Lords, we may as well leave the job alone." This sort of feeling is not merely entertained by Nonconformists in the House,' he continued, 'it is held even more strongly by many Churchmen who know the feeling of their Nonconformist supporters.'[43]

Lloyd George loyally supported the Education Bill against attacks by nonconformists from one side and on the other, surprisingly, from Catholics who complained that the population requirement for extended facilities was too high. He narrowly defeated a resolution condemning the measure in the National Council of Free Churches and reminded his Welsh constituency that it was necessary to balance the continuation of Cowper-Temple instruction with concessions to the Catholics.[44]

The Education Bill passed its third reading in the House of Commons on 30 July with the Irish Nationalists voting against it. Before parliament recessed on 4 August the House of Lords gave the bill its second reading with, however, clear warning from Lord Lansdowne that the upper house would deal with the measure in the autumn session which would begin on 23 October.

In mid-August Lloyd George took his family, including Margaret for the first time, and his brother, on a voyage to Lisbon. With £2,000 per year he now had money, although his upper deck suite was partly by courtesy of Owen Philipps, Liberal MP for Pembroke and Haverfordwest, who was a director of several steamship companies.[45] He was back in time for the Eisteddfod, which he never missed, and on 29 September he visited Llanelli in Llewelyn Williams's constituency to rouse support for the government. Here he solicited applause for the Liberal program and hisses for the House of Lords as an obstacle to all progressive legislation. The Education Bill if not passed now would nevertheless be passed someday, he predicted, 'when the House of Lords was sleeping, as it frequently does.'

Because Lloyd George had included in his list of measures that the House of Lords had vetoed one which in truth they had already passed, he became involved in an acrimonious and entertaining public correspondence with Lord Lansdowne carried on in letters to *The Times*. Evidently this correspondence drew the King's attention to the fact that one of his own ministers had criticized the House of Lords. As a result Campbell-Bannerman, who had buried his adored wife scarcely two months before and was recovering from a heart attack, received another royal complaint about his President of the Board of Trade. This time he defended Lloyd George with some spirit and received warm thanks from Lloyd George for the 'kind way' he had rebuked him.[46]

But a more serious issue emerged in October. Only a few days earlier, on the eve of the reassembly of parliament, the Court of Appeal had reversed the finding of a lower court which had forbidden the West Riding Local Education Authority to withhold from the salaries of teachers in four denominational schools pay for that portion of their time used in giving sectarian religious instruction. By its reversal, in effect by agreeing with the local authority, the Appeals Court judgement practically had nullified the 1902 Act, Lloyd George told Herbert Lewis the day before. But he found now, to his astonishment, that the Board of Education was going to appeal to the House of Lords although the matter had never come before the Cabinet. Lloyd George said he understood that Morant, to save his creation, the 1902 Act, had induced Birrell to ask the Prime Minister for the right of appeal by getting the Archbishop of Canterbury to talk to Birrell. No wonder, he concluded, Morant was known in the Board of Education as 'the serpent,' but how humiliating for the Liberals.[47] Lloyd George emphasized the unwisdom of an appeal in a letter to the Prime Minister the following day dealing with the King's complaints. It was wanted only by 'officials at the B of E, on behalf of the Church schools. The Education Bill is now at a critical juncture' and nonconformist discontent was already well-known. The Lords' amendments, said Lloyd George, would require all possible influence with free churchmen. 'We are frittering away that influence by helping the clergy out of a difficulty in which their own frauds have put them.'[48] Nonetheless, the Cabinet approved the appeal that day and early in December the House of Lords, predictably, reversed the Court of Appeals, reinstating the original judgement against the West Riding County Council.

At almost the same time, on 6 December, the upper chamber passed the third reading of its own version of the Education Bill. The peers, for practical purposes, had rewritten the measure. Clause 4, extended facilities, was changed to apply to rural as well as urban areas and was made obligatory as well upon the councils, while the proportion of parents needed to obtain extended facilities was reduced from four-fifths to two-thirds. Equally, the Lords went further than Balfour had ever dared to go by providing ordinary facilities for denominational teaching two days a week in board schools as well as in transferred schools. On the other hand, Lloyd George's Council for Wales, on a motion from Lord Cawdor, was deleted from the measure after an extended debate which consisted mostly of abuse of Lloyd George. Three of the four Welsh diocesans voted to drop the council. St. Asaph abstained.[49] What had come to the upper chamber as a replacement for Balfour's act had become, in two weeks, an extension of it.

Lloyd George had promised Campbell-Bannerman that he would make no more public attacks on the House of Lords, but the mutilation of the Education Bill, even though he had predicted precisely this fate for such a broad measure, and one may suspect the almost disdainful excision of the central Council for Wales, evoked a new outburst on 1 December before the Palmerston Club at the Randolph Hotel in Oxford. This time the burden of the address was the threat of constitutional change. Balfour had dared the government to dissolve the House of Commons on the question of education. Such a proposal, said Lloyd George, from a man who had given the electorate no hint of his own education bill, was intolerable. Was there, he asked, any suggestion to dissolve the House of Lords?

> If the House of Lords persisted in its present policy, it would be a much larger measure than the Education Bill that would come up for con-
> sideration. It would come up on this issue, whether the country was to be governed by the King and his peers or by the King and the people.[50]

The reference brought this time a truly angry letter from Knollys. 'His Majesty feels that he has a right, and it is one on which he intends to insist, that Mr. Lloyd George shall not introduce the sovereign's name into those violent tirades of his....' Campbell-Bannerman this time defended his colleague stoutly. (It should be noted that only the week before the House of Lords had given an easy second reading to Lloyd George's Merchant Shipping Bill.) The President of the Board of Trade, wrote the Prime Minister, was distraught and angry about the Lords' treatment of the Education Bill, which it had 'turned upside down.' He could not restrain himself. However the introduction of the reference to the King was only to avoid disrespect that would accrue from the suggestion that the nation was governed by the peers and the people alone. The Prime Minister pointedly did not say that such outbursts would never occur again. Rather he hinted that they might.[51]

What was to be done about the House of Lords was a question for the future. The present problem was an Education Bill now again before the House of Commons that belonged to nobody, certainly not to the government and probably in no real sense to the House of Lords. The crux of the argument against the Lords' changes lay in the situation of teachers in the transferred schools now to be under public authority, who would be asked to teach a creed in which they perhaps did not believe. Although they could not be required to do so, a refusal, it was argued, would incur the displeasure of the head teacher and cause difficulty when appointments were renewed. There appear to have been a number of members of the Cabinet who favored surrender to the Lords' ultimatum, with perhaps a few face-saving compromises. The loss of a major bill for a party in its first parliamentary session, that had been in opposition for a decade and without effective governing power for more than two, was an unhappy prospect. Lloyd George thought otherwise. At the end of 1908, after the Lords' peremptory destruction of the chief measure of that session, the Licensing Bill, Lloyd George told Robertson Nicoll that he had proposed a dissolution over education. That 'was the minute for attack. We should have won easily—with a few insignificant electoral casualties...& we...could have gone on passing Licensing Bills and real Education Bills.'[52]

However, indeed as Lloyd George well knew, Liberal nonconformists were sharply divided on the bill, feeling it had been unsatisfactory from the beginning and the Lords had only made it more so. A dissolution was out of the question, wrote Robert Perks to Rosebery on 24 November when the Lords were in the midst of the amending process. The bill, he said, 'is hated by the Noncons and creates no enthusiasm....Even among Liberals...if there were an appeal to electors the Free Church ministers would refuse to take the field.'[54]

The Cabinet's rejection of Lloyd George's advice to take the contest with the upper chamber to the country may have been wise, but it clearly heeded his advice on the critical issue of the Lords' amendments. He, evidently alone, drove the Cabinet into resistance to the Lords on the central matter of denominational teaching by lay teachers. The date is unclear, probably the Cabinet of 5 December when Campbell-Bannerman reported to the King that 'a protracted conversation...on the position of teachers in the non-provided schools' had occurred. 'The question really centres on this.'[55] A number of his colleagues, evidently among them John Burns, wanted to give in to the opposition on this matter. At this point Lloyd George made a speech, the only one, he insisted, that he had made in Cabinet. 'I did not threaten to resign,' he told Herbert Lewis three weeks later when the two were at Biarritz.

> I have never done that. I spoke quietly but as gravely and impressively as I could, and they saw I meant it. I recalled the action of the Cabinet in 1870 [evidently the surrender of Gladstone's government on Clause 26 of the Forster Education Bill which allowed school boards to pay childrens' tuition at voluntary schools. This aroused much anger among nonconformists. [Among the attackers was Joseph Chamberlain.] And I reminded them that although the government survived until 1874 there was no life in it and it was the defection of the Nonconformists which chiefly caused its ruin at the polls. At this a vehement 'hear! hear!' came from CB....

'The Members of the Cabinet', he continued,

> were rather apt to run down the Nonconformist leaders and to regard them as extreme and impracticable men, and I told them that I had been in touch with them all along, that they were not merely interested in Education from the Nonconformist point of view, but were Liberals keenly anxious that the Government should live, and that the Government had no more loyal supporters. This carried the Cabinet. If I had

not made that speech they would have given way all along on the question of teachers.[56]

Lloyd George was in the habit of dramatizing the importance of a single occurrence or decision to make it the sole efficient cause of some event. Whether his speech converted the Cabinet, as he supposed, it is nevertheless certain that the demise of the Liberal Education Bill came over the issue of denominational instruction by lay teachers.[57] Although the House of Commons rejected all the Lords' amendments in a single resolution on 12 December, the two sides had already begun private negotiation aimed at compromise which would save the bill. These negotiations, at Lord Crewe's house in Curzon Street, in which Lloyd George did not participate, ended in failure on the morning of 19 December over the Liberal refusal to compromise on teachers. 'I fully hoped that the Govt. would make some material concessions,' wrote a disappointed Archbishop Davidson to Francis Knollys that day. 'But they thought it impossible to do so, frankly avowing that it was the opinion of the Nonconformist extremists which rendered it impracticable for them.'[58] One item which the Liberals were, however, willing to sacrifice was Lloyd George's Welsh council.[59]

Later that day the House of Lords voted to insist upon its amendments and the next day, 20 December, Campbell-Bannerman announced the bill would be dropped.

The Education Bill was dead but Lloyd George was able to resurrect the part in which he had the greatest interest, the separate government of Welsh education. Well before the Lords had finished with the bill he had been proposing that the government do administratively, for Wales at least, what it was not able to do by legislation. The possibility of such a change came with the removal of Birrell, who before Christmas was told he was to be transferred to Ireland. Knowing that he would soon depart, he gave consent for the creation of a Welsh department within the Board of Education.[60] On 17 January, before the Caernarvon Liberal Association, in the course of what came to be known for other reasons as the 'guard room speech' Lloyd George, after discussing the loss of the Welsh education council in the bill, announced that 'the government, however, mean to do their best to circumvent the House of Lords' petty and spiteful piece of vandalism.'[61]

The idea of a Welsh enclave within his department was not well received by Morant. Writing to Arthur Ponsonby, Campbell-Bannerman's secretary, about the sort of person needed to replace Birrell, he recommended 'the firm handling of Wales, not giving in to Lloyd George, is one of the earliest things needed. Give us therefore a hard and careful worker and a brainy handler of Parliament...if you don't want the Govt to suffer very seriously.'[62] But the new President, Reginald McKenna, born a Congregationalist, MP since 1895 for North Monmouthshire, and, at this stage, an ardent Welsh nationalist, was not likely to rescind favors to Lloyd George.

The new Welsh department was not the council for Wales made up of nominees of Welsh education authorities that had been envisioned in the 1906 bill. Basically it was a separate inspectorate for the principality, similar to the office for which Lloyd George had negotiated with Balfour. But it was to get its own permanent secretary who reported directly to the President, so removing Wales from the pernicious influence of R.L. Morant, and it would be on the reports of the Board of Education inspectors that schools were deemed efficient, so qualifying for Treasury grants. Best of all the patronage belonged entirely to Lloyd George.

He began to deal with appointments, evidently with some relish, almost as soon as he returned from Biarritz, indeed before McKenna's appointment was announced and only seven days after McKenna had learned by letter from Campbell-Bannerman—who spent the entire month of January at Belmont Castle—that he was to go to the Board of Education.[63]

On 19 January, at Criccieth, Lloyd George offered his old friend, one-time election agent, and law partner of Herbert Lewis, A.T. Davies, the headship of the new Welsh department. Three days later Davies visited Morant in London. After a long conversation he succeeded in extracting recognition that he would rank as a permanent secretary at a salary of £1,200, £500 less than Morant himself earned.[64] Lloyd George spent much time in the next three weeks, usually with the cooperation of Herbert Lewis, considering other appointments to the Welsh department.[65] The other critical appointment was that of the Chief Inspector. For this post Morant had proposed Owen M. Edwards. Edwards had held for a few months Tom Ellis's seat in Merioneth, after the latter's death until the election of 1900. However, his suitability for the inspectorate derived from his eminence as a scholar of Welsh history and culture. Since 1889 he had been a fellow of Lincoln College, Oxford, although he sturdily maintained his Welsh identity and did much of his writing in Welsh.

Lloyd George was not enthusiastic about Edwards, feeling that he was insufficiently Welsh and snobbish. There was a strain of pettiness, indeed vindictiveness, in Lloyd George, which contrasted sharply with his usual easy good humor and lack of personal affectation. As he told D.R. Daniel, when he and Maggie had been at Oxford with Sir John Rhys, Edwards had never 'even invited them over for so much as a cup of tea.' One may also suspect that if Morant approved of Edwards, for Lloyd George he was the wrong man. Nevertheless, Edwards was appointed, according to Daniel because he and Llewelyn Williams were able to convince Lloyd George that the presence of so distinguished a figure would give the Welsh department the prominence it needed. (Edwards, however, declined to work under Davies and insisted on receiving the same salary 'co-equal and co-etcetera!' snorted Morant.)[66] The new office was announced on 12 February to the general applause of the Welsh press and to general criticism elsewhere that the government was allowing Lloyd George to construct a personal political machine.[67] It was the first administrative recognition within Whitehall of the uniqueness of Wales, a practice that would be repeated with national health insurance. The Welsh inspectorate still exists.

More important, for Lloyd George the Welsh department concluded the educational revolt. Something, not much perhaps, had been accomplished to justify the sacrifices of 1904 and 1905. Even though the Liberal government would continue under McKenna and under his successor, Walter Runciman, to try to do something for the state schools, and St. Asaph would introduce his Freedom of Contract Bill again in 1908, Lloyd George was not involved although he saw Bishop Edwards regularly and was apparently consulted about the bill.[68] Nonetheless, so far as Lloyd George was concerned the crusade against denominational education was at an end and even when, as Prime Minister, he undertook a full scale reform of the British education system as a central part of his program to build a better Britain, his President of the Board of Education, H.A.L. Fisher, discreetly left the sectarian problem alone.

III

In the political catechism of Welsh nonconformity, the indivisible trinity consisted of education reform, Church disestablishment and temperance legislation. Each of these matters was addressed in turn by the Liberal government that came to power in December 1905 and in each case complicated and time consuming legislation was blocked by a House of Lords secure in the knowledge that the issues involved were of no interest to the public at large. Politically, the causes were linked. The frustration over the Education Bill in 1906 revived enthusiasm for disestablishment, which had tended to languish during the education revolt. Similarly, because it would have deprived the Church of its schools, many Welsh dissenters and indeed many Churchmen had seen the 1906 Education Bill as a step toward disestablishment. Now that the Church had kept its schools the attack on the structure itself was renewed.

For Lloyd George disestablishment was, and always had been, a secondary and slightly false issue. As early as his first election campaign he had tried to avoid the matter until called to order by Evan Jones. Subsequently of course he spoke on it many times but usually as a way of drawing attention to Wales and of attacking the Church. At best it was a problem that should be solved with Welsh Home Rule. But for the present, for the Liberal government, it was potentially an explosive issue either to be buried or sterilized. It promised nothing but profitless and losing battles. It could hardly be an issue to take to the people of England. English nonconformists, as Lloyd George would continually remind his country-men, were only slightly interested in it and would resent Welsh preemption of parliamentary time which should belong to the larger issues of education and licensing. In a speech during the election campaign he had routinely promised that disestablishment would remain a part of the Liberal program, but as he was speaking in Evan Jones's Moriah Chapel in Caernarvon, he could hardly say less. Pressure for disestablishment, when the Liberal government came to power, proceeded not from Lloyd George but from D.A. Thomas supported by Sam Evans and Ellis Griffith, who argued that if a bill were ever to pass the Lords it would have to come to the upper chamber early in the government's life. After two or three years such a measure would have no chance.[69]

Lloyd George was anxious to avoid any fight over disestablishment. When he learned of Thomas's demands, in order to forestall potential embarrassment for a government already struggling to assemble an unwieldy Education Bill, he moved quickly, and as usual privately, to make an agreed settlement. On 21 February 1906, as soon as parliament assembled, he saw his friend Bishop Edwards to ask whether the Welsh Church would accept 'a very mild and kindly Disestablishment Bill.' He had as yet nothing in writing, St. Asaph reported to Archbishop Davidson that day, but roughly it amounted to an arrangement that the Church should retain everything—buildings, houses, glebe etc.—but not tithes. 'The terms,' he continued, 'are of course very much more favorable than Mr. Asquith's former Bill and the Bishop believes that Mr. Lloyd George would rather like to get disestablishment carried with a minimum of friction.'[70]

Davidson was cautious, but not unfriendly. The next day the three men met in the Bishops' Robing Room of the House of Lords and Lloyd George asked what the Archbishop would think of a royal commission on the state of the Church in Wales. Would the Church cooperate and suggest members?[71] This had not been mentioned the previous day although it may have been in Lloyd George's mind from the beginning. Both sides, for different reasons, were anxious to delay action, but Lloyd George did not want the government to appear to be leaving the field open for the initiative of D.A. Thomas.[72]

Davidson again was cautious, but soon agreed to a commission and the Cabinet approved it two weeks later.[73] The 'Royal Commission on the Church of England and other religious bodies in Wales and Monmouthshire' was announced in May, although it did not begin work until October. Lloyd George was active in the selection of its members, which numbered four Churchmen among whom were Lord Hugh Cecil and Frank Edwards and four Nonconformists including Sam Evans. The chairman was the Rt. Honourable Sir Roland Vaughan Williams, a Lord Justice of the Court of Appeal since 1897, but a man of rigid legal mind and although technically a Welshman, he lacked any sense of nonconformist grievances.

The result was disaster. Sir Roland determined, evidently at the beginning, that the commission had been charged with investigating the state of the Welsh Church, not with Welsh chapel complaints against it. Particularly it had not the task of drafting a disestablishment bill. (Its terms of reference were: 'To report the origin, amount and nature...of properties of the Church...and work done by Churches of all denominations...and the extent to which the people avail themselves of such provisions....')[74] Congregations were not allowed to present their case against the Church, and the Chairman, when not silencing his colleagues, disrupted proceedings with irrelevant asides and reminiscences.

Through the winter of 1906 and 1907 as the Education Bill languished and died, there were increasing complaints in the Welsh press about the royal commission: that the figures it would gather about the numbers in chapel congregations would be incorrect and that the government had no intention of bringing forward a disestablishment bill.

So far Lloyd George was not touched. His undoubted ministerial success, which earned him even the reluctant admiration of a *Times* leader on 30 January 1907, the announcement of the Welsh Department of Education, and his ambitious legislative program for the coming year, made him the clear success of the new administration. Wales still was proud of him. Yet there was manifest a rising disenchantment toward the government, in Wales over the meandering royal commission, and in England over the apparent inability of the Liberals to solve the education problem. The erosion of Liberal authority, from the pinnacle of 1906 to a near stalemate with the Unionists four years later, began in the spring of 1907. Lloyd George was not the cause of this decline but as he had been a highly visible figure in mobilizing nonconformist support so, as free church frustration mounted, he had to assume a share of the odium accruing to the government.

The issues need careful definition. English and Welsh nonconformists agreed that the government had failed, but not upon what its failures were. The Welsh, after the end of 1906, were almost entirely concerned with disestablishment. The English, on the other hand, cared at bottom very little about the Welsh Church and wanted instead to continue the battle for education reform while doing something about temperance. Lloyd George's opinions on these matters have been discussed. For him the education battle was over, disestablishmentarians were a noisy nuisance, and drink, although a matter about which he did have personal convictions, was politically unprofitable. But the common objection to all action on any nonconformist demand, English or Welsh, was the barrier of the House of Lords. The fact that none of the free church issues was popular enough generally to provide a platform on which to challenge the peers, the nonconformists, with that obtuseness common to single-issue enthusiasts, seemed unable to understand. Lloyd George, who had expressed similar disregard for political realities in the middle nineties, spent much time during 1907 and the spring of 1908 loyally attempting to restrain importunate free churchmen both in Wales and in England. In doing so he earned for himself, eventually, a certain amount of unpopularity among groups accustomed to regarding him as their champion.

He began his explanation in a speech at a Liberal meeting in Caernarvon on 17 January 1907 in honor of his forty-fourth birthday. Here he devoted most of his time to the customary denunciation of the Lords for their 'spiteful vandalism' against the Education Bill, but at this time also he made the announcement already mentioned that separate treatment of Welsh education would be achieved anyway. However, knowing that the King's Speech, set for 12 February, would contain nothing on disestablishment, he concluded with a courageous warning to his countrymen to keep peace on the subject.

> The fact was that Wales would not get a dog's chance of fair play from the Lords. They hated its Radicalism, they despised its Nonconformity and they could indulge their scorn freely because Wales was so small (loud cheers). And he would say this to his fellow countrymen, if they found the government manoeuvering their artillery into position for leading an attack on the Lords, the Welshmen who worried them into attending anything else until the citadel had been stormed ought to be put in the guardroom. (Laughter and Cheers)[75]

The 'guard room speech' evidently shocked no one at the time of its delivery. The *British Weekly* did not even notice it and by itself it caused Lloyd George little of the trouble he thought fit to allow Herbert DuParcq to assign to it in 1912.[76] But neither was it forgotten. By summer, as the Campbell-Bannerman government floundered, attempting, and failing, to implement the step by step policy in Ireland, to improve the situation of tenants in Scotland, and to breathe some life into a measure to reverse by statute the West Riding judgement, Wales was forgotten and Lloyd George's apparent unwillingness to direct the government's attention to the principality recalled his indiscretion.

Trouble began for the Campbell-Bannerman government on 26 February, when, on the same day that McKenna introduced his Education Bill to exempt councils from paying the cost of denominational teaching, the Liberals lost an important by-election in the nonconformist stronghold of Brigg, Lincolnshire to a Unionist who, worse, was an outspoken tariff reformer. The seat, which had been staunchly Liberal since its creation and had been held through the disasters of 1895 and 1900 by a well-known Quaker, H.J. Reckitt, who won by nearly two thousand in 1906, was lost with a substantial drop in the Liberal vote brought on, it was reported, by defections among the Methodists who feared Home Rule.[77] Then, as if to prove that Brigg was no accident, the voters of London on 2 March dismissed the Liberal majority on the London County Council. Both defeats, asserted the *British Weekly*, showed the defection of nonconformity.[78]

Lloyd George had been the subject of grumbling, but no worse, in Welsh religious and political meetings through the late winter and spring while Welsh Members of Parliament attempted meekly to extract from the Prime Minister some promise on disestablishment. Meanwhile the royal commission inched along, ignored by most Englishmen except for a regular letter in the *British Weekly* from the Reverend H. Elvet Lewis. The storm broke at the end of April. Lewis's letter on the twenty-fifth, after a series of surprisingly moderate reports, contained an outspoken attack on the commission. The same issue of the *British Weekly* reported that three of the four nonconformist members, including Sam Evans, had resigned in protest against the behavior of the chairman. (In fact the three had ceased attending meetings more than a week earlier.)

The collapse of the investigation into the Welsh Church brought the royal commission to the notice of English nonconformity in a way its slow progress had never done. Lloyd George felt obliged to deny that he was responsible for the commission. The blame lay with Asquith. The *British Weekly* remarked that his Welsh supporters would be 'relieved' to know this. However he did agree that Vaughan Williams's interpretation of the terms of reference was correct.[79] He had attempted some mediation on the commission before his friends' resignation, but his letters show him almost entirely preoccupied with the work of his department with the result, among other things, that he failed to attend the annual meeting of the Liberation Society in early May.

Parliament reassembled after the Whitsun recess on 27 May. Before the recess Campbell-Bannerman had announced he would make a major statement on parliamentary business which rumor immediately interpreted as an announcement that a number of bills would be dropped. (The Cabinet had been unhappily discussing for weeks the lamentable progress of the 1907 legislative program, the Prime Minister insisting nevertheless that there would be no autumn session.) Attention focused on the McKenna Education Bill. On 30 May the *British Weekly* sounded the alarm with a round-up of nonconformist press denunciation about the failure to solve the education problem and featuring an unprecedented front page leader entitled 'Losing of the Legions.' This article, almost a declaration of war upon the Campbell-Bannerman government, called for a revolt of nonconformist MPs and warned the Liberals that 99% of the 8 million nonconformists in the country voted in their interest. Yet the government paid no attention to nonconformist politicians and failed even to distribute honors to nonconformist citizens.[80]

The Prime Minister's statement followed the publication of the *British Weekly*'s warning by only three days. Delivered with the devastating simplicity of which Campbell-Bannerman was capable, it was a candid admission that in many ways his government, so far, had failed, although he promised more action in the next session. He recited the program outlined in the King's Speech, licensing, Irish self-government, and land valuation. These bills were now to be withdrawn or, in the case of licensing, held over until the next year. Among those withdrawn was McKenna's Education Act although again with the promise of a major bill in 1908. Disestablishment was not mentioned.[81]

The astonishing admissions of 3 June, drove the *British Weekly* and Wales into a fury directed this time at Lloyd George. He had not been mentioned by name in the 'Losing of the Legions' but he emerged the next week in a second front page editorial, two pages long, entitled 'Grabbers and Nippers,' as the man responsible for the government's surrender.

'If there were a general election tomorrow,' the *British Weekly* began, 'the Government would be beaten.' How could the Liberals have become so weak in eighteen months? The answer was that they were frightened of the House of Lords. The blame, by implication, lay with the man who at one time made nonconformist grievances the central issue of his political life, David Lloyd George. Now he was a nipper, not a grabber. He had betrayed Wales.

> Where is Wales today? What change has come over the scene? What has been done about education? What is the position of the Welsh revolt? What about disestablishment? Mr. Lloyd-George is a supremely clever man with a quite ecclesiastical turn for manoeuvre. He has done brilliantly in his department, but what has he done for Wales? Well, he has given Wales the Welsh Commission, a boon the Principality is deeply pondering. What was his action about the Welsh Council in the Educational discussion? Mr. Lloyd-George is detained by mysterious providences from appearing at Non-conformist gatherings now-a-days, but he will have to explain himself to the nation that has so trusted him. If Wales is satisfied there is no more to say, but is there one Welshman who believes the present Government will take up Disestablishment? Perhaps it may be thought on reflection that Mr. Lloyd-George and the Government have nipped rather than grabbed the Welsh problem.[82]

Campbell-Bannerman was clearly oblivious to the storm he had raised in the nonconformist community. On 11 June he innocently replied to a question from Ellis Griffith asking for a promise on disestablishment for next year by saying that he could not 'hold out any expectation' of such a measure, nor would he say that other legislation would not take precedence.[83] A few days later he said the same thing again to a delegation of Welsh Members of Parliament. Griffith replied to these rebuffs with a long letter to the *British Weekly* attacking the Prime Minister, although not Lloyd George.[84] There were many other letters in the following weeks.

Lloyd George had to try to repair the damage. On 24 June he replied to what was probably a solicited letter from the Reverend H. Elvet Lewis, a comrade from the Cymru Fydd days, with a strong affirmation that the government did indeed care about disestablishment and that if parliament ran its normal course such a bill would be put through the House of Commons. However, all questions would have to wait upon the House of Lords. He emphasized that his letter had been shown to the Prime Minister, who agreed that it accurately reflected his views.[85] In addition, he began again to speak publicly avowing the government's interest in disestablishment.[86] More important perhaps, he undertook to cultivate the friendship of William Robertson Nicoll.

The support of Nicoll's *British Weekly* became such an important weapon in Lloyd George's political arsenal in the years between 1907 and 1914 that one wonders how he could have been so casual about it before. He had known Nicoll at least since 1902 and possibly before that, even though the *British Weekly* in common with many other free church papers was a strong supporter of the South African War and, through the agency of Robert Perks, the impresario of English nonconformity, a follower of Rosebery. The paper had reported Lloyd George's adventures, not always uncritically, during the education revolt and had applauded his appointment to the government. However since December 1905, except for his interventions on the Education Bill, Lloyd George had sought to disentangle himself from nonconformist and Welsh affairs. But he had found, by the summer of 1907, that even if he wished to remove himself from Wales, Wales would not let him go. The immensely powerful pastoral establishment in his country, with the dual voices of press and pulpit at its disposal, which for so many years he had flattered, now regarded him as a hostage for the government's behavior. His name flew about congregational meetings and abusive letters deluged the Welsh and English nonconformist press.

This outrage was not dangerous to Lloyd George. In terms of his entire life it represents only the stress of his transition from the Welsh Parnell to the national radical hero he would be in the next half decade, the prophet of the New Liberalism, who as Chancellor of the Exchequer would try to put life into a dispirited Liberal party. But as he sought to make a place for himself in the British national political world, he needed a constituency. There were plenty of examples of solitary radicals: Labouchere, Dilke, and since 1906, Chiozza Money, who were listened to with respect in the House of Commons, but who had little influence within the party. Nicoll could give him influence. Nonconformity, temperance, social reform, and attention to what was coming to be called 'the condition of the people question' fitted neatly together and involved no sharp break from his former concerns. The *British Weekly* had a circulation of 100,000, nearly twice that of the *Daily News* when he had negotiated for its purchase, and four times the sale of

J.A. Spender's powerful *Westminster Gazette*. Since 1902, after the death of Hugh Price Hughes of the *Methodist Times*, it had become the bible of English free churchmen.

Nicoll was a comparatively easy conquest who possessed a vanity that equalled, and probably resulted from, his political influence. On 16 July, Herbert Lewis recorded that Lloyd George had told him as the two were standing in the aye lobby of the House of Commons that the proprietor of the *Western Mail* had warned some days earlier that Lloyd George should look after Robertson Nicoll, who was feeling neglected. Soon after this, Lloyd George remarked, he had found out that Nicoll had invited him to dinner and that he either had forgotten to reply, or accepting, had forgotten to go. This slight, Lloyd George decided, was the cause of the 'Losing of the Legions.'[87]

Lloyd George quickly made amends. 'Been lunching with Robertson Nicoll,' he wrote Maggie on 31 July. 'He is most friendly. Told me I was the only Minister who had made a reputation as a Minister and that everyone was talking of me as the next Liberal Prime Minister. He had great contempt for Ellis Griffith and for all Welsh MPs—even poor Herbert Lewis. Said I was the only man amongst them. He had seen Elfed [the Rev. H. Elvet Lewis] yesterday and Elfed had told him, apropo of the Welsh disestablishment agitation, "you may depend upon it, the Welsh people won't give up Lloyd George lightly—they are proud of him & besides they have no substitute" [in Welsh] Pretty good isn't it?'[88]

Besides suggesting that Lloyd George himself was not entirely immune to flattery, his meeting with Nicoll at the end of July produced useful political information which he enlarged upon a few days later to Herbert Lewis. Nicoll had told him, he reported, that the *British Weekly* had received many bitter and abusive letters about him, unsigned, and so unprinted. The editor urged that the government at least should introduce a disestablishment bill. He, Nicoll, would be satisfied with that.[89]

Parliament, in 1907, did not rise until 28 August and Lloyd George was fully engaged until the end with his Patents and Limited Partnership Bills. In the second week of September he took his family to the Alpine resort of St. Gervais in the French Department of Haute Savoie. It was the last holiday that the seven would enjoy together. This was for Lloyd George a short vacation. By the end of the month he was back in England attending to Robertson Nicoll. He needed support. The Welsh nonconformist world was in an uproar.

While he was away the *British Weekly* had published a long letter from J. Morgan Jones of Cardiff, the President of the Calvinistic Methodist Assembly, announcing a 'Welsh National Convention' to assemble in the huge Wood Street Chapel in Cardiff on 10 October and to be sponsored by all Welsh denominations. All free churchmen were invited to attend and protest the failure of the government to disestablish the Welsh Church.[90] Lloyd George did not 'pooh pooh' the Welsh convention as Beriah Evans suggests.[91] Although the protest was ostensibly aimed at the Liberal government, he was, as he knew, involved. It was far too reminiscent of similar meetings he had organized himself to make, indeed, the same demands. His reports from Wales were not reassuring. There exists in his file a letter from J.H. Roberts who evidently was attempting to water down the resolutions of denunciation that were being prepared. He reports having a 'trying time,' although the government had 'a few friends' who 'may have gained a point.' But, he concluded, 'W.H. Hughes [secretary of Lloyd George's Welsh National Liberal Council] writes expressing the hope that we will not go to the convention!'[92]

Lloyd George had already summoned Robertson Nicoll to Routh Road and had stated his case in a long interview. After the usual reciprocal compliments, Lloyd George telling Nicoll that the *British Weekly* was the first thing he read when he returned (this was quite true, he never missed an issue) he reiterated his assertion that there need be no anxiety about disestablishment beyond that which arose from the House of Lords. He reminded Nicoll of his letter to Elvet Lewis which had been approved by the Prime Minister. He would not accept that the government had defaulted on its pledges. The House of Lords' action on the Education Bill had upset the timetable. The Education Bill itself had been the greatest measure of disestablishment and disendowment ever introduced. Also, Welsh nonconformists should stop abusing the Welsh MPs. They had no power. In 1894 they could bring down the government, but not now. 'Who are their allies?' Lloyd George asked rhetorically. 'No one.' And most of all, he concluded, Welsh nonconformists should remember that by their clamor for disestablishment they risked alienating English nonconformists who looked forward still to a revision of the Education Act, which was now under consideration in the Cabinet.

Evidently Lloyd George said more than appeared in the interview. Nicoll commented rather smugly in his 'Notes of the Week' column, calling attention to the interview on another page, that he would not be surprised if Lloyd George would soon say that a disestablishment bill was being prepared.[93]

Lloyd George's frankness had considerable effect in Wales. The Reverend H.M. Hughes of the Welsh Congregational Union, who himself had been a leader in the denunciation of the royal commission, wrote to Lloyd George on the day the interview appeared to say that the warning was 'just what was needed to counteract "schemes" and machinations of two or three persons who have tried in every way to stir up a revolt.' Hughes had obtained an invitation for Lloyd George to attend the convention and hoped that the President of the Board of Trade would come.[94]

Conflicting advice or not, Lloyd George intended to go to the convention but not, if he could help it, empty handed. From Criccieth a few days later Lloyd George wrote to the Prime Minister to ask for some sort of a promise on the Church and Wales. There would be 'a conference on disestablishment on Thursday.' Welsh agitation was becoming 'menacing'; however, all the nonconformist ministers, he continued innocently, were great admirers of Campbell-Bannerman. Everything was among friends. No one was seeking a quarrel. Nevertheless, he thought there was a 'good deal to be said' for the agitation. It had been going on, after all, since about 1865 and now the Welsh felt they were being put off. Therefore, as he had been 'invited' to attend he asked for a 'strong letter' with a 'clear declaration' from the Prime Minister that he intended to push for disestablishment before the present parliament was dissolved.[95]

Campbell-Bannerman was not impressed. He replied tersely: 'You may repeat what I said to the deputation last session', that the government desired to deal with the question but cannot because of the crisis between the two Houses.[96]

Lloyd George had asked H.M. Hughes to arrange a meeting with the leaders of the convention, of which Hughes was one, on the day before the meeting. Accordingly on Wednesday, 9 October, he was in Cardiff and, on Beriah Evans's record, promised the committee, quite without authorization, that a disestablishment bill would be introduced no later than 1909 unless the session was 'occupied by issues concerning the House of Lords, or the reform of the electoral law.'[97] He thus was able to water down substantially the official resolution of condemnation that was to be put before the meeting the next day.

However, on this occasion the usual tactics of compromise and squaring did not work. Lloyd George saved the government from a serious public defeat only by one of the greatest speeches of his life and in doing so vanquished his old nemesis Evan Jones. The meeting according to all accounts was the largest and most representative ever held in Wales, with over two thousand people present. After the committee's resolution had been put, with tepid cheering, the patriarch of Welsh chapels, Evan Jones, arose. 'The veteran warrior of a hundred battles', Elvet Lewis reported in his letter to the *British Weekly*, received wild applause which continually interrupted him when he began to speak. 'If there were four George's,' he declared 'I would still say, don't be sheep.' The Liberal government had consistently ignored the claims of Wales and the Prime Minister treated the demand for disestablishment as if he had first heard of it. Finally Jones moved to amend the resolution before the meeting to say that no person who did not put disestablishment and disendowment in the 'forefront of his programme' should be 'adopted...for a constituency in Wales.'

This resolution, the exact repetition of the motion Evan Jones had put at Rhyl nearly two decades before, which then had brought Lloyd George meekly to heel, caused hysterical applause. Lloyd George as he usually did had intended to speak last, but now he was forced to reply. He began amiably and undramatically as always. He was there, he said amid laughter, 'to face the music.' The Reverend Evan Jones had referred to 'an uneasiness in men's minds...he was not surprised to hear it (hear hear). He welcomed and rejoiced in it.'

'The Rev. Evan Jones said that he was angry at the treatment which had been accorded to the question of disestablishment by the Prime Minister and asked why he did not say it was part and parcel of the Liberal programme, but that is exactly what he did say.' If there was to be any domestic legislation, he promised, in the fourth session, disestablishment would be a part of it. 'You be fair to me, we will be fair to you.'

At this point Evan Jones interrupted to ask whether, should the bill not have been introduced when the government dissolved, the question of disestablishment would be put before the country. 'Certainly' replied the junior member of the Cabinet. Jones sat down, apparently satisfied and in fact defeated.

At last Lloyd George moved to his peroration, perhaps the most famous he ever delivered in Wales.

Just recognize our difficulties.... No man gives his best to a people who distrust him, who, the moment difficulties arise, assail him with suspicion. You have got to trust somebody. [A voice: 'Lloyd George' cheers] Let me say this to you: if you can find a better go to him, but in the meantime don't fire at us from behind. [Now his voice began to quiver as if he were choked with emotion.] Who said that I was going to sell Wales? Seven years ago there was a little country which I never saw, fighting for freedom, fighting for fair play. I had never been within a thousand miles of it, never knew any of its inhabitants. Pardon me for reminding you, I risked my seat. I risked my livelihood — it was leaving me. [A voice: 'You risked your life.' A roar from the meeting. By this time the audience was on its feet, some members were cheering, some including the speaker were sobbing.] Yes I risked my life. Am I going to sell the land I love? [A breathless silence, then in Welsh] God knows how dear Wales is to me!

Instantly the two thousand were on their feet again, but not in applause, Elvet Lewis reported to the *British Weekly*, rather in awe. Many were crying outright. 'The ranks are now closed' concluded Elvet Lewis, 'a fighting nerve has been restored to the rank and file; the leader is back with the strains of a great triumph to reassure him.... he left the platform more than ever the people's leader.'[98] Afterwards Ellis Griffith tried to remind the convention that Lloyd George had insulted Wales in the guard room speech, but the audience was leaving. There was nothing more to say. Lloyd George had defeated the Welsh revolt and had freed himself from the menace of chapel politics represented by Evan Jones, who nevertheless, eighteen months later, became the first Welshman to be elected president of the National Council of Free Churches.

Perhaps D.A. Thomas best understood what had happened, that Wales had now lost control of Lloyd George forever. On 17 October he published a two page article in the *British Weekly* entitled 'Wales and Mr. Lloyd George.' Beginning with the always ominous affirmation that he and the the Member for Caernarvon District had been good friends for many years, he recalled Lloyd George's fight for disestablishment in 1894 and the resulting embarrassment to 'poor Tom Ellis.' It was in poor taste therefore, 'to threaten the Guard Room to other Welshmen when they follow, far behind, the example he set in earlier days.'

The convention, in effect, had been a failure, said Thomas. He did not doubt that Lloyd George loved Wales, but perhaps 'George loves not Wales the less though he may love ambition more.' Nor would they recapture Lloyd George. 'The statesman seated in the Cabinet Council can not help regarding things from a different point of view to that of a politician when climbing the ladder. From the higher and more secure level of Cabinet eminence things often look smaller and of less consequence than from the lower rungs.' The Member for Caernarvon District dwelt now in another part of the forest, away from his old friends. He might love them still, but he would speak henceforth with a different voice and say other things. 'Mr. Lloyd George,' concluded Thomas, 'is human, I say it with all respect, very human. With Emerson he has long thought consistency to be the hobgoblin of little minds.'[99]

The Cardiff speech did not silence Welsh cries for disestablishment, but for Lloyd George they were now out of date and irrelevant. A year later, when he was now Chancellor of the Exchequer, D.R. Daniel informed him that Ellis Griffith had announced he would 'raise a storm in Wales' if the government did not take action on disestablishment in 1909, he laughed:

> He doesn't understand how to raise a storm, and what's more import-
> ant, he doesn't know what to write on the banner. He imagines that the
> old question we had in 1894—Disestablishment—would do now as then,
> not remembering that fifteen years have now gone by and a new nation
> and new questions have come to the surface. The nation does not look at
> disestablishment now as it did then. All is now social questions and if Ellis
> Jones Griffith had any gumption at all he'd have put those on his
> banner and turned to the workers and quarrymen as he does—but he
> hasn't got the ability and he would have given quite a lot to worry the
> Government. But he doesn't know the signs of the times.[100]

Lloyd George would still attend the disorderly meetings of the Welsh MPs, but his contempt for most of them was no less because he now controlled them. He watched carefully over Welsh patronage. He always visited Wales during the Whitsun recess—he began his new house in Criccieth the next year in 1908—and his doings were duly recorded in Welsh newspapers. But the newsmen important to him now were in England: George Riddell, A.G. Gardiner, Robert Donald of the *Daily Chronicle*, Massingham, C.P. Scott, and above all Robertson Nicoll for whom he obtained the long coveted knighthood in 1909. To be sure he kept in his mind the issues he had learned as a young man in North Wales, pensions and especially land reform, but he would think of them in national terms. He maintained his nonconformity, like his Welshness, as a symbol of political uniqueness. It testified that he was not of the establishment, as his national origins meant he was not English. Moreover nonconformity provided a link to the pacifists, to the social radical dissent of the North of England, to the trade unionists, to the Cadburys and the Rowntrees, and to the *Manchester Guardian*. Wales always provided him with a reference point and it gave him the ideological baggage he would carry for the rest of his long life. But it would control him no more. He had escaped.

IV

Back in London, Lloyd George wrote on 17 October to Campbell-Bannerman in Scotland a slightly smug letter confirming his victory. Cardiff, he reported, 'went very well.' 'You will not be troubled by Welsh disestablishment any more this session,' although the government would be pressed when planning next year's program. It might be well, he suggested, perhaps remembering his promise to the convention's executive committee, to get it out of the way in 1909.[101] Then he passed to another subject of which the newspapers were already full, the threatened national railway strike.

The possibility of a stoppage of railway transport throughout Great Britain had been apparent for many weeks before the meeting at Cardiff and Lloyd George's concern about it began at least in the middle of September. His involvement in the dispute was brief, dramatic, and effective, but as was frequently the case with him, his work was less in solving the problem than in heading off the immediate crisis. Nonetheless, in avoiding for the moment what uniformly was expected in those days to be an unmitigated public disaster, Lloyd George elevated himself to the status of national hero. His participation gave him the reputation of a mediator and conciliator of genius whose talents were to be called upon in the future many times, perhaps too often, to extract the government from tight places.

The origins of the railway dispute of 1907 deserve a brief notice, not only because Lloyd George would be dealing with the same problem many times throughout his ministerial career, but because the railways presented an example of the malaise that had begun to affect much of British heavy industry in the years before the war.

British railways were old; the track network was substantially completed by the 1860s. Moreover they were heavily, some would say over, capitalized. Then as regulation of rates began in the last quarter of the nineteenth century, the weight of the top-heavy capital structure put pressure on dividends which in turn made it difficult for the over two hundred railway companies in Britain to raise new money for improvements. The pressure to save money fell upon the railwaymen in the form of low wages, which had increased only five per cent in twenty years, leaving the railwaymen, by 1907, with earnings lower than in any similar skilled heavy industry.[102] The railway companies had always responded by saying that the railways were in the nature of a public service giving the men stability of employment, and privileges such as uniforms and free travel, not enjoyed by workers in more precarious private employment.

Whether or not the railwaymen believed this, the fact was that union organization came late to the railways. Although the Amalgamated Society of Railway Servants (ASRS) was founded in 1872 as an early attempt at industrial 'all grades' organization, it grew very slowly in the next quarter century. At the turn of the century the unions could claim only 60,000 members out of 600,000 men employed in the industry. Its status was further diminished by the establishment of the Amalgamated Society of Locomotive Engineers and Firemen (ASLEF) in 1880 which included only the 'footplate men', the highest paid in the industry, and challenged ASRS's claim to speak for all railway workers. The weakness of the ASRS was further compounded by the inability of the central organization to control its branches. One example of this was the disastrous Taff Vale strike of August 1900 that resulted in an award of £32,000 in costs and damages against the ASRS.

The Taff Vale decision, finally confirmed by the House of Lords in 1901, was reversed by the Campbell-Bannerman government in 1906 with the Trade Disputes Act, which made unions immune from suits for damages resulting from industrial action. During the passage of this liberating measure the General Secretary of the ASRS, Richard Bell, was at work on a comprehensive program for his union which aimed at setting wages, hours, and working conditions for everyone employed by British railway companies. There was an element of competition in this. Bell was under pressure to show that his union was a genuine alternative to the ASLEF. Indeed the hostility between the two organizations seriously weakened his bargaining position in the fall of 1907. Bell, who had become General Secretary of the ASRS in 1897, was the man largely responsible for freeing the union from its quarter century of impotence. He was in addition one of the two candidates supported by the Labour Representation Committee to be elected to the House of Commons in 1900. But he was also a cautious and conservative man whose relations with the rest of the Labour party were virtually dissolved by 1907.[103] Under the protection of the new Liberal legislation he set about rebuilding his union. Between November 1906, when he announced his 'all grades' program, and the summer of 1907, he approached British railway companies three times proposing negotiation upon its points. Only the North Eastern, whose Managing Director until the previous year had been Sir Edward Grey, agreed even to talk. Early in September, Bell announced he intended to ask his members to approve a nationwide railway strike to secure recognition of his union.

Lloyd George was genuinely unprejudiced on the matter of the railway dispute, or rather he saw difficulties on both sides. The railways represented monopolies created by acts of parliament, the privileges of which the companies exploited while failing to perform the duties required by public service. The companies were unpopular with many younger Liberals who hoped to see them nationalized, a point of view Lloyd George supported although less from radical conviction than from his observation of the rapid improvement of European state-owned systems resulting from easy access to capital.[104] Worse, he thought, the misbehavior of British railway companies would soon make it impossible to pass even the simplest private measures for their benefit through the House of Commons. In April 1907, he had warned the Cabinet that contributions by railway and some dock companies had helped to finance the recent Moderate (i.e. Unionist) victory in the London County Council. 'It is evident,' he wrote, 'that the action of the companies is so keenly resented by many members of the House that unless something can be done to ensure it will not be continued, there is some danger that private bills containing valuable proposals for providing new facilities for public and for trade, affording employment for labour, may be postponed or wrecked.'[105]

Yet on the other hand, he detested strikes, and would continue to do so. 'They do not settle the justice or injustice of any point in dispute,' he told the diners at the Royal Sportsman Hotel in Caernarvon after he had received the Freedom of the City on 13 March 1908. 'They settle probably the strength of the parties who engage in them, exactly as any other war would.' Those who suffered, he contended, were less the strikers, organized and with strike pay, than the small businesses in the neighborhood which depended upon the firm involved in the dispute, and their employees and their families. 'Really,' he concluded, 'it is time in a civilized country where there is the reign of law, where there is a sense of justice, that there should be something better than the brute machinery of either strikes or lockouts to settle disputes. The little that I have ever seen of strikes has given me a horror of them, and that entered into the administration of my office.'[106]

Richard Bell's announcement in September that he intended to consult his union about a general railway strike made the long-simmering dispute a national crisis. The Board of Trade had the power to conduct mediation, but, as the Penrhyn stike had shown, this was impossible without the consent and good will of both sides. However, the alternative, a stoppage of all transportation, loomed as a national disaster. Britain had never experienced such a thing. Although the ASRS enrolled by 1907 only about one-sixth of all railway employees, this proportion now was growing rapidly and constituted, as Bell always made clear in speeches, the skilled workers in the shops, the switchmen, and the guards. The unorganized were the unskilled laborers in rural areas. Some action now was required.

Lloyd George recalled later to Lucy Masterman that the senior advisors at the Board of Trade were unanimously against interference in the strike and hence his intervention in it was an act of great courage or foolhardiness. On the other hand his file contains a letter from Sidney Buxton, the Postmaster General, whose department had only recently recognized the post office clerks' union, telling him that he must take action. Otherwise 'the fat is in the fire.' There might, thought Buxton, be some way of gaining recognition for the ASRS while saving the face of the railway companies.[107] As an added motive to become involved it should be noted that John Clifford was thundering support for the railwaymen from his pulpit in Westbourne Park Chapel. In addition, Lloyd George's parliamentary secretary, Hudson Kearley, also records that he told the President he must step in.[108] In any case, at the end of September, with his mind preoccupied by the Welsh revolt, Lloyd George determined also to try and settle the railway dispute. On 30 September he wrote to Campbell-Bannerman at Belmont warning him not to make a general appeal to the workers, in fact to make no statement of any kind.[109] After his return from Wales, in the letter reporting on the Cardiff speech, he outlined his plans to the Prime Minister who remained in Scotland. Of the two sides, probably the more vulnerable was the companies. Their weakness lay in their unpopularity in the press, in the House of Commons, and among the population at large. It would be easy and politically rewarding, he knew, to coerce the companies by legal action. The directors so far had been 'insolent,' Lloyd George told Campbell-Bannerman and he feared they might refuse to negotiate. He wanted 'to clear his lines of action' with the Prime Minister. He intended to invite the railway directors to see him the next week. The government ought to make up its mind that there would be no strike. It would be disastrous for trade, which currently was doing well compared with America and Germany, and would cause unemployment.

Therefore, he told Campbell-Bannerman, the final threat would be parliamentary action. If the directors refused to negotiate, the government must be prepared as a final step to make arbitration compulsory in all disputes which the Board of Trade thought important. Lloyd George emphasized that this injunction was aimed at the companies rather than at the unions. Negotiations after all were what Bell had been asking for and he wanted to be able to assure the General Secretary that 'the Government will take a strong line.'[110]

He asked for an answer immediately, which evidently he received, for on the twenty-first he wrote confidently to his brother William: 'The railway strike is demanding all my attention. Things are going well so far. Whatever happens I am coming out on top of this business. I can see my way clear right to the station. Conciliation first but failing that the steamroller. The Companies must give way on that point I am definite.'[111]

Throughout the negotiations, the threat of compulsory arbitration was Lloyd George's final weapon, the 'steamroller.' The companies always argued that any worker grievances were already adequately heard and that they did not need a third party, a union or a Board of Trade arbitrator, coming between them and their men. On the other hand they were equally aware of the low esteem in which they were generally held.

The critical meeting, foreshadowed in Lloyd George's letter of 17 October, occurred on the twenty-fifth between Lloyd George and a large number of railway directors. The several accounts of this conference agree that Lloyd George was charming and conciliatory.[112] He did not use the streamroller nor did he disclose the other piece of important information that he almost certainly possessed by this time: that Bell was not going to press the companies for formal recognition of the union. This concession, according to George Askwith, at that time Assistant Secretary at the Board of Trade for Railways, had been conveyed to Lloyd George by himself, although Askwith is unclear about when he did it. In fact the date is of no importance. Lloyd George would not have revealed it on 25 October under any circumstances.[113] Rather at this meeting Lloyd George dilated upon the evil effects to the nation that would accrue from a general railway strike, which the directors, with a little flexibility, had in their power to avoid.[114]

His interview with the directors was 'most satisfactory,' Lloyd George reported to the Prime Minister that day. The directors, who in fact had held a preliminary meeting at Euston Station where they agreed not to concede anything, were 'a little hostile at first but came around.'[115] He now had a plan for settling the dispute and had asked the directors for the names of six of them for further negotiation.[116] He was less modest in his letter to William. 'An excellent beginning. They all almost fell on my neck including Lord Claud Hamilton Chairman of the Great Eastern....I have won their confidence and that is almost everything. You never saw anything like the change in their demeanour. I have asked them to consider my proposals to appoint six of their number to meet me about them....I am sanguine of good results.'[117]

So far he had addressed the directors only by appealing to their sense of public duty, reminding them of the disastrous effects of a strike. However he knew, and certainly the directors knew, that a strike by the railway servants would not be supported by the locomotive engineers and firemen, ASLEF, whose secretary, Albert Fox, absolutely opposed the 'all grades' movement of the ASRS.[118] A strike was possible, but a successful one was unlikely. To this extent Lloyd George's position was weakened.

There existed a deadline for extracting some concessions from the companies. On 3 November, the ASRS intended to hold a rally at the Albert Hall where Richard Bell would read the results of the ballot, which, all reports indicated, would be heavily in favor of a strike. After this it would be difficult to avoid setting a date for industrial action even though Bell himself certainly knew the risks involved and was eager for compromise.

Lloyd George increased the pressure on the directors by inspiring an article in the *Daily Mail* on 29 October calling for compulsory arbitration in railway disputes. 'That fixed them,' he wrote to his brother. Two days later he met the directors again for the entire day. 'In the morning I had to threaten them. Told them that there must not be a strike on any account.' Evidently the breakthrough came on 31 October, for the next day Lloyd George met both Bell and the directors, separately, and was able to send William a copy of the provisional agreement.[119]

The dramatic climax of Bell's campaign for union recognition duly arrived on 3 November with a giant rally in the Albert Hall and the announcement of the results of the strike ballot. As expected the figures were heavily in favor of a work stoppage. Of about 100,000 ballots sent out, 76,825 were for a strike.[120] Lloyd George had visited the Prime Minister that afternoon, presumably to reassure him about the outcome of the ASRS meeting. The next day he was at Downing Street again to give him the terms of the settlement.[121] Finally, on 5 November, while Lloyd George was telling the Cabinet that a settlement would almost surely be announced the next day, Richard Bell was convincing his union executive committee to postpone a decision on the date for a strike by saying he would meet Lloyd George at the Board of Trade at 3:30 p.m. the following day. He did not tell them, evidently, that he had already agreed provisionally to a settlement.[122]

The signing took place on 6 November. Lloyd George met the six directors at 11:30 in the morning and Bell and his executive committee at 3:30 in the afternoon. At this meeting he hit upon, it would seem for the first time, a tactic that would become characteristic with him for many years both when he was a mediator and when he was a party to negotiations, the declaration of a sudden need for haste. Everything must be finished soon or unimaginable castastrophes would occur. The directors wanted to consult their shareholders, Lloyd George recalled to Lewis on 9 November. Would not Bell then have to refer the scheme to his shareholders, the union, asked Lloyd George? This delay would make agreement impossible. The document must be signed at once.[123] The six company representatives quickly signed the agreement before them.

This was not, it should be emphasized, an agreement with the union but rather with the Board of Trade attested to by Lloyd George, Hudson Kearley, Hubert Llewellyn Smith, the Permanent Secretary at the Board of Trade, and George Askwith.[124] In the afternoon the unions received the same treatment. Lloyd George told them that he had obtained the directors' assent only 'with much difficulty.'[125] There was no opportunity for discussion, testified J.H. Thomas, four years later, before the royal commission on the working of Lloyd George's plan. The agreement had to be concluded immediately.[126] And so it was. Within twenty minutes, it was reported, the six union men signed and, like the directors, only with Lloyd George, Kearley, and the Board of Trade officials. The two sides never met.

The two identical documents, subscribed by the railway directors and the union officials with the Board of Trade, pledged only that the 'undersigned' were ready 'to adopt a system of Conciliation and Arbitration' in the settlement of problems of wages, hours and working conditions. There was no mention of the railway union.[127] The system which the two sides agreed to adopt, worked out by H. Llewellyn Smith, appeared as an annex to the signed agreement.[128] It provided for a network of 'conciliation boards' made up of railway employees and management with an appeal, first to 'sectional boards,' then to a 'central board' and beyond that to an arbitrator. In deference to the companies' sensibilities about remaining in touch with their men free of outside interference, the scheme stipulated that representatives on the boards would be company employees, although as Lloyd George pointed out to his brother, this did not exclude union men. Nevertheless the scheme rigorously avoided any suggestion that in the adjudication of grievances, the union constituted a bargaining agent. Indeed, as the scheme provided permanent representation for the men in a system of grievance machinery, an article in *The Times* immediately after this settlement, written by 'a Chief Railway Official' (evidently Lord Claud Hamilton) argued that there was no need any longer for the union to exist.[129]

Lloyd George's settlement was greeted publicly with loud congratulations in the press and in the political world. Part of this joy represented a universal feeling of relief that the nation had been spared the unknown horror of a general railway strike, but partly also, particularly among politicians and the politically knowledgeable segments of the upper classes, there was an apparent sense of wonder, almost of unbelief, that the Welsh savage, the rebel, the thief of property, the lawbreaker, the pro-Boer, had been able, with patience, amiability, and the strictest impartiality, somehow to save the nation. Congratulations poured in on Lloyd George from all sides. 'The papers,' he wrote to his brother, 'without distinction of party wild with enthusiastic and amazed satisfaction. I had great difficulty in getting the Directors to sign but they behaved well. The King has written expressing his delight.'[130] Knollys had written also to Campbell-Bannerman reporting that the monarch had heard personally from a railway director who said that his colleagues were most satisfied with the President of the Board of Trade, finding him absolutely impartial without any bias toward the men.[131]

On 12 November Lloyd George attended a grand reception at Windsor to meet the German Emperor, William II. Here he was the lion of the evening to the exclusion of Campbell-Bannerman who also attended. The Emperor congratulated Lloyd George upon his handling of the railway strike and showed considerable knowledge of the Merchant Shipping Act passed the year before. 'He was with me three times as long as he was with the P.M. He said he had heard of me from Herr Balchin, the great German Shipowner, the greatest in the world [surely this is Albert Ballin, chairman of the Hamburg-America line and a most important supporter of the rapidly growing Imperial Navy]. Balchin, he told me, had a tremendous opinion of me. He said that whenever I came to Germany, I would receive a great reception.' However by the end of the evening Lloyd George had concluded that both King Edward and the Kaiser were anti-labor. He ended his letter with the remark, 'I came away hating all Kings.'[132]

Notwithstanding his grudge against monarchs, Lloyd George clearly enjoyed the glory of his accomplishment, but what he had produced was not the 'landmark' settlement it has been termed.[133] He had accomplished only one thing: he had averted a national railway strike. He had not created workable grievance machinery. His greatest accomplishment in the negotiations was to be found not, as he thought, in inducing the directors to appoint a negotiating committee, but in convincing the honest Richard Bell that the ramshackle hierarchy of grievance committees was the equivalent of union recognition and a victory sufficient to warrant calling off the strike. The fact is that the conciliation machinery never worked. The companies found endless ways to hinder its operation. Within three years Bell was replaced as General Secretary by the more pugnacious J.E. Williams and as MP for Derby by J.H. Thomas. When Bell signed Lloyd George's scheme Lord Claud Hamilton told a royal commission with evident satisfaction, 'his doom was sealed.'[134]

Only three weeks after his sensational rescue of the country from the dislocation and discomfort of a railway stoppage, while he was still enjoying the unaccustomed experience of good will pouring in upon him from all sides, Lloyd George was struck by the most devastating personal tragedy of his life, the sudden death of his second child and eldest daughter, Mair Eluned. Mair had been born on 2 August 1890 and had grown to adolescence as her father's favorite. All accounts of her describe a sweet, gentle, pretty, rather quiet child who in country walks in Wales and in the garden at Routh Road was always at his side and whose great pleasure was to accompany him on the piano in evenings of song. She was a student at Clapham High School and was acquainted there with a slightly older girl, Frances Louise Stevenson, who would later enter the Lloyd George family as a tutor for the youngest daughter, Megan.

On 25 November, Lloyd George received a note from his secretary at the Board of Trade, John Rowland, saying that Mrs. Lloyd George had informed him that she would not be coming to town that day because Mair had returned from school feeling unwell.[135] The complaint turned out to be an inflamed appendix which ruptured before it could be removed. Mair died on the afternoon of 29 November after an unsuccessful emergency operation performed in the parlor of the Routh Road house.[136]

Lloyd George was crushed, yet also, in a way, enraged. Why should this calamity have befallen him? What blind malevolent demon had contrived to destroy his happiness at a moment when he was at the pinnacle of personal achievement? He seems to have brooded upon the nexus between his triumph in the railway dispute and the loss of his daughter. He described his reflections in a letter to William over six years later when his brother had lost an infant son.[137] There was a childish selfishness in his grief that precluded much sympathy for other members of his family who also suffered. His wife, he told Frances Stevenson many years later, showed no emotion at the tragedy and seemed 'to recover from the blow very easily.'[138] He could make no decisions and take no responsibility. William, whom he summoned to London on the morning of the 29th but who arrived some hours after Mair's death, took him to the Board of Trade the next day, there to attend to him while others prepared to ship his daughter's body to Wales.[139] William then returned to Wales to make the funeral arrangements while Lloyd George and Herbert Lewis traveled down on 2 December in the Royal Saloon that the Great Western had put at their disposal.[140] Among other things the weight of his pain was such that he would not return to Routh Road. Indeed, as Frances Stevenson records, he avoided visiting the area for many years.[141] Accordingly, Maggie, with William's help, set to work to dispose of the old residence. The two soon found another place, No. 5 Cheyne Place in Chelsea where however he would live only a few months.[142]

The funeral in Criccieth took place at 11:00 in the morning of 3 December. Herbert Lewis records that besides the family and two or three friends from the town, only himself, Alfred Thomas, William Jones and Llewelyn Williams attended. In the afternoon, Lloyd George, Lewis, and William Clark from the Board of Trade took a six mile walk. 'Spent the evening at Garthcelyn [William George's handsome house in Criccieth] in conversation. [They sought to divert the current of LG's thought.] Laughter and tears were very near one another, and in the midst of it he had to leave us for a while. He returned and kept us all amused and interested with a brilliant flow of literary historical and reminiscent talk.'[143]

The next day Lloyd George was in Manchester settling a wage dispute brought on by a demand from the cotton fine spinners for an increase in wages. While he was there he wrote Maggie the most consoling letter of which, perhaps, he was capable. Nonetheless the emphasis was on himself. Although he complimented her upon her bravery, while condemning his own 'turbulent and emotional nature,' he continued: 'We must help each other not to brood....we did our best. It was the decree of fate which millions beside ourselves are now enduring. What right have we to grumble?' Perhaps Mair's death 'will prove to be the greatest blessing that has befallen us & through us the multitude who God has sent me to give a helping hand out of misery and worry a myriad worse than ours.'[144]

On the day after Mair's funeral, Rendel had written inviting the Lloyd Georges to come and stay at Cannes. Lloyd George had been there many times before. There was an upstairs sitting room Rendel reminded Lloyd George, and 'you know how quietly we live.' He could stay until 10 January.[145] Lloyd George did not accept this kindness, perhaps because Maggie did not want to go, but a few days later he agreed quickly to occupy a villa in Nice offered him by Florence, Lady Nunburnholme whose own husband had died only a month before and whose family, presumably, would not be in residence while Lloyd George was there.[146] He could bring friends and it was near a golf course. Lloyd George took up this invitation and wrote to Herbert Lewis demanding that he come. He would be leaving Friday (20 December). 'Follow as soon as you can. I need you badly. I am depressed—tortured with grief. I hope your cold is off. Take care!'[147]

Lloyd George drove to Nice from Boulogne with Hudson Kearley, Richard and William and Kearley's two sons. While he was gone his letters to the family were in the tone of self reproach that he generally adopted when writing to Wales from abroad: having left he was miserable that he had done so. For example, from Lyon: 'Looking forward to getting letters from home when I reach Nice. They will be like balm to my burning wound. It's a shame I should be expecting consolation from you whom I ought to be it to your poor sore heart: that I do miss you—never have I missed you more.'[148]

A substantial group assembled in Nice over the holidays and Lloyd

George embarked on a round of visits and dinners which began on Christmas Eve, hours after his party arrived. Faithful Herbert Lewis came in on 27 December. Lord and Lady Rendel were at Cannes. In addition to several others there were Charles Henry, a wealthy Jewish merchant and copper importer of whom Lloyd George would see a good deal in the next few years, and his wife, Julia Lewisohn of New York.

While Lloyd George was in Nice the question of the increase in his salary, which he himself had clearly initiated over a month before, came to a head. In the aftermath of the railway dispute he apparently inspired letters to newspapers proposing that the lowly status of the Board of Trade, and the salary of its President, be raised in gratitude for his work as the savior of the nation. Three letters to this effect in almost identical wording appeared in *The Times* within two weeks.[149] By the time these letters were published Mair had died, adding sympathy to the weight of Lloyd George's case. Before he left for the continent Lloyd George spoke to Asquith, and perhaps to Rendel. In any case both men sent notes to the Prime Minister suggesting that something be done.[150] Asquith added however in his letter that John Burns had heard of the proposal and had demanded equal treatment. Also, Walter Runciman, who had replaced McKenna as Financial Secretary to the Treasury at the beginning of the year, learned of Lloyd George's maneuverings. On 18 December he wrote a hot letter to Lloyd George saying that he had heard of the intrigue and was 'offended.'[151] This almost inevitable departmental jealousy effectively killed any possibility of raising the official status of the Board of Trade, but the Prime Minister still desired to help Lloyd George personally. There was a proposal to buy the freehold of the Cheyne Place house. Some 'good friends,' Maggie wrote on 24 December, wanted to contribute the necessary £3,000. 'People gave Tom Ellis his lease & he had not done 1/3 what you have done for Wales....'[152] Campbell-Bannerman also asked his secretary Arthur Ponsonby to write to Herbert Lewis asking him to intimate to Lloyd George that 'a few friends' had suggested making 'some provision for Lloyd George's family.' Lewis carried out this delicate commission in Nice and recorded in his diary that his colleague was in doubt. He did not want to prejudice his independence, but was indeed worried about his family. His legal practice had been knocked to pieces by the Boer War and had not revived.[153]

In the end Lloyd George rejected the offer. He perceived easily the difference between a public reward for good service coming to him through the Board of Trade and a private stipend from party funds passed to him under the table, even though no doubt the purse would be made up of contributions from such honorable men as Alfred Thomas, Rendel, and perhaps the Prime Minister himself. No one coveted money, or rather the convenience and ease that money brought, more than he. He accepted favors, gifts, and tips gratefully. He allowed Dalziel and Charles Henry to pay for holidays, and George Riddell to buy him a car and build him a house, and was flattered by it all. But more than anything, he valued his career, in which his chief asset was political independence. He would give his cleverness and oratory to a man, a cause, or to the Liberal party, but he would not sell them. Hence he wrote to Maggie on 10 January:

I am not going to accept the charity of the Party, come what may. I have made up my mind not to. Tom Ellis did it and was their doormat. I mean to fight my way myself. This is an offer made to me because they find the jealousies and rivalries are so great that they cannot raise the status of my office & C.B. wants to do something for me. It is very kind of him but I won't have it. I'll take my chance & I know I can rely on your help.[154]

On the whole, Lloyd George enjoyed himself at Nice where he stayed until the middle of January. There were conversations with Lewis about politics and business to worry about at the Board of Trade. After the settlement of the cotton fine spinners dispute, the cotton ring spinners in Oldham began wage agitation. Llewellyn Smith undertook to handle this himself, much to Lloyd George's anger. The problem was settled without government intervention but as the tart correspondence with his perm-anent secretary suggests, Lloyd George's thoughts were moving back into their accustomed channels. Nevertheless it is unfair to say that the wound of Mair's departure healed entirely. He spoke of her often in later years to Frances Stevenson and came to feel that he was the only one who remembered her. Occasionally some location or event would remind him of her, resulting in a tearful letter to his stoic wife.

V

Lloyd George's departmental work at the Board of Trade during his two and a quarter years in that office constitutes a segment of his career that usually receives little attention from historians and biographers. To be sure it is always agreed that he displayed at this time an unexpected virtuosity at conciliation, and an aptitude for the unspectacular work of bill briefing and minute preparation which, with his good humor and courtesy, won general applause. His bills, Merchant Shipping, Patents, and the Port of London, were useful and timely and were passed with a minimum of friction. Altogether it is held that he showed rare talents and substantially forwarded his career. But nevertheless, intrinsically the Board of Trade appears as an aberrant period, with little connection to what came before or afterward. It is a topic that almost elicits the biographer's apology.

In fact Lloyd George's first administrative tenure provided him with a crammer's course in executive methods which he would use again in 1915 and 1916, in the national, not the party interest, in founding the Ministry of Munitions. Besides the talent he discovered in himself for management of men and for private negotiation, he learned also that he could master mechanical and technical subjects, and more important that he could meet on equal terms men with business and engineering backgrounds who understood these things. 'Before I went to the Board of Trade,' he told Charles Masterman several years later, 'I do not mind telling you I was in a blue funk. I thought "Here am I, with no business training and I shall have to deal with all these great businessmen." But I found them children.'[155] There was an element of hyperbole in this as with many things Lloyd George said of his early life. But of lasting importance was the fact that he discovered a class of wealthy men among whom were many—although not the railway directors—whose energy and imagination, contempt for amateurism, and willingness to take risks were like his own. As his distrust of the higher civil service increased in the years ahead, the sense that businessmen had the qualities that the official establishment lacked grew also. His wholesale introduction of businessmen into government service during the war was the revolutionary consequence.

Far more apparent in those years, indeed soon the talk of the civil service, were Lloyd George's unconventional methods of work. His lack of order amazed those around him. It is a myth that he never wrote cabinet papers, as it is untrue that he wrote no letters. But it is quite clear that the systematic study of an issue through research and blue books, he found tedious. Yet when the time came for him to meet a delegation, as with the railway directors, or to speak in parliament, his mastery of detail, and more important his understanding of what was significant in the problem, always impressed his listeners. Without any systematic knowledge except of land law, he had no preconceived opinions about issues external to his own experience, but he had an almost intuitive sense of the essence of a matter. He could divine almost immediately what a deputation, or a political enemy, was trying to accomplish and what data he needed to make an argument. Then he could easily send someone to find the relevant facts. From the beginning of his time in parliament he had employed his brother to record for him particularly flagrant examples of landlord or Church abuse. When attacking Chamberlain he sent Harold Spender to Somerset House to dig up connections between Joe and Kynochs, or, after Marconi, to get the names of Tory ministers who were also company directors. Even on those occasions when his instincts were wrong, his facts usually were right.

In general Lloyd George learned the things he felt he needed to know from people, not from books. He learned of course upon the civil servants around him, but he learned also from deputations. As his importance grew, particularly after he became Chancellor of the Exchequer, he collected around himself a body of younger men, some lower rank civil servants such as J.S. Bradbury and W.J. Braithwaite. But the more important advisors were new Members of Parliament among whom for a long time the most influential were Charles Masterman and Christopher Addison. These men were his eyes and ears. They researched the mechanics of his proposals, they assisted him before delegations, they answered questions in the House of Commons, and, endlessly, they discussed with him the problems and the ramifications of his projects.

All of this makes it difficult, when discussing Lloyd George's prewar legislation, to assign an author to a given provision, or even to account in every detail for the shape of a bill as it emerged from parliament.[156] Sometimes the measure itself had changed beyond recognition. What had sprung from Lloyd George's mind like a rabbit from a hat could emerge from the parliamentary mill several years later as a camel.

Lloyd George's peculiar form of legislation, inspiration molded by convenience and consensus, did not appear in its mature form until after he became Chancellor of the Exchequer, but the technique was clear in his first initiative at the Board of Trade, the Merchant Shipping Bill. And his undoubted success with the measure, dealing with matters of which he knew nothing, commended the method for the future.

In a sense Lloyd George inherited the Merchant Shipping Bill. The problems it addressed were of long standing and had been the subject of official investigations in 1903 and 1905. He was at work on the measure within days after his return from Wales after his reelection.[157] Among Lloyd George's first acts was an invitation to representatives of British shipowners to meet at the Board of Trade and to discuss with him the terms of his bill. To their astonishment he brought the group back a second time, still before the bill was introduced, to comment upon the provisions of a draft which he distributed.

The problem of the British merchant shipping industry was that while Britain, since the 1870s, had been progressively improving by law the levels of safety and comfort aboard ships of the merchant navy, the conditions of work of seamen on cargo vessels had not kept pace with improving conditions among the British working class generally. As a result the proportion of native born on British ships was falling rapidly, their places being taken by foreigners and by East Indians, always referred to by the English colloquialism of 'lascars.' The employment of foreigners was regarded as undesirable in itself and the limited ability of many non-English sailors to understand commands given in English was clearly detrimental to safety.

But on the other hand the bill's goals: a substantial tightening of requirements for accommodation, food, and amenities for the crew, more stringent stipulations for storage of cargo and for life saving equipment, and for lowering the load line, would lessen British competitiveness in carrying the world's freight. British ships found unseaworthy, even under existing regulations, it was well known, were regularly sold to foreign buyers who undercut British freight rates. The solution was to apply new regulations to ships of foreign registry touching at ports under British jurisdiction.

Lloyd George introduced the Merchant Shipping Bill on 20 March in a speech, as would be usual for him, which told less of the contents of the measure the House was invited to approve, than of the illnesses of the shipping industry that it was supposed to remedy.[158] He reported routinely the next day to his wife that he had received a 'chorus of approbation from all sides of the House' and that both 'Shipowners and Sailors blessed the Bill.'[159] Nonetheless he had created a small sensation, of which he may not have been aware, by saying that he hoped the bill would have no opposition and that it would be handled by the Committee on Trade where he 'would be sorry' if the whips were used.[160]

The willingness to throw the bill to the parliamentary wolves and to take his chances with the result was an unusual step. 'Mr. Lloyd George's dismissal of responsibility is a little odd and scarcely complimentary to the nurseling,' commented *The Times* the next day in a friendly but patronizing lead article.[161] In fact it was an unavoidable risk. He had had no time in the weeks before its introduction to assess, even had he known them, the multitude of vested interests involved. Thus the architect would have to work as the structure was being built.

Between 27 March when the Merchant Shipping Bill received its second reading, again unopposed, and 22 November when it received its third reading, Lloyd George met deputations. He never refused to meet one, he proudly told a deputation of shipowners on 3 August, reminding them that he had taken the unusual step of seeing some of their number even before the bill was framed. Never, he said, had there been a bill upon which there was so much consultation.[162] (The complaint of this deputation was that the provisions to restrict employment of foreign sailors would raise wage costs. The eventual compromise allowed the employment of foreigners with an examination in the English language.)

'Nothing could have been more skilful than his handling of the diverse elements of a committee,' commented J.A. Spender who had the opportunity to observe Lloyd George in action in the settlement of the railway strike.

> He always mastered his subject before hand, but though he knew exactly what he was driving at he kept his intentions veiled until his opponents had been driven three-fourths of the way he wanted them to go; then he cut off their retreat.... He had an almost uncanny way of persuading men in opposite camps that they really meant the same thing—which were the things he wanted them to mean—and before a few weeks were over the supposedly irreconcilable differences of opposing groups were dissolving into incredible unity.[163]

There were, nevertheless, surprises. The most significant of these proceeded from the evolution of technology. Since the original plimsoll load lines were introduced in 1875, the world's merchant fleets had become largely steam powered. Thus a steamship could heavily overload herself in a foreign port, but by using perhaps two hundred tons of bunker coal during her inward voyage she would be in compliance with safety requirements when she entered British waters. The stipulations of British law could not be applied to foreign ships loading in foreign ports; Lloyd George had not realized this and the eventual solution was to raise slightly the load line for British ships, which caused some loud criticisms in labor circles. Indeed the proceedings in committee show that Lloyd George's most frequent opponent was J. Havelock Wilson of the National Seamen's Union.[164] Unquestionably, the Merchant Shipping Bill appealed far more to shipowners than to labor and Wilson denounced Lloyd George in precisely these terms on the third reading.[165]

On the other hand the political effect of the measure was to provide evidence for a story, which all Unionists affected to believe, that Lloyd George was a crypto-tariff reformer. The regulation of foreign shipping differed very little, it was argued, from the regulation of foreign trade.[166]

By the time the Merchant Shipping Bill left the House of Commons, where on the third reading it earned Lloyd George a handsome accolade from the previous Unionist Parliamentary Secretary of the Board of Trade, Andrew Bonar Law, the measure had grown from 43 clauses to 85.[167] The bill was preeminently the product of a consensus of interests for which Lloyd George had been the referee; it belonged to no single person. Nonetheless, quite properly, Lloyd George received the credit. The shipowners were delighted. He was toasted at dinners of the shipping associations in Liverpool and Newcastle. Even *The Times*, which as late as October had compared him to an educated Black African who, when caught in the frenzy of a tribal dance, was likely to take off his clothes, admitted three months later that it now perceived 'more sober and statesmanlike qualities.'[168]

Undoubtedly his success in the first year at the Board of Trade, and perhaps the realization that of the twelve pieces of legislation promised in the King's Speech, the only ones to become acts, except for the Trade Disputes Bill, would be his, prompted Lloyd George to formulate an ambitious legislative program for 1907. In early November 1906, even before the Merchant Shipping Bill had cleared the House of Commons, he put before the Cabinet a memorandum on the sorry state of the London dock companies who were too poor to carry out necessary improvements of their facilities, with the result that London's share of the United Kingdom's shipping had been declining for 15 years. The need for a public port authority, with access to capital, to own and expand the docks was urgent. A strong Royal Commission had recommended it as long ago as 1902 and virtually nothing had been spent on the docks or river since. The House of Commons had recognized this in a resolution the previous March which, Lloyd George noted, he had himself supported.[169] Even though his memoranda asserted that the assumption of the London docks by a public authority would not be a considerable project, the Cabinet thought otherwise and put it off until the fall of 1907.

By that time Lloyd George was immersed in the Welsh revolt and the railways crisis. Then he was distracted by the death of Mair and his month in Cannes. Negotiations with the dock companies, although begun in August 1907, were made more difficult by the reluctance of the companies to explain their records which were, in any case, so badly kept as to be nearly useless. Eventually, at Kearley's suggestion, a formal audit of the dock companies' books was undertaken by Sir William Plender, an eminent accountant, whom Lloyd George would employ on other occasions.[170] Lloyd George's papers suggest that he was not actively involved and that he used Kearley and Sir Edwin Cornwall, a Fulham coal dealer, as negotiators with the dock companies.[171] The Cabinet committee on the Port of London Bill was not appointed until 6 November, the day the railway crisis ended.[172]

Lloyd George finally introduced the Port of London Bill on 2 April 1908, the day after Sir Henry Campbell-Bannerman told the King that he intended to resign.[173] Eleven days later his connection with it was severed when he went to the Exchequer.[174]

Within a month after he had first submitted the proposal for a Port of London Authority Lloyd George came forward with a full list of smaller measures.[175] The list included eight measures of which four were subsequently introduced and became law. All were concerned with business and commerce, none of general application, but all were immensely complicated and technical. In some cases they were the result of recommendations made years earlier by departmental or parliamentary committees. For Lloyd George they would require time, energy and study. Of the four which became law one dealt with employers' liability carriers, which had proliferated since the Workmen's Compensation Act, requiring them to make the same £20,000 deposit and publish the reports stipulated for life companies. A second companies bill required firms to provide the government and the public with information on its directors and its balance sheet unless this were already available by prospectus. The other two concerned patents. One was simply a consolidation of existing patent law, but the second, which was Lloyd George's major accomplishment of the 1907 session, included a very large number of changes in patent procedure, making applications easier and cheaper, the terms clearer, and most important, in Clause 15, providing that after four years any patent held but not worked in the United Kingdom could, upon application, be revoked.[176] This previous loophole in British patent law had benefitted particularly German chemical firms and was an important reason for the backwardness of the United Kingdom dye industry.

The Patents and Designs Bill revived the rumors which the Unionists, with wicked glee, had begun to circulate the previous year: that Lloyd George was at heart a tariff reformer. After all, said Bonar Law on 17 April, the President of the Board of Trade had admitted that the United States had no such provision in its law. But then, he continued, there was no need for it. If the United States government wanted to ensure that a particular device was manufactured within the nation, tariffs would see that it was done.[177] The President of the Board of Trade only wished to protect British industry from unfair competition 'which is the only kind of protection with which the opponents of the Government have any sympathy. Now in this Bill, which the Right Hon. Gentleman was piloting through the House he had gone a long step further, for he had undoubtedly, in principle, sapped the foundations on which the whole of our fiscal system was based. (ministerial cries "No")'[178]

Bonar Law was no more than half serious, but the notion that somehow Lloyd George could be captured for protection continued to circulate among Unionists for a number of years. In fact he had no economic doctrines, or, more accurately, he had only the emotional baggage he had brought from Wales, a hatred of privilege, a love of the land, and his peculiar social and political, agnostic nonconformity. But it is no more possible to classify him as a tariff reformer, or for that matter a free trader, than it is to discover in him principles on imperialism or socialism. Because he belonged to a party that chose to uphold free trade, he would denounce protection enthusiastically, but he would have thought it ridiculous that some tenet of Cobdenite orthodoxy forbade the government to protect the British merchant marine or the British chemical industry. A workable plan was worth more than a shipload of doctrine.

How seriously Lloyd George took the protectionist jeers can only be speculated upon, although he made few speeches outside of Wales in 1907 in which he failed to provide some testimonial to his loyalty to free trade. As he well understood, Bonar Law was only engaging in the popular game of political repartee and on the whole had supported warmly the Shipping and Patent Bills. In the course of the next few years the two men would become close political, if not personal friends, a connection of vast importance for Lloyd George's later career.

Lloyd George's work, especially in the dismal parliamentary year of 1907, was a spot of cheer for the Liberals. In addition to the Patent Bill, passed with general approbation, he put through a more controversial measure which had grown out of some changes made by the Merchant Shipping Bill. This measure, the Merchant Shipping (Tonnage Reduction for Propelling Power) Bill, limited to 55% the deduction from nominal gross tonnage allowed in steam ships for engine space for the purposes of docking and pilotage charges. The bill, which was put together by select committee, under H.J. Tennant, without Lloyd George's participation, was necessarily a compromise. But it stirred a good deal of hostility among docking interests and pilot associations in the Southwest, who employed the notorious Taff Vale Railway director, Owen Beasley, as their parliamentary agent. His influence was reflected in some wrecking amendments in the House of Lords.[179]

Similarly the Companies Bill, requiring greater publicity about particulars of smaller firms, was not universally popular. Lloyd George, who through July had been crowing regularly to Maggie about the unprecedented success of his legislative package, encountered in August a flurry of angry, but disorganized opposition. There was, he thought, a feeling that at least one of his bills should be destroyed. On the other hand the solid support of the British shipping industry he had earned with the previous Merchant Shipping Act and friendship of the larger British commercial and industrial interests, derived from both the Patent and the Companies Bills, carried him through. Such magnates as Lord Nunburnholme of the Wilson Line, the owner of the largest private fleet in the world, in whose villa he had stayed in Cannes, or Sir Christopher Furness of Furness-Withy, or Robert Houston of the Houston Line were unlikely to allow measures they themselves had helped to shape either in delegation or parliamentary committee to be defeated by a clique of Bristol and Cardiff dock owners whose most visible spokesman in the House of Commons was D.A. Thomas. Lloyd George's consensus politics neatly eviscerated the potential opposition. Each bill had a strong lobby on its behalf, in both parties and in both houses.[180]

VI

Unquestionably Lloyd George made a spectacular success in his first ministerial office. Not only had he forced a nearly moribund department to produce a fountain of long demanded legislation, but he had proved to be an invaluable handyman for the Cabinet at large, fixing or squaring, somehow patching up, embarrassing disfunctions in the national economic machinery. He had, in addition, moved less publicly to improve British commercial intelligence by a voluntary wage census begun early in 1906 which was soon supplemented by legislation for a compulsory national census of production in 1907. Meanwhile he had begun to expand the very limited number of British commercial attachés resident abroad and he worked to see that business intelligence from around the world was promptly collated and published. His models frequently cited in these endeavors were Germany and the United States.

Lloyd George's contribution, by the end of 1907, was the more visible when measured against the misfortunes of the rest of the Campbell-Bannerman administration. Education, temperance, Welsh disestablishment, land reform, old age pensions, and Irish settlement, all ancient problems, were still unfulfilled promises. The House of Lords still blocked the way.

In January 1908, in quick succession the Liberals lost two by-elections. One, Hertford, Ross, a Liberal Unionist stronghold won only in the landslide of 1906, was understandable, but the other, Devonshire, Ashburton, had been solidly Liberal since 1885. 1908 would be a busy year with an autumn session. If the government were to make a reputation it would have to be made then. Licensing, a final settlement of the tortured education question, and old age pensions, all had been promised at one time or another during the 1907 session. Then, as parliament met at the end of January 1908, the Prime Minister was stricken again with heart trouble. On 12 February he made his last speech in the House of Commons and attended his last Cabinet meeting. He returned to his room in Downing Street which he would not leave again alive. He delayed resigning chiefly because he had promised the King that the Monarch's holiday at Biarritz should not be interrupted. But on 1 April he wrote the King saying that he intended to ask to be relieved of his office and he telegraphed his formal resignation on 3 April. On the sixth King Edward summoned H.H. Asquith to Biarritz where he was named Prime Minister on 8 April. Campbell-Bannerman died two weeks later.

Because of the protracted nature of the Prime Minister's last illness the negotiations and intrigue surrounding the construction of a new Cabinet had begun much earlier. Asquith was the natural, and probably the inevitable, successor, although since the autumn of 1907, when C.B.'s deteriorating health had become public knowledge, the radical and nonconformist press had treated his translation to the prime ministership as much less than a foregone conclusion.[181] Nonetheless, after the first week of March Asquith was discussing future Cabinet appointments with the clear assumption that he would become Prime Minister.

No decision was as important as the one regarding the office he was himself vacating, the Exchequer. Second in rank in the Cabinet, the Chancellor ought to balance, rather than complement, the Prime Minister. Asquith had functioned in this way under Campbell-Bannerman. Nonetheless it appears that Asquith had 'half offered' the Chancellorship to R.B. Haldane early in March.[182]

A more serious claimant for the Exchequer, one who seemed afterwards unable to accept the fact that somehow he did not have it, was John Morley. The direct evidence is to be found in a curious interview which Morley recorded in his *Recollections*, unfortunately not dated, in which the Prime Minister designate inquired whether Morley had any views on his position in the new Cabinet. Morley replied that he supposed his seniority gave him a claim on the Exchequer but that he would rather stay at the India Office and take a peerage. If this modest request was supposed to put pressure upon Morley to seek something better, it failed. Asquith questioned why anyone would want a peerage, but said nothing about a new post.[183]

Yet after the new Cabinet was announced, Morley wrote to Lord Minto, Viceroy of India, saying that Asquith had pressed the Exchequer upon him and that he had declined on account of age.[184] On the other hand Morley intimated to Charles Hobhouse in July 1908 that he had been offered the Exchequer but in a form he would not accept. Then 13 years later in January 1921, he told John Morgan that he had not been offered the

Exchequer, but that he would have resigned if Haldane had received it; '...it would recreate the ascendancy of the old Liberal League,' he recalled saying. 'Whereupon Asquith said, "then I'll send for Lloyd George."'[185]

Morley's love of gossip was equalled only by his vanity. He obviously was anxious to avoid the appearance of having been passed over and for whatever reason Lloyd George was willing to accommodate him. Hence all of Lloyd George's official biographies state flatly that the Exchequer was offered to Morley first and this must be taken as the version Lloyd George chose to make public.[186] Nevertheless, very early in the period of Cabinet negotiation, only six days after the King had intimated to Asquith that he would be called upon should Campbell-Bannerman resign, Lloyd George told Herbert Lewis that Asquith, that day, had offered him the post providing only that the Prime Minister would himself introduce the 1908 budget.[187]

In his interview with King Edward on 4 March, Asquith had indicated that he might keep the Exchequer himself, for a time at least. Clearly he soon thought better of this plan—the results of Gladstone's experiment were not reassuring. More important, as his prime ministership represented a move to the 'right' in the Cabinet, it was necessary to have a Chancellor of the Exchequer on the 'left.' The Cabinet should not be all of one color.

However, there is a strong indication that the chief alternative to Lloyd George was neither of the men named so far but Reginald McKenna whose abilities Asquith had come to admire at the Treasury and who had the necessary radical qualifications. This could account for the story in Lord Esher's journal that he had been told, again by Morley on 9 April, that Lloyd George had finally confronted Asquith while he was still searching for an alternative to the India Secretary: 'Lloyd George "put a pistol to Asquith's head," and asked for the Ch. of the Ex. with the threat of resignation. He had previously, however, told Morley that he was about to do this, but only if J.M. waived his claim. This he instantly did.'[188] The consideration of McKenna probably accounts for Lloyd George's threat of resignation. McKenna's appointment, a man junior to Lloyd George both in the House of Commons and in front bench experience, would be unacceptable. Morley, of course, is far from the ideal historical source but the story of Lloyd George's threat is confirmed by others. 'Lloyd George,' concluded E.T. Raymond (i.e. E.R. Thompson, editor of the *Evening Standard*) 'contrived to make it clear that peace could only be purchased at a price.'[189] Better support for this thesis appears in a congratulatory letter from J.L. Garvin to McKenna in May 1915 when the latter finally achieved the Exchequer. 'I wasn't as surprised as some,' wrote the editor of the *Observer*, 'for I knew how near you came to the Chancellorship in 1908....'[190] Even earlier, Almeric Fitzroy, pondering Asquith's almost notorious flabbiness of will in the early months of the 1910 session, remarked in his diary about the Prime Minister's 'surrender to Lloyd George as Chancellor of the Exchequer when McKenna was his own choice.'[191]

Evidently Lloyd George had his interview with Asquith on Friday, 3 April. The next day Asquith heard from the King that Campbell-Bannerman had resigned and the following afternoon, Sunday, 5 April he left for the Continent. He kissed hands at about ten o'clock in the morning on 8 April and that afternoon at the Hotel Du Palais at Biarritz he wrote to Lloyd George inviting him formally to become Chancellor of the Exchequer.[192]

> The offer which I am privileged to make, is a well-deserved tribute to your long & eminent service to our party, and to the splendid capacity which you have shown at the Board of Trade.
> I know from experience, both the attractions and the difficulties of the Exchequer. It is one of the most thankless & the most full of opportunities, in the whole government.

The Prime Minister concluded by saying that he would introduce the 1908 Budget.[193] Lloyd George received this important message on 10 April, and, after trying unsuccessfully to telephone his brother, he wrote him the next day: 'I am the Chancellor of the Exchequer and consequently second in Command in the Liberal host....I am to see the P.M. this afternoon to discuss further arrangements although there really is nothing further to discuss we settled everything last Friday week [3 April].' The list would be announced on Monday (13 April). Asquith, he continued, would introduce the budget for which he was most grateful. He concluded: 'there is great sadness for me in the promotion. It is so hard that my little girl should have been taken away before these events which would have given her such joy.'[194]

This letter concealed a serious problem that had appeared the previous evening. Asquith had arrived back in London a little before six in the evening of 10 April. There he discovered to his fury that after two days of well-informed speculation the *Daily Chronicle* had published on 8 April, the day he kissed the King's hand, a full and accurate list of the new Cabinet. He took no action that evening but his wife Margot, whose delight in intrigue was fuelled rather than dampened by her husband's political success, wrote immediately to Churchill naming Lloyd George as the source and charging the new President of the Board of Trade with the task of uncovering the plot.

> 20 Cavendish Square
> Private
> Dearest Winston,
> I am told Lloyd George dines with you tonight. I wish you wd speak to him & tell him quite plainly that the staff of the *Daily Chronicle* have given him away to 3 independent people (better praps keep McKenna's name out) Mr. Nash & Runciman. Quite simply told them both that Lloyd George had given them the list. The only man the King resented at all (dont say this to a living soul not even to Henry please) was Lloyd George wh seemed so odd! Ld Knollys knows it was LG who split & says the King will be furious. Lloyd George's best chance if he is a good fellow, wh I take yr word for, is not to lie about it when H speaks heavily to him but to give up his whole Press Campaign; he will be done as a dog if he goes on. I think you might ease him & the Cabinet if you do this courageously. The Editor as well as others told Nash do yr d-dest. Ive just driven H from the station & he said to me 'he hoped to God Winston would give it him'. He is perfectly furious.
> Yrs.
> Margot Burn this[195]

Churchill carried out this delicate commission, evidently without naming Lloyd George's accusers, and wrote to Asquith at midnight.

My dear Asquith,
I broached the matter to Lloyd George. He denies it utterly. I told him that you had said you learned that several colleagues thought he was responsible; But that you had no knowledge yourself. He intends to speak to you tomorrow on the subject, & I have told him he can quote me as having put the question. It will be a good opportunity for a talk.
I hope you will let me know if it turns out that you want to replace Kearley at the Board of Trade. I have preserved the silence of an oyster upon minor appointments.[196]

The next day Lloyd George wrote Asquith from Cheyne Place accepting the Exchequer and also defending himself angrily and at length against the charges of breach of trust.

Dear Prime Minister,
I thank you for the flattering proposal contained in your letter & even more for the flattering terms in which it is conveyed to me. The condition you impose as the next Budget relieves me of a great anxiety & I gladly acknowledge its fairness. I shall be proud to serve under your Premiership and no member of the Government will render more loyal service & support to his chief.
Winston told me last night that some of my colleagues had rushed to you immediately on your arrival with the amiable suggestion that I had been responsible for the publication of the Cabinet list. I need hardly tell you that I felt very hurt at the accusation & I think I ought to know who it is amongst my colleagues who deems me capable of what is not merely a gross indiscretion but a downright discreditable breach of trust. Men whose promotion is not sustained by birth or other favouring conditions are always liable to be assailed with unkind suspicions of this sort. I would ask it therefore as a favour that you should not entertain them without satisfying yourself that they have some basis of truth. In this case there is not a shadow of truth in the insinuation & I am ashamed to think that it should be even necessary to say so.[197]

Asquith replied the same day in a conciliatory letter which showed him fully recovered from his anger of the previous evening.

My dear Lloyd George,
I was glad to receive your cordial acceptance of my offer, & I reciprocate your wish and belief that our co-operation will always be of the closest.
I confess that I was a good deal annoyed to find, on my way home, that a substantially accurate forecast of the proposed changes in the Cabinet was published the 'Chronicle' on the very morning on which I was first to submit them to the King.
On my arrival here I was told by more than one colleague (there is no use in giving names) that it was reported that the editor of the paper vouched you as the source of his information, & finding from Winston that you were to dine with him last night I suggested that he should inform you of what was being said. I need not say that I accept without

reserve your disclaimer. The press in these days is ubiquitous, difficult to baffle, and ingenious in drawing inferences from silence as well as from speech.[198]

Lloyd George was clearly most upset by this misadventure. His anger and sense of persecution were clear in his letter to Asquith. Even John Burns who saw him at the National Liberal Club that evening noted in his diary that Lloyd George 'appeared anxious.' Burns, who apparently was the only Liberal in politics who did not read the *Chronicle* and who could be depended upon to be misinformed on any topic, recorded also that he expected Lloyd George to go to the Home Office.[199] Although Asquith seems to have forgotten the episode quickly, echoes of it lingered in Lloyd George's relations with his colleagues in the Cabinet. He had asked Asquith for the names of his informants and was refused, but probably he soon discovered who they were, no doubt from Churchill. One must imagine that Mrs. Asquith's special insistance in her letter to Churchill that Lloyd George not learn that McKenna was involved proceeded from her knowledge that McKenna realized he had been considered, and passed over, for the Exchequer and was not entirely consoled even with the glittering post of the Admiralty. He certainly would have taken particular pleasure in reporting Lloyd George's indiscretion to the Prime Minister. Similarly Lloyd George would regard anyone who told tales about him as an enemy. This, to be sure, is speculation based upon scanty evidence. But what followed is clear. After Lloyd George came to the Exchequer relations between himself and McKenna, which had been reasonably good before, cooled immediately. This was not the result of struggles over the naval estimates which did not begin until 1909. Inevitably Churchill, who had been a friend of McKenna, was drawn in and the breach widened further when Churchill replaced McKenna at the Admiralty in the fall of 1911.[200] In the years to come, McKenna, who was widely respected, not least by the Prime Minister, for his precision of mind, clarity, and industry, would become a dangerous enemy at a time when Lloyd George needed all the friends he could collect.

The question must be answered as to whether Lloyd George was in fact guilty of passing information about the Cabinet to the *Daily Chronicle*. There is no clear evidence, but the circumstances, and Lloyd George's behavior on other occasions, strongly suggest that he did.[201] It is hardly likely that the story given in Margot Asquith's letter was fabricated. McKenna and Runciman certainly were not fond of the new Chancellor but Vaughan Nash bore him no ill will, was a close friend of Harold Spender, and had no reason to fabricate a tale.[202] On the other hand Lloyd George surely was not the only source for the story. Many politicians liked to reveal facts to newsmen which are flattering to themselves.

In any case he was now Chancellor of the Exchequer, a post he would hold for over seven years. In terms of legislation, of settling the lines of evolution of domestic British institutions, he accomplished in those years some of the most important work of his life. But he succeeded also in dispersing the atmosphere of good will that had settled around him at the Board of Trade. He became again the most controversial man in politics, fighting new battles that involved this time not only Wales but the entire nation.

6 The Exchequer, the Liberal Crisis and the Budget, 1908

Asquith's new government, announced in the newspapers on Monday, 13 April 1908 inherited from the Campbell-Bannerman administration a gigantic burden of unfinished business, made up chiefly of promises to importunate nonconformists. Among these the most pressing were the unsolved, and as it turned out unsolvable, problem of education, now in its third year and still outstanding at the end of the session, and the reduction of public house licences. This latter had already been announced as the major legislative project for 1908.

The Licensing Bill of 1908 had been introduced on 27 February, by Asquith himself, in the waning days of the previous Cabinet. Its underlying goal was the recovery for the community of the de facto right to extinguish public house licenses at the time of their annual renewal. Legally, such licenses existed only at the pleasure of the local authorities, but custom and public opinion had established in them a property right which might not be appropriated without compensation. Balfour had put this consensus into law in 1904 with the creation of a fund for the purchase of such licenses: 'The Brewers' Endowment Bill' or the 'Publicans' Pension' as Lloyd George had variously described it.

The Liberal bill, although a lengthy and complex instrument, was basically a statement that after 14 years licenses would again be terminable without compensation in a variety of carefully defined circumstances: the number of premises and population within given areas, local opinion, the behavior of the licensee. Although it represented, particularly in its local option provisions, a point of view to which he subscribed, Lloyd George was not involved in the planning of the Licensing Bill, which was in the rather inept hands of the Home Secretary, Herbert Gladstone.

From its introduction the bill brought the government widespread unpopularity. Like the Education Bill, it was a clumsy measure. The nonconformists, to whom it was supposed to appeal, reinforced by a substantial contingent of radical reformers who saw drink as a large impediment to national efficiency, all objected to the long delay in its effective date. Working class voters, not to mention the Irish, opposed the bill on principle. Less than a month after its introduction, the lessons of the Ashburton and Ross by-election defeats in January were repeated by a rebuff in Peckham, Camberwell, where on 24 March a Liberal winning margin of 2,339 in 1906 became a losing margin of 2,494 in an uproarious campaign that turned entirely on the temperance issue. The Liberal candidate suffered a carnival of abuse and insult while the Unionists won simply on the slogan 'Thou shalt not steal. There is no time limit to that'.[1] Here was a bill which the Lords could feel perfectly safe in rejecting, by which, indeed, they would earn themselves a measure of popularity. They lost no time in doing so at the end of November.

In 1908 the Licensing Bill and its defeat were politically important. But historically, this rebuff represents only the dying spasms of orthodox nineteenth-century nonconformity, whose insistence upon the enactment into law of its social and religious principles and whose antagonism for the Irish had drained the Liberal party of its energies since Gladstone's first administration. For the future, and for Lloyd George, the measure that symbolized the transition to the New Liberalism, of which he would become the high priest, was old age pensions. This ancient promise of both parties was finally announced in the King's Speech on 29 January 1908 and Asquith outlined the terms of the proposed measure in his budget speech on 7 May, carefully making clear that this gratuity to Britain's elderly came from a generous party which had gone through 'the last election entirely unpledged in regard to this matter.'[2] Asquith put Lloyd George in charge of the bill the next day although the Chancellor of the Exchequer had taken no part in the preparation of the measure and was not even a member of the Cabinet committee which dealt with it. Nevertheless the Old Age Pension Act, the lessons learned from it, its cost, the political pressures that determined its shape, and indeed its popularity, would affect profoundly Lloyd George's political strategy during the next four years. Accordingly, a word is necessary about the background of the bill.

The beginnings of serious pension agitation in the 1890s have been discussed. The first front bench politician to be intimately associated with it was Joseph Chamberlain and his failure to make good on his promises had provided Lloyd George with much ammunition. Lloyd George himself had not overlooked the political appeal of pensions and had been a member of the Chaplin Committee, one of the last of the several bodies to consider them. However, the Member for Caernarvon District was never involved closely enough with pensions to encounter serious problems about their cost. He had always waved the matter aside with the suggestion that pensions could be paid for by rates on landed estates, or by the Church, or by any other body that deserved to be plundered.

Yet pensions would not have become the political necessity that they were by 1906 without the revolution in public attitudes in the years after the South African War over national efficiency, and the eruption of the 'condition of the people' question. This profound change in the national mood, partly a reaction to jingoistic imperialism, partly a search for national renewal, partly a fear of racial degeneration, had touched Lloyd George, as his speeches in the spring of 1903 showed, even though it had hardly modified his program. Rather he saw that the reforms that he had long demanded, land valuation and leasehold franchise, pensions and license reform, now had a wider appeal. No man in British politics was less affected than Lloyd George by ideology, but no man was more sensitive to the changing political currents that ideology could bring.

The election of 1906 showed what had happened. Not only did it put in power a Liberal government pledged to reform education, to restore the right to strike, and to maintain free trade. It brought also into the House of Commons and into the political and journalistic world around it, a generation of young Liberals for whom radical social reform and interventionist politics were a creed. Many of these men had scarcely left the universities at the time the South African War broke out. In their backgrounds were the writings of T.H. Greene, J.A. Hobson, and L.T. Hobhouse, experience in the slums, often at university settlements, and frequently also work in journalism under the patronage of C.P. Scott, J.L. Hammond, A.G. Gardiner or H.W. Massingham. To them the South African War had been an abomination and imperialism a crime as it had been to Campbell-Bannerman and John Morley. But where to the older official Liberal generation reform, with peace and retrenchment, meant temperance, disestablishment, secular education, abolition of the House of Lords veto or one man one vote, for the new Liberals reform was, as it was styled, 'social,' meaning the care of children and the aged, a graduated income tax, work for the unemployed, and land valuation, taxation, and nationalization. The new men attended the austere salons of Sydney and Beatrice Webb, looked approvingly, if uncomprehendingly, upon the trade unions and were well aware of the power of the working class vote and of the appeal of tariff reform. They supported measures for school meals in 1906 and the medical inspection of school children in 1907. Most important, many of them had included proposals for old age pensions in their election addresses.[3]

Lloyd George was in no way a part of this assemblage although Churchill could be counted an honorary member. He contributed his own influential reflections to its general stock of ideas in 'The Untrodden Field in Politics,' which appeared in the *Nation* in March 1908. But just a week before he refused to accept the Local Government Board on the plea that he detested and knew nothing about social reform.[4] During 1906 and 1907 Lloyd George was preoccupied at the Board of Trade, and with the Welsh Church and with education. He apparently did not become acquainted with the most visible member of the young Liberal radicals, Charles Masterman, until he went to the Exchequer and then probably the introduction came through Churchill who was for a time Masterman's close comrade and from whom he received instruction in reform. Lloyd George received responsibility for old age pensions not because of any previous connection with the proposal but because the measure had been framed in the Treasury and because, to ensure its passage through the House of Lords, pensions were designated in the King's Speech as being part of the 'financial arrangements' for the coming year. In effect the Old Age Pension Bill, although physically separate, was a section of the Finance Bill of 1908.[5]

The fact that Lloyd George had nothing to do with the framing of the pension bill would become a matter of great importance for the future. To be sure he believed thoroughly in its political timeliness. 'It is time we did something that appealed straight to the people—it will, I think help to stop this electoral rot, and that is most necessary,' he wrote to his brother on 6 May after Asquith had announced the terms of the scheme in his budget address.[6] And he had understood longer than most of his colleagues the threat to Liberalism from demagogic Unionism hawking cheap social welfare to the masses at the price of import duties. But nevertheless he had no personal commitment to the details of the bill. Well before pensions went into effect he came to feel that the tax supported measure was a mistake: that it was carelessly drawn, that it would complicate Liberal financial problems to the point of imperilling free trade and that the pension provision was so narrow that its extension was inevitable. Finally he knew that if free trade finance were to be saved, the extensions would have to be paid for by beneficiary contributions.

The measure upon which Lloyd George opened debate on 15 June 1908 represented the most meagre possible response to the conflicting pressures for old age pensions of the last decade. By and large the bill was based upon the estimates generated by previous investigating committees, particularly that of Sir Edward Hamilton's committee which had looked into the possible cost of the five shilling pension at age 65 recommended by the Chaplin Committee. Most of the work had been done by Roderick Meiklejohn, Asquith's secretary. No investigation by independent actuaries was made. The government never considered a universal pension of the sort proposed by Charles Booth. Rather it hedged eligibility around with a variety of restrictions, good civic behavior, ability to stay off the poor law, evidence of thrift (but, on the other hand, not too much thrift for an income above 10s a week would also make an applicant ineligible).[7] After reviewing the figures and solely to reduce costs, Asquith raised the pensionable age from 65, which the pension reformers demanded, to 70 and reduced the amount payable to eligible married couples from 10s to 7s 6d. The number of pensioners in the first year would not exceed 500,000, he assured the King on 1 May, 1908 when the Cabinet approved the bill. Nor would the cost be more than £6,500,000 although, he admitted, all figures were 'highly conjectural.'[8]

Even though Lloyd George was dubious about the pension bill while admitting its political utility, it still cost too much and did too little. Soon after the bill was approved by the Cabinet, in his first Cabinet paper as Chancellor of the Exchequer, he questioned the Prime Minister's assertions on the cost. 'I regard the estimate of 6 millions for the cost of old age pensions in the first year as a minimum rather than a maximum,' he wrote. 'If any of the allowances or corrections which we have made should not be realized, or if, during the passage of the Bill, we should have to make further concessions, the costs may turn out to be nearer 7 millions.'[9]

By this time he was already looking beyond the slim provision of a 5s pension at age 70 to what would become within the next few years the gigantic structure of national insurance. The germ of this was apparent in a conversation with D.R. Daniel during the Easter week recess which had begun on 14 April 1908, the day after the new Cabinet was announced. During a morning walk at Criccieth he mused aloud to Daniel:

> After all, in my opinion, old age is not the hardest burden...lonely and sad though the old may be, the way to carry it is not far, the old only has his own burden to carry. The tragedy that appeals most to me is seeing the workman whose strength is ebbing gradually, and yet

because of his family burdens has to go every day to the quarry or factory. Seeing his wife and children before him when he should be resting. A little rest for three to six months in some healthful place under care and nursing would put him back on his feet, but he cannot do anything but press on until he falls into the pit, leaving his wife and family at the mercy of the parish. That is the class I'd like to do something for if I could. I am glad that one helps the old—but this sort of thing is far more important.[10]

Lloyd George rarely came as close as this to unmixed philanthropy. Unquestionably his sympathy for the poor, particularly the working man or more often his widow and children, was perfectly genuine—he loved children, perhaps even more after Mair's death—but usually involved was a reciprocal anger at privilege and inherited wealth. More typical was his declaration, six months later, also at Criccieth, when he repeated virtually the same speech to Herbert Lewis with more characteristic additions.

Take...the man who works at Llechwedd Quarry. He risks his life. Our servant, Sarah, received a telegram to say her father had been killed at the quarry. He was a fine old boy. The death rate at that quarry. What does he get for his work? 25s a week, often having to live away from home in uncomfortable lodging or barracks. When there is no work it means starvation. And what about the owner of the quarry? The man who does not work? He has a beautiful house with gardens and ornamental grounds that extend for miles. Even that is not enough for him. He must have another house at Caernarvon—twenty miles away. There is no justice in it. It is not divine justice, it is not human justice.[11]

Despite Lloyd George's opinion of it, the Old Age Pension Bill involved a prodigious commitment for the future. Lloyd George understood this and made it the theme of his introductory speech on the second reading of the bill. He repeated almost exactly his soliloquies to Daniel and Lewis quoted above. The scheme, he said

is an incomplete one; we say it is a beginning and only a beginning but a real beginning. We do not say it deals with all the unmerited destitution in this country. We do not even contend that it deals with the worst part of that problem. It might be held that many an old man dependent upon the charity of the parish was better off than many a young man, broken down in health, or who cannot find a market for his labour. The provision which is made for the sick and unemployed is grossly inadequate in this country, and yet the working classes have done their best during fifty years to make provision without the aid of the State. But it is insufficient. The old man has to bear his own burden; while in the case of a young man who is broken down and who has a wife and family to maintain, that suffering is increased and multiplied to that extent. These problems of the sick, of the infirm, of the men who cannot find means of earning a livelihood though they seek it as if they were seeking for alms, who are out of work through no fault of their own, and who cannot even guess the reason why, are problems with which it is the business of the State to deal; they are problems which the State has neglected too long.[12]

The Unionist reception of this measure was curious. On one hand the opposition questioned continually the uncertain projection of the cost of the scheme offered by Asquith and Lloyd George. Balfour scoffed at the Prime Minister's complacent assurances during his budget statement that the number of pensioners would not exceed 500,000 and the cost would be around £6 million. The Prime Minister, he jeered at Lloyd George, had told the House of Commons several times that he knew where the money would come from. But evidently he had not told the Chancellor of the Exchequer.

> I think that this is carrying secrecy too far. I think that in the comity of the Cabinet the late Chancellor of the Exchequer should have told the present Chancellor of the Exchequer how, within the limits of free trade finance, £6,500,000 are to be found in the next year and £7,500,000 the year after. It is not going to be £7,500,000 either. If my interpretation of the situation is correct you will get to £11,500,000 almost immediately, and how within the limits of free trade finance are you to get £11,500,000?[13]

As an example of what he meant the leader of the opposition pointed out that pensions, set to begin on 1 January, 1909, would apply to all born in 1839. In Ireland there had been no civil registration of births until 1865. (Parish registration before that time had been in the hands of the Church of Ireland, which the majority of the nation did not attend. Roman Catholic parochial registers were haphazard and incomplete.) He proposed that a man whom he called O'Grady who had left Cork thirty years ago and had worked since on the London docks would neither know, nor have any proof, that he had been born in 1839. He would have no proof of age.

> Why should he have proof? I do not think I should know my own age if it were not that tactless friends are constantly reminding me of it. Most assuredly a dock labourer who left Cork thirty years ago may very well be excused if he has not proof of age, since he was born in a country where there is no registration of births at the time he was presumably born.[14]

Although he 'rejoiced in the policy of pensions' Balfour concluded, he did not believe the government's predictions of their cost nor that they could be supported by the present fiscal system.

Balfour, on the third reading debate, had summarized neatly the entire weakness of the pension program. Asquith, in innocent optimism which Lloyd George loyally repeated during his speeches on the bill, assumed that for a variety of reasons far fewer than the number eligible would apply for pensions in the first year and indeed in the second. *The Times* observed the next day that Lloyd George's anger at Balfour and his failure to deal with Balfour's estimate of pension costs suggested that he probably agreed.[15] In fact Lloyd George had admitted as much ten days before. In a joking remark during the committee stage, which caused him immense trouble in the next few months, he conceded that he had no idea where he would find the money for pensions.

The public show in the House of Commons reflected a consensus among both tariff reformers and Unionist free traders that the cost of pensions would destroy within the next few years free trade finance. Chamberlainites ironically welcomed pensions as a way of demonstrating the necessity of broadening the tax base.[16] St. Loe Strachey, the editor of the *Spectator* and the increasingly lonely voice of Unionist free trade, condemned pensions out of hand as destroying the moral fibre of the nation, leading directly to protection. Strachey carried on a busy correspondence with the equally isolated Lord Rosebery in which the two reinforced each other's fears of the danger of an open-ended Treasury commitment which pensions constituted to the citizenry of the nation. Rosebery accurately predicted the effect of pensions in his speech upon the bill in the House of Lords on 20 July. He quoted the 'intrepid editor' of a 'great weekly journal' who warned that if pensions did not lead to protection they would lead to such taxation as to 'make many converts to protection.'[17]

Rosebery's speech prompted a widely noted lead article in *The Times* entitled 'Fiscal Questions' which sneered at the uncertainty the Liberals increasingly displayed about the cost of pensions. Lloyd George had hinted on the first reading that after the first couple of years he did not know where the pension money would come from and later, on 29 June, in an ill-advised remark that would become famous, he said:

> I have no nest eggs. I have got to rob somebody's hen roost next year. I am on the lookout which will be the easiest to get and where I shall be least punished, and where I shall get the most eggs, and, not only that, but where they can be most easily spared, which is another important qualification.[18]

Old age pensions, *The Times* declared, showed free trade finance 'in extremis.' Income tax was already at wartime levels and the indirect tax base was demonstrably too narrow. 'Gradually, and no doubt at first dimly and confusedly, the nation is getting to see that the system is in fact bankrupt.'[19]

Eventually Strachey provoked Asquith, who alone in the British political world seemed to think that pensions would be inexpensive. The Prime Minister sent the editor a stern letter admitting that the danger to free trade existed theoretically, while insisting that it would be surmounted. The *Spectator*, said Asquith, seemed to be 'losing its way—and I might add its head—in the whole domain of finance.'

> I have realized from the first that if it could not be proved that Social Reform (not socialism) can be financed on Free Trade lines, a return to Protection is a virtual certainty. This has been one of the mainsprings of my policy at the Exchequer. I prepared the way by steadily reducing the principal of the debt—at the cost of the taxpayer and by means of war taxes—till I have brought it at the end of this year to the level of 20 years ago…Old age pensions were inevitable. I have secured an ample fund to meet them without any extra taxation.[20]

Several historians, misreading Asquith's perpendicular handwriting, Robert Scally and Alfred Gollin in particular, have made a mystery of this relatively straightforward letter by seeing 'virtual certainty' as 'moral certainty.'[21]

Nevertheless, in simplest terms, Asquith was wrong and Balfour right.

Asquith had promised the King in his Cabinet letter of 1 May and had repeated in his announcement of pensions during the Budget speech a few days later that not more than 500,000 people would take up pensions during the first year and that the cost would be no more than £6 million or £6,500,000 after the elimination of the marriage reductions. Lloyd George had repeated this optimistic estimate on the second reading.[22] Asquith seems to have based these assurances on the experience of New Zealand where a relatively low percentage of those eligible, for reasons of indolence or ignorance, had applied for pensions in their initial year and he took for granted, indeed founded the government's financial planning upon, the assumption that the British experience would be similar. The figures at the end of the first financial year tell the story clearly enough. On 31 March 1910, the number of pensions in force, instead of 500,000, was 699,352 and their cost was not £6,500,000 but £8,500,000, more than the price of four dreadnoughts. Perhaps most significant was the fact that while 44.7% of those over 70 had applied in England and Wales and 53.8% of those eligible received pensions in Scotland, 98.6%, virtually every person in the appropriate age group, was receiving a pension in Ireland.[23] By 1912 the cost of pensions was nearly £12 million.

I

The Old Age Pension Bill received the Royal Assent on 1 August 1908 and on that day parliament adjourned until 12 October. In passage, the bill had been altered in two major ways. The reduced pension for married couples, who together would have received 7s. 6d. instead of the 10s. that would have been due them if living apart, was removed. This was estimated to cost £400,000 a year. Lloyd George accepted this amendment with a rather excessive show of reluctance, as a means, he explained to his brother the next day, of preventing Liberal reformers from abolishing the provision that disqualified for pensions anyone who had received poor law relief in the past two years.[24] On the other hand he gladly assented to the introduction of a variable scale for eligibility which provided in place of the flat rate of a 5s. pension for anyone earning less than £26 per year, a full pension only to those who received less than £21 per year with gradually smaller amounts for larger incomes down to 1s. per week for those with as much as £31 10s. He had proposed this in the cabinet but was opposed by Asquith. Now that he was in charge of the bill, he said, he could do as he liked. In fact this amendment which had been expected to cost £100,000 a year may have saved a considerable sum. Only about 8% of those eligible applied for pensions at the reduced rates and the number of people accepting the 1s. and 2s. pensions which were available to persons above the old maximum of £26 was minute, amounting only to about 15,000 people in the entire United Kingdom.

Yet, stingy as it was, the Old Age Pension Act of 1908 remains of seminal importance as a factor in Lloyd George's decisions in the year to come. Well before the bill had passed the House of Commons he had begun to regard it as a disaster. He had been unable to find any reasonable estimates of its cost after coming to the Exchequer, he told A. T. Davies.[25] Strachey had heard the same. 'I am told that Lloyd George is in despair as to where he is going to get his money,' wrote Strachey to Rosebery in a congratulatory letter after the latter's speech in the House of Lords on the pensions bill, 'and I do not wonder because unless he juggles the national finance next year he will have to find at least 15 million more money; and even if he juggles he will only put off the day of reckoning till the year after.' Strachey concluded, after reporting some gossip from Treasury civil servants about the Chancellor's inadequate financial sense, that he had heard the Liberal Chief Agent, Robert Hudson, say that the next budget might double the tax on incomes over £5,000 and triple it on incomes over £10,000.[26]

In the next few years, as the cost of pensions grew and his annual battles with the services became fiercer, Lloyd George's conviction that tax-supported pensions had been a mistake increased to a passion. At Brighton on 21 May 1909, D.R. Daniel recorded 'L.G. very critical of O.A. Pen. scheme says it will cost £11 million to give pensions to people of 70. With £15 million "I could have given something far greater which would have sheltered thousands more especially the needy."'[27] In a conversation with Arnold White in September 1911, when he was at work on national health insurance—and by which time the cost of old age pensions had grown to nearly £10 million—he remarked that if half the money 'squandered' on pensions had been spent on housing some people might have been helped.[28]

Similarly W.J. Braithwaite, the principal architect of national health insurance, recalled Lloyd George's constant recollections of his agony over costs during the passage of the pensions bill. The Liberals had got into a 'panic' over pensions. There was no professional actuarial work. Everyone was free to propose amendments expanding the program. This had taught Lloyd George, Braithwaite concluded 'what the cost of free grants could be, and turned his mind to contributory insurance.'[29]

During the second reading address, on 15 June, as a part of his declaration that pensions for the aged were only the beginning of the attack on pauperism, Lloyd George had pointed to the example of Germany which had 'a prosperous scheme for old age, for infirmity, for sickness, and unemployment,' all paid for by insurance.[30] Germany possessed, of course, in 1908 the world's largest and oldest system of compulsory contributory insurance, covering sickness, old age, infirmity and some dependents' welfare. Lloyd George surely must have been aware of her progress in this respect for many years. Any discussion of pensions always invoked the German example. Yet clearly he had not studied the system closely, for contrary to his assertion just quoted, the Kaiser's empire offered no unemployment insurance. Indeed the Imperial Labour Department had determined, after an intensive investigation of the problem in 1906, that compulsory unemployment insurance was not feasible.

Lloyd George learned by observation and conversation; it would not be too much to say that he formulated ideas by talking. An interest in the example of the German system of national insurance meant, therefore, a trip to Germany. This journey was of singular importance for Lloyd George, not only because it provided him with a platform from which to sell to the nation welfare programs based upon beneficiary contribution, which hitherto he had always opposed. It also coincided with the beginnings of the desperate naval race with Germany in which Lloyd George was already both emotionally and politically involved.

For the Chancellor of the Exchequer as well as for the Cabinet the two great imponderables in the next several years were dreadnought class battleships and pensions. Ironically, new naval construction and care for the aged were about equal in cost, between £8 and £10 million, and rising each year. In the summer of 1908, as each day produced new miseries over the prospective cost of pensions, there appeared alarming and rather unexpected reports of rapidly increasing German warship construction which began to turn what had hitherto been only a major domestic political embarrassment into a potential crisis.

In 1908, naval competition with Germany was just a decade old and during this time the latter had raised her navy from a position inferior to Russia's to one second only to Great Britain. Until 1906 this challenge was less dangerous than it appeared because of the Royal Navy's immense superiority in tonnage already in commission. To overtake Britain before that time, matching ship for ship, would have been well beyond Germany's physical shipbuilding facilities as well as beyond the limited and rather primitive financial resources of the Imperial government. However, on 10 February 1906, Britain's comfortable advantage disappeared with the launching at Portsmouth by Edward VII of the *Dreadnought*, a battleship so much faster and so heavily armed as to make obsolete any existing capital ship in any navy in the world, including Great Britain's. Henceforth the Royal Navy's margin of superiority over Germany was one ship. The naval race was now a dreadnought race.

The technological revolution brought by the *Dreadnought* did more than destroy Britain's lead in the naval competition with Germany. Far more important from Lloyd George's point of view it made the race much more expensive. The *Dreadnought* had cost nearly twice as much as ordinary pre-*Dreadnought* battleships, about £2,000,000 instead of £1,000,000. (The last ships laid down before the war, the Queen Elizabeths, were approaching £3,000,000.) In addition the new ships carried a much larger complement of men, nearly 1,000 instead of 700, who had to be recruited, fed, paid and pensioned.

Germany's immediate response to the *Dreadnought* was to install more heavy guns on conventional battleships then under construction. But her serious challenge, which brought on the 'naval scare' of 1909 and which, along with pensions, made Lloyd George's first budget the unprecedented attack upon wealth that it was, appeared only in 1908 with the passage by the Reichstag in February of an amendment to the basic Navy Law of 1900 providing for the laying down of four new dreadnoughts each year for the next four years with a reduced rate thereafter. The Navy Law Amendment of 1908 was received within the British service community as little less than a declaration of war. Until nearly the end of 1907 Sir John Fisher, the First Sea Lord, whose creation, so much as it belonged to any one man, the *Dreadnought* was, had been assuring the government and the nation at large that the British fleet had made a tremendous leap forward. Germany was now hopelessly surpassed.[31] During the same year Campbell-Bannerman had allowed Asquith to reduce the debt, holding down service estimates, while, following his own inclinations, engaging Britain actively in an attempt at armament limitation at the Hague Peace Conference. Here the Germans had resisted absolutely all attempts at compromises in weaponry. The law of 1908 seemed to show now that British restraint the previous year had been, if not a mistake, at least unproductive.

The terms of Germany's new program had been made public on 18 November 1907. Considering all that would blow up over the Kaiser's naval construction plans within the next few months, the Admiralty's estimates for the 1908-09 financial year were modest, one dreadnought only, barely enough to keep British armor plate shops at work.[32] Nevertheless, in early February, reformers in the Cabinet, evidently with the mild approval of Campbell-Bannerman and with Lloyd George as spokesman, caused an uproar demanding still further cuts in the estimates which the Cabinet in fact had already approved. According to Lord Esher, Lloyd George with Harcourt, McKenna, Burns, and apparently Lord Crewe, pushed their resistance to the point of resignation. This led to a famous confrontation between the economizers and Sir John Fisher, in which the First Sea Lord scoffed at their threats of leaving the government and retorted that if the cuts they demanded were made the result would be, on the other hand, the resignation of the Board of Admiralty, and, he observed tartly, it would be a good deal more difficult to replace the Board of Admiralty.[33]

The revolt soon burned out, settled as one of his last official acts by the dying Prime Minister, who convinced Haldane to give up some money from the Army, and the First Lord to reduce slightly the Navy estimates, although not those for new construction. Its importance, besides introducing Lloyd George to the redoubtable Jackie Fisher whose path he would cross many times in the future, lies in the demonstration it provides of Lloyd George's usual prewar attitude toward military expenditure, even before he became Chancellor of the Exchequer. More important it shows as a corollary that he was, on the whole, far less suspicious of Germany than many of his colleagues. This would change and he would attempt to gloss over his early attitudes in his *War Memoirs*, emphasizing instead the sturdy pugnacity he displayed, for example, to the German ambassador in asserting Britain's absolute determination to maintain naval superiority. There is certainly no reason to question his patriotism, and his sympathy for the German position rose and fell several times in the years before the war. Nevertheless in 1908, in private battles in the Cabinet, and in semi-public ventures into personal diplomacy, he attempted to establish an understanding with Germany which would make the ruinous cost of pensions, as he saw them, easier to bear.

'I mean to cut down army expenditure...' he wrote to his brother on 12 May 1908 a few days after he had been put in charge of the pension bill. 'I am not going to increase taxation to pay Old Age Pensions until I have exhausted all means of reducing expenditure. I have told the Prime Minister he must help me. He promises to do so, and my difficulties over Old Age Pensions are now much less than they seemed a week ago.'[34]

He continued to fight for economy within the Cabinet through the summer. Relations with the service ministers, McKenna and Haldane, already cool, chilled still further.[35] A preliminary climax in this campaign was a ringing battle in the Cabinet on 2 July over the disposal of a substantial sum paid to the Exchequer by the Indian government for defense services provided by Britain, which Haldane hoped to use for the purchase of artillery ranges for the new Territorial Force. 'The Chancellor of the Exchequer,' wrote Asquith to the King, 'was very adverse [sic] to allocating for this purpose any part of the fund...he pointed out with great force the need for the Treasury to utilize for general purposes in the existing financial situation any funds that are legally at its disposal. A warm discussion ensued...' but in the end Asquith supported Lloyd George although Haldane was allowed to borrow money for the ranges.[36]

Possibly this defeat elicited the letter from Haldane to Asquith on 9 August that may be the embryo of the 1909 budget. After a general discussion of policy, directed mainly at ensuring that John Burns should be forced to take some action on reform of the Poor Law, Haldane suggested that the need for money might make necessary substantially higher direct taxes in the next year. Even Liberal principles should not stop the Hegelian flow of history.

> We have not stumbled into the introduction of an Old Age Pension system, nor into the increase of the proportion which direct bears to indirect taxation. These two changes are Reforms which the True Spirit has called us for as definitely as it called for Electoral Reform in 1832.

He urged Asquith to form a Cabinet Committee on taxation with himself as Chairman.[37]

Haldane had not mentioned Lloyd George but the proposal to establish a Cabinet committee in the Chancellor's area of administration suggested doubts about his capacity. Asquith was receiving caveats from other quarters. Charles Hobhouse, Lloyd George's own Financial Secretary at the Treasury, recorded in his diary that his chief's 'contempt for details and ignorance of the common facts of life make him a bad official.' Since the end of June, on the Prime Minister's instructions, Hobhouse had been visiting Asquith weekly so that the latter could learn the financial position of the government over which he presided.[38]

Lloyd George was rapidly losing, indeed by summer had already lost, most of the stock of political good will that he had accumulated during the years at the Board of Trade. Those inside the Cabinet, Haldane, McKenna, Hobhouse, Burns, the new junior whip, J.A. Pease, detested his seeming idleness and irresponsibility, his endless conspiracies with Churchill (who, if possible, was disliked even more), his publicity-seeking flirtations with newspapers, and his ability to bully the Prime Minister.[39] In the rest of the political world, the opposition already suspected the Chancellor's patriotism as manifested by his unwillingness to find the money to keep Britain strong and by his flirtations with socialists. Some people think he 'will move to the extreme left and play up to the wild men,' wrote the powerful tariff reform editor of the *National Review*, Leo Maxse, to Bonar Law on 5 June after noting that Lloyd George and Churchill were planning a further 'joint intrigue,' to make more raids on the service estimates. He was building a base to 'secure the reversion of the premiership. He will require very careful watching and I hope we shall not be too indulgent. We have all been very kind about his Board of Trade administration—perhaps too kind but that is no reason to tolerate any treacheries at the Exchequer.'[40]

In contrast to Haldane, Lloyd George seems still to have hoped, at least into the autumn, that by sensible economies in service spending he could avoid large new taxes. He told Herbert Lewis early in September that although he expected to impose a direct tax on landowners that could be deducted from the rent they received from farmers, he did not believe in a supertax on income. The rich could always avoid it by apportioning their wealth among nominees.[41] Three days earlier he had written to Robert Chalmers:

> My mind has been working on a Land Tax—either uniform or gradu-
> ated according to size of estimates. A special tax on ground rents and
> on all land situated within the area of towns or within a certain distance
> of towns—graduated according to size of towns. I feel that if there is to
> be an extension of the pension system on contributory lines the
> property which is improved by the labour of the community should
> contribute its share. Mining royalties ought also to be taxed for the
> same reason. I have also a proposal to make about the taxation of
> wasteland.[42]

Clearly at this time he was concerned with the increased costs of arms and domestic social reform. The simplest way to reduce military expenditure was to reduce the need for it by an accommodation with Germany. Already there was a crisis. McKenna, on 4 May 1908, had accepted the Admiralty board recommendation of four dreadnoughts to be laid down under the 1909 budget and, if the maintenance of the Admiralty standard of two keels to one seemed to warrant it, six. This was 'the greatest triumph I have ever known,' John Fisher wrote to Lord Esher the next day. 'This is what I suggest you impress on Lloyd George: *let there be no misunder-standing about two keels for one in dreadnoughts!*'[43] Lloyd George, therefore, in the summer of 1908, as an exercise in personal diplomacy and in angelic innocence of the sacred preserves he invaded, sought compromise.

Precisely what he aimed at is unclear, but in the last two weeks of July he obviously tried to send the German Emperor a signal that a body of opinion existed in Britain which, while entirely patriotic, held Germany to be neither offensive nor unfriendly and did not wish the naval competition to continue. One may speculate that he was influenced by the famous nine-page letter the Kaiser had sent Lord Tweedmouth, then First Lord of the Admiralty, on 16 February just after the Lloyd George/McKenna revolt on the 1908-09 estimates. Although the letter was first of all an attack on Esher, it contained also assertions of only the warmest feelings for Britain, insisting that she should not see a threat in German naval construction.[44] The Kaiser, as Lloyd George and the world knew, was suspicious, hyper-sensitive, and jealous, but he was also demonstrably impatient with convention, impulsive, and eager to be seen as a man of action—in these things, not unlike Lloyd George himself. Lloyd George had met him only a little more than six months before, and had been awarded an extended interview and an invitation to visit Germany. It clearly occurred to him that a trip to inspect German insurance could provide also the opportunity for another amiable conversation with the Kaiser but concerning battleships rather than railway workers. In any case the upshot was a lunch with the German Ambassador in London, Count Paul Metternich, on 14 July 1908 at Sir Edward Grey's residence. Metternich stated in his memorandum of this conversation that Grey had invited him. This does not exclude the possibility that Lloyd George asked Grey for an opportunity to meet the German representative although subsequently Lloyd George denied this.

In the course of the conversation Lloyd George insisted that Britain would never permit Germany to obtain naval superiority and that he, as Chancellor of the Exchequer, would gladly borrow £100,000,000 if necessary to maintain his country's position. He repeated this statement to Lord Esher, to Esher's delight, knowing perhaps that it would be conveyed to the King.[45] This item is one of the few firm statements about the conversation to appear in Lloyd George's first account of the talk written evidently at the time he first projected his war memoirs in the middle 1920s.[46] However, after having included his own recollection of the conversation, Lloyd George printed in full the report that Metternich transmitted to the Kaiser two days later. This shows that he said a good deal more. He proposed also private negotiations aimed at slowing the rate of naval construction, Metternich reported. Lloyd George expected this 'would contribute more quickly to reassure public opinion than any political action could.' Metternich then continued quoting Lloyd George:

> We should find them on this side [i.e. Britain's] most ready to meet us half way in establishing a joint basis for curtailment of fleet building on both sides. The introduction of Dreadnought type had been a great mistake from the English side. The Government here would give every possible guarantee that no new type would be introduced if we could come to an understanding. He had very much regretted that the correspondence between His Majesty the Kaiser and Lord Tweedmouth had not been published at the time. From that correspondence the friendly feeling of His Majesty the Kaiser for England would have become clear to the public and he would also have seen in His Majesty's letter a justification for entering into a confidential discussion with us about naval expenditure. If he had at the time had the responsibility for State Finances he would indeed have insisted in the Cabinet on the publication of the correspondence. A conference at the Hague was not the proper way to reach curtailment in naval expenditure. If as he fervently hoped, it should ever come to this, it must not be tried in an official manner, such as with an exchange of notes. Unofficial confidential discussions which must not be made public at all, would, if an understanding between England and our selves in this matter were at all possible, be more likely to conduce the desired end.[47]

This was not the end. Lloyd George lunched with Metternich again on 28 July, this time, according to Lloyd George, at Metternich's invitation. (Lloyd George confuses many events of these two meetings in his recollections about them.) Here he produced again the familiar argument for a mutually agreed naval holiday, adding that the expenditure for a navy would encourage tariff reformers in Britain and supporters of military conscription, but insisting also that his country would do whatever was necessary to insure its security. Lloyd George implies in his own statement about these meetings that the second interview was acrimonious, that he insisted that Britain would never surrender to German coercion. 'The luncheon party,' he concluded his account, 'was not, I fear, a success.'[48]

Nevertheless that evening he continued his campaign with an ardent plea at Queen's Hall for an understanding with Germany, an event not mentioned in his memoirs. There was no basic conflict between the two nations, he insisted. The naval race indeed was Britain's fault. Constantly interrupted by suffragettes, he began by reminding a packed hall of the Old Age Pensions Bill, which had just passed the House of Lords. 'My Principle is, as Chancellor of the Exchequer, less money for the production of suffering, more money for the reduction of suffering.' There was no purpose in the naval race. Britain was Germany's best customer. 'Why should they want to kill us?' Moreover Germany bought £30,000,000 of goods from Britain. 'Why should we want to kill them? What folly, what stupidity this is....'

> We had an overwhelming preponderance at sea which would have secured us against any conceivable enemy, but we were not satisfied. We said 'let there be Dreadnoughts'. What for? We did not require them. Nobody was building them, if anyone had started building them, we, with our greater shipbuilding resources could have built them faster than any other country in the world.

Britain had the two-power standard which gave her security, but Germany's army was smaller than the combined forces of France and Russia. In effect she had no two-power standard. 'Do not forget that when you wonder why Germany is frightened at alliances and understandings and at the mysterious writings which appear in the press.'[49]

Lloyd George was sharply attacked in a *Times* leader the next day. After commenting favorably on an address by Sir Edward Grey, the paper declared that the Chancellor of the Exchequer's speech was 'singularly reckless and inopportune.'[50] This called forth a rebuttal from Lloyd George, as such criticism usually did, in which he amplified his charges. Germany was less to be blamed than Britain, he wrote, for Britain had a fleet more than twice the size of any other nation. Germany was understandably nervous with an army far smaller than the combined forces of her two potential enemies.[51]

Two days later he departed for Germany in the company of Harold Spender and Mr. and Mrs. Charles Henry, who evidently paid for the trip.[52] In his memoirs Lloyd George states that he had discovered 'recently' that Metternich, after the first conversation, had recommended that his government give Lloyd George 'every consideration' during his travels in Germany and that he had learned also that the Emperor had prepared to invite him to an audience but, on the urging of the Imperial Chancellor Bernhard von Bülow, the invitation was never issued. Lloyd George insists, of course, that he knew nothing of this arrangement at the time.[53]

Nevertheless the evidence suggests that the solicitation of such an interview was from the beginning the principal reason for his trip. Spender frankly affirms this in his memoir. Most of the trip was occupied with insurance, he admitted, but

> a deeper scheme was on foot, which was nothing less than the persuading of the Germans to come to a compromise with England over the bitter competition in armaments....I remember that Lloyd George often discussed this matter with me, and we got into the habit of calling it 'the plan.'

There were people in England, he thought, who wanted war, but his mission 'was in accordance with the general policy and the strong desire of the Cabinet for a peaceful understanding...' with Germany. Some people, concluded Spender, thought he was attempting to split Grey and Asquith.[54]

The party entered Germany on 6 August and first visited Frankfurt, staying at the house of Francis Oppenheimer, the British Commercial Attaché, who was a friend of Rufus Isaacs and also, apparently, of the Henrys. Through Oppenheimer Lloyd George met Dr. Ralph Oeser, correspondent for the *Frankfurter Zeitung*, whom he asked to arrange an interview with Chancellor Von Bülow. The English group remained several days in Frankfurt, but Bülow declined to meet the Chancellor saying, according to Oeser, that it would cause 'national excitement' and, indeed, left Berlin for his estate at Norderney.[55]

As it turned out, during his stay in Germany Lloyd George met no one more exalted than the Vice Chancellor for the Interior, Theobald von Bettmann Hollweg, within whose province fell the Imperial insurance administration. Bettmann Hollweg, with an English wife and a son at Oxford, was no Anglophobe, but he clearly had instructions not to discuss naval matters with Lloyd George and became excited and angry when the Chancellor of the Exchequer repeated his standard proposals for a private Anglo-German naval conversation.[56]

The Chancellor supplemented his private efforts by further public attempts to open a channel of communication. On 12 August the *Neue Freie Presse* published in Vienna an interview with the British visitors at Carlsbad in which Lloyd George reminded the Germans that a naval understanding would allow both nations to spend more on social reform. He did not, he declared, believe that such an understanding could be concluded immediately but something needed to be done to dissipate the mutual apprehension that gripped both countries. England had of course a two-power standard for her own defense, but her fleet need not grow endlessly. He himself had recently protested against the inflammatory language of anti-German journals in his own country, but equally the Germans should abandon their suspicions that Britain was trying to isolate her. 'We must work,' he emphasized, 'for the conclusion of an entente between England and Germany in order that we may be able to devote ourselves wholly to the tasks of peace, of progress, and of social reform...there must be an end of the evil game of setting England and Germany upon each other like two dogs.'[57]

A week later, as it was becoming clear that Lloyd George would see no person more important than Bettmann Hollweg, Harold Spender, who accompanied Lloyd George, gave a statement to the *Berliner Tageblatt* saying that Lloyd George 'would willingly and only too gladly, enter into... discussions with official circles if only the latter would give him the opportunity.'[58]

These two statements, and the hysterical protests in the French press that followed, awakened the holidaying Cabinet in Britain to the consequences of allowing the Chancellor of the Exchequer to go abroad unsupervised.[59] Asquith had to return from Arran and on 20 August sent Lloyd George a telegram telling him not to approach the Emperor on the naval question as his Imperial Majesty had grown sensitive about it.[60] Lloyd George replied innocently the next day: 'I do not propose approaching anyone on an international question. I am confining my investigation to invalid and other pensions....'[61] On that date too Lloyd George gave a statement to the press saying the same thing: that he had no interest in anything beyond the scope of his own office. 'It must be observed however,' commented *The Times*'s Berlin correspondent, 'that Mr. Lloyd George might have preserved a more strict incognito without prejudice to the objects of his inquiry.'[62]

However, the next day Spender's frank request on Lloyd George's behalf for an interview, made in the *Berliner Tageblatt*, was reprinted in the *Daily Telegraph*. This evoked more, indeed harsher, remarks about Lloyd George allowing himself to be interviewed through a low-ranking newspaperman. Grey simultaneously had sent a telegram, Charles Hardinge reported to the King, saying that as he 'appeared to be devoting more of his time in matters affecting the Foreign Office than to the study of the workings of old age pensions in Germany...the question of naval armaments was not to be discussed by him during his stay in Berlin nor any other subject of that kind.'[63] The King, who had just seen William II himself at Kronberg and had found him unwilling to discuss naval compromise, responded from Marienbad complimenting the undersecretary on his memorandum of their meeting and added: 'It is a mercy that we have you as Under-secretary at the Foreign Office and that Lloyd George and Churchill do not occupy that position! I cannot conceive how the Prime Minister allows them ever to make speeches on foreign affairs concerning which they know nothing....'[64] On 14 August, Churchill had spoken at Swansea urging good feeling and military accommodation toward Germany. Lloyd George sent him a telegram of congratulation from Hamburg saying that the Germans were immensely pleased. The two insurgents however were condemned together in a leader in *The Times*.[65]

Lloyd George returned from Germany on 26 August. He said nothing in subsequent interviews about his diplomatic activities there nor did he answer any of the outraged press commentary about his behavior.[66] There is nothing about the diplomatic side of his trip in his *War Memoirs* nor in any of the postwar publications concerning him over which he had any control. One can understand, if not approve, his attempts later to suppress the details of a courageous, if inept, campaign to slow the disastrous naval race with Germany. Obviously, as the man who won the war, he had a natural inclination to appear also as the man who had foreseen and helped to prepare for the war. The standard recitation of his interview with Metternich, as he told Esher and Churchill and recorded in his memoirs, speaks only of the warning that he would borrow £100,000,000 if necessary to retain British naval supremacy.[67] It may be suspected that the long transcripts of his conversations with Metternich, which modify rather sharply his earlier recollections of the two interviews, would not have been printed had not the great German collection of diplomatic documents *Die Grosse Politik* appeared between 1922 and 1927, thus laying him open to contradiction. Surely he never wished to be remembered as the man who thought the *Dreadnought* had been a mistake.

The purpose of this excursion into the dimensions of Lloyd George's inexact recollections of his motives and activities before the war has been partly to emphasize what a thunderclap to the Germans was his warning in July 1911 in the Mansion House Speech that the Kaiser's empire must be prepared to deal with Britain unless she ceased to bully France in Morocco. That the man who had pleaded passionately, almost abjectly, three years earlier for a crumb of German cooperation so that Britain would spend less on warships should calmly threaten war was almost beyond belief. In his own memoirs Lloyd George underrates the magnitude of the alteration in the German perception of himself.

But secondly, because Lloyd George willed it so, scholars have seen the trip to Germany almost entirely in terms of what immediately followed, the beginnings of national insurance. From this came the universal assumption that the scheme was founded upon the German program. This is mistaken. So far as there was any model for national health insurance, it was the British friendly society movement and even this pattern was largely submerged by the time the measure was enacted at the end of 1911. The Germans of course provided no plan for unemployment insurance.

To be sure Lloyd George had visited the Imperial Insurance Office in Berlin where everyone was impressed by his now famous quickness of perception and understanding. He had his conversations with Bettmann Hollweg, whom he found competent but not impressive, and he spoke to trade union and socialist leaders. Nevertheless, when after an interval of two years during which the nation determined the status of the House of Lords, he returned to social insurance, he sent inland revenue expert William John Braithwaite to Germany to look at insurance again.

However, the German trip must be reviewed from one other, and for Lloyd George very personal, point of view. Whether he realized it or not he had made himself appear silly to the Germans and worse to many of his colleagues, not only because it was a clumsy and amateurish excursion into a world of which he knew little, but because of the tawdry nature of the group he took with him. The Chancellor remained the subject of unfavorable comment within the inner circles of the Cabinet for weeks after he returned. On 4 October J.A. Pease, then a Junior Whip who saw the Prime Minister every day, recorded in his diary:

> We then had a long talk on Lloyd George's relations with Mrs. Charles Henry. I assured him I thought the scandal was founded on a platonic relationship due to a pushing American heiress'[?] desire to get on socially – Asquith said his visit to Berlin as a Peace promoter and to secure reduction of navy was mistimed. [Later Margot joins and 'dwelt

upon Lloyd George's failure a probability at the Exchequer'.] The Emperor only laughed at Ll. George motoring tour and he became ridiculous going round with the Henrys and Harold Spender. He and Edward Grey had concocted a really strong telegram stopping him from making an ass of himself, which they sent to him, on his arrival at Berlin through the Embassy. We then had a chat on Lloyd George's limitations — his laziness, which was such a trouble to Sir George Murray — I alluded to his continual interviews with Churchill, but I thought there was really no intrigue but Winston in many ways was a child. Asquith agreed and said Lou Lou Harcourt was not in the group and he would like to have given him the promotion to the Home Office.[68]

A year later Lucy Masterman noted that Lloyd George's name was still linked romantically with Mrs. Henry but wrote also that Mrs. L.G. had said there was nothing to it. They had been invited once to stay with the Henrys but he had declined to go and was rude to Mrs. Henry. Equally after the January 1910 election when he and Masterman toured the continent Henry was pointedly not invited 'or else we should have to take Mrs. Henry which would be Hell.'[69]

Pease continued to poison Asquith's mind against the Chancellor through the autumn. At the end of October, as industrial unemployment was beginning to trouble the government he recorded that Sir Christopher Furniss, about to retire from political life but willing to put £2 million into fifty shipping orders to help unemployment if it would help the party, would obviously want 'a pat on the back and would look to a peerage.' The Prime Minister was unable to see him and asked Pease to telephone Lloyd George. 'I found the latter was away as usual — playing golf at Walton Heath! Idle dog that he is.' Later he asked Asquith if Lloyd George was loyal. 'It had been suggested in more than one quarter (J. Burns for one) he was afraid of next year's budget, that Winston was intriguing for a dissolution in the spring.'[70]

II

Lloyd George arrived in Southampton from Bremen aboard the *Kronprinz Wilhelm* on 26 August. He immediately took the boat train to Waterloo accompanied by a correspondent from the *Daily News* who was probably Harold Spender. His praise of Germany was lavish.

> I never realized on what a gigantic scale the pension system is concocted. Nor had I any idea how successfully it worked. I had read about it, but no amount of study at home or reports and returns can convey to the mind a clear idea of all that state insurance means to Germany. You have to see it before you can understand it. It touches the German people in well nigh every walk of life. Old age pensions form but a comparatively small part of the system: does the worker fall ill? State insurance comes to his aid. Is he permanently invalided from work? Again he gets a regular grant whether he has reached the pension age or not.

Lloyd George was asked whether he had changed his mind on non-contributory pensions. He answered that he had not and concluded by saying he was not sure whether German pension methods could be adapted to Great Britain, but in any case he intended to study Belgian and Austrian pension systems as well.[71]

The other newspapers received a more formal statement emphasizing that he had gone to Germany with no aim except to see whether contributory insurance for old age, invalidity and sickness could be 'grafted' onto a non-contributory system. However he noted that he had been unable to get any information on unemployment insurance.[72]

Before the end of August Lloyd George had returned to Wales. He attended as usual the national Eisteddfod at Llangollen where he stayed with the Bishop of St. Asaph. Churchill joined them for a few days during the festival. Churchill's growing friendship for Lloyd George at this time remained something of a junior-senior relationship. He did not yet address him as 'David' in letters. When the two were walking, attended by D.R. Daniel, Churchill burst out: 'You are much stronger than I: I have noticed that you go about things quietly and calmly, you do not excite yourself, but what you wish happens as you desire it: I am too excitable, I tear about and make too much noise.'[73] By 12 September he was back in London to attend Churchill's wedding to Clementine Hozier at which St. Asaph officiated. (Randolph Churchill in the biography of his father states that he does not know why St. Asaph was asked to perform the ceremony.)[74]

After the wedding Lloyd George offered Lord Riddell an equally candid estimate of Churchill. 'He is a remarkable person, quite a phenomenon. When discussing him, Lloyd George said laughing that he had never met anyone with such a passion for politics. Even at his wedding Winston commenced talking politics to L.G. in the vestry! L.G. says Winston has amazing industry. His valet calls him at 5 or 6 o'clock, and then he sits up in bed and writes articles, speeches, etc.'[75]

Since the summer, Britain, and indeed the rest of Europe, had been afflicted with a growing problem of unemployment, the impact of the Rich Man's Panic of the previous year in the United States. No good statistics existed to measure it except the incomplete reports of some trade unions which kept records of the situation of their own membership, but sporadic outbreaks of violence among jobless men in industrial centers testified to the existence of serious hardship.[76] Already in March, in what may be thought of as his personal manifesto as a social reformer, Churchill had identified unemployment as the 'untrodden field of politics.' In a singularly important letter to the *Nation* he diagnosed a social sickness that was creeping over Britain that would kill old Liberalism unless the party responded. Like Lloyd George he identified its cause as the plague of Chamberlainism, a new Toryism which sought to draw the masses toward import duties by offering counterfeit social reform. Advanced Liberalism, he concluded, echoing Lloyd George's thesis, must respond or disappear.[77]

The month before the *Westminster Review* had printed a remarkable article saying much the same, which could have been written by Lloyd George himself. Entitled 'Liberalism Without Ideas' it warned that the Unionists were stealing social reform. Even if they did not mean it they had the catch words. The party needed a new radical program like the one with which Chamberlain had revived it in 1885. 'Will no Liberal hand,' it asked, 'be stretched out to pick up the torch which he upheld so bravely in the old days...?'[78]

Here was the challenge Lloyd George and Churchill determined to take up. Clearly the two men had discussed the unemployment problem at length in Wales in the early days of September. In the conversation with J.H. Lewis on 8 September, when Lloyd George had described his feelings about the plight of the ordinary worker as opposed to the elderly, he outlined a program of compulsory unemployment insurance based upon the trade unions and covering about 5 million men. He assumed an average unemployment of 3-4%. The plan would pay a benefit of 10s. a week and would require a fund of £5 million from the workers and a further £2 million from the state.[79] He was still pondering this when he returned to London in October, except that in place of administration through trade unions he thought now of a network of trade boards.[80] Eventually the formulation of unemployment insurance went to Churchill who was already at work, with the help of William Henry Beveridge, on a plan for labor exchanges.

However, before Lloyd George left Wales he spoke at Swansea on 1 October announcing that the expansion of the pension program was about to begin. Nothing he said at this time was new and the address, like his speech at Newcastle in April 1903, was presented as the program of the Liberal party, not of Lloyd George alone. Nevertheless, the Swansea statement was not a proposal but a declaration that the New Liberalism was about to begin and here he used those words for the first time.

He began with the frank statement that the government which had come to power three years earlier had not been allowed fairly to complete the task for which it was chosen and, with an oblique reference to the rising sense of frustration within the party which would become more evident by the end of the year, he admitted '...we would have done more but for the malignant destructiveness of the House of Lords. Three of the greatest measures the government labouriously carried through the Commons have now been slaughtered in the charnelhouse across the road, and the Lords are now menacing the life of the fourth.' Echoing Churchill's letter to the *Nation* he explained the evolution of his party.

> The old Liberals in this country used the natural discontent of the people with poverty and precariousness of the means of subsistence as motive power to win for them a better, more influential, more honourable status in the citizenship of their native land. The new Liberalism, while pursuing this great political ideal with unflinching energy devotes part of its endeavour also to the removing of the immediate causes of discontent. It is true that men cannot live by bread alone. It is equally true that a man cannot live without bread. Let Liberalism proceed with its glorious work of building up the temple of liberty in this country, but let it also bear in mind that the worshippers of that shrine have to live. It is a recognition of that elemental fact that has promoted legislation like the Old Age Pensions Act but it is just the beginning of things. We are still confronted with the more gigantic task of dealing with the rest— the sick, the infirm, the unemployed, the widows and the orphans.

No country can lay any real claim to civilization that allows them to starve. Starvation is a punishment that society has ceased to inflict for centuries on its worst criminals, and at its most barbarous stage humanity never starved the children of the criminal.

I have had some excruciating letters piled upon me, more especially during the last year or two from people whose cases I have investigated — honest workmen thrown out of work, tramping the streets from town to town, from one workshop to another, begging for work as they would for charity, and at the end of the day trudging home tired, disheartened, and empty handed, to be greeted by faces, and some of them little faces, haggard and pinched with starvation and anxiety. The day will come, and it is not far distant, that this country will shudder at its toleration of that state of things when it was rolling in wealth. I say again, that apart from inhumanity and its essential injustice, it is robbery, it is confiscation of what is the workman's share of the riches of this land. During years of prosperity the workman has helped to create these enormous piles of wealth which have accumulated in the country since the last period of depression. Hundreds of millions are added to the national wealth during the cycle of plenty. Surely, a few of these millions might be spared to preserve from hunger and from torturing anxiety the workmen who have helped to make that great wealth.[81]

Lloyd George had poured out what had been distilling in his mind for the past six months. Many of the metaphors, for instance of the unemployed workman begging for work as he would for alms, had been tried out already on Daniel and Lewis, no doubt on Churchill and many others. He had listed also the components of the great national insurance program which, with old age pensions and land reform, constituted the New Liberalism. He concluded with a candid political warning as to how all this would be achieved. If the House of Lords declined to allow the Liberals to invite the working men of the nation to the full benefits of citizenship '...Then we shall invite the electorate of this country to arm us with the authority to use the most effective means for removing this senseless obstruction from the path of progress. Whatever befalls Liberalism at the next election, I feel sure that with such a record as this the democracy will turn again with renewed hope and confidence to the great party which served it so loyally, so effectively, and so jealously in the days of its power.'[82]

By the time Lloyd George spoke at Swansea whispers about a compulsory social insurance program were already passing through the narrow world of British trade union and friendly society leadership. Evidently even before he left for Germany Lloyd George had talked briefly with the parliamentary agents of the National Conference of Friendly Societies, W.G. Bunn and William Marlow, and had assured them that the government would do nothing to harm the admirable organizations they represented. He knew as well as anyone the story of the friendly societies' destruction of Chamberlain's contributory pension scheme in the 1890s. If pensions were to be extended to the sick, disabled, and widows and orphans, as he had said was inevitable, and if the scheme were to be contributory as was absolutely necessary, he would have to win somehow the cooperation of the provident organizations, whose suspicion of all government intrusions into their field of activity was nearly pathological. His glowing statements after his return about German state insurance, which was entirely government operated, had frightened them. A few days later they were appalled at the announcement by David Shackleton to the Trades Union Congress at Nottingham on 10 September that the Home Secretary, Herbert Gladstone, intended to appoint a royal commission on state insurance.[83]

At some time toward the end of September Marlow wrote to Lloyd George reminding him of his earlier promises. Noting Shackleton's speech to the TUC, he asked, in tangled syntax, what were the government's intentions. 'In the face of press notices that you are strongly in favour of the German system of State Insurance, I venture to say that the remarks made to Mr. Bunn and I when we were received by you at the Treasury are based upon knowledge of our work during the past 50 to 100 years, against the week's mission in Germany that has completely altered the opinions you then expressed.' Any system of state insurance he continued, would 'kill' the 4,100,000 member friendly society movement. Therefore representatives of the societies should be members of any royal commission. Would Lloyd George see to it?

Lloyd George responded quickly inviting Brothers Marlow and Bunn and the President of the National Conference of Friendly Societies, George Wilde, to breakfast at No. 11. Here, apparently, they were assured that he had nothing but the warmest feelings for the great provident societies, and, more important, that he intended there would be no royal commission.[84]

Three days after the meeting with the friendly society officials, at a large breakfast in Downing Street Lloyd George met, probably for the first time and almost certainly at the behest of Churchill, Sidney and Beatrice Webb.[85] Also included in this gathering were Churchill, Haldane, and Harold Cox, Liberal MP for Preston, an expert on insurance and the only Liberal to vote against the Old Age Pension Bill on the third reading. The Webbs attempted to explain that compulsory insurance with or without friendly society cooperation would destroy the societies. Worse, from their point of view, it was undesirable because it contradicted their fundamental principle of relief conditional upon good behavior. Evidently at this meeting Lloyd George sensed quickly that there was little the couple could tell him and talked more than was his custom. Unlike Churchill, he usually was a good listener. The Webbs came away from the meeting with the sense that Lloyd George was a less attractive personality than the President of the Board of Trade, 'more of the preacher, less of the statesman.'[86] The Webbs were not consulted again until 1911 and eventually were reduced to insinuating their proposals into the Cabinet through Haldane. Lloyd George went back to the friendly societies.

There were four more meetings with larger groups of society representatives on 27 October, 17 November, 1 December, and 15 December. Out of these gatherings came what may be termed the first plan of national health insurance, which was at this point called however, 'invalidity and disability etc. pensions.' The scheme settled upon at the end of 1908 was based entirely upon the friendly societies. It would require all members of the British working population not already in a society to join one and to subscribe for a statutory minimum benefit in return for a small payment that would be withheld from wages and which would be subsidized by the employer and the state. The plan proposed a 5s weekly benefit for sickness, disability, and widowhood, with a further 1s 6d per week for each child.

These were admittedly niggardly benefits, about half the amount the societies normally provided. For the societies the more important provisions were that their existing membership, or anyone else prosperous enough to join as a private member and to insure for the usual society benefits, would not have their contributions withheld from wages but would pay the societies directly while retaining the employer and state subsidies. In effect the societies would gain from the requirement that the poorer three-fifths of the working class would be required to join with an outside subsidy while their existing well-to-do members could remain undisturbed. The stipulated payments under the government plan thus were kept low to encourage the better type of member to subscribe privately for larger benefits and to make possible also a relatively small contribution.[87]

A second important point about the first health plan worked out in 1908 was that it confined itself entirely to the true, permanent, voluntary, provident societies. It stipulated that the societies should be registered, permanent, organizations, with reserve funds capable of actuarial valuation and above all, that they be self governing and not for profit. Accordingly it excluded, on one side, all the innumerable neighborhood and village sick clubs which provided medical care, usually from a local doctor under contract, and a sickness benefit in return for a small payment in the neighborhood of a penny a week. Ordinarily at the end of the year these clubs would dissolve, divide up whatever sums remained, and start again. Uncle Lloyd had belonged to a sick benefit club in Llanystumdwy, Lloyd George recalled to D.R. Daniel, 'and they held a decent dinner once a year.'[88] On the other hand he told A.G. Gardiner the same story and said the club went bankrupt.[89] These clubs, from the friendly society point of view, were the outlaws of the provident world. Many were insolvent and offered substandard medical care, while their members were at the mercy of dishonest or ignorant officers. But of much more importance, the first insurance program excluded also the huge profitmaking industrial insurance companies and the so-called 'collecting' friendly societies. There is no evidence that in 1908 this prohibition was aimed specifically at commercial insurance. The industrial insurance industry sold only funeral benefits, policies payable on the death of the insured to provide a decent burial and to save the deceased from the potter's field. They were not interested in health insurance. Industrial insurance was nonetheless an enormous and hugely profitable enterprise with the Prudential being the largest and best known. (The 'collecting' friendly societies, of which only three, the Royal Liver, the Liverpool Victoria and the Scottish Legal were large enough to be important, were organized as friendly societies to take advantage of the stamp and other tax exemptions available to the registered friendly societies. Being without shareholders they were run for the benefit of their officers and agents but their operation and political outlook were identical to the rest of the industry.)

By agreement between the Chancellor and the society representatives, who included at the end of the series of meetings, in addition to Bunn and Marlow, R.W. Moffrey, parliamentary agent of the largest society, the 700,000 member Manchester Unity of Odd Fellows, the first plan was submitted to actuaries for a cost analysis. The societies made clear at this point that they were absolutely uncommitted to participation in any plan.[90] After the last meeting, on 15 December, the first phase of the evolution of national insurance ended. The actuarial report did not appear until March 1910.

By mid-December 1908, Liberal politics were in turmoil and the party's spirits were near desperation. On 24 November, meeting at Lansdowne House, after a good lunch and some desultory conversation about field sports, the Unionist peers determined to reject the Licensing Bill to which the House of Commons had devoted thirty-one and a half days.[91] Three days later, almost without debate, the House of Lords declined to give the measure a second reading.

This was not a gesture of opposition, rather of contempt. But the blow was more devastating for being almost unexpected. Balfour, to be sure, had given some thinly veiled warnings about the bill during the summer, but the bishops had spoken in its favor, and Asquith had written contentedly to the King in July that he could expect the bill for signature in the autumn session.[92] In October, precisely to mollify the House of Lords and in the face of strenuous nonconformist objection, the delaying period for the compulsory, unreimbursed, extinction of pub licenses was extended from 14 to 21 years.[93] Most members of the government, not to mention many peers, would have been in their graves before any harm was done.

The summary dismissal of the chief government measure of the 1908 session brought derision from the Unionist press, sharp warnings from the Liberal papers, and caused variously anger and despair among the members of Asquith's Cabinet. All of this was compounded by the breakdown at almost the same time of the negotiations with Church leaders over an educational settlement and the consequent withdrawal, early in December, of the fourth and last Liberal education bill. Even the lift provided by the undoubted popularity of the pension program, soon to begin, seemed to evaporate. Inevitably there were proposals that the government resign, but after an extended discussion on 9 December, the Cabinet agreed unanimously to remain in office although Asquith admitted to the King that the members were not yet able to reach a conclusion upon what to do next.[94] He emphasized however that a warm and protracted discussion on future policy took place.

Unlike Churchill, who was outraged at the Lords' action although his convictions about the evils of drink were hardly pressing, Lloyd George seemed unconcerned. He told both Daniel and Riddell that he planned a Thanksgiving service at the Treasury. He was looking forward to taxing the trade, he wrote to his brother, and the rejection provided the opportunity for some 'exquisite plans,' for outwitting the upper house in the budget.[95] Even though Riddell reports that he was told after the Cabinet meeting on 9 December when the government considered their position, that of the three members in favour of an early dissolution, two were Lloyd George and

Churchill, the evidence at hand shows precisely the opposite.[96] The letters and statements by the two men and letters about them by others uniformly suggest that both believed resignation in December 1908 would be a fatal mistake. Each saw that the days of licensing, education, and Church reform were over. These issues did not stir the soul of the British nation as Hugh Price Hughes had done in 1890 when, with shouting and vituperation, he forced Gladstone to break with Parnell. That era had passed. The Liberal administration of 1905 had squandered three years and much of its political capital trying to soothe the nonconformist conscience with measures that were essentially of another day.

The great uprising of 1906 somehow had failed, wrote A.G. Gardiner five years later. 'Protection would be the mould into which the future would run.'

> For three years it seemed that the opportunity had been lost. It is true great things were accomplished. United South Africa was founded and Old Age Pensions were granted. But we had opened up no new horizons. We were still in the old prison and the Lords held the key of the gate. The country was turning against the Liberal Party in weariness and were beginning to calculate when the election would come, and by how much the Liberals would lose. Mr. Chamberlain had made his bid. For the moment he had failed, but if his bid remained without challenge, if Liberalism could offer no alternative policy, then his future was assured.[97]

The man who saved British Liberalism, wrote the editor of the *Daily News*, was the Chancellor of the Exchequer, David Lloyd George. The party could no longer fight its battles on the grave of dead Gladstonianism. To have a parliamentary record, to win elections, to defeat the House of Lords, it had to have a policy. This Lloyd George had offered at the critical Cabinet meeting of 9 December. 'No dissolution—at least not before the Budget is over,' Lloyd George wrote his brother that day. 'The Prime Minister has approved my plans as they are now. I was with him now. "Budget Sensational."'[98] Certainly Lloyd George had been dropping hints of his plans to the press all that week. On Monday, 7 December, two days before the Cabinet, *The Times* in a full column of political notes had announced what became, indeed, the government program. There would be no dissolution and the list of proposals to be enacted before an election included as major items: land valuation, increased license duties, a graduated income tax, labor exchanges, invalidity and unemployment insurance.[99]

Lloyd George had discussed all of this at length with Churchill. The budget's immunity to tampering would provide the first opportunity to establish a Liberal reputation for accomplishment. Lucy Masterman, dining with Churchill (the Mastermans, married only the previous June, were still far closer to Churchill than to Lloyd George), found him so enraged he could hardly speak. Stabbing furiously at his bread he growled '"we shall send them such a Budget in June as shall terrify them, they have started the class war, they had better be careful." I asked him how long he thought the Government had to live. "If they thurvive the next Budget, two or three years. That'll be the tetht."'[100] Charles Masterman himself was not enthusiastic about deferring the battle until the Liberal record was established. Like many of the younger radicals of the party he wanted to begin the struggle with the House of Lords immediately. Writing a month later to congratulate his friend Arthur Ponsonby, Campbell-Bannerman's former secretary who had succeeded his master in Stirling District in May, upon a speech demanding 'resistance and defence' against the peers, he concluded: 'I may come out—on these lines— even now—I think I shall, if they decided on this insane George and Winston policy of hanging another 2-3 years.' What did Ponsonby think about an anti-peers amendment to the address 'to force the pace,' to 'dig'm out'?[101]

Two days after the 9 December Cabinet, Asquith announced at the National Liberal Club essentially what had been decided so far: there would be no dissolution, the government would take its case to the people at a time of its own choosing, not at a moment settled by Lord Lansdowne. But the House of Lords was now, he said, the 'dominating issue in politics' and the budget would be used to circumvent the upper chamber. 'Finance,' said the Prime Minister in conclusion and without specifying what measures he had in mind, 'is an instrument of great potency and also great flexibility (cheers) and it may be found, in some directions at any rate, a partial solvent of what, under existing constitutional conditions, would be otherwise insoluble problems'.[102]

At this point the question must be addressed as to whether Asquith or Lloyd George anticipated that the budget would provoke a House of Lords veto and whether they deliberately framed an instrument to cause such a determination. The matter is old, but not quite dead. Lloyd George said, of course, after the event that he had expected precisely what happened. He told Randolph Churchill this in the 1930s and was evidently telling other men the same thing long before that.[103] Not long after the passage of the Parliament Act, H.W. Massingham wrote: 'Those who knew Mr. Lloyd George's mind in those days [1909] knew also that he foresaw and planned a first rejection by the Lords and endorsement by the country, and a following attack on the Veto in which the peers were bound, whatever their tactics, to succumb.'[104] But Lloyd George's own accounts of his past motives, activities, and thoughts usually are the stuff of which legends are made, not histories. It must be noted in contradiction that in the foreword to an edition of his speeches published in August 1910, in effect before the passage of the Parliament Act, he was at pains to make clear that he had not tried to challenge the Lords. The budget was not an 'electioneering expedient.' The speeches printed in the book, he said, showed 'that the ideas which found form in the Finance Bill of 1909 had been in my mind years before the present Liberal Government was even in sight.' Moreover, this preface was dated 'Criccieth, August 1910' at the time, in fact, when he was preparing a proposal for a party coalition precisely to avoid a collision between the houses. (It should be remarked that the first speech which he considered to be part of the People's Budget was the Newcastle Address of 4 April, 1903.)[105]

Still there is contemporary evidence that the possibility of a Lords' veto was, at least, considered by some men. Asquith told J.A. Pease on 8 December that the rejection of the Licensing Bill was the most outrageous thing the Lords had ever done and the two men then discussed what would happen if the Lords threw out the budget. 'Keep it in the back of your mind,' confided Asquith finally, 'that we may have a dissolution next July if they do.'[106] On the same day Charles Hobhouse, who from his office at the Treasury knew better than anyone what Lloyd George was planning, grumbled in his diary:

> If the Cabinet give Ll.G. his way, he will find the money for next year which will probably be £12 millions in excess of this year's requirement by lowering the range of income tax so as to fully tax with incomes of £500, by a surtax on incomes over £5,000; by a 2/-capital tax on non-agricultural land: and by high licenses and increase on tea. Such proposals, if propounded to the country, ought to ensure the rejection of the Budget by the Lords, and force a dissolution, and ensure our irretrievable defeat.[107]

More important, Lloyd George evidently appreciated also the possibility of a peers' veto. At Liverpool, ten days after Asquith's address in the National Liberal Club, he challenged the peers to contest with the Liberals the issue of tariff reform. After some jokes about the rapid aging that had appeared in the population, particularly in Ireland, since the advent of old age pensions, he echoed the Prime Minister's assertion that the battle with the Lords would begin only when his side was ready and not when 'King Lansdowne' wanted it. But 'unless I am mistaken, before we are done we shall shatter the throne of this most uninteresting of all pretenders.' The Lords, he continued, now have a 'straight issue.... The Budget has got to go on sometime next year and if they want to put the alternative of taxing bread, by all means let them do it. I shall be perfectly prepared to take the opinion of my part of the world upon that proposal.... Free institutions of free trade, or, on the other hand, privileges and protection, taxes on bread, meat, and timber.... That is surely a straight issue,' he said rising to his peroration, 'and this is the issue, if the Lords want to stake their privileges on it, by all means let them do it.'[108]

These were strong words and they thrilled the Liverpool Liberals, but they also accurately defined the central point of contest in what would become the People's Budget. Its essence for the opposition was not really land taxes or, more important, land valuation. Much as the Lords hated these proposals they had little meaning for the nation at large. Moreover they were not new. Measures on these lines had appeared in the last three sessions and Lloyd George's commitment to land reform, of course, went back to his days in Criccieth. Nor was it the heavy taxes Lloyd George laid upon public houses. The central issue was the ability of free trade finance to counter the dynamism of the tariff reform revolution that was sweeping the Unionist party. If the budget won, Chamberlainism was dead. The tariff reformers, Lloyd George wrote to J.A. Spender in May 1909, 'are convinced that if this Budget goes through their cause is lost.'[109] Although its founder lay now crippled in a bath chair in Edgbaston, the new Unionism, demagogic, violent and reckless, had so far defeated the old Liberalism. The budget was the first installment of the New Liberalism. Lloyd George intended that the opposition should appreciate the challenge.

It does not follow that anyone wished, or expected, the Lords to throw the budget out.[110] In late November, just after the veto of the Licensing Bill, Riddell recalls Lloyd George ridiculing the idea that the peers would ever do the same to a budget.[111] 'Do you think they are mad?' snorted F.E. Smith to Lloyd George when the two discussed the question.[112] 'I learn that Lansdowne in private utterly scouts the suggestion that the Lords will reject the budget bill,' Churchill declared to Asquith late in December 1908. 'On this assumption you will, I presume, be making your plans for two more complete sessions.'[113]

This letter from the President of the Board of Trade to the Prime Minister, and a second on 29 December, are of special importance because they provide evidence, albeit at second hand, of the sequence of the political strategy which Lloyd George and Churchill discussed nearly every day. Lloyd George would make a statement on insurance in the budget speech, Churchill wrote, and he was himself working on both labor exchanges and unemployment insurance. But, he thought, unemployment insurance ought to wait until 'Lloyd George has found a way of dealing with infirmity or (wh. is possible) has found that there is no way.' Eventually unemployment insurance could be presented either as a part of an infirmity insurance bill or as a part of labor exchanges. 'This is the course of action wh. Lloyd George and I, after much debating, think best, and I should like to know what view you take upon it.'

'There is a tremendous policy in Social Organization,' he continued to the Prime Minister three days later:

> The need is urgent & the moment ripe. Germany with a harder climate and far less accumulated wealth has managed to establish tolerable basic conditions for her people. She is organized not only for war, but for peace. We are organized for nothing except party politics. The Minister who will apply to this country the successful experiences of Germany in social organization may or may not be supported at the polls, but he will have left a memorial which time will not deface of his administration. It is not impossible to underpin the existing voluntary agencies by a comprehensive system — necessarily at a lower level — of state action. We have at least two years. We have the miseries which this winter is inflicting upon the poorer classes to back us. And oddly enough the very class of legislation which is required is just the kind the House of Lords will not dare to oppose. The expenditure of less than ten million a year, not upon relief, but upon machinery, & thrift stimuli would make England a different country for the poor. And I believe that once the nation begins to feel the momentum of these large designs, it will range itself at first with breathless interest & afterwards solid support behind the shoulder of the Government. Here are the steps as I see them.
>
> 1. Labour Exchanges & unemployment insurance:
> 2. National Infirmity Insurance etc:
> 3. Special Expansive State Industries — Afforestation — Roads:
> 4. Modernized Poor Law i.e. classification:
> 5. Railway Amalgamation with State Control Guarantee:
> 6. Education compulsory till 17.

I believe there is not one of these things that canot be carried & carried triumphantly & that they would not only benefit the state but fortify the party. But how much better to fail in such noble efforts, than to perish by slow paralysis or windy agitation.

I say—thrust a big slice of Bismarckianism over the underside of our industrial system, & await the consequences whatever they may be with a good conscience.[114]

The burden of these letters, taken together, would appear to be that while the Lords would allow the budget to pass, the Liberals might be upset over one of the reform measures that Churchill and Lloyd George had concocted. If so the Liberals would have at hand the admirable issue of popular welfare versus the Lords. Alternatively, if nothing happened and the parliament of 1906 lived until the end of the 1910 session or into the spring of 1911, the party would have in place a full grown welfare record upon which to appeal for support.

Churchill was quite specific about this strategy in a letter to Massingham three weeks later. The Licensing Bill had been unpopular throughout England, he wrote. The Lords, who always acted upon excellent canvassing information, gained strength by rejecting it. The circumstances of the Education Bill were similar although he and Lloyd George had been willing to fight in January 1907. However today, said Churchill, 'I do not perceive a single argument for that course [resignation] except the Chinese—that you should commit suicide on the doorstep of the man who has wronged you.' Now men of whom Massingham approved had some power.

Very large plans are being industriously and laboriously shaped. They will certainly be brought forward. They may even acquire a national momentum. Two complete Sessions will be needed to produce and to finance them. They are worth doing for their own sake, whatever the upshot. I do not think the Lords will interfere with any of them. I am sure they cannot do so without coming near to creating that conjunction of forces which is most dangerous to them. Anyhow I would back them cheerfully with our political existence.

There is no reason why controversial political bills should not meanwhile move forward to the climax together—like a volley of grapeshot—in the last weeks of 1910. Then indeed—life or death, but with a chance of victory; and for something worthy of the effort and the risk.[115]

III

The story of the formulation of the 1909 Budget has its beginnings in the attempt to build a record for a desperate and dispirited Liberal party and in the need to find money for the unexpected costliness of old age pensions. Then, just at the end of 1908, a third element appeared. This was the frightening news, first discussed in the Cabinet early in December, that the Germans, far from reducing their rate of dreadnought building seemed to be accelerating the rate of construction of the ships in their 1908 program and worse, were letting contracts for the 1909 program even before the money for them had been appropriated by the Reichstag.[116] By 1912 Germany, it appeared, would have not 13 but at least 17 dreadnoughts, three-fourths the number possessed by Britain. Fisher's proportion of two keels for one was in danger.

The Cabinet discussed the new developments at length in a two-day meeting on 18 and 19 December and for the next few weeks concerned itself with little else.[117] While in Wales in September, Lloyd George, at Churchill's behest, had telegraphed McKenna urging the Admiralty to anticipate ship construction under the 1909 program. Could ships not yet authorized be contracted for immediately in order to alleviate unemployment in Scotland and the North, he asked? McKenna replied with a substantial essay on the logistics of warship construction. New designs for every ship took six months. He would do nothing without the approval of the Prime Minister. And anyway, he implied, it was none of Lloyd George's business.[118] Lloyd George sent McKenna a stinging and insulting reply and eventually Churchill, on his honeymoon, had to write McKenna saying that the idea was his and that he was concerned about distress around his new constituency in Dundee.[119] McKenna replied less tartly to Churchill, but the result was gossip in the Treasury, noted by the malevolent Charles Hobhouse in his diary, that Lloyd George was encouraging ministers to spend money so that he would have an excuse for extra taxation in the coming year.[120]

Despite what he proposed to McKenna, in the Cabinets of 18 and 19 December Lloyd George doubted the veracity of the Admiralty's intelligence. Warmly supported by Churchill he denounced the Board of Admiralty and Sir John Fisher who, he argued, could force the naval attachés in Europe to provide any sort of data he needed.[121]

McKenna, it will be remembered, had approved the previous spring the Sea Lords' estimates for the 1909 budget which included four dreadnoughts, or six if necessary. The whole thing, Lloyd George felt, was a cheap trick to show that six capital ships were now vital. After two days of wrangling Asquith characteristically proposed approving four dreadnoughts and adjourned debate on the other two until after the Christmas holidays. On 25 December Lloyd George left for Cannes. There on 3 January he wrote to Churchill from the Hotel Prince De Galles that he had heard from his secretary at the Treasury that the Admiralty wanted now, not six, but eight dreadnoughts in the 1909-10 program. 'I feared all along this would happen,' he told his friend. 'Fisher is a very clever person & when he found his programme in danger he wired Davidson [assistant private secretary to the King] for something more panicky — & of course he got it.'[122]

By the time the Cabinet reassembled late in January the press was printing alarmist stories about the increasing speed of German construction and of the resultant need for a larger British program, while the opposition in the House of Commons, aroused by information supplied from the Board of Admiralty, had begun to shout for eight dreadnoughts. The Cabinet itself was hopelessly split and McKenna, as he told G.M. Trevelyan many years later, was on the verge of resignation.[123]

Yet already Lloyd George was changing his position. On 24 January, he and a number of other ministers attended a seminar in which the Sea Lords gave details of the new evidence on Germany's shipbuilding capacity.

Lloyd George clearly was impressed and upbraided McKenna, unfairly, for not having informed the Cabinet before.[124] From this change in his opinion emerged the famous compromise of four dreadnoughts immediately and four others sanctioned but deferred. Lloyd George did not propose this to the Cabinet but sought approval first from Asquith. In a long letter on 2 February he warned the Prime Minister that the struggle over dreadnoughts was tearing the party to pieces. Invoking the names of Churchill and Morley in support, he argued that the bulk of the party took seriously the pledges of 1906 'to reduce the gigantic expenditure on armaments built up by the recklessness of our predecessors....But if Tory extravagance on armaments is to be exceeded, Liberals who have nothing to hope from this Parliament in the way of redress of their grievances will hardly think it worthwhile to make any effort to keep in office a Liberal Ministry.' Yet, he continued, if the allegations about the growth of the German program were true, the Admiralty proposals were hopelessly inadequate. 'The essential vice of the Admiralty plan is that it is a purely hand-to-mouth program unsuitable for any emergency. It is a poor compromise between two scares—the fear of the German navy abroad & the fear of the Radical majority at home.' What the Germans in fact were doing was to move forward the construction of already authorized battleships to relieve unemployment. 'This is the real explanation of the "anticipation" which has so thoroughly scared the Admiralty.' This was a good plan, he said, recalling his unpleasant exchanges with McKenna in September.

The core of Lloyd George's proposals was a long range program, sanctioned by parliament, with construction scheduled over a period of years. This would alarm neither the Germans nor the economists at home.[125]

Asquith considered the proposal for six days, talked with Crewe who approved, and answered on 8 February urging Lloyd George to develop his proposal. At the same time he deplored the tumult in the press. Lloyd George now answered immediately. He too deplored the press excitement but noted that the Unionist press 'the *Times*, the *D.T.*, *The Observer*... seemed to have been fully informed as to what was going on [within?] the Cabinet weeks ago.' He was glad to see that there was now the prospect of an agreement. 'I feel sure that a programme measured out over a period of years will give confidence to the public while it is more likely to win support on our side as being in fact more sober and restrained and not so menacing to the hope of those who are looking forward to great schemes of social reform.' As a postscript he added a draft public statement of his proposal which in fact contained the substance of the settlement that eventually occurred. 'H.M.G. may later in the financial year 1909-10 consider it desirable to make preparation for rapid construction, coming in a part of the following financial year, of further ships.' The government would ask parliament for special powers which could include, for the 1909-10 financial year, the amassing of gun mountings, guns, armor, and machinery for shipbuilding 'with a view to rapid construction of four more ships.'[126] Here was the essence of the compromise that emerged a month later, which Churchill described in his memoirs with more humor than accuracy: 'In the end a curious and characteristic solution was reached. The Admiralty had demanded six ships: the economists offered four: and we finally compromised on eight.'[127]

Lloyd George's proposal matched what Admiralty intelligence in fact professed to believe the Germans were doing: collecting material, particularly the complicated and rapidly evolving components of gun laying and fire control and the great naval rifles themselves, of which the dreadnoughts carried twice as many as previous battleships, so seriously straining both British and German manufacturing capacity. Yet aside from the technology, for Lloyd George the advantages of a delayed commitment to four more dreadnoughts were to be found in the time lag between the authorization of a ship and the beginning of the expenditure of any considerable sum of money upon it. McKenna had carefully explained in his letter in September that unless a ship were to be built from existing plans, in which case the benefits of new technical developments were lost, design took at least six months. Hence the cost of any ship begun late in the 1909-10 budget year, even though legally a part of that year's program as the Admiralty insisted the extra four must be, would fall almost entirely in the following fiscal years. The 1910-11 budget could take care of itself.

Lloyd George brought his proposal before the Cabinet on 15 February. As Asquith reported it to the King after outlining the divisions in the Cabinet—Churchill, Harcourt, Burns and Morley on one side; Grey Runciman, Crewe and Buxton on the other—'The Chancellor of the Exchequer, while siding personally with the former opinion, suggested as a compromise the adoption of a programme (sanctioned by act of Parliament) spread over a certain number of years, and so arranged as more or less to equalize the burden of expenditure. The Prime Minister, Lord Crewe and Sir Edward Grey were all disposed[?] to support[?] a settlement along these lines if the details could be satisfactorily arranged....' McKenna was opposed, but Asquith appointed a committee of himself, Lloyd George and Morley to interview again the Board of Admiralty.[128]

Asquith was not happy with this compromise, which he felt was forced upon him by the visible pacifism of the bulk of the Liberal party and by the press, among whom Lloyd George had far too many friends. 'The economists are in a state of wild alarm,' he wrote to Margot on 20 February, 'and Winston and LlG by their combined machinations have got the bulk of the Liberal press into the same camp....They...go about darkly hinting at resignation (which is bluff)...but there are moments when I am disposed summarily to cashier them both.'[129]

But on the other hand, neither were the Liberal radicals nor the Sea Lords content. Fisher wrote to McKenna on 21 February also hinting at resignation and demanding concrete assurances.[130] Eventually McKenna promised the First Sea Lord that the pledge would be explicit, enacted by parliament, and that the extra ships even though laid down in March 1910 would be a part of the 1909-10 program and would not diminish the following year's construction. Even so Fisher wrote back to McKenna: 'We are placing our whole and sole trust in you that these two jugglers don't outwit us.'[131]

The economists were equally discontented, if more polite. On 18 February J.A. Spender wrote to Lloyd George denouncing the postpone-ment of the extra dreadnoughts. Either the ships existed or they did not. The whole thing was 'a transparent shuffle.' Nevertheless the economizers should not resign he concluded. 'You and Winston are wrong in talking and thinking as if your remaining within the government would be surrender.'[132]

With everyone against it the compromise was bound to succeed.[133] On 5 March the Prime Minister told the Cabinet that the Sea Lords would sign the estimates—he did not specify how reluctantly. It was agreed that four dreadnoughts would be authorized imediately and laid down in July and October 1909 and that the collection of components would begin for the construction of four more to be laid down in April 1910 so that twenty dreadnoughts would be in commission by April 1912.[134] The agreement was published on 5 March on page 226 of the estimates, in almost precisely the words of Lloyd George's original draft of 8 February.[135]

The Cabinet had spent the latter part of January, all of February, and the first week of March wrestling with the Board of Admiralty. It did not begin to consider the budget until 18 March. In simplest terms what became the Finance Bill of 1909 may be considered as two distinct measures, one concerning revenue and one dealing with politics. As a revenue measure the problem was relatively straightforward although devastatingly large. Existing taxation would provide £148,300,000 in 1909-10. Hence with an estimated expenditure of £164,100,000 the Exchequer was left with a deficit of between £16 and £17 million. The two largest new items were, of course, £8 million for old age pensions (which itself turned out to be not enough) and £3 million for new warship construction (this in addition to sums necessary to continue work on four unfinished dreadnoughts and battle cruisers laid down between 1907 and 1909).[136] Two thirds of the deficit was to be covered by a large increase in income tax, a rise in the standard rate, and more important for the future, a supertax to be levied against incomes larger than a stipulated figure. However, the innovation, the revolution of the Budget of 1909, lay not so much in the graduated rate of income tax as in the resort to direct taxes, almost alone, to cover the huge new spending plans. In 1909 income tax became, and has remained, the first, rather than the last, tool of British fiscal policy.

British financial custom, and indeed Liberal Gladstonian principle, had always held that the income tax was a dangerous innovation, liable to abuse, to be regarded as a temporary expedient, annually renewed, and never allowed to become the principal basis for government finance. The amounts collected by the Board of Inland Revenue which generally dealt with direct taxes ought never to exceed the returns from the Board of Customs and Excise in indirect taxes. Indeed one of the many appeals of tariff reform would have been the strengthening and maintenance of this balance. (During the nineteenth century customs and excise normally provided about two-thirds of the government income and even after Harcourt's death duties and the South African War direct taxes reached no more than equality with indirect.)

Soon after the Liberals came to power, in May 1906, a select committee had been appointed to investigate the possibility of a progressive income tax and in November 1906 had reported favorably. But despite this support Lloyd George clearly was not enthusiastic and he approached the matter most reluctantly. Even after he became Chancellor of the Exchequer he had emphasized to Herbert Lewis that he thought a supertax impracticable and, as was noticed by many during the debate on old age pensions, he had cheerfully admitted many times that he did not know how he would pay for them. During the winter of 1908 and 1909 most of the energy that was not devoted to resisting John Fisher or playing golf in Cannes was applied to reflections on land taxes, not income taxes. In his letter to the King on the last day of March, Asquith informed Edward VII that the Cabinet had not yet heard the Chancellor's proposals on taxation although Lloyd George had promised a paper on the subject.[137]

Lloyd George's income tax proposals finally were embodied in two short memoranda from Robert Chalmers and John Bradbury outlining a scheme for an extra levy of between 6d and 1s in the pound, falling on all taxpayers earning more than £5,000 but with some portion of their income, between £2,000 and £3,000, to be deducted. Chalmers may be regarded as the father of progressive tax rates, Lloyd George later told D.R. Daniel. He was the only member of the Treasury staff to support the idea. In his memorandum he devoted most of his time to a justification of the equity of an increased tax rate on wealthier citizens. Chalmers's central point, aimed obviously at the Prime Minister and suggesting some collaboration with Lloyd George, was that the super tax could not be regarded as an innovation because a precedent existed in Asquith's 1907 Budget with the abatement to 9d in a pound allowed for earned income. Unearned income, in effect, had been subject to a 3d 'super tax.' However, the strongest argument for the proposal, of no less force for being buried in Chalmers and Bradbury's statistics, was the fact that a tax on incomes over £5,000 would affect, on Bradbury's figures, only ten thousand taxpayers while, at the rate of 6d. on the pound on the portion of individual income over £3,000, as it was eventually set, it would produce when fully collected £2,600,000.[138]

Over the first weekend in April, the Cabinet, as Asquith recited to the King, was almost entirely occupied by continuous discussion of the financial plans of the Chancellor of the Exchequer. On Tuesday, 6 April, the members agreed to a financial package that included 6d on incomes over £5,000 and also an increase of 2d on unearned income over £700, thus increasing Asquith's differential from 3d to 5d, and adding 2d (i.e. from 12 to 14d in the pound) to the tax on all incomes earned or unearned over £3,000. All together these would produce about £4,500,000. Increases in estate and legacy rates might produce £4,500,000 and a new tax on public house licenses, collected by Customs and Excise but based upon the value of the premises, in fact an income tax, another £2,500,000. With relief of £10 for children under 16 years of age for less affluent taxpayers and certain other deductions the value of the package was about £10,200,000, of which only £3,400,000 would come from indirect taxes.[139]

Asquith's support was of the greatest importance, Lloyd George reported to his brother on the evening of 6 April. The Cabinet was strongly divided.[140] To D.R. Daniel at the end of May, with the struggle in parliament already under way, Lloyd George was far more explicit. Asked how the Budget had fared in the Cabinet he replied 'The battle in the House of Commons is as nothing compared with That!' He got no help from Burns.[141] Only Churchill, and above all the Prime Minister, supported him. Of

Asquith he could not say too much. 'He has, like me, come from among the ordinary people....He hadn't perhaps, like myself, had experience of the worker's life, his house and fare, not at all, till he came to his present high position.' But he understood. Yet also, Lloyd George admitted, he knew Asquith did not like unpleasantness in the Cabinet and would always stop it. Hence Lloyd George would stage a row and win in this way.[142]

In the budget Lloyd George increased the productivity of the income tax by about 50%, from about £30 million where it had stood quite constantly since the turn of the century to £45 million in the first normal year after the Budget of 1909. Similarly, in the year before the war, the surtax produced a little more than 6% of all income revenue. Afterwards it produced regularly over 20% of a much larger total.

Here lies the revolution, as opposed to the rhetoric, associated with the Budget of 1909. The income tax was no longer the financial supplement that since Peel it technically had been. The traditional restraints were now gone. It could be raised to any level. 'The income tax,' said Lloyd George bluntly in his budget address, 'imposed originally as a temporary expedient, is now in reality the centre and sheet anchor of our financial system.'[143]

These considerations sharpened the distinction between Liberal and Unionist policy. The differences were not only the immediate ones of how to pay for pensions and dreadnoughts, although assuredly this was the immediate issue. For the future the departure made in 1909 was of prodigious importance. Britain would become the quintessential high income tax country among major nations of Europe.[144] Moreover tax policy henceforth would be a class issue in politics in a way it never before had been. Tariff reform, whatever its imperfections, promised benefits for everyone and demanded contributions from all. The progressive income tax, on the other hand, particularly when coupled with an income transfer agency such as old age pensions, divided the nation into two groups: those who paid money in and those who received it. Balfour seized upon this central fact with devastating simplicity in the debate upon the budget resolutions. Noting that Lloyd George had pointed out that the liability for super tax would be £5,000 rather than £3,000 because with the former figure he would have to deal with only ten thousand people instead of twenty-five thousand, the leader of the opposition said: '...It is very easy for a Chancellor of the Exchequer in a democratic constitution to throw a very great burden on a small number of people who themselves for the very fact that they are a small number of people have very little practical power of making their voice heard.'[145] Balfour's philosophic insight was impeccable. The battle of the Budget of 1909 developed as a war upon the rich. British politics henceforth were to be the story of class politics.

If for the future of Britain, the innovation of the progressive tax rate was of great significance, for Lloyd George in 1909 this part of the budget represented only a solution to an immediate political problem and the super tax was nothing more than the most expedient method of attack, pitting the many against the few. He would display the Liberal party as the party of the masses and unmask the magnates of Britain as selfish cowards who demanded battleships to protect their wealth but who were unwilling, on the other hand, to pay for them. The other area of the budget, however, the land taxes, was founded in his own background. The campaign for land reform was one of the very few projects in his political life to which he held a real and genuine personal commitment. Since the beginning of his public career, the landlord, the owner of the Church and the school, the bully of voting tenants, the collector of rents and royalties, had been his enemy. Protected by a tax system of incredible antiquity—the parish quotas for the old land and property tax had been fixed in 1798—and by a rating system that imputed value only to improvements while laying the burden of rates upon the occupier rather than the owner, the landlord, as Lloyd George endlessly reiterated, made no contribution toward the welfare of the community in which he lived and which gave his property value. English land law was probably the only field of politics in which Lloyd George possessed extensive systematic knowledge. Nevertheless, he had always approached land reform, as he approached most social issues, with loud public denunciations of the evils attendant on the land monopoly with very little indication of what he proposed to do about it.

Lloyd George's first exposition of his plans for land tax appeared in a Cabinet memorandum of 5 December 1908 entitled 'The Imposition of a National Tax on Land Values.' Its author was Edgar Harper, the statistical officer of the London County Council.[146] This was supplemented the next month by a description of the method of assessment and taxation of real property in the City of New York by Lawson Purdy of that municipality's Department of Taxation.[147] Basically Lloyd George proposed a tax of ld in the pound on the capital value of all land worth more than £50. This levy would be paid by the ground rent owner, not by the occupier, and would be based upon the value of the land alone. The key to any proposal for land reform, and central to Lloyd George's plans as they developed in the next few years, was the accomplishment of a national valuation of real property separate from any improvement of buildings, based upon the site value alone. The separate assessment of lands and improvements was a common demand of land reformers of every school and bills to authorize such valuation had appeared in the King's speeches in 1907 and 1908 but had been caught and destroyed by the House of Lords.

The fact is that valuation of all British land, separate from improvements, was for Lloyd George of far greater importance in the Budget of 1909 than any particular form of land taxation. Valuation was the key to all other reform: to the setting of agriculture and building grants, to the enfranchisement of leaseholders, and of course to any of a dozen forms of land taxation or rating. Once some estimate of the wealth tied up in land was obtained, methods of redistributing it could be devised. Lloyd George made his intentions clear in a memorandum circulated on 13 March as the Cabinet was about to take up the budget. His two objects he said were first to obtain a valuation in the United Kingdom and second to raise revenue from land taxes, which he estimated would come to about £500,000 in the first year although more in subsequent years. But, he made clear, the taxes themselves were of subsidiary importance and were in the budget only to justify the provision for valuation. 'It is now clear,' he continued, 'that it would be impossible to secure the passage of a separate valuation bill during the existence of the present Parliament owing to the opposition of the Lords, and therefore the only possible chance which the Government have of redeeming their pledges in this respect is by incorporating proposals involving land valuation in a Finance Bill.'

> On the other hand, it must be borne in mind that proposals for valuing land which do not form part of a provision for raising revenue in the financial year for which the Budget is introduced would probably be regarded as being outside the limits of a Finance Bill by the Speaker of the House of Commons. I have consulted Sir Courtenay Ilbert on the subject, and he is distinctly of the opinion that, unless it is contemplated to raise substantial revenue during the year, valuation clauses would be regarded by the authorities of the House as being a fit subject for a separate Bill, and not for a Finance Bill.

Therefore some sort of land taxes, almost any sort of taxes, would have to be included.[148]

Nevertheless, it was the taxes rather than the valuation that stirred up opposition in the Cabinet and in the party at large. They had to be justified separately. Lloyd George's notes for his speech to the Cabinet, probably of 18 March when he introduced his land proposals, dealt mostly with valuation as a political weapon against the Lords, but emphasized nevertheless that the money from the land taxes would be extremely valuable.

> —want revenues—want millions more next year—just in that position where an extra £500,000 makes all the differences between screwing estate duties or income tax to a point where they will appear oppressive —incidental advantage of the first magnitude—Enables us to legislate on one of the greatest questions submitted to the country despite the House of Lords. This is what really makes our supporters so keenly desirous for it
> —how do we stand in reference to the H. of Lords?
> —education—temperance—land valuation thwarted checkmated beginning to look silly
> menace followed by inaction or rather by action on something else country sees this—produces a sense of our ineptitude & impotence short of dissolution we can only walk round the Lords by means of our financial powers.
> Licensing—but this imperfect remedy—even if it be a remedy valuation we can completely circumnavigate them.[149]

The taxes described in the memorandum of 13 March have excited a good deal of interest among historians. But in fact Lloyd George did not take them seriously. In the future the valuation would provide many options and that was the important goal. For the moment the taxes were merely camouflage. 'I knew the land taxes would not produce much,' he remarked to Lord Riddell in May, 1912 when the two were discussing the second phase of land reform, the land campaign. 'I only put them in the Budget because I could not get a valuation without them.'[150]

The various land duties suggested influence from many schools of land reformers although Lloyd George had himself referred to all of them many times before. The sole expert help that he received, outside the Treasury, beginning what would become in the next few years an important association for him, was from Charles Masterman. Masterman was a member of the United Committee for the Taxation of Land Values and had indeed made the pursuance of the government commitment to site value taxation a condition for his acceptance of office at the Local Government Board in 1908.[151] Together with Robert Chalmers in the Treasury Masterman may be regarded as the efficient author of the land clauses of the Finance Bill.[152] There is no evidence to support the assertion in the Hobhouse diary that Hobhouse and Haldane helped Lloyd George.[153]

Of the five land taxes proposed three were relatively straightforward: a duty of 1s in the pound on the value of mineral property and on present ground rents from improved property, with 1d (later reduced to 1/2d) on the capital value of undeveloped land worth more than £50. Two others were far more complicated and, like the duty on undeveloped land, depended entirely upon completion of the national valuation. The first was the tax of 1s in the pound on the assessed capital value of improved sites. There would be various deductions from this levy, such as the old land and property tax, but when it was complete it could, potentially, bring in a huge amount. Finally Lloyd George proposed a tax of 20% on the increased value of any real property sold or inherited after 30 April 1909 and a similar tax of 10% on any profit accruing to a ground rent owner at the termination of a lease. In the case of land owned by corporations, where death did not occur, the inheritance duty would be levied in 1914 and every 15 years thereafter. The increment value tax made necessary, Lloyd George explained later, the tax on the value of unimproved property. While the latter would not be very productive financially, it was necessary to ensure an honest valuation for the purposes of the former. Valuation in the beginning would have to be accomplished on the basis of estimates furnished by the landlords themselves. He was interested only in land held near cities, for speculation, not genuine agricultural land. The unimproved property tax would prevent landowners from assigning an excessive valuation to their holdings in order to escape the increment duty. Each tax would facilitate the working of the other like, he said, a scissors.[154]

In the Cabinets of 18 and 19 March Lloyd George's colleagues immediately leaped upon the land taxes. The most unpopular were the levies on ground rents and on the capital value of land and clearly reflected opinions outside the government among wealthy Liberals. Soon after the return from the Christmas holidays Asquith had begun to receive letters, whether solicited or not he did not say, from Liberal supporters in the House of Commons. On 22 January the Prime Minister circulated printed extracts of three of these, authors unnamed, among the Cabinet finance committee which was by this time struggling, apparently unsuccessfully, to induce Lloyd George to produce a definitive set of tax proposals. Lloyd George evidently did not take the finance committee seriously—it was made up almost entirely of men with whom he was already on bad terms, McKenna, Haldane, and Loreburn. Nevertheless he knew well enough the problems that could accrue through a revolt of the rank and file of the party. He had organized several of these himself. The letters, quoted in Asquith's memorandum, were frank and caustic. 'You and Lloyd George don't know whether you are trying to raise revenue, bring land onto the market, or be like Henry George,' wrote one Liberal, described only as a well known West Country landlord.[155] But the substance of all three letters was that the taxes on capital values and ground rents would destroy all the relief given by the Agricultural Rating Act, would devastate Liberalism in the countryside, and worst of all would violate existing leases which specified uniformly that taxes and rates on the ground were the obligation of the occupier, not the owner.

Lloyd George undertook to answer these letters, point by point, in an ill-tempered and uncharacteristically long memorandum. He tried to show that the party was already pledged to land value taxes, but that he would be willing to exclude agricultural land from the capital value tax. As for existing contracts Robert Peel had specified in 1842 that existing contracts would not stand in the way of the collection of the property tax and that anyway the writers of the letters were hardly unprejudiced witnesses. He knew who they were and they were all opulent landlords.[156]

This battle of memoranda obviously affected the struggle in the Cabinet on 18 and 19 March, but it meant more than that. There were, according to the yearbook of the Land Nationalization Society, 130 Members of Parliament who were members of the association.[157] Certainly there were several hundred other young Liberals who counted some sort of land reform among their various causes although many, Masterman for example, belonged to more than one organization. (The *Liberal Yearbook* for these years shows nine societies associated with the Liberal party that featured land reform of some kind prominently among their goals.) Yet Lloyd George, at this stage at least, was only imperfectly aware of the latent hostility toward land taxes among the older members of his party. '...there are at the outside,' he wrote in his memorandum to the Finance Committee, answering the letters Asquith had circulated, 'six members of the Liberals' side of the house who oppose it [the taxation of land values] in principle. They have never mustered more than three in the Division Lobby when the Government proposals bearing on this subject have submitted to the House.'[158] In his long conversation with Daniel four months later, he was only slightly more realistic, admitting when Daniel asked him whether a number of rich Liberals did not disapprove, that there were some. There was for example 'Sir T.W. [Thomas Whittaker] who can't care less how I treat the publicans, but Oh Injustice once I touch his leaseholds, or the properties of his companies.' On the other hand John Brunner was very helpful. At this point Maggie interjected to say that the rich hated John Brunner.[159]

According to the account he gave to Herbert Lewis, Lloyd George was able to push the land clauses through the Finance Committee by simple bullying: challenging the Lord Chancellor, Loreburn, whose radical credentials were at least as good and far older than Lloyd George's, 'you were concerned for your friends the Dukes,' and with similar charges for the other members of the committee.[160] But this was not possible in the full Cabinet. At its second discussion of the budget on 19 March, the Cabinet rejected his proposals for levies on improved land and ground rents, leaving only the taxes on unimproved land and upon the increment after sale or transfer, and the mineral rights duties.[161] The stated objection was, as it had been in all previous discussions, that taxes on ground rent owners of improved property contravened existing leases.

Here opened a substantial philosophical breach, never satisfactorily closed during the debates on the 1909 Budget and so providing the initial impetus for the second phase of the land reform program which opened with the so-called land campaign in 1912 and ended in the disastrous Budget of 1914. How were the older members of the Liberal party, who had considered the Irish Land Acts socialism, who had pushed Gladstone to announce the abolition of the income tax in 1874, who saw reform as extension of the franchise or Welsh disestablishment, to regard an attack on property, the most elemental of human rights? The Liberal 'cave' that began to form early in the year, grew to about thirty after the budget was presented. Many of its members were of the Liberal League such as Robert Perks and several were former Unionists who had become Liberals over tariff reform, among them Ivor Guest whom Lloyd George only four years earlier had helped to sponsor in Cardiff. Most were old, some nearing the end of their parliamentary life. Most were wealthy. All in all they were a group the Liberals might hesitate to offend. In 1909 the 'cave' represented a protest rather than a threat, but as land reform revived after the constitutional struggles of the next two years and after the great Liberal majority of 1906 was reduced in the elections of 1910, it presented a danger that could not be ignored.[162]

Necessarily, the growth of a Liberal opposition to land reform involves the question of what Lloyd George intended with the land clauses. If he did not think the specific taxes in the budget were of much importance, what did he expect to accomplish with the valuation for which the taxes were a cover? The answer is that in 1909 probably he was not sure. He was, as always, working toward a goal which might be defined as a revival of rural Britain. (Even though land reform was clearly also an urban issue, Lloyd George usually thought in terms of the countryside.) But his route there he did not yet know. Eventually, probably through conversations with Charles Masterman, he would come to learn that the best use for valuation of improved sites lay not in revenue for the Treasury but in rating by local authorities, thus shifting the burden of rates from the tenant to the landlord and expanding also the financial resources of county and borough government. He received a deputation of municipal officials in mid-March who protested the land tax and insisted that any levy on site values belonged to them as a rate.[163] This may account for his first proposal, which was to give one half of the produce of the land taxes to the municipalities. All this was reinforced by Charles Masterman who had explained in a letter to Asquith of 15 January 1909 that moving assessments from building to site value 'was the only way that relief can come to such forlorn districts as West Ham' (his constituency). In addition Lloyd George may have noticed the significant conclusion by the assessor of New York, Lawson Purdy, that in his experience the assessment of the site 'on the whole does not increase rentals but decreases selling value.'[164] This combination of site value rating for improved property, the fixing by tribunals of lower farm rents which would be based upon the real, not the speculative, value of land, and the increasing of agricultural laborers' wages based upon the farmer's lower rent cost, would become by 1912 the land program. To all of it the land valuation of 1909 was central. Lloyd George did not have the finished program in his mind at that time, yet the land campaign had begun.

In the midst of budget preparations, on 12 March, only days before he presented the land clauses to the Cabinet, Lloyd George appeared in court to press a suit for libel against the popular and conservative Sunday paper, the *People*. In early January, while Lloyd George was at Cannes, the journal had published a series of items of gossip which, while not naming him, had made clear that a prominent politician was about to be called as a corespondent in a divorce suit and that friends had found an 'alternative' solution.[165] John Rowland, Lloyd George's secretary, no doubt at the Chancellor's suggestion, had consulted George Riddell, who advised Lloyd George not to take legal action but agreed to go to see W.T. Madge, Managing Director of the paper to try to get an apology and possibly a nominal sum.[166] Evidently Riddell's mission was unsuccessful for in March the suit came to trial with Rufus Isaacs leading for Lloyd George and Raymond Asquith and F.E. Smith as juniors. Edward Carson and Edward Duke represented the *People*.[167] Lloyd George was present with Maggie at his side, after, according to his son, a morning of tearful pleading in which he vowed his career would be ruined if she did not appear.[168] There were no fireworks; Lloyd George swore that there was not a word of truth to the allegations. Carson without cross-examination said his client agreed and was prepared to pay £1,000. The money eventually financed a new village institute in Llanystumdwy which Maggie later opened with appropriate ceremonies. When Lloyd George next appeared in the House of Commons he was received with cheers on all sides.[169]

This cannot be the entire story. Lloyd George seemed to be unable to avoid trouble of this kind. The previous summer, on 29 July, the *Bystander* had published an even less circumstantial item that there had been rumors that the new Chancellor of the Exchequer was having problems with women. This could have referred to the German trip which would commence two days later and which included Mrs. Charles Henry. In any case the editor of the *Bystander*, appalled at what appeared in his paper, paid £300 without any legal action. But neither article provided much more than innuendo and in the *People* article, evidently the more serious, he had not been named. Subsequently Lloyd George biographers have said that the aggrieved husband, whoever he was, had been bought off for £20,000.[170] But there was no reference to this in either article nor at the trial.

On the other hand, both reports could have been a reflection of some larger current story. Isaacs's opening remarks had specified that rumors had been in circulation for some time and reports had appeared in colonial newspapers. More significant, there are a few bits of evidence that Lloyd George had been troubled for several years by a fairly consistent whispering campaign of the sort about which he complained after the Edwards case. Riddell, who acted as an intermediary on such occasions, told A.J. Sylvester many years later that he had first met Lloyd George at the house on

Wandsworth Common, the simple furnishing of which he described accurately in his diary, when he had gone there to advise Lloyd George about a libel case.[171] As Lloyd George left this house after Mair's funeral in December 1907, the contemplation of a legal action at least two years before the *People* case indicates a continuing problem. J.A. Pease furnished more direct evidence when he told Asquith on 15 February 1909, after the *People* article, that gossip asserted that his Chancellor of the Exchequer was either suffering from or subject to blackmail and that increasingly his 'position was making things unpleasant.'[172] The question remains: for what was Lloyd George being blackmailed, in whose marriage had he intruded? The *People* article did not make clear when the event occurred but the description suggested the Edwards case. William George says flatly that the *People* libel was a revival of the Edwards affair of 1897.[173] If this is so the reported £20,000 payment represented a new fact that may provide the reason for the attempt at extortion. The basic charge, that Lloyd George had been cited by Dr. Edwards, was hardly unknown, but the reason for the husband's startling withdrawal of the charge against Lloyd George, even after obtaining his wife's confession, had remained a mystery. One could also question whether Mrs. Edwards's physician's appearance a year later asking for the intervention of the Queen's Proctor before the decree was made final had not been occasioned by some evidence of collusion that had turned up. This was the ordinary reason for the intervention of that official. Lloyd George of course had a good deal of evidence to disprove any wrongdoing with Kitty Edwards on the night of 4 February 1896, but the payment of £20,000, if it were true and public, would have convinced many people that he had something to hide, a misdeed which had occurred perhaps on another night. It could have been a cause for blackmail. All of this, of course, is speculation. Nevertheless the evidence asserts that something was afoot, that Lloyd George had been aware of it for several years, and that as in 1897 and 1898, he had been unable to find anyone to take to court. Then the *People*, having heard perhaps some, but not all, of the story had published an incorrect version allowing him legally to clear his name without admitting all the facts. He had tried unsuccessfully to do this at the second Edwards hearing and he and Isaacs would use essentially the same stratagem again in March 1913 in the suit against *Le Matin* during the Marconi affair.

Lloyd George would have more narrow escapes, none, given the brittleness of Edwardian propriety, with more potential for political devastation. A society that saw little ethical connection between private behavior and public good form would react in horror at official public notice, such as a divorce case, of a breach of the latter, while ignoring entirely the former. Many of the men who cheered Lloyd George in the House of Commons at his plucky and clever defense of himself were not his friends, as their public outcry over the Marconi shares, when he was in truth innocent, would show. Some may have reflected that they were more fortunate only by the grace of God.

IV

Lloyd George began his budget speech at 3:10 in the afternoon on 29 April. He spoke until a little after 8 o'clock with an interval of thirty minutes' rest. It was the longest budget speech since Gladstone's first of 1853 and, from all accounts, the worst in history. Lloyd George 'can make a vulgar but effective speech,' wrote Hilaire Belloc, at that time Liberal member for Salford South, to Maurice Baring. 'Why on earth he had gone to pieces like that no one can make out. He spoke like a man in the last stages of physical and mental decay. One could hardly hear his voice. His speech was read from beginning to end from typewritten notes and was simply deplorable. It lasted four hours, of which quite two and one half consisted of long stupid paragraphs about the rich being rich and the poor being poor.'[174] Belloc, who found the actual tax proposals excellent, insisted that his reaction was the general one.

However, as Belloc emphasized, Lloyd George's budget address was far more than an account of Britain's finances. It was a statement of the New Liberalism, a program for the future which dealt with matters only marginally concerned with taxation and expenditure.[175] He began naturally with a statement about dreadnoughts—four dreadnoughts cost 2d on the income tax for each of two years—but moved quickly to social and land reform, sickness and invalidity insurance, unemployment insurance, and land development. All of these, he reiterated, were a natural outgrowth of old age pensions. The aged were not the only sufferers of deprivation, so were the sick and disabled, the widowed, the underpaid and the unemployed. Germany had already shown what could be done. So far he had said all of this before many times. It was a summary of a dozen previous speeches and conversations with Churchill. The reference to Germany was followed however by some news. Why should Britain not use the German plan? Because 'at the present moment there is a network of powerful organizations in this country...which have succeeded in inducing millions of workmen to make systematic provision for the troubles of life....No scheme would be profitable, no scheme would be tolerable, which would do the least damage to those highly beneficent organizations. On the contrary it must be the aim of every well-conducted plan to encourage, and, if practicable, as I believe it is, to work through them.'[176] The government, he said, was already in communication with the friendly societies and other bodies. (Soon after the introduction of the budget, Lloyd George sent letters to the presidents of the major friendly societies inviting each of them to read his flattering references to their organization in the budget speech and promising again that his invalidity scheme would only strengthen them. He suggested they announce to their organizations at the annual meetings that negotiations with the government had begun.)[177]

Among all Lloyd George's proposals for future action mentioned in his speech, the one derived most clearly from his personal experience, his 'pet child' as he described it to Sir John Brunner, was the development commission.[178] As usual, he was majestically eloquent about the potential benefits of systematic improvements of the nation's resources, but beyond afforestation, he was mysterious about what he proposed to do, except that a board would be established with £200,000 taken from unspent departmental balances to do something. '...the grant will be utilized in the promotion of schemes...for...development of the resources of the country. It will include besides forestry expenditure upon scientific research in the interest of agriculture..., the encouragement and promotion of cooperation, the improvement of rural transport...and measures for attracting labour back to the land by small holdings or reclamation of wastes....'

> We have, more especially during the last sixty years, in this country accumulated wealth to an extent which is almost unparalleled in the history of the world, but we have done it at an appalling waste of human material. We have drawn upon the robust vitality of the rural areas of Great Britain, and especially of Ireland, and have spent its energies recklessly in the devitalizing atmosphere of urban factories and workshops as if the supply were inexhaustable. We are now beginning to realize that we have been spending our capital at a disastrous rate, and it is time we should make a real, concerted, national effort to replenish it.

There was wasted land and wasted lives, idle land in the hands of idle men.

This was not rhetoric. These evil equations he believed existed. His words about the development commission could have been used as an introduction to the Bedford and Swindon speeches of 1913 announcing the land program. Indeed they would have fitted into the Limehouse and Newcastle addresses later in 1909. In the progressive income tax and the super tax Lloyd George found money to pay for pensions and dreadnoughts, in the duties on pub licenses he kept the Liberal government's promise to nonconformists, invalidity and unemployment insurance gave the Liberals a program, but land reform and development were his own. Here was the project he would return to after the crowded years of 1910 and 1911 and which would occupy him until the war.

Austen Chamberlain's response to Lloyd George in the evening of 29 April was openly conciliatory, even admiring. 'With a good deal' of what the Chancellor of the Exchequer said, 'and with a great number of the objects which he has set before the House I, for one, heartily sympathize....'[179] However, with the beginning of formal debate upon the budget resolutions on 3 May, Balfour took up the challenge implied in Lloyd George's explanation. The budget was, as the Chancellor had stated in his speech, a war budget, it was the war of the many against the few, said Balfour in a statement of unusual violence.

> You have apparently made it your principle to distinguish arbitrarily between one kind of property and another. So blind and ignorant are you of the fact that it is impossible to attack one kind of property... without throwing a shade of fear...and suspicion over every other class of property. Much of the evil you have done has been done even by the fact of your proposals. Whatever the House may do with them, even the fact that you have proposed them...has disturbed the mind of everybody who reflects on the many conditions on which an individualistic society, so long as it lasts, can alone flourish. Your scheme is arbitrary and unjust...by the very proposals you have made you have given a shock to confidence and credit, which will take a long time to recover.[180]

Lloyd George was under no illusions about Unionist intentions, although he usually reserved his invective for public speeches while retaining his characteristic courtesy and amiability within the House of Commons. This was not ordinary party warfare. The opposition intended to win, and indeed felt they must win. But meanwhile there were many, within the government as well as out of it, already anxious for compromise.[181] In his long conversation with Llewelyn Williams and D.R. Daniel at Brighton on 21 May, already cited, when the debate on the budget resolutions was coming to an end, Lloyd George wondered aloud, whether, even at this early date, the budget could go though intact. Williams asked whether there would be pressure on the House of Lords to veto it. (Immediately after the budget speech, the Chairman of the Tariff Reform League, Lord Ridley had stated that while he did not wish to forecast any decisions, the House of Lords had never before interfered with financial matters because the government was conducted by 'sane men, but now there was a House of Commons controlled by a pack of madmen and they had to take different measures.')[182] Lloyd George, wrote Daniel, replied to Williams:

'Yes, as much pressure as the extremists can put. That's their hope. Whether they can carry Balfour as far as that we don't know yet. He knows full well what that means, in confusion for the country and to his party if it comes into power and what it means to the House of Lords in the end, but when you get a solid bloc of a party wanting authority they are none too careful of their methods ....'
Bonar Law told Lloyd George the other day that putting a tariff at once in their first session would be their plan .... From all this it is fairly clear that their force would be put at once to destroy the Budget somehow, at once. 'They see,' said G, 'that now's their chance for tariff reform. That little devil (that's the word) [presumably Bonar Law] will have ten million next year to bribe the electorate with, by all manner of social reforms and relief from taxation. They will see that this budget will if carried be a complete vindication of free trade.'

Lloyd George added that he wished John Bright were available to arouse the country.[183]

Whether or not Lloyd George was absolutely a convinced free trader may be a matter for conjecture. But there can be no doubt that in 1909 he was certain that the mutilation of his budget in the House of Commons would result in the triumph of tariffs, the end of the New Liberalism, and most important the destruction of land reform. With import duties the Unionists could match the appeal of his own program with a variety of welfare measures equally tempting to the working class, while dropping the land program. His sense of popular politics told him that for the ordinary voter there was little difference between Chamberlainite Unionist democracy and radical reforming Liberalism. For the future health of Liberalism, after the budget, he needed another issue.

These speculations impel one toward the conclusion that his public campaign for the budget, which began in late July with the famous Limehouse speech, may have been designed precisely to force the Lords to throw out the budget, so allowing him to shift the emphasis in party debate from the relatively straightforward one of progressive income taxes versus import duties to the more favorable ground of the peers against the people. Such was J.A. Spender's opinion after the event. Had the budget been in Asquith's hands, he wrote, it would have been passed after protest. But the volleys of gratuitous insults that began at Limehouse 'drove the Tory party off its mental balance.'[184] Charles Masterman, although with a different view of the outcome, concurred. 'Fortunately, from our point of view insane counsels prevailed,' his wife recalled him saying years later.

> If the House of Lords had passed the budget in December instead of forcing an election which compelled them to pass it three months later, the Liberal Party would have been like a beetle on its back. We had entered into a streak of bad unemployment. The slogan 'tax the foreigner' would no longer have been dominated by the slogan 'God gave the land to the people.' Half the electors hated an Education Bill, almost all the electors hated the Licensing Bill—distrustful of a raid on the working man's beer.
> We were losing every by-election and had nothing to offer except Welsh Disestablishment, which would have put the lid on as far as England and Scotland were concerned. The Conservatives would have been returned with a great majority in 1910. England would have become a protection-ist instead of a free trade country....'[185]

Masterman's recollection after years of electoral ill-fortune may have been unduly pessimistic. Almost certainly Lloyd George's own reflections by the middle of July were otherwise. The budget was an excellent electoral weapon, generally its most popular features were those that the Lords liked the least and, as the months passed, Liberal prospects, as by-elections showed, were improving. 'Members tell me that it [the budget] has put new heart into the Party and that they find a change in the tone of their meetings', he wrote to J.A. Spender on 24 May, two days before the Finance Bill was introduced. 'I hear also from the other side that their efforts to decry it at public meetings are a complete failure, that they can arouse no indignation except among very wealthy people on the platform and that the Tariff Reformers are especially depressed as they are convinced that if the Budget goes through their cause is lost.'[186] Lloyd George of course was always full of optimism and confidence about his own projects but the tone of the letter to Spender is generally confirmed by Arthur Lee, Conservative Member for Fareham since 1901, who was in some demand in the summer of 1909 as an anti-Budget speaker. Lee recalls that he learned early it was never wise even before normally anti-budget audiences, to mention Lloyd George's name. It always evoked a cheer and made the meeting hostile.[187]

Lloyd George's opinion was not, however, shared within the leadership of the Liberal party. The Finance Bill received its second reading on 10 June and went into committee on 21 June. Lloyd George allowed the land clauses to be taken first. During the committee stage protests from bankers, landowners, brewers, and indeed disaffected Liberals filled the news-papers. Lord Rothschild, a former Liberal MP, had written Asquith denouncing the measure a month earlier. In June he presided over a huge demonstration of outraged City merchants and traders and earned himself a rebuke from Lloyd George for trying to be a dictator. As summer began, consideration of the budget proceeded at a hesitant shuffle. On 16 June Lloyd George had asked for support of the Cabinet to set a time schedule, 'the guillotine', for the disposition of clauses, but was almost unanimously refused. Only Churchill supported him.[188] On using the guillotine he had written to his brother: 'The Prime Minister is for it but I shall have trouble with the rest of my colleagues who hate the budget and would very much like to see it killed by time but they won't, as the party is behind me.'[189] There was continuing pressure within the Liberal leadership upon the Chancellor to lighten the budget by dropping the land clauses. On 13 July he made his only important concession by permitting an amendment to exempt agricultural land from the increment duty although it remained subject to valuation.[190] 'Squared the agriculturalists, Liberal and Irish, this morning,' wrote Lloyd George to his brother, 'so we are a happy family once more.'[191] This, as *The Times* noted the next day, reinforced the speculation that the increment tax, the proceeds from which would now be very small, was in fact of minor importance in comparison to the valuation.[192]

After this small concession of 13 July, lobby and press gossip suddenly began to predict that the Lords would reject the budget. There may have been a reason for this rumor. A few days earlier Balfour had written Strachey, guardian of the soul of the most stern and unbending Tories, asking for constitutional precedent concerning the Lords' power over money bills. Strachey replied on 9 July making a difficult distinction, based upon a statement by Gladstone in 1861, between a tax, that is a tax in being which the upper chamber could not touch, and a tax bill which they might.[193]

The critical decision, perhaps the most important determination made upon the budget, came in the Cabinet of 16 July when J.A. Pease, the Chief Whip, asked Lloyd George to drop at least some of the land clauses. The Chancellor, said Pease, was asking the Commons to do more than it could and the opposition was attempting to force a guillotine so that they could resist it. Could not at least the undeveloped land tax be dropped? Lloyd George replied promptly that he would rather resign, 'as usual' remarked Pease.[194] There may have been more to the exchange than this. Burns's diary entry of the same meeting records that Asquith was stirred to intervene. Burns felt that the Prime Minister 'at last…realized the situation but that it may be too late.' 'We are in rough waters,' Asquith told Burns later.[195]

Burns was, to be sure, the last member of the Cabinet to comprehend anything, but on this occasion he may have perceived dimly what was clear to everyone else: that the Lords might in fact veto the budget, that there would be an election and that the Liberals might be turned out. (On 16 July, although after the Cabinet meeting, Lord Lansdowne, the Unionist leader in the upper Chamber, made the first intimation about the Lords' future action on the budget: that they would not 'swallow it without wincing.')

These were, indeed, rough waters. Some of the acutest Liberal thinkers predicted, as the Unionists had been saying since the beginning of 1909, that in a general election Balfour's party would be returned with a comfortable majority.[196] Among the faint hearts was J.A. Spender whose influence with the Prime Minister was powerful and well known and who was himself now concerned that the land clauses would ensure the budget's rejection, bringing down the government. Very likely he had heard of the Cabinet decision on the land taxes and certainly had become aware, as were many others, of Asquith's uncharacteristic indecisiveness and weakness at Cabinet meetings.[197] After the 16 July Cabinet, Lloyd George wrote to Spender warning that continued pressure in the Cabinet and press to drop that part of the bill that evoked the most popular enthusiasm would cause him to resign. No doubt, he continued, Spender had heard, as had everyone, the rumors of the last two or three days that the Lords would take action. No matter, he said.

> I do not agree with you that we ought never have introduced the Land Clauses in the fourth Session. The Party had lost heart. On all hands I was told that enthusiasm had almost disappeared at meetings, and we wanted something to rouse the fighting spirit of our forces. This the Land proposals have undoubtedly succeeded in doing.

Within the budget, he continued, the land clauses will make the Lords hesitate. All the other taxes injured someone, some vested interest. 'The Cabinet after months of deliberation and discussion decided to introduce them in the Finance Bill of this year. The fight has been conducted for three months on the merits and demerits of these taxes.' They were the only things that were popular, Lloyd George concluded. Without them the Lords could throw out the budget with impunity.[198]

This letter may be read in two ways. As would be usual for Lloyd George, he may have been trying to soothe Spender, to induce him to believe that everything was in strong hands and to invite him to stop bothering Asquith and the public with cowardly advice that threatened the Chancellor's support in Cabinet on the one matter he cared about. Or, it may be that for once Lloyd George was saying precisely what he believed: not only was the budget, particularly the land clauses, popular, but they were so popular that the Lords would fear to veto the Finance Bill as they had surrendered on the Trade Disputes Bill. There was other evidence to reinforce this last speculation. The Liberals enjoyed in July a remarkable series of by-election victories, Yorkshire, Cleveland on 9 July, Mid-Derbyshire on 15 July, Dumfries District on 20 July and Derbyshire High Peak on 22 July. These were all, to be sure, Liberal seats in 1909. Cleveland was a Pease pocket borough while Dumfries was Loreburn's old seat, and the winner in Mid-Derbyshire was in fact a Labourite, although there was no Liberal intervention. Also in every case the Liberal majority of 1906 was reduced. Rather, the cause for rejoicing came not from the fact that the Liberals had won great victories, but that they had won at all. In contrast, in 1908 and during the first three months of 1909, the government had lost more than nine seats without taking any from the opposition.

One could surmise then that in the weeks between the end of May and the end of July Lloyd George had begun to believe, even if his colleagues did not, that he had in the Finance Bill an election-winning instrument and that it would not be necessary to wait, as he and Churchill had felt at the beginning of the year, to challenge the House of Lords on the wider field of social reform. If so he obviously meant exactly what he had said to Spender, that the Unionists would fear now to challenge the budget, that they would fear to lose the subsequent election. If then the budget was so popular that the Lords were frightened not to approve it, the same budget could win an election if the Lords could be induced to reject it. This reasoning may account for the violent departure of the Limehouse speech on 30 July. He intended to make it impossible for the Lords to approve the budget and to make certain that the British nation understood that any rejection was not merely a blow at the Liberal government but worse, a selfish and unconstitutional arrogation of powers that belonged to the people as a whole. The Lords, not the budget, would be the issue in the future election campaign.

The Limehouse speech, given before an audience of 4,000 at the 'Edinburgh Castle,' a pub which had become a mission hall, in London's East End, represented a raising of the stakes in the political game the Lords had played with the Liberals since 1906. At once a threat and a challenge, its essence was a warning that an unconstitutional action by the peers would affect not only the political world but the structure of society. He seemed at least to threaten class warfare and in these terms he was understood.

Lloyd George took a good deal of time preparing his public addresses and finished usually by virtually memorizing them, depending upon his actor's instinct to make them sound spontaneous. However, he did not begin work on the Limehouse speech until after the High Peak election and in fact referred to it at the beginning of his address.[199] He referred also to a second event which fortuitously occurred just before the speech, the announcement by McKenna in the House of Commons on 26 July that the second group of four dreadnoughts authorized but deferred in the 1909 budget would be laid down by April 1910.

These would cost money, said Lloyd George in his opening remarks; four dreadnoughts needed £8 million. The 'miners and weavers of Derbyshire and Yorkshire, the Scotchmen of Dumfries, who like all of their countrymen know the value of money, they all drop in their coppers. We went round to Belgravia, and there has been such a howl ever since that it well nigh deafened us.'

This was the theme of the speech: the poor were willing to pay their share of taxes, the land-owning aristocracy were not. By and large the Limehouse speech consisted of lurid examples of how landlords defrauded the community through profits in sales and leases of land and minerals. He described the money made on the Hackney marshes where land rated at £2 or £3 per acre was eventually sold for housing at two, three, six or eight thousand pounds an acre. (Frequently Lloyd George was imprecise with figures, regarding them as adjectives.) 'Who made that golden swamp?' he cried.

> Was it the landlord? Was it his energy? Was it his brains—a very bad lookout for the place if it were—his forethought? It was purely the combined efforts of all the people engaged in the trade and commerce of the Port of London—trader, merchant, shipowner, dock labourer, workman —everybody except the landlord....
> That is now coming to an end. On the walls of Mr. Balfour's meeting last Friday were the words, 'We protest against fraud and folly.' So do I.

These things I tell you have only been possible up to the present through the 'fraud' of the few and the 'folly' of the many. What is going to happen in the future? In the future those landlords will have to contribute to the taxation of the country on the basis of the real value—only one half penny in the pound! Only a half penny! And that is what all the howling is about.

In turn he outlined the working of the undeveloped land tax, the increment value duty, the lease reversion and mineral taxes. Describing lease reversion he illustrated the distinction he always insisted upon between the idle, despicable, wasteful, landlord and the self-made businessman, no matter how rich. Here he specified the individuals involved.

There is the famous Gorringe case. In that case advantage was taken of the fact that a man had built up a great business. The landlord said in effect. 'You have built up a great business here; you cannot take it away; you cannot move it to other premises because your trade and goodwill are here; your lease is coming to an end, and we decline to renew it except on the most oppressive terms.' The Gorringe case is a very famous case. It was the case of the Duke of Westminster. Oh, these dukes how they harass us!
Mr. Gorringe had got a lease of premises at a few hundred pounds a year ground rent. He built up a great business there as a very able businessman. When the end of the lease came he went to the Duke of Westminster, and he said, 'will you renew my lease? I want to carry on my business here.' The reply was, 'Oh, yes, I will; but only on condition that the few hundred pounds a year you pay for ground rent shall be in the future £4,000 a year.' In addition to that Mr. Gorringe had to pay a fine of £50,000, and to build up huge premises at enormous expense, according to plans approved by the Duke of Westminster.
All I can say is that—if it is confiscation and robbery for us to say to that Duke that, being in need of money for public purposes, we will take ten % of all you got, for those purposes, what would you call his taking nine-tenths from Mr. Gorringe?

He cited this difference again in a striking illustration of the tax on mineral royalties.

The capitalist risks, at any rate, the whole of his money; the engineer puts his brains in; the miner risks his life. Have you been down in a coalmine? I went down one the other day. We sank down into a pit half a mile deep. We then walked underneath the mountain and we had about three quarters of a mile of rock and shale above us. The earth seemed to be straining—around us and above us. You could see the pit-props bent and twisted and sundered, their fibres split in resisting the pressure. Sometimes they give way, and then there is mutilation and death. Often a spark ignites, the whole pit is deluged in fire, the breath of life is scorched out of hundreds of breasts by the consuming flame. In the very next colliery to the one I descended, just a few years ago,

300 people lost their lives in that way; and yet when the Prime Minister and I knock at the doors of these great landlords, and say to them: 'Here you know these poor fellows who have been digging up royalties at the risk of their lives, some of them are old, they have survived the perils of their trade, they are broken, they can earn no more. Won't you give us towards keeping them out of the workhouse?' They scowl at us. We say, 'only a ha'penny, just a copper.' They retort, 'you thieves!' And they turn their dogs onto us, and you can hear their bark every morning. If this is an indication of the view taken by these great landlords of their responsibility to the people who, at the risk of their life, create their wealth, then I say their day of reckoning is at hand.

'The ownership of land is not merely an enjoyment,' he concluded, 'it is a stewardship.'

We are placing burdens on the broadest shoulders. Why should I put burdens on the people? I am one of the children of the people. I was brought up amongst them. I know their trials; and God forbid that I should add one grain of trouble to the anxieties which they bear with such patience and fortitude. When the Prime Minister did me the honour of inviting me to take charge of the national Exchequer at a time of great difficulty, I made up my mind, in framing the Budget which was in front of me, that at any rate no cupboard should be barer, no lot should be harder. By that test, I challenge you to judge the Budget.[200]

To say that the Limehouse speech was a shock would be a monumental understatement. It evoked near-panic among the Unionists and, as important, among the Liberals. The first use of what would become a repeated theme for cartoonists appeared in *Punch* the next week, showing a preadolescent Lloyd George in sailor suit, urged on by an infant Churchill, driving a bathing machine filled with agitated and timorous elderly Liberals into deep water. Asquith, whose official point of view was that the peers would never commit the political crime of a veto, wrote Lloyd George a strong letter saying that the King was upset, warning him especially against provocation and vindictiveness, and saying that he had received angry comments from many Liberals. Lloyd George immediately wrote the King a long letter hardly mentioning the speech but defending the budget, reminding the King that he had explained it to His Majesty on two occasions, and ending with the complaint that people were always saying unpleasant things about him while he had been a model of sweetness and accommodation in the House of Commons.[201] The King replied on 7 August pointing out first of all that he had not complained about the budget but the Limehouse speech and agreeing that his Chancellor of the Exchequer had shown 'patience and perfect temper in debate.' But as an individual holding office under the crown, as opposed to a private member, he could not use language which 'was calculated to set class against class and to inflame the passions of the working and lower orders against people who happen to be owners of property.'[202]

This of course was not the first time Edward had complained of Lloyd

George's oratory, but hitherto he had objected to violence of language against the House of Lords or to references to the monarchy itself. At Limehouse Lloyd George was no more abusive than on many other occasions, nor had he expressed any opinion that many Labour members would not have found routine. The King, nevertheless, was perfectly correct; his Chancellor was indeed appealing to popular instincts of economic selfishness, calling for an attack on landlords, and he was doing this, not during an election campaign in an obscure constituency in Wales, but in the capital, before a huge working class audience, on behalf of the principal government measure of the parliamentary session. The government seemed to be sponsoring revolution and Citizen Lloyd George was in charge of the tumbrils.[203]

While the King was concerned basically with the propriety of the Limehouse speech the Unionists were concerned with its effect. Lloyd George had challenged them to meet his wager on the popularity of the land clauses, or conversely, on the unpopularity of the landlords. His sense of Unionist misery was clear in his letters to his brother in the next few days.

> 3 August 1909: I hear that reports are coming into Tory headquarters from all parts of the country and that the Budget is popular.
> Rutherford, M.P. for Liverpool here now and telling me my Land Clauses were very popular. General feeling is that they will make a show of fight and then collapse. They are raging over Limehouse, but our fellows most enthusiastic. Prime Minister going to Birmingham to address a great Budget meeting. Arthur Chamberlain taking the chair [Arthur Chamberlain was still chairman of Kynoch's and a dedicated Liberal].
> 4 August 1909: Lord Northcliffe came to see me last night. He is, as you know, the Proprietor the *Daily Mail* and *Times*. He told me that the Budget has completely destroyed the tariff reform propaganda in the country. He said they had all miscalculated about the popularity of the Land Clauses. He wants to trim. Glad to hear M. had a good night. [M. was Mary Ellen, Lloyd George's sister who was ill with cancer].
> 17 August 1909: Things going well. Both in the House and outside. In the country it is a 'mighty running wind' sweeping before it all opposition. I hear from all parts of the country startling accounts of the changes affected by the Budget in public opinion. There is undoubtedly a popular rising such as has not been witnessed over a generation. What will happen if they throw it out I can conjecture and I rejoice at the prospect. Many a rotten institution, system and law will be submerged by the deluge. I wonder whether they will be such fools. I am almost wishing they should be stricken with blindness.[204]

'Those fools,' he remarked to Lucy Masterman about the House of Lords, 'won't realize that they have got the middle classes against them now. Every tradesman, everyone who has had to build a house or wishes to enlarge his garden, has got a grievance against the town landlord.'[205]

The visit of Northcliffe on 3 August, to which he had referred, was an event of contemporary significance, besides providing the starting point for an important but uneasy association between the two men. Lloyd George had invited the publisher to come to see him only a little more than a month earlier. Northcliffe, knowing that Lloyd George collected newspaper publishers, had declined. Now, after the Limehouse speech, he appeared promptly. Even though Lloyd George remarked later that a conversation with Northcliffe was like taking a walk with a grasshopper he had, in company with most politicians, a high regard for the newspaperman's sense of the drift of public opinion. Lloyd George gave Northcliffe a peek at some proposals for the Development Board which the House of Commons had not yet seen and the publisher of *The Times* and the *Daily Mail* went away delighted. *The Times*'s first leader on the speech had called for the Lords to reject the budget, but the day after Northcliffe's meeting with Lloyd George the 'Political Notes,' column remarked that public sentiment was moving inexorably in favor of the budget, 'a change comparable only to the turn of the tide upon an estuary when moored boats swing slowly around.' It commented further that the High Peak election had been more important than people were aware of at the time.[206] Lloyd George cited this assessment in his letter to the King the next day.

Whether, in the weeks that followed, Northcliffe believed he was creating public opinion or following what his astute perceptions showed already to be the trend is really unimportant. Both *The Times* and the *Daily Mail* noted and enlarged upon the Unionist disarray. Liberal papers, of course, were saying the same in stronger terms. A leader from the *Daily News* on 6 August was entitled: 'In Full Flight: Panic Among the Opposition,' and the next day: 'What Will the Tories Do?' Similarly Unionist papers were denouncing *The Times* and the *Daily Mail* for 'panic in the face of Jack Cade.'[207]

Much of this, to be sure, constituted newspaper froth, yet as was, and is, frequently the case, it reflected, even diminished, the reality. The Unionists whose enthusiastic revival had seemed so certain eight months before were now divided. On one hand were old Tories, many of them aristocratic landlords, some of whom indeed were tariff reformers, who disliked the land clauses and thought in vague terms of some sort of Lords' amendment. On the other hand were the younger Chamberlainites who saw the budget as the end of protection and of their campaign to regenerate Britain and the Unionist party. The Chamberlainites, mostly commoners, passionately wanted a general election on the fiscal issues as a whole and regarded the land clauses as a red herring.[208] Chamberlain himself, from the first, wanted uncompromising resistance.[209] He intended the election to be a referendum on tariff reform. Balfour's problem lay not in his doubts about the constitutional propriety of vetoing the budget but in the wisdom of throwing the party into the arms of the Chamberlainites. An election victory would be their victory, but a loss would be his and would damage the entire Unionist party, not to mention the House of Lords. Intellectually he could accept import duties as a painless way of raising money and as a useful political warcry and had admitted this privately since at least the previous spring.[210] What he could not accept, philosophically, perhaps emotionally, were the whole hog tariff reformers, their reckless demagoguery, their revolutionary commitment, their impatience with political tradition, usage and compromise. These things to him were the core of the

English parliamentary genius. No doubt he knew his world was dying, but his failure to come to terms with this New Toryism cost him the party leadership two years later.

The brilliance of Lloyd George's strategy at Limehouse lay in his sense of the Unionist dilemma. He understood Balfour intuitively, as, one may suspect, Balfour understood him. The Unionist leader had detected and denounced the appearance of class-based politics even as Lloyd George began the process in his budget speech. At Limehouse, Lloyd George made clear that the cause to be put before the country was not the classless issue of tariff reform but the selfishness of the landlord. He comprehended the inherent popular appeal of the protection campaign and had been warning his party of the danger since 1903. Now, in the land clauses, Lloyd George found the alternative. These were not a red herring, at least land valuation was not, but bred in his bones. Nevertheless, possibly to his own surprise, suddenly they were popular. The Lords, after all, had twice rejected valuation bills in previous years and no one had noticed. Now, when the Lords rejected them again they would provide the basis for an attack on the upper chamber.

Finally he had made it impossible for the budget to be approved. The Lords alone might force the issue. The threat of valuation had set off alarm bells among Britain's great landowners. In the third week of August, Lord St. David, who as John Wynford Philipps had been Liberal MP for Pembrokeshire until 1908 and still was a trusted supporter, warned Lloyd George that backwoods peers were turning up in unprecedented numbers for the single reason of hewing down the budget.[211] Lloyd George clearly was hearing the same from other sources. Hobhouse records that the Chancellor told him that Lansdowne had, in effect, apologized to the Archbishop of Canterbury, who was against rejection, saying that the backwoodsmen 'were too many for him and he should have to give way.'[212] The Unionists were in the desperate position of having to force an election they could not be sure of winning. Surrender was no longer an option.

When, precisely, Balfour decided that the Lords must veto the Finance Bill, and that it must be rejected, not amended, is a matter of considerable debate among historians.[213] A clear terminal date is the third week of September when he told Austen Chamberlain that if the Lords did not exercise their veto he would resign leadership of the party.[214] But there were whispers of such an outcome well before the end of August, as Lloyd George had noted in a letter to his brother on 17 August, and on 8 September the Cabinet discussed formally a memorandum by George Murray on the financial implications of a rejection of the Finance Bill.[215] It does not do to proclaim, as does Lloyd George's most recent biographer after devoting a chapter to Limehouse, that the speech produced only an eddy in the current flowing toward rejection.[216] Whether or not Lloyd George's address was the sole efficient cause or the largest among several related events of early August, it remains, nevertheless, the opening gun in the tremendous constitutional and political battle that destroyed the political power of the House of Lords and the commanding parliamentary position of the Liberal party, opened the door for Irish Home Rule, and brought Britain and Ireland to what appeared to be, by the end of July

1914, the verge of civil war.

Immediately after the Limehouse speech Balfour came under pressure within the party to resist surrender at all costs. The day following Northcliffe's interview with Lloyd George, the publisher received a long letter from J.L. Garvin, the editor of the *Observer*, which paper Northcliffe had bought in 1905 and would own until 1911, affirming in the strongest terms that the options now were either resistance or collapse. Garvin feared the latter, which would he thought devastate the party for a generation. The danger of the present budget would grow greater, not less, in the future. The execution had to take place now.

> The Government is of course less unpopular than last year. If they pass the Budget substantially as it stands they will have secured a Parliamentary triumph as brilliant as any in our recollection. They will be more popular and powerful than at any single moment since the General Election. They will have given us a knock-out blow. The Unionist Party will appear, by contrast, beaten, impotent and ridiculous....The methods of this Budget might be quite as audaciously applied in 1911 as now, and the possibilities of a campaign of promises...are simply limitless...men like Lloyd George and Winston Churchill will do anything to win. Upon the lines of the Budget they will keep on winning if we submit now....England with the last Constitutional safeguard destroyed at home, with the cause of Imperial Union killed in the sight of the Colonies, with direct taxation heaped up on home capital and enterprise, would be a socialist republic in everything but name.

The budget as a whole would have to be rejected. To delete only the land clauses would be to fight the election on the single issue of landlord greed whereas the genuine alternatives were tariff reform and social reform. 'Dukes should be warned to keep off the grass.' Garvin concluded by noting that Asquith would speak in Bingley Hall in Birmingham on 17 September. Balfour should follow him and declare the Unionist policy of tariff reform, social reform, and naval supremacy.[217]

Northcliffe immediately sent this letter on to Balfour who replied on 10 August, thanking Garvin for his letter and for the subsequent article in the *Observer* on 8 August. He would go to Bingley Hall the week after Asquith if it could be secured, so Garvin's 'advice on this point has not been thrown away....'[218]

Balfour was able to arrange for Bingley Hall on 22 September. After a long letter from Joseph Chamberlain had been read to general cheering, he embraced tariff reform, a little stiffly, saying that it was the alternative to 'the bottomless confusion of Socialistic legislation.'[219]

Balfour's letter to Garvin was written on 10 September, the day after the House returned to the Finance Bill following three weeks devoted to other business. On 9 September Lloyd George had announced some amendments to the land clauses. The changes themselves were minor: a tax on landlord's royalties in working mines and quarries in place of the duties on minerals still in the ground; provision for the state to bear the cost of land valuation and for appeals to the high court against assessments; and finally the exemption from the undeveloped land duty of any land upon which £100 had been spent in the last ten years. This last change rendered the return from the undeveloped land tax negligible and erased further the cosmetic that the tax had provided for valuation. Thus it seemed to prove the charge already circulating that valuation had been 'tacked' onto the budget to secure a House of Lords veto. Uncharacteristically Balfour lost his temper. No one knew, he exploded, even how much the undeveloped land tax now would bring.

> This is not a tax to get money, it is a tax to get votes. It is a tax cynically put forward as a tax which is going to catch votes because it affects the few and leaves the many untouched. A more contemptible calculation, a more preposterous method of dealing with great interests under the guise of meeting the nation's necessities never was presented by any Statesman of whom this country has any record whatever.[220]

The next day he returned to the subject.

> We are not dealing with finance. We are not dealing with the methods for meeting the financial strain to which this country is subject. We are dealing with schemes, be they good or bad, which have not the character of financial provision, but of social revolution.... There is no national crisis. We admit your need for money, but this money will not enable you to pay the smallest of your debts. I do not, of course, deny that, as far as individual hardship is concerned, the proposals of the government are intended to diminish that hardship.... But we cannot consider that in isolation. We have to consider the whole scheme of which this is a part. And doing my best to consider the whole scheme, I say this is not a Finance Bill at all. I believe it is unconstitutional and I believe it is unwise and I shall vote against this resolution....[221]

Adding to the evidence that the second week of August may have been the critical period for determining the Unionist response to Lloyd George's budget, Balfour's private secretary, John Sandars, received on 8 August a gloomy report from the Chief Whip, Sir Alexander Acland-Hood, on the state of constituency parties which presumably he quickly passed on to the leader of the opposition. The document did not mention the Limehouse speech, and indeed generally dealt with events before the speech, but it emphasized that with the budget the Unionists had lost the initiative, that a Liberal renaissance was in progress, and that Lloyd George's exploitation of what was in fact only a minor corner of the Finance Bill now made action by Balfour imperative. The Whip's statement was no more than a short professional summary of Garvin's 14 page work of intuition which Balfour had received three or four days before. The Unionist problems were:

> Disappointment at High Peak
> The idea that in the House we have been fighting the battle of the big landlords (especially urban) only
> The temporary eclipse of tariff reform by the Budget
> The loss of nerve by Northcliffe, which has reacted on our own people,

and given the notion that the Budget is enthusiastically supported
in the Country
The eight Dreadnoughts

Balfour must take up tariff reform. If he did so the Unionists might win 320 seats.[222] Three days later, the Liberal Whip, J.A. Pease, as unrealistic as Acland-Hood, predicted for Asquith a Liberal-Labour majority of 40 over the Unionists and Irish together.[223]

The evidence then is that within two weeks after Limehouse, Balfour decided that the challenge of the budget would have to be met even at the risk of a constitutional rupture. He told Esher as much over lunch in November. 'Anyhow, from the opening days of the controversy,' Esher recorded in his journal, 'certainly from the day of Lloyd George's Speech at Limehouse, the fate of the budget was sealed.'[224] Balfour could reflect that he had fought Lloyd George over education and had won. He would do it again dragging along the reluctant sections of his party, the Unionist free traders, and the nervous peers and bishops who hated the budget but disliked even more a constitutional fight. Once the battle began, he carried it forward with the same implacable determination he had displayed in his contest to save Church education, probably increased by his need to ensure that the victory, when it came, would be his and the party's, and not belong only to the tariff reformers. Hence, in the next few weeks, he was careful to emphasize unity. At Bingley Hall his acceptance of tariff reform was measured. Stragglers had to be rounded up. The Archbishop of Canterbury, for example, who was much opposed to a Lords' veto, received from Sandars a letter reminding him that should he accede to the House of Commons' right to attach irrelevant material to a budget, the Chancellor of the Exchequer might well disestablish the Church of England in the same way, perhaps by taxing all Church revenues at fifty per cent.[225]

Thus, until unity was achieved, Unionist intentions remained hidden. Through September and October Lloyd George pressed the bill to create his development board and presided, day after day, on the committee stage of his budget, always, as Burns described in his diary, in his 'small, elusive, smiling, acquiescent manner a limit to which has not yet been reached....'[226] But the new tone of the opposition was clear.

The Cabinet of 8 September, which had considered for the first time as a body the possibility of the rejection of the budget, discussed the subject, not reported to the King, of the political tactics to follow a veto. There would be an election, but not until January by which time the new register could be ready. There was no longer any need for haste. According to Almeric Fitzroy, whose Cabinet secrets now came usually through the Lord President, Lord Wolverhampton (Henry Fowler), an argument developed over the strategy of attacking the House of Lords as opposed to defending the budget. Lloyd George and Churchill, as usual alone, were in favor of the former. Over the protests of the two miscreants, the Cabinet eventually agreed to postpone a decision until Lord Rosebery's speech at Glasgow, scheduled for 11 September.[227]

Lloyd George had breakfasted that morning with his old friend from the early years of Welsh politics, A.H.D. Acland, who brought him comforting reassurances of the popularity of the land clauses, 'the country is aflame.'[228] Evidently the two also discussed the Liberal political strategy, for a week later Acland wrote Lloyd George a letter urging him in old-fashioned political terms not to make the House of Lords an electoral issue. He would rather see the election fought on an honest and straight-forward question of the budget, free trade, and the government's record. The veto would be included only as one of a long list of 'crimes' of the upper chamber.[229]

One cannot avoid the sense that in the latter days of September and in early October 1909, some portions of the political world of Great Britain in both parties suddenly began to recoil from the disaster to which they were committed, even as they rushed toward the precipice. Lloyd George was forcing on his own terms a battle over the House of Lords against Unionists of whom many were at least reluctant to die for import duties. Equally he was dragging with him a large body of unwilling soldiers in his own party who, even if happy to shake their fists at the House of Lords from the security of the trenches, had no wish to take the field under the banner of land reform. The overturn of centuries of traditions would throw the constitution itself into a void. To make an institution of government an issue of contention, rather than a man or a party, was to turn the clock back to 1688: if the Lords today, why not the King tomorrow? Among the fainthearted were the Unionist leadership in the House of Lords and Unionist free traders everywhere, probably Asquith and certainly many of his colleagues in the Cabinet who saw the Prime Minister's weakness as responsible for the budget, and the King. On the other side were backbench Tory peers, who met on 28 September and decided, as St. David had warned Lloyd George would happen, that the budget must be killed.[230] In the House of Commons the fighters were the 1906 generation of radical MPs, and Lloyd George, Churchill, and Arthur James Balfour and the Chamberlainites. Recklessness was pitted against caution, the bloody-minded against the soft-headed. On 6 October, the King saw Asquith at Balmoral and asked whether he might see Balfour and Lansdowne. Asquith quickly assented and agreed to allow the King to say that if the budget were not rejected he would ask for a dissolution in January anyway.[231] The next day Asquith wrote Lloyd George telling him of the interview with the King and enjoining him, as he was speaking at Newcastle two days hence, to do nothing to endanger the monarch's negotiations and to proceed on the assumption that the budget would be approved.

For Lloyd George the time for compromise with the Lords had long passed. A warning that he should not interfere with sensitive mediation was unwelcome and to be ignored. As he wrote his brother after the Newcastle speech of 9 October, those who, after making a challenge, try to hang back are cowards. 'They all realize,' he said, '—both sides—that they must fight now or eat humble pie and that will be difficult for a proud tho' pusillinous [sic] aristocracy. I deliberately provoked them to fight. I fear me they will run away in spite of all my pains.'[232]

The Newcastle speech offered indeed deliberate provocation. Limehouse had attacked landlords in general; the grievance was the monopoly of land. At Newcastle, before an audience of over five thousand at the Palace Theatre, Lloyd George narrowed the charge to the House of

Lords, noble landlords who were corrupting Britain's constitutional democracy to protect their wealth.

He began by putting his address neatly in context with a reference to his previous speech in Newcastle on 4 April 1903, when he had attacked landlords and royalty owners. His campaign for land reform, he made clear, had not begun with the 1909 budget.

Generally the Newcastle speech followed the good against evil construction that Lloyd George ordinarily used except that he concentrated on a single aspect of his budget, land valuation, and the upper chamber was symbolized by a particularly greedy and stupid species of peer, 'the Dukes.' 'What is the chief charge against the budget by its opponents?' he asked.

> That it is an attack on industry and an attack on property! I am going to demonstrate to you that it is neither. It is very remarkable that since this attack on industry was first promulgated in the House of Commons trade has improved.... Only one stock has gone down badly—there has been a great slump in dukes. They used to stand rather high in the market, especially the Tory market, but the Tory press has discovered that they are of no value.
>
> The dukes have been making speeches recently. One especially expensive duke made a speech, and all the Tory Press said, 'Well, now, really, is that the sort of thing we are spending £250,000 a year upon?' Because a fully equipped duke costs as much to keep up as two 'dreadnoughts' and they are just as great a terror, and they last longer. As long as they were content to be mere idols on their pedestals, preserving that stately silence which became their rank and their intelligence, all went well, and the average British citizen rather looked up to them, and said to himself, 'well, if worst comes to worst for this old country, we always have got the dukes to fall back on.'
>
> The chief objection of the great landlords to this Budget lies in the fact that it has great valuation proposals. Why do they object to valuation? Well, I will tell you why. It goes to the very root of all things in the land question. There has never been a public undertaking in this country, municipal, State or industrial, there has never been an enterprise but that the landlord has generally secured anything from four to forty times as much for the value of the land as its agricultural price.... The moment they ask for that land its value goes up enormously. Every trick and chicanery of the law, and there are many of them as my brothers in law to the right can testify, every one of these is exhausted in order to prove that this worthless land has an enormous hidden value....

As always he emphasized that the land monopoly defrauded not only the poor, but honest industry as well.

> What have we in trade, in business, in commerce, in industry? If you want to found a new business or extend an old one, the charges for land are extravagant, especially if you want to extend because you are there. A trader who has been building up a business in a particular locality, who by years of care and industry and a good deal of anxiety and worry has been building up a business gradually year by year—he

cannot carry his trade away as if it were a coster's barrow and plant it in the next street; he has to get his extension where he is. Then comes the landlord, who has done nothing, and demands the highest price he can possibly extort. I can give you many cases of the kind. I have my bag full of them, sent to me from all parts of the country, with full particulars.

Hence the need for State valuation.

On one hand was the Goliath of landlordism, mouthing hypocritical patriotism and pseudo-democracy, and on the other was the sturdy young David asking simply that his opponents support the institutions they professed to honor.

When I come along and say, 'here, gentlemen, you have escaped long enough, it is your turn now; I want you to pay just 5 per cent on the £10,000 odd.' 'Five per cent,' they say to me. 'You are a thief; you are worse, you are an attorney; worst of all, you are a Welshman.' That is always the crowning epithet. Well, gentlemen, I do not apologize; I could not help it, and I do not mind telling you that if I could I would not. I am proud of the little land among the hills. But there is one thing I should like to say. Whenever they hurl my nationality at my head, I say to them, 'You Unionists! You hypocrites! Pharisees! You are the people who in every peroration—well, they have only got one—always talk about our being one kith and kin throughout the Empire from the old man of Hoy down to Van Diemen's Land in the South.' And yet if any man dares to aspire to any position, who does not belong to the particular nationality which they have dignified by choosing their parents from, they have no use for him. Well, they have got to stand the Welshman this time....

What will the Lords do? I tell you frankly it is a matter which concerns them far more than it concerns us. The more irresponsible and feather-headed among them want to throw it out. But what will the rest do? It will depend on the weather. There are some who are not fair weather sailors, and they will go on. But poor Lord Lansdowne—with his creaking old ship and his mutinous crew—there he is, he has got to sail through the narrows with one eye on the weather glass and the other on the forecastle.

Let them realize what they are doing. They are forcing a revolution, and they will get it. The Lords may decree a revolution, but the people will direct it. If they begin, issues will be raised that they little dream of. Questions will be asked which are now whispered in humble voices, and answers will be demanded then with authority. The question will be asked whether five hundred men, ordinary men chosen accidentally from among the unemployed, should override the judgement—the deliberate judgement—of millions of people who are engaged in the industry which makes the wealth of the country.

That is one question. Another will be, Who ordained that a few should have the land of Britain as a perquisite? Who made ten thousand people owners of the soil, and the rest of us trespassers on the land of our birth? Who is it who is responsible for the scheme of things whereby one man is engaged through his life in grinding labour to win a bare and precarious subsistence for himself, and when at the end of his days, he claims at the hands of the community he served a poor pension of 8d a day, he can get it only through a revolution, and another man who does not toil receives every hour of the day, every hour of the night, whilst he slumbers, more than his poor neighbour receives in a whole year of toil? Where did the table of that law come from? Whose finger inscribed it? These are the questions that will be asked. The answers are charged with peril for the order of things the Peers represent; but they are fraught with rare and refreshing fruit for the parched lips of the multitude who have been treading the dusty road, along which the people have marched, through the dark ages which are now merging into the light.[233]

It may be too much to say that the Limehouse and Newcastle speeches alone caused the dissolution of the old deferential traditions of Westminster politics, but all the newspapers in the autumn of 1909 recognized a new temper in public affairs and filled their pages with denunciations of Lloyd George as a Jacobin revolutionary. In one sense the budget itself had begun the process of class struggle, as Balfour clearly perceived. Yet probably it was inevitable after the establishment of household franchise. Certainly Chamberlain understood this and had begun to act upon it, and the budget was Lloyd George's reaction to Chamberlainism. But in the years afterwards, Limehouse and Newcastle were the points that were remembered. For Liberal radicals the speeches meant a revival of party enthusiasm.

Even some Gladstonians approved it guardedly. Lloyd George was vulgar, mused Lord Rendel in a letter to Stafford Howard in February 1910, but he said things that needed to be said. His coarseness was no worse than Tory half-truths. He was scurrilous but not cowardly. 'It was rather harsh of him to tilt at the dukes. Of course there are good dukes and bad dukes. But there is no Liberal duke and it was time to shake up England a little about dukes—I let alone duchesses.'[234] For the Unionists, Limehouse and Newcastle marked the breakdown of the upper class agreement on the restraints and responsibilities of power. 'The whole political atmosphere has changed since Limehouse, Newcastle, etc.,' wrote Henry T. Eve, a Unionist land expert who had been commissioned by the Chairman of the Party, Arthur Steele-Maitland, in June 1912 to develop a response to the renewed land campaign, 'and I suppose it is the fact of history that when once the respect of one class for another is gone, there is no halting place. It is either there or it is gone—like a pebble thrown in a pond.'[235]

The ripples spread ever outward. One evidence of their effect may have been that hundreds of simple citizens, men and women, were moved to write Lloyd George between the years of 1909 and 1914. These letters, often scratched painfully on school tablet paper, frequently in pencil, are touching reminders of the place he held in the popular mind. He had become a working class messiah who had been put on earth or 'specially raised up' to help the common folk. Scores of people remembered his birthday, but many asked for advice on personal matters. Some pleaded for money. Always it was implied that the Chancellor of the Exchequer, unlike anyone else, would understand the writer's problem. Until the advent of Frances Stevenson, Lloyd George regularly threw away letters from grander sorts, but these halting testimonials he saved.

On the eve of the Newcastle speech, on 8 October, parliament had recessed for ten days. After a short holiday on the continent Lloyd George returned to Wales and then was back in London for the report stage of the Finance Bill which began on 19 October. On the 21st, in a graceful gesture, he entertained Balfour at the annual dinner of the Welsh antiquarian society of Cymmrodorion. On 28 October Almeric Fitzroy learned, to his dismay, that the Lords indeed would reject the budget.[236]

The Clerk of the Privy council did not suggest a reason for this abrupt decision but the coincidence of a surprising Unionist victory in Bermond-sey, Southwark on that day must be noted. Heavily working class, Bermondsey was a famous swing constituency. It had supported the winning party by a decent majority in every general election since its creation in 1885. The Liberal margin in 1906 had been 53% of the votes cast. Now on 28 October the Unionists easily recaptured it, increasing their 1906 vote by over 1,200, enough to have defeated the Liberals in the previous general election.

Whether Bermondsey was the cause, Fitzroy's news was accurate. In his Cabinet letter of 3 November, the day before the Finance Bill finally cleared the House of Commons, Asquith admitted to the King that a veto now was 'generally regarded as possible.'[237] In the next two weeks the Cabinet pondered the financial dislocations that would ensue from the dissolution of parliament when the provisional collection of income taxes and tea duty would become illegal. After considering and rejecting a short bill, strongly opposed by Lloyd George, simply declaring existing taxes collectable (which the Lords might have rejected also), the government determined instead to depend upon borrowing, the suspension of payments to the sinking fund, and a bill in the new parliament making all tax collections retroactive to the dissolution of the old one. The only irretrievable loss would be the interest on the short term debt. The responsibility for any disruption of the financial markets would lie with the upper chamber.

Finally on 16 November, Lansdowne, nervous and ill at ease as Almeric Fitzroy described him, announced that he intended to move the rejection of the Finance Bill on the second reading. 'Well, the Lords have made up their minds,' exulted Lloyd George in a letter to Maggie that evening. 'The Lord hath delivered them unto our hands. That is my feeling. The budget is quite safe as far as its leading features are concerned. We may have to come to terms with the Irish but that won't touch land.'[238]

Lansdowne moved his amendment on 22 November. It called for a general election before the approval of the Finance Bill. The next day he told Crewe, the Liberal leader in the Lords, that so many peers wanted to speak against the bill that debate would have to be extended from the four days already scheduled.[239] Finally, after six days of speeches filled with many disparaging references to Limehouse and Newcastle, just before midnight on 30 November, the House of Lords declined a second reading, 350 to 75. In doing so the peers disdained a last minute warning from Rosebery, who often said sensible things at the wrong time, that the Lords were doing precisely what their enemies wished them to do and that it would be well for the upper chamber to save its veto for more important issues like Irish Home Rule.[240] (Rosebery also said foolish things. On 11 September in Glasgow he had seemed to add his weight to the veto forces by describing the budget as a 'revolution without popular mandate' and so had contributed to the rejection he now sought to forestall.) Lloyd George had done his work well. 'Liberty,' he mused at a luncheon at the National Liberal Club three days later, 'owes as much to the foolishness of its foes as it does to the sapience and wisdom of its friends.'[241] Lansdowne, even had he been the man to do so, and Balfour with all his skill, could hardly have stifled this Vesuvius of lordly outrage. Peers who dreamed of seeing the Chancellor of the Exchequer torn apart by a pack of foxhounds—the 'Mad Mullahs', Lloyd George styled them on 3 December—were not prepared to heed the counsels of political prudence or even self-preservation. As Lord Camperdown advised them, their lordships should throw out the bill and 'let the consequences take care of themselves.'

7 The Struggle with the Lords, National Insurance, Agadir, 1910-12

In the midst of the fight over the budget, ten days after Limehouse, on 8 August 1909 Lloyd George's sister, Mary Ellen, for whom Mair Elunid had been named, died in Criccieth of cancer. Lloyd George had been rather frightened of her as a boy and became impatient with her fundamentalist puritanism as he grew older. But she was a kindly aunt for his children and a friend of Maggie's, which he reluctantly acknowledged. She had married Philip Davies, a sea captain, and ordinarily lived with her brother William at Garthcelyn. At her death she was 47 years old.

While he had made appropriate comments on the reports from his brother about her condition, usually at the end of letters, during the summer of 1909, he did not express much concern. However when the telegram from the faithful William arrived, while Lloyd George and Charles Masterman were dealing with a deputation, he asked to be excused for a moment. Later he showed Masterman the telegram which read '...do not think of us. Do not let this private grief make you pause in the great work you are doing for the downtrodden and the poor.' By this time he was in tears.[1] He made a flying trip to Criccieth for the funeral, but nonetheless he was off to Brighton as usual the next weekend with the Mastermans, gaily stopping the car at intervals at newsagents to try and buy a copy of the *British Weekly*.[2]

In these years the connection with Criccieth was becoming more stable and yet more distant. Soon after he became Chancellor of the Exchequer, Lloyd George began to plan a new house to replace the semi-detached villa on the Portmadoc road. By the autumn of 1908 the plans were complete; he told Lord Riddell he could not afford more than £1,200. By 1910, when he moved in, it had cost, according to his statement to the Marconi Committee, a little more than £2,000. The house was situated on the hills behind Criccieth offering a magnificent view of the bay; it provided space for the gardens that Maggie loved, but, like all Lloyd George's other domestic arrangements, it was simple, a little austere, and totally without style. He called it Brynawelon, 'Hill of Breezes.' In fact it was Maggie's house, not his, nor did he claim it. Even though Mair's grave is in the cemetery only a little way further down toward the village, he chose when his time came to be interred not in Criccieth but on the banks of the Dwyfor in Llanystumdwy. Nevertheless there were now six bedrooms for guests and in the next few years, between 1910 and 1914, Lloyd George's London cronies, Masterman, Churchill, Isaacs, and their families, were visitors. From their notes and recollections, the historian is provided with a glimpse of Lloyd George's domestic life, uncolored by his own imagination, before his family began to fall apart. 'Every chick and child in the village knew and hailed him when he went about,' wrote Lucy Masterman in August, 1911. 'A more serious grievance was the fact that every Welshman he had ever known considered that he had a right to call upon him and have an unlimited interview. The result was that his house became a regular centre for tourists, and I hardly ever remember seeing it without one or two people peering at him though the trees.'[3] Similarly he knew everyone.

Yet despite all his protestations in public about his Welshness, he found the returns to the land of his youth difficult. Mrs. Masterman was with him when a letter arrived from Megan, at that time nine years old, containing some sweet peas and an earnest plea that her father not require her to come to London. Megan liked Criccieth, he told Mrs. Masterman. 'All the children do.' Then, suddenly dropping his head into his hand, he added 'I hate it.' 'That, of course,' Lucy reflected, 'is on account of his dead child.'[4] Still, another less trying connection with Wales appeared when, upon the death of his old opponent Sir John Puleston in October, 1908, Lloyd George, to no one's surprise, was appointed on 10 November Constable of Caernarvon Castle.

I

There are times in history when forces beyond human control seem to overpower the course of events. It is as if some huge clockspring wound ever tighter through generations suddenly slips its balance wheel and sets the hands on the face spinning. The flow of events speeds up. One feels this uncontrolled acceleration in the approach of some modern wars but particularly in the story of British politics between the end of 1909 and August of 1914, after which equilibrium in Britain was violently restored by the onset of a greater, foreign, catastrophe, although even then the latent energy of the spring was not yet exhausted.

Lloyd George sensed intuitively that both parties had lost control of the political game in which they were engaged, that the game had acquired a life of its own. He tried to change the rules with a party coalition. But the prejudice of faction, and mistrust of Lloyd George himself, were not so easily turned aside. Nor of course was he ever, even in this endeavor, entirely selfless. There were immediate and important parliamentary advantages for him. Nonetheless he did offer to compromise on nearly every issue dividing Westminster Palace. When his plan was rejected, even though graver minds than his by now saw the same catastrophe, the furies took control again.

After the House of Lords' defeat of the budget, parliament was prorogued on 3 December with polling ordered for the last two weeks of January. The election in Caernarvon District was set for 22 January 1910. Lloyd George's opponent was H.C. Vincent, the mayor of Bangor, a man with unimpeachable Welsh credentials who was able to attract local and national support—Lord Penrhyn and F.E. Smith on 29 December—in a way that R.A. Naylor had never done.[5] Like the unfortunate Naylor, however, his meetings were often interrupted. Lloyd George himself spent little time in the constituency. He made an extended tour through South Wales speaking for D.A. Thomas in his new constituency of Cardiff, his last contest, and for

Alfred Mond in Swanseatown among others.[6] He spoke as well in Devon and Cornwall, in Reading twice for Rufus Isaacs, and in London. In between times he darted back to Caernarvon District, fretting about the canvass, encouraging his supporters, and denouncing the House of Lords.[7]

His speeches if read together contain a single theme: that the House of Lords was responsible for all the evils abroad in the land. It was the House of Lords, he told nonconformists, that prevented justice to free churches. It was the House of Lords, he said in coastal towns, that would destroy the budget, bring tariffs to Britain, lower wages and force honest working men to eat black bread and horsemeat like the protectionist Germans. It was the House of Lords, he declared in rural districts, that prevented the development of the countryside. In cities the House of Lords drove up rents and by interfering with the largesse of social welfare envisioned in the budget kept invalid working men and their helpless widows locked up in the workhouse. The sermon was adapted to the audience before him, but the text was always the same.[8] These addresses were not restatements of Limehouse and Newcastle, which were public challenges to the peers. The speeches of December and January 1909-10 were not designed to provoke the nobility but to persuade the nation that the peerage was the enemy, not so much of the Liberal party as of the people themselves. A gargantuan banquet had been spread for the people, but the peers barred the door.

Lloyd George's polling day was about midway through the election period. He was reelected on a slightly reduced margin, some of which surely was due to a more capable opponent than he had faced in 1906. The figures were: Lloyd George 3,183, H.C. Vincent 2,105, majority 1,078.

Nationally the Liberals did far less well. At the time of the dissolution the party held 373 seats representing a net loss of 12 at by-elections, plus the secession of a number of Lib/Labs to the Labour whip. (Several Liberal seats were vacant.) When the polls closed they returned to Westminster with 275 seats while the Unionists held 273. Moreover the Labour party, which had held 46 seats at the time of the dissolution, returned only 40 with a loss of over one per cent of the votes per candidate in contested seats. Everywhere, even if seats were not lost, Liberal majorities were down. In Falmouth, the incumbent, Sir John Barker, the department store owner, for whom Lloyd George had spoken eloquently, was defeated. In Plymouth, where he had assured the meeting that Sir Francis Drake would never have allowed the House of Lords to force freeborn Englishmen to eat horseflesh instead of roast beef, the two Liberals scraped home with a margin of 311 as against 2,367 in 1906. Perhaps most disturbing was the fact that while the government, and indeed also the Labour party, polled almost exactly the number of votes nationally that they had won in 1906, the Unionists increased their 1906 total by 28% or 675,443. Moreover the Liberals had only one unopposed return in January 1910 in contrast to 27 in 1906 and were better organized than the party had been for decades. In gaining an approximate equality of seats, the Unionists received 234,306 more votes than the Liberals.

It is not clear whether tariff reform, or the budget, or the House of Lords won or lost many seats. The constituency map of Great Britain and Northern Ireland after the January 1910 election resembles closely the map after the Khaki Election of October 1900.[9] The Unionists recaptured the southeast agricultural and urban districts, although they did not sweep London as in 1900, and the rural areas of the West Midlands. The party, in effect, recovered most of the seats it had lost in 1906. Whether this was the result of the popularity of the idea of import duties on agricultural products, or the unpopularity of land taxes in rural areas as had been predicted in January 1909, or the true blue Conservatism of countrymen, 'the finest brute votes in Europe,' is difficult to say. Louis Harcourt, one of Lloyd George's most violent, but secret, enemies wrote to Asquith at the end of the polling period saying that the Chancellor's speeches which excited either 'alarm' or 'disgust' were probably responsible for the heavy losses in the South.[10]

The preceding paragraph must not be allowed to diminish the magnitude of Lloyd George's achievement between January 1909 and January 1910. When compared with the panic a year earlier after the defeat of the Licensing Bill, the standoff of 1910 was a victory. 'If we had gone to the country then [January 1909] we should have been out by a majority of not less than one hundred,' wrote J.A. Spender to Bryce on 3 February 1910. 'Since then we have been steadily reviving thanks to the Budget. ...for this Lloyd George deserves much credit, since he showed real grit and courage in making a new departure at an unpromising moment.'[11] Similarly D.R. Daniel had recorded on 29 October: 'G's' budget has forced a wave of new life into the Liberal Party. Before this the party was fading, its leaves beginning to shrivel and a fall in every election and G has revived it from the jaws of the grave....The truth is the Socialist Party has been rather alarmed to see G taking the wind out of their sails.'[12]

Certainly a factor which cannot be ignored in Lloyd George's successful appeal in the last half of 1909 was the Budget League. This was organized in June as an officially independent body although operating, in fact, as an arm of the whip's office. Because of the hard work and genius for publicity of its secretary, Sir Henry Norman, who indeed lost his own seat in January 1910, Liberal election machinery functioned better than it had for many years.[13] Lloyd George had no formal connection with the league except that it sponsored speaking engagements for him, Limehouse and Newcastle for example, as it did for other ministers. Haldane, sick through much of the autumn, was President, and Churchill, Chairman. But two of Lloyd George's closest journalistic lieutenants, Masterman and Harold Spender, were paid public relations assistants cranking out columns of handouts for newspapers and writing speeches.[14] More to the point, Lloyd George saw to finances. The league never seemed to lack for money, Spender recalled.[15] Lloyd George by this time was well acquainted in land reform circles and was able to obtain substantial sums from Joseph Fels, the American soap manufacturer and land reformer.[16] He also obtained funds from English sources and was accused to his face by Pease of promising honors in return for support of the league.[17] Whether or not this was true, Harold Spender names Alfred Mond, a sincere land reformer, as the largest contributor to the league, and certainly Mond became a baronet in 1910 receiving at the same time a translation from the most uncertain borough of Chester City to the safe Liberal haven of Swanseatown.[18] If 'Ll.G. has anything to say about it,

Jack Pease will not be Whip in the coming Parliament,' wrote Lucy Masterman some time in January 1910. He was 'one of the very few people whom George thoroughly hates.'[19] As it turned out Pease was himself defeated at Saffron Walden and Asquith replaced him as whip with Alexander Murray, Master of Elibank, on 10 February 1910 so bringing an important new face into Lloyd George's circle.

Shortly before the election Lloyd George and George Riddell had agreed that the result would be, as it turned out, a virtual tie between the two parties.[20] This prediction represents a retreat from Lloyd George's remarkably rosy anticipations of two months earlier when he wagered a pound with Sir Joseph Lawrence, a Unionist MP, that the Liberals would have a margin of 90 excluding the Irish.[21] This was within the range of Pease's estimate of September of a majority of 40 over the Unionists and Irish together.

The whip's predictions may account for the remarkable lack of concern manifested by the Liberal leaders in the weeks leading up to the election over the possibility that in case of a close vote the government would be prisoners of the Irish. As this was the result, the government faced, even before parliament met, a towering crisis of political strategy that drove it within days after the polling to the verge of resignation. Hence relations with the Irish deserve some brief review. Asquith had promised at the beginning of the campaign that the new Liberal parliament would pursue Home Rule, but this affirmation was more or less routine among Liberals, intended to secure Irish votes for Liberal candidates in British constituencies. Certainly nothing that the Liberal government had done between January 1906 and January 1910 would have suggested even to the most optimistic member of John Redmond's party that the Liberals were preparing to reestablish a parliament on College Green within the foreseeable future. But the leverage accruing from the new situation was clear. On 9 February, even before the last votes were counted in Orkney and Shetland, T.P. O'Connor sent to Lloyd George, just returned from a visit to Nice with Masterman and Charles Henry, a solemn warning: 'I have grave news to give you. I have seen all our friends here and I find them unanimous in saying that they must oppose the budget unless it be preceded by the announcement of a measure limiting the legislative and financial veto of the House of Lords, this to be linked with a guarantee that it would pass into law that same year.'[22] The following day in Cabinet, Asquith read a similar letter from O'Connor to John Morley, and on the next day, 11 February, after a truculent speech by John Redmond at the Gresham Hotel in Dublin which carried the message that would become the Irish slogan for the next few months, 'no veto, no budget,' the outlook seemed incredibly gloomy. If Redmond adhered to his position, and the Unionists chose to work with him, Asquith wrote the King on 11 February, the budget would be defeated in the House of Commons.[23]

Repeatedly in the next few weeks Irish pressure came close to disrupting the newly elected government. The constituents of the problem were several. With the balance of the major parties nearly equal, even with the support of 40 Labourites, the Liberals depended for their majority upon the support, or at least the acquiescence, of the 82 Irish, of whom about 70 were followers of John Redmond and the rest, divided over everything except Home Rule, followers of William O'Brien. Second, precipitating the problem, Asquith incautiously had announced in the opening speech of the election campaign on 10 December at the Albert Hall that his government 'would not submit again to the rebuffs and humiliations of the past four years' and 'would neither assume nor hold office again unless we can secure the safeguards which experience shows us to be necessary for the legislative utility and honour of the party of progress.'[24] To the political world this meant that the Prime Minister had asked, or at least intended to ask soon, as a condition of taking office after the election, for a promise from the King to appoint a sufficient number of peers to allow the passage of a bill reforming either the composition or the powers of the Lords. What no one knew, evidently not even the Cabinet until after the election, was that on 15 December, immediately after this speech, Edward VII had sent Knollys to tell the Prime Minister that he would decline to accept advice to create peers until after a second general election.[25] Thus, Redmond's demanded promise of the passage of a House of Lords reform bill was impossible to give, even had the members of the government been willing to accept the stigma of dictation from the Irish.

Yet, third, the threat of an Irish vote against the budget, 'no veto, no budget,' was no bluff. The Unionists would be delighted to assist. A defeat now in the Commons would justify the action of the House of Lords. More important Redmond was absolutely in earnest, nor was his threat the product of blind vindictiveness. Contrary to what many historians have assumed, he had no fear of turning the Liberals out. The Liberals were most unpopular in Ireland. Redmond did not think that Asquith, Grey and Haldane were committed to Home Rule, although be believed Lloyd George and Churchill were. There was 'no good to be got by keeping Asquith in office,' Redmond told Wilfred Scawen Blunt on 13 February, 'or anything much to be feared by letting Balfour into office. Unless the Liberal party could abolish the Lords' veto there was as much to be hoped from the Tories as from them.' He would trust Asquith only if he made a public promise to obtain guarantees 'in so many words.'[26] Indeed it is one of the supreme ironies of modern British history that the normal allies of the Irish Nationalist party were not the Conservatives, with whom they agreed upon clerical education, licensing, occupier land purchases, local government reform, and even tariffs, but rather the Liberals, the party of secular education, temperance, and Parnell-murdering nonconformity. Redmond understood this himself and had offered the Earl of Dudley (Balfour's last Lord Lieutenant) an exchange of support on tariff reform for Home Rule.[27]

Fourth was the fact that the Irish disliked the budget on its own terms, and the Chancellor of the Exchequer to which it belonged, nearly as much as did the Unionists. Particularly they objected to the licence and spirit duties which hit publicans and distillers, the most important financial supporters of the Nationalist party. Lloyd George had held a long interview at No. 11 on 26 August 1909 with the Nationalist leadership after which Redmond believed that the Chancellor had agreed to certain concessions in the licence duty, but which afterwards were withdrawn.[28] The result was anger and a sense of frustration among the Irish which continued through the rest of 1909 and was quite evident in the conversations that began now in February 1910.[29] The Irish in 1909 in fact had opposed the second reading of the Finance Bill and had abstained on the third reading. After the January election they were in a position of power and would not be put off again.

Finally, there was a wide difference of opinion upon what to do about the House of Lords. By and large the senior men of the Cabinet, led by Grey, wanted to alter the composition of the upper chamber to make it more representative while leaving it the substance of power. Their fear was of a single chamber legislature. This solution would have elicited sympathy among Unionists and within the Lords themselves, but would have been time consuming. The alternative, the quick solution, favored by the radicals in the Cabinet and in the party and demanded by the Irish, was the simple elimination of the upper chamber veto, making the Lords subordinate to the House of Commons and in the last analysis powerless in the face of a determined lower chamber. Lloyd George by instinct was in favor of the latter plan but, as always, he was far more concerned to see the crisis ended so that the government could move forward to more popular issues.

The early days of February 1910 witnessed a decline in Asquith's well-known powers of leadership and decision. He seemed fuzzy and unsure in the Cabinet. His public speeches were hesitant and rambling. There were rumors that he might retire. After a long Cabinet on 12 February in which the group miserably debated the alternatives, which seemed to be either surrender to the Irish or a defeat on the budget and a second election, Asquith announced he would see Redmond the next day. In the event it was not he but Lloyd George who met Redmond and O'Connor.[30] On 12 February Lloyd George outlined a plan for putting the budget without the whiskey duties and a bill dealing with the Lords through the parliamentary process at the same time, with the veto bill going to the upper chamber first where, upon its rejection, there would be an election, probably in July. Lloyd George and the new Chief Whip, Alec Murray, interviewed Redmond again, this time with Dillon, on 17 February, slipping away secretly through the tradesman's entrance during the Prime Minister's dinner at Wimborne House.[31] There is no record of what transpired but the conversations were clearly unproductive for after the meeting Redmond wrote to Lloyd George admitting the impasse. 'We stand, I am sorry to say, where we did at the commencement of our interchange of opinion some days ago,' the Irish leader concluded. Would Lloyd George show the note to the Prime Minister?[32]

Worse was to come. Four days later Asquith, nervous and embarrassed, in what Murray considered the 'worst speech I ever heard him make' admitted to an astonished House of Commons during the debate on the address that he did not have, and had not sought, assurances from the King on the creation of peers.[33] He had not said, he lamely insisted, that 'the Liberal Ministry ought not to meet the new House of Commons,' without 'guarantees' from the monarch.[34] Unfortunately, as anyone with a copy of *The Times* for 11 December would have known, this was exactly what he had said except that instead of the word 'guarantees' he had used the word 'safeguards.' Other ministers, including Lloyd George, had said the same thing.

After Asquith's confession of 21 February, relations between the Liberal government and the Irish were frozen and the Liberal party in the country, in C.P. Scott's words, was in 'confusion and despair.'[35] Redmond, who had followed Asquith on the twenty-first, announced angrily that the Irish had not supported the Liberals in the election because of the Prime Minister's declaration for Home Rule, but precisely because of the promise 'not to hold or assume office,' which he had now withdrawn. In fact here lay the essence of the problem. At issue was the position of the monarch. Asquith could not make a public promise to the Irish on whether the King, in a hypothetical situation, would take a step of very dubious constitutional propriety. Yet the Irish were requiring that the Prime Minister bring the crisis to a head before the Finance Bill was approved, simply to find out. There seemed to be no escape.

By 25 February the government was on the verge of resignation. Lloyd George told Lewis that evening at a Welsh dinner that but for Churchill and himself the Cabinet would have returned its seals that afternoon. The government, he said, was living from hand to mouth. Ministers were staying in their departments and not thinking about Cabinet matters.[36]

In his disastrous speech of 21 February, Asquith, holding out a compromise to the Irish, had announced that the government would proceed with the House of Lords question by the formulation of resolutions on the relationship between the two houses which would be later embodied in a bill. At the same time, the Prime Minister had announced that until the Easter recess on 24 March the government would preempt all the time of the House for the passage of financial measures necessary to legalize the Treasury borrowing of the last few months. He described the resolutions briefly a few days later, telling enough to indicate that they would deal with the upper chamber's veto and that reform would be left to 'a subsequent year.'[37] Redmond, following him, challenged him again to state whether, if the resolutions were thrown out 'or hung up' in the Lords, he would ask for guarantees on the creation of peers.[38]

Here the crisis lay through the next month while the House of Commons toiled with expedients for funding the spending that had occurred since the previous November. (It should be noted that the government requested spending authorization for six weeks only so that if it were turned out the incoming Unionists would be not only without money to run government departments, but without the votes to extract it from the House of Commons.) Before the House reassembled on 29 March, Grey wrote to the Prime Minister saying that he would resign unless there were a serious attempt at reform. Runciman, McKenna, and perhaps Haldane, would go with him.[39]

The second stage of the crisis began on 29 March when the veto resolutions were put before the House of Commons and ended on 14 April, when, as if by magic, the problem was solved. A central element of the difficulty of this period lay in the fundamental misapprehension of the Cabinet, shared it seems by historians since that time, that Redmond really cared a great deal about the whiskey taxes, admittedly most unpopular in Ireland, and would have been willing to forego his opposition to the budget if they were dropped. Charles Hobhouse, whose ability to collect misinformation in his early days in the ministry nearly equalled that of Burns, went about saying this even after the crisis was over.[40] Redmond denied this again and again. On 16 March, in Newcastle, he expressly contradicted the idea. The Irish, he said, would 'not let go their grip on the Budget before they knew what was going to happen to the Veto.'

> Some people seemed to imagine that their attitude on the matter was governed by certain taxes in the Budget. The Irish, they said, did not like the whiskey taxes. Well, they did not and there were other taxes they did not like, but he vehemently denied that their attitude on the Budget was governed by those considerations. On behalf of the Irish Party he offered in the House of Commons to accept the budget in one hour tomorrow... without change of one comma so long as they had assurance that the Government would be able to deal effectively with the House of Lords.

He would not hesitate to defeat the budget and was not afraid of a general election.[41] He repeated virtually the same statement in Liverpool four days later.

Nothing could be clearer than that. The heir to the mantle of Butt and Parnell would not be seduced from his duty by the promise of pennies off a glass of whiskey. Yet there was the smaller group, the independent O'Brienite nationalists, whose separate existence dated only from the 1910 election and whose differences with Redmond's party, although involving a large amount of personal animosity, included also a wider concern for Irish taxation and land reform. During March Lloyd George, with the authority of the Cabinet, sought to separate the two groups, promising the repeal of the whiskey duties and an increase in the land purchase fund in return for O'Brienite support. His intent, made obvious in a bitter speech by William O'Brien on 18 April, was to detach the independents from the Redmondites by offering these concessions, sure to be popular in Ireland, which the majority of the nationalists could then be said to have refused.[42]

Evidently it was the breakdown of negotiations with O'Brien, never more than a forlorn hope, that convinced Lloyd George the solution lay elsewhere.[43] It was useless to try to bribe Redmond with a gift he did not want. Contrary to what the Cabinet believed, he now himself regarded the whiskey taxes as 'trivial.'[44] This conviction, however, he kept from the Cabinet, all of whom, except Churchill, had in any case not yet agreed to suffer the indignity of repealing the taxes, which were most popular with the radicals in the party. Then on Tuesday, 12 April, Lloyd George announced primly that he and 'his advisors' had decided that from a fiscal point of view the deletion of the whiskey tax was quite impossible.[45] He made clear what no one had understood before: that from the government's point of view the whiskey duties were more valuable in fact in the budget than out of it, but only if they were accompanied by a declaration from the Prime Minister about the creation of peers. If the Prime Minister would not agree, reported Alec Murray, who parenthetically had become since appointment the second in Lloyd George's tiny group of Cabinet supporters, the Chancellor would resign and join the Irish.[46] The scene, according to Lucy Masterman was of 'joy and astonishment...caused by this refusal to be dictated to by the Irish....' But then immediately and dramatically came the question of guarantees. 'The decision,' Lloyd George declared, 'could not be put off any longer. The Irish would not put the government out on the whiskey tax.' To do so would be to alienate the priests and the whole body of English radicals. But:

> They would put it out for refusing to ask for guarantees and for not carrying out its own declared policy; though the whiskey tax might be the motive of the rank and file. The rank and file of the Liberal party would undoubtedly be in sympathy with the Irish on the subject of the guarantees, even if, under pressure of the Whips, they voted in the Government lobby. If a declaration was made on guarantees, the Irish could not possibly vote against it, and 'Redmond, if he wished to turn them out, would have to do so unashamedly on the whiskey tax, where the rank and file would be dead against them.'
> Suddenly the whole opposition in the Cabinet collapsed, the government agreed to the double declaration, keeping the whiskey tax and giving the promise of the guarantee policy, and to let Redmond do his best or worst.[47]

Lloyd George had stampeded the Cabinet into making most of the declarations that the Irish demanded. Asquith now would have to reaffirm his dishonored statement of 10 December. Murray, who suggests that it was he who convinced Lloyd George that the whiskey duties were irrelevant for the Irish, no matter what the Cabinet believed, realized the simplicity of the solution.

> I never saw a set of men more relieved than the members of the Cabinet on its breakup. Why in Heaven's name they could not have come to this decision two months earlier and saved all this pother, I for one cannot understand. There is no doubt they were tired and overworked and overanxious and weighed down with the extraordinary responsibilities that faced them. Moreover, it is a Cabinet composed of men of many striking personalities and men of strong mind and independence of thought and action, and this factor no doubt is one of the contributory causes of delay in their decision. But when such a decision is taken, it is of immeasurably more value and strength than one of a one-man, invertebrate, jellyfish Cabinet, such as Arthur Balfour loved to gather around him.[48]

How distressed and divided the Cabinet had been was evident in Asquith's letter to the King on 13 April covering three consecutive days of Cabinet meetings. He was still unsure that a coalition of the Irish and Unionists might not yet defeat the budget and therefore

> a crisis of an unexampled and most embarrassing kind would arise. How is Your Majesty's government to be carried on? By whom? With what Parliamentary majority? Or is the country after an interval of barely three months, to be plunged again into the turmoil of and expense of a general election with the disturbance of trade and the embitterment of feeling which inevitably accompany an appeal to the people?
> It is an acute sense of these public disadvantages and dangers, and not any desire to prolong their official life, which under existing conditions is

far from being a bed of roses, that has [had?] induced Your Majesty's ministers to authorize the Chancellor of the Exchequer to interchange views with the leaders of the two sections of the Nationalist Party. From the first, both were made clearly to understand that the Chancellor had no authority to offer concessions or to make bargains. He was simply to invite an expression of their views, and to discuss the scope and relative importance of their objections to the Budget as it stands.

The result of these conversations however had been small and the Cabinet were unanimously of the opinion that the transformation of what was in 1909 made a permanent tax, into a temporary tax, would be a modification of the framework of the budget which would not be consistent with their promises.

Asquith, as can be seen, was not entirely candid with the King. He emphasized Irish dislike of the budget, which was incidental, and said nothing of Redmond's demands for guarantees. But whatever the reasons, the message was unchanged: '. . . it is possible, and at this moment not improbable, that as a consequence the Nationalists may on Monday combine with the opposition to defeat the government.' But there was one other thing he said in conclusion.

> The Cabinet have determined that if the resolutions carried by the
> Commons are rejected or laid aside by the Lords, it would be their duty
> at once to tender advice to the Crown as to the necessary steps—whether
> by the exercise of the prerogative or by a referendum ad hoc, or other-
> wise to be taken to ensure that the policy approved by the House of
> Commons by a large majority should be given statutory effect in this
> Parliament.

If they did not receive agreement they would resign or advise a dissolution, but there would be no dissolution except 'under such conditions as would secure in the new Parliament that the judgement of the people expressed at the elections would be carried into law.'[49] Asquith now had demanded the promise the King already had vowed he would not give without a second election.

The next day in the House of Commons, during the last day of debate on the House of Lords resolutions, Asquith pronounced the fatal words. Balfour, guessing what was coming, obtained an order from the Speaker to prevent the announcement during ordinary business, but with the final vote on the resolutions and after the Parliament Bill in which the resolutions were embodied received its first reading by title only, he rose, at 11:00 p.m. on a motion to adjourn. In half a dozen sentences he ended the crisis. If the government he said were not in a position to ensure that statutory effect was given to the resolutions just approved 'we shall either resign our offices or recommend a dissolution of Parliament.' But the government would not recommend a dissolution 'except under such circumstances as will secure in the new Parliament the judgment of the people as expressed in the election will be carried into law.'[50]

As Asquith's letter to the King indicated, no one was sure that a promise only to seek guarantees upon the threat of resignation from a stubborn

King would satisfy Redmond. Reluctance to offend English noncon-formists, who had so often insulted the Irish, over whiskey might not be enough to ensure Redmond's support of the budget. Redmond suggested cheerfully after the Prime Minister's statement that he was satisfied, but the critical day remained Monday, 18 April, when the Prime Minister put down the guillotine resolution to govern the passage of the reintroduced Finance Bill. At this time O'Brien made his violent statement charging the government in general and Lloyd George in particular with deception and falsehood on the whiskey tax. Redmond followed him saying that the Nationalists had decided, only that afternoon, to support the guillotine resolutions. He added that although he would have preferred to block the budget until he saw what the Lords did with the veto resolutions, and that the Prime Minister had promised less than the Irish wanted, an attempt to hold up the Finance Bill now would hurt rather than help the campaign for Home Rule. Last of all, he emphasized that until his party had met that afternoon no one in London could have told how the Irish would vote. There had been no bargain.[51] When the House divided the guillotine resolution passed with a majority of 93. The Redmondites solidly supported the resolution and the O'Brienites equally unanimously opposed it. The Lords approved it the next day without a division. Finally on 29 April, exactly one year after Lloyd George's original budget statement, the Finance Bill of 1909 received the royal assent.

Asquith's previous letters had given the King no intimation of his government's change of position on guarantees. Indeed, in Biarritz, Edward probably received the newspaper report of Asquith's announce-ment of 14 April and the Cabinet letter warning of it at the same time. His biographer describes him as 'cruelly depressed,' although he discounts rumors that the shock caused his death three weeks later. Knollys, almost hysterical with fury, wrote to Esher that if he were King he would abdicate rather than agree to the creation of peers.[52] Nevertheless, a step had been taken. Another imperative directing the course of political events was now in place. As the Lords' veto of the Finance Bill had caused the elections, the elections had given the Irish their leverage. Redmond used his power with great skill, refusing to be bought off by sudden concessions on the same whiskey taxes which had been refused him the previous autumn. Lloyd George eventually had convinced the Cabinet that the guarantees would have to be reissued. But in so doing the government now committed itself to the next step in the inexorable process, the struggle with the House of Lords and, beyond that, to a parliament in Dublin whose jurisdiction not all Irishmen would accept.

Asquith continually asserted that there was no bargain with the Irish. In the technical sense, that the Irish gave nothing except support for the 1909 Finance Bill, this was true. (Balfour styled it a 'quasi bargain.') As his letter to the King of 13 April testified, the Prime Minister was not even sure, on that day, that the Irish finally would support the Finance Bill. But he underestimated Redmond's singlemindedness, and wittingly or not, he had traded away his freedom of action. Nor did he see that on 14 April he had planted the seeds of revolution in Ulster, the wild harvest Lloyd George one day would have to reap.

II

Just before midnight, on 6 May, King Edward VII, who had returned from Biarritz only on 27 April, expired. In those nine days he had made no promise on the creation of peers. On the contrary, on the day he returned, at a secret conference at Lambeth Palace, Balfour had agreed to take office should the Liberals resign in the face of the King's refusal to participate in the coercion of the upper chamber.[53]

To Lloyd George, the King's death was more a surprise than a shock. His relations with the throne had been patently bad in the past few years, but he was accustomed to abuse and Edward at least was a known quantity. The possibility of his death 'never entered our calculations,' he wrote Maggie on 8 May, adding solemnly, 'we reckoned without taking the Great Ruler into account.'[54] The Great Ruler may or may not have been a Unionist, but the opposition took advantage of His intervention and the accession of a new King to divert the impending collision between the two houses. The idea of an interparty conference on the House of Lords originated with J.L. Garvin, editor of the *Observer,* who proposed a 'Truce of God' in a leader in his newspaper on 8 May.[55] Within a few days it was accepted, a little warily, by leaders on both sides of the house. Lloyd George was willing, if not anxious, to go along. He could see as well as anyone the web of contingent promises in which the government was caught and, even if other party leaders were distrustful, his nature and political style leaned toward private accommodation and compromise when an intractable issue was at hand. Through W.T. Stead he encouraged Garvin to push along with his proposal.

Lloyd George also may have been impelled toward the idea of a conference for more practical reasons of Liberal advantage. He distrusted the new King on the question of the House of Lords, according to Lucy Masterman, and wanted a delay to mark time.[56] One may suspect he had little hope that the conference, by itself, would accomplish much. But to proceed with the Parliament Bill and force a general election in late July, which Asquith had promised not to call without royal promises, was to court disaster. To some extent Asquith's statement of 14 April had been a bluff of which George V, perhaps from ignorance, apparently was not frightened. These are not speculations. Within days after the succession of the new king, Asquith had received a note from Arthur Bigge, the new King's private secretary, saying that any agreements made with the dead King were not binding on the new one.[57]

The Cabinet agreed formally upon a conference (soon to be styled the 'Constitutional Conference') on 6 June and on 9 June Asquith wrote to Balfour requesting a meeting. The first meeting occurred in the Prime Minister's room in the House of Commons on 17 June. The Liberal delegation consisted of Asquith, Lloyd George, Augustine Birrell, the Irish Secretary, and Lord Crewe. The opposition was represented by Balfour, Austen Chamberlain, Lansdowne, and Lord Cawdor, Lloyd George's most implacable Welsh foe and Balfour's confidant and advisor during the education struggle. This was not a strong delegation; it was reminiscent of Balfour's Cabinet, made up largely of cronies and containing only the intellect of its leader. (Cawdor had been Balfour's fag at Eton as Balfour was Lansdowne's.) Lloyd George later told Charles Masterman that the only person he could deal with was Balfour and conversely that Balfour usually addressed his remarks to Lloyd George.[58]

Between 17 June and 29 July, after which parliament rose, the conference met 13 times. It did not convene again until 11 October when there was a week of sessions and another adjournment to the beginning of November, in all 22 meetings.[59] Generally the Constitutional Conference belongs to the wider story of politics of the prewar period although Lloyd George's part in the deliberations was substantial. Nonetheless, it is apparent that he soon was discontented. Asquith proposed at the beginning that the conference address the matter of Lords' reform by separate consideration of methods of dealing with financial, ordinary, and special or organic (i.e. constitutional) legislation. The pitfall within this sensible suggestion lay not in how each category should be dealt with—no one quarreled with the assertion that approval of money bills was the prerogative of the House of Commons alone—but with the definition of each type of measure. Within a short time, by the end of the first series of meetings, it was clear that the question of whether Home Rule, even though never mentioned, was organic or ordinary legislation would eventually break up the conference.

From Lloyd George's point of view the value of the conference resided in its potential as a vehicle for the mediation of issues dividing the parties. Even though he had denounced the House of Lords for years he disliked wrangling about institutional structures or parliamentary techniques in the abstract. Theories about legislative practice bored him. What mattered was not how the government operated, but what got done. And above all, obscuring all the earnest conversation, Asquith's inexorable logic and Balfour's dialectical brilliance, loomed the single overarching and invisible fact of Home Rule for Ireland. Only if the conference could agree on that would it succeed. If not, it would fail.

Lloyd George atempted to force this truth upon his colleagues at the last meetings of the first session, on 27 and 28 July, when he proposed a definition of organic legislation which would include only questions dealing with the monarchy, the protestant succession, the House of Lords, and the relationship between the two houses, in effect pertaining only to con-clusions achieved by the conference itself. Home Rule thus would be treated as ordinary legislation.[60] This excursion nearly disrupted the meetings. Probably it was now that Lloyd George determined that if British politics were not to dissolve into open warfare in which nothing would be accomplished, a wider settlement, including not only Home Rule and tariff reform but his own social and land program, would have to be achieved. Here almost certainly lay the origins of the famous proposal for coalition between the two major parties which Lloyd George drafted within the next two weeks at Criccieth, finally dated 17 August. This remarkable document of 29 typescript pages seems at first to be so out of step with the increasing ferocity of Georgian partisan warfare that recent historians have explained it as evidence of some fascination for coalitions secreted within its author.[61] Yet basically the Criccieth proposal was simply another manifestation of Lloyd George's usual way of conducting political business through conciliation and mutual accommodation, always aiming at circumventing the single issue enthusiasts who tended to dominate both parties. But more significantly the coalition memorandum stands as an earnest attempt, even at the ultimate sacrifice of his own office, to avert the impending crisis over Home Rule and to solve, should he remain in the government, a serious, immediate and practical problem in social insurance.

In his *War Memoirs* Lloyd George uses the coalition memorandum, like his account of his conversations with the German ambassador in 1908, as evidence of his steady concern for British military preparedness.[62] As a result, his description of the proposal dwells almost entirely upon a few sentences suggesting that Britain might adopt the Swiss militia system of military training. This was in fact a minor point in the document. The near breakdown of the Constitutional Conference was clearly the occasion for his proposal. The Conference would never arrive at a settlement of the Lords issue without an agreement on Home Rule, yet, he could reason, a settlement of substantive issues within a two party ministry would make a conclusion on the Lords unnecessary. The power of the House of Lords was irrelevant if work somehow could be done. A point not noticed by the many historians who have commented upon, but apparently not read, the coalition memorandum is that the one issue never mentioned in the 17 August document was the upper chamber veto.[63] However, the central theme of the coalition proposal was neither the impasse over the House of Lords nor the call for national security, but the pressing need for joint action by both parties on domestic reform, to 'liquidate the arrears of reform, to repair the deficiencies of our national system...which, if much longer neglected, may end in national impoverishment, if not insolvency.' These were murky generalities of the sort Lloyd George usually employed when working his way toward a plan for action—a litany of problems rather than solutions. In the memorandum itself eight of the twelve items specified for attention, and the ones discussed in by far the greatest detail, concerned domestic social and economic reform, essentially the existing program of the New Liberalism. Lloyd George had set his heart on this program and saw it in danger of being destroyed, as had been the Welsh nationalist reform program nearly two decades earlier, by the battle over Home Rule. Again, as in the 1890s, 'Ireland blocked the way.'

Immediately after the House recessed on 2 August, with six weeks of fruitless discussion behind him, Lloyd George retreated to Criccieth. Here, walking through the meadow and woodland between his house and Llanystumdwy three miles away, he described to D.R. Daniel his hopes for what might lie beyond the Constitutional Conference. He spoke in some detail of his earnest desire for a settlement between the parties. 'I could see,' wrote Daniel,

> without his guessing I was judging him that he was in this discussion with an honest mind and quite patriotic intentions. I noticed this many times in the conversation when he could not be intending to mislead me in my mind. It was quite clear that he thought there were potentialities of a Grand Coalition Government on the doorstep, with the great aim before it of tackling the great social questions that were now ripe for settlement. But to effect such a consummation G was quite aware that the spirit of

self-effacement was necessary. G thought that he could himself bring Balfour around to this. 'Tackle him' I think were his words. 'What a large amount of solid work could be done,' said G 'about five or ten years before another party could arise!' Balfour as Prime Minister in the Lords, Asquith as Leader, Austen Chamberlain as Chancellor if he desired it—self-denial is essential—combined with a genuine endeavour to settle the questions of poverty, intemperance, land and other mighty problems. G showed himself to be quite ready for the sacrifice. His talk was dominated by the spirit of reform, the enthusiasm of humanity, his soul is still young. He has immense amounts of hope....[64]

This talk, as the two men walked along the bank of the Dwyfor near a spot where, as Lloyd George pointed out, Churchill had once fallen in and nearly drowned—a feat that would seem impossible except as a deliberate act of self-immolation—revealed Lloyd George at his most idealistic. There is no reason to suppose that he meant less than he said, even though he often used men such as Daniel, or Herbert Lewis, or Masterman, as targets for the verbal formulation of his ideas. The burden of this meaning was that British affairs were at an impasse. The Constitutional Conference, even if it solved the problem of the House of Lords, would lead only to a further more dangerous and more prolonged strife over Ireland. To restore movement and action to politics the great parties must end the struggle and cooperate, take the initiative from the extremists on both flanks, and concentrate upon the national welfare.

This resolve is manifest in the introduction to the coalition proposals of 17 August which provides also a succinct and honest exposition of Lloyd George's view of two-party democratic politics. Parties, he wrote, explaining a truth that he understood well from experience, are not dominated by their majority centers but by their radical fringes.

> Extreme partisans supporting the government often drive it against its better judgement to attempting legislation on lines which are the least useful in dealing with a question. As a rule the advanced sections of a Party, being propagandist, are the most active, the best organized, the most resolute, and therefore the most irresistible. Joint action would make it possible to settle these urgent questions without paying undo regard to the formulae and projects of rival faddists.

Joint action, he contended, was the more imperative because of the present equality between the parties in the House of Commons.

> If you have a hostile party with nearly half the nation amongst its organized supporters waiting to take advantage of every slip, no ministry will be disposed to take unnecessary risks, and often the unpopular section of a project has to be ruthlessly cut out, in order to save the remnant, although that section may be essential to a complete and successful treatment of the subject.

'A government with a small majority,' he continued,

> has only to alienate a comparatively small number of the electorate in the country in order to incur defeat, and an Opposition has only to win the support of the same number in order to oust their opponents from

power. Thus often the least responsible, the least well-informed and the most selfish amongst the electorate may have a decisive view in determining the issues upon which the whole fortunes of the British Empire may depend. If joint action between the Parties could be negotiated, these undesirable elements would sink to their proper significance as factors.

This is a corollary of the two preceding propositions. No settlement is possible without exciting a good many ill-informed prejudices, some of them with an historical basis. They cannot be argued with, they cannot always be voted down; but they are extremely pernicious in their influence upon the settlement of a difficult and complex problem. Separate action means that a Party in opposition is driven into enlisting the support of these prejudices, whether it wishes to do so or not: the more extreme men amongst their own supporters on the platform and in the press always take advantage of these elements, however enlightened the view the Party leaders may take.

All of this applied obviously to the Home Rule issue. If there remained any question that Lloyd George was willing to compromise in this area he removed it in an addendum to the paragraph dealing with what he styled 'Imperial Problems.' Here, after remarking that schemes for defense and economic improvement of overseas territories were particularly appropriate for adjudication in a coalition ministry, he concluded with one of the few nominal references in the memorandum. 'In this connection, the settlement of the Irish question would come up for consideration. The advantages of a non-Party treatment of this vexed problem are obvious. Parties might deal with it without being subject to embarassing [sic] dictation of extreme partisans, whether from Nationalists or Orangemen.' He elaborated on this in early October in discussing his memorandum with F.E. Smith. The Liberal Party, he said, was 'pledged to Devolution in some form or another and could not abandon the pledge, but if a scheme agreed on between the two great Parties were rejected by the Irish, the Liberals would then wash their hands of the whole affair and leave the Irish to stew in their own juice.'[65]

Although outflanking the Irish was evidently in Lloyd George's mind when he wrote the coalition memorandum, the bulk of the document was a plea for help on social reform combined with attractions for the Unionists in the form of proposals for compromise on tariff reform, compulsory military training, and consolidation of the empire. However these, in every case except one, were discussed in the most ambiguous terms as 'topics to be investigated' or 'questions...not to be shirked.' He supplied a little more detail in a supplementary memorandum dictated on 20 October after the Unionist leadership had seen the original document and evidently had pressed him for specific proposals.[66] The second memorandum can be taken as a measure of the distance Lloyd George would have gone in negotiations to obtain Unionist support for land reform and insurance. On tariffs he suggested immediate colonial preferences for any goods that were currently paying duty and an investigation into the tariff system, which, he stipulated in conversations with Austen Chamberlain, would be required to finish its work in six months. He promised that he would support 'all necessary steps to be taken for the defense of the empire at home and abroad' which would be coupled, however, with attempts at international understanding in order to reduce the expenditure on arms. The Welsh Church would have to be disestablished, but this could be done on the more generous terms of the Irish Church settlement of 1869, with a referendum before any action. On Home Rule, Lloyd George invoked Chamberlain's plan of 1886, in effect his own favorite, Home Rule All Round.

These were astounding concessions and after being amplified in conversations with Unionist leaders some of the latter were led to ask Balfour how Lloyd George could justify them to his own people. To this the leader of the opposition replied sensibly that that was Lloyd George's business, not theirs.[67] Still, the coalition proposals were intended first of all to buy Unionist help for the New Liberalism and most of the items discussed or mentioned were those with which Lloyd George had been involved since his entrance into parliament. Besides disestablishment, he proposed education reform along the lines of the bill of 1906, licensing, land reform generally within the terms of his development scheme, systematic aid for public housing, (a matter with which he would concern himself more and more frequently henceforth), action to overhaul the poor law and to relieve unemployment, and finally, in by far the longest and most detailed single item in the 17 August document, Lloyd George asked for help in protecting his plan for invalidity and widows' pensions from the intrusions of the industrial insurance industry.

The long paragraphs on, insurance (although for some reason under the heading of 'unemployment') are in such contrast to the murky formlessness of the rest of the memorandum that they seem to belong to a different document. In them Lloyd George attempted to explain a matter which at the time he did not quite understand but which represented a clear and present crisis. It had nothing to do with political principles, the future regeneration of Britain, or the increasing virulence in British national politics. Rather he hoped to use a party coalition to circumvent the threat to his social insurance program from the nation's commercial insurance industry. And, as it turned out, the failure of the Criccieth proposals caused a major overhaul in the structure of the insurance program, opening it in operation to forms of abuse that seriously reduced its utility and resulted in permanent harm to the friendly societies, whom Lloyd George had promised always to protect. As such this part of the coalition proposal was of much importance and requires some explanation.

It will be recalled that the conferences with the friendly society leaders in the last three months of 1908 had produced the skeleton of a plan of insurance-based pensions, offered through friendly societies, for sick and disabled workmen and for widows and orphans. The plan was to be compulsory upon all manual workers employed for weekly wages and for all others earning less than £160 per year. (i.e. the beginning level of liability for income tax). Most important, the basic pension was very small, only 5s per week (approximately one quarter of an unskilled worker's weekly wage, although agricultural wages were less) and less than half the benefit usually paid by friendly societies in sickness claims to their ordinary members. Lloyd George's agreement with the societies, constantly reiterated, was that his scheme would strengthen them, not compete with them. The low benefits were designed to induce the 6 million members of the British working class who were not currently members of the societies and who would now be required to register with one, to insure individually through a society for extra benefits. (These features of the original insurance plan answer the question of why the Lloyd George scheme offered workers of varying incomes only equal benefits. The assumption was that private insurance would provide income-related payments. The original Beveridge plan included these same provisions only to have them cut out in the National Insurance Bill of 1946.)

The first scheme of insurance was finally submitted to actuaries on 20 April 1909. By this time it had grown to include medical care by doctors under contract to the friendly societies, a maternity benefit, and sanatorial care for tuberculosis. As has been seen, Lloyd George announced the plan in grand but vague terms in his 1909 budget statement nine days later and wrote to the societies in the summer of 1909 urging them to commend the principle of state insurance to their annual conferences. Finally in his 1910 budget address on 30 June, he stated that a bill for invalidity insurance as well as unemployment insurance would be put down in 1911.[68] Meanwhile, on 21 March, he received the report of the actuaries.[69]

At some time during the summer of 1910, Lloyd George learned that the insurance program as presently planned would be opposed by industrial insurance, one of the wealthiest and potentially the most influential concentrations of commercial and financial power in the United Kingdom. The term 'industrial insurance' referred specifically to the sale of 'funeral benefits', that is life insurance policies carrying a face value of at most £10 or £15 intended to provide the deceased with a respectable funeral and to save him from the unspeakable degradation of the potter's field. On this narrow basis had been built a huge, incredibly profitable commercial interest with, in 1910, 40 million policies outstanding worth well over £300 million, nearly half the national debt, and a premium income of over £15 million per year. All of this was handled by an army of some seventy thousand collector-salesmen who visited nearly every working class household in the nation to collect personally the weekly one or two penny premium which gave industrial insurance its peculiar characteristic. (It was often designated 'collecting insurance'.)

Although there were scores of industrial insurance companies, only twelve, of which nine were limited companies and three collecting friendly societies, conducted well over 90% of the business. By far the largest company was the Prudential which accounted for perhaps two-fifths of the business of the entire industry.[70]

The army of agents was the secret of the political power of the commercial insurance industry. Collecting the premiums on 40 million funeral policies gave the agents access to the working class of Great Britain. The lobbying influence of commercial insurance was therefore more than the power of established wealth. The collectors were a fully developed core of political canvassers of a kind a Liberal or Unionist election agent could only admire. Moreover, this was an army with a particular financial interest in the struggle. The high commissions and new business bonuses involved in the sale of funeral benefits offered a sharp, unabashed, persuasive young man of working class background the opportunity to earn as much as £3 or £4 per week income—an amount enjoyed by only one person in six in pre-World War I Britain. Such an interest was worth protecting. Even though their agents were likely to be radical-Liberals in politics, to be members of the National Union of Assurance Agents, and to have no particular love for the company that employed them, the insurance industry leaders received the full cooperation of their outdoor staff in the struggle that developed over national insurance.

To the individual agent the total amount of contributions due him for policies outstanding was termed in the trade his 'book'. The value of the book would normally be between £4 and £10 per week. However, the agent's commission was calculated not on the theoretical amount of the book, but on the amount of weekly collections, which in a poor neighborhood would never be the full amount of the book, and agents continually asserted that they lent their own money for premiums when a customer had no pennies in the sugar bowl on the parlor mantelpiece. The book constituted the agent's equity in his business. It was the accumulation of his goodwill with his customers. Books could be bought from agents changing companies, or they could be built up from nothing. A few particularly persuasive solicitors of new business devoted themselves to building up books on commission for other agents, or for sale. The sale price of a book might be between twenty and forty times its face. Although it was never calculated officially the total value of the books of seventy thousand collecting agents could not have been less than £15 million, and was stated by David Lloyd George in the coalition memorandum to be twice this amount. Here was a vested interest that could not be ignored and which was in a position to protect itself.

Technically Lloyd George's program did not compete with industrial insurance. The conferences of 1908 had expressly agreed to exclude funeral benefits, partially in order to avoid arousing outside protests, but particularly because friendly societies offered funeral benefits also. The difficulty in the summer of 1910 arose however over widows' and orphans' pensions, instigated, it would appear, not by the insurance companies themselves but by the collecting salesmen, the outdoor staff. Although the date is uncertain, Lloyd George interviewed representatives of the agents probably in June, and learned to his surprise of their opposition to the still-secret terms of the invalidity insurance program. (Lloyd George made no reference to widows' pensions in discussing his insurance program in the budget statement on 30 June, which suggests that the meeting with the insurance agents had already occurred. Henceforth he always described it as a plan of 'insurance for invalidity, disability, etc.' Etcetera meant pensions.) At the meeting the agents announced baldly that they and the companies they represented would resist any government payment contingent upon the death of a worker, not only a funeral benefit, but a widow's pension or any other benefit that would lessen the bereaved's financial difficulty. Their political influence was quite clear. In

418

the homes they visited they were looked upon, they said, as advisors, counselors and friends. No government, particularly a Liberal one, could oppose them.

Lloyd George obviously was unfamiliar with the business of collecting insurance. In the only account of the meeting, written unfortunately twenty years later, he was reported to have suggested that perhaps the government could offer compensation to the agents for the loss in their books. No doubt 'a few tens of thousands would settle the matter. He was told to his surprise that in one great Society alone, adequate compensation would amount to between two and three million pounds.'[71] Widows' and orphans' pensions would have to be taken from the bill.

Here then was the origin of the long, rather unclear paragraphs that form the central part of the coalition memorandum. Insurance, said Lloyd George, 'illustrates one of the difficulties that must necessarily be encountered by every Government that attempts to grapple with it without first securing the cooperation of its opponents.'

The hardest case of all is that of the man who dies in the prime of life leaving a widow and young children. She suddenly finds herself without adequate means, very often with all her means exhausted by medical and funeral expenses, face to face with the task of having not merely to attend to her household duties and the bringing up of the children, but also with that of earning a livelihood for herself and for them. In Germany they contemplate adding provision for widows under these conditions to their ordinary invalidity insurance. It is comparatively easy to set a system of that kind in Germany; but, here, one would have to encounter the bitter hostility of powerful organizations like the Prudential, the Liver, the Royal Victoria [sic], the Pearl and similar institutions, with an army, numbering scores if not hundreds of thousands, of agents and collectors that make a living out of collecting a few pence a week from millions of households in this country for the purpose of providing death allowances [Royal Liver and Liverpool Victoria]. The expenses of collection and administration come to something like 50% of the total receipts, and these poor widows and children are by this extravagant system robbed of one half of the benefit which it has cost the workman so much to provide for them. Sometimes these agents and collectors sell their books and sub-let them and make hundreds of pounds out of the transactions, all at the expense of the poorest and most helpless creatures in the land. This system ought to be terminated at the earliest possible moment. The benefits are small, costly and precarious, for, if a man is unable, owing to ill-health, or lack of employment, to keep up his payments his policy is forfeited. State insurance costs 10% to administer, and, in as much as the state and the employer both contribute, either the premium is considerably less, or the benefits are substantially greater than with the Insurance Companies. But, however desirable it may be to substitute State Insurance, which does not involve collection and therefore is more economical, any Party that attempted it would instantly incur the relentless hostility of all these agents and collectors.

They visit every house, they are indefatigable, they are often very intelligent, and a Government which attempted to take over their work without first of all securing the cooperation of the other Party would inevitably fail in its undertaking; so that, if a scheme of national insurance is taken in hand by any Party Government, it must be confined to Invalidity, and the most urgent and pitiable cases of all must be left out. I may add that compensation on an adequate scale is well-nigh impossible, in as much as it would cost something like 20 or 30 millions at the very least to buy off the interest of these collectors, and such a payment would crush the scheme and destroy its usefulness. On the other hand the agents cannot be absorbed into the new system there being no door to door collection contemplated. This is an excellent illustration of the difficulty of dealing with some of these problems except by joint action.

These passages excited no interest among the Unionists; Austen Chamberlain, who understood the ways of the commercial world better than most of his colleagues, recalled two years later only that there was 'some vague reference to Insurance, which, if done by common agreement could be done better and cheaper than by one party.'[72] Nevertheless, had Lloyd George been able to face the challenge of industrial insurance, instead of surrendering to it, national insurance in Great Britain, as will be seen, would have evolved as a vastly different program.

III

Within days after the coalition memorandum was complete, but before he had shown it to anyone, Lloyd George and Charles Masterman traveled to southern Austria and then by car to northern Italy for a short holiday. Masterman by now was a constant companion and Lloyd George, for some time, had been trying to bring him to the Treasury in place of Charles Hobhouse, who himself wanted to move. But Asquith, who depended upon Hobhouse to keep him informed of what his Chancellor of the Exchequer was doing, refused to agree to the exchange.[73]

Masterman was then 36, the son of an impecunious but devout evangelical family. He had attended Christ's College, Cambridge on a scholarship, winning a double first in Natural and Moral Science. After leaving university, he settled in a slum dwelling in Camberwell, there to work among the poor and to publicize their condition in the *Daily News* and the *Nation*. Throughout his life Masterman was afflicted with an overwhelming sympathy for the helpless. This philanthropy, reinforced by an uncompromising high Churchmanship learned at Cambridge, provided the spur for his political career, but turned him also into an almost pathological depressive as he came to realize how little he could do to change the world. He was a brilliant writer and reporter on social subjects. His best book, a classic dissection of Edwardian society, *The Condition of England*, went through six editions between 1909 and 1911. Lord Beaverbrook thought him one of the two best journalists in England; the other was Churchill. And like Churchill, although a good performer in the House of Commons, he was a poor constituency man. Churchill was arrogant, unfriendly, and without small talk. Masterman was pessimistic and ironic. Not surprisingly when Masterman entered the House of Commons in 1906 he and Churchill became close comrades.[74] Less than a year apart in age, considered equally odd, both married in 1908 notably handsome women who were also contemporaries. The two couples were identified socially, while the two men, as supporters of Lloyd George, began to rise together in Liberal affairs. Even when he was at the Local Government Board under Burns and, after July 1909 at the Home Office under Herbert Gladstone and Churchill, Masterman had provided Lloyd George with expert, confidential, and above all politically oriented, advice of the sort the civil service could not offer. Thus Masterman was an unofficial parliamentary secretary long before he finally came to the Treasury in February 1912, to manage national health insurance.

For Lloyd George the continental trip, which catered mainly to Masterman's religious interests, was hardly a success. He disliked the Passion Play at Oberammergau and was interested in gondolas but not churches in Venice.[75] In any case, the holiday was cut short because of an invitation Lloyd George had received just before he departed to attend the Royal Family at Balmoral from 5 to 12 September. (The invitation had been delayed while the King ascertained whether by inviting Lloyd George he would be required also to invite Churchill whom he could not stand.) Lloyd George found the King friendly and unassuming, although uninstructed, while the atmosphere in the royal household was simple and familylike. Everyone, he noted, was eager to make him welcome.[76] Yet he soon became lonely. He wrote Maggie a long letter about Mair urging that flowers be planted on her grave until the headstone was ready. His mind could not lose his memory of her, he concluded. 'She dwells in it night and day and will until I join her and I don't care how soon that comes.' Well before his stay was over he hated Balmoral.[77]

After leaving Balmoral and before his return to Criccieth for the usual autumn visit, Lloyd George spent a few days in London quieting a storm that had blown up over the first step in the process of land valuation, the infamous Form IV. This document, to provide information for the increment value tax, had been sent out by the Treasury to all landowners at the end of August. Although it contained mostly questions that ratepayers had answered for years it went this time not to occupiers but to groundrent owners. As a result there was loud complaint in the newspapers, references to the Spanish Inquisition, and cartoons of honest John Bull spending hours which were needed for the harvest torturing himself to provide numbers for blockheaded civil servants.[78]

As yet Lloyd George had shown the coalition memorandum to no one, but after his return to Criccieth he prepared to test it on Winston Churchill. Churchill had been cruising the eastern Mediterranean on the yacht of Maurice DeForest, the natural and adopted son of Baron Hirsch. Churchill returned in the third week of September to find a letter from Lloyd George confirming a previous invitation and emphasizing that consultation between the two men was now urgent. '...our real danger,' wrote Lloyd George,

is that the government will drift along without any clear definite policy or

421

purpose. I am perfectly certain that our more important associates have no plan of operations in their mind. This aimlessness, if persevered in, means utter disaster.[79]

As he recounted the story to Riddell a year later, with the customary theatrics, he made his proposal to Churchill on the Criccieth golf course in Clementine Churchill's presence. There were two alternatives; coalition to

settle old outstanding questions, including Home Rule, and govern the country on middle lines acceptable to both parties but providing measures of moderate social reform. The other, to formulate and carry through an advanced land and social reform policy. Mrs. Winston, who was there, always a more sound radical than her husband said, 'I am for the second.' Winston replied, 'I am for the first!' I [LG] shall never forget the incident. We were playing golf at Criccieth. Winston forgot all about the game and has never forgotton our conversation.[80]

Churchill was clearly enthusiastic at the idea of a grand coalition.[81] Like Lloyd George he was impatient with party scruples that hindered action although he was for a moment put off by the suggestion that he might not be a member of the new government. Masterman, on the other hand, predictably, was pessimistic. Radical principles meant much to him. A coalition with the Unionists was a pact with the devil.[82] Probably on Churchill's recommendation, the first Unionist to see the coalition proposal was Churchill's close friend F.E. Smith, Unionist Member for Liverpool, Walton. Smith's passionate intelligence and love of political adventure had put him among the leaders of the Tory radicals since his election in 1906. A coalition for action suited him perfectly and by 20 October he wrote to Austen Chamberlain urging the proposal upon him. As a strong tariff reformer he immediately fastened upon the possibilities for colonial preference on existing duties suggested by Lloyd George as the bait that would attract most Unionists, as indeed it did. '…concessions to colonies on the basis of existing duties and a real and firm inquiry of which Lloyd George has said he would gladly follow if it recommends change,' wrote Smith to Chamberlain, means 'vindication of your father's pre-science.'[83] By the date of this letter Chamberlain clearly had seen the coalition memorandum himself. Similarly, some time in the week of 9 through 15 October Lloyd George took it to Asquith and perhaps earlier, evidently on 12 October, to Balfour. Meanwhile he authorized Smith to discuss it with Bonar Law.[84] Initially he reported finding much agreement although leaders in both parties asked for more detail.[85]

By the beginning of the fourth week of October letters discussing the proposal flowed back and forth among major figures on both sides of the House. Grey and Crewe wrote to Asquith strongly, almost desperately, supporting the proposal as the last Liberal alternative, the last chance for political stability. 'I have thought for some time,' wrote Crewe on 22 October, 'that we have got not far from the end of our tether as regards the carrying of large reforms….' The previous day he had written to Lloyd George in almost the same gloomy terms. Grey, four days later, was even more discouraged and apocalyptic.

> If the conference breaks up without agreement, I foresee the break-up
> of the Liberal Party and a time of political instability, perhaps of chaos, to
> the great detriment of the country. The other party of course is
> paralyzed and useless. But behind us there are explosive and violent
> forces which will split our party....[86]

Although Asquith later declared he had not taken the coalition seriously, he could hardly have failed to be impressed by these warnings from the two men in the Cabinet he trusted most and, as his biographer admits, he supported it at least mildly.[87]

On 17 October, as the discussions on the coalition proposal approached their peak, Lloyd George delivered an uncharacteristically mild speech at the City Temple under the auspices of the Liberal Christian League, theoretically a non-political body. In it he retreated markedly from the theme he had maintained since 1903: that social reform was a Liberal monopoly and that the Unionist pretensions in this direction were a shoddy fraud upon the working class. The address was in effect a public manifestation of the atmosphere of private compromise he had attempted to create in the Criccieth memorandum. Above all it represented an outstretched hand to the Chamberlainites. Reversing everything he previously had maintained, he admitted that the agitation for tariff reform was a sincere and honest, if misguided, attempt to call attention to the economic and social difficulties of the nation. Even if the solution was wrong, the member for West Birmingham had done a real service in pointing to the existence of the problems of distress. All the industrial nations of Europe and North America, he announced at the beginning, suffered, amidst great wealth, the problem of destitution and of the social unrest that accompanied it. The best one could say of Britain was that there had been no bread riots so far.

> Both parties admit the salient facts; neither party is satisfied with present
> conditions; and they are agreed in this, at any rate—that those conditions
> stand in urgent need of mending. The presence of a mass of remediable
> poverty is common ground to both parties; there is no recognizable
> section in this country who now contend that all is well; there is no
> section of any consequence that will contend that the state cannot assist
> effectively in putting things right.
> I am not a tariff reformer; all the same, I recognize that Mr. Chamberlain's
> historic agitation has rendered one outstanding service to the cause of
> the masses. It has helped to call attention to a number of real crying evils
> festering amongst us, the existence of which the governing classes of this
> country were ignorant or overlooked. We had all got into the habit of
> passing by on the other side.

He concluded with a virtual restatement of the introduction to his coalition memorandum.

> What is to be done? Once more I agree with Mr. Chamberlain that
> whatever is done, the remedy must be a bold one. Our efforts hitherto
> have been too timid, too nervous, achieving no great aim. Before we
> succeed in remedying one evil, fresh ones crop up. We are hopelessly in

423

arrears. The problem has to be considered on a great scale. The time has come for a thorough overhauling of our national and Imperial conditions. That time comes in every enterprise—commercial, national, and religious; and woe be to the generation that lacks the courage to undertake the task. I believe the masses of the people are ready for great things; nay, they are expecting them.... My counsel to the people would be this—let them enlarge the purpose of their politics and, having done so, let them adhere to that purpose with unswerving resolve through all difficulties and discouragements until their redemption is accomplished.[88]

Most of the speech was a catalogue of the familiar problems of excessive armament, poverty, destitution in old age, and of a need for land reform, all of which had appeared in the coalition memorandum. But, as in the memorandum, he did not insist that only the Liberal party could solve the problem. The City Temple speech provides a perfect early example of a political tactic that Lloyd George would use frequently in the future: an appeal over the heads of politicians to the people when he was faced by a parliamentary stalemate.

The Constitutional Conference and the coalition proposal fell together. Certainly the latter could never have succeeded after the collapse of the former. Lloyd George states in his memoirs that the movement toward a union of parties was destroyed by Lord Chilston, who, as A. Akers Douglas, had been Unionist Whip from 1892 to 1895 and Balfour's Home Secretary after the reconstruction of the Cabinet in 1902.[89] Balfour told Lloyd George, evidently at an early meeting in the coalition negotiations, that to assess the political response of the party rank and file to a coalition he would have to consult the former Chief Whip. Garvin, at the same time, was hammering at Balfour to accept the proposal and predicting doom if he did not.[90] Chilston evidently reported that lower levels of the party would oppose the idea. That, Lloyd George recalled, was the end of it.

The demise of the coalition proposal was not so simple as Lloyd George, twenty years later, allowed it to appear. He states also that he had secured the firm adhesion of the Liberal leaders before approaching Balfour, which was clearly not the case. Balfour, first of all, certainly had known of the coalition proposal before Asquith and second, although Asquith may not have so ridiculed the idea as he later suggested he had done, it would seem too much to say that he ever 'regarded the proposal with considerable favour' as Lloyd George states. One may assume further that even 'considerable favour' would have been severely diluted had he known that in the hypothetical distribution of offices, Lloyd George had destined him for the House of Lords.[91] One may be confident that in his conversations with the Unionists, Lloyd George exaggerated the support his plan commanded among his colleagues.

Still, Balfour desperately wanted to save the House of Lords and in this he was supported by Garvin and many others who also would have compromised on some form of devolution in order to retain the second chamber veto. In his anxiety to avoid constitutional change Balfour had written to Esher on 9 October a letter, apparently for transmission to Knollys and the King, suggesting that the monarch dismiss Asquith on his own initiative and appoint as Prime Minister an elderly non-party dignitary, perhaps Rosebery, who would then advise an election.[92] As this occurred only a few days, evidently three, before the leader of the opposition learned of the coalition memorandum, the proposal probably attracted him as a possible detour from the inevitable collision he foresaw. Moreover, he was attracted enough by the coalition proposal to suggest to Lloyd George, after reporting that sentiment in the lower ranks of the party was against a union and that he could not be a Peel to his party, that perhaps the coalition might go forward if the two of them stood aside. Telling Frances Stevenson of this later, Lloyd George said that he immediately agreed but that subsequently Balfour drew back.[93] Very likely it was Balfour who asked Lloyd George to draft the second, slightly more detailed, memorandum that appeared on 29 October.[94] Two days before Balfour had reported to Austen Chamberlain that Lloyd George had asked to see him on Monday (31 October) and probably the supplement was prepared for this meeting.[95] The 29 October memorandum bears the stamp of Balfour's questioning. First of all, he no doubt asked, what about the House of Lords? What of the peers' veto? Lloyd George disposed of this easily by the statement: 'The Constitutional Question to be settled substantially on the terms of the August memorandum,' which of course had ignored the constitutional question entirely. No doubt many of the other points of the 29 October memorandum had been conceded already in Lloyd George's conversations with the Unionists: an inquiry into tariffs with immediate colonial preferences on imperial goods presently dutiable, devolution all round and more attention to defense (although there was no mention of compulsory military training in the second memorandum). Again there was a statement on national insurance and widows' pensions. These constituted real concessions and, as the Unionists noted, were probably more than Lloyd George could have sold to his own party. One is left to wonder whether any Liberals other than Masterman ever saw the second document. Masterman himself objected to the colonial preferences and Lloyd George admitted that he had no 'free trade conscience' like his friend. The principle was defensible he agreed, but not sacred.[96]

With both sides anxious, if for different reasons, for a compromise, the meeting of 31 October (or 1 November) was critical. Lucy Masterman's unvarying woolliness on dates leaves the time of the interview uncertain. Indeed there may have been two. She gives, nevertheless, the impression that the discussion centered chiefly on ways to keep the Constitutional Conference alive rather than on the coalition specifically. Generally the two men discussed the size of the Liberal majority in the House of Commons that would be required to override a House of Lords veto, in the case of a combined session to which the Lords would send a representative delegation of one hundred to sit and vote with the full House of Commons.[97] Various formulae for choosing the contingent could require between forty and sixty extra Liberals.

Indeed it made little difference whether Lloyd George and Balfour, sitting in the plain Office of Works furniture at 11 Downing Street, debated the House of Lords or the coalition: the issue remained Irish Home Rule. If the conference fell over the establishment of a Dublin parliament, Lloyd George's proposal would go with it. If, on the other hand, a union of parties was achieved, the Constitutional Conference was redundant, but still Home Rule remained. On this matter Lloyd George was willing to compromise but Balfour could concede nothing. His whole history, he told Austen Chamberlain, 'forebade his being a party to any form of Home Rule, though younger men,' he added philosophically, 'less involved in the controversies of '86 and '93 might be free to contemplate what he could not accept.'[98]

One scholar states there was a second meeting on 8 November between the two men upon whom as Lloyd George, and evidently Balfour also, believed the conference depended.[99] This is possible but necessarily it was brief for the Constitutional Conference met also on that day. In any case on 8 November Asquith forwarded to Lloyd George an undated note from Balfour admitting that he believed there was no use in continuing meetings. The Unionist leader added that he was sorry 'and had hoped for better things.' No doubt the two sides should meet again to draft a public statement.[100]

Although there were two more conference meetings, this was the end. The downhill roll toward collision commenced again, its momentum hardly interrupted. The best political minds of the age could contrive neither a solution to the problem of the House of Lords nor a party union that might have saved the upper chamber. Balfour conferring with his niece and biographer many years later laughed at Lloyd George's attempt to find a compromise and saw in it a symptom of his want of principle.[101] This was unfair, not only because Balfour himself was ready enough to compromise to rescue the House of Lords, saving only the Irish union, but also because in his recollections he misrepresented Lloyd George's stated perception of the dilemma. 'Principles mean nothing to him—never have,' he told Mrs. Dugdale. 'His mind doesn't work that way, it's both his strength and his weakness. He says to himself at a given moment: "Come on now—we've been squabbling too long, let's find a reasonable way out of the difficulties."'[102] Yet compromise in politics is hardly lack of principle. Rather it is the grease without which wheels would not turn at all. Moreover Lloyd George, in the introduction to the coalition memorandum, had warned as clearly as he could that both parties were losing their grip on events, that without an agreement between the central core of moderate men of good will the extremists would, indeed in the name of principle, drive parliamentary government to chaos. Grey, Crewe, Garvin and others, each had said the same to their leaders. For Lloyd George the only principle was a government with the power and the will to act, not the conservation of any particular political institution. For this he had pleaded in the coalition memorandum.

Two days after Balfour's note to Asquith the Constitutional Conference assembled briefly for the last time and later, still on 10 November, Asquith reported the failure of the conference to the full Cabinet. According to J.A. Pease, Lloyd George explained that Balfour and Chamberlain had been anxious for an agreement and that Lansdowne and Cawdor would have come along. The problems in the party were Halsbury and Londonderry.[103] This is confirmed to some extent by a conversation between Hobhouse and Lloyd George in Rendel's villa on the Riviera in March 1911. Although

Hobhouse apparently confused the Constitutional Conference meetings with the discussion on a coalition, he recorded that at a meeting at Lansdowne House a substantial body of the Unionist leadership had accepted Welsh disestablishment, colonial preference, and devolution. Only Halsbury and Londonderry objected, refusing any form of Home Rule while wishing to keep tariff reform an issue. The two were able to carry the meeting against Balfour who left the room, Lloyd George reported, 'looking white as a sheet.'[104]

On 10 November, the Cabinet, at the urging of Alec Murray, determined upon an immediate general election, before the end of the year, even though conventional political wisdom dictated that a stale register always harmed the Liberals. (The Liberals were unprepared in other ways. In December 1910, the party left 94 of the 456 seats in England uncontested, the Unionists only 20.) On 11 November, and again on 16 November Asquith visited the King, first at Sandringham and then at Buckingham Palace, to advise a dissolution and to extract the promise on the creation of peers that had so long eluded him. At the second interview, reminding George V of the statement of 14 April, the Prime Minister obtained His Majesty's promise, for the time being to be kept entirely secret, that if the Liberals were returned with an 'adequate majority' the King would create a sufficient number of peers to pass a parliament bill limiting the Lords' veto. This guarantee, given only reluctantly by George V, became the subject of much royal unhappiness later when the King discovered that Francis Knollys had incorrectly assured him that there were no alternatives to the agreement Asquith demanded. Knollys told the King that Balfour would decline to form a government should the King refuse peers and Asquith resign. In fact Knollys knew, as the King did not in November 1910, that Balfour had agreed at the Lambeth Conference on the previous 29 April to take office under these circumstances. Edward VII had been informed of Balfour's commitment the day before he died.[105] George's reaction to his secretary's lack of candor, when he discovered it, caused Knollys's resignation in 1913. Nonetheless Asquith now had the King's promise in his pocket and parliament was dissolved on 28 November. The first contests occurred only five days later.

Lloyd George expected the election to continue the stalemate between the parties. 'It looks like ending "as we were". As you know that was my bet,' he wrote to Maggie on 14 December.[106] Alec Murray, the Chief Whip, had expected an increased majority of perhaps twenty-five which may account for his eagerness for an early election.[107] Lloyd George's own election date was early in the period. His opponent was Austen Lloyd-Jones whom he defeated on Saturday, 10 December, by 3,112 to 1,904, a majority of 1,208. He toured his constituency for only three days, Wednesday, Thursday and Friday, before the poll. There was, as now seemed to be the rule, some disorder during the contest. Supporters of the unfortunate Mr. Jones were hustled and booed by local quarrymen.[108] He spent much time, as usual, in South Wales and spoke also in Scotland for his friend Alec Murray and for a new Liberal candidate, Donald Maclean. The target of his attacks, as in January, was the House of Lords.

For the Liberals the election of 1910 was a straightforward repetition of the previous January. The intervening months had neither settled old issues nor raised new ones. No seats had changed hands at by-elections. The only Liberal matter before the voters remained the Parliament Bill and the iniquities of the House of Lords. Lloyd George had set the tone in a rousing address before an audience of five thousand at the Paragon Music Hall in Mile End Road, on 21 November, when he returned to the oratory of class bias of Limehouse and Newcastle.[109] Asquith echoed his charges in only slightly better taste at Hull four days later.

The Unionist campaign, however, altered dramatically when Balfour, at the Albert Hall on 27 November, proposed that 'the principles of tariff reform' be submitted to a referendum. He offered the suggestion, as he admitted, with very little reflection and had consulted privately only with Lansdowne. Even though he meant in fact that only food taxes, the so called 'Imperial Preferences' would be subject to popular vote, in view of the fact that the use of a referendum for the solution of difficult problems was generally under discussion, this retreat on tariff reform divided again the Unionist party into two warring factions. In 1903 Joseph Chamberlain had split the party. Since 1906 Balfour, with much help from Lloyd George, seemed to have reunited it. He had accepted, the Chamberlainites believed, the notion that the future of the party and the regeneration of Britain lay within the program of tariff reform. Now he was drawing back.

Balfour was under pressure from a small but influential section of his party led by J.L. Garvin to drop, at least for the moment, his advocacy of import duties on food, on the argument that the prospect of higher food prices was causing unhappiness in working and lower middle class constituencies, particularly in the North. In order to save the House of Lords and the Union, food taxes would have to be dropped. Tariffs on manufactures, which the foreigner would pay, could be kept.[110] Whether these electoral calculations were correct, whether consumer votes won in the North if food taxes were dropped would be balanced by those won in the rural areas of the South if they were kept, is unimportant here. The significance of the Albert Hall declaration lies less in the damage done to Unionist voting prospects than in the harm it did to A.J. Balfour himself.

He apologized promptly to Austen Chamberlain and received on 6 December a relatively good-tempered letter assessing the electoral effects, but other members of the party were less forgiving and Chamberlain wrote nearly thirty years later that he was 'broken hearted.'[111] At the end of his life, Leopold Amery, who was defeated for Bow and Bromley in a seat previously held by a Unionist, retained his bitterness.[112] More important for the future was a scathing attack on the former Prime Minister in the pages of the influential tariff reform journal the *National Review*, in which its editor, Leo Maxse, predicted that the 'Albert Hall Blunder' not only might cost Balfour his party leadership, but that he would be succeeded by Bonar Law.[113]

The result of the election, as Lloyd George had predicted, was continued stalemate: the Liberals held 272 seats, the Unionists the same. The Irish Nationalists retained their leverage with 84 and Labour kept 42.

On 20 December, immediately after the last contest, Lloyd George departed for the south of France to be joined after Christmas by the

Mastermans, Alec Murray and the new Attorney General, Sir Rufus Isaacs.[114] Lloyd George took this trip every year during the Christmas recess but on this occasion he had been ordered by his doctor, G.W.F. Macnaughton, to rest. Through the autumn he had been bothered again by his throat and in fact one of the very few days in his constituency during the election had been spent at home in Criccieth because of it.

Although supposed to convalesce, Lloyd George could never remain inactive for long, nor, even though he had been to the Riviera many times by now, did he find it easy to remain in one place. He settled first at Hotel Cap Martin and then, soon after the new year, he took his party, in a car lent him by Joseph Pulitzer of the *New York World*, to the Hotel Des Anglais at Nice. Here, on 3 January, the group was joined by Sir John Bradbury, at this time a principal clerk at the Treasury, and William John Braithwaite, an assistant secretary in Inland Revenue. Braithwaite had just completed a four day survey of the German insurance scheme, undertaken at Lloyd George's request. That afternoon on the pier at Nice, with the band playing in the background, he made his report and serious work began on what would become the National Insurance Act of 1911.

IV

While easier to explain, it would be untrue to say that social insurance grew out of the reform ideology of the Edwardian period. Lloyd George's mind simply did not work that way. The immediate impulse came from what he regarded, as did everyone, to be the inevitable extension of old age pensions. Invalidity and widows' pensions could not be borne by existing taxation. The cost would be too huge. In some way they would have to be financed by the beneficiaries of the system. But a contributory system had problems of its own. Joseph Chamberlain's first proposal for a contributory system on the German model had been decisively vetoed by the friendly society movement, an opponent that even he could not overcome. Tariff reform, Chamberlain thought, would provide the solution. The beneficiaries would indeed pay for the program but through import duties, not through direct contributions collected in competition with the provident societies. This connection between tariffs and social reform Lloyd George had extracted from Chamberlain in his dramatic attack, in the 'illimitable veldt' speech in the House of Commons, on 22 May 1903. In it lay the Chamberlainite challenge to the New Liberalism.

Lloyd George's solution was only a variation of the original plan: a basic system of contributory invalidity and widows' pensions insurance which bought off friendly society opposition by making the societies the administrative and fiscal agents of the state scheme. In addition his plan would cover only the three-fifths of the British working class who were not members of friendly societies but who with a state subsidy would be encouraged to join. He had, he believed, squared the societies, but in the summer of 1910 the industrial insurance industry appeared with new objections to the widows' pensions which were for Lloyd George the most important part of the program. Had the coalition proposal succeeded, the political power of the collecting agents would have been neutralized. But when the proposal died in early November the problem had to be faced.

Industrial insurance could not be defeated; it had to be bought off.

Some of what happened in the crowded weeks between mid-November and mid-December is uncertain. During much of the time Lloyd George was not in London and no work could be done. In the Mile End Road speech of 21 November he had made the now routine promises about insurance in a way that suggested that widows' pensions remained part of the plan. All now was arranged, he announced, for insurance of two million men against unemployment and of 'fifteen millions of work people—men and women—against the anxiety, the distress, that comes to households when the breadwinner's health breaks down.' All the money was in place, everything was set to begin, and so on. He had not mentioned widows' pensions to be sure, but he had not done so publicly anywhere since the meetings with the industrial insurance men of the previous summer.

There were as yet no details of the insurance scheme available to the public, but suddenly, at the end of November, the British industrial insurance world was awash with a wave of rumors of a government plan that would compete with and destroy the funeral benefit business. What the insurance men had heard is not entirely clear. Certainly no new decisions had been made on the insurance scheme. Indeed it seems to have progressed little since the actuaries' report of the previous spring. (There may have been some anger in industrial insurance circles resulting from Lloyd George's refusal to meet some of their representatives after he had interviewed, earlier in the month, an important delegation from the 700,000 member Manchester Unity of Odd Fellows.)[115] Nonetheless, the editor of the *Insurance Mail* later declared that word had come to him on 26 November 'on exceptional authority that the government intended to introduce a State-aided scheme which was practically industrial life assurance.'[116]

In the next few days there appeared a series of newspaper articles, none with much detail, about secret government schemes to harm the industrial insurance industry, which were coupled also with stories of angry reaction in the industry itself. The immediate result was a disingenuous letter from Lloyd George to the insurance world, dated 1 December, saying that government proposals would not interfere in any way with industrial insurance. 'The proposed benefits,' wrote Lloyd George, choosing his words carefully, 'do not include the provision of a funeral benefit or any immediate money payment on the death of a contributor or his relatives nor, of course, will there be any endowment of children on reaching a certain age....I have given a pledge on behalf of the Government that no scheme dealing with sickness and invalidity will be submitted to the House of Commons until all societies having any interest in the matter have been consulted.'[117]

Lloyd George's letter, on the eve of the general election, did nothing to quiet the disturbance. The editor of the *Insurance Mail* speculated that the Chancellor might be lying. The key words 'immediate money payment on death' did not exclude a widows' pension and a funeral benefit could be introduced later. In any case the insurance collectors themselves, with evidently some urging from their employers, continued a campaign already begun to collect pledges from parliamentary candidates promising to 'oppose any measure of State insurance which is likely prejudicially to affect' industrial insurance 'or to jeopardize the livelihood of the very many thousands of persons engaged in the business of industrial life assurance.'[118]

This campaign received little notice in the London press although insurance journals watched it closely.[119] The results were precisely as Lloyd George predicted in the Criccieth memorandum. The agents found pledges easy to obtain and eventually received promises from 490 MPs to guard insurance interests.[120] Widows' and orphans' pensions would have to be dropped. Lloyd George was faced by a parliamentary force even more powerful than the friendly societies.

Although Lloyd George had foreseen this possibility in his coalition proposal in August, he could not have known of the effectiveness of the insurance agents' canvass of parliamentary candidates before he left for the continent. Evidently he made no decision on pensions until after his return. (The *Nation*, which included several helpers in insurance planning among its staff, confidently described the old pre-industrial insurance plan as the coming scheme of insurance on 7 January 1911.)

Lloyd George returned from the south of France at the beginning of the second week of January. He scheduled immediately a series of conferences with the friendly societies and, for the first time, with representatives of the industrial insurance companies.[121] But his throat had not improved during the sojourn on the Riviera and was now worse than before.[122] As a result he departed again for Criccieth leaving Rufus Isaacs, Masterman, Bradbury and Braithwaite, to deal with the deputations. Hence he missed the meeting with the industrial insurance men on 12 January at which the fate of widows' pensions, and indeed the shape of what would soon be styled officially 'national health insurance,' was decided. (The title was Braithwaite's, who argued that as insurance against death was life insurance, so insurance against sickness should be health insurance.)

The group on 12 January represented the twelve biggest industrial insurance offices which were in those days styled the 'Combine' and are known today as the Associated Offices. Their spokesman, who appeared first at this time, was a chubby smiling little solicitor for the Royal London Mutual who would eventually attach himself to Lloyd George, entering parliament with a coupon in 1918, later transferring his allegiance to Neville Chamberlain, and ending his days as Winston Churchill's wartime Chancellor of the Exchequer: Howard Kingsley Wood.[123] No doubt it was Kingsley Wood who made clear that industrial insurance now had enough support in the House of Commons to resist any attempt to found a state scheme of widows' and orphans' pensions. However, and perhaps more important, the government learned at this time also that industrial insurance would demand the right, to be exercised or not, to enter health insurance on equal terms with the friendly societies. This came as a surprise. No one had considered before that collecting insurance would be interested. The industrial insurance companies did not offer sickness payments. The collecting friendly societies, as required by law, did so, but discouraged its purchase most successfully. Nonetheless, their demand to be allowed to enter health insurance administration if they wished could no more be resisted than their insistence upon dropping pensions. Eventually, at a large meeting at the Hotel Albion in Brighton on the weekend of 18 and 19 February, Lloyd George determined, to the fury of the friendly societies, that the bill would have to be framed so as to allow subsidiary organizations of the industrial companies to administer the plan.[124] Still Braithwaite and Bradbury hoped to impose regulations for representation of the insured and for democratic government of the societies, routine in true friendly societies, that would effectively, if informally, exclude the funeral benefit industry.

However, the effect on health insurance of dropping widows' pensions was vast. At one stroke their deletion had reduced the cost of projected benefits by about fifty per cent. All other benefits now could be raised. On the day after the meeting with the leaders of the Combine, Bradbury wrote to the actuaries asking for an estimate of the effect of increasing the weekly sickness benefit from 5s to 10s.[125] This seemingly useful change altered, as it turned out, the entire character of health insurance. Instead of providing a state program with benefits at less than subsistence level, which would encourage new contributors becoming members of friendly societies to insure for extra benefits, the plan now offered benefits that equalled those the societies already gave. In place of a two tier scheme, with the friendly societies at the top, health insurance became what the societies had feared from the beginning: a state medical plan which the societies were allowed to help administer, but one which their former members would now be required to join. Only the most loyal, or the most affluent, friendly society member would remain within their ranks.[126] The final blow came in the autumn when the societies, fighting to the end, lost their monopoly in the administration of the scheme with the admission of industrial insurance.

Through the first three months of 1911, while bargaining with industrial insurance was in process and while Braithwaite and Bradbury were struggling to put together a workable plan, constantly distracted by peremptory and often contradictory instructions from their minister, who was himself seldom in evidence, Lloyd George sought for ways to strengthen the parliamentary position of the health insurance proposals. His thoughts apparently continued to run in the direction of outflanking the insurance industry by an agreement with the opposition to treat insurance as a non-party measure. Such an agreement would secure a friendly hearing in a select committee, a procedure Lloyd George had used to great advantage at the Board of Trade, and allow, perhaps, widows' pensions to be put back in. Finally, he hoped to increase his plan's popularity by linking it with unemployment insurance which at that time was expected, incorrectly, to have great public appeal. (He toyed also with a plan to offer old age pensions at age 65 to all contributors who had been members of the scheme for twenty years.) The joining of the two insurance plans as parts I and II of what would become the National Insurance Bill of 1911, and the select committee procedure, were approved at the first Cabinet meeting of the new year on 20 January.[127]

At the same time he attempted to get control of unemployment insurance using Alec Murray as an intermediary with the Prime Minister. He gave his friend a long, and generally untruthful, story about the origins of unemployment insurance. He, Lloyd George, had studied unemployment insurance plans on the continent (there was no compulsory unemployment insurance anywhere in 1908) and when he returned after thinking about it for a month, in a 'weak moment' had told Churchill about them. The latter then had produced his own bill which Lloyd George found unsatisfactory in many, unspecified, ways. Now, with Churchill transferred to the Home Office, and with Sydney Buxton caring for unemployment insurance, it would be desirable to combine the two measures in a single proposal.[128] All of this was grossly unfair to Churchill who had published his 'untrodden fields' article on unemployment while Lloyd George was still occupied by the Port of London Bill and had produced his first Cabinet Paper on the subject at the end of November 1908, before Lloyd George had even finished his original series of conferences with the friendly societies.[129]

Nevertheless, Murray saw Asquith and reported that 'your idea of lumping the insurance bills in one measure pleased him very much and I am sure he will agree to your select committee suggestion. I gave him your hint about Sydney Buxton.'[130] What this bit of intrigue was supposed to accomplish, beyond allowing some of the expected glamour of unemployment insurance to accrue to the health scheme, is not entirely clear. Lloyd George indicated to Murray he wanted to unify the two plans and continued to talk about it, but he took no steps in this direction in the next few months although there were a few joint meetings between the Treasury and the Board of Trade. Churchill overstated what was happening when he wrote unhappily to his wife on 22 April: 'Lloyd George has practically taken over unemployment insurance to his own bosom & I am I think effectively elbowed out of this large field in which I consumed thought and effort.'[131]

At the same time Lloyd George sought to reawaken the comradeship with the Unionist reformers that had evaporated at the end of the Constitutional Conference. On this Asquith was unenthusiastic. When Lloyd George asked the Prime Minister in mid April for permission to see Balfour about it privately, Asquith had wondered 'why divide the credit?'[132] However, during that month Waldorf Astor, a strong supporter of reform, replaced Northcliffe as the proprietor of the *Observer*, allowing that paper's editor, J.L. Garvin, to throw himself again into the congenial role of mediator between the parties.[133] Garvin went to breakfast at No. 11 on 5 May the day after the insurance bill was introduced and provided a welcoming leader in his Sunday edition calling for cooperation 'to organize the vital efficiency of the mass of the nation' while reminding his readers that contributory insurance was first proposed by Joseph Chamberlain. More important, he informed Balfour through Sandars, as Lloyd George certainly had intended he should, of the Chancellor's fear of popular opposition to his bill and of his desire for the agreement 'of the best men of both parties.'[134] These phrases, reminiscent of the Criccieth memorandum, suggest a characteristic turn of the Chancellor's mind. Vested interests that could not be bought off had to be faced by the united determination of the few responsible politicians of both parties.

In the end nothing came of Lloyd George's second approach to the Unionists. Although Austen Chamberlain liked the insurance plan immediately and a number of the younger Unionists, including Waldorf Astor and Stanley Baldwin, organized in the Unionist Social Reform Committee, genuinely attempted to put forth constructive suggestions, Balfour himself realized soon after its introduction that national insurance's massive complexity and wide application afforded many opportunities for trouble-making and so declined to take any responsibility for it.[135] Eventually, the hostile Unionist response meant also the end of the plan to handle health insurance in the intimacy of a select committee. Instead the measure had to be debated in the public arena of a Committee of the Whole.

Even though Lloyd George was constantly troubled by his throat during the spring of 1911, so that he spent much time away from London at Criccieth, Brighton, and Beachborough, the estate of Sir Arthur Markham near Folkestone—he complained that he had to get away because when he was near business he could not help talking—and despite the fact he had also to prepare the 1911 budget involving the usual fights with McKenna, the outline of the insurance bill was ready for the Cabinet at the end of March.[136]

The plan that the Cabinet considered on 5 April was in most, although not all, respects embodied in the bill Lloyd George introduced on 4 May. But more important it contained certain anticipations by Lloyd George of changes he expected to make during passage. He was, in effect, adhering to his now standard parliamentary style. A measure going before parliament was not a finished work but a piece of raw material which would be chiseled and shaped according to the political forces that it encountered and the compromises he would be required to make. Hence, the insurance scheme described in the memorandum of 30 March merits some discussion at this point. Most of the points of contention that grew up around the national health insurance program were foreseen by Lloyd George in his Cabinet Paper.

In essence the new health scheme was now a plan of state insurance to be administered by any private, non-profit, agency that cared to apply for official approval. These were eventually given the name of 'approved societies.' They could be friendly societies, trade unions, employer sponsored benefit clubs, cooperatives, or specially established subsections of industrial insurance companies. All working people over age 16 and under 65, ten million men and four million women, earning less than the lower limit of the income tax, £160 per year, would be required to join one of the societies. (The scheme was later amended to include any manual worker even if he were liable for the income tax.) For his weekly premium of 9d, (8d for women) the contributor received unlimited general practitioner care from a physician employed by the approved society, 10s per week (7s 6d for women) for 13 weeks (later increased to 26 weeks) during sickness, and 5s per week for an unlimited period if he were chronically disabled. Finally each society was required to contribute 1s per member per year into a fund to provide sanatorial care for tuberculosis. (Later a maternity benefit of 30s paid to the wife of a contributor was added.)

The 9d weekly contribution was to be made up of 4d (3d in the case of women) from the workman's wages, 3d added by the employer, and 2d from the government, making the famous '9d for 4d' of which Lloyd

George, to the fury of the Unionists, continually boasted. Contributions were to be remitted by the employer who would deduct the workman's 4d from wages, add his own 3d, and convey the money to the insurance fund by means of revenue stamps purchased at the post office. These stamps, when affixed to a card belonging to the workman, represented the contributor's equity in the insurance fund. The government would pay its 2d, actually two-ninths of the cost of benefits, directly to each approved society.

Each society would be responsible for its own fund and for the maintenance of benefits to its own members, but the scheme provided that the government would protect each society against the actuarial disadvantage of admitting the older members who would be compulsorily insured under the scheme by the creation of an artificial claims reserve, the so-called 'reserve values.' The reserve values, in reality a debt created by the admission of older lives for whom no contributions had been paid in youth to cover the claims of old age, was part of the cost to national health insurance of Braithwaite's insistence upon an accumulating, or funded, scheme. The alternative, a lateral, or 'dividing out' plan in which contributions would be immediately paid out in benefits, has been the rule in all compulsory national insurance in Britain and abroad since the original scheme. Indeed in 1911 unemployment insurance was planned to operate on the dividing out principle. Nonetheless, in March, shortly before the presentation of the Cabinet memorandum, Braithwaite convinced Lloyd George that a conventional, interest earning, accumulating plan was required. This was, in fact, a mistake, despite Braithwaite's assertions to the contrary, and the cause of many difficulties of which reserve values, never redeemed, were only one.[137]

One of Braithwaite's principal arguments for a funded system of insurance was his insistence that such a plan would increase both the power and responsibility of the approved societies. In his mind these were to be only the old friendly societies and trade unions. Lloyd George's Cabinet memorandum contained a long list of provisions dealing with the government of societies specifying absolute, and local, control by membership with which, he expected, industrial insurance would be unable or unwilling to comply. 'It must be remembered,' the memorandum explained, that the scheme

> will be open to Trade Unions, Industrial Insurance Companies, Superannuation Funds established by Employers, Collecting Societies which are only in name Friendly Societies, and all sorts of other associations of persons, to apply for approval as an Approved Society. The conditions as to 'self-government,' 'not working for profit,' and 'election of Committees,' have been drawn so as to cover cases of this kind.[138]

These intentions, in the event, were not fulfilled. The great undercover defeat in the last stage of the passage of the bill, the insurance industry's second act of defiance, forced Lloyd George to change the rules for approval, as it had forced him to drop widows' pensions.

A more open and longer lasting struggle flared up with the medical profession. This would become a major threat to national health insurance, not to the passage of the bill, but afterwards to the establishment of the program. The administration of medical care had hardly been considered during the early stages of planning and had not indeed been part of the scheme during the conferences with friendly societies in 1908. The assumption was that medical service would be provided by doctors under contract to friendly societies on the terms that were already in force for their members.

'I have interviewed a large number of doctors on the medical side of this scheme,' Lloyd George told the Cabinet.

> They all agree in denouncing the present system of medical relief as organized by the Friendly Societies. Doctors employed by these Societies are paid an inclusive fee of (say) 4s per member. This fee covers drugs and the cheaper medical appliances. This fee is obviously insufficient, and the medical profession are up in arms against it. I am assured that it has resulted in handing over this class of practice entirely to more incompetent members of the profession, who shun the more costly drugs however necessary they be to effect a cure, and habitually deceive their patients by plying them with water charged with pure colouring matter possessing no curative properties....
>
> I should like to see the whole of the medical work under the scheme undertaken by the Health Committee and I have no doubt that is what will ultimately ensue. But compulsorily to transfer the medical work now undertaken by Friendly Societies, Medical Clubs and Works Clubs to the Health Committee would at this stage provoke formidable opposition.
>
> I propose, however, to give these Societies the option of handing over this part of their duties to the Health Committee, the latter charging them 5s per member. Even then there would be a deficit. I propose that this should be shared between the State and the Local Authority; the latter can well afford it, for the scheme must effect a considerable saving in medical charges now falling on the rate. The compulsory character of the scheme secures a contribution of 5s a head from that class of population who now, having the Society to fall back upon in case of illness, resort to the poor law both for medicine and maintenance.[139]

These paragraphs, Braithwaite records, were dictated by Lloyd George himself after the memorandum was substantially finished.[140]

The only doctor who knew the details of the insurance scheme was Arthur Newsholme, Chief Medical Officer of the Local Government Board. John Burns' diary shows that he and Newsholme discussed the plan with Lloyd George repeatedly in the days before Lloyd George submitted his memorandum to the Cabinet. Newsholme was a former medical officer of health and a strong supporter of any plan for social medicine. Moreover, he was, at this stage of his career, a friend and confidant of the Webbs who, at a breakfast with Lloyd George, Masterman and Braithwaite, on 28 February had first suggested that Lloyd George consult some medical officers of health. (The breakfast itself was not a success. Sidney Webb was rude to Lloyd George and condemned the funded scheme that Braithwaite was recommending while Mrs. Webb terrified the proper Braithwaite himself by lecturing to him about syphilis.

Lloyd George determined to avoid consulting the Webbs again.) It was certainly Newsholme who provided the inspiration for the Local Health Authority, giving national health insurance what slight orientation it had toward public preventive medicine, and probably he suggested also the establishment of the medical research committee which eventually became the Medical Research Council. Finally, no doubt Newsholme first warned Lloyd George that the medical profession would resist employment by friendly societies and that a capitation fee of 4s per patient was too low.[141]

Lloyd George himself did not favor a capitation fee, a method of payment which, by making the doctors' income proportionate to his popularity among the insured, in effect to his willingness to sign certificates permitting his patients to draw sickness benefits, would promote malingering. A 'certain method of repressing malingering would be to encourage a system of salaried doctors' his Cabinet memorandum concluded.

> Free choice of doctors promotes malingering. This is the experience of Germany. It is equally the experience of our Friendly Societies. The medical profession like it, and we shall have to encounter a certain measure of opposition amongst a class of doctors if we set our face against free choice. I would not recommend the Government to forbid it altogether, but rather to make arrangements in the Bill which will tend gradually and eventually to eliminate it. This, I hope, will be accomplished if we can make it worth the Friendly Societies' while to transfer the duty of providing medical relief for their members to the Health Authority proposed to be set up by this Bill. As the leaders of the Friendly Societies are fully alive to the inroads made on their funds by this evil and to the extent to which it is fostered by free selection of doctors, they will not be averse to a restriction of this right.[142]

These paragraphs proposing what could have become a state medical service would have astounded later critics of the insurance scheme who denounced David Lloyd George for ignorance of the broader aspects of public health and for excessive obeisance to the sensibilities of the medical profession. Lloyd George, as always, was feeling his way along, confiding to the Cabinet the shape into which he hoped to see his measure evolve and holding himself in readiness to seize political opportunities. In none of his projects, health insurance least of all, did he ever suggest, or believe, that he had produced the ideal scheme. 'One thing people do not understand about me,' said Lloyd George to Riddell, referring to the incomplete state of the Insurance Act after passage, 'is that I am a patient man. I can wait. I am very patient. I can bide my time.'[143] Nothing was perfect, but then nothing was ever finished.

The Cabinet had its first discussion of health and unemployment insurance on 5 April. In view of the criticism that Lloyd George's plan received from his colleagues later, Asquith's description of its initial reception may be worth recording. 'After a searching examination,' Asquith wrote the King, 'the Cabinet expressed warm and unanimous approval of the main and governing principles of the scheme which they believe to be more comprehensive in its scope and more provident and statesmanlike in its machinery than anything that has hitherto been attempted or proposed.' Then followed a discussion of unemployment insurance and the Prime Minister concluded proudly: 'The two schemes taken together with the Old Age Pensions Act, will, in the opinion of the Cabinet, form the largest and most significant measure of social reform yet achieved in any country.'[144]

V

The Cabinet finally approved health insurance on 11 April and on 4 May at a little after 4.00 p.m. Lloyd George introduced part one of the National Insurance Bill.[145] In a low, almost inaudible voice—his throat was still troublesome—he explained that the aim of the measure was to provide the benefits of friendly society membership to the three-fifths of the working population not presently protected by these admirable organizations. He noted the publication of the majority and minority reports of the Royal Commission on the Poor Laws and tried to suggest that health insurance was a response to these recommendations, although it was nothing of the kind, and he asked again for non-party consideration of the bill. He found encouragement in Austen Chamberlain's answering speech which admitted that the bill represented an occasion 'when for all too brief a moment the housebreakers among his colleagues are silent and the Right Honourable Gentleman is allowed to turn to constructive work. I venture to say he will not appeal in vain to any section of the House....'[146] 'The Tories will regret their proceeding of today,' observed Robertson Nicoll who, with Riddell, came to hear Lloyd George introduce his bill. 'They have given away the whole show and acted like idiots. L.G. called his Bill a non-party and noncontroversial measure. We shall see.'[147] Nicoll's political instincts, as usual, were excellent. Lloyd George renewed his search for good will after the bill was finally published on 9 May and members discovered its length and complexity. He ordered Braithwaite to sit in the House of Commons lobby to explain difficult points and he proposed during the second reading the appointment of an all party conference that could agree on noncontroversial amendments. But the search for accommodation came to nothing. On 1 June Balfour courteously but firmly declined any compromise.[148]

The insistence upon confrontation was not entirely the fault of health insurance. On 26 May the Parliament Bill had reached the House of Lords and the last phase of the battle over the peers' veto began. In such an atmosphere any friendly compromise was difficult for Balfour. But probably more important, by the end of May it had become clear to the Unionist back bench that the insurance scheme had many enemies in the country and remarkably few friends. Working men generally disliked the contributory feature. The small friendly societies feared extinction. Worst of all, the hostile industrial insurance industry had found that it had an ally in the medical profession.

As Lloyd George had anticipated in his memorandum of 30 March, the doctors were enraged at the provision in the bill making them employees of approved societies. 'Club practice,' with all its overtones of corruption, the solicitation of patients, underpayment, and officiousness by dignitaries of local societies, was detested by the British Medical Association and feared by new physicians who saw in it a job of last resort. Until the publication of the bill on 9 May the medical profession had known little about the scheme. They may have been put off by the publication in both *The Times* and the *Manchester Guardian* on 4 January 1911, of reports that the insurance plan would offer no medical benefit because the relatively high £160 limit would deprive many doctors of private patients. The appearance of identical reports in two usually well-informed journals suggests a deliberate leak of misleading information rather than the reprinting of speculation. But, more to the point, during the planning of the bill Lloyd George appears also to have avoided the profession. Although he told the House of Commons in 1912, at the height of the doctors' revolt, that he had met the medical profession four times in March and April 1911, the *British Medical Journal* insisted that he had seen the B.M.A. only once for just an hour immediately before the bill was introduced.[149] It may be imagined that Lloyd George counted his interviews with Dr. Newsholme as professional consultation.

In any case, the medical reaction to Lloyd George's presentation of the health insurance scheme was immediate and violent. The *British Medical Journal*, which published a mildly approving editorial on 13 May, taken almost verbatim from Austen Chamberlain's speech, was deluged with abusive letters.[150] Some of this outrage was caused by a clear mistake during the 4 May speech when Lloyd George referred to raising the capitation payment to doctors under the plan 'to' instead of 'above' 4s, but much of it proceeded from the specification of approved society administration of the medical benefit.[151] The B.M.A. Council immediately ordered a special meeting of the association to convene at the end of May and asked Lloyd George to receive a deputation at this time. The Chancellor requested that he instead be allowed to speak to the meeting. Here then, on 1 June in the examination hall of the Royal College of Physicians, he played the card he had shown the Cabinet on 5 April. Setting two pressure groups against each other he proposed the transfer of the medical benefit from the despised approved societies to statutory local health committees. In one of his most effective speeches he convinced the profession that a change which he had already decided upon privately was really a symbol of his good will. For years, he announced, he had been a careful student of the conditions of medical practice, and the doctors had a genuine grievance.

> I can tell you this: that I am entirely with you in this...and if you can persuade the House of Commons to consent to the transfer of the whole medical attendance, including maternity, to the local health committees you will find me an enthusiastic supporter of that proposal. (Loud applause.) But you must remember there are two sides to this question, and that the approved societies will not readily resign this power. You have brought a good deal of pressure on me during the last few days and I want you to transfer that pressure from me to the House of Commons. I am entirely of your view as to this; I do not believe you will ever get a satisfactory medical service until you do transfer it to the local commit-tees.[152]

For the moment Lloyd George had captivated the doctors. 'I was one of those present when the Chancellor met the delegates of the British Medical

Association,' wrote a well-known specialist, Dr. Herbert Woodcock.

> The bright-eyed, alert, popular politician, courageous, ready and good humoured, was a glorified example of the witty businesslike market practitioner compelling his wares on a circle of admiring but doubting critics. He was just the man to make us forget that the Cabinet Minister in charge of the Bill is a man who has to strive strenuously to pass his measure whatever its value. This particular Bill however, was a bad one.[153]

Before the doctors adjourned, however, they recovered enough to pass six resolutions, immediately dubbed the 'Six Cardinal Points', detailing changes they demanded in national health insurance. These six cardinal points would become the center of the struggle with the medical profession in 1912.

Lloyd George's warning about friendly society opposition to the transfer away from themselves of the control of the doctors with their power of certification of illness was partly rhetoric. One large centralized society, the Hearts of Oak, had never employed doctors, had used salaried sickness visitors to prevent malingering and had already proposed to the Chancellor that it give up the medical benefit. More important, the industrial insurance companies, which had determined by this time that the protection of their funeral benefit business required their participation in health insurance administration, had no interest in the management of medical care. Thus the Chancellor was presiding over, and probably had already foreseen, the formation of an alliance between the medical profession and industrial insurance that the friendly societies could not resist. On 1 August the House of Commons on a technically free vote removed the medical benefit from the control of the approved societies and vested it with the local health committees.[154] At the same time, as a reward for help on the medical benefit by industrial insurance, the doctors in turn supported the deletion of a requirement for local management committees for contributors. This, one of Braithwaite's chief ideas for making life difficult for industrial insurance, would have allowed any 250 contributors in any locality who belonged to an approved society without branches, in effect to all but true friendly societies, to take over and supervise local administration, thus eliminating any need for collectors in the work of health insurance.

The fact of a bargain was confirmed, with clear satisfaction, by Kingsley Wood in an interview with the *Insurance Mail*. Insurance companies, he said, would now be able 'to escape the interference of local tradesmen with our methods of conducting the State sickness insurance scheme. We get this concession by placing in the hands of the local health committee the administration of the medical benefit provided in the Bill, a matter that has just been dealt with by the House of Commons.'[155] The doctors did not want to work for the approved societies; the insurance industry did not want the local management committees. The two died together. It was at about this time that Braithwaite recalls Kingsley Wood leaning over to him and muttering: 'We have got Ll.G. there (putting his thumb on the desk) and shall get our own terms!'[156]

The last weeks of July and the early days of August may count as a new phase in the troubled period of British prewar political history. On 20 July Asquith announced in a letter to Balfour and Lansdowne that he had received a promise from the King to act upon advice to appoint enough peers to pass the Parliament Bill. On 10 August the House of Lords agreed not to insist upon its amendments to the bill, thus allowing the House of Commons' version to pass into law. The subsequent anger among Unionists came to be focused upon the party leader A.J. Balfour and was articulated in October in a furious article in Leopold Maxse's *National Review* entitled 'The Champion Scuttler' signed by 'B.M.G.' which was understood to mean 'Balfour Must Go.'[157] On 8 November Balfour announced he had resigned the leadership of the Unionist party.

Parallel to these public events, political opposition to national health insurance stiffened. Friendly society anger over the transfer of the medical benefit provided a convenient weapon for the angry Unionists who wished to attack health insurance without seeming to oppose it in principle. Evidence was pouring in from all sides that the bill was not popular even with the working men and women it was supposed to protect. Balfour, in his last days as leader, had remained uncertain about the profit of all-out opposition, but his departure, and the succession of Andrew Bonar Law, brought a distinct hardening of the Unionist attitude, carried to the extent of granting subsidies from the whip's fund for demonstrations against the bill.[158]

The increasing belligerency of the opposition in the House of Commons was evident in the prolonged committee stage of the bill. By the end of July only a dozen of the bill's 87 clauses had been cleared and it was obvious that the measure could not be carried before adjournment. As Lloyd George wrote to Maggie on 31 July the alternatives were sitting until the end of September or an early recess and another autumn session. He had, he concluded, no preferences 'as long as the Bill goes through this year.'[159] A few days later the Cabinet determined upon an autumn sitting with a timetable for committee debate.

Among the most serious troublemakers in committee were a small faction of the left wing of the Labour party, Keir Hardie, Philip Snowden, and George Lansbury, whose agitation both inside and outside the House of Commons provided a stimulus for the rising unpopularity of health insurance. Contributory welfare, they shouted, was a tax on poverty. A gesture toward labor was necessary and the appropriate instrument was at hand, salaries for Members of Parliament. On 21 December 1909 the House of Lords in the so-called 'Osborne Decision' had held unanimously that trade unions could not use funds compulsorily collected from their members for political purposes, including the payment of salaries to Labour party MPs. Twenty-four Members found their support reduced or ended. The Liberal alternatives were either a reversal of the Osborne Decision by statute or, preferably, salaries for members of the House of Commons, which fulfilled an ancient radical demand going back to the Chartists. Lloyd George himself had long supported salaries. His own impoverished circumstances in his first fifteen years in London were reason enough. But he had as well a typically practical political point of view. Payment would reduce trade union control, he told the Cabinet in July

1910, when the Osborne Decision was under discussion. In Wales the best labor men were shut out by union dictation. Only wild men, he said, perhaps with Keir Hardie in mind, had a chance at Labour seats.[160] There had been suggestions of a Liberal party bargain with the Labour party: support for national health insurance in exchange for payment of MPs.[161] In fact this appears to have been little more than coincidence. The Liberals had long urged payment—it had been an item in the Newcastle Programme of 1891—and Lloyd George, as will be seen, had announced it for the session during the Budget Address on 16 May at a time when he still hoped to see the National Insurance Bill pass as an agreed measure. Moreover the Labour party as a whole accepted, if not welcomed, the insurance scheme while joining the Liberals in regarding their radical fringe as hooligans. Lloyd George himself made no mention of an agreement in the letter to his wife after his introduction of the payment resolution on 10 August, noting only that the Tories also congratulated him and that he had made, as usual, the best speech of his life.[162] His explanation of the proposal was founded upon what was certainly his only creed for Members of Parliament, that they must maintain their independence. They owed loyalty only to their constituency.[163] So far as a bargain existed it turned not on health insurance, but, as several Unionists hinted, on the Liberal desire to retain the friendship of labor while allowing the Osborne judgement to stand.[164]

The only evidence of any connection between payment and labor support for insurance appears in a letter from Alec Murray to Lloyd George on 5 October during the recess, in which the Chief Whip reported that now that salaries were in place, Ramsay MacDonald, the Labour party leader, 'and his friends' would support health insurance. Included was a letter of the previous day from MacDonald promising help from most of his party on the coming guillotine resolution, 'at the outside three Members may do the contrary.'[165] But this note does not suggest a contract. The payment resolution had been passed two months before. Rather at most it suggests Alec Murray's speculation about MacDonald's motives. In any case Lloyd George remained unsure of Labour support and even less sure of MacDonald's place in the byzantine structure of the party. He ate lunch with the Labour party insurance committee the following week and reported to Maggie that the party would indeed support the closure resolution. 'They have at last made up their minds to fight Hardie, Snowden and Lansbury. They had an actuarial report [paid for by Lloyd George] which completely supports my scheme.'[166]

In fact the serious objections to health insurance came not from the Labour party but from the Irish. On the last day of the recess and the day before Asquith was to introduce the all-important closure resolution, William O'Brien of the independent Nationalists sent Lloyd George a stiff letter demanding that the medical benefit for the other island be dropped and that contributors themselves be given the money otherwise paid to doctors and allowed to make their own arrangements for medical care. The Irish worker, added O'Brien, already had available free doctor's care from the Poor Law and the voluntary hospitals. The real terror in Ireland was unemployment. The Chancellor, he concluded, ought not to doubt the unpopularity of national health insurance in Ireland. The measure should be left to a free vote.[167] O'Brien did not speak for the whole of the Irish party but the discontent manifest in his letter was genuine enough. Lloyd George received more like it from other Irishmen and eventually also a memorandum from the Redmondites demanding the elimination of the Irish medical service.[168] As a result, in the resumed committee stage, the Irish medical benefit was deleted from the bill, the Irish worker's contribution was reduced from 4d to 3d and his employers' from 3d to 2½d. The Irish demanded also, and received, separate administration for their island. This concession to the Irish caused a clamor for a complete reconstruction of the administration of the scheme along national lines. The single board of health commissioners was superseded by four national committees for each of the three kingdoms with, to John Burns's anger and disappointment, a separate body for Wales.[169] Lloyd George promptly filled the Welsh National Insurance Commission with supporters from the principality. His old friend from the education revolt, Alderman T.J. Hughes of Cardiff, became Chairman. Perhaps as important, beginning a new association for Lloyd George, was the appointment of a young lecturer at Glasgow University, Thomas Jones of Rhymney, as Secretary.

When on 21 November the National Insurance Bill emerged from its committee stage of 29 days it had grown from 87 clauses to 115 with nine additional schedules. Besides the changes in administration already noted and the removal of the medical benefit from the approved societies to the local health committees, Lloyd George had been forced to permit free choice of doctor. Any doctor who chose could put his name on the local health committee panel list and so announce his availability for insurance practice. These changes had completely antagonized the friendly societies upon which Lloyd George's original conception had been founded. The societies were now in open rebellion and the Chancellor's main supporters, as the bill moved toward passage, became the industrial insurance interests, the Combine.

The Combine had determined early in June that industrial insurance had better find a place for itself within the national health insurance administration. This decision, announced by Arthur Henri of the Liverpool Victoria at the end of June, precipitated an unprecedented lobby campaign to force the amendment of the requirements for approved society self-government and voluntary administration that Braithwaite had embedded in the bill. The elimination of the local management committees was an early victory.[170] This underground struggle continued through the summer and autumn and came to a climax at an acrimonious meeting at the Treasury on 19 October.[171] Here the men of the societies and industrial insurance faced each other for the only time. At the annual friendly society conferences in the previous month, health insurance and its ministerial sponsor had come under increasingly violent denunciation and there were many demands that the provident movement withdraw from the scheme altogether. However, this threat was not real. The societies could not compete against a subsidized state scheme. They were trapped within the plan they had helped to found but could no longer control.

Lloyd George realized this well enough. With the big guns of industrial insurance behind him he did not need to fear the well-known, but old fashioned, lobby influence of the societies.[172] If necessary the Chancellor could run health insurance with the funeral benefit industry alone and the provident movement would decay. Accordingly, on 19 October, he gave industrial insurance what it wanted, the deletion of the remaining clauses requiring self-government for approved societies.[173]

Health insurance was now safe, but many men felt betrayed. Braithwaite recorded his anger in his diary. Self-government should be a legal, not a political matter.

> ...From this moment, at the bottom of my heart, I lost a great deal of my interest in the bill. I regarded the whole transaction as a betrayal of the spirit of the bill, for whilst these collecting Societies were entitled to come in, they should have done so under control and not as controllers. The fight lost that day [it had really been lost some months before in the House of Commons], will have to be renewed at some time in the future, when Industrial Insurance is either bought out or confiscated.[174]

The insurance world, conversely, was completely satisfied with a task well and fully completed. 'The Chancellor has made a good bargain with our industrial insurance institutions,' declared the *Insurance Mail* the following week, 'and thus has the support of 100,000 practiced insurance men. He need fear no threats. We believe he will stick to his bargain with us, and we believe the sick clubs know he will. It is this knowledge that has cleared the air.'[175]

But even as the last serious obstructions were cleared during the final days of the autumn recess, the Liberals were learning, as they had feared for weeks, that Lloyd George's project was a political millstone. In quick succession, on 13 and 22 November, two solid Liberal seats at Oldham and South Somerset were lost. Worse, as the dull and fruitless committee stage under the guillotine wore on, denunciation and opposition moved from the narrow arena of the House of Commons to the newspapers and the public platform. On the day of the South Somerset defeat Lloyd George had rejected an amendment put down by the opposition that would have made insurance optional for household servants. He had argued that to permit this would be virtually to exclude serving girls from insurance, for their mistresses could easily influence them. In anticipation of the rejection of this amendment the *Daily Mail* early in the month had called for correspondence on the subject of the insurance of domestic servants. By the twenty-first it reported that 'never in its history' had it received so much correspondence. A 'Litchfield Matron' wrote that the Chancellor 'forgets that if he gets his silly Insurance Bill through Parliament he has to meet a whole army of indignant women who will simply laugh in his face and refuse to obey him.' A Kensington mistress 'of twenty years experience' said: 'We are ready to fight for our homes. My orderly life shall not be interfered with and upset by a tyrannical law.' A St. Johns Wood matron wrote that insurance contributions were really being used to pay old age pensions.[176]

As the end of the month approached *The Times* noted that the Unionists were reported as being 'snowed under' by letters and postcards of protest against national health insurance. Ten mail sacks on 28 November, nine on

29 November. This, said the journal, represented an informal referendum against national health insurance.[177]

At issue specifically was the affixing of the revenue stamps to the insurance cards which the law made the responsibility of employers of domestic servants. The result was the famous anti-stamp licking campaign. The 29th of November saw the climax of the anti-stamp licking campaign with the well-known Albert Hall rally in which mistresses and maids were invited by the *Daily Mail* to come and demonstrate that they would not submit to tyranny. The vitality of British democracy was manifest by the appearance of the dowager Countess Desart and her maid on the same platform. *The Times* reported that the vast auditorium was filled and thousands of women stood outside. 'The night was raw and foggy but it made no difference. The girls were determined to show their feelings on a matter which they consider vitally affects their interests....' Before the meeting an organist maintained enthusiasm by playing popular airs. Unfortunately he hit upon 'March of the Men of Harlech.' 'Immediately', reported the *Times* correspondent, 'there was a tornado of hissing which changed to enthusiastic cheers as the music of "Rule Britannia, Britons never shall be slaves" broke upon the ears.' Lady Desart made the address of the evening, concluding a violent attack upon the Welsh Chancellor of the Exchequer with the reminder that

> England...never did nor never shall
> Lie At the Proud Foot of a Conqueror.

The meeting concluded with fiery speeches from a number of other titled ladies and from Hilaire Belloc. It passed a carefully worded resolution protesting at health insurance only as it applied to domestic servants and condemning the armies of politically appointed inspectors who would soon invade the homes of freeborn Englishmen to force housewives to lick stamps for Lloyd George. The only untoward occurrences were persistent questions from the floor demanding to know why the Unionists had not come out flatly against health insurance.[178]

The Albert Hall rally seriously worried the government. 'There can, I think, be no doubt that the insurance Bill is, (to say the least) not an electioneering asset,' wrote Asquith to Crewe the next day.

> The *Daily Mail* has been engineering a particularly unscrupulous crusade on behalf of mistress and maid and one hears from all constituencies of defections from our party of the small class of employers. Nor is the situation likely to improve a year hence, when the contributions are in full blast, and the 'benefits' remote and sporadic. The Lords will not reject the Bill and it seems doubtful now whether they will seriously amend it. A 'wash our hands' policy seems likely to be foreshadowed.[179]

Although there were suggestions after the rally that the next logical step was straightforward refusal to pay the national insurance contribution, and Lady Desart established the 'Tax Defence Association' in South Molton Street which continued well into the spring of 1912 to collect pledges to disobey the law, the anti-stamp licking campaign was over. Fatuous it had been, but it represented a genuine and wide-spread discontent that was confirmed again on 20 December with the third Liberal by-election loss in six weeks, this time in North Ayrshire. Just four days earlier the National Insurance Bill had received the Royal Assent. 'I think Lloyd George and co. are doing all they can to help us,' exulted Henry Chaplin to Bonar Law on New Year's Eve. 'Quite apart from party prospects—what with Labour unrest at home—and affairs abroad in so many different parts of the world, the general atmosphere seems to me to be created to say the least of it. With all good wishes....'[180]

VI

During the oppressively hot summer of 1911 Britain enjoyed two immense public spectacles: the coronation of George V and Queen Mary on 22 June and, the more impressive for its innovation, the investiture of the seventeen-year old Prince of Wales at Caernarvon Castle on 13 July. The idea of a formal investiture in Wales occurred first to the Bishop of St. Asaph soon after Lloyd George had become Constable of Caernarvon Castle. He suggested it to his friend who quickly agreed.[181] The ramifications of such a venture for the promotion of Wales and Welshness were limitless, as Lloyd George saw. St. Asaph then went off to the British Museum to discover what in fact took place at an investiture.[182] George V heartily approved the idea, not least, according to his son's recollection, because it would smooth his way with Lloyd George. The royal proclamation announcing the event was published on 4 February 1911.

Usual memories of the investiture include the hazy heat and the enormous crowds of people, most of whom never saw the ceremony that took place in the inner bailey of Caernarvon Castle, which had been partly restored for the event. Lloyd George sensibly arranged for an appearance and speech in Castle Square before the investiture at which the young prince, to the crowd's delight, pronounced in Welsh taught him by Lloyd George: 'All Wales is a sea of song' and 'Thanks from the bottom of my heart to this old land of my fathers.'

Lloyd George kept modest his own participation in the ceremony. He fully understood that his presence would distract attention from the royal family.[183] The Chancellor was visible only in the parade to Castle Square in which he rode in an automobile with Alec Murray and later when, as Constable, he handed the keys to the King as the royal party entered the castle at the Water Gate. But he found places for his friends. The Welsh bishops were in evidence but Evan Jones, appropriately, opened the religious ceremony with a long and stirring prayer. Churchill proclaimed the royal titles with much gusto.[184] The prince, who had not relished the proposal for an investiture in the first place, remained friends with Lloyd George until well after his abdication as king.

Later Lloyd George told George Riddell a charming story illustrative of the character of George V, with whom, so far, he was still on good terms. During the preparations for the investiture he was at a dinner at Buckingham Palace when the King asked him: 'When are you coming to teach that boy of mine Welsh?' Lloyd George replied that he had not been invited, at which the King said he did not need an invitation. For some days nothing happened and then Lloyd George received a note from the palace saying that as he was clearly busy the Prince would come to Downing Street for his instruction, which he did.[185]

The peaceful and happy celebration in the sweltering sunshine of North Wales occurred at the opening of the Agadir crisis, by far the gravest international confrontation of the prewar period. Agadir meant far more than the dispatch of a virtually unarmed, 1,000 ton, German naval vessel with a complement of 125 men to an unknown port in southern Morocco. At this time Britain took a long step toward the involvement in the French defense plans that would require intervention in the First World War. More important, for Lloyd George the crisis provided an opportunity for his first official excursion into foreign and military affairs from which, unlike his amateur and unwanted attempts in 1908, he emerged a national, if controversial, champion. Finally, the effect of the crisis was to spur the Cabinet and the heads of the services towards substantive and concrete planning for Britain's part in a war between France and Germany. In all this Lloyd George was closely involved as a spectator and as a participant. He knew, and discussed at length with Churchill, the Army's expectations of sending an expeditionary force to France in the event of an attack by Germany. He knew also that the French counted upon such a force to the point of refraining from offensive operations in Belgium in order to ensure British participation.[186] He knew that Brigadier Henry Wilson, the Director of Military Operations, expected the German attack to come through Belgium. He urged Asquith to dismiss McKenna from the Admiralty and appoint Churchill in his place.

Taken together, the secret planning sessions and the Cabinet changes of August, September and October of 1911 are of far greater significance than the public international confrontation between France and Germany in July. One cannot avoid the impression that some of Britain's foremost politicians, Grey in the lead strongly supported by Churchill and Haldane with Asquith trailing more reluctantly behind, all driven along by Henry Wilson, came at this time to the conclusion that in the event of a German attack upon France Britain would have to act whether or not the Germans invaded Belgium. The implications for Britain of a defeated, bloodied, and pauperized France, reduced in size and stripped of her colonies, were too terrible to contemplate. Britain would face alone a German-dominated and organized Europe. What would the dreadnought competition be like then? Who would secure the seas? What would become of free trade and Britain's commercial predominance? Could the empire, indeed the home islands, be defended? In all of this the question of Belgium was hardly raised except amid speculation that she might be afraid to resist the German armies. As a consequence, during the gloomy Bank Holiday weekend at the end of July 1914, although many members did not know it, the Cabinet was debating a decision that for practical purposes had already been made and in which Lloyd George had participated. His behavior at that time, his reluctance to commit himself publicly until the Germans had in fact invaded Belgium, his willingness to consort with the pacifists in the Cabinet, need to be judged against the fact that he knew and accepted the assumption that although the Germans would indeed attack France through Belgium, Britain would have to intervene in any case.

As he was preparing to conduct his annual battle with McKenna over naval estimates in January 1911, Lloyd George had complained that he was uninformed on foreign policy questions which affected the budget, but which were familiar to other ministers who came to him for money. Could he be allowed to read Foreign Office dispatches? In the end he was not included in the routing of Foreign Office papers but Asquith, in a characteristic gesture, established a foreign affairs subcommittee of the Cabinet to which Lloyd George was appointed. At this time Grey was attempting, half-heartedly, to negotiate some kind of a naval agreement with Germany that would abate the naval contest. Lloyd George enthusiastically supported this departure and used information gained from the committee when he began his fight with McKenna.

His argument was that relations with Germany were improving and that the inflated navy estimates of the past two years could now be reduced. After what Asquith described to Pease as a 'breeze' in his presence on 16 February at which Lloyd George offered to resign and, according to Lloyd George, Asquith demanded McKenna's resignation instead, he and his antagonist agreed upon a formula by which Lloyd George would approve the expenditures necessary to complete construction in progress in return for a promise by McKenna to save £4,400,000 in the fiscal years 1913 and 1914 and keep the estimates at £4 million.[187] The Cabinet approved the arrangement on 1 March.[188] Nonetheless the bitterness between the two had been further exacerbated. In a long letter to McKenna, who was being bombarded by warnings from Fisher in Switzerland to beware of the 'Welsh Lyre,' Lloyd George could not resist one more shot at the First Lord. There were, he admitted, problems with the economists on one side and 'scaremongers' on the other and he knew that McKenna was aware that German shipbuilding was not as advanced as had been thought. 'There is a much better feeling with Germany now. Grey feels very sanguine that we may be able to secure an understanding as to slowing down. This wd. save tremendously in 1913-14.' He hated to be Shylock and would interpret the First Lord's undertaking reasonably and fairly in 1913-14 but he 'would not assent to its cancellation…you…undertook to "deliver the goods" & I earnestly trust you will not reopen a lawyer's controversy now because of an unfounded apprehension that the Cabinet will treat your failure to comply with your agreement harshly even if you have sincerely endeavored to carry it out.'[189] This agreement has been noted at length because when Churchill became the First Lord it would become the focus of an even more bitter controversy over the estimates.

Lloyd George presented the budget of which these figures were a part on 16 May, less than two weeks after the introduction of the National Insurance Bill. In an address that attracted relatively little attention, he announced with obvious satisfaction that naval expenditure had reached a peak and would now begin to subside.[190] The 1911-12 year, he announced, would see the completion of the four extra battleships that had been the center of the 1909 naval scare. The estimates of £44,300,000 would not be repeated and he warned members not to attempt to increase expenditure on national insurance. On the other hand old age pensions would cost £12,415,000.[191] He did not remark that this figure was precisely twice Asquith's estimate.

However his most interesting announcement was that the budget resolutions shortly would be amended to allow the payment of £400 per year to Members of Parliament. It was nothing new, Lloyd George assured the House. All other countries did it and Asquith had mentioned it before the December election of the previous year.[192]

Lloyd George's comfortable assurances of a return to fiscal normality were exploded less than six weeks after he spoke by the news on 1 July that Germany had sent a gunboat, the *Panther*, to the port of Agadir on the south coast of Morocco, ostensibly to protect German interests there, but in fact to challenge France whose troops earlier in the year had occupied the Moroccan capital of Fez. Germany was motivated less by a wish to protect Morocco than by the desire to enforce its demand for compensation in French Africa in the negotiations with France already begun. Britain's interests were two: some alarmists saw a danger in the German possession of a port near Britain's South Atlantic trade routes. But more important, Britain had undertaken by treaty in 1904 to support any French attempt in the future to establish in Morocco a protectorate which would give her the position there that Britain held in Egypt. This acquiescence, however, had been kept secret since 1904, was generally unknown at the time of the crisis and in fact was not made public until 11 November, 1911 when the confidential clauses were published by *Le Temps*. As a result, patriotic outrage in Unionist newspapers was matched by assertions among the radical Liberal press and platform that the French/German squabble was none of Britain's business. The Royal Navy could not expect to control every port in the world. After the arrival of the *Panther*, Grey, whose commitment to France was nearly absolute, obtained Cabinet permission to convey Britain's alarm to Germany, which he did in a terse interview with Metternich on 4 July. Britain he said would not recognize any new arrangements upon which she had not been consulted.[193] For two weeks there was no German reply but plenty of newspaper reports that the German fleet had mobilized, was cruising alone in the North Sea, and that British intelligence had lost contact with it. After the Cabinet returned from the Prince of Wales's investiture, Grey determined he would wait no longer. On 19 July he wrote to Asquith saying that if he had not heard from Germany by Friday, 21 July, he would tell Metternich that Britain 'must become a party to the discussion of the situation,' between Germany and France and that to underscore her concern Britain would also send a ship to Agadir.[194]

On the afternoon of 21 July, after he had told the Cabinet of what he intended to say to Metternich, Grey was informed, to his surprise, that Lloyd George had come to the Foreign Office to see him. He was to make a speech as Chancellor of the Exchequer at the Lord Mayor's dinner for the Bankers' Association at the Mansion House that evening. He proposed to add his own public warning to the private rebuke Grey intended to deliver to the German Ambassador that afternoon. Lloyd George had his statement written out. Grey welcomed the Chancellor's support, confirmed that there had been no word from Germany, looked carefully at the sentences before him and evidently rewrote some of them. (Grey does not mention in his memoirs any consultation with Asquith, although Lloyd George affirms that he had previously seen the Prime Minister.)[195]

The conference with Grey was prolonged. Lloyd George, usually prompt to the minute on public occasions, arrived at the Mansion House half an hour late only to have his introduction interrupted by a young man in evening clothes proclaiming the rights of women. By and large the speech gave the City bankers the emollient reassurances they annually expected and received on such occasions. The government cared for nothing but economy; the insurance bill would not raise taxes; and Sir Edward Grey's negotiations for an arbitration treaty with the United States testified to Britain's pacific and merciful attitude toward the world. Then slowing suddenly, and beginning to read, he concluded:

> But I am bound also to say this—that I believe it is essential in the highest
> interests, not merely of this country, but of the world, that Britain should
> at all hazards maintain her place and her prestige amongst the Great
> Powers of the world. Her potent influence has many a time been in the
> past, and may yet be in the future, invaluable to the cause of human
> liberty. It has more than once in the past redeemed Continental nations,
> who are sometimes too apt to forget that service, from overwhelming
> disaster and even from national extinction. I would make great sacrifices
> to preserve peace. I can see that nothing would justify disturbance of
> international good will except questions of the gravest national moment.
> But if a situation were to be forced upon us in which peace could only be
> preserved by the surrender of the great and beneficent position Britain
> has won by centuries of heroism and achievement, by allowing Britain to
> be treated where her interests were vitally affected as if she were of no
> account in the Cabinet of nations, then I say emphatically that peace at
> that price would be a humiliation intolerable for a great country like ours
> to endure. National honour is no party question. The security of our
> great international trade is no party question; the peace of the world is
> much more likely to be secured if all nations realize fairly what the
> conditions of peace must be. And it is because I have the conviction that
> nations are beginning to understand each other better, to appreciate each
> other's points of view more thoroughly, to be more ready to discuss
> calmly and dispassionately their differences, that I feel assured that
> nothing will happen between now and next year which will render it
> difficult for the Chancellor of the Exchequer in this place to respond to
> the toast proposed by you, my Lord Mayor, of the continued prosperity
> of the public purse.[196]

The usual accounts of this speech assert that the assembled bankers took no note of Lloyd George's challenge to Germany, but *The Times* transcript shows that he was interrupted three times by cheers. It noted also that he read this passage although he had memorized the rest of the speech.

Why had Lloyd George done this? No one suggests that the causes for this intervention lay anywhere but within himself, although Churchill, who had seen him on the morning of 21 July, relates that he encouraged the Chancellor to take the step, while the wording of the statement itself is reminiscent of Grey's letter to Asquith of 19 July.[197] Moreover, Churchill states flatly that he and Lloyd George had discussed the worsening international situation many times during the previous weeks and had sensed themselves drifting from the pacifist wing of the Cabinet with which normally both were allied. But Churchill insists that until the morning of 21 July he had no idea what position his friend would take. On that day he found 'a different man.'

> His mind was made up. He saw quite clearly the course to take. He knew what to do and when to do it. The tenor of his statement to me was that we were drifting towards war. He dwelt on the oppressive silence of Germany so far as we were concerned. He pointed out that Germany was acting as if England did not count in the matter in any way; that she had completely ignored our strong representation; that she was proceeding to put the most severe pressure on France; that a catastrophe might ensue; and that if it was to be averted we must speak with great decision, and we must speak at once.[198]

For Churchill himself the events of the summer of 1911, following the *Panther*'s arrival at Agadir, were critical. He moved quickly and permanently from the pacifist to the interventionist camp within the Cabinet, a change that would only be confirmed, and was not caused, by his appointment to the Admiralty in October. One may speculate that his conversation, his eloquence, and his wide knowledge of military affairs, influenced Lloyd George.

However, Lloyd George rarely took new positions without earnest consideration of contingencies and consequences. The Mansion House statement was a departure not only from the attitudes toward Germany held as recently as the previous spring during the budget struggles, but from the pacifist radical Liberal coalition in the House of Commons and the country with which he usually associated. All of this had to be explained. He could not move too far from his usual constituency too quickly. These factors may account for the extraordinary letter received on 21 July by C.P. Scott, editor of the *Manchester Guardian*, senior official of the Liberal organization in that city and national custodian of the radical conscience. Scott had been a Liberal MP from 1895 until 1905 and Lloyd George had written many articles for his paper, so the two surely were acquainted. But even though the *Guardian* generally supported Lloyd George, Scott's stiffbacked independence kept him from the intimacy enjoyed by many other editors. For weeks the London correspondent of the *Guardian*, R.H. Gretton, had been attempting unsuccessfully to interview Lloyd George on the insurance bill, and Scott himself, at the urging of Lord Loreburn, the senior pacifist in the Cabinet, had tried to see Asquith about Agadir just the day before, on Thursday, 20 July, only to be told by the Prime Minister that he was fully committed.[199] Then on Friday afternoon, through Gretton who still had not been able to see the Chancellor himself, Scott received a note from Lloyd George inviting him to breakfast the next morning and begging him not to write anything 'about the German business' until the two had talked. He received in addition a note from Asquith inviting the editor to see him after he was finished with the Chancellor.[200]

Accordingly, the next day Scott traveled back to London and at breakfast with the Chancellor, with Churchill seconding, he received the full force of

Lloyd George's famous charm. 'They were all civil and apologetic for bringing me up,' Scott wrote in his diary. 'Churchill said to Lloyd George that I ought to be kept constantly informed as to all important matters. Lloyd George said that was just what he tried to do and rather reproached me for not coming to him sooner now.'

Lloyd George rather laid it on about 'Manchester Guardian'—it would smash party if we and the Government were at odds. 'Manchester Guardian' he had found much more considered in Germany than any other Liberal paper and if we let Government down in international controversy it would be inferred that they had no sufficient backing in the country and give a dangerously false impression of their actual determination which up to a certain point was fixed and practically unanimous, Loreburn being the only exception.

Lloyd George spoke warmly of Grey and said he was very good in showing him (Lloyd George) everything and that he (Lloyd George) had got him only yesterday to modify his dispatch (to Berlin). A dispatch had also been sent to our ambassador at Paris instructing him to inform the French Government that we were not prepared to give them support in regard to the French Congo....

Asquith was quite conscious of the anti-Germanism of the Foreign Office staff and was prepared to resist it. But neither he nor Grey nor himself (Lloyd George) would consent to hold office unless they were permitted to assert the claim of Great Britain to have her treaty rights and her real interests considered and to be treated with ordinary diplomatic civility as a Great Power. The whole correspondence would have hereafter to be published and it would be fatal even to our party interests if it should be found that we had not maintained the clear rights and dignity of the country.

I of course agreed with him about this. I do not think it conceivable that Germany should resist such a demand temperately pressed, but the question was what interests we had for which in the last resort we were prepared to go to war and was the prevention of a German naval station at Agadir one of them. I got no clear answer to this.

Repeatedly in the course of the conversation Lloyd George spoke of France's weakness and terror in the face of Germany. She had her eyes ever fixed on 'those terrible legions across the frontier'. 'They could be in Paris in a month and she knew it.' Then Germany would ask not 200 millions but 1,000 millions as an indemnity and would see to it that France as a Great Power ceased to exist. This was real danger that Prussia (and it was Prussia really, not Germany, which was in question) should seek a European predominance not far removed from the Napoleonic.

***

The present German Chancellor he described as a coarse bully and said his opinion of the Emperor had considerably changed since he had found he was the sort of man thoroughly to enjoy this person's company, drinking quantities of beer with him and roaring over the smutty stories which formed the staple of his conversation. He did not tell me his authority for all this. The impression I got was that he is not immune from microbe of Germanophobia.

He was very much down on Loreburn whom he described as 'petulant, unreasonable' and always 'rubbing Grey the wrong way', practically alone in the Cabinet. When I spoke of the Cabinet as a 'Liberal League Cabinet' he repudiated the description—there had been a great change in the last year or two. I said no doubt the Radicalism of the party was influencing the Government; he suggested that it was rather the Budget that had done it.[201]

This interview has been quoted at length, first, because it emphasizes the one great underlying fact, rarely expressed, but paramount in all consultations about a Franco-German conflict both in 1911 and in 1914: that most British leaders believed that without their country's help France would be quickly overrun. Arguably Lloyd George's assertion to Scott contained more than a little rhetoric, but others more expert than he, Kitchener for example and Col. Repington of *The Times*, held the same opinion.[202] Second, for Lloyd George personally, the interview on Saturday morning, 22 July, demonstrates the care, critical in July and August of 1914, that he took to avoid moving too far from his main base of political support. He could agree with men such as Scott, or Morley, or Loreburn, and the millions of Liberal voters like them, that international understanding was preferable to war. War was an immoral act, abhorrent to Liberal principles. Certainly old age pensions were preferable to dreadnoughts. Yet the principles of nationhood, Welsh or British, were likewise absolute. Britain should not suffer insults from German Junkers any more than Welsh nonconformists should be bullied by Anglicized gentry. These sentiments, of course, were personal and the assortment of middle-class, well-to-do, non-Welsh, politicians, journalists, and philanthropists who supported his projects, the Ponsonbys, Buxtons, Cadburys, Nevinson, Brailsford, Gooch, Rowntree, L.T. Hobhouse and H.W. Massingham, and of course C.P. Scott, did not share or understand them. As a result, a startling pronouncement such as the Mansion House speech had to be carefully qualified afterwards. He needed to insist that he was not a tool of a Liberal League-dominated Cabinet, that the German menace was real, and that his outburst involved no departure from principle.[203]

The aftermath of the Mansion House speech brought Lloyd George into intimate contact for the first time with the high matters of diplomacy and defense. The crisis did not end with Lloyd George's warning on 21 July or with the German Ambassador's angry response four days later on 25 July, as Grey suggests, a little too innocently, in his memoirs.[204] Indeed the repercussions from Agadir, the escalation of British planning for war, the consequent huge increase in German naval construction, the resulting creation of the new Home Fleet concentrated at Scapa Flow and the subsequent commitments to France to defend the Channel, made intervention in 1914 all but inevitable. In these affairs Lloyd George was a witness and a participant. His knowledge of the British involvement with French defense and of the Army's expectations about German strategy in an attack on France was far greater than that possessed by the rest of the pacifist wing of the Cabinet. He certainly hoped to avoid war, and tried sincerely and vigorously to hold down naval expenditure in 1913 and 1914, but equally he understood well before the fatal summer Bank Holiday weekend of 1914 that Britain would have to go to war. But he did not say so.

The Mansion House speech caused surprise and anger in Germany which did not subside.[205] The first important German response came on 25 July in a long and angry interview between Grey and Metternich in which the latter concluded: 'If the British Government...should have had the intention to embroil the political situation and lead toward a violent explosion, they could not have chosen a better means than the speech of the Chancellor of the Exchequer, which took so very little into account, with regard to Germany, the dignity and place of a Great Power which the Chancellor of the Exchequer claimed for England in that speech.'[206] Grey considered this conversation so alarming that he sent messengers to find Churchill and Lloyd George to summon them to the Foreign Office to warn that the fleet might be attacked at any moment. Similarly in Germany about two weeks later after a banquet, Sir Edward Goschen, the British Ambassador, recorded in his diary: 'The Emperor took me aside and gave me a good doing for ¾ of an hour. He was rampant about Lloyd George's speech and our interference—and said that without that Germany and France would have arranged matters long ago. I reminded him of Agadir and we had some warm work: he abused us like pickpockets. And said that if France didn't give him the compensation he wanted he would have every French soldier out of Morocco by force if necessary.'[207] More ominously, at Hamburg only two weeks later on 27 August, William II announced there would be large increases in German naval construction 'so that we can be sure that nobody will dispute our rightful place in the sun.' It seems clear that Lloyd George's speech, not on account of anything it contained, but because it was public and because of what Lloyd George represented in British politics, prolonged rather than moderated the Agadir crisis. The French press leaped forward joyfully to attack Germany, while German papers replied. Had Germany indeed been prepared to make concessions, none was possible now.[208]

The Kaiser's attack upon Goschen on 12 August may have caused Asquith's summons, at Wilson's and Haldane's suggestion, of a special meeting of the Committee of Imperial Defence which the Prime Minister set for 23 August after parliament had risen. Curiously, the invitations were sent more than a week before that date, on 15 August, and a number of known pacifists in the Cabinet, Loreburn, Harcourt, and Crewe, who usually attended, were not invited, while Morley who regularly attended was known to be leaving London. On the other hand Lloyd George and Churchill attended for the first time. (The Prime Minister was the only permanent member of the C.I.D. He could invite whom he pleased.) Kitchener was invited but refused to come because he was sure the Germans would walk through the French 'like partridges' and wanted no part of any decision.[209] Besides the Prime Minister, Grey, Haldane, and McKenna, the Director of Military Operations, Brigadier Henry Wilson, and the First Sea Lord, Sir Arthur K. Wilson, with some other officers and Sir Maurice Hankey, were present.

Officially the meeting had been called to explain to senior Cabinet members the Army's and Navy's plans to aid France in the event of war. Unofficially it may have been Asquith's, or particularly Haldane's, way of bringing to light the fact that the Admiralty had no plan at all, at least none outside the brain of the First Sea Lord.[210]

The man who dominated the 23 August meeting at No. 2 Whitehall Gardens, and who perhaps more than any other person except possibly Grey himself, made Britain's support of France in 1914 inescapable, was Henry Hughes Wilson. A highly political soldier, Ulsterman, ardent Unionist, clever, articulate, affable and caustic, his career would be entwined with Lloyd George's until Wilson's assassination on the steps of his house in Eaton Place at the end of June 1922, just four months before Lloyd George resigned the Prime Ministership. Wilson had always taken for granted that the chief German thrust toward France would come through Belgium in massive force aiming at Paris, but turning as far north as Brussels. In such an attack a British army of five or six divisions would be lost and the only importance of a British contribution on land would be in the stiffening of French morale. However in April 1911 he revised this most accurate calculation and determined that the Germans would remain south of the Sambre-Meuse Rivers, crossing thus only the southeastern one-third of Belgium. As this area contained only thirteen roads, as he knew from bicycling over it, which could carry only three divisions each, the whole German force invading Belgium would now be reduced to at most 40 divisions. If, in this case, the French deployed about one half their army, 37 to 39 divisions, to the west of the Ardennes, six British divisions on the French-Belgian border around Maubeuge would provide approximate equality in numbers and allow the British to attack across the German supply train as they entered France. Now, in effect, a British force, even six divisions, was no longer simply an enhancement of French morale but the 'deciding factor.'[211] As one may imagine Wilson understood well, the new predictions made British involvement inevitable. A French defeat became Britain's responsibility.

All of this, and more, Lloyd George heard on the morning of 23 August. Belgium would surely be invaded although there was much doubt about whether she would resist. Churchill pressed strongly the point that he had made in a memorandum of 13 August, submitted to the C.I.D. and to the Prime Minister, that the Germans would invade the north of Belgium as well as the southeast. Lloyd George and Churchill's questions were directed again and again to the problem of what would happen if France were not able to hold the line at the frontier and had to retreat south. Where should the British Army go? McKenna innocently proposed that the British Army be placed under French command. Churchill and the soldiers nearly exploded.[212] Nonetheless, Wilson insisted, as his most important point, that British divisions should be in Maubeuge on the Belgian border by the fourteenth day and deployed by the seventeenth.[213]

In the afternoon session, which received the Admiralty statement from A.K. Wilson, the Cabinet members learned that the Navy had no plans for war beyond the defense of the British Isles and, after the German fleet was neutralized, the seizure of islands off the German coast and the threatening of the Kiel Canal and Wilhelmshaven. This would have required at least one division of soldiers, and military transport, all of which were needed for France. One of the generals called it 'madness.' Admiral Wilson had no plans for transporting the British Army to France. He did not doubt that the Navy could do it, although perhaps not within the time required, but in any case he did not expect Britain to fight that sort of war.[214] His presentation was woolly and rambling. The politicians, as well as the soldiers, were outraged.

Hankey's biographer may be overstating the effect of this meeting by saying that Britain was commited to war henceforth, but there can be no question, and all accounts agree, that Henry Wilson's suave and persuasive presentation on 23 August had a profound effect upon his audience and Lloyd George.[215] The Chancellor's interjections at the meeting, his subsequent correspondence with Churchill and, perhaps most of all, his support of Churchill, now an avowed interventionist, for the Admiralty testified to his acceptance of the inevitability of a British declaration of war in case of a German attack on France.

Haldane relates in his autobiography that he told Asquith after the meeting that unless changes were made at the Admiralty and better communications established he could not continue at the War Office. (McKenna had stated at the beginning of the meeting that he was hearing for the first time of the plan to send six divisions to France in case of an outbreak of war.)[216] Haldane followed this with a letter in the same tone which suggested also that he become First Lord.[217]

After the meeting, Lloyd George left London for Criccieth, agitated and unhappy. On 25 August he wrote Churchill a gloomy letter fearing that war would come and that Britain would not be prepared. British participation, he proposed, should be in Belgium rather than France. There is

> another position we ought to reconnoitre. What about Belgium? 150,000 British troops supporting the Belgian army on the German flank would be a much more formidable proposition than the same number of troops extending the French line. It would force the Germans to detach at least 500,000 men to protect their lines of communication. The Anglo-Belgian army numbering 400,000 men would pivot on the great fort at Antwerp. The command of the sea would make that position impregnable. Is there no way open to us to sound out Belgium. She does not want Germany as a neighbour on the Congo as well as a tenant of Liege and possibly of Antwerp. Send this along to Grey with your views. But let me hear from you also. I am inclined to think the chances of war are multiplying.... 'Be ye therefore ready.'[218]

Churchill concurred in the Antwerp policy, urging pressure on Belgium to defy Germany, and showed Lloyd George's letter to both Grey and Wilson, each of whom replied.[219] This series of letters continued into the middle of September after Lloyd George left Criccieth for Balmoral to serve again as Minister in Attendance upon the King. They are of interest not only as evidence that the two men took for granted British participation in the war in case of a German attack (which during these weeks seemed imminent as the Germans concentrated troops around Malmedy on the Belgian border), but also that the two, far from regarding Belgium as an excuse for British intervention, sought for a way to enforce Belgian resistance should she decide, as many expected, not to fight Germany.

(Grey had suggested at the C.I.D. meeting that the Belgians would 'avoid committing themselves as long as possible in order to try and make certain of being on the winning side.')[220]

Lloyd George left Criccieth for London on 12 September, dining with Churchill that evening. Churchill reported to Wilson that he and the Chancellor had agreed that the DMO's proposal of simultaneous mobilization with the French and the dispatch of all six divisions to the continent was vital.[221] The next day, Lloyd George saw Wilson himself. Wilson's record of this interview further amplifies the Chancellor's views.

> I had a long talk with Lloyd George who was passing through London on his way up to Balmoral. I impressed on him the value of a friendly Belgium, the absolute necessity for our mobilizing the same day as the French, and of our sending the whole six divisions. I think he agreed with all this. He was quite in favour of war now. I asked him if he would give us conscription, and he said that, although he was entirely in favour of a ballot he dare not say so until war broke out, which I told him was too late. He told me Lord K. had told him the French army was rotten and ours not much better. What a d...d fool that man is.[222]

As he had the year before, Lloyd George hated the duty at Balmoral. 'I am not cut out for court life,' he reported to Maggie. 'The whole atmosphere reeks of Toryism. I can breathe it & it depresses and sickens me. Everybody very civil to me as they would be to a dangerous wild animal whom they fear & perhaps just a little admire for its suppleness and strength. The King is hostile to the bone to all who are working to lift the working man out of the mire.' He would be glad when he could leave.[223]

Nonetheless, the stay at Balmoral had one significant consequence. Lloyd George arrived on 14 September just as A.J. Balfour, still Unionist leader, was about to depart, but in time for the two to have a long talk. Lloyd George thought it important enough to report it to Maggie. 'Had a long chat with Balfour before he left this morning. We are all concerned about the foreign situation which is worsening.'[224] And to Churchill: 'I had a long talk with Balfour. He is very much worried—as you are—about the Navy. He is by no means happy about the Admiralty. He has no confidence in Wilson's capacity for direction and leadership. He thinks the Admirals too cocksure. If there is war he [Balfour] will support us.'[225]

Evidently Lloyd George astounded Balfour, and indeed the King, with his animosity toward Germany. More than a month later Balfour exclaimed to Austen Chamberlain upon the Chancellor's bellicosity. '"Germany," Lloyd George had said to Balfour, "meant war; wouldn't it perhaps be better—to have it at once?" and so on. Balfour was "rather shocked" by his violence.'[226] These same strong words, and indeed the same reaction to them, were related by George V, no pacifist, to Churchill who followed Lloyd George at Balmoral.[227]

These reports, flying around the close world of Westminster Palace, as Lloyd George surely knew they would, betrayed a new man. More accurately this was a facet of Lloyd George's character that had always existed unobserved. He had always hated privilege and had sympathized with the underdog; now Britain was the underdog. 'People think,' he told

Lucy Masterman a few days after the Mansion House speech, 'that because I was a pro-Boer I am anti-war in general; and that I should faint at the mention of a cannon! I am not against war a bit. I like the Germans but I hate the Junker caste.'[228] He said virtually the same thing to Riddell at about the same time, when he believed, or pretended to believe, that the Germans were attempting to force his dismissal as they had evicted Foreign Minister Delcassé from the French Cabinet during the first Moroccan crisis. 'The nation should know what the German attitude of mind is. The policy of the jack boot won't do for us. I am all for peace, but I am not going to be jack booted by anybody.'[229]

Lloyd George left Balmoral on 18 September with Alec Murray for a tour of Scotland which included Skibo Castle, Sutherland, the estate of Andrew Carnegie.[230] Returning from the north he saw Grey at Fallodon and Asquith at Archerfield in East Lothian over the weekend of 23-4 September. While at Archerfield, as he related to Riddell later in Churchill's hearing, he urged the Prime Minister to appoint not Haldane but Churchill to the Admiralty.[231] On 26 September he was back in London.

As it happened, Asquith had written McKenna a few days before he met Lloyd George complaining in severe terms of slackness at the Admiralty. The War Office could get no replies on transport plans, all admirals were away on vacation, said the Prime Minister.[232] At the end of September Churchill, with Haldane, was invited to Archerfield and offered the Admiralty, which he immediately accepted.[233] A full ten days later Asquith wrote to McKenna to tell him in only slightly courteous terms that he must leave the Admiralty, but could go to the Home Office.[234] McKenna, whose ignorance of the amount of earth that had dissolved beneath his feet since 23 August is beyond belief, now hastened to Archerfield. There on 20 October he underwent a painful interview with the Prime Minister. He asked to keep his post. He asked for delay: his health, the estimates, perhaps the crisis would be ended by the first of the year. Asquith replied that health could be a reason for the change and the new First Lord should handle the estimates.[235]

This unhappy episode would not be germane to the career of Lloyd George were it not that at this conversation between McKenna and the Prime Minister the massive changes which had occurred since the Mansion House address were brought into focus. The usual explanation for Churchill's translation to the Admiralty has been that he would preside over the creation of a Navy planning board. As Arthur K. Wilson resisted a planning board, Churchill's appointment would involve also the retirement of the First Sea Lord. This may indeed have been Asquith's own reason for the replacement of McKenna; certainly it was the burden of Haldane's original criticism. However, the discussion at Archerfield turned not on Admiralty organization but on the issues turned up on 23 August: the fundamentals of defense policy, a 'Continental strategy' as opposed to a 'blue water' or 'Baltic strategy,' Britain's way of fighting war since the days of the elder Pitt. Early in the conversation McKenna admitted that he 'abhorred the use of British troops in France.' Britain ought not to encourage France. He feared Churchill's plan. It was politically wrong and strategically bad. Its very existence encouraged the French. In all this lay the implication, which Asquith quickly detected, that the Prime Minister was a weak leader. The French would never be encouraged so long as he was Prime Minister, he retorted. He resented the notion that he was a mere figurehead 'to be pushed along against his will.' Lloyd George might be able to do this with insurance, but not in the case of war.[236] In his classic history of the Royal Navy Arthur Marder finds it remarkable that this interview, of which he prints a portion, dealt only with high strategy and not with Admiralty reorganization. But Marder had not seen the Churchill-Lloyd George correspondence or the Hankey diaries. Instead he suspected Asquith was being devious, although he agreed that McKenna himself believed he was being replaced because he opposed the commitments to France.[237]

In fact Asquith was not being devious and McKenna was quite right. Asquith was surely thinking only of the Moroccan crisis in his conversation with McKenna, and not contemplating an irrevocable commitment to France for the future, but the changes of 1911 made a British refusal to aid France in 1914 virtually unthinkable, as McKenna sensed. For ever after he insisted to anyone who would listen, that he had been sacked by a cabal of warhawks in the Cabinet, not for refusing to reorganize the Admiralty, but for opposing the Continental strategy. Only Haldane, he said, put it about that he had resigned over transport plans.[238]

In fact the Cabinet had been overtaken by the imperatives of war planning. If in order to save France, six British divisions had to be deployed before Maubeuge by the seventeenth day, the provision of transportation and the mobilization of the Navy had to begin immediately upon a German declaration of war. Hence the planning had to be done before the war. This meant a First Lord and a First Sea Lord sympathetic to a Continental strategy. The replacement of McKenna and A.K. Wilson and the provision of a British force in France could not be separated. In 1914 the British Cabinet's alternatives were constrained by the tactical objectives of its military planners in exactly the same way that German diplomacy was stifled by the Schlieffen Plan.

The Agadir crisis ended with the signing of a German-French accord on 4 November which provided the Germans with substantial compensation in the French Congo. But the poison spilled upon international friendships and on relationships among Liberals in Britain remained. Grey, with whom Lloyd George had formed a close friendship, was gloomy about the future of diplomacy. 'A patched-up peace between France and Germany, violent animosity worked up against us in Germany for the sake of January elections there, and a large increase in naval expenditure is not a pleasant prospect, but that is the way things are tending' was his report to Asquith of a conversation with Lloyd George in Aberdeen when the latter was on his way to Balmoral.[239] This unhappy forecast was fulfilled two days later in a private dispatch from the naval attaché in Berlin, Admiral Hugh Watson, who reported reliable information from the highest authorities that as a result of the Agadir affair German dreadnought construction would be greatly increased by an amendment, in 1912, to the basic navy law.[240] The shadow cast by Lloyd George's address at the Mansion House continued to lengthen.

More immediately troubling, and with greater effect on Lloyd George, was the revolt among the radical pacifist Liberals both within and without the government. A group led by Morley and Loreburn disrupted Cabinet meetings on 1 and 15 November demanding to know the nature and importance of the military conversations with France. Apparently Loreburn was the first to learn of the C.I.D. meeting and heard of it, to his anger, from Alfred Lyttelton, a Unionist.
[241] This row, in which McKenna joined the rebels and Lloyd George supported Grey, centered almost entirely on the revelations of the 23 August meeting of the C.I.D. and resulted in a resolution prohibiting further plans for cooperation with France without direction from the Cabinet. 'Asquith, Grey, Haldane, Lloyd George and Churchill thought they could boss the rest of us but were mistaken,' wrote an exultant rebel, J.A. Pease, in his diary.[242]

At the same t' ¬ Henry Wilson heard from Haldane a different report. After complimenting the D.M.O. on his performance on 23 August, Wilson wrote, the War Secretary observed that there had been a 'serious disagreement in the Cabinet.'

> Asquith, Haldane, Lloyd George, Grey and Winston on one side,
> agreeing with my lecture on August 23rd, whilst Morley, Crewe,
> Harcourt, McKenna and some smaller fry were mad that they were not
> present August 23 (McKenna of course got kicked out for his pains) and
> were opposed to all ideas of war and especially angry with me....
> The Govt fear there may be a split but Haldane told me that he had
> influenced Asquith that if there was a change in policy he would go.[243]

Meanwhile, the newspapers in the country upon which Lloyd George usually depended began to condemn his speech of 21 July for having provoked a crisis between Britain and Germany where none had existed before.[244] Even the *British Weekly*, staunchly imperialist during the South African War, took up the attack. Lloyd George clearly had seen his important friend Robertson Nicoll before the Mansion House speech and had silenced him, as he had mollified C.P. Scott, for Nicoll's paper carried no mention of the Chancellor's challenge to Germany the following Thursday. However, in the autumn, as other Liberal papers began to question Britain's growing stiffness toward its North Sea neighbor and equally the unseemly friendliness with France, the *British Weekly* began, a little more mildly, to participate. For the *British Weekly* and others the target was Grey, rather than Lloyd George, although the Chancellor's speech, it reminded its readers, 'is not forgotten.'[245] Rumors of a promise of 150,000 troops to France were circulating. Was there a secret treaty?[246] In the last weeks of the year a concerted 'Grey Must Go' campaign developed among Liberal-radicals of all sorts from Lord Courtney and Ellis's patron, Sir John Brunner, to A.G. Gardiner and Dr. John Clifford. Brunner sponsored a conference on Anglo-German understanding. Courtney founded a Liberal foreign policy committee to keep an eye on jingoes in the Cabinet and the Foreign Office. Even the faithful Harold Spender was affected: '...the British Foreign Office, being manned almost exclusively by members of our aristocracy,' he wrote to the German historian, Erich Eyck in December 1911, 'does not represent either the tone or the spirit of the Liberal party.'[247]

This was danger from a quarter Lloyd George could not ignore. While he courageously stood by Grey in private, he did not speak when Grey made a rather surly defense of his policies in the House of Commons on 27 November. More to the point he took care to dine regularly with Nicoll and Scott and continued in the following years his campaign for the reduction of military and naval expenditure with an energy and forthrightness that endangered his friendship with Churchill. Most important, he was careful not to anticipate again public reactions in foreign affairs. There was no Mansion House address in late July 1914. Lloyd George carefully avoided public statements and allowed himself to attend meetings of anti-war ministers while awaiting the invasion of Belgium he knew would come. Unquestionably he honestly hoped for peace and wanted to avoid provocation but he had made his mind up in 1911 and had taken his stand with the interventionists.

'Don't ever forget to teach your children to keep alive the memory of Lloyd George who by his timely speech has saved the peace of Europe and our good name,' wrote Grey's private secretary Sir William Tyrrell to Cecil Spring-Rice, then Minister to Sweden, in the anxious first week of August 1911.

I shall never forget the service rendered by him. His courage was great as he risked his position with the people who have mainly made him.
His cooperation with the Chief is delightful to watch. I breakfasted with him last week and I was struck by his 'flair' in foreign politics. From your and my point of view his is as sound as a bell and it hardly needed the Germans to undeceive him.[248]

VII

In the midst of the Moroccan crisis, during the tangled early weeks of August as the peers wrestled with the Parliament Bill and their consciences and Lloyd George fought health insurance through the Committee of the Whole, Britain faced still another emergency in the form of a general railway strike. In one sense the railway disturbance was simply a manifestation of general labor unrest that plagued the nation during the hot summer of 1911, but historically it represented in fact a continuation of the drive begun by Richard Bell in 1907 to gain recognition for the Amalgamated Society of Railway Servants. Lloyd George's settlement had averted the earlier strike but the conciliation boards were not the equivalent of recognition and never worked. By August of 1911 the railwaymen's discontent, stimulated by a national dock strike, was causing a rash of unofficial stoppages.

Probably Asquith caused the strike with his intransigence, first on 16 August by promising the railway companies that the government would undertake to keep the lines open, with troops if necessary, and the next day by saying the same to the union executive committee while offering only a royal commission to look into the work of the conciliation committees. This the workers' representatives rejected and Asquith immediately left them for a country weekend muttering, as G.R. Askwith reports: 'Then your blood be on your own head.'[249] Such a challenge the union leaders, who themselves indeed feared a strike, had to accept. The result was issuance of an order for a general railway stoppage which began the next day on 18 August and included this time both the Amalgamated Society of Railway Servants, the engineers and firemen, and the other two smaller railway unions.

Lloyd George was appalled when he heard what the Prime Minister had done. 'They are going to strike,' he exclaimed to Charles Masterman, who himself was fully occupied with the last phases of the dock strike, 'and I could have stopped them if I had been there.'[250] Urged by Masterman and Isaacs to intervene, he sent Ramsay MacDonald to round up whatever members of the railway union executive committees were still in London.

Most of the negotiations occurred on Saturday, 19 August. On that day Lloyd George saw the railway directors and elicited a promise that all workmen would be taken back without reprisals and that representatives of the companies would meet the union secretaries. This still was not formal recognition, but resembled it. The unions were more difficult. The leaders, who had worried that the response to a call for a strike would be meagre, discovered to their joy that north of Liverpool and Nottingham not a goods train was running, although on the other hand south of London traffic was almost normal. Lloyd George explained that the royal commission Asquith had promised was not a device for deferring action, but would be a small group (eventually it was five) with instructions to report quickly. He reminded the union leaders that the employers had agreed to meet union representatives. Nonetheless at dinner with Masterman at the National Liberal Club on Saturday evening, after the two sides at last had met, he was in despair. 'The men are the damndest fools,' Masterman recalled him exclaiming. 'I have got them everything they want and they are now sticking out for recognition before the strike ends! It is not possible.'[251]

That evening, Saturday, he met the union representatives again. He argued that if the royal commission did not find the conciliation boards satisfactory, it would have no option but to recommend direct negotiations between employers and the unions, which would constitute recognition. But his most important weapon, brought out with elaborate injunctions to secrecy, was a whisper about the dangerous international situation, Agadir. The appeal to patriotism evidently was effective.[252] In reality, Lloyd George had nothing to offer. He could not force the employers to bargain with the unions, although he could, and apparently did, hint that the government might permit fares to rise allowing an increase in wages.[253] Nor could the government bring an end to the increasingly violent strike which, with two men killed by troops in Llanelli in Wales on 19 August, seemed to be in danger of spreading.

Yet with his genius for conciliation, his ability to convince each side it would eventually get what it wanted, his good humor and patience, even without anything to offer, he had succeeded after Asquith had failed. The Prime Minister had sought precise delineation of the issues. Lloyd George simply blurred them while promising goodwill. But by 21 August the men were back at work. 'Hardest struggle of my life, but I won,' he wrote to Maggie Saturday evening. 'I cannot even now recognize how. As someone said "It is a miracle" & really it looks like it.'[254] More colorful was his appearance later that evening at the War Office where Haldane sat waiting unhappily for news of further confrontations between troops and strikers. 'Suddenly,' Haldane told Austen Chamberlain, 'Lloyd George burst into our room exclaiming, "a bottle of Champagne! I've done it! Don't ask me how, but I've done it! The strike is settled!" And,' concluded Haldane, 'from that day to this I have never known and none of his colleagues have ever known how it was done.'[255] In fact, after the royal commission reported on 20 October, Lloyd George's settlement appeared more miraculous than ever. The commission proposed some changes in the cumbersome machinery of the conciliation boards but pointedly did not recommend recognition of the union. The railway workers had nothing to show for their strike.

Lloyd George received an unusually fulsome letter of thanks from a relieved Asquith, which cited the 'indomitable purpose,' 'the untiring energy,' and 'matchless skill' the Chancellor had brought to the settlement of the 'formidable problem,' and a similar, more dignified, note from the King.[256] But repercussions of the strike and of his service to the Prime Minister were not yet ended. The following week he denounced Keir Hardie in the House of Commons for having stated in a speech that Asquith had threatened to shoot every striker in order to keep the railways open. The issue at hand was the incident at Llanelli on 19 August where a train had been stopped, the engine driver severely beaten, and troops attempting to disperse the mob were attacked, after which two men had been shot. Keir Hardie attempted to convey the notion that Asquith had announced at his meeting with the union secretaries on 17 August that he would order this. Lloyd George began a withering cross-examination which eventually reduced the Member for Merthyr to silence. None of his embarrassed colleagues, except Will Thorne, rose to defend him.[257] There 'is no word in the category of parliamentary language to describe such conduct' was Lloyd George's most vivid phrase, widely quoted in the next few days.[258]

Lloyd George's loathing of the Independent Labour party radicals remained with him through his active political career. They were more than just a political annoyance in the passage of health insurance. Their 'Red Socialism' harmed the labor movement, particularly Welsh miners, he told Arnold White a few weeks later. He denied he had sought the support of any of them and looked forward to the day when Hardie would be ejected from Merthyr. He could be defeated, Lloyd George said, 'by any good Liberal speaker who can speak both languages.'[259] Keir Hardie, for his part, continued for years to insist that the Agadir crisis and the railway strike were linked; that Lloyd George had conspired to protect at once British investments in Morocco and the dividends of railway shareholders.[260]

In the final week of August Lloyd George was able, at last, to leave London for Criccieth, with the Mastermans following. A new member of the household, Lucy Masterman noted in her diary, was a tall, pretty young woman, Frances Stevenson, who was Megan's temporary holiday governess. For some weeks Lloyd George had been unhappy at his youngest daughter's summer isolation in Wales. She will forget 'all she has learned from Miss James,' he wrote to Maggie on 18 July. 'Either she must get a temporary governess who can take her over the holidays and there are plenty now that the schools are breaking up or she must come up here...and go to Beachborough where she can get the benefit of tuition with the Markham children.' Nor, on second thought, he added a week later, did he want Miss James's sister 'if she is as surly as Miss James.'[261]

(He continually worried about the moral welfare of his children, particularly the girls. Six months later he was nervous about Olwen, then nineteen. After naming some people she was not to see, he lectured Maggie: 'Olwen is at a dangerous age and ought to be talked to—however disagreeable a task it may appear. *This is the mother's charge* [underlined twice] . . . I know the world and girls must be looked after.')[262]

The unpleasant Miss James's replacement had graduated recently from Royal Holloway College and was teaching at Allenswood, a girls' school in Wimbledon. She had attended Clapham High School with Mair and had come to Lloyd George's attention through the recommendation of that institution's headmistress. Lloyd George talked to her at the end of July and soon she was on the train for Wales. Here she was welcomed as a member of the family, Lucy Masterman noticed, commenting on the total lack of snobbery and condescension in either Lloyd George or his wife.[263]

Mrs. Masterman thought Miss Stevenson 'a very nice girl, slightly bitten with suffragettism, about which George never fails to rag her.'[264] Nevertheless she fitted well into the disorderly ménage. The two women and Megan went to the beach every day while the Chancellor gave his time alternately but irregularly to Christopher Williams who was painting his official portrait and to W.J. Braithwaite, who had come down to try to work on health insurance. In the long and unusually sunny afternoons there were picnics and extended walks, often over Ellis-Nanney's land. 'If we kept the law about trespassing when we were children, we should have nowhere to play but the dusty high road,' Lloyd George observed to Mrs. Masterman. She continued: 'I never remember during all our visit passing a "trespassers will be prosecuted" notice, without him remarking "I hate that sort of thing."'[265]

Lloyd George was of course corresponding with Churchill about Morocco at this time and although evenings were occupied by games and singing at the piano there was also much conversation about Germany, during which Mrs. Masterman noticed the Chancellor's anti-Junker, although not anti-German, prejudice. 'One evening I remember things were so lively that George got out the map of the frontier prepared by the military authorities showing the great fortresses and describing the Germans' probable line of advance which would be through Belgium, avoiding if possible Lille [sic Liege], which General Wilson had calculated could withstand the Germans, forcing them to stay south of the Meuse, and attacking any totally unfortified part further north—the ancient cockpit of Europe.'[266]

Lloyd George remained in Criccieth until the end of the second week of September when he left for Balmoral. In October Megan enrolled as a weekly boarder at Allenswood where Miss Stevenson was teaching, making necessary regular visits to Wimbledon for conferences. Soon evolved a ripening friendship with his daughter's tutor, who also visited Lloyd George in London, observed him in action in the House of Commons, and allowed him to take her to dinner at Gatti's.

During October and November he was fully occupied with the frantic last stages of the insurance bill, but when parliament rose on 16 December, with health insurance safely on the statute book, Lloyd George departed quickly for Wales. After some speeches in Cardiff, and a day in London, he left England at the first of the year for Lord Rothermere's villa at Cap Martin where he was joined by Rufus Isaacs, Alec and his brother Arthur Murray. He returned to England at the end of January.

While Lloyd George rested in the sunshine of southern France his supporter and critic, H.W. Massingham, the spiritual godfather of the New Liberalism, published in the *Nation* a remarkable estimate of his success and failure since he became Chancellor of the Exchequer. More significantly he combined with it a warning that the Chancellor might yet become a danger to the party of which he was a member and that both he and his works, important as they were, were less than popular.

> Mr. Lloyd George has arrived at a stage of a distinguished man's career when the world begins to ask of him—What will he do next? The pause does not occur at a specially high point of popularity. That was reached the evening of the passing of his great Budget. The rude stroke which dissipated the growing Tory reaction made Mr. George the most popular figure in politics since Mr. Chamberlain. Men saw in it, and rightly, that the strategy which secured it had also meant and obtained a still greater victory—the overthrow of the House of Lords.... The Budget was part of a constructive policy, the most acceptable phase of which had already been accomplished by the Prime Minister. Insurance was bound to come; not as a decree of the Caucus, but as a first charge on the scheme of taxes initiated in 1909. And insurance could not in the nature of things rival old age pensions, either in its appeal to sentiment or in immediate, substantial, social benefits. Fiscal exigency and opinion, especially Conservative opinion, both decreed that sick and unemployment insurance should be on the contributory model. The Opposition, having fixed this principle in the public mind, took the meanest use of its electoral disadvantages....

> For the moment, therefore, this brilliant career hangs in the air. For the next session Mr. George, like the stars in another and a kindred world, will be 'resting.' He is, as I have said, almost completely detached. The Insurance Bill comes of no school; it is pure empiricism; vaguely Socialistic in conception, individualist as to nine-tenths of its machinery and method. Its author has swept it through Parliament by a coup de main. But now a different task awaits him. Is the Budget of 1909 to have the sequel which its author designed? The sequel is the transformation of British agriculture through the three roads of the reform of the land laws and land taxation, the further reform of housing, and the State's control of the railway system. It is safe to say that only the Liberal and Labour Parties can achieve this change, working through the best constructive minds in our politics and the richest stores of personal energy. The fall of the House of Lords was not a mere political event; it was the beginning of a new economic order.

Meanwhile, neither Mr. Lloyd George's friends nor his enemies would care to dispute their tacit agreement that he is the most interesting figure in British politics.... He is something newer, or older still than Chamberlain for in spite of his place of birth and his adaptability to town life, he is of the country and the hills. The small farm and the small chapel formed him, just as even now they form two-thirds of the directing forces of Liberalism and Labour. No special culture was added such as Mr. Chamberlain's association with Unitarianism, or the transplanting of the Prime Minister from Yorkshire to London to Jowett and Balliol, or Mr. Burns's early travels and adventures as a skilled craftsman. Welsh blood, Welsh poetry, Welsh sentiment, Welsh religion, Welsh refinement and subtlety, had to make up for the absence of all foreign enrichments of character and intellect. It is as if a whole people had come to flower in a single personality....

All his gifts are in their way Napoleonic. They make Mr. George a general of the utmost value to his own side and the most dangerous genius to his adversaries. What is not Napoleonic in him, as a statesman and a manager of men, is his indifference to the traditional side of politics; to the influence of the past, and the vengeance that things established take upon those who handle affairs empirically. These things are not, at present at least, on the mental horizon of the most naturally gifted man of his time. Perhaps he is as yet too young in heart, too self-confident, to feel them. In this sense, rather than in the more conventional meaning of the phrase, the Chancellor is not a man of principles. Nor is he specially a man of ideas. He is rather a great and not always calculable natural force, thrown into a medium where his mental swiftness often yields him — easy — too easy — victories. He is wholly attached by birth and feeling to popular causes. But he is deeply in love with expedients, and fascinated at times with their superficial advantages. He takes freely from many sources of political inspiration — Liberalism, Socialism, even Imperialism, and gives back his adaptive and energetic spirit and his unequalled capacity for action. No career in English politics has marched so fast since the days of Pitt; and none has seemed so lightly planted in the soil from which it has made such astonishing growth.[267]

References

Introduction, pp. 11-25

1. Albert James Sylvester, *Life with Lloyd George,* London, 1975, p. 95, 27 April 1933.

2. J.H. Lewis Papers, National Library of Wales 10/230. Conversation with Lloyd George, 8 September 1908.

3. Frank Harris, *Latest Contemporary Portraits,* New York, 1927, pp. 242-3.

4. See: *Transactions of the Honourable Society of Cymmrodorion,* 1971, p. 85.

5. D.R. Daniel, Memoir, National Library of Wales, I, p. 10.

6. Maurice V. Brett, ed., *The Journals and Letters of Reginald, Viscount Esher* (London: 1934), III, 61.

7. *Sunday News,* 13 June 1926, quoted in John Campbell, *The Goat in the Wilderness,* London, 1977, pp. 150-1.

8. *Observer,* 12 November 1961.

9. Harold Spender, *The Fire of Life, A Book of Memories,* London, n.d. [1926], p. 377-8.

10. F.E. Hamer, ed., *The Personal Papers of Lord Rendel,* London, 1931, pp. 177-8.

11. *Observer,* 12 November 1961.

12. Harold Spender, *The Prime Minister,* London, 1920, p. 354.

13. Lucy Masterman, Typescript Diary, II, p. 23, 'Brighton'. In the possession of Neville Masterman.

14. Official Report, House of Commons Debates, Series 5, XXXII (11 December 1911), cols. 1938-9.

15. Lucy Masterman, *C.F.G. Masterman,* London, 1939, p. 211.

16. W.D. Rubenstein, *Men of Property, The Wealthy in Britain Since the Industrial Revolution,* London, 1981, p. 175n.

17. See: Isabel Emmett, *A North Wales Village, A Social and Anthropological Study,* London, 1964.

18. Only 4.2% of the holdings in Caernarvonshire were owned by their occupiers in the 1880s as opposed to 10.4% for the rest of Wales and 16.1% for England. John Davies, 'The End of the Great Estates and the Rise of Freehold Farming in Wales,' *Welsh History Review,* VII (December, 1974) 2, 212.

19. The 1901 Census showed that 90% of the population in Caernarvon spoke either Welsh alone or Welsh and English. The figure was 95% in Merionethshire. Although Henry Pelling notes that the ability to speak Welsh seems to correlate more closely with Liberal voting than with nonconformity, this would be, in fact, difficult to prove. There was no religious census in Wales between 1851 and 1905, but a comparison of the incidence of the use of the Welsh language and nonconformity taken county by county would appear to show that the two coincide

almost exactly. On this see Michael Kinnear, *The British Voter,* London, 1968, pp. 134-7; Henry Pelling, *Social Geography of British Elections, 1885-1910,* London, 1967, p. 347.

20. David Williams, *Modern Wales,* London, 1950, pp. 223-4, 242.

21. See T. Jones Hughes, 'Aberdaron, the Social Geography of a Small Region in the Lleyn Peninsula,' in Elwyn Davies and Alwyn D. Rees, eds. *Welsh Rural Communities,* Cardiff, 1962 p. 164; See also Reginald Coupland, *Welsh and Scottish Nationalism,* London, 1954, p. 218.

22. See Kenneth O. Morgan, 'Welsh Nationalism; The Historical Background' *Journal of Contemporary History* VI, 1971, 1. 153-72.

23. See for instance: C.J. Wrigley, *David Lloyd George and the British Labour Movement,* Brighton, 1976, pp. 7-8, 19.

24. Edward David, ed, *The Diaries of Charles Hobhouse,* London, 1977, p. 98, 30 October 1910.

25. J.H. Lewis Papers, NLW 10/230. By far the best source for Lloyd George's father and mother is W.R.P. George, *The Making of Lloyd George,* London, 1976, pp. 36-55.

26. Uncharacteristically, Lloyd George in 1939 objected to the publication of the fact that his mother had been in service. W.W. Davies's excellent biography of him. Sylvester *Life with Lloyd George,* pp. 223-4.

27. See William George, *My Brother and I,* London, 1958 p. 93.

28. W.R.P. George, *L.G.,* pp. 48-51.

29. *Ibid* pp. 56-57.

30. *Ibid,* p. 62.

31. Richard Lloyd George, *My Father, Lloyd George,* New York, 1961, p. 19.

32. Census, 1871, *British Parliamentary Papers,* Population, XVII, Irish University Press, Shannon, pp. 578-9.

33. Each of these cities gained about 3% in population in the decade of the sixties. Criccieth reached 5,870 in 1871 and Pwllheli 6,754. *Ibid.,* XVI, p. 131.

34. *Ibid.,* XVIII, pp. 600-1.

35. Williams, *Modern Wales,* p. 260. The Rev. Michael D. Jones of Bala reported that upon one large, unnamed estate with 150 tenants, the five who voted Liberal were given notice to quit the next day and nine others who had declined to vote had their rent raised. *Parliamentary Papers,* Government Elections, IV, Select Committee on Parliamentary and Municipal Elections, 1868-69, IVP Minutes of evidence, p. 287.

36. *Ibid.,* 244-66.

37. County franchise after 1832 included, beside the ancient forty shilling freehold, a vote for £50 tenants at will. This had been inserted in the Reform Bill by the Tories precisely to permit landowners to control county voting over the heads of independent farmers. For an excellent description of the militancy of the sixties see Kenneth Morgan, *Wales in British Politics,* Cardiff, 1970, pp. 20-1.

38. There were reports from Merioneth, where W.W.E. Wynne's son, W.R.M. Wynne, was returned against David Williams, although with a reduced majority, that tenants, now prudently voting Tory, had had their rent reduced. Select Committee, op. cit., p. 287.

39. The local story was that the second reform act had given control of the county to the quarrymen at Ffestiniog and that Wynne had withdrawn rather than face certain defeat. *Ibid.,* p. 288. Kenneth Morgan suggests that the effect of the 1867

reform was negligible in the counties although in fact the proportion of electors in the population more than doubled in Caernarvon, Merioneth, and Denbigh. Morgan, *Wales,* p. 21.

40. A quarter century later the issue remained fresh. See the testimony before the 'Royal Commission on Land in Wales and Monmouthshire,' *C.7439,* 1894.

41. Morgan, *Wales,* p. 26. Reference to evictions in Wales does not appear in the Select Committee evidence. There are no good reports that any evictions occurred in Caernarvonshire. Wales, in fact, was ignored in the final report of the Select Committee.

Chapter 1, pp. 27-76

1. William George, *My Brother and I,* London, 1958, p. 24.

2. *Ibid.,* p. 25.

3. William George, *Brother,* p. 33. See also Richard Lloyd George, *My Father, Lloyd George,* New York, 1961, pp. 30-1.

4. W.R.P. George, *The Making of Lloyd George,* London, 1976, p. 135.

5. On Uncle Lloyd's political advice, see: W. George, *Brother,* pp. 27-30.

6. J.H. Lewis Papers, 10/230 unsorted, National Library of Wales, Diary, 4 December, 1907.

7. He wrote a 41-page precis of Green's *History of England.*

8. W. George, *Brother,* p. 41.

9. *Ibid.*

10. W.R.P. George, *L.G.* pp. 76-77.

11. See for instance his comments to Lucy Masterman, in the summer of 1911. Lucy Masterman, *C.F.G. Masterman,* London, 1939, p. 211.

12. *Review of Reviews,* XXX, September, 1904, pp. 369-79, 'Mr. Lloyd George, Chieftain of Wales'.

13. William's son reports his father dwelling unhappily on the incident at the age of 101, a few months before he died. W.R.P. George. *L.G.,* pp. 74-5.

14. This turns up in many early biographies by contemporary journalists. The first reference seems to have been in an article in 'M.A.P.' [Mainly About People] 10 September 1898. See also Beriah Evans, *The Life Romance of Lloyd George,* London, n.d [1916], p. 17.

15. James Marchant, *Doctor John Clifford,* London, 1924, p.225.

16. See: John Grigg, *The Young Lloyd George,* London, 1973, p. 31.

17. See: 'Lloyd George,' *Review of Reviews,* September, 1904, pp. 369-79.

18. In an excellent volume on Lloyd George's career until 1914 that counts to some extent as a primary source for his early life, William Watkin Davies, who grew up in Criccieth early in the twentieth century, sees the memory of early deprivation as an important component of Lloyd George's adult character. It led to a narrowness that caused him to deny any sort of virtue even to the most innocent parts of certain institutions such as the squirearchy and the Church. W.W. Davies, *Lloyd George, 1863-1914,* London, 1939, pp. 82-3.

19. W. George, *Brother,* p. 44.

20. J. Hugh Edwards, *David Lloyd George,* London, n.d. [1913], I. 26-7.

21. W.R.P. George, *L.G.,* p. 74.

22. Masterman, *Masterman*, p. 209.

23. A.J.P. Taylor, ed., *A Diary by Frances Stevenson*, London, 1971, p. 7, 27 November, 1915.

24. W.R.P. George, *L.G.*, p. 97.

25. W. George, *Brother*, p. 113.

26. W.R.P. George, *L.G.*, pp. 77-8, 103.

27. W. George, *Brother*, p. 54.

28. More than half a century later Lloyd George recalled that the news of his success in the Preliminary Law Examination brought the 'most memorable day' of his life. Taylor, ed., *Stevenson Diary*, p.268, 1934.

29. W.R.P. George, *L.G.*, p. 86; W. George, *Brother*, p. 109. W.R.P. George, Lloyd George's nephew suggests that his uncle collected in addition industrial insurance premiums for Mr. Holl, who also taught him shorthand. In view of his later collision with the collecting insurance industry, this would have been an interesting coincidence.

30. W.R.P. George reflects that David's first 18 months as articled clerk were most crucial in his development as a politician and statesman and that too much emphasis has been placed on conversations in the village smithy at Llanystumdwy, and with Richard Lloyd. W.R.P. George, *L.G.*, p. 83. It should be noted that emphasis on Llanystumdwy came from the adult Lloyd George himself.

31. W. George, *Brother*, p. 108. William George dates this passage 24 September, 1879, but the correct date must be 1878. David was well acquainted with Portmadoc by the next year, attending and speaking at the debating society although not yet a member, and much interested in girls. In addition comparisons between William George's rendering of other letters and those reproduced by his son suggest that the earlier year was not correct. The above diary entry is not reproduced in W.R.P. George's book but the letter that William George, the father, prints before and after it do appear and are dated by W.R.P. George, 3 September and Tuesday, 8 October, 1878 while William George dates each of them 1879. W.R.P. George, *L.G.*, pp. 84-6. Furthermore these letters refer to untidy mortgages and to David's first shorthand lesson. Lloyd George began to use shorthand in his journal in 1880, which he could hardly have learned with four months' intermittent tuition. Moreover, Lloyd George frequently identified his entries by days of the week; the entry to the shorthand lesson, Tuesday, 8 October, 1878 is correct. It is likely that most of the diary entries on page 108 of *My Brother and I* should read 1878 rather than 1879.

32. W.R.P. George, *L.G.*, p.87.

33. W.R.P. George, *L.G.*, pp. 104-5.

34. Fifty years later, writing his *War Memoirs*, he joked about the military training he received. David Lloyd George, *War Memoirs* (Boston:1933), I, p. 340.

35. Sunday, 29 June, 1884. W.R.P. George, *L.G.*, p. 105.

36. Taylor, ed., *Stevenson Diary*, p. 77.

37. Masterman, *Masterman*, p. 209, Diary, August, 1911.

38. George, Lord Riddell, *War Diary*, London, 1933, p.350, August 1918.

39. W.R.P. George, *L.G.*, p. 108; W. George, *Brother*, p. 75, et seq.

40. See L. G. to Margaret Lloyd George, 4 December 1907, printed in Kenneth Morgan, *Lloyd George Family Letters, 1885-1936*, Cardiff, 1973, p. 149.

41. D.R. Daniel, 'Memoirs of David Lloyd George,' Vol. II, p. 34, Daniel MS, NLW 2913, TS.

42. W.R.P. George, *L.G.*, p. 106.

43. *Ibid.*, pp. 82-3.

44. W. George, *Brother*, p. 108.

45. Herbert DuParcq, *The Life of David Lloyd George*, London, 1913, I. 33-4.

46. W.R.P. George, *L.G.*, pp. 92-4. 29 of the 33 seats in Wales and Monmouthshire fell to the Liberals.

47. W.R.P. George, *L.G.*, p. 102.

48. W. George, *Brother*, p. 114.

49. The entire letter is printed in DuParcq, *L.G.*, I, 35-6.

50. See William George's remarks late in life to his son, W.R.P. George, *L.G.*, p.97. On the other hand see also William George's testimony on Ellis-Nanney before the Royal Commission on Land in Wales and Monmouthshire. *C. 7439*, 1894, pp. 494-51, 491, 510. See also Brian L. James 'The Great Landowners of Wales of 1873', *National Library of Wales Journal*, XIV (Summer, 1966), 3, 301-20.

51. W.R.P. George, *L.G.*, p. 95.

52. *Ibid,* p. 96.

53. *Ibid.*

54. See for instance: DuParcq, *L.G.*, I, 76.

55. W.R.P. George, *L.G.*, p. 98.

56. *Ibid,* p. 100.

57. *Ibid*, p. 101.

58. *Ibid*, pp. 105-7.

59. DuParcq, *L.G.* I, 45.

60. W.R.P. George, *L.G.*, p. 104. (n).

61. DuParcq, *L.G.*, I, 42.

62. W.R.P. George, *L.G.*, pp. 12-3.

63. See W. George, *Brother*, pp. 82-4; W.R.P. George, *L.G.*, pp. 115-7. On both occasions David received also small presents from Mr. Casson.

64. W.R.P. George, *L.G.*, p. 117; Peter Rowland in *David Lloyd George*, London 1975, p. 37 states that he attempted to take the final examination on 16 and 17 January 1884, just before his 21st birthday, but that he was prevented by the Law Society authorities. This is unlikely. Lloyd George had been able to begin serious study only in late November, but more important, the term of his articles did not expire until January 25.

65. W.R.P. George, *L.G.*, p. 118.

66. W. George, *Brother*, p. 135.

67. W.R.P. George, *L.G.*, p. 120.

68. *Ibid.*

69. William refers to this briefly in W. George, *Brother*, p. 134.

70. W.R.P. George, *L.G.*, pp. 120-1.

71. W. George, *Brother*, p. 135.

72. See his description of the case to Lucy Masterman in, *Masterman*, p. 210.

73. See: Isabel Emmett, *A North Wales Village, A Social Anthropological Study*, London, 1964, p. 69.

74. W.R.P. George, *L.G.*, p. 123; DuParcq, *L.G.*, I. p. 45.

75. W.R.P. George, *L.G.*, p. 134.

76. This point is excellently made in Jane Morgan, 'Denbighshire's Annus Mirabilis: the Borough and County Elections of 1868,' *Welsh History Review*, VII (June, 1974), I, 63-4, 86-7.

77. See obituary of Gee and article in: *Times*, 29 September 1898.

78. Gee Papers, NLW, 8130D/500, 29 January, 1895.

79. Morgan, *Letters*, p. 116, LG to MLG, 29 September, 1898.

80. See W. H. Crowhurst, 'The Established Church in the Village', *Contemporary Review*, XLVII, November 1885, 676-92.

81. For background to the so called Tithe War see: *C.5195*, 'Report of an Inquiry as to Disturbances Concerned with the Levying of the Tithe rent charge in Wales,' 1887; R. E. Prothero, *The Anti Tithe Agitation in Wales*, London, 1889; J.P.D. Dunabin, *Rural Discontent in 19th Century Britain*, London, 1974, pp. 27 et seq., 286-91.

82. *C.5195*, p. 4.

83 *Ibid.*, pp. 82-6.

84. For an excellent newspaper description of a typical Lloyd George impromptu, open-air, anti-tithe meeting, held at a fair in Lleyn in July, 1887 see: DuParcq, *LG*, I, appendix, pp. 201-4.

85. Evans, *Romance of Lloyd George*, p. 44.

86. LG to Thomas Ellis, 19 May 1887, quoted in Kenneth Morgan, *Wales in British Politics, 1868-1922*, Cardiff, 1970, p. 86.

87. *C.5195*, p. 149.

88. Alfred G. Edwards, *Memories*, London, 1927, pp. 130-2; Prothero, *Anti-Tithe*, pp. 4-5. This view is essentially followed by J. P. D. Dunabin, *Discontent*, p. 291.

89. Davies's description of his first meeting with Lloyd George in the back parlor law office at Criccieth is printed in DuParcq, *L.G.*, I, 49-51.

90. DuParcq, *L.G.*, I, 46.

91. *Ibid.*

92. *Ibid.*, p. 48.

93. W.R.P. George, *L.G.*, pp. 129-30.

94. See DuParcq, *L.G.*, I, 76-7 and LGP, H of L A/6/2/1.

95. W.R.P. George, *L.G.*, p. 131; see also Dr. R. D. Evans's recollections of the conversation in Edwards, *L.G.*, II, 135-6 with a slightly different story about the railway station.

96. W.R.P. George, *L.G.*, pp. 130-2.

97. *Ibid.*, p. 133.

98. There are many sketches of Ellis, see particularly, Neville Masterman, *The Forerunner, The Dilemmas of Tom Ellis, 1859-1899*, Llandybie, 1972, pp. 84-5. For the opinion of a contemporary see Frank Harris, *Contemporary Portraits*, Second Series, New York, 1919, p. 263 et seq.

99. Masterman, *Ellis*, p. 84.

100. W.R.P. George, *L.G.*, p. 132.

101. 'Mr. D. Lloyd George, M.P.', *British Monthly*, June, 1904, TS copy in LGP, H of L, A/12/1/69.

102. Ellis Papers, NLW, 678, LG to Ellis, 12 June 1886.

103. Neal Blewett, *The Peers, the Parties, and the People*, London, 1972, pp. 10-11.

104. *Liberal Yearbook*, 1887, p. 143.

105. W.R.P. George, *L.G.*, pp. 152-3. Lloyd George had helped to frame the constitution of the league the previous year. See Lloyd George to Howell Gee, 7 November 1887, *Ibid.*, pp. 163-4.

106. He asked D. R. Daniel on 14 June 1888 to join him in Llandybie where he was trying to form a branch of the land league. Daniel Memoir, NLW p. 16, LG to DR Daniel, 14 June 1888.

107. Morgan, *Letters*, pp. 20-1, Diary, 4 September 1887.

108. Daniel Papers, NLW 2912, Daniel Memoir, II, pp. 6-8.

109. Daniel Memoir, Vol. I. p. 1.

110. LGP, NLW, 20443A, M.S. Diary, 27 June 1887. For the newspaper account of the meeting see DuParcq, *L.G.*, I, p. 204.

111. Daniel Memoir, II, p. 1. Daniel to Ellis, 22 October 1887.

112. *Ibid.*, p. 5.

113. *Ibid.*, p. 19, LG to D. R. Daniel, 10 March [20], 1890.

114. W.R.P. George, *L.G.*, p. 156.

115. Daniel Memoir, II, p. 16, LG to Daniel, 5 July 1888.

116. *Ibid.*, p. 18, LG to Daniel, 17 July 1888.

117. DuParcq, *L.G.*, 82-3; Daniel Memoir, II, p. 18.

118. Quoted in DuParcq, *L.G.*, I, p. 82.

119. *Ibid.*, p. 83.

120. W.R.P. George, *L.G.*, p. 58.

121. *Ibid.*, p. 129.

122. See 'Mr. Lloyd George, Chieftain of Wales', *Review of Reviews* XXX (September, 1904), 371; Masterman, *Masterman*, p. 181.

123. For Lloyd George's comments on his nomination see: W.R.P. George, *L.G.*, p. 158; LGP, NLW, 2044A, LG Diary, 3 January 1889.

124. W.R.P. George, *L.G.*, p. 99.

125. *Ibid.*, p. 106.

126. *Ibid.*, p. 115.

127. *Ibid.*, pp. 106-136.

128. *Ibid.*, p. 136.

129. *Ibid.*, pp. 138-9.

130. *Ibid.*, p. 140. Diary, 25 August 1886.

131. Morgan, *Letters*, p. 16.

132. W.R.P. George, *L.G.*, p. 140.

133. W. George, *Brother*, p. 98. Diary, 1 October 1886.

134. W.R.P. George, *L.G.*, p. 141. Morgan, *Letters*, p. 17.

135. W.R.P. George, *L.G.*, pp. 142-3, undated.

136. LGP, NLW, 20303C/21, LG to MO, postmark 6 January 1887.

137. Morgan *Letters*, pp. 18-19, undated.

138. W.R.P. George, *L.G.*, p. 146. LG Diary, 22 March 1887.

139. *Ibid*, p. 144.

140. Morgan, *Letters*, p. 14, undated. W.R.P. George suggests this letter was sent at the end of January, 1887. W.R.P. George, *L.G.*, pp. 144-5.

141. LGP, NLW, 20403C/37, LG to MO, n.d. [Summer, 1887].

142. W.R.P. George, *L.G.*, p. 148, Diary, 7 September 1887.

143. Morgan, *Letters*, p. 20, Diary, 30 August 1887.

144. LGP, NLW, 20443A, MS diary, 19 September 1887.

145. *Ibid.*, Diary, 5 October 1887.

146. Morgan, *Letters*, p. 21, Diary, 1 November 1887. Richard Lloyd George's recollection that Richard Owen's opinion of his father was changed by his vigorous attack on the magistrates in the Llanfrothen burial case and in the Nantille lake case is clearly in error. Both of these trials occurred after Lloyd George was married. Richard Lloyd George, *My Father, Lloyd George*, London, 1960, p. 37.

147. LGP, NLW, 20403C/39, LG to MO, n.d., postmark 9 November 1887.

148. W. George, *Brother*, p. 99, Diary, 20 January 1888.

149. See the report in the *Carnarvon Herald* quoted in DuParcq, *L.G.*, I, 80; W. George, *Brother*, p. 100, diary, 24 January 1888.

150. W.R.P. George, *L.G.*, p. 159. His father, Thomas Acland, was one of Gladstone's oldest friends.

151. W.R.P. George, *L.G.*, p. 160. On Acland and Ellis see: Masterman, *Ellis*, pp. 115 et seq.

152. *North Wales Observer*, 5 April 1889, in LGP, H of L, A/6/3/3.

153. Lloyd George to Schnadhorst, 27 April 1889 in W.R.P. George, *L.G.*, p. 161.

154. *Carnarvon Herald*, 15 February 1889, in LGP, H of L, A/6/3/2.

155. Evans, *Romance of Lloyd George*, p. 48.

156. *Carnarvon Herald*, 18 October 1889, in LGP, H of L, A/6/3/7.

157. W.R.P. George, *L.G.*, pp. 165-6.

158. DuParcq, *L.G.*, I, p. 89.

159. Masterman, *Ellis*, pp. 135-6.

160. Daniel Memoir, I, p. 29. Daniel describes the frequent assertions, often made by Lloyd George himself, that Mrs. Lloyd George supported his political career, as 'twaddle.'

161. Emyr Price, 'Lloyd George and the By-election in the Carnarvon boroughs,' *Caernarvonshire Historical Society, Transactions*, XXXVI (1975), 140-2.

162. W.R.P. George, *L.G.*, p. 169.

163. Quoted in Masterman, *Forerunner*, p. 139.

164. Evans, *Romance of Lloyd George*, pp. 54-5. Evans recalls that in Nevin where the Free Baptists were mostly Conservative, Lloyd George could not find a person even to escort him to meetings. *Ibid.*, p. 56.

165. *Cardiff Times*, 29 March 1890 in LGP, NLW, 20457D.

166. *Ibid.*

167. See lead articles on the politics of the election, *Liverpool Daily Post*, 12 April 1890, in LGP, NLW, A/6/4/8.

168. See William George's diary comments in W.R.P. George, *L.G.*, p. 169. 7 April 1890.

169. The address is printed in full in DuParcq, *L.G.*, I, 95-6.

170. *Carnarvon Herald*, 28 March 1890 in LGP, H of L, A/6/4/2.

171. DuParcq, *L.G.*, I, 98-9; *Times*, 8 April 1890.

172. *South Wales Daily News*, 3 April 1890, in LGP, NLW, 20457D.

173. *The Times*, 27 March 1890; Morgan, *Letters*, p. 24, 7 April 1890. As it turned out he received a good majority in Caernarvon but lost heavily in Bangor. *British Weekly*, 18 April 1890.

174. Lloyd George, *Father*, pp. 42-5.

175. *Carnarvon Herald*, 11 April 1890 in LGP, H of L, A/6/4/7.

Chapter 2, pp. 77-148

1. D.A. Hamer, *Liberal Politics in the Age of Gladstone and Rosebery*, Oxford, 1972, pp. 30-31.

2. J.H. Lewis Papers, National Library of Wales 10/231, Diary extract, 8 January 1905.

3. W.R.P. George, *The Making of Lloyd George*, London, 1976, p. 172; See also, Neville Masterman, *The Forerunner, The Dilemmas of Tom Ellis*, Llandybie, 1972, p. 141.

4. Masterman, *Ellis*, pp. 139-40.

5. In *Dod's Parliamentary Companion* for 1890-91 he listed himself as a: 'Welsh Nationalist supporting Home Rule, temperance, disestablishment and other items in the programme of the advanced Liberal Party.'

6. Letter by 'Cymro,' 'The Caernarvon By-election', *British Weekly*, 10 April 1890.

7. 'Shall We Send Or Go?' *North Wales Observer and Express*, 2 May 1890. For an extended discussion of the Rhyl meeting see: J. Hugh Edwards, *The Life of David Lloyd George* (London: n.d.) [1913] III, 6-9.

8. 'Welsh Members and Disestablishment', *North Wales Observer and Express*, 25 April 1890.

9. 'The Welsh Gladstonians,' *Times*, 28 May 1890.

10. The incident became famous in the political world. Alfred Thomas reminded Lloyd George of it in a letter fifteen years later. Lloyd George Papers, House of Lords, A/1/7/1, Alfred Thomas to LG, 4 October 1905.

11. George, Lord Riddell, *War Diary*, London, 1933, p. 66, 7 March 1915.

12. By far the fullest account of the Hawarden incident, and of its effects on Lloyd George, appears in Edwards, *LG*, III, 10-16. Edwards knew Lloyd George well, was involved in the Welsh nationalist movement and was elected Liberal Member of Parliament in 1910.

13. Kenneth Morgan, *Lloyd George Family Letters*, Cardiff, 1973, p. 26. See also the remarks on this in William George, *My Brother and I*, London, 1958, p. 156.

14. Brunner to Ellis, 13 February 1891 in: Stephen Koss, *John Brunner, Radical Plutocrat*, Cambridge, England, 1970, p. 171.

15. L.A. Atherley-Jones, *Looking Back, Reminiscences of a Political Career*, London, 1925, p. 87.

16. *The Times* quoted only the remarks of the chairman of the meeting, Henry Campbell-Bannerman, and did not name Lloyd George as part of the program.

17. *North Wales Observer*, 16 May 1890. Herbert DuParcq, *Life of David Lloyd George* (London: 1913), I, 104, and subsequent biographers have assumed this speech was lost. The complete text appears in the *North Wales Observer and Express*.

18. Morgan, *Letters*, p. 26, undated. Rendel was far too upright a man to lavish insincere flattery, but the person who heard the speech and who had reported to Rendel, almost certainly Ellis Griffith, privately had reported the speech a failure. Masterman, *Ellis*, p. 141; see also, Morgan, *Letters*, pp. 25-6.

19. A.J.P. Taylor, ed., *A Diary by Frances Stevenson*, London, 1971, p. 268, Diary, 10 April 1934.

20. For the speech see: *Manchester Guardian*, 5 June 1890.

21. *Cambrian News*, 13 June 1890 in LGP, H of L, A/6/4/14.

22. Morgan, *Letters*, pp. 27-8, LG to MLG, 5 June 1890.

23. Lord Moran, *Churchill*, Boston, 1966, p. 392.

24. Harold Macmillan, *The Past Masters*, New York, 1975, p. 58.

25 J.H. Lewis Papers, NLW, 10/231, diary extract, undated.

26. Beriah Evans, *The Life Romance of Lloyd George*, London, n.d. [1916], pp. 7-9.

27. *Hansard, Parliamentary Debates*, 3rd Series, CCCXLIII (24 April 1890) col. 1284.

28. DuParcq, *LG*, I, 122.

29. *Hansard*, CCCXLV (5 June 1890) cols. 78-100.

30. Edwards, *LG*, III, 23-24.

31. DuParcq, *LG*, I, 108-9.

32. Letter to the *Carnarvon Herald*, 13 June 1890 in LGP, H of L, A/6/4/15. H.J. Ellis-Nanney promptly announced that he would not seek to reimburse himself from his tenantry for the cost of the tithe.

33. *North Wales Observer*, 11 July 1890, in LGP, H of L, A/6/4/19.

34. On the Carlton Gardens meeting see Lloyd George's comment in: Morgan, *Letters*, p. 28 and 'Gladstone and the Welsh Liberals,' *British Weekly*, 20 June 1890.

35. *Hansard*, CCCXLV (13 June 1890) col. 873.

36. DuParcq, *LG*, I, 109.

37. *Hansard*, CCCVLIII (13 August 1890) cols. 904-6.

38. *Ibid.*, col. 910.

39. DuParcq, *LG*, I, 102.

40. *St. Helen's Newspaper and Advertiser*, 4 October 1890, in LGP A/6/4/22.

41. See *Carnarvon Herald*, 14 November 1890.

42. Stephen Koss, *Nonconformity in Modern British Politics*, London, 1975, p. 27.

43. Quoted in DuParcq, *LG*, I, 110.

44. Lloyd George Papers, NLW, 20407C/141, Lloyd George to Margaret Lloyd George, 25 November 1890.

45. Morgan, *Letters*, p. 40; DuParcq, *LG*, I, 117. Evidently these were two different letters of the same date. Twenty years later George Riddell recorded in his diary that Lloyd George 'still seemed to have a weak place' for Parnell and that the then Chancellor of the Exchequer had discovered that Joseph Chamberlain had paid Captain O'Shea £5000 to bring the divorce case. British Library, Add. MS 62970, Riddell Diaries, TS, 10 Feb 1912.

46. T.E. Ellis Papers, National Library of Wales, 682, Lloyd George to Ellis, 27 November 1890.

47. Quoted in Hamer, *Liberal Politics*, p. 31.

48. LGP, NLW, 2047C/119, LG to MLG, 31 July 1890.

49. DuParcq, *LG*, I, 118.

50. On this change see: Masterman, *Ellis*, pp. 146-7.

51. Morgan, *Letters*, p. 40.

52. For Lloyd George's comments on his work see: DuParcq, *LG*, I, 122-3.

53. Gee Papers, National Library of Wales 8310D/498, LG to Gee, 2 February 1891.

54. Ellis Papers, N.L.W., 683, LG to T. Ellis, 11 April 1891.

55. *Ibid.*

56. DuParcq, *LG*, I, 124-5, inaccurately dated; see *Hansard*, CCCLI (18 March 1891), cols 1340-42.

57. Gee Papers, N.L.W. 8310D/498, LG to Gee, 2 February 1891.

58. Letter, 21 June 1891 in DuParcq, *LG*, I, 121.

59. *Hansard*, CCCLIV (23 June 1891) cols. 1301-3, 1315-23.

60. See: Edwards, *LG*, III, 50-1.

61. *North Wales Observer*, 11 January 1889; *Liverpool Mercury*, 4 January 1889, in LGP, NLW, 20457D.

62. *Cambrian News*, 24 June 1891, *LGP*, NLW, 20457D.

63. DuParcq, *LG*, I, 130-2.

64. See: Edwards, *LG*, III, 54-6. According to A.G. Edwards, Bishop of St. Asaph, the Welsh MPs led by Osborne Morgan had successfully resisted a religious census in Wales to be taken as part of a national census of 1891.

65. Masterman, *Ellis*, 163-4.

66. Quoted in Edwards, *LG*, III, 59-60.

67. D.A. Thomas was listed as one of the eleven millionaires who died in Britain in 1918, leaving an estate of well over £1 million. W.D. Rubinstein, 'British Millionaires, 1809-1949,' *Bulletin of the Institute of Historical Research*, XLVII (November, 1974), 215.

68. Ellis Papers, NLW, 685, LG to Ellis, 21 December 1891.

69. *North Wales Observer and Express*, 13 May 1892.

70. Evans, *LG*, pp. 62-3.

71. As soon as the *Genedl* was purchased he began to publish in it long letters that were virtually a regular column of political commentary and by 1892 he was contributing frequently to the 'Welsh Lobby Notes' for the Wales edition of the *Manchester Guardian*. However, his letters home suggest that in this case he was as interested in the money he earned, £57-12-0 in 1893, as in the good press he gave himself.

72. *Hansard*, CCCLVI, (29 July 1891) col. 694.

73. LG Papers, NLW, 20408C/178, LG to MLG, 30 July 1891.

74. *Hansard*, CCCLVI (4 August 1891) col. 1215.

75. *Hansard* Series 4, I (23 February 1892) cols. 1071-6. See also 'The Church in Wales,' *The Times*, 24 February 1892.

76. *Hansard*, IV (28 April 1892) cols. 1593-1601.

77. *Times*, 29 April 1892.

78. *Hansard*, IV (28 April 1892), cols. 1601-08.

79. Morgan, *Letters*, pp. 48-9, LG to MLG, 29 April 1892.

80. *Hansard*, IV (20 May 1892) cols. 1454-5.

81. *Hansard*, V (2 June 1892) col. 518.

82. *The Times*, 17 September 1891.

83. Quoted in Hamer, *Liberal Politics*, p. 32.

84. Quoted in Kenneth Morgan, *Wales in British Politics, 1868-1922*, Cardiff, 1970, p. 117.

85. *Ibid*.

86. LGP, NLW, 20409C/219, LG to MLG, 31 March 1892.

87. Morgan, *Letters*, p. 53, LG to MLG, 30 May 1892.

88. LGP, NLW, 20410C/252, LG to MLG, 2 June 1892. On Lloyd George's patriotism see quotations in: W.R.P. George, *Lloyd George Backbencher*, Llandysul, 1983, p. 85.

89. LGP, NLW 20409C/231, LG to MLG, 3 May 1892.

90. *Ibid*., NLW 20410C/243,4, LG to MLG, 7,9 June 1892.

91. Quoted in Edwards, *LG*, III, 79.

92. See letter to *The Times*, 26 April 1892.

93. See letters on the election in Wales, *British Weekly*, 21, 28 July 1892.

94. *Ibid*., 21 July.

95. LGP, NLW 20410C/260,2, LG to MLG, 20,23 June 1892. On the importance of Evan Jones in 1892 see also: Edwards, *LG*, III, 8, 82.

96. Gee Papers, NLW 8310D/499, LG to Gee, 12 July 1892.

97. LGP, H. of L., A/7/1/27, *Carnarvon Herald*, 24 June 1892.

98. *Carnarvon Herald*, 1 July 1892; Beriah Evans, *LG*, p. 63.

99. 'Nonconformity in the General Election' and 'Welsh Notes' *British Weekly*, 14 July 1892. D.A. Thomas had to write to *The Times* on 21 July 1892 denying that Wales had thrown over Home Rule in the election, as was being charged by the Church party.

100. *British Weekly*, 28 July 1892. See William George's comments on this speech: W.R.P. George, *LG*, p. 97.

101. See Edwards, *LG*, III, p. 93.

102. John Morley, *The Life of William Ewart Gladstone*, New York, 1911, III, 490; Masterman, *Ellis*, pp. 175, 180.

103. Evans, *LG*, p. 68, 75. Evans states that they met at his house in Caernarvon.

104. Masterman, *Ellis*, p. 182.

105. *Morning Leader*, 8 February 1893, in LGP, H of L, A/7/2/4.

106. D.R. Daniel, Memoir, I, 13, NLW. He followed this with a milder letter, expressing similar sentiments, to Sam Evans, W.R.P. George, *LG*, p. 99.

107. LGP, NLW, 20410C/2733,4, LG to MLG, 9, 10 August 1892.

108. Gladstone to Harcourt, 18 July 1892, quoted in Morgan, *Wales*, p. 134.

109. Masterman, *Ellis*, pp. 189-90. Masterman incorrectly states that Gladstone intended to stay with Watkin William Wynn.

110. *Times*, 13 September 1892.

111. *Ibid*.

112 *Times*, 14 September 1892.

113. 'Mr. Gladstone and Welsh Rents,' *Times*, 22 September 1892. Harcourt assumed the same thing. Harcourt to Gladstone, 23 November 1892, quoted in Morgan, *Wales*, p. 125.

114. Catherine Gladstone to 'Dear Friend,' (Ellen Rendel), 13 September 1892 in F.E. Hamer, ed. *The Personal Papers of Lord Rendel*, London, 1931, p. 201.

115. *Ibid.*

116. David Lloyd George, *War Memoirs* (Boston, 1933), I, 5-7.

117. LGP, NLW, 20410C/238, LG to MLG, 29 October, 1892.

118. LGP, NLW, 20410C/283, 20411C/316, LG to MLG, 12 November 1892, 5 January 1893.

119. Koss, *Brunner*, 1970, p. 53.

120. LGP, NLW, 2041C/354, LG to MLG, 16 August 1983.

121. LGP, NLW, 20411C/375,6,7, LG to MLG, 19, 21 September 1983.

122. LGP, NLW, 20462C/2392, T.J. Hughes to LG, 4 October 1893.

123. LGP, NLW, 20411C/497, LG to MLG, 21 December 1893.

124. *Hansard*, IX (23 February 1893), cols 204-87. A quarter century earlier in the months before Irish disestablishment, the number of compensatable Church appointments had risen by nearly 50%.

125. Quoted in DuParcq, *LG*, I, 156.

126. *Ibid.*, 157.

127. Morgan, *Letters*, p. 60.

128. LGP, NLW, 20411C/339, LG to MLG, 12 July 1893.

129. Morgan, *Letters*, pp. 60-1, The complete text of the letters between Gladstone and the Welsh MPs is printed in Alfred G. Edwards, Archbishop of Wales, *Memories*, London, 1927, pp. 155-7.

130. Edwards, *Memories*.

131. LGP, NLW, 20411C/350, LG to MLG, 8 August 1893.

132. Ellis Papers, NLW, 687, LG to Ellis, 2 January 1893; LGP, NLW, 20411C/344, LG to MLG, 24 July 1893.

133. *British Weekly*, 24 August 1893.

134. Thomas's position in this first attempt at revolt and in others in the next two years is full of ambiguity. In an interview given to the *British Weekly* only a few days before, but after the South Wales Liberal Federation resolution, he had called upon all Welshmen to support Home Rule. *British Weekly*, 24 August 1893.

135. These votes are listed in Morgan, *Wales*, p. 140. The *British Weekly*, however, reported on 7 September 1893 that Lloyd George's motion was supported by 17 votes, in effect a majority of all Welsh MPs.

136. LGP, NLW, 20411C/362, LG to MLG, 1 September 1893.

137. See: Morgan, *Wales*, 139-41.

138. *Ibid*, 141. More pointed see Llewelyn Williams, 'Political Life,' in Margaret, Viscountess Rhondda, ed., *D.A. Thomas, Viscount Rhondda*, London, 1921, p. 64. This is an important but unreliable source. Williams was at this time a young journalist and a devoted follower of Lloyd George. He would be closely involved in the Cymru Fydd movement. But by the time he wrote his essay for the Rhondda biography he hated the man who was then Prime Minister.

139. *British Weekly,* 15 February 1894.

140. LGP, NLW, 20412C/392-6, LG to MLG 1,2,3,4,5 January, '1893' 1894.

141. Rendel to Humphreys-Owen, 4 March 1894. Quoted in Morgan, *Wales,* p. 142.

142. For a more favorable view of Gladstone's attachment to Wales see: Kenneth Morgan, 'Liberal Nationalists and Mr. Gladstone,' *The Transactions of the Honourable Society of Cymmrodorion, 1960,* pp. 36-52.

143. Ellis Papers, NLW, 686, LG to Ellis, 11 August 1892.

144. LGP, NLW, 20462C/2360, Rosebery to LG, 7 March 1894.

145. *North Wales Observer,* 23 March 1894, *Times,* 17 March 1894, in LGP, H of L, A/7/3/7.

146. On anti-Parnellite poverty see: F.S.L. Lyons, *John Dillon,* London, 1968, pp. 162-3.

147. *Hansard,* XXXII, (12 March 1894) col. 32.

148. *Ibid.* (13 March 1894) col. 208; *Times,* 14 March 1894.

149. John Viscount Morley, *Recollections* (New York: 1917), II, p. 11.

150. *British Weekly,* 12 April 1894.

151. *Times,* 13 April 1894.

152. Williams, 'Political Life' in *Rhondda,* ed., *Thomas,* p. 66; Masterman, *Ellis,* p. 205.

153. *North Wales Observer,* 20 April 1894 in LGP, H of L, A/7/3/8; *British Weekly,* 19 April 1894; Edwards, *LG,* III, 98.

154. Harold Spender, *The Prime Minister,* London, 1920, p. 104.

155. *British Weekly,* 19 April 1894.

156. Masterman, *Ellis,* p. 206.

157. Peter Rowland, *David Lloyd George: A Biography,* New York, 1976, p. 105.

158. Edwards, *LG,* III, p. 106.

159. *Ibid.*

160. LGP, NLW, 20412C/422, 3, LG to MLG, 27, 30 April 1894.

161. *Hansard,* XXIII (30 April 1894) cols. 1690-1702. His chief source for statistics, an excellent one in a field with little solid data, was Thomas Darlington, 'Church and Nonconformity in Wales,' *Contemporary Review,* LXV (May, 1894) 649-61.

162. Morgan, *Letters,* p. 70.

163. T.E. Ellis Papers, NLW, 1411, J.H. Lewis to Ellis, 'Sunday evening' 6 May.

164. *New York Herald,* 21 January 1880.

165. For a long discussion see: Edwards, *LG,* III, 106-122.

166. Quoted in: DuParcq, *LG,* I, 164.

167. *Ibid.*

168. Morgan, *Letters,* pp. 71-2; *British Weekly,* 24 May 1894.

169. Morgan, *Letters,* pp. 72-3.

170. Masterman, *Ellis,* pp. 68-9.

171. *Times,* 24 May 1894.

172. 'Political Notes,' *Times,* 25 May 1894.

173. Morgan, *Letters,* pp. 72-3, LG to MLG, 23, 25 May 1894; *Times,* 23 May 1894.

174. 'Political Notes,' *Times*, 26 May 1894; *Carnarvon Herald*, 1 June 1894 in LGP, H of L, A/7/3/18.

175. LGP, NLW, 20413C/444, LG to MLG, 29 May 1894.

176. *Caervarnon Herald*, 1 June 1894 in LGP, H of L A/7/3/19.

177. LGP, NLW, 20413C/445, LG to MLG, 30 May 1894.

178. Morgan, *Wales*, p. 145.

179. *Times*, 15 November 1934.

180. Morgan, *Letters*, pp. 74-5.

181. Ellis Papers, NLW, 1410, J. H. Lewis to Ellis, 1 June 1894.

182. Quoted in Masterman, *Ellis*, p. 205.

183. See Masterman, *Ellis*, pp. 204-5; Morgan, *Letters*, p. 68, LG to MLG, n.d. 6 April 1894.

184. LGP, NLW, 2046C/ 2366, W.T. Stead to LG, 1 June 1894; *Review of Reviews*, IX (May, 1894), 451.

185. Morgan, *Wales*, p. 161.

186. J.H. Lewis Papers, NLW, 3/10, LG to Lewis, 22 June 1894.

187. Morgan, *Wales*, p. 105.

188. Masterman, *Ellis*, pp. 103-5. Although its hero was Tom Ellis, he appears to have had no connection with the journal.

189. For the constitution see: LGP, NLW, 20455E/2170.

190. Williams, 'Political Life,' in Rhondda, ed., D.A. Thomas, p. 72.

191. Evans, *Romance of Lloyd George*, pp. 68-73.

192. J.H. Lewis Papers, NLW, 10/2305, unsorted, LG to Lewis, 31 October 1894.

193. LGP, NLW, 20413C/476, LG to MLG, 5 October 1894.

194. *Western Mail*, 29 September 1894 in LGP, H of L, A/7/3/28.

195. LGP, NLW, 20462C/2325, Lewis Harcourt to LG, 29 September 1894.

196. *Carnarvon Herald*, 12 October 1894; *North Wales Observer*, 19 October 1894. In LGP, H of L, A/7/3/33, 36. See also Morgan, *Wales*, p. 149. Edwards, *Memories*, p. 162.

197. 'Editorial Note' *Young Wales A National Magazine for Wales*, I (January, 1895) 74.

198. *Ibid.*, p. 17.

199. Morgan, *Wales*, p. 162.

200. *Western Mail*, 4 January 1895. As the paper cared neither for Thomas nor Lloyd George it provides, perhaps, a better source for the struggle between the two than the *South* or *North Wales Observer*.

201. Williams, in, Rhondda, ed., *Thomas*, p. 72.

202. *British Weekly*, 10 January 1895.

203. J.H. Lewis Papers, NLW, 10/230 unsorted, Lewis to Rosebery.

204. Llewelyn Williams Diary, MSS, in the possession of Neville Masterman.

205. *Times*, 19 January 1895. He did however, while in Cardiff, take the opportunity to praise the 'Young Wales Movement' to the students at University College, Cardiff.

206. A week later, in the Cabinet on 25 January, Rosebery and Harcourt, agreeing for once, refused Morley's demand that Irish Home Rule again be given

precedence over Welsh disestablishment in the Queen's Speech. T.W. Heyck, *The Dimensions of British Radicalism: The Case of Ireland, 1874-95*, Urbana, 1978, p. 228.

207. Even some of the new Liberal peers created by Gladstone on the eve of Home Rule, who had supported the Irish measure from personal loyalty to the G.O.M., were opposing the new 'collectivist tyranny' of the House of Commons manifested by the disestablishment, and particularly the disendowment, of the Welsh Church. Lord Stanmore to Gladstone, 10 May 1894, 5 July 1895. Paul Knaplund, ed., *Gladstone—Gordon Correspondence, 1851-96*, Philadelphia, 1961, pp. 109, 111.

208. Edwards, *Memories*, p. 175.

209. The *British Weekly* was outraged at Rosebery's predictions that the House of Lords would veto disestablishment. *British Weekly*, 24 January 1895.

210. *Hansard*, XXXI (21 March 1895) col. 1574. Endowments made since 1703 produced only £13,000. Edwards, *Memories*, p. 160.

211. Masterman, *Ellis*, pp. 214-5; Williams, 'Political Life,' Rhondda, ed., *Thomas*, pp. 66-7; Morgan, *Wales*, p. 149.

212. Edwards, *Memories*, pp. 169-70.

213. On the Bangor scheme see: *Church Times*, 25 January 1895; Morgan, *Wales*, p. 148; Masterman, *Ellis*, p. 210.

214. Edwards, *Memories*, p. 170.

215. *Church Times*, 8 February 1895. Evidently this letter was to be private, but the editor published it in his paper. See: *Church Times*, 22 February 1895.

216. See A.G. Edwards to Randall Davidson, 21 February 1906. In G.K.A. Bell, *Randall Davidson, Archbishop of Canterbury*, London, 1938, p. 504.

217. *Church Times*, 15, 22 February 1895.

218. *Hansard*, XXXII (26 March 1895), col 247-59.

219. Llewelyn Williams Diary, 26 March 1895.

220. A.G. Edwards, *Handbook of Welsh Church Defence*, London, 1895, p. 43.

221. *Manchester Guardian*, 6 April 1895.

222. *Ibid.*

223. 'Welsh Notes,' *Manchester Guardian*, 9 April 1895. In a letter to Maggie a few days later, Lloyd George mentioned having written this column.

224. 'Welsh Notes' *Manchester Guardian*, 17 April 1895. The author of this column is unknown.

225. LGP, NLW, 20414C/542, LG to MLG, 8 April 1895.

226. *South Wales Daily News*, 10 April 1895.

227. *Ibid*, 11, 13 April 1895.

228. *Ibid.*, 17 April 1895.

229. Llewelyn Williams Diary, 17 April 1875.

230. *Western Mail*, 18 April 1895.

231. *Western Mail*, 19 April 1895.

232. *Western Mail, South Wales Daily News*, 19 April 1895.

233. *Manchester Guardian*, 2 April 1895.

234. 'Note on the National Convention,' *Young Wales*, May, 1895, 120-2.

235. *Ibid.*, p. 117.

236. 'Welsh Notes,' *Manchester Guardian*, 23 April 1895.

237. For the Bala speech see Masterman, *Ellis*, pp. 135-7.

238. LGP, NLW, 20414C/584, LG to MLG, 20 April 1895.

239. Morgan, *Letters*, pp. 84-5.

240. *South Wales Daily Post*, 24 June 1895.

241. *Carnarvon Herald*, 28 June, 5 July 1895.

242. *Hansard*, XXXIII (20 May 1895) cols 1632-4.

243. Morgan, *Wales*, pp. 152-3.

244. Morgan, *Wales*, p. 153. Nineteen Welsh MPs supported the government.

245. *South Wales Daily News*, 6 June 1895 in LGP, H of L, A/8/1/15.

246. H.H. Asquith, *Fifty Years of Parliament* (London: 1926), I, 230. On the same day, 20 June, Lloyd George reported to William that Asquith had accepted his amendment. W.R.P. George *LG*, p. 174. See *Church Times*, 14 June 1895 quoting Henry Labouchere in *Truth*. See also: *Times*, 22 May 1895.

247. *British Weekly*, 27 June 1895.

248. This account is based upon the version of events given in the *Liverpool Mercury*, 6 November 1895 in LGP, H of L, A/8/1/46, 'Political Bickering.' See also: Morgan, *Wales*. p. 157.

249. *Hansard*, XXXIV (18 June 1895) col 1396.

250. *Ibid.*, col 1405.

251. *Times*, 19 June 1895.

252. *Hansard*, XXXIV (20 June 1895) cols. 1598-1615; *Church Times*, 28 June 1895.

253. Asquith to Ellis, 20 November 1895, quoted in Morgan, *Wales*, pp. 157-8.

254. See: A.G. Gardiner, *The Life of Sir William Harcourt*, London, 1923, II, 362; J.L. Garvin, *The Life of Joseph Chamberlain*, London, 1933, II, 603-4.

255. Peter Stansky, *Ambitions and Strategies, The Struggle for Liberal Leadership in the 1890s*, Oxford, 1964, pp. 164-7. Henry Lucy's often quoted remark that a faction of Welsh Members were determined to wreck the government simply contradicts the radical strategy. Henry W. Lucy, *Memories of Eight Parliaments*, New York, 1908, pp. 146-7.

256. Robert Rhodes James, *Rosebery*, New York, 1963, p. 378.

257. Masterman, *Ellis*, pp. 216-7.

258. Lord Crewe, *Lord Rosebery*, London, 1931, II, 391.

259. Evidently to pin this down he had told the *Carnarvon Herald* the previous autumn that he would not regret leaving the House of Commons. Cited in DuParcq, *LG*, I, 168.

260. Bryn Roberts Papers, NLW, 318, J. Bryn Roberts to W. Huw Roland 13 July 1895.

261. Eighteen months earlier, before the Royal Commission on Welsh Land, William George and David Jones of Llangybi had taken care to blacken the character of Ellis-Nanney as one of the cruellest of the landlords during the eviction of 1868-69. *C: 7439*, 'Minutes of evidence taken before the Royal Commission on Land in Wales and Monmouthshire,' 1894, pp. 494, 503, 512.

262. 'A bluenose Meth,' was Lloyd George's estimate of Jones, 'but a good fellow in spite of that.' LGP, NLW, 20415C/594, LG to MLG, 8 November 1895.

263. See Morgan, *Letters,* p. 86. William George to LG, 13 July, LG to MLG, 5, 12 July. See also LGP, NLW, 20462C/2357, Robert Roberts to LG, 6 July 1895; W. Jones to Robert Roberts, 5 July 1895. Roberts was Lloyd George's agent.

264. LGP, NLW, 20414C/561, LG to MLG, 14 July 1895. Bryn Roberts was making similar statements about Lloyd George's chances.

265. *Ibid.,* /562, LG to MLG, 16 July 1895.

266. Edwards, *LG,* III, 124.

267. *Ibid.,* p. 123.

268. LGP, H of L, A/8/1/26, *North Wales Observer,* 12 July 1895.

269. Morgan, *Letters,* pp. 87-8, LG to MLG, 24 July 1895. He nevertheless did go to speak for Morgan.

270. LGP, H of L, A/8/1/38, *North Wales Observer,* 16 August 1895; 'National Self-Government for Wales,' *Young Wales,* pp. 231-34 in LGP, NLW, 20455E/2171.

271. Edwards, *LG,* III, 131-2.

272. *British Weekly,* 31 October, 7 November 1895.

273. *Baner ac Amserau Cymru,* 30 July 1895 reprinted in *Carnarvon Herald,* 2 August 1895, LGP, H. of L., A/8/1/35.

274. Morgan, *Letters,* p. 88, LG to MLG, 27 August 1895.

275. A.T. Davies, *The Lloyd George I Knew,* London, 1948, pp. 30-1. This book is less interesting than it ought to be and is full of inaccuracies, Lloyd George at the Board of Trade in 1902 for example. On the narrow escape see: A.J. Sylvester, *The Real Lloyd George,* London, 1947, p. 184.

276. These men have been frequently confused. See for example, John Grigg, *The Young Lloyd George,* London, 1973, p. 224. W.R.P. George, *LG,* p. 183.

277. LGP, NLW, 20415C/590, LG to MLG, 2 September 1895.

278. *Ibid.*

279. See: Morgan, *Wales,* p. 156. The first article in a series appeared on 25 September.

280. Gee Papers, NLW, 8310D/501, LG to Thomas Gee, 9 October 1895.

281. LGP, NLW, 20462C/2315, B.G. Evans to LG, 15 November 1893.

282. See: W.R.P. George, *LG,* p. 75, W. George to Evans, 12 February 1894 and LGP, NLW, 20461C/2275, W. George to LG, 18 February 1894.

283. J.H. Lewis Papers, NLW 10/230, LG to Lewis, 11 December 1895.

284. *Ibid,* 3/19, LG to Lewis, 31 December 1895.

285. Ellis Papers, NLW, 690, LG to Ellis, 4 November 1895.

286. LGP, NLW, 20415C/294, LG to MLG, 8 November 1895.

287. 'The Attack on Mr. Lloyd George, "Y Goleuad" Vanquished,' *North Wales Observer,* 15 November 1895, in LGP, H of L, A/8/1/48. The letter itself is in the Lloyd George Papers, NLW, 20415C/592.

288. LGP, NLW, 20415C/601, LG to MLG, 16 November 1895.

289. *Manchester Guardian,* 12 November 1895.

290. John Bryn Roberts Papers, NLW, 325, E.W. Evans to Roberts, 9 November 1895. See also: Roberts to Sir Henry Fowler, 5 October 1895, *Ibid.,* NLW, 332; R.H. Morgan to Roberts, 5 October 1895, NLW, 323.

291. For a discussion see: Morgan, *Wales,* pp. 157-8.

292. Speech at Newbridge, 2 November 1898, in *South Wales Daily News*, 3 November 1898 in LGP, H of L, A/8/4/28.

293. Morgan, *Letters,* p. 91.

294. Interview with the *Merthyr Times* at Treharris, 23 November 1895 in LGP, H of L, A/8/1/50.

295. Morgan, *Letters,* pp. 91-2.

296. Morgan, *Letters,* p. 91.

297. Lewis Papers, NLW, 10/230, LG to Lewis, 5 December 1895. See also LG to MLG, 12 November, 17 December 1895 in Morgan, *Letters,* pp. 90-93.

298. LG to MLG, 20, 21 November 1895, 15 January 1896, Morgan, *Letters,* pp. 91-2, 94.

299. Lewis Papers, NLW, 10/230, unsorted, LG to Lewis, 4 January 1896.

300. LGP, NLW, 20416C/632, LG to MLG, 11 January 1896.

301. *Ibid.,* 20416C/633, LG to MLG, 12 January 1896.

302. *Ibid.,* 20416C/634,635,636, LG to MLG, 13, 14, 15 January 1896.

303. *Young Wales,* II (January 1896), 24.

304. J.H. Lewis Papers, NLW, 3/19, LG to Lewis, 16 January 1896.

305. See letter: LG to MLG, 16 January 1896, Morgan, *Letters,* p. 94 and Llewelyn Williams' report in *Young Wales* II (January 1896) 24.

306. Llewelyn Williams, 'Through Welsh Spectacles,' *Young Wales,* II (January 1896), 31; LGP, NLW, 20416C/638, 639, LG to MLG, 18, 19 January 1896.

307. John Jones, 'Mr. D. Lloyd-George, MP. As the apostle of Welsh Nationalism,' *Young Wales,* II (August 1896), 196.

308. Spender, *Prime Minister,* p. 113.

Chapter 3, pp. 149-214

1. Lloyd George Papers, National Library of Wales, 20418C/800, LG to MLG, 28? May 1897.

2. Alfred T. Davies, *The Lloyd George I Knew,* London, 1948, pp. 27-8. Much of Lloyd George's nervousness about money may have come from Maggie who was notoriously tight-fisted. A result may have been her rather austere household. Frances Stevenson, not to be sure a friend, reports a saying in 1915 that 'she would rather go without food than pay for it.' A.J.P. Taylor, ed., *A Diary By Frances Stevenson,* London, 1971, p. 40, 4 April 1915.

3. *Carnarvon Herald,* 4 January 1898; *North Wales Observer,* 20 May 1898.

4. J. Hugh Edwards reports that Lloyd George told him, evidently in 1896 or 1897, that Harcourt had said Lloyd George would surely receive an appointment when the Liberals returned to power. Lloyd George, Edwards continued. said he was much cheered by this as 'his spirit had been bruised by the bickerings…of his own countrymen…and his motives…impuned.' Edwards says also that he heard through W.T. Howells, Unionist MP for Denbigh district, that Balfour had made virtually the same prediction early in 1897. J. Hugh Edwards, *The Life of David Lloyd George,* London, n.d. [1913], III, 146-7, 180. Certainly the radical press was saying the same. Three or four years earlier no one would have suggested such a thing.

5. Neville Masterman, *The Forerunner: The Dilemmas of Tom Ellis 1859-1899,* Llandybie, 1972, p. 242.

6. Masterman, *Ellis,* pp. 242-3. See also: Kenneth Morgan, *Lloyd George Family Letters,* Cardiff, 1973, p. 99, LG to MLG, 14 February 1896.

7. *Hansard,* XL (30 April 1896) cols 237-42.

8. *Ibid.,* cols 237-42; 14 May 1896, cols. 1344-50; *South Wales Daily News,* 30 November 1896, 11 January 1897 in Lloyd George Papers, House of Lords, A/8/2/21, A/8/3/5.

9. *Hansard,* XL (14 May 1896) cols 1344-50; Morgan, *Letters,* p. 102, LG to MLG, 14 May 1896.

10. *Ibid.,* col 1349-53.

11. *Hansard,* XLI (21 May 1896) cols 150-54.

12. LGP, H of L, A/8/2/14, *North Wales Observer,* 29 May 1896; LGP, NLW, 20417C/699, LG to MLG, 2 June 1896.

13. Dennis Gwynn, *The Life of John Redmond,* London, 1932, p. 89.

14. *Hansard,* XL (12 May 1896) cols 1220-24.

15. He had made such a statement in Manchester early in January but it had gone unnoticed. *Church Times,* 10 January 1896.

16. *Times,* 16,18,21 May 1896; *Church Times,* 29 May 1896.

17. The *British Weekly* 14 May 1896 however placed much of the blame for the death of Home Rule on the Archbishop of Westminster, Herbert, Cardinal Vaughan. *British Weekly,* 21 May 1896.

18. See his remarks on Dillon to George Riddell, *More Pages From My Diary,* London, 1934, p. 187, 16 November 1913.

19. *Times,* 23 May 1896.

20. *Hansard,* XLVIII (16 March 1897) cols 784-6.

21. *Hansard,* LIII (17 February 1898) cols 975-6. It should be noted that Lloyd George's speech was denounced by the Solicitor General for Ireland and the Member, since 1892, for Dublin University, Edward Carson as well as by Morley and R.B. Haldane.

22. *Hansard,* LVI (19 April 1898) cols 479-488.

23. *Hansard,* LXII (18 July 1898) cols 141-48.

24. *British Weekly,* 21 July 1898.

25. Morgan, *Letters,* p. 114, 17 August 1898.

26. J.H. Lewis Papers, National Library of Wales, 10/231, Diary, 3 October 1898.

27. *Hansard,* LIII (11 February, 1898) cols 371-82.

28. *Ibid.,* cols 377-9.

29. See: *British Weekly,* 17 February 1898.

30. *South Wales Daily News,* 3 November 1898, in LGP, H of L, A/8/4/28.)

31. Quoted in Herbert DuParcq, *The Life of David Lloyd George,* London, 1913, I, 171n.

32. Quoted in Edwards, *LG,* III, 145.

33. Quoted in DuParcq, *LG,* I, 178.

34. LGP, NLW, 20417C/726, LG to MLG, 26 July 1896.

35. LGP, NLW, 20417C/737-747, LG to MLG, 22 August—29 September 1896.

36. Stephen Koss, *The Rise and Fall of the Political Press in Britain,* Chapel Hill, 1981, p. 334 and private communications. See also *Times,* 17 June 1935.

37. Max, Lord Beaverbrook, *Politicians and the War,* London, 1960, p. 423.

38. *Hansard,* XXXII (29 March 1895) cols 531-9.

39. William George, *My Brother and I,* London, 1958, p. 195.

40. J.H. Lewis Papers, NLW, 3/19, LG to JHL, 27 October 1896, Criccieth. Lloyd George's letter and Dr. Edwards's conciliatory but guarded reply appear in W.R.P. George, *Lloyd George, Backbencher,* Llandysul, 1983, pp. 213-4.

41. *Ibid.,* LG to JHL, 'Sunday' 31 October 1896, Criccieth.

42. *Times,* 19 November 1897.

43. LGP, NLW, 20462C/2392, LG to W. Bowen Rowlands, 12 November 1896.

44. Morgan, *Letters,* p. 107, LG to MLG, 1 December 1896.

45. Gee Papers, National Library of Wales, 8306D/86, LG to Thomas Gee, 18 December 1896.

46. LGP, NLW, 20462C/2391, LG to Marton Woosnam, 28 December 1896.

47. *South Wales Daily News,* 6 February 1896; *Carnarvon Herald,* 7 February 1896 in LGP, H of L, A/8/2/6,7.

48. LGP, NLW, 20416C/647, LG to MLG, 30 January 1896. Letter quoted in Du Parcq, *LG,* I, 172.

49. LGP, NLW, 20416C/648, LG to MLG, 6 February 1896.

50. W.R.P. George *LG,* p. 212.

51. *Times,* 20 June 1897.

52. W. George, *Brother,* p. 197, 'undated postscript' evidently 19 June 1897.

53. LGP, NLW, 20461C/2277, W. George to LG, 27 July 1897.

54. W. George, *Brother,* p. 197-198.nd [late July].

55. *Times,* 19 November 1897. Inexplicably Lloyd George's son states that his father took the stand and cleared himself by showing that he was in the House of Commons on 4 February. Richard Lloyd George, *My Father, Lloyd George,* New York, 1961, p. 63.

56. LGP, NLW, 20461C/2282, W. George to LG, 21 October 1897.

57. W.R.P. George, *LG,* p. 224.

58. See Lloyd George letter to William George, undated, 'Saturday' correcting the *Carnarvon Herald* story of the trial and see William George's letter to the newspaper. W. George, *Brother,* pp. 199-200.

59. See Lloyd George letter in the *Times,* 29 November 1897, thanking the Carnarvon Borough's Liberal Association for its resolution of support. Also printed in the *Carnarvon Herald,* 3 December 1897 in LGP, H of L, A/8/3/30. There were many newspaper statements of congratulation.

60. Roy Jenkins, *Sir Charles Dilke,* London, 1958, pp. 215-370. For the best discussion of the legal aspects of the case see: Edward Marjoribanks, *For the Defense: The Life of Sir Edward Marshall Hall,* London, 1929, pp. 51-4. It should be noted that the Queen's Proctor in the Dilke action had briefed Sir Walter Phillmore, whose junior in the case was Bargrave Deane. For details of this action see: *Times,* 17 June, 20 June 1899.

61. Morgan, *Letters,* pp. 111-2, LG to MLG, 19, 21 August 1897.

62. The Marquis of Reading, *Rufus Isaacs,* London, 1942, I, 178.

63. Edwards, *LG,* III, 126-33; Morgan, *Letters,* pp. 99, 101, LG to MLG, 18 February, 3 March 1896.

64. Morgan, *Letters*, p. 99, LG to MLG, 18 February 1896. The 'Radical Committee,' whose leading members were Charles Dilke and Henry Labouchere, was a slightly amorphous body of backbench Liberals. Attendance at meetings varied widely. Fifty MPs, among 177 Liberals in the House of Commons, was large.

65. *Times*, 'Political Notes', 24, 25 March 1896.

66. Morgan, *Letters*, p. 102, LG to MLG, 24 March 1896. Ironically Spicer had been chairman of the 16 January meeting at Newport.

67. *Times*, 29 May, 1896; 'The Place of National Self-government in the Next Liberal Programme,' *Young Wales*, III (January, 1897), 11-15.

68. LGP, NLW, 20416C/673, LG to MLG, 6 March 1896.

69. LG to William George, 27 February 1896 in Du Parcq, *LG*, I, 152.

70. *Times*, 20 May 1896.

71. Morgan, *Letters*, pp. 100, 101, LG to MLG, 6 March 1896; LG to William George, 21 March 1896 in Du Parcq, *LG*, I, 152. Redmond was impossible; in any case he controlled only twelve votes.

72. *Times*, 29 May 1896.

73. See Du Parcq, *LG*, I, 175-6.

74. See: D.A. Hamer, *Liberal Politics in the Age of Gladstone*, Oxford, 1972 p. 231-2, 249. See also on Rosebery, *Times*, lead article, 25 March 1896.

75. Gee Papers, NLW, 8306D/86, LG to Gee, 18 December 1896.

76. LGP, NLW, 20416C/679, LG to MLG, 19 March 1896.

77. *Rhyl Record and Advertiser*, 9 January 1897 in LGP, H of L, A/8/3/4; Morgan, *Letters*, p. 108, LG to MLG, 5 January 1897.

78. *Carnarvon Herald*, 2 April 1897 in LGP, H of L, A/8/3/4.

79. *North Wales Observer*, 24 September 1897 in LGP, H of L, A/8/3/18.

80. *Times*, 26 May 1897.

81. On Thomas's resignation see: Morgan, *Letters*, pp. 109-10, LG to MLG, 11, 12, 25, 27 May 1897.

82. Gee Papers, NLW, 8310D/502, LG to Gee, 20 October 1897.

83. *South/Wales Daily News*, 4 December 1897 in LGP, H of L, A/8/3/31.

84. *Times*, 5 February 1898; *British Weekly*, 10 February 1898.

85. *South Wales Daily News*, 1 August 1899 in LGP, H of L, A/9/1/19.

86. *Liberal Yearbook*, 1905 et seq.

87. *Times*, 16 February 1898; see also Morgan, *Wales*, p. 167.

88. J.H. Lewis Papers, NLW, 10/231, Diary 14 February 1898. Lewis's 'Diary' is made up of extracts of conversations with Lloyd George recorded on any scrap of paper available and subsequently transcribed by typewriter. Probably he intended to write a biography of his friend.

89. Kenneth Morgan, *Wales in British Politics*, Cardiff, 1970, pp. 167-70, 205-8.

90. *Times*, 19 May, 1899; DuParcq, *LG*, I, 189-90; Morgan, *Wales*, p. 178.

91. On the origins of the dispute see: David Williams, *A History of Modern Wales*, London, 1950, p. 243.

92. *Hansard*, XLV (28 January 1897) cols 691-762.

93. See: Morgan, *Letters*, pp. 108-9, LG to MLG, 19, 25, 26, 29 January 1897.

94. 'You will like him,' he told Maggie, 'I should like Burns to be received as well as we can possibly afford...' But there was no need for her to bring in wine. Burns was a teetotaler. LGP, NLW, 20418C/778, 781, LG to MLG, 27 April, 30 April 1897.

95. *North Wales Observer,* 7 May 1897, in LGP, H of L, A/8/3/12.

96. Masterman, *Ellis,* pp. 237-8.

97. Gee Papers, NLW, 8306D/87, LG to Gee, 16 December 1897.

98. Morgan, *Letters,* p. 116, LG to MLG, 29 September 1898.

99. Joseph Chamberlain Papers, University of Birmingham, JC11/6, Chamberlain to Salisbury, 3 January 1899; JC5/5/81, Chamberlain to Balfour, 2 February 1899; C.A. Whitemore 'Is the Unionist Party Committed to Old-Age Pensions?' *National Review,* XXXIII, July 1899, 713.

100. *Hansard,* LXIX (22 March 1899) cols 68,81.

101. Morgan, *Letters,* pp. 117, 118, LG to MLG, 21, 26 July 1899.

102. For a recent example see: Chris Wrigley, *David Lloyd George and the British Labour Movement,* Hassocks, 1976, pp. 33-6.

103. 'Report from the Select Committee on the Aged, Deserving, Poor, Minutes of Evidence,' 1899, *Parliamentary Papers,* 296, Vol. VIII, 1896 Irish University Press Series, Poor Law, Vol. XXX, pp. xxxviii-xlii.

104. *Ibid.,* p. 215, Appendix 21, 'Memorandum by Mr. Lloyd George M.P.'

105. Morgan, *Letters,* p. 118, LG to MLG, 25 July 1899.

106. *Liverpool Mercury,* 17 July 1899, in LGP, H of L, A/9/1/18. The speech is printed in the appendix of DuParcq, *LG,* I, 224-8.

107. On the Welsh reaction to the war see: Morgan, *Wales,* pp. 178-9.

108. See: J.W. Auld, 'The Liberal Pro-Boers,' *Journal of British Studies,* XIV, May 1975, 2 100-1.

109. Frederic Whyte, *The Life of W.T. Stead* (London: 1925), II, 172.

110. See for example, John Grigg, review of Kenneth Morgan, *Lloyd George Family Letters, Listener,* 89 (March 1973), 314.

111. DuParcq, *LG,* II, 214.

112. Keir Hardie, never one to admit that any man's conscience was more tender than his own, was highly critical of Lloyd George's approval of the annexations at the end of the war and of his admiration for certain British generals, Kitchener for one. Kenneth Morgan, *Keir Hardie, Radical and Socialist,* London, 1975, p. 123.

113. LGP, H of L, I/2/2/73, William George to Harold Spender, 18 May 1917.

114. For example: *Times,* 5 January, 7 December 1901.

115. Lucy Masterman, T.S. Diary, undated, apparently 1908. In the possession of Neville Masterman.

116. DuParcq, *LG,* II, 216.

117. *North Wales Observer,* 13 October 1899 in LGP, H of L, A/9/1/20.

118. See: John, Viscount Morley, *Recollections* (New York: 1917), II, 86.

119. LGP, NLW, 20461C/2278, William George to LG, 29 September 1899. Beriah Evans had resigned as editor of the *Genedl* in 1895 but clearly had returned.

120. Morgan, *Letters,* p. 123, LG to MLG, 2 October 1899.

121. Quoted in W. George, *Brother,* p. 177.

122. *Hansard,* LXXVII (27 October 1897) cols. 782-4. See also his letter to Maggie, Morgan, *Letters,* p. 124.

123. J.H. Lewis Papers, NLW, 10/230, unsorted. LG to Lewis, 31 October 1899. In fact the Boers took about 1,000 prisoners who were subsequently paraded through Pretoria.

124. Morgan, *Letters*, p. 125, LG to MLG, 2 November 1899.

125. Cory Hall, Cardiff, 6 November 1899, Nonconformist Political Council, *South Wales Daily News*, 7 November 1899, in LGP, H of L, A/9/1/23.

126. Carmarthen Town Hall, 27 November 1899, *The Welshman*, 1 December 1899 in LGP, H of L, A/9/1/25.

127. Quoted in DuParcq, *LG*, 223.

128. See Bentley B. Gilbert, 'The Grant of Responsible Government to the Transvaal, More Notes on a Myth,' *Historical Journal*, X(1967)4, 457-9.

129. *New Liberal Review*, I (February 1901)1,1.

130. *Times*, 17 November 1900.

131. The last suggestion is prompted by a fascinating aside in E.T. Raymond (Edward Raymond Thompson), *Man of Promise, Lord Rosebery, A Critical Study*, London, 1923, p. 197 in which Raymond hints that Harmsworth was behind Rosebery. At the time this book was published Rosebery was still alive and Thompson was editor of the *Evening Standard*, just acquired by Lord Beaverbrook, and so was in a position to know secrets. Rosebery and Harmsworth were near neighbors in Berkeley Square and often walked together.

132. Riddell, *Diary*, p. 64, May 1912; Taylor, ed., *Stevenson Diary*, p. 300, 29 January 1935.

133. Quoted in DuParcq, *LG*, II, 220-3.

134. *North Wales Observer*, 19 January 1900 in LGP, H of L, A/9/2/4.

135. *Hansard*, LXXVII (6 February 1900) cols. 758-67.

136. *Hansard*, LXXX (19 March 1900) col. 1266.

137. W. George, *Brother*, p. 179 LG to WG, undated.

138. *Ibid.*, 22 March 1900.

139. *Western Mail*, 6, 10 April 1900 in LGP, H of L, A/9/2/11, 12.

140. See his description to his brother, W. George, *Brother*, p. 178, LG to WG, 7 March 1900.

141. *North Wales Observer*, 13 April 1900 in LGP, H of L, A/9/2/13.

142. *North Wales Observer*, ibid. William George's account of the meeting, even though he states he attended it, varies considerably from the newspaper report and does not mention the attack on Lloyd George. The description suggests that William George confused it with the Glasgow meeting on 6 March. William George, *Brother*, pp. 179-80.

143. J.H. Lewis Papers, NLW, 10/230. LG to Lewis, 19 April 1900, 'Criccieth.'

144. *North Wales Observer*, 27 April 1900, in LGP, H of L, A/9/2/15.

145. Edwards, *LG*, II, 210.

146. See: J.A. Spender, *The Life of the Rt. Hon. Sir Henry Campbell-Bannerman*, London, 1923, I, 278-84.

147. LGP, NLW, 204620/2388, John Dillon to 'Mr. Durkin,' 2 October 1900.

148. W. George, *Brother*, p. 182, LG to WG, 27 June 1900.

149. *Western Morning News*, 6 July 1900 in LGP, H of L, A/9/2/16.

150. Quoted in DuParcq, *LG*, II, 232.

151. Spender, *CB*, I, 286.

152. *Hansard*, LXXVII (25 July 1900) cols. 1199-1213.

153. The letter is fully reproduced in: Frederick Maurice, *The Life of Lord Haldane of Cloan*, London, 1937, I, 105-6.

154. *Times*, 27 July 1900.

155. H.G.C. Matthew, *The Liberal Imperialists*, London, 1973, p. 62, Perks to Rosebery, 27 February 1901.

156. Edwards, *LG*, I, 204.

157. See: Clyde Trebilcock, 'A Special Relationship—Government Rearmament and the Cordite Firms' *Economic History Review*, XIX (1966), 364-79.

158. *Times*, 13 August 1900. Letter from Onlooker.

159. Julian Amery, *The Life of Joseph Chamberlain*, London, 1951, IV, 21-22; Diana W. Lang, *Mistress of Herself: Biography of Mary Endicott Chamberlain*, Barre, Mass, 1965, p. 136. J.L. Garvin, *The Life of Joseph Chamberlain* (London: 1934), III, 606, Letter to Jesse Collings, 10 October 1900.

160. Harold Spender, *The Fire of Life, A Book of Memories*, London, n.d. [1926], pp. 60-2.

161. Garvin, *Chamberlain*, III, 616-7; Amery, *Chamberlain*, IV, 20-21; DuParcq, *LG*, II, 300.

162. See for example, G.E. Raine, *The Real Lloyd George*, London, 1913, pp. 52-70, 140-157. This was evidently written as a reply to DuParcq.

163. W.S. Churchill to Rosebery, 4 October 1900 in Randolph S. Churchill, *Winston S. Churchill*, I, Companion Volume 2, 1206.

164. Morgan, *Letters*, pp. 125-6, LG to MLG, 3,7 August 1900; *Carnarvon Herald*, 3, 10 August in LGP, H of L, A/9/2/18, 19.

165. Morgan, *Letters*, p. 126, LG to MLG, 20 August 1900.

166. Morgan, *Letters*, pp. 126-7, LG to MLG 20, 31 August 1900. The only national daily paper not supporting the war was the *Manchester Guardian*.

167. *Ibid.* W.R.P. George reports on the strength of a letter from Sir John Gorst to Lloyd George dated 'January 1900' that Lloyd George had become interested in the *Daily News* a year earlier. Almost certainly this is the result of an incorrect date, Gorst forgetting, as Lloyd George frequently did also, the New Year had passed. W.R.P. George *LG*, pp. 311-2.

168. *North Wales Observer*, 11 January 1889, in LGP, NLW, 20457D.

169. J.H. Lewis Papers, NLW, 3/19, LG to Lewis, 20 September 1900 'Conway.'

170. *Ibid.*, LG to Lewis, 26 September 1900.

171. *North Wales Observer*, 28 September 1900, in LGP, H of L, A/8/2/28.

172. Quoted in W. George, *Brother*, p. 190. As these statistics evidently dealt with the entire five years of the Salisbury parliament through most of which South Africa was hardly important, the exercise was misleading.

173. *Carnarvon Herald*, 21 September 1900, in LGP, H of L, A/9/2/25, 27.

174. Morgan, *Keir Hardie*, p. 23.

175. *North Wales Observer*, 5 October 1900, in LGP, H of L, A/9/2/34.

176. H. Lloyd Carter to Robert Roberts, 3 October 1900, LGP, NLW, 2389.

177. Harold Spender, *The Prime Minister*, London, 1919, 126-7.

178. J.H. Lewis Papers, NLW, 10/230, LG to Lewis, nd [13 April 1894].

179. Auld, 'Pro-Boers', *JBS*, XIV, 2, 100-1.

180. 'Mr. Lloyd George, Chieftain of Wales,' *Review of Reviews*, September 1904, in LGP, H of L, A/12/2/42.

181. Auld, 'Pro-Boers', *JBS*, XIV, 2, 93.

182. J.A. Spender, 'The Patriotic Election—and After,' *Contemporary Review*, LXXVIII (November 1900) 746-60.

183. John Wilson, *A Life of Sir Henry Campbell-Bannerman*, New York, 1973, p. 338.

184. *Ibid.*, 340. Beatrice Webb, *Our Partnership*, London, 1948, 201-3, 7 October, 9 December 1900.

185. *Times*, 11 December 1900.

186. Quoted in Spender, *CB*, I, 316-8.

187. *Times*, 15 February 1901.

188. Quoted in Matthew, *Liberal Imperialists*, p. 61.

189. British Library, Add. MS 45987, Herbert Gladstone Papers, vol III, CB to H. Gladstone, 15 February 1901.

190. Quoted in Spender, *CB*, I, 321-2.

191. *Wolverhampton Express and Star*, 24 April 1901 in LGP, H of L, A/10/1/8.

192. D. Lloyd-George, MP., 'The Stagnation of Business in the House of Commons,' *New Liberal Review*, I (May 1901), 4,458-63.

193. Spender, *Fire of Life*, p. 115.

194. Spender, *CB*, I, 355-6; Wilson, *CB*, 348-9. Emily Hobhouse herself recalled later that he seemed profoundly moved during their talk and murmured the phrase 'methods of barbarism' to himself. Quoted in *Ibid.*, p. 348.

195. *Hansard*, XCV (17 June 1901) cols 541-73.

196. *Liverpool Daily Post*, in LGP, H of L, A/10/1/18.

197. Webb, *Partnership*, p. 217, 9 July 1901.

198. Quoted in Keith Robbins, *Sir Edward Grey*, London, 1971, pp. 90-91. On Lloyd George leadership see also: W.R.P. George, *LG*, pp. 334-5, LG to W. George, 5 July 1901.

199. Webb, *Partnership*, p. 218.

200. Sydney Webb, 'Lord Rosebery's Escape From Houndsditch', *Nineteenth Century*, L (September 1901), 366-86. Campbell-Bannerman came to consider Webb as the 'chief instructor of the Liberal imperialists.' Campbell-Bannerman to Herbert Gladstone, 18 December, quoted in Spender, *CB*, II, 14.

201. *Times*, 20 June 1901.

202. *Review of Reviews*, September 1904.

203. Strachey Papers, House of Lords, S/13/13/2. Harold Spender to St. Loe. Strachey, 'April 1913'.

204. Richard Lloyd George, *Father*, p. 73. However, the children were back in London in April of 1902 at the time of Megan's birth.

205. *Newcastle Daily Leader*, 28 August 1901, in LGP, H of L, A/10/1/23.

206. *Sheffield Independent*, 15 July 1901, in LGP, H of L, A/10/1/20.

207. *Pontypridd Chronicle*, 20 July 1901, in LGP, H of L, A/10/1/21; *Times*, 13 June 1901.

208. *British Weekly,* 6 June 1901.

209. Spender, *Prime Minister,* p. 120.

210. LGP, NLW, 2462C/2292, Cadbury to LG, 18 December, 1900. This letter is one of the few references to the *Daily News* transaction in the Lloyd George Papers.

211. Spender, *Fire of Life,* pp. 108-9.

212. Spender reports that the paper lost £10,000 in the course of its attack on the concentration camps during the autumn of 1901. Spender, *Fire of Life,* p. 113. For a discussion see Stephen Koss, *Fleet Street Radical, A.G. Gardiner and the Daily News,* London, 1973, pp. 40-44.

213. Quoted in Koss, *Fleet Street Radical,* p. 43.

214. LG to Lewis, 2 December 1901, J.H. Lewis Papers, NLW, 3.19.

215. *Carnarvon Herald,* 14 February 1902, in LGP, H of L, A/10/2/8.

216. Morgan, *Letters,* p. 128-9 LG to MLG, 10 March 1902.

217. LG to MLG, 17 April 1902, *Ibid.,* p. 133.

218. *Times,* '1901 Review of the Year,' 31 December 1901.

219. *Times,* 13 June 1901.

220. Quoted in DuParcq, *LG,* II, 310-11.

221. On the visit see: Perks to Asquith, 2 January 1902, Asquith Papers, Bodleian Library, Vol. X, ff 46-8.

222. *Hansard,* CI (20 January 1902) col 397.

223. *Hansard,* CI (21 January 1902) cols 537-43.

224. See for example John Grigg, *Young Lloyd George,* London, 1973, p. 291.

225. See LG to MLG, 5, 11, 17 March 1902 in Morgan, *Letters,* p. 126, 129, 130.

226. H.J. Wilson to LG, 22 January 1902 in LGP, H of L, A/1/12/1.

227. *Times,* 22 January 1902.

228. *Liverpool Daily Post,* 23 January 1902, in LGP, H of L, A/10/2/5; *British Weekly,* 23 January 1902.

229. 'Below the Gangway,' *New Liberal Review,* III, March 1902, 14, 251-7.

230. Campbell-Bannerman to Ripon, 24 January 1902, in Wilson, *CB,* p. 384.

231. Matthew, *Liberal Imperialists,* p. 84 and note.

232. J.H. Lewis Papers, NLW, 10/231, Diary extract, 16 February 1902.

233. *Times,* 15 February 1902.

234. *Times,* 17 February 1902; for a fuller statement see *Daily News,* 17 February 1902 in LGP, H of L, A/10/2/9.

235. *Times,* 21 February 1902.

236. Matthew, *Liberal Imperialists,* pp. 84-86.

237. LG to MLG, 11, 12 March 1902, in Morgan, *Letters,* p. 129.

238. *Hansard,* CV (20 March 1902) cols 591-4, 638-58.

239. *Birmingham Daily Post,* 19 December 1901 in LGP, H of L, A/10/1/12. The bulk of this speech is printed in DuParcq, *LG,* II, 301-3.

240. *Bristol Daily Mercury,* 7 January 1902 in LGP, H of L, A/10/2/1; David Lloyd George, MP, 'Lord Rosebery and Peace' *New Liberal Review,* III (January 1902), 767-74.

241. *Ibid.,* p. 774.

242. Lucy Masterman, T.S. Diary, p. 17.

243. DuParcq, *LG*, II, 262-3.

244. *Birmingham Daily Mail*, 16 December 1910. See the summary of press comment in DuParcq, *LG*, II, 279-83.

245. Lucy Masterman, T.S. Diary, I, p. 16.

246. J.H. Lewis Papers, NLW, 10/231, diary extract 2 January 1902. This account of events given Lewis two weeks later seems to be the earliest Lloyd George version of the story now in existence.

247. DuParcq, *LG*, II, 287-91. DuParcq's story, with times of day and other private details, shows much evidence of having been written by Lloyd George himself.

248. Lloyd George later told Lord Riddell there were no policemen in the hall, which contradicts other accounts and leaves unanswered the question of why he was not killed immediately when the mob attacked the platform. Riddell, *More Pages*, p. 154. *Diary*, 26 May 1913.

249. J.H. Lewis Papers, Diary extract, 2 January 1902.

250. W. George, *Brother*, p. 185.

251. See: *Review of Reviews*, October 1904.

252. Taylor, ed, *Stevenson Diary*, p. 300, entry 29 January 1935.

253. J.H. Lewis Papers, NLW, 10/231, diary extract 20 June 1905.

254. A spurious photograph of Lloyd George in police uniform was hawked around Birmingham after the event. William George took the seller to court winning £50 and an apology. LGP, H of L, I/2/2/1, William George to Lloyd George, 14 February 1902.

255. Amery, *Chamberlain*, IV, 21-2.

256. *Times*, 19 December 1901.

257. *Times*, 21 December 1901.

258. J.H. Lewis Papers, diary extract, 20 January 1902.

259. *Times*, 21 December 1901.

260. 'Outis,' 'Hopes and Fears for the Liberal Party,' *New Liberal Review*, V, (April 1903) 27,307.

261. Morgan, *Keir Hardie*, pp. 132-135.

Chapter 4, pp. 215-284

1. Stephen Koss, *Nonconformity in Modern British Politics*, London, 1975, p. 38.

2. *Hansard*, CV (24 March 1902) col. 855. In Wales the balance was more even. There were 840 voluntary schools, mostly Anglican and Roman Catholic, with about 96,000 students. There were relatively few nonconformist voluntary schools. In addition there were 821 board schools with an attendance of 171,500.

3. George Kekewich, 'The Church and the Education Act,' *Contemporary Review*, LXXXIII (May 1903), 779-86.

4. Quoted in Bernard M. Allen, *Sir Robert Morant*, London, 1934, p. 153.

5. Julian Amery, *The Life of Joseph Chamberlain*, London, 1951, IV, 482.

6. Almeric Fitzroy, *Memoirs*, London, n.d. [1925], I, 72, Diary, 20 January 1902.

7. Elie Halevy, in a rare mistake, suggests that the 'option' applied only to the council assumption of the board schools. Elie Halevy, *Imperialism and the Rise of*

Labour, London, 1961, p. 202. This rather important error has become part of the literature. For example see: John Grigg, *Lloyd George, The People's Champion,* Berkeley, 1978, pp. 23-4.

8. *Hansard,* CV, (24 March 1902) cols. 846-68.

9. *Times,* 25 March 1902. At the time Balfour introduced it, the Education Bill had not been printed.

10. Kenneth Morgan, *Lloyd George Family Letters,* Cardiff, 1973, pp. 131-2, LG to MLG, 24 March 1902.

11. *Hansard,* CV (24 March 1902) cols. 950-53.

12. *British Weekly,* 27 March 1902.

13. *Lincoln Leader,* 13 December 1902 in Lloyd George Papers, House of Lords, A/10/2/41.

14. See his speech to the Welsh Baptist Union at Rhyl on 30 September 1895 in *Carnarvon Herald,* 4 October 1895 in LGP, H of L, A/8/1/41.

15. *Manchester Guardian,* 2 March 1903.

16. For discussion see: *British Weekly,* 3 April 1902.

17. *North Wales Observer,* 23 January 1903 in LGP, H of L, A/11/1/2.

18. For example: Lloyd George Papers, National Library of Wales, 20461/C, W. George to LG, 6 May 1902.

19. This had long been Rendel's fear also. LGP, H of L, A/1/7/1, Rendel to Alfred Thomas, 27 September 1905.

20. Lloyd George to Robertson Nicoll, 19 July, 1902, quoted in Koss, *Nonconformity,* p. 48.

21. See: H.C.G. Matthew, *The Liberal Imperialists,* London, 1973, pp. 94-7.

22. See: J.A. Spender, *The Life of the Right Hon. Sir Henry Campbell- Bannerman,* London, 1924 I, 294.

23. *Hansard,* CVII (8 May 1902) cols. 1110-1111.

24. *British Weekly,* 12 June 1902.

25. Matthew, *Liberal Imperialists,* p. 95 and note.

26. *Carnarvon Herald,* 16 May 1902, in LGP, H of L, A/10/2/23.

27. *Carnarvon Herald,* 30 May 1902, LGP, H of L, A/10/2/26.

28. Freeman Freeman-Thomas to LG, 179 Trinity Road, Wandsworth, 4 December 1902, LGP, H of L, A/1/9/1; LG to MLG, 4 December 1902 in Morgan, *Letters,* p. 138; *North Wales Observer,* 8 December 1902 in LGP, H of L, A/10/2/40.

29. Months earlier *The Times* had remarked that the government would be happy to withdraw the optional feature. *Times,* 2 April 1902.

30. *British Weekly,* 17 July 1902.

31. *Times,* 10 July 1902.

32. *British Weekly,* 24 July 1902.

33. *Lincoln Leader,* 13 December 1902 in LGP, H of L, A/10/2/41.

34. *British Weekly,* 23 October, 6 November, 23 December 1902.

35. *British Weekly,* 23 December 1902.

36. 'Characters in Outline, Lloyd George,' *Speaker,* 8 November 1902.

37. *Hansard,* CXV (3 December 1902) cols. 1173-4. Lloyd George reported this accolade to Maggie in the same letter in which he told her of being summoned to see

Rosebery. LG to MLG, 4 December 1902, Morgan, *Letters*, p. 138. Harold Spender reports that Balfour was the first to recommend to Campbell-Bannerman that Lloyd George should be in the next Liberal Cabinet. Harold Spender, *The Prime Minister*, London, 1920, p. 136. The Welsh delegation had entertained Balfour at a dinner in the Irish Dining Room in Westminster Palace on 28 October.

38. British Library Add MS. 49774, Balfour Papers, Vol. XCII, Chamberlain to Balfour, 4 August 1902.

39. *Hansard*, CXI (22 July 1902) cols. 925-45.

40. *British Weekly*, 24 July 1902.

41. *Manchester Guardian*, 4 September 1902; Morgan, *Letters*, p. 138, LG to MLG, 4 September 1902. In fact the strikers' case was somewhat prejudiced by the fact that about two-thirds of them had already found other work and by the slipshod accounting of their secretary, D.R. Daniel, who despite incomparable journalistic skill was unable to tell what had happened to the money already sent. *Manchester Guardian*, 16 September 1902.

42. In the first two, safe Conservative or Liberal Unionist seats had been lost to the government since the introduction of the bill, and at Sevenoaks on 21 August, a Conservative majority of 4,800 had been reduced to 891.

43. *British Weekly*, 11 September 1902.

44. *British Weekly*, 2 October 1902.

45. *Hansard*, CXVI, (11 November 1902), col. 663.

46. Lloyd George's political mentor Michael Davitt, although no longer in parliament, had recently written urging the Irish to defect. *British Weekly*, 9 October 1902.

47. *Manchester Guardian*, 7 October 1902. In Vaughan's defense, it should be noted that he afterwards regretted the use of the phrase 'triumph over Nonconformist opposition ...' John George Snead-Cox, *The Life of Cardinal Vaughan*, London, 1910, II, 136-8.

48. *Times*, 13 October 1902.

49. *British Weekly*, 13 November 1902.

50. *Hansard*, CXIV (12 November 1902) cols 766-9. On November 11 Balfour had moved a closing resolution to speed up the passage of his bill.

51. *British Weekly*, 27 November, 4 December 1902.

52. Quoted in Kenneth Morgan, *Wales in British Politics*, Cardiff, 1970, p. 187.

53. See his explanation to Herbert Lewis, quoted in Morgan, *Wales*, pp. 186-7.

54. *Hansard*, CXV (25 November 1902) cols. 401-2.

55. *Ibid*, col 439-40.

56. Lloyd George's two early biographers, DuParcq and Edwards, who were subject to his influence, make much of his eagerness to compromise and of his fellowship with Lord Hugh Cecil but they gloss over his failure at this time to make good on his promise to compromise. Herbert DuParcq, *Life of David Lloyd George*, London, 1913, II, 343-5; J. Hugh Edwards, *The Life of David Lloyd George*, London, n.d. [1913], IV, 9-11.

57. Rendel Papers, NLW, Vol 2, 145, A. C. Humphreys-Owen, 27 December 1902.

58. *Times*, 31 December 1902.

59. *South Wales Daily News*, 21 January 1903; *North Wales Observer*, 23 January 1903 in LGP, H of L, A/11/1/1,2. The address itself is printed in DuParcq, *LG*, II, 412-16.

60. *Ibid.*, p. 415.

61. The *Manchester Guardian* had advocated this exchange since the summer. *Manchester Guardian*, 23 July 1902.

62. He retained this conviction throughout the education struggle. See: Arthur Richmond, *Another Sixty Years*, London, 1965, pp. 29-30.

63. W.R.P. George, *Lloyd George, Backbencher*, Llandysul, 1983, pp. 372-4; Alfred George, Archbishop Edwards, *Memories*, London, 1927, pp. 190-1.

64. Edwards, *LG*, IV, 26. On Llandrindod Wells see also: W.R.P. George, *LG*, pp. 375-7.

65. *Church Times*, 6 March 1903; George G. Lerry, *Alfred George Edwards, Archbishop of Wales*, Oswestry, 1940, pp. 82-3.

66. LGP, H of L, A/2/8/14, 'The Education Act, 1902, Proceedings of a Conference held at the Westminster Palace Hotel on Tuesday, March 24th, 1903 between Representatives of the Voluntary Schools of the Diocese of St. Asaph and Representatives of the County Councils of Wales, Private and Confidential' 28 pages.

67. *Ibid.*, p. 16.

68. *Ibid.*, p. 26.

69. *Ibid.*, pp. 17-18.

70. See his speech to the Montgomeryshire Liberal Association on the eve of the diocesan meeting. *Montgomeryshire Express*, 21 May 1903 in LGP, H of L, A/11/1/30. See his letter to William after the Westminster Palace conference. W.R.P. George, *LG*, p. 377.

71. J.H. Lewis Papers, NLW, 3/19, LG to JHL, 21 April 1903.

72. *Church Times*, 22 May 1903. Letter from a 'Cardiffian.'

73. *British Weekly*, 23 April, 7 May 1903; *Church Times*, 1, 22 May 1903.

74. Matthew, *Liberal Imperialists*, p. 234 and n.

75. *South Wales Daily News*, 20 May 1903 in LGP, H of L, A/11/1/37.

76. *Pilot*, 30 May 1903, LGP, H of L, A/11/1/40.

77. In the spring of 1904 he noted that among 307 school board districts in Wales and Monmouthshire, just 54 provided systematic non-sectarian instruction and only 17 gave an examination. This was not religious neutrality but paganism. *Hansard*, CXXXIV (9 May 1904) col. 707.

78. *South Wales Daily News*, 4 June 1903 in LGP, H of L, A/11/1/41; *Manchester Guardian*, 4 June 1903.

79. *Carnarvon Herald*, 12 February; *Herts Advertiser and St. Alban's Times*, 13 February 1902 in LGP, H of L, A/12/1/16,17.

80. Bernard Holland, *The Life of Spencer Compton, Eighth Duke of Devonshire*, London, 1911, II, 372-5.

81. Morgan, *Letters*, p. 140, LG to MLG, 23 December 1903.

82. Allen Sykes, *Tariff Reform in British Politics*, Oxford, 1979, pp.74-5; Richard Rempel, *Unionists Divided. Arthur Balfour, Joseph Chamberlain and the Unionist Free Traders*, Newton Abbot, 1972, pp. 83-85.

83. W.S.C. to Lord Hugh Cecil, 1 January 1904, in Randolph S. Churchill, *Winston S. Churchill*, II, Companion Volume 2, 1, 281-2. Churchill himself supported Balfour's bill loyally and opposed concession. 'You do not make friends of

enemies,' he had said at Accrington on 3 October, 'by making enemies of your friends,' *Manchester Guardian*, 4 October 1902.

84. *Nineteenth Century*, LV (January 1904), 42.

85. *Carnarvon Herald*, 29 January 1904, in LGP, H of L, A/12/1/12.

86. T.J. Hughes, 'The Proposed Educational Concordat: A Nonconformist Reply,' *Nineteenth Century*, LV, (March 1904), 399.

87. Morgan, *Letters*, p. 140, LG to MLG, 23 December 1903.

88. Edwards, *Memories*, p. 195.

89. Perks to Rosebery, 1 April 1904, quoted in Koss, *Nonconformity*, p. 66.

90. Morgan, *Letters*, p. 140, LG to MLG, 1 January 1904.

91. *Hansard*, CXXIV (9 May 1904) cols 704-22.

92. Interview, *Carnarvon Herald*, 13 May 1904, LGP, H of L, A/12/1/56.

93. DLG to WG, undated, (Spring, 1904) in William George, *My Brother and I*, London, 1958, p. 171.

94. Edwards, *Memories*, p. 195.

95. Eluned E. Owen, *The Later Life of Bishop Owen, A Son of Wales*, Llandysul, 1961, II, 43-48.

96. It may have been on this occasion when the Member for Caernarvon District, to his brother's horror, was reported to have accepted communion from the Bishop's hand. W. George, *Brother*, p. 169.

97. LGP, H of L, A/2/8/21, 'Proposal Towards an Interim Concordat in Wales, Confidential,' 4 pages, n.d., printer's mark shows September 1904.

98. 'David and the Philistines,' *Sunday Sun*, 10 January 1904 in LGP, H of L, A/12/1/7.

99. Religious Census of 1905 and Language Census of 1911. Michael Kinnear, *The British Voter*, London, 1968, pp. 134-136.

100. *Yorkshire Daily Observer*, 3 March 1904, in LGP, H of L, A/12/1/22.

101. *South Wales Daily News*, 10 March 1904 in LGP, H of L, A/12/1/25. Throughout Wales the progressives, before the election, had held 543 seats to 252 for the sectarians. By late summer, with a few contests to be decided, the figures were 649 to 153. *Times*, 29 August 1904.

102. Harold Spender, *The Fire of Life*, London, n.d. [1926], p. 180. Quoted in Edwards, *Lloyd George*, IV, 39.

103. W. Lewis Jones, 'The Education Crisis in Wales,' *Independent Review*, II (March 1904), 2, 283-96.

104. *Hansard*, CXXXI (14 March 1904) cols. 1004-1015. After this address Lloyd George and Bishop Owen met in the House of Commons lobby and chatted in most friendly terms—however, to a nearby reporter's despair, in Welsh. *Morning Leader*, 16 March 1904 in LGP, H of L, A/12/1/33.

105. *Western Mail*, 15 March 1904 in LGP, H of L, A/12/1/31.

106. W.R.P. George, *LG*, p. 389. P.R.O. Cab. 37/69/42 'Welsh Education', 17 March 1904, 'Ldy'.

107. P.R.O. Cab. 37/67/76, 'Education Situation in Wales,' 24 November 1903, 'Ldy'.

108. P.R.O. Cab. 41/28/22, A.J.B. to Edw VII, 21 November 1903.

109. The report provides a useful source on the way in which the Welsh revolt was

conducted at the local level. *P.P.* LXXV, 'Report of a Public Enquiry held under Section 16 and 23 of the Education Act of 1902 and Section 73 of the Elementary Act, 1870 by A.T. Lawrence, K.C. at Carmarthen on the 24th and the 25th of March 1904,' 1904.

110. *Hansard*, CXXXIII (26 April 1904) col. 1204.

111. Owen, *Owen*, pp. 50-1.

112. *Hansard*, CXXXVIII (15 July 1904) cols 206-7.

113. 'How the Coercion Act Is To Be Met,' *North Wales Observer*, 6 May 1904 in LGP, H of L, A/12/2/52.

114. Balfour had warned the King in July that the Unionist backbench was unhappy and restive, making parliamentary business difficult. Cab. 49/21/28, A.J.B. to Edw VII, 26 July 1904.

115. *Hansard*, CXXXIX (5 August 1904) cols. 1221-1268.

116. See comments of the *Manchester Guardian*, 6 August 1904.

117. *Times*, 10 August 1904. As the meeting was supposed to be secret *The Times*'s penetration of it caused something of a sensation. Even the *Manchester Guardian*, which followed Lloyd George's doings closely and which was usually privy to his plans, was reduced to quoting *The Times* article. *Manchester Guardian*, 11 August 1904.

118. J.H. Lewis Papers, NLW, 10/231 diary extract, 10 August 1904.

119. 'Mr. Lloyd George: Chieftain of Wales.' *Review of Reviews*, XXX, (September 1904), 267.

120. *Daily News*, 17 September 1904 in LGP, H of L, A/12/2/15.

121. *Times*, 11 August 1904. On *The Times*'s leader see 'The Rising Power of Mr. Lloyd George,' *Western Mail*, 15 August 1904 in LGP, H of L, A/12/2/7.

122. But in October, contrary to many other writers, Henry W. Lucy, the dean of lobby correspondents, declared that the sense of the House of Commons was that Lloyd George was not yet ready for Cabinet office. 'The Next Liberal Ministry,' *Nineteenth Century*, CVI (October 1904), 684.

123. *Manchester Guardian*, 4 September 1904.

124. Morgan, *Letters*, p. 141, LG to MLG, 15 September 1904.

125. B.L. Add. MS 49787, Balfour Papers, Vol CV, R.L. Morant to A.J. Balfour, 17 September 1904.

126. *Ibid*, R.L. Morant to A.J. Balfour, 19 September 1904. W.R.P. George, *LG*, 396.

127. *Ibid.*, A.J. Balfour to R.L. Morant, 21 September 1904.

128. *Ibid.*, R.L. Morant to A.J. Balfour, 3 October 1904.

129. *South Wales Daily News*, 7 October 1904 in LGP, H of L, A/12/2/21.

130. *Manchester Guardian*, 7 October 1904.

131. On this see: 'The Welsh Revolt: Surveying the Battleground,' *Times*, 29 August 1904.

132. *Manchester Guardian*, 6 October 1904.

133. See: 'Welsh Revolt, Merionethshire,' *Times*, 24 September 1904; *Manchester Guardian*, 3 October 1904; Alfred Thomas Davies, *The Lloyd George I Knew*, London, 1948, pp. 46-7. Davies was at this time a law partner of Herbert Lewis.

134. 'The Position of the Teachers,' *South Wales Daily News*, 6 October 1904 in LGP, H of L, A/12/2/19.

135. J.H. Lewis Papers, NLW, 10/230, Lewis to LG, nd.

136. Cab 37/72/124, 'The Situation in Wales,' Memorandum by Lord Londonderry and Sir W. Anson, 7 October 1904.

137. Cab 37/72/124, 'Course to be pursued in connection with Welsh Education and the application of the Defaulting Authorities Act,' 9 October 1904, AJB.

138. *Manchester Guardian*, 26 October 1904.

139. B.L., Add. MS, 49787, Balfour Papers, Vol CV, J.St. David to R.L. Morant, 15 October 1904.

140. *Church Times*, 4 November 1904. Bishop Owen suggested that the Welsh bishops' meeting had been called at his request. Balfour's prior knowledge of it indicates that this could not have been the case.

141. *Manchester Guardian*, 22 October 1904.

142. *Church Times*, 4 November 1904.

143. *Manchester Guardian*, 26 October 1904.

144. *Church Times*, 4 November 1904.

145. Owen, *Owen*, p. 73.

146. DuParcq, *LG*, IV, 36-7.; Spender, *Prime Minister*, p. 135; Frank Owen, *Tempestuous Journey*, New York, 1955, p. 130.

147. *Manchester Guardian*, 21 November 1904; *Cambridge Independent Press*, 2 December 1904 in LGP, H of L, A/12/2/50.

148. *South Wales Argus*, 27 October 1904, in LGP, H of L, A/12/2/36.

149. See for example, St. Asaph to the *Manchester Guardian*, 5 November 1904.

150. *Church Times*, 6 January 1905.

151. *Ibid.*, 11 November 1904.

152. *Ibid.*, 3 February 1905.

153. *Times*, 27 February 1905.

154. *Hansard*, CXLVI, (13 May 1905) cols 374-9.

155. *Ibid.*, CXLV (17 April 1905) cols 310-11.

156. *Ibid.*, CXLVI (13 May 1905) cols. 363-98.

157. *Ibid.*, CL (25 July 1905) cols. 178-9.

158. *P.P.* Cd. 2783 'Report of the Board of Education for the Year 1904-5,' 22 November 1905, Accounts and Papers, XXVII, 1906.

159. *Church Times*, 25 August, 1 September 1905.

160. *British Weekly*, 2 March 1905.

161. *Hansard*, CL (1 August 1905) cols. 1206-26.

162. Arthur Porritt, *The Best I Remember*, New York, 1923, pp. 95-6.

163. Beriah Evans, *The Life Romance of Lloyd George*, London, n.d. [1916], pp. 135-7; see also: Margaret, Viscountess Rhondda, *D.A. Thomas, Viscount Rhondda*, London, 1921, p. 79.

164. LGP, H of L, A/1/3/2, Evan R. Davies to LG, 3 Routh Road, Wandsworth, 15 January 1905.

165. Gibson Bowles, an old Unionist friend of Lloyd George's, repudiated by his constituency, had discussed his unhappy situation while at Minton in January. See: Morgan, *Letters*, p. 141, LG to MLG, 4 January 1905. Bowles eventually became a Liberal.

166. Koss, *Nonconformity,* p. 166.

167. A.S.T. Griffith-Boscawen, *Fourteen Years in Parliament,* London, 1907, p. 344.

168. *Christian World,* 2 March 1905.

169. *Christian World,* 9 March 1905.

170. *Ibid.*

171. *British Weekly,* 9 March 1905.

172. LGP, H of L, A/1/15/8, Thomas Law to LG, 8 March 1905, 9:40 a.m.

173. *British Weekly,* 16 March; *Manchester Guardian,* 10 March 1905.

174. Porritt, *The Best I Remember,* pp. 97-98.

175. *Christian World,* 9 March 1905.

176. *Church Times,* 1 September 1905.

177. *Church Times,* 8 September 1905.

178. *Church Times,* 29 December 1905.

179. Llewelyn Williams in Rhondda, *Thomas,* p. 79; Davies, *Lloyd George,* p. 47; *Church Times,* 3,10,17 March 1905; LG to MLG, 25 August 1905 in Morgan, *Letters,* p. 143.

180. Davies, *LG,* p. 48.

181. See: 'Wales in 1905,' *Times,* 1 January 1906.

182. See: *P.P.,* Cd. 2947, 'Board of Education, Statement showing the number of voluntary schools in England and Wales, 31 July 1904,' Accounts and Papers, XC, 1906; Cd. 3219, 'Board of Education, Statement showing the number of voluntary schools, 1 January 1906.' Accounts and Papers, XC, 1906.

183. See for example, J.A. Lovat-Fraser, 'The Right Hon. David Lloyd -George,' *National Review,* (January 1908), 807-8.

184. *Times,* 25 July 1903.

185. *Hansard,* CXXVI (5 August 1903) col. 1579.

186. *Carnarvon Herald,* 13 May 1904, in LGP, H of L, A/12/1/57; 'Extract of message sent to a Liberal meeting held in Colwyn Bay to discuss the Education Bill,' 9 March 1906, MS. in *Ibid.* A/2/9/1.

187. P.R.O. Cab. 41/29/21, AJB to Edw VII, 21 June 1904. On 30 October 1903 he wrote to his brother that Morant had said Wales would get educational autonomy. W.R.P. George, *LG,* p. 384-5.

188. David Lloyd George, 'The Welsh Political Programmes,' *Independent Review,* III, 12 (1 September 1904), 486.

189. Because Alderman Hughes, the leader of the education revolt in the South, was a solicitor in Bridgend which was also the site of the Glamorgan County Lunatic Asylum, Thomas usually satirized Lloyd George's threat to close schools as the 'Bridgend policy.' Rhondda, *Thomas,* p. 78. Both Llewelyn Williams and Beriah Evans agreed that it was the member for Merthyr working through friends in the Carmarthen County Council who ended the prospects for a Welsh joint education committee. *Ibid.,* p. 79; Evans, *Romance,* p. 136.

190. Leslie Wynne-Evans, 'The Genesis of the Welsh Department, Board of Education, 1906-07,' *Transactions of the Honourable Society of Cymmrodorion,* 1970, 195-228.

191. Quoted in: Peter J. Randall, 'The Origins and Establishment of the Welsh Department of Education,' *Welsh History Review,* VII (December 1975), 4, 454.

192. The biography of Morant by Bernard M. Allen says almost nothing about the Welsh revolt.

193. LGP, H of L, B/2/9/2, 'First Draft of a Clause Proposed to be inserted in the Education Bill for the establishment of a Welsh National Council for Education in Wales,' 20 March 1906.

194. *Times*, 24 January 1906.

195. See: W. Watkin Davies, *Lloyd George, 1863-1914*, London, 1939, pp. 223-4.

196. Winston Churchill to Lord Hugh Cecil, 1 January 1904, R.S. Churchill, *W.S. Churchill*, II, Companion Volume 1, 284.

197. Speech at the meeting of the Newcastle Liberal Association, Palace Theatre, Newcastle, 4 April 1903, *Newcastle Daily Leader*, 6 April 1903 in LGP, H of L, A/11/1/26. This speech appears in full in DuParcq, *LG*, IV, 617-26.

198. B. Seebohm Rowntree, *Poverty: A Study of Town Life*, London, 1901.

199. Sir John E. Gorst, *The Children of the Nation*, New York, 1907. Churchill had visited Gorst in Egypt where he was staying with his son, the High Commissioner, in December 1902 to get information for the biography. Soon the two were joined in opposition to tariff reform.

200. 'Miles,' 'Where to Get Men,' *Contemporary Review*, LXXXI (January 1902), 78-86.

201. Major General Sir John Frederick Maurice, 'National Health, A Soldier's Study,' *Contemporary Review*, LXXXIII (January 1903), 41-56.

202. Cd. 1501, 'Report of the Inspector General of Recruiting,' 1903.

203. *Hansard*, CXXII (22 May 1903) cols 1541-1549.

204. Rempel, *Unionists Divided*, pp. 32-4.

205. *Hansard*, CXXII (22 May 1903) col. 1553.

206. *Ibid.*, CXXIII, (28 May 1903) cols. 165-70.

207. See: Beatrice Webb's comments on the effect of Booth's conversion. Beatrice Webb, *Our Partnership*, London, 1948, p. 279. Diary entry, 20 December 1903.

208. *Aberdeen Free Press*, 14 November 1903; *Falkirk Herald*, 21 November 1903 in LGP, H of L, A/11/2/38, 42.

209. H.W. Massingham, 'The Need for a Radical Party,' *Contemporary Review*, LXXXV (January 1904), 12-23.

210. *Daily News*, 8 January 1904 in LGP, H of L, A/12/1/3.

211. LGP, NLW, 20462C/2287, Campbell-Bannerman to LG, 20 November 1903.

212. *Times*, 8 January 1904.

213. *North Wales Observer*, 28 October 1892, in LGP, H of L, A/7/1/4.

214. *Manchester Guardian*, 7 November 1904.

215. Philip Poirier, *The Advent of the Labour Party*, New York, 1958, pp. 182-93.

216. See: Alfred Havighurst, *Radical Journalist, H.W. Massingham*, Cambridge, 1974, pp. 129-131.

217. LGP, NLW, 20463C/2436, J.L. Wanklyn to LG, 1 January 1904.

218. Churchill, *Churchill*, II, Companion Volume 2, 3413, WS Churchill to Thomas, 4 May 1904; Thomas to WSC, 5 May 1904.

219. *South Wales Daily News*, 28 May 1904, in LGP, H of L, A/12/1/63.

220. Quoted in Rhondda, *Thomas*, p. 158-62.

221. *Manchester Guardian*, 19 October 1904.

222. Keith Robbins, *Sir Edward Grey*, London, 1971, p. 112.

223. Churchill, *Churchill*, II, 251.

224. For example at Huddersfield, 6 May 1905. *Manchester Guardian*, 8 May 1905.

225. Lloyd George to William George, 8 September 1905 quoted in William George, *Brother*, p. 6.

226. *Fife Free Press*, 28 October 1905 in LGP, H of L, A/13/2/8.

227. *Glasgow Herald*, 2 November 1905 in LGP, H of L, A/13/2/11.

228. W. George, *Brother*, pp. 87-90.

229. Spender, *Campbell-Bannerman*, II, 189-91.

230. Gainford Papers, Nuffield College, Box 37, J.A. Pease Diary, 11 December 1905.

231. *Manchester Guardian*, 8 December 1905.

232. W. George, *Brother*, p. 206.

233. Wilson, *Campbell-Bannerman*, p. 435.

234. *Manchester Guardian*, 8 December 1905.

235. Wilson, *Campbell-Bannerman*, p. 443.

236. J. Hugh Edwards, *LG*, III, 60-1.

237. Daniel, Memoir, I, 1908. This was unfair and not strictly true. In fact Lord Penrhyn had refused an offer of arbitration by the Board of Trade.

238. W. George, *Brother*, p. 207. LG to WG.

239. Webb, *Partnership*, p. 326, Diary, 15 December 1905.

Chapter 5, pp. 285-334

1. J. Hugh Edwards, *The Life of David Lloyd George*, London, n.d., [1913], IV, 65.

2. J.H. Lewis Papers, National Library of Wales, 10/230, diary extract, 30 December 1906.

3. W. Watkin Davies, *Lloyd George, 1863-1914*, London, 1939, p. 251. During the railway strike in 1907, when Lloyd George was constantly attended by reporters, Frank Dilnot, himself a journalist, noted that not only did the President of the Board of Trade stop at the entrance of his building to exchange banter, itself unheard of for a Cabinet member, but when the November weather turned inclement, he invited the reporters inside. Frank Dilnot, *Lloyd George, The Man and His Story*, New York, 1917, pp. 63-4.

4. Almeric Fitzroy, *Memoirs*, London, n.d., [1925], I, 390, 14 December 1909.

5. Beriah G. Evans, *The Life Romance of Lloyd George*, London, 1916, p. 142.

6. *Ibid.*, p. 141.

7. 'Conference on National Insurance Bill, Clause 18,' 19 October 1911 (Transcript from shorthand notes), p. 20, W.J. Braithwaite Papers, British Library of Political and Economic Science, Part I 'Memoirs, 1910-11'.

8. *Carnarvon Herald*, 13 November 1903 in Lloyd George Papers, House of Lords,, A/11/2/35.

9. *North Wales Observer*, 17 June 1904, in LGP, H of L, A/12/2/68.

10. *Manchester Guardian*, 30 December 1905.

11. *Manchester Guardian*, 22 December 1905.

12. *Manchester Guardian,* 20 December 1905.

13. *Manchester Guardian,* 29 December 1905.

14. *Western Mail,* 12 October 1906, in LGP, H of L, B/4/2/28. Most of this speech, without however any indication of the auspices under which it was given, is printed in Herbert DuParcq, *The Life of David Lloyd George* (London: 1913), IV, 627-31. W.S. Adams, in his article in *Past and Present* in 1953, which in many ways establishes the beginning of the new scholarship on Lloyd George, suggests that the 11 October speech marks the beginning of Lloyd George's campaign for social reform. This clearly is in error. At Cardiff Lloyd George was noting only that the advent of the party simply made more necessary than ever the program he had been putting forward since the spring of 1903. William S. Adams, 'Lloyd George and the Labour Movement,' *Past and Present,* February 1953, 55-64.

15. *Times,* 23 October 1906. With only two exceptions, his speeches in the House of Commons during 1906 dealt entirely with Board of Trade matters or education.

16. William George, *My Brother and I,* London, 1958, p. 207. *Hansard* shows that A. Akers-Douglas, who followed him, commented upon his moderation, but records no cheer. *Hansard,* CLII (26 February 1906) cols. 873-5.

17. *Times,* 27 June 1906.

18. Stephen Koss, *Nonconformity in Modern British Politics,* Hamden, Connecticut, 1975, pp. 227-8.

19. Lloyd George was a member of the Cabinet committee although Almeric Fitzroy observed that he spent most of his time writing letters. Fitzroy, *Memoirs,* I, 281.

20. G.K.A. Bell, *Randall Davidson, Archbishop of Canterbury,* London, 1938, pp. 516-7.

21. *Ibid.,* pp. 516-7.

22. P.R.O., Cab 41/30/50, CB to Edw VII, 21 March 1906.

23. P.T. Forsyth, 'The Catholic Threat of Passive Resistance,' *Contemporary Review,* LXXXIX (April 1906), 562-67; Cab 41/30/50,51, CB to Edw VII, 21, 24,26 March 1907.

24. A. Lawrence Lowell, *The Government of England,* New York, 1919, II, 319.

25. *Hansard,* CLXI (17 July 1906) col. 50.

26. Quoted in Leslie Wynne-Evans, 'The Genesis of the Welsh Department, Board of Education,' *Transactions of the Honourable Society of Cymmrodorion,* 1970, 207.

27. J.A. Spender, *Life, Journalism and Politics,* New York, n.d., [1927], I, 157-8.

28. *Ibid.,* p. 158.

29. *South Wales Daily News,* 5 March 1906 in LGP, H of L, B/4/2/3.

30. *South Wales Daily News,* 29 March 1906 in LGP, H of L, B/4/2/4.

31. Extract of message sent to Liberal Meeting in Colwyn Bay, 9 March 1906 in LGP, H of L, B/2/9/1.

32. *Hansard,* CLXV (21 November 1906) cols. 795-802.

33. A.J. Balfour at the Cambridge Guildhall, *Times,* 7 May 1906.

34. *Hansard,* CLVI (8 May 1906) cols 1174-8.

35. *Hansard,* LCXI (17 July 1906) cols. 53-61.

36. LG to W. George, 18 July 1906 quoted in W. George, *Brother,* p. 208; See also: *Times,* 18 July 1906.

37. Sidney Lee, *King Edward VII* (London: 1927), II, 456.

38. British Library, Add. MS 41239, Campbell-Bannerman Papers, Vol. XXXIV, Lloyd George to Campbell-Bannerman, 19 July 1906.

39. Add. MS 41207, CB Papers, II, LG to CB, 20 July 1906; *Ibid.*, Knollys to CB, 20 July 1906.

40. Sir George Kekewich, Morant's predecessor as Permanent Secretary at the Board of Education and in 1906 Liberal Member of Parliament for Exeter City, described the Education Bill in his memoirs as 'thoroughly bad.' He recalls that he wished that he could have voted against it. George W. Kekewich, *The Education Department and After*, London, 1920, pp. 266-7.

41. Quoted in DuParcq, *LG*, III, 455.

42. J.H. Lewis Papers, NLW, 10/230 Lewis to LG, 8 April 1906.

43. Lewis to LG, 9 April 1906, quoted in Koss, *Nonconformity*, pp. 79-80.

44. Lloyd George to Walter H. Hughes, Bangor, *Times*, 20 January 1906; Koss, *Nonconformity*, p. 79.

45. Lloyd George to MLG, 1 August 1906 in Kenneth Morgan, *Lloyd George Family Letters*, Cardiff, 1973, p. 146

46. Lee, *Edward VII*, II, 456-7; B.L. Add. MS. 41239, CB Papers, Vol. XXXIV, LG to CB, 22 October 1906.

47. J.H. Lewis Papers, NLW, 10/231, 21 October 1906.

48. LG to CB, 22 October 1906, CB Papers, op. cit.

49. *Hansard*, CLXV (21 November 1906) cols. 781-997.

50. *Oxford Chronicle*, 7 December 1906 in LGP, H of L, B/4/2/40.

51. B.L. Add. MS., 41207, CB Papers, II, Knollys to CB, 3 December 1906; CB to Knollys, 4 December 1906. These letters are printed in full in J.A. Spender, *The Life of the Right Hon. Sir Henry Campbell-Bannerman*, London, 1924, II, 314-17.

52. LG to Nicoll. 21 December 1908, quoted in Koss, *Nonconformity*, p. 99.

53. Randolph Churchill, *Winston Churchill*, Boston, 1967, II, Comp. Vol. 2, 872-3.

54. Quoted in Koss, *Nonconformity*, p. 83.

55. P.R.O. Cab. 41/30/78, CB to Edw VII, 5 December 1906.

56. J.H. Lewis Papers, NLW, 10/231, 29 December 1906.

57. Lord Newton, *Lord Lansdowne*, London, 1925, p. 356.

58. Quoted in John D. Fair, *British Interparty Conferences*, Oxford, 1980, p. 74.

59. Charles Petrie, *The Life and Letters of the Right Hon. Sir Austen Chamberlain*, London, 1939, I, 195. See also: Newton, *Lansdowne*, pp. 356-7. It should be noted however that Balfour packed the Unionist delegation against compromise. The hardline Welsh Churchman Lord Cawdor was present, but the Duke of Devonshire was excluded.

60. See McKenna's statement: *Hansard*, CLXXI (13 March 1907) col. 104.

61. *Times*, 18 January 1907.

62. Ponsonby Papers, Bodleian Library, MS Eng Hist, C654,f3, R.L. Morant to A. Ponsonby, n.d.

63. Stephen McKenna, *Reginald McKenna*, London, 1948, p. 43.

64. A.T. Davies, *The Lloyd George I Knew*, London, 1948, p. 51.

65. J.H. Lewis Papers, NLW, 10/230, a series of unsorted letters.

66. Fitzroy, *Memoirs*, I, 318-9.

67. See: *Hansard*, CLXX (27 February 1907) col. 44.

68. Bell, *Davidson*, 531; Eluned E. Owen, *The Later Life of Bishop Owen*, Llandysul, 1961, II, 113-4.

69. Owen, *Owen*, pp. 81-2.

70. Quoted in Bell, *Davidson*, p. 504.

71. *Ibid.*, p. 505.

72. Owen, *Owen*, pp. 81-2.

73. Bell, *Davidson*, p. 505.

74. Cd. 5432, Report, 'Royal Commission on the Church of England in Wales,' XIV, 1, 1910.

75. *Times*, 18 January 1907.

76. DuParcq, *LG*, III, 464-7.

77. Koss, *Nonconformity*, p. 86.

78. *British Weekly*, 7 March 1907.

79. *British Weekly*, 2 May 1907.

80. *British Weekly*, 30 May 1907.

81. *Hansard*, CLXXV (3 June 1907) cols. 320-30.

82. *British Weekly*, 6 June 1907.

83. *Hansard*, CLXXI (11 June 1907) col. 1247.

84. *British Weekly*, 4 July 1907.

85. LGP, H of L, B/1/8/2, LG to Elvet Lewis, 24 June 1907.

86. During one of these addresses in July before a small audience at the New Reform Club at 10 Adelphi Terrace, the *British Weekly* reporter, to his astonishment, saw Lloyd George sinfully smoking a cigarette. *British Weekly*, 4 July 1907. The New Reform Club was a nebulous, short-lived, group, one of a number which Lloyd George chose to patronize from time to time as a platform for speeches. He was a member of the Reform Club but rarely used it and referred to the New Reform as the 'real Reform Club.' There is a letter in Herbert Lewis's papers dated only a few days before the speech referred to here. 'To the Reform Club, 30 June 1907: I resign now and forever. D. Lloyd George.' J.H. Lewis Papers, NLW, 10/230. This peremptory note either was not sent or Lloyd George rejoined the Reform Club, because he resigned a second time early in 1913.

87. J. H. Lewis Papers, NLW, 10/231, diary extract, 16 July 1907. One problem with this story is that the proprietor of the *Western Mail*, now George Riddell, who would also become an intimate of Lloyd George, records that he came to know Nicoll only in 1908. George, Lord Riddell, *More Pages From My Diary*, London, 1934, p. 1, October 1908.

88. LGP, NLW, 20428C/1247. This letter, in slightly abbreviated form, appears in Morgan, *Letters*, pp. 147-8.

89. J.H. Lewis Papers, NLW, 10/231, Diary extract, 7 August 1907.

90. *British Weekly*, 26 September 1907.

91. Evans, *Lloyd George*, p. 121.

92. LGP, NLW, 20462C/2355, J.H. Roberts to LG, 3 October 1907.

93. *British Weekly*, 3 October 1907.

94. H.M. Hughes to LG, 3 October 1907, Quoted in Koss, *Nonconformity*, p. 94.

95. BL Add. MS 41240, CB Papers, XXXV, LG to CB, 6? Oct., 1907.

96. *Ibid.*

97. Evans, *Lloyd George*, p. 110.

98. *British Weekly*, 17 October 1907. See also: *Times*, 11 October 1907; *South Wales Daily News*, 11 October 1907 in LGP, H of L, B/5/1/23. The best description of Lloyd George's histrionics, even though it deals mostly with the peroration, is: Edwards, *LG*, IV, 83-6. Almost certainly Edwards, still a journalist, was present.

99. *British Weekly*, 17 October 1907.

100. D.R. Daniel, Memoir, National Library of Wales, 2915, I, p. 14.

101. B.L. Add. MS 41240, CB Papers, Vol. XXXV, LG to CB, 17 October 1907. Later in the winter of 1908 at dinner at No. 11 with Daniel and Llewelyn Williams, he denied that he had made any pledge except to bring a bill in the present parliament. D.R. Daniel, Memoir, NLW, I, p. 21. Nonetheless on 21 April 1909, with the now three year old royal commission still unable to produce a report, the government redeemed Lloyd George's unauthorized promise and put down a Disestablishment and Disendowment Bill. It was introduced by the new Prime Minister himself who had no intention of proceeding with it. Lloyd George took no part in its preparation.

102. The average wage for men on the railways was 26s 9d per week to be compared with 32s 5d in engineering or 33s in the building trades. Indeed they earned 3s 9d less than tramway and bus operatives. Department of Employment, *British Labour Statistics, Historical Abstract, 1886-1968*, London, 1971, pp. 95-96. These detailed statistics collected by the Board of Trade as part of Lloyd George's industrial census in 1906-7 unfortunately were not published until 1912-13 and so were not available during the first railway dispute when most figures came from the union.

103. See: Kenneth Morgan, *Keir Hardie*, London, 1975, p. 127-8.

104. *Hansard*, CLXIII (11 February 1908) cols. 1639-42.

105. PRO, Cab. 37/90/116, 'DLG' 'Subscriptions by Railway and other Companies for election purposes.' n.d. [April 1907].

106. *Times*, 14 March 1908.

107. LGP, NLW, 20462C/2289, Buxton to LG, 24 September 1907.

108. Hudson Kearley, Viscount Devonport, *The Travelled Road*, Privately Printed, n.d. [1930], p. 129.

109. B.L., Add. MS 41240, CB Papers, XXXV, LG to CB, 30 September 1907.

110. *Ibid.*, LG to CB, 17 October 1907.

111. LG to W. George, 21 October 1907 in W. George, *Brother*, p. 212.

112. See: LGP, H of L, B/1/1/6/C and /7, Herbert Maxwell (a director) to LG, 25 October 1907; Mark Lockwood (a director) to LG, 26 October 1907. This file contains also a note from W.H. Clark, Lloyd George's secretary, to Lloyd George, who at this time was spending weekends in Brighton, saying that Lockwood and Bell would meet at the Board of Trade on Tuesday, 29 October. If this transpired it was the only time the two sides conversed.

113. George, Lord Askwith, *Industrial Problems and Disputes*, London, 1920, reprinted 1971, p. 121.

114. Herbert Maxwell, *Evening Memories*, London, 1932, pp. 305-6; Devonport, *Road*, pp. 129-30.

115. Maxwell, *Memories*, p. 305.

116. B.L. Add. MS. 41240, CB Papers, XXXV, LG to CB, 25 October 1907.

117. LG to W. George, 25 October 1907 in W. George, *Brother*, p. 212.

118. See *Times*, 4 November 1907.

119. W. George, *Brother*, p. 212.

120. *Times,* 4 November 1907.

121. *Times, Ibid;* W. George, *Brother,* p. 212.

122. Cab. 41/31/35, CB to Edw VII, 5 November, 1907; Philip S. Bagwell, *The Railwaymen,* London, 1963, p. 268.

123. J.H. Lewis Papers, NLW, 10/230, diary entry, 9 November 1907.

124. The documents, and a short history of the dispute, are printed in: *Parliamentary Papers,* Cd. 4254, 'Report of Strikes and Lockouts and on conciliation and arbitration boards in the United Kingdom,' 1908.

125. Bagwell, *Railwaymen,* p. 272.

126. *PP.,* Cd. 6014, 'Minutes of Evidence taken before the Royal Commission on the Railway Conciliation Arbitration Scheme of 1907,' 1912-13, p. 73 evidence, 11 August 1911.

127. Cd. 4254, 'Report of Strikes and Lockouts.'

128. Askwith, *Industrial Problems,* p. 122.

129. *Times,* 8 November 1907.

130. LG to W. George, n.d. [7 November 1907], in W. George, *Brother,* p. 213.

131. B.L. Add. MS 41208, CB Papers, Vol. III, Francis Knollys to CB, 7 November 1907.

132. LG to W. George, 13 November 1907 in W. George, *Brother,* p. 213.

133. For example: E.H. Phelps Brown, *The Growth of British Industrial Relations,* London, 1965, p. 302.

134. Cd. 6014, 'Minutes of Evidence,' p. 391, 18 September 1911. Bell has been officially excised from British labor histories. When mentioned he is called simply a traitor. Bagwell, *Railwaymen,* says only that he 'resigned' in December 1909. In 1910 he was given a job in the Labour Exchange administration of the Board of Trade.

135. LGP, H of L, I/2/1/20 J Rowland to LG, 25 November 1907.

136. The correct date of her death is 29 November, not 30 November as is recorded in DuParcq and many subsequent works. See *Times,* 30 November 1907.

137. W. George, *Brother,* pp. 217-8.

138. A.J.P. Taylor, ed., *A Diary by Frances Stevenson,* London, 1971, p. 260, diary extract, 10 March 1934.

139. W. George, *Brother,* p. 215.

140. J.H. Lewis Papers, NLW, 10/230, diary extract, 2 December 1907.

141. Taylor, ed., *Stevenson Diary,* p. 4, diary extract, 9 October 1914.

142. LGP, H of L, I/2/2/5, W. George to LG, 22 December 1907; *Ibid.,* I/1/2/7,8, MLG to LG 'Sunday.'

143. J.H. Lewis Papers, NLW, 10/230, diary extract, 3 December 1907.

144. LG to MLG, 4 December 1907 in Morgan, *Letters,* p. 149.

145. LGP, H of L, I/4 (unsorted) Rendel to LG, 4 December 1907.

146. See LG to MLG, 5 January 1908 in Morgan, *Letters,* p. 150.

147. J.H. Lewis Papers, NLW, 10/230, LG to Lewis, 17 December 1907. He invited also St. Asaph and McKenna.

148. LGP, NLW, 20428C/1275, LG to MLG, 23 December 1907.

149. *Times,* 6,10,17 December 1907.

150. Rendel to CB, 18 December; Asquith to CB, 23 December 1907, in John Wilson, *A Life of Sir Henry Campbell-Bannerman*, New York, 1973, p. 609.

151. LGP, H of L, B/1/5/1, Runciman to LG, 18 December 1907.

152. LGP, H of L, I/1/2/10, MLG to LG, 24 December 1907.

153. J.H. Lewis Papers, NLW, 10/231, diary extract, 4 January 1908.

154. LG to MLG, 10 January 1908 in Morgan, *Letters*, p. 151. It should be noted that in 1909 Churchill carried the Board of Trade Act permitting the salary of the President, excluding the incumbent, to be raised as it was when Sydney Buxton became President.

155. Lucy Masterman, *C.F.G. Masterman*, London, 1939, p. 177.

156. There is no certain story, for example, of the origins of the Medical Research Committee (now the Medical Research Council) which was founded by the National Insurance Act, even though the official historian of this important body made a serious attempt to discover whose idea it was. A. Lansborough Thomson, *Half A Century of Medical Research*, London, 1973, I, 11-15.

157. B.L. Add. MS 41239, Campbell-Bannerman Papers, XXXIV, LG to CB, 9 February 1906.

158. *Hansard*, CLIV (20 March 1906) cols. 237-53.

159. LG to MLG, 21 March 1906 in W. George, *Brother*, p. 208.

160. *Hansard*, CLIV (20 March 1906) col. 253.

161. *Times*, 21 March 1906.

162. *Times*, 4 August 1907.

163. Spender, *Life*, I, 157.

164. See: *P.P.* 1906, H of C Paper 202, 'Report of the Standing Committee on Trade on the Merchant Shipping Act's Amendment (No. 2) Bill with Proceedings of the Committee.'

165. *Hansard*, CLXV (22 November 1906), col. 1045.

166. This point of view has been adopted by a recent historian who finds that Lloyd George's legislation at the Board of Trade was designed to win the friendship of protectionists and give him a place between, or above, political parties. Robert J. Scally, *The Origins of the Lloyd George Coalition*, Princeton, 1975, pp. 139-41. Unfortunately Scally uses the Assay of Foreign Watchcases Act as an example of protectionist legislation. In reality by releasing foreign watchcases from hallmark requirements fixed for British watchcases, this measure's effect was the opposite.

167. *Hansard*, CLXV (22 November 1906), cols. 1054-7.

168. *Times*, 31 October 1906; 30 January 1907.

169. PRO, Cab. 37/85/8, 'Port of London,' 2 November 1906.

170. Devonport, *Road*, pp. 135-8.

171. Cornwall was Timothy Davies' predecessor as Mayor of Fulham and would become a member of the Port Authority. He eventually succeeded C.F.G. Masterman as manager of national health insurance.

172. See: LGP, H of L, B/2/7a/4, 'Port of London, Revenue of Proposed Port Authority,' unsigned, E. Cornwall, 18 December 1907; LGP, NLW, 20455E/2174, 'Memorandum of Conversation between Mr. Farrer of the Board of Trade and Sir Edgar Speyer of the Dock Companies. '21/8' 1907, MS transcript of conversation 'secret' annotated, 'Mr. Farrer thought you might like to see this. L1.S.'

173. *Hansard*, CLXXXVII (2 April 1908) cols. 708-12.

174. For the origins of the Bill itself see: *P.P.* XCIII, 1908, H of C Paper 109, 'Port of London Bill, explanatory memorandum,' April 1908. When the authority finally took over the docks in March, 1909, Lloyd George's Parliamentary Secretary at the Board of Trade, Hudson Kearley, became its first chairman.

175. PRO, Cab. 37/85/91, 'Preliminary Note on Certain Legislation which the Board of Trade Propose to Introduce,' 3 December 1906.

176. P.P. III, 1907, 'Patents and Designs (Amendment) Bill as amended in Committee,' 1907.

177. *Hansard*, CLXXII (17 April 1907) cols. 1049-50.

178. *Ibid.*, col. 1051.

179. See LG to W. George, 16 August 1907 in W. George, *Brother*, p. 211. On the origins of the Tonnage Bill see: *P.P.* VI, 507, 1907, 'Report and Special Report from the Select Committee on the Merchant Shipping (Tonnage Deduction for Propelling Power) Bill with a transcript of proceedings.'

180. See LG to MLG, 8, 23 August 1907 in Morgan, *Letters*, pp. 148, 149.

181. See: Stephen Koss, *Asquith*, New York, 1976, pp. 86-8. Kearley reports that Lloyd George told him during the trip to Cannes after Mair's death that John Morley was intriguing to introduce Earl Spencer as Campbell-Bannerman's successor. Kearley, *Road*, pp. 143-4.

182. See Haldane's letter to his mother of 17 March, quoted in Bruce Murray, *The People's Budget*, Oxford, 1980, pp. 64-5. There is in Maurice's biography of Haldane a portion of a letter saying: 'I have firmly decided to stay at the War Office and see my task through.' This may have been by way of explanation. Frederick Maurice, *Haldane* (Westport, Conn: 1970), I, 225. In any case Haldane's goal was the post of Lord Chancellor.

183. John, Viscount Morley, *Recollections* (New York: 1917), II, 251.

184. Stephen Koss, *Morley at the India Office*, New Haven, 1969, p. 61. Koss dates this Morley-Asquith interview as 6 April. However by this time all appointments were settled.

185. John H. Morgan, *John, Viscount Morley*, Boston, 1924, p. 48. To further complicate things Morley told Lord Esher on 11 February he 'would like to be Prime Minister himself.' Maurice Brett, ed., *Journals and Letters of Reginald Viscount Esher* (London: 1934), II, 303, 11 February 1908.

186. DuParcq, *LG*, III, 505; Edwards, *LG*, IV, 96-7; Harold Spender, *The Prime Minister*, New York, 1920, p. 149.

187. J.H. Lewis Papers, NLW, 10/231, 10 March 1908. Churchill was offered, and refused, the Local Government Board three days later.

188. Brett, *Esher Journals*, II, 303, 10 April 1908.

189. E.T. Raymond, *Mr. Lloyd George*, New York, 1922, p. 111.

190. Quoted in McKenna, *McKenna*, p. 227.

191. Fitzroy, *Memoirs*, I, 400-1, 6 April 1910.

192. The dating in Spender's biography is incorrect. J.A. Spender and Cyril Asquith, *Life of Herbert Henry Asquith* (London: 1932) I, 197.

193. LGP, NLW, 20462C/2285, Asquith to LG, 8 April 1908. On the same day he wrote Churchill offering him the Board of Trade.

194. LG to W. George, 11 April 1908, quoted in W. George, *Brother*, p. 220.

195. Churchill, *Churchill* II, Comp Vol 2, 771-2, Margot Asquith to WSC, n.d. [10 April 1908].

196. *Ibid.*, 772, Churchill to Asquith, 10 April 1908 midnight.

197. Asquith Papers, Bodleian Library, Vol. XI, LG to Asquith, 11 April 1908.

198. LGP, NLW, 20462C/2286, Asquith to LG, 11 April 1908. There exists in the Lloyd George papers the draft, on Board of Trade stationery, of an indignant reply to this letter which evidently was not sent.

199. B.L. Add. MS 46,326, Burns Papers, Diary, 11 April 1908.

200. Churchill, *Churchill*, II, Comp Vol 2, 928, Churchill to Morley, 23 December 1908. McKenna had offered, during the Cabinet making, to give up the Admiralty if Churchill wanted it.

201. Lord Esher recorded in his journal on 10 April 1910 that he had heard that the *Chronicle* story was 'attributed to Lloyd George' as it was a newspaper 'with which he was connected.' Brett, ed., *Esher Journals*, II, 303.

202. Runciman was reported to have threatened resignation if Lloyd George went to the Exchequer. Emmott Papers, quoted in Michael G. Fry, *Lloyd George and Foreign Policy*, Montreal, 1977, I, 81-2.

Chapter 6, pp. 335-398

1. On the Peckham by-election see: C.F.G. Masterman, *The Condition of England*, London, 1911, p. 109-12. The Unionist winner was H.C. Gooch, the brother of Liberal MP G.P. Gooch who was one of the 1906 generation of young radicals.

2. *Hansard*, CLXXXVIII (7 May 1908) col. 465.

3. On the New Liberals in parliament see for example: 'The New Parliament,' *Speaker*, XIII (24 February 1906) 496-7; 'The Government and Social Reform,' *Speaker*, XIII (3 March 1906), 514-5; C.F.G. Masterman, 'Liberalism and Labour,' *Nineteenth Century*, LX (November 1906), 706-18; C.F.G. Masterman, 'Politics in Transition,' *Nineteenth Century*, LXIII (January 1908), 1-17. For the bible of this group, essentially the new Liberal manifesto, see: C.F.G. Masterman, ed., *The Heart of the Empire*, London, 1901.

4. *Nation*, 7 March 1908.

5. *Hansard*, CLXXIII (29 January 1908) col. 4.

6. LG to W. George, 6 May 1908 in William George, *My Brother and I*, London, 1958, p. 220.

7. P.R.O., Cab. 37/85/96, R.S. Meiklejohn, 'Old Age Pensions,' 14 December 1906.

8. P.R.O., Cab. 41/31/54, Asquith to Edw VII, 1 May 1908; see also Asquith Papers, Bodleian Library, Papers on Old Age Pensions, 'Old Age Pensions, Report of Committee of Cabinet', April 1908.

9. P.R.O. Cab. 37/93/62, 'The Financial Situation—this year and next.' D. Ll.G., 18 May 1908.

10. D.R. Daniel, MS, National Library of Wales, 2915.

11. J.H. Lewis Papers, National Library of Wales, 10/230, diary extract, 8 September 1908.

12. *Hansard*, CXC (15 June 1908) col. 585.

13. *Hansard*, CXLCII (9 July 1908) cols. 184-85.

14. *Ibid.*, col. 175.

15. *Ibid.*, cols. 187-93; *Times*, 10 July 1908. After receiving the census figures of 1911, J.S. Bradbury noted dryly that 201,783 pensions were being paid in Ireland alone while census figures showed, even without regard to any statutory

disqualifications, that there were only 191,720 persons over seventy in the entire island. P.R.O.,J.S. Bradbury Papers, T 170/5, undated memorandum.

16. For example: Leopold Maxse, 'Episodes of the Month,' *National Review*, XLIX (March 1907), 20.

17. *Hansard*, CXCII (22 July 1908) col. 1384.

18. *Hansard*, CXCI (29 June 1908) cols. 395-6.

19. *Times*, 23 July 1908.

20. Strachey Papers, House of Lords, S/11/6/6, Asquith to Strachey, 9 May 1908.

21. Robert J. Scally, *The Origins of the Lloyd George Coalition*, Princeton, 1975, pp. 137-8; Alfred Gollin, *Proconsul in Politics*, London, 1964, p. 152.

22. *Hansard*, CXC (15 July 1908) col. 571.

23. See: *Whitaker's Almanack*, 1911, p. 458; Noel A. Humphreys, 'Old Age Pensions in the United Kingdom,' *Journal of the Royal Statistical Society*, LXXIV (December 1910), 73-4.

24. LG to W. George, 25 June 1908 in W. George, *Brother*, p. 221.

25. Alfred T. Davies, *The Lloyd George I Knew*, London, 1948, p. 63.

26. Strachey Papers, H of L, S/12/7/12, Strachey to Rosebery, 23 July 1908.

27. D.R. Daniel Memoir, NLW, I, p. 33.

28. Austen Chamberlain Papers, Birmingham University, AC 9/21, White to Austen Chamberlain, 4 October 1911.

29. Henry N. Bunbury, ed., *Lloyd George's Ambulance Wagon, The Memoirs of W.J. Braithwaite*, London, 1957, p. 71.

30. *Hansard*, CXC (15 June 1908) col. 574.

31. See: Arthur J. Marder, *From the Dreadnought to Scapa Flow*, London, 1961, I, 135-6.

32. See: 'Report to the First Lord on the Navy Estimates of 1908-09, by the Sea Lords,' 3 December 1907, quoted in *Ibid.*, p. 137.

33. Maurice V. Brett, ed., *Journals and Letters of Reginald, Viscount Esher*, London, 1934, II, 281-84, 7 February 1908. It should be understood that Admiralty estimates, unlike others, were formulated a year ahead of the budget of which they would be a part and were presented not only by the First Lord but by the Board of Admiralty as a whole. The Chancellor of the Exchequer usually received them in draft early in the autumn before other departmental estimates. Finally, and most important, unlike the practice at the War Office, whatever compromise emerged from the Cabinet had by custom to be approved not only by the responsible minister, the First Lord, but to be initialled also by the Sea Lords before it was included in the budget.

34. LG to W. George, 12 May 1908 in W. George, *Brother*, p. 221.

35. Beatrice Webb, a close friend of the Secretary of State for War, referred to him as Haldane's 'bete noire.' Beatrice Webb, *Our Partnership*, London, 1948, p. 411, diary, 19 May 1908.

36. P.R.O., Cab. 41/31/64, Asquith to Edw VII, 22 July 1908.

37. Asquith Papers, Bodleian Library, Vol. XI, Haldane to Asquith, 9 August 1908.

38. Edward David, ed., *Inside Asquith's Cabinet, The Diaries of Charles Hobhouse*, London, 1977, p. 73, 5 August 1908.

39. Asquith had written McKenna on 4 July, saying that he was 'growing sceptical...as to the whole "Dreadnought" policy,' and invited McKenna to agree. McKenna, the opponent of armament in February, was by this time the virtual slave of the

Board of Admiralty. McKenna Papers, Churchill College 3/3/2A, Asquith to McKenna, 4 July 1908.

40. Bonar Law Papers, House of Lords, 18/6/66, Maxse to A. Bonar Law, 5 June 1908.

41. J.H. Lewis Papers, NLW, 10/230, 8 September 1908.

42. LG to R. Chalmers, 5 September 1908, in Anver Offer, *Property and Politics, 1870-1914,* Cambridge, 1981. p. 323.

43. Fisher to Esher, 5 May 1908 in John, Baron Fisher, *Memories,* London, 1919, p. 186. See also Marder, *Dreadnought,* I, 142.

44. The letter, and Tweedmouth's reply, including the small 1908-9 naval estimates which parliament had not yet seen, were suppressed at the time but finally appeared in the *Morning Post* on 30 October 1914.

45. Brett, *Esher Journals,* II, 329-30, Journal, 23 July 1908.

46. David Lloyd George, *War Memoirs* Boston, 1933, I, 12-14.

47. Lloyd George, *War Memoirs,* I, 19-20.

48. *Ibid.,* I, 14.

49. *Times,* 29 July 1908.

50. *Ibid.*

51. *Times,* 30 July 1908.

52. Spender calls Lloyd George the 'travelling guest of Henry.' He does not mention that Mrs. Henry accompanied the party. Harold Spender, *Prime Minister,* London, 1920, p. 150.

53. Lloyd George, *War Memoirs,* I, 27-8.

54. Harold Spender, *Fire Of Life,* London, n.d. [1926] p. 162.

55. Francis Oppenheimer, *Stranger Within,* London, 1960, p. 183. After the war Oeser confirmed publicly at a Democratic party meeting that he had approached Bulow on Lloyd George's behalf. 'Missed Opportunity,' *Times,* 17 January 1921.

56. Lloyd George, *War Memoirs,* I, 28-9. There is evidence that Spender was encouraging Lloyd George in these excursions. With others of the radical pacifist wing of the Liberal party he shared a suspicion of the anti-Germanism of the permanent officials in the Foreign Office and may have hoped to use his friendship with the Chancellor to circumvent them.

57. J. Hugh Edwards, *The Life of David Lloyd George,* London: n.d. [1913], IV, 100-2.

58. Quoted in M.L. Dockrill, 'David Lloyd George and Foreign Policy Before 1914,' in A.J.P. Taylor, ed., *Lloyd George, Twelve Essays,* New York, 1971, p. 9.

59. *Daily News,* 19 August 1908.

60. Asquith Papers, Vol. XI, Asquith to LG, 20 August 1908.

61. *Ibid.,* LG to Asquith, 21 August 1908.

62. *Times,* 22 August 1908.

63. Randolph Churchill, *Winston Churchill,* Boston, 1967, II, Companion Volume 2, 836, Hardinge to Edw VII, 24 August 1908.

64. Quoted in Philip Magnus, *King Edward VII,* New York, 1964, p. 411.

65. *Times,* 17 August 1908.

66. See for example: *National Review,* LII (October 1908), 13-14.

67. Winston S. Churchill, *The World Crisis,* New York, 1924, I, 51-52.

68. Gainford Papers, Nuffield College, Box 38, J.A. Pease diary, 1908-1911, 4 October 1908.

69. Lucy Masterman, T.S. Diary, Chap. 2, pp. 12-13, Chap. 3, pp. 17-18.

70. Gainford Papers, Pease Diary, 30 October 1908. Furniss duly received his peerage in 1910.

71. *Daily News,* 27 August 1908.

72. *Times,* 27 August 1908.

73. D.R. Daniel, Memoir, I, NLW, p. 15.

74. Churchill, *Churchill,* II, 265.

75. George, Lord Riddell, *More Pages From My Diary,* London, 1934, p. 1, diary, 'October 1908.'

76. The Board of Trade's Abstract of Labour Statistics showed trade union unemployment in October 1908 to be 9.5% compared to 4.2% in October 1907.

77. *Nation,* 7 March 1908.

78. 'A Radical of '85', 'Liberalism Without Ideas,' *Westminster Review,* CLXIX (February 1908), 137-50.

79. J.H. Lewis Papers, NLW, 10/230, diary 8 September 1908.

80. Riddell, *More Pages,* pp. 3, diary 'October 1908.'

81. Speech at Swansea, 1 October 1908, reprinted in Herbert Du Parcq, *The Life of David Lloyd George* London, 1913, IV, 638-44.

82. *Ibid.,* p. 644.

83. *Times,* 11 September 1908. Shackleton said that Gladstone had told him of his intention in a letter which he had received since the conference convened. Quite possibly this was the result of a hint to Gladstone by John Burns who was becoming increasingly jealous of Lloyd George's leadership in social reform.

84. Reprinted: Resolutions of the Annual Meeting of the National Conference of Friendly Societies. 14-16 October 1909, Report of the Parliamentary Agents, p. 26.

85. On Churchill's brief friendship with the Webbs see: Bentley B. Gilbert, 'Winston Churchill versus the Webbs,' *American Historical Review,* LXXI (April 1966), 3, 846-62.

86. Webb, *Partnership,* p. 417, diary, 16 October 1908.

87. Delegate Minutes, Hearts of Oak Benefit Society, 1910-12, London, 9 July 1911, W.G. Bunn 'Original Scheme of State Insurance,' pp.35-7.

88. D.R. Daniel Memoir, NLW, I, p. 18.

89. Alfred G. Gardiner, *Pillars of Society,* London, 1913, p. 290.

90. Independent Order of Odd Fellows, Manchester Unity, Report to Annual Movable Conference, Central Baths Hall, Bradford, by R.W. Moffrey, 5 May 1909, p. 136.

91. Richard, Lord Willoughby DeBroke, *The Passing Years,* London, 1924, pp. 246-7.

92. P.R.O. Cab. 41/31/62, Asquith to Edw VII, 8 July 1908.

93. On the consideration of this change see: Gainford Papers, J.A. Pease diary, 13 October 1908.

94. P.R.O. Cab. 46/31/72, Asquith to Edw VII, 9 December 1908.

95. W. George, *Brother,* p. 222, LG to William George, 25 November 1908. Riddell, *More Pages,* p. 10, diary, 24 November 1908.

96. *Ibid.,* p. 13, diary, 10 December 1908.

97. Gardiner, *Pillars,* p. 287.

98. W. George, *Brother,* p. 222, LG to W. George, 9 December 1908.

99. *Times,* 7 December 1908.

100. Lucy Masterman, *C.F.G. Masterman,* London, 1939, p. 114.

101. Arthur Ponsonby Papers, Bodleian Library, MS Eng Hist, C657, ff 184-5, Masterman to Ponsonby, 'Monday' 21 December 1908.

102. *Times,* 12 December 1908.

103. Churchill, *Churchill,* II, 312.

104. 'The Position of Mr. Lloyd George,' *Nation,* 6 January 1912.

105. David Lloyd George, *Better Times,* London, 1910, p. vii.

106. Gainford Papers, Nuffield College, Pease Diary, 8 December 1908.

107. David, ed., *Hobhouse Diary,* p. 74, diary, 8 December 1908.

108. *Times,* 22 December 1908.

109. LG to J.A. Spender, 24 May 1909, Quoted in Richard Kezirian, 'David Lloyd George and the Origins of the British Welfare State,' Unpublished Ph.D. dissertation, 1976, U. of Cal., Santa Barbara, p. 93.

110. Asquith, for example, made clear during the discussions of the 1909 legislative program that he did not wish to plan for an autumn session. P.R.O. Cab. 41/32/1, Asquith to Edw. VII, 26 January 1909.

111. Riddell, *More Pages,* p. 10, 24 November 1908.

112. LG to W. George, 1 May 1909 in W. George, *Brother,* p. 226.

113. Churchill to Asquith, 26 December 1908 in Churchill, *Churchill,* II, Comp. Vol. 2, 860.

114. Churchill to Asquith, 29 December 1908, *Ibid.,* 863.

115. Churchill to H.W. Massingham, 22 January 1909, *Ibid.,* 873.

116. For the evidence see: Marder, *Dreadnought,* I, 151-5.

117. P.R.O. Cab. 41/31/74, Asquith to Edw VII, 19 December 1908.

118. LG to McKenna, n.d. [10 September 1908], McKenna Papers, Churchill College, 3/20/2; McKenna to LG, 12 September 1908, LGP, H of L, C/5/12/1.

119. McKenna Papers, *Ibid.,* 3/20/8,9,10, Churchill to McKenna, 19 September 1908.

120. David, ed., *Hobhouse Diaries,* p. 74, 17 November 1908. One must question the overall quality of many of Hobhouse's early diary reports.

121. See: Lloyd George to W.S.C., 21 December 1908 quoted in Churchill, *Churchill,* II, 497.

122. LG to W.S.C., 3 January 1909 in *Ibid.,* 498.

123. G.M. Trevelyan, *Grey of Fallodon,* New York, 1937, p. 241-2.

124. Memorandum by John Jellicoe, quoted in Marder, *Dreadnought,* I, 161.

125. LGP, H of L, C/6/11/2, LG to Asquith, 2 February 1909.

126. LGP, H of L, C/6/11/5, LG to 'P.M.', 8 February 1908.

127. Churchill, *Crisis,* I, 33.

128. P.R.O., Cab., 41/32/4, Asquith to Edw VII, 15 February 1909.

129. Quoted in J.A. Spender and Cyril Asquith, *The Life of Lord Oxford and Asquith,* London, 1932, I, 254.

130. McKenna Papers, 6/2/09, Fisher to McKenna, 21 February 1909.

131. Quoted in Stephen McKenna, *Reginald McKenna*, London, 1948, pp. 82-83.

132. British Library, Add. MS. 46388, Spender Papers, Vol. III, J.A. Spender to LG, 18 February 1909.

133. Uncharacteristically Asquith, in a letter to Margot on 25 February, attempted to steal for himself the credit for the Chancellor's ingenious settlement. Quoted in Spender, *Asquith*, I, 254.

134. P.R.O. Cab. 41/32/5, Asquith to Edw VII, 5 March 1908.

135. Quoted in Marder, *Dreadnought*, p. 162. To no one's surprise the second four ships were authorized by McKenna on 26 July.

136. See: P.R.O. Cab. 41/32/10, Asquith to Edw VII, 31 March 1909. Cabinets of 30, 31 March.

137. P.R.O. Cab. 42/32/10.

138. P.R.O., Cab. 37/99/57, 'Super Tax,' 31 March 1909. However for the 1909 Budget, because of difficulties in establishing the system of collection, Lloyd George calculated super tax revenue would be only £500,000. This figure was continually attacked in the House of Commons as an underestimate, as indeed it turned out to be.

139. Asquith to Edw VII, 6, 7 April 1909. These letters have been omitted from the Public Record Office index of Cabinet letters although the documents themselves exist at Windsor.

140. W. George, *Brother*, p. 223, 6 April 1909.

141. In his diary, Burns admitted he disliked the Budget and its author. B. L. Add. MS. 46,327, Burns Papers, Diary, 1 April 1909.

142. D.R. Daniel, Memoir, I, 21 May 1909.

143. *Official Report, House of Commons Debates*, Series V, Volume IV (23 April 1909), col. 507. Churchill put it more succinctly: 'The state will ask not only "how much have you got?" but, "how did you get it?"'

144. The proportion of individual earnings taken by income tax in Britain was nearly twice as high in 1978 as that of any other member of the E.E.C., except Ireland, and it provided more than twice as great a proportion of government revenue as in West Germany and France. John D. Hey, *Britain In Context*, Oxford, 1979, pp. 152-3.

145. *H of C Deb.*, IV (9 May 1909), col. 755-6.

146. P.R.O. Cab. 37/96/161.

147. P.R.O., Cab. 37/97/9, 'The Taxation of Land Values in New York,' 29 January 1909.

148. P.R.O. Cab., 37/98/44, D Ll-G, 'The Taxation of Land Values,' 13 March 1909.

149. LGP, H of L, C/26/1/2.

150. Riddell, *More Pages*, p. 65, diary, 27 May 1912.

151. Masterman, *Masterman*, p. 121, Masterman to Asquith, 15 January 1909.

152. *Ibid.*, p. 129-30, 31 May 1909 (misdated 1908).

153. David, ed., *Hobhouse Diaries*, p. 76, diary, 7 March 1909.

154. *H of C Deb.*, IV (29 April 1909), col. 540.

155. P.R.O., Cab., 37/97/10, 'Taxation of Land Values,' P.M., 22 January 1909. In the covering note Asquith declared that he was 'neutral' on the matters under discussion.

156. P.R.O., Cab., 37/97/16, 'Taxation of Land Values,' D. Ll.G., 30 Jan uary 1909, 6 pages.

157. Quoted in: H.V. Emy, 'The Land Campaign,' in Taylor, ed., *Twelve Essays*, 1971, p. 42.

158. P.R.O., Cab., 37/97/16, 29 January 1909.

159. D.R. Daniel Memoir, I, p. 32, 21 May 1909.

160. J.H. Lewis Papers, NLW, 10/230 conversation, 28 February 1909.

161. P.R.O., Cab., 41/32/7, Asquith to Edw VII, 19 March 1909.

162. Bruce K. Murray, *The People's Budget*, Oxford, 1980, pp. 180-84.

163. *Times*, 19 March 1909.

164. P.R.O., Cab., 37/97/9, 'Taxation of Land Values in New York,' 21 January 1909, p. 7.

165. *People*, 3 January 1909.

166. LGP, NLW, 20463C/2423, Rowland to LG, nd.

167. *Times*, 13 March 1909; *People*, 14 March 1909.

168. Richard Lloyd George, *My Father Lloyd George*, New York, 1961, pp. 111-2.

169. W. George, *Brother*, p. 223, LG to W. George, 16 March 1909.

170. This statement appears in Lloyd George, *My Father*, p. 111 and Donald McCormick, *The Mask of Merlin*, London, 1963, pp. 310-11, who says also that the woman was an actress but gives no source.

171. Colin Cross, ed., *Life with Lloyd George, The Diary of A.J. Sylvester*, London, 1975, p. 101, diary, 6 October 1933; Riddell, *More Pages*, pp. 4-5.

172. Gainford Papers, J.A. Pease diary, 1908-11, 15 February 1909.

173. W. George, *Brother*, p. 201.

174. Robert Speaight, *The Life of Hilaire Belloc*, New York, 1957, p. 233.

175. *H of C Deb.*, IV (29 April 1909), cols. 472-549.

176. *Ibid.*, col. 485.

177. Annual Statement, Hearts of Oak Friendly Society, Minutes of Annual Meetings, 1909, p. 67. In this connection it should be noted that Churchill's planning for unemployment insurance was far more advanced than Lloyd George's for invalidity insurance. Churchill however had agreed not to introduce his measure until 1910 although he insisted that Lloyd George mention unemployment insurance in the budget speech. LGP, NLW, 20462C/2294, WSC to LG, 8 April 1909.

178. Stephen Koss, *Sir John Brunner, Radical Plutocrat*, Cambridge, 1970, p. 206.

179. *H. of C. Deb.*, IV, (29 April 1909) cols. 549-50.

180. *Ibid.*, (3 May 1909), cols. 755-6.

181. Almeric Fitzroy, *Memoirs*, London: n.d. [1925], I, 377, diary, 3 May 1909.

182. *Times*, 3 May, 1909.

183. D.R. Daniel, Memoir, I, 21 May 1909, pp. 31.

184. J.A. Spender, *Life, Journalism and Politics*, New York, n.d. [1927], I, 231.

185. Masterman, *Masterman*, p. 134, undated.

186. B. L. Add. MS. 46388, J.A. Spender Papers, III, LG to Spender, 24 May 1909.

187. Arthur, Viscount Lee of Fareham, 'A Good Innings and A Great Partnership,' privately printed, 1939, I, 402.

188. David, ed., *Hobhouse Diaries*, p. 78, 17 June 1909.

189. This letter is dated 12 July, but evidently should be dated 12 June, W. George, *Brother*, p. 228.

190. *H of C Deb.*, VII (13 July 1909), cols. 1878-83.

191. W. George, *Brother*, p. 228, 13 July 1909.

192. *Times*, 14 July 1909.

193. Strachey Papers, H of L, S/2/4/14, Strachey to Balfour, 9 July 1909.

194. Gainford Papers, Box 38, J.A. Pease diary, 16 July 1909.

195. B. L. Add. MS. 46327, John Burns diary, 16 July 1909.

196. The trend in by-elections of 1908 would have given the Unionists a majority of 150 although the Conservative central office expected officially only twenty. Neal Blewett, *The Peers, The Parties and the People, The General Elections of 1910*, London, 1972, p. 62.

197. The summer of 1909 saw the appearance of one of Asquith's periodic bouts with alcohol which caused much comment even among men who admired the Prime Minister greatly. See: David, ed., *Hobhouse Diary*, p. 79, diary, 1 July 1909; Fitzroy, *Memoirs*, p. 382, diary, 1 September 1909.

198. B. L., Add. MS. 46388, J.A. Spender Papers, III, LG to Spender, 16 July 1909.

199. On 25 July he wrote Maggie complaining that he had been too busy to think about the speech. 'That's serious,' he concluded. LGP, NLW, 20429C/1299.

200. The Limehouse speech is printed in full in DuParcq, *LG*, IV, 678-85.

201. LGP, H of L, C/5/5/1, LG to Edw VII, 5 August 1909. The copy of this letter in the Lloyd George papers contains corrections in what appears to be Asquith's manuscript.

202. *Ibid.*, C/5/5/2, Edw VII to LG, 7 August 1909.

203. See, for example, *Punch*, 18 August 1909.

204. W. George, *Brother*, p. 230.

205. Masterman, *Masterman*, p. 143.

206. *Times*, 2, 4 August 1909.

207. Quoted in Alfred Gollin, *The Observer and J.L. Garvin*, London, 1960, p. 107 and note.

208. Leopold Amery, *My Political Life* (London: 1953), I, 343.

209. J. Amery, *The Life of Joseph Chamberlain* (New York: 1969), VI, 935-7.

210. Blewett, *Peers*, p. 64.

211. The original letter is lost, but Lloyd George's reply makes its contents clear. LGP, NLW, 20462C/2362, LG to St. David's, 26 August 1909. Blewett has calculated that two-thirds of the peers voting against the budget owned more than five thousand acres. Blewett, *Peers*, p. 77.

212. David, ed., *Hobhouse Diaries*, p. 80, 31 October 1909.

213. Blanche Dugdale confesses that the moment of decision was 'unmarked.' Blanche Dugdale, *Arthur James Balfour* London, 1936, II, 57.

214. A. Chamberlain to Mary E. Chamberlain, 20 September 1909, quoted in J. Amery, *Chamberlain*, VI, 937.

215. P.R.O. Cab. 37/100/121, 7 September 1909; P.R.O. Cab. 41, Asquith to Edw VII, 8 September 1909. This letter does not appear in the Public Record Office

index. See also Lloyd George's letter to William, 8 September 1909, W. George, *Brother*, p. 230.

216. John Grigg, *Lloyd George, The People's Champion*, Berkeley, 1978, p. 217.

217. Gollin, *Garvin*, p. 109-110.

218. *Ibid.*, p. 113.

219. *Times*, 23 September 1909.

220. *H. of C Deb.* IX (10 August 1909), col. 313.

221. *H of C Deb.* IX (11 August 1909), col. 438. Asquith, who was not easily shaken, referred to the 'unusual vehemence' of Balfour's remarks. *Ibid.*, col. 314.

222. Murray, *People's Budget*, pp. 212-3.

223. Gainford Papers, Pease diary, 6 September 1909.

224. Brett, ed., *Esher Journals*, II, 421.

225. G.K.A. Bell, *Randall Davidson, Archbishop of Canterbury*, London, 1938, p. 595.

226. B. L. Add. MS 46327, John Burns Diary, 3 September 1909. During one late session Churchill was detected on the Treasury Bench with pink pajamas rolled up under his suit.

227. Fitzroy, *Memoirs*, I, 383, 8 September 1909.

228. LG to W. George, 8 September 1909 in W. George, *Brother*, p. 230.

229. LGP, NLW, 20463C/2393, A.H.D. Acland to LG, 16 September 1909.

230. Magnus, *Edward VII*, p. 437.

231. *Ibid.*, p. 437.

232. LG to W. George, 19 October 1909 (perhaps misdated) in W. George, *Brother*, p. 232.

233. DuParcq, *LG*, IV, 686-96.

234. F.E. Hamer, *The Personal Papers of Lord Rendel*, London, 1931, p. 234.

235. Quoted in Offer, *Property and Politics*, p. 379.

236. Fitzroy, *Memoirs*, I, 385.

237. P.R.O. Cab. 41/42/40, Asquith to Edw VII, 3 November 1909.

238. LG to MLG, 16 November 1909 in Morgan, *Letters*, pp. 151-2.

239. P.R.O. Cab., 41/32/42, Asquith to Edw VII, 24 November 1909.

240. *Official Report, House of Lords Debates*, Series V, IV (24 November 1909), col. 953.

241. DuParcq, *LG*, IV, 697-8.

Chapter 7, pp. 399-466

1. Lucy Masterman, *C.F.G. Masterman*, London, 1939, pp. 138-9.

2. Lucy Masterman, Typescript diary in the possession of Neville Masterman, pp. 1-2.

3. Masterman, *Masterman*, p. 212.

4. Masterman, Typescript diary, Chap. VIII, p. 10, dictated 31 July 1911.

5. *Times*, 30 December 1909.

6. See *Times*, 22,23,24 December 1909.

7. See his remarks on the unsatisfactory canvass, LG to MLG, 12 January, 1910 in Kenneth Morgan, *Lloyd George Family Letters*, Cardiff, 1973, p. 152; and his speech to

Criccieth Liberals, *South Wales Daily News*, 30 December, 1909 in LGP, H of L, C/33/2/32.

8. A number of these speeches are reprinted in Herbert DuParcq, *The Life of David Lloyd George* London, 1913, IV, 707-65.

9. See the excellent maps in Michael Kinnear, *The British Voter*, London, 1968, pp. 26-33.

10. Asquith Papers, Bodleian Library, Vol. XII, Harcourt to Asquith, 26 January 1910.

11. Quoted in Bruce K. Murray, *The People's Budget*, Oxford, 1980, p. 259.

12. Daniel, Memoir, National Library of Wales, I, p. 35.

13. For example the party's principal pamphlet, 'The People's Budget', was dated 20 November, 1909, which was two days before Lansdowne moved his amendment of rejection of the budget.

14. See: Murray, *Budget*, pp. 188-90.

15. Harold Spender, *The Prime Minister*, London, 1919, p. 163.

16. Mary Fels, *Joseph Fels, His Life-Work*, New York, 1916, p. 146.

17. Gainford Papers, Nuffield College, J.A. Pease Diary, 3 December 1909.

18. Harold Spender, *Fire of Life*, London, n.d. [1926], p. 138.

19. Masterman, Typescript Diary, Chap. III, p. 18.

20. George, Lord Riddell, *More Pages From My Diary*, London, 1934, p. 18, 'January 1910.'

21. Randolph Churchill, *Winston Churchill* Boston, 1967, II, Comp. Vol. 2, 102-8, Sir Joseph Lawrence to J.S. Sandars, 20 November 1910.

22. LGP, H of L, C/6/10/3, O'Connor to LG, 9 February 1910.

23. P.R.O. Cab. 41/32/46, Asquith to Edw VII.

24. *Times,* 11 December 1909.

25. Philip Magnus, *King Edward the Seventh*, New York, 1964, p. 441.

26. Wilfred Scawen Blunt, *My Diaries* London, 1919, II, 289.

27. *Ibid.*

28. Dennis Gwynn, *The Life of John Redmond*, London, 1932, pp. 162-5.

29. See LGP, H of L, C/6/10/1, 2, T.P. O'Connor to LG, 25 September, 30 October 1909.

30. PRO. Cab., 41/32/46, Asquith to Edw VII, 11 February 1910.

31. Arthur Murray, *Master and Brother*, London, 1945, p. 47.

32. LGP, H of L, C/7/3/2, Redmond to LG, 17 February 1910.

33. Murray, *Master*, p. 39.

34. *Official Report, House of Commons Debates*, XIV (21 February 1909), col. 55.

35. Churchill, *Churchill*, II, Comp Vol 2, p. 977, C.P. Scott to W.S.C., 24 February 1910.

36. J.H. Lewis Papers, National Library of Wales, 10/231, Diary, 25 February 1910; P.R.O. Cab., 41/32/51, Asquith to Edw VII, 25 February 1910.

37. *H of C Deb.*, XIV (28 February 1909), col. 594-5.

38. *Ibid.*, cols. 605-6.

39. Grey to Asquith, 25 March 1910 in Keith Robbins, *Sir Edward Grey*, London, 1971, p. 216.

40. See: Edward David, ed., *Inside Asquith's Cabinet, The Diaries of Charles Hobhouse,* London, 1977, p. 89, 16 April 1910.

41. *Times,* 17 March 1910.

42. *H of C Deb.,* XVI (18 April 1910), cols. 1739-1751. on the O'Brien negotiations see Hudson, Lord Devonport, *The Travelled Road,* privately printed, n.d. [1930], pp. 190-7.

43. *Ibid.*

44. Masterman, Typescript diary, Chapter IV, pp. 5-10.

45. *Ibid.*

46. Murray, *Master,* p. 46.

47. Masterman, *Masterman,* p. 162. Mrs. Masterman is maddeningly unclear on dates but this is certainly either the Cabinet of 12 April or of 13 April.

48. Murray, *Master,* p. 46. There are many versions of this crisis. Generally courtesy to Asquith and/or the King renders them incomprehensible. See for example: R.J. Scally, *The Origins of the Lloyd George Coalition,* Princeton, 1975, pp. 169-70.

49. This extremely important Cabinet letter does not appear in the List and Index Society Calendar of Cabinet letters at Windsor. It is to be found however in Asquith Papers, Bodleian Library, Volume V, Asquith to Edw VII, 13 April 1910.

50. *H of C Deb.,* XVI, (14 April 1910), cols. 1547-8.

51. *H of C Deb.,* XVI (18 April 1910), cols. 1762-4.

52. Magnus, *Edward VII,* pp. 453, 457.

53. *Ibid.,* p. 454.

54. Morgan, *Letters,* p. 152.

55. Alfred Gollin, *The Observer and J.L. Garvin,* London, 1960, pp. 185-6.

56. Masterman, *Masterman,* p. 163.

57. Quoted in Scally, *Lloyd George Coalition,* p. 181.

58. Masterman, *Masterman,* p. 163.

59. The best recent study of the Constitutional Conference appears in John D. Fair, *British Interparty Conferences,* Oxford, 1980, pp. 77-102; see also Corrine Comstock Weston, 'The Liberal Leadership and the Lords' Veto, 1907-1910,' *Historical Journal,* XI (1968), 3, 508-37. Each account uses extensively the notes of the conference kept by Austen Chamberlain, which, with some memoranda by Lansdowne, constitute the principal written record of the proceedings.

60. See: Fair, *Conferences,* pp. 89-90.

61. See for example: Scally, *Lloyd George Coalition,* passim. In fact Lloyd George thought so little of the coalition memorandum that within two years he could not find either of the two copies he had made. Bonar Law Papers, House of Lords, 31/1/3 Austen Chamberlain, 'Memorandum of a Conversation with Winston Churchill,' 27 November 1913.

62. David Lloyd George, *War Memoirs* Boston, 1933, I, 31-9.

63. The coalition memoranda, one of 17 August and a second, shorter, explanatory document of 29 October, are in LGP, H of L, C/16/9/1,3. The two have been reprinted in Scally, *Lloyd George Coalition,* p. 375-86. The reprint in John Grigg's biography of Lloyd George omits, without indication, a substantial portion of the first document. Although there are several typewritten drafts of the memorandum in the Lloyd George papers, the composition appears to have been very much his own. Even the final draft contains several misspellings and inaccurately used words

and displays the aimless wandering between passive and active voice that was characteristic of his writing.

64. D.R. Daniel Memoir, National Library of Wales, Vol. II, pp. 32-4.

65. Austen Chamberlain, *Politics From Inside,* London, 1936, p. 287.

66. On the preparation of this document, which she assumes is the original coalition memorandum, see: Lucy Masterman, *Masterman,* pp. 170-2.

67. Chamberlain, *Politics,* p. 293.

68. *H of C Deb.,* XVIII (30 June 1910), cols 1141-2.

69. Much of this document is printed in: Henry N. Bunbury, ed., *Lloyd George's Ambulance Wagon, The Memoirs of W.J. Braithwaite,* London, 1957, pp. 73-6.

70. For data on the movement in 1910 see: *Whitaker's Almanack,* 1911, pp. 351-3.

71. G.B. Wilkie, *The Nationalization of Insurance,* London, 1931, p. 36.

72. Chamberlain, *Politics,* p. 292.

73. Gainford Papers, Nuffield College, J.A. Pease Diary, 3 November 1910; David, ed., *Hobhouse Diaries,* p. 87, 20 February 1910.

74. The two seemed to be almost sentimental friends, reflected Beatrice Webb after entertaining them together in March 1908. Beatrice Webb, *Our Partnership,* London, 1948, p. 404.

75. Masterman, *Masterman,* pp. 169-70.

76. Morgan, *Letters,* p. 153.

77. LGP, NLW, 20429C/1336,1337; Masterman, *Masterman,* p. 170.

78. See: Anvér Offer, *Property and Politics, 1870-1914,* Cambridge, 1981, p. 364.

79. Churchill, *Churchill,* II, Comp. Vol. 2, 1023-4, LG to WSC, 25 September 1910.

80. Riddell, *More Pages,* p. 277, 2 July 1912.

81. See his bread and butter letter to Lloyd George. Churchill, *Churchill,* II, Comp. Vol. 2, pp. 1024-5, 6 October 1910.

82. Masterman, *Masterman,* pp. 164-5.

83. Earl of Birkenhead, *Frederick Edwin, Earl of Birkenhead* London, 1933, I, 205.

84. Chamberlain, *Politics,* p. 286, Chamberlain to Cawdor, 21 October 1910.

85. LGP, H of L, C/4/1/1, LG to Crewe, 20 October 1910.

86. Asquith Papers, Vol XII, Crewe to Asquith, 22 October; Grey to Asquith, 26 October 1910.

87. Roy Jenkins, *Asquith,* London, 1964, p. 217.

88. DuParcq, *Lloyd George,* IV, 766-75.

89. Lloyd George, *War Memoirs,* I, 36.

90. Gollin, *Garvin,* 213-5, 223-6.

91. Lloyd George, *War Memoirs,* I, 34; Chamberlain, *Politics,* p.293.

92. Maurice V. Brett, ed., *Journals and Letters of Reginald Viscount Esher,* London, 1934, III, 148, Esher to Stamfordham, 28 December 1913.

93. A.J.P. Taylor, ed., *A Diary by Frances Stevenson ,* London, 1971, p. 9, 2 November 1914.

94. LGP, H of L, C/16/9/3, untitled, 'Dictated 29 October 1910.'

95. Chamberlain, *Politics,* p. 289, Balfour to Chamberlain, 27 October 1910.

96. Masterman, *Masterman,* p. 175.

97. *Ibid.*

98. Chamberlain, *Politics,* p. 293.

99. Scally, *Lloyd George Coalition,* p. 209; Masterman, *Masterman,* p. 175.

100. LGP, H of L, C/6/11/8, Asquith to LG, 8 November 1910.

101. Blanche E. Dugdale, *Arthur James Balfour,* London, 1936, II, 77.

102. *Ibid.*

103. Gainford Papers, Nuffield College, J.A. Pease Diary, 1908-11, undated diary entry.

104. David, ed., *Hobhouse Diaries,* pp. 100-1, 2 March 1911.

105. See: Roy Jenkins, *Mr. Balfour's Poodle,* London, 1954, pp. 177-8.

106. Morgan, *Letters,* p. 154.

107. Masterman, *Masterman,* p. 176; David, ed., *Hobhouse Diaries,* p. 99, 20 December 1910.

108. *Times,* 12 December 1910.

109. *Times,* 22 November 1910.

110. See: Gollin, *Garvin,* pp. 245-7; Neal Blewett, *The Peers, The Parties and the People,* London, 1972, pp. 180-81.

111. Chamberlain, *Politics,* p. 195.

112. Leopold Amery, *My Political Life,* London, 1953, I, 365-6.

113. 'Episodes of the Month,' *National Review,* LVI (January 1911), 709-732. The entire section, usually reporting on current events in general, was devoted to this topic. Charles Hobhouse also speculated that the Albert Hall speech might cost Balfour his leadership. David, ed., *Hobhouse Diaries,* p. 99, 20 December 1910.

114. LGP, NLW, 20429C/1349, LG to MLG, 17 December 1910.

115. *Times,* 3, 26 November 1910.

116. *Insurance Mail,* 17 December 1910.

117. *Ibid.*

118. *Financier,* 2 December 1910.

119. *Assurance Agents Chronicle,* 10 December, 1910; *Insurance Mail,* 17 December 1910.

120. *Insurance Mail,* 24 June 1911.

121. LGP, NLW, 20430C/1350, LG to MLG, 9 January 1911.

122. *Ibid.*

123. On the leaders of the Combine see; Bunbury, ed., *Braithwaite Memoirs,* pp. 96-98.

124. *Ibid.,* pp. 113-5.

125. Braithwaite Papers, Library of Economic and Political Science, Part II, Item 9, J.S. Bradbury to G.F. Hardy, 13 January 1911.

126. See the bitter comments of W.G. Bunn, 'Original Scheme of State Insurance,' 9 June 1911, delegate minutes, Hearts of Oak Benefit Society, p. 37. For a reaction to Bunn's revelations see: the Reverend J. Frome Wilkinson, 'The National Insurance Bill,' *Contemporary Review,* C (October 1911), 501-18.

127. Asquith Papers, Vol. VII, Asquith to George V, 20 January 1911; see also Gainford Papers, J.A. Pease Diary, 20 January 1911.

128. Murray, *Master,* pp. 88-9.

129. PRO Cab. 37/96/159, 'Unemployment Insurance: Labour Exchanges,' 30 November 1908.

130. LGP, NLW, 20463C/2445, Murray to LG, 24 January 1911.

131. Churchill, *Churchill*, II, Companion Volume 2, 1069, W.S.C. to C. Churchill, 22 April 1911.

132. J.H. Lewis Papers, NLW, 10/231, diary, 17 April 1910.

133. See: Gollin, *Garvin*, pp. 326-332.

134. Quoted in Scally, *Lloyd George Coalition*, p. 219.

135. See: Bunbury, ed., *Braithwaite Memoirs*, pp. 173-4. On Chamberlain's view of the scheme see: Chamberlain, *Politics*, pp. 336-8.

136. PRO, Cab. 37/106/40, 'Insurance Scheme, D. Ll.G.,' 30 March 1911.

137. Bunbury, ed., *Braithwaite Memoirs*, p. 127.

138. PRO, Cab. 37/106/40, 'Insurance Scheme' 23 pp., p. 10.

139. *Ibid.*, p. 18-19.

140. Bunbury, ed., *Braithwaite Memoirs*, p. 141.

141. Christopher Addison's view of himself as the chief interpreter of medical opinion to the Exchequer is certainly overstated. Christopher Addison, *Politics From Within* London, 1924, I, 20-1.

142. PRO, Cab. 37/106/40, pp. 22-3.

143. Riddell, *More Pages*, p. 54, 17 April 1912.

144. PRO, Cab. 41/33/9, Asquith to George V, 5 April 1911.

145. *H of C Deb.*, XXV (4 May 1911), cols. 609-45.

146. *Ibid.*, col. 645.

147. Riddell, *More Pages*, p. 33, misdated 12 December 1911.

148. *H of C Deb.*, XXVI (1 June 1911), cols. 1229-36.

149. *H of C Deb.*, XXXVIII (6 May 1912), cols. 178-9; *British Medical Journal*, Supplement, 17 June 1911, p. 441.

150. *British Medical Journal*, 13, 20, May 1911, pp. 1137, 1191-4.

151. *H of C Deb.*, XXV (4 May 1911) col. 629.

152. *British Medical Journal*, Supplement, 3 June 1911, p. 354.

153. Herbert DeCarle Woodcock, *The Doctor and the People*, London, 1912, p. 77.

154. *H of C Deb.*, XXIX (1 August 1911), col. 318.

155. *Insurance Mail*, 12 August 1911.

156. Bunbury, ed., *Braithwaite Memoirs*, p. 168.

157. *National Review*, LVIII (October 1911), 241-49.

158. See, British Library, Add. MS., 49736, Balfour Papers, CIV, Chamberlain to Balfour, 16 October 1911, Balfour to Chamberlain, 17 October 1911. See also Bonar Law Papers, H of L, 24/5/149, A. Steel Maitland to Bonar Law, 20 December 1911. Two doctors had asked for, and evidently received, £200 to canvass for a doctors' boycott of health insurance.

159. LGP, NLW, 20430C/1363, LG to MLG, 31 July 1911.

160. Gainford Papers, J.A. Pease Diary, 6 July 1910. Eventually, in November 1910, the Cabinet determined to introduce legislation allowing unions, under certain restrictions, to establish political funds. David Marquand, *Ramsay MacDonald*, London, 1977, pp. 123-4.

161. See for example, C.J. Wrigley, *David Lloyd George and The British Labour Movement*, Hassocks, 1976 p. 39.

162. Morgan, *Letters*, p. 157, LG to MLG, 10 August 1911. This was also the day of the critical House of Lords vote on the Parliament Bill. Lloyd George wrote the next day of the Liberal victory with deep satisfaction: 'The dream…of generations at last realized….So pleased I am responsible for it. The Budget did it.' *Ibid.*, 11 August 1911.

163. *H of C Deb.*, XXIX (10 August 1911) cols. 1375-6.

164. See for example Arthur Lee, in *Ibid.*, cols. 1388-9.

165. LGP, H of L, C/6/5/5, Murray to LG, 5 October 1911. In fact the majority of the Labour party was interested chiefly in a reduced contribution from badly paid workers. Braithwaite had already proposed this in February and it was eventually included. Bunbury, ed., *Braithwaite Memoirs*, pp. 196, 246-7.

166. Morgan, *Letters*, p. 160, LG to MLG, 11 August 1911.

167. LGP, H of L, C/6/9/11, O'Brien to LG, 24 October 1911.

168. See Bunbury, ed., *Braithwaite Memoirs*, p. 222.

169. B.L., Add. MS. 46333, Burns Papers, diary, vol. 53, 24, 27, 29 November 1911. The National Insurance Commission in Wales assumed duties Burns had expected would be left to the Local Government Board. The bill was changing so fast, noted Burns in his diary, that he could not recommend a pamphlet about it that was more than a week old.

170. *Assurance Agents' Chronicle*, 1 July 1911.

171. See: Bentley B. Gilbert, *The Evolution of National Insurance in Great Britain*, London, 1966, pp. 358-63, 369-83.

172. See the clear warning to the friendly societies, probably written by Masterman, 'Insurance and Disablement,' *Nation*, 14 October 1911.

173. Braithwaite Papers, L.S.E., Part I, 'Memoirs 1910-12,' Part I, Part 3 'Conference on National Insurance Bill (Clause 18)' 19 October 1911 ('Transcript from Shorthand Notes of R.D. Shedlock.')

174. Bunbury, ed., *Braithwaite Memoirs*, p. 212.

175. Lead article 'Gathering Up the Threads,' *Insurance Mail*, 28 October 1911.

176. *Daily Mail*, quoted in *Westminster Gazette*, 21 November 1911.

177. *Times*, 29 November 1911.

178. *Times*, 30 November 1911.

179. Asquith Papers, Vol. XLVI, Asquith to Crewe, 30 November 1911.

180. Bonar Law Papers, H of L, 24/5/166, Chaplin to A.B.L., 31 December 1911.

181. A.G. Edwards, *Memories*, London, 1927, p. 245.

182. LGP, NLW, 20463C/2424., St. Asaph to LG, 23 March 1911. In this letter the bishop described one of his few bits of evidence, a miniature showing Prince Henry kneeling before James I and receiving a gold rod about two and a half feet in length.

183. W. Watkin Davies, *Lloyd George, 1913-1914*, London, 1939, p. 381. Davies was a boy in Criccieth who knew Lloyd George and attended the investiture.

184. *Times*, 14 July 1911. See also: Churchill, *Churchill*, II, Comp. Vol. 2, 1099, W.S.C. to Clementine, 14 July 1911.

185. B.L. Add. MS 62970 Riddell Diaries, TS, 24 February 1912.

186. General Henry Wilson recalls asking General Ferdinand Foch in January 1910, what he would consider the smallest British military force that would be of any

practical use. 'One single private soldier,' Foch immediately replied, 'and we would take good care that he was killed.' C.E. Callwell, *Field Marshal Sir Henry Wilson, His Life and Diaries* London, 1927, I, 78-9.

187. Gainford Papers, Pease Diary, 16 February 1911; LGP, H of L, C/5/12/6, McKenna to LG, 16 February 1911. See Lloyd George's description of the meeting in Trevor Wilson, ed., *The Political Diaries of C.P.Scott, 1911-1928,* Ithaca, New York, 1970, pp. 39-41, 17 February 1911.

188. Asquith Papers, Vol. VII, Asquith to King George V, 1 March 1911.

189. McKenna Papers, Churchill College, 3/20.

190. *H of C Deb.*, XXV (16 May 1911) cols. 1849-70.

191. *Ibid.*, col. 1853.

192. *Ibid.*, cols. 1854-5.

193. Grey of Fallodon, *Twenty-five Years* New York, 1925, I, 214-5.

194. G.P. Gooch and H. Temperley, ed., *British Documents on the Origin of the War* London, 1932, VII, pp. 377-8, (hereafter, BDOW) Grey to Asquith, 19 July 1911.

195. Grey, *Twenty-five Years*, I, 116-7.

196. *Times*, 22 July 1911.

197. Winston Churchill, *The World Crisis* New York, 1924, I, 42-3. Grey's letter to the Prime Minister also would seem to dispose of A.J.P. Taylor's assertion that the Mansion House speech was directed at France rather than at Germany. A.J.P. Taylor, *The Struggle for the Mastery of Europe*, Oxford, 1954, p. 471 and n.

198. Churchill, *World Crisis*, I, 43.

199. Lloyd George customarily released news through Spender, now of the *Morning Leader*, and P.W. Wilson of the *Daily News*.

200. David Ayerst, *The Manchester Guardian*, Ithaca, New York, 1971, pp. 349, 365-6.

201. Wilson, ed., *Scott Diaries*, pp. 46-8, 22 July 1911.

202. Masterman, *Masterman*, pp. 214-5.

203. Scott, as he had been requested, published no leader on the Mansion House address on Saturday morning. On Monday, however, the *Guardian* carried a carefully balanced statement agreeing that 'vital interests' had to be defended but that France should not be encouraged to believe Britain supported her imperial designs without reservation. Several other non-conformist and Liberal papers were as cautious and equally anti-French. *British Weekly*, 3, 31 August 1911. The Unionist press routinely applauded the new Lloyd George. See: *Times*, 22 July 1911; *Nation*, 6 January 1912; *British Weekly*, 23 November 1911; Ayerst, *Guardian*, pp. 367-8; Alfred Havighurst, *Radical Journalist, H.W. Massingham*, London, 1974, p. 205.

204. Grey, *Twenty-five Years*, I, 220-3.

205. For a recent discussion of German press comment see: Paul Kennedy, *The Rise of the Anglo-German Antagonism, 1860-1914,* London, 1980, pp. 447-50.

206. Grey to Edward Goschen, 25 July 1911, in Grey, *Twenty-five Years*, I, 222.

207. Christopher M.D. Howard, ed., *The Diary of Edward Goschen, 1900- 1914,* London, 1980, p. 212, 12 August 1911.

208. See for example, Goschen to Grey, 26, 29 July 1911, BDOW, VII, 4204, 407.

209. Brett, ed. *Esher Journals*, III, 58, 6 September 1911; S.R. Williamson, *The Politics of Grand Strategy*, Cambridge, Mass. 1969, pp. 187-8.

210. Arthur Marder, *From the Dreadnought to Scapa Flow* London, 1961 I, pp. 244,246.

211. PRO, Cab., 2/2/9, 'Committee of Imperial Defence, Minutes of 114th Meeting,' 23 August 1914, p. 5; Williamson, *Grand Strategy*, p. 169 and n.

212. Cab. 2/2/9, 'C.I.D. Minutes,' p. 8.

213. *Ibid.*, p. 7. Wilson, in fact, had assured the French military attaché, Major Victor Huguet, that this would be the case. Williamson, *Grand Strategy*, p. 173.

214. 'Minutes of C.I.D.,' pp. 11-14.

215. Stephen Roskill, *Hankey, Man of Secrets* New York, 1970, I, 103.

216. 'Minutes of C.I.D.,' p. 2.

217. R.B. Haldane, *An Autobiography*, London, 1926, p. 277; Sir Frederick Maurice, *The Life of Viscount Haldane of Cloan*, London, 1937, I, 283-4.

218. LGP, H of L, C/3/5/6, LG to W.S.C., 25 August 1911.

219. Churchill, *Churchill,* II, Comp. Vol. 2, pp. 1116-19, WSC to Grey, 30 August, Grey to WSC, 30 August, WSC to LG, 31 August 1911.

220. 'Minutes of C.I.D.,' p. 5.

221. Imperial War Museum, The Diaries of Field Marshal Sir Henry Wilson, 13 September 1914. This passage does not appear in Wilson's published diaries.

222. Imp War Mus, Wilson Diaries, 14 September 1911. The last line is omitted from the published diaries.

223. Morgan, *Letters,* pp. 158-9, LG to MLG, 16 September 1911.

224. LGP, NLW, 20430C/1384, LG to MLG, 14 September 1911.

225. Churchill, *Churchill,* II, Comp. Vol. 2, 1125, LG to W.S.C., 15 September 1911.

226. Chamberlain, *Politics,* p. 363, 23 October 1911.

227. Churchill, *Churchill,* Comp. Vol. 2, 1128, WSC to Clementine, 24 September 1911.

228. Masterman, *Masterman,* p. 199. Mrs Masterman mistakenly places the speech at the Guildhall.

229. Riddell, *Pages,* pp. 21-2 (end of July).

230. See his note to Megan; Morgan, *Letters,* p. 159.

231. Riddell, *Pages,* p. 25, 'November 1911.'

232. McKenna Papers, Churchill College, 4/1/2, Asquith to McKenna, 18 September 1911.

233. Churchill, *Crisis,* I, 66-7.

234. McKenna Papers, 4/1/3, Asquith to McKenna, 10 October 1911.

235. McKenna Papers, 4/2/1, MS note of meeting at Archerfield, 20 October 1911. See also 4/1/8, McKenna to P.M., 17 October 1911; 4/1/10, P.M. to McKenna, 18 October 1911.

236. *Ibid.* 'Notes'.

237. Marder, *Dreadnought,* p. 251.

238. See: David, ed., *Hobhouse Diaries,* pp. 111-12, 20 February 1912; Riddell, *More Pages,* p. 175, 29 September 1913; George, Lord Riddell, *War Diary,* London, 1933, p. 13, 15 August 1914.

239. Asquith Papers, Vol. XIII, Grey to Asquith, 13 September 1911.

240. Marder, *Dreadnought,* p. 233.

241. Wilson, ed., *Scott Diaries,* p. 62, 23 October 1914.

242. Gainford Papers, Pease Diary, 1 November 1911 and marginal note, 24 October

1911; PRO Cab. 41/53/628, Asquith to George V, 2 November 1911; B.L. Add MS, 46,333, John Burns Diary, 15 November 1911; David, ed., *Hobhouse Diaries,* pp. 107-8, 16 November 1911.

243. Callwell, *Wilson,* I, 106-7.

244. See: A.S. Morris, *Radicalism Against War,* Totowa, New Jersey, 1972, pp. 248-51; Havighurst, *Massingham,* pp. 204-8.

245. *British Weekly,* 9 November 1911.

246. *Ibid.,* 23, 30 November 1911.

247. Quoted in Frank Eyck, *G.P. Gooch,* Atlantic Highland, N.J., 1982, p. 138. For a general discussion see: Morris, *Radicalism,* pp. 250-72.

248. Steven Gwynn ed., *The Letters and Friendships of Sir Cecil Spring-Rice,* London, 1929, II, 163, 1 August 1911.

249. G.R. Askwith, *Industrial Problems and Disputes,* London, 1920, p. 74.

250. Masterman, *Masterman,* p. 204.

251. *Ibid.*

252. M.A. Hamilton, *Arthur Henderson,* London, 1938, pp. 87-8.

253. Philip S. Bagwell, *The Railwaymen,* London, 1963, p. 298.

254. Morgan, *Letters,* p. 158, 19 August 1911.

255. Chamberlain, *Politics,* p. 437, March 1912.

256. LGP, H of L, C/6/11/9, Asquith to LG, 20 August 1911; NLW, 20463C/2045, George V to LG, n.d.

257. *H of C Deb.,* XXIX (22 August 1911) cols. 2345-54.

258. *Ibid.,* col. 2347.

259. Austen Chamberlain Papers, University of Birmingham, AC9/21, Arnold White to Austen Chamberlain, 4 October 1911.

260. Kenneth Morgan, *Keir Hardie,* London, 1975, pp. 243-4.

261. LGP, NLW, 20430C/1359, 1362, LG to MLG, 18, 26, July 1911.

262. LGP, NLW, 20431C/1405, LG to MLG, 12 January 1912.

263. Lucy Masterman, T.S. Diary, IX, p. 25; see also Frances Stevenson, *Lloyd George, The Years That Are Past,* London, 1967, pp. 41-7.

264. Lucy Masterman, T.S. Diary, p. 18.

265. Masterman, *Masterman,* p. 211.

266. *Ibid.,* p. 213.

267. H.W.M., 'The Position of Mr. Lloyd George', *Nation,* 6 January 1912.

Bibliography

Primary Sources

1. Letters and manuscript collections

Asquith Papers, Bodleian Library.

Balfour Papers, British Library.

Bonar Law Papers, House of Lords Record Office.

Braithwaite Papers, London School of Economics.

Burns Papers, MS Diaries, 1908-14, British Library.

Campbell-Bannerman Papers, British Library.

Chamberlain, Austen, Papers, University of Birmingham.

Daniel, David R. 'Memoir of David Lloyd George,' TS, 98pp., National Library of Wales.

Ellis, Thomas Edward, Papers, National Library of Wales.

Gainford Papers, MS Diaries of Joseph A. Pease, 1908-11, 1911-15, Nuffield College.

Gee, Thomas, Papers, National Library of Wales.

Gladstone, Herbert, Papers, British Library.

Lee, Arthur, Viscount Lee of Fareham, 'A Good Innings and a Great Partnership, being the Life Story of Arthur and Ruth Lee,' 3 vols, privately printed, 1939, House of Lords Record Office.

Lee Papers, House of Lords Record Office, Lloyd George file, unsorted.

Lewis, John Herbert, Papers, National Library of Wales.

Lloyd George Papers, House of Lords Record Office, National Library of Wales.

Masterman, Lucy, Diary, TS, Churchill College, Cambridge.

McKenna Papers, Churchill College, Cambridge.

Ponsonby, Arthur, Papers, Bodleian Library.

Reading Papers, India Office Library.

Rendel Papers, National Library of Wales.

Ripon Papers, British Library.

Roberts, John Bryn, Papers, National Library of Wales.

Samuel Papers, House of Lords Record Office.

Spender, John A., Papers, British Library.

Strachey Papers, House of Lords Record Office.

Williams, Llewelyn, MS Diaries, National Library of Wales.

Wilson Papers, Imperial War Museum.

2. Unpublished official documents
   Cabinet Papers, Public Record Office.
   Ministry of Social Security Bill File, National Insurance, 1911.
   Prime Ministers' Letters.

3. Published documents
   Gooch, George Peabody, and Temperley, Harold., eds. *British Documents on the Origins of the War* (London: 1932) VII, VIII.
   Hansard, Parliamentary Debates, Fourth Series.
   House of Commons Papers.
   Official Report, House of Commons Debates, Fifth Series.
   Official Report, House of Lords Debates, Fifth Series.
   Parliamentary Papers.

4. Newspapers and periodicals
   Assurance Agents' Chronicle
   British Medical Journal
   British Weekly
   Cambrian News
   Cardiff Times
   Carnarvon Herald
   Christian World
   Church Times
   Contemporary Review
   Daily Chronicle
   Daily Mail
   Daily News
   Financier
   Insurance Mail
   Journal of the American Medical Association
   Manchester Guardian
   National Insurance Gazette
   Nation
   National Review
   New Liberal Review
   New Statesman
   Nineteenth Century
   North Wales Observer (and Express)
   People
   Review of Reviews
   Roundtable
   Saturday Review
   South Wales Daily News
   Speaker
   Spectator
   The Times
   Western Mail
   Westminster Gazette
   Westminster Review
   Young Wales, A National Magazine for Wales

5. Contemporary pamphlets, polemical material, personal sketches and reference works
   Churchill, Winston Spencer, *Liberalism and the Social Problem*, London, 1909.
   _____*The People's Rights*, London, 1909, reprinted 1970.
   Dictionary of Welsh Biography, 1959.
   Dod's Parliamentary Companion, passim.
   Edwards, Alfred George, *A Handbook of Welsh Church Defence*, London, 1895.
   Gardiner, Alfred G., *Pillars of Society*, London, 1913.
   _____*Prophets, Priests and Kings*, London, 1908.
   Guedalla, Philip, ed., *Slings and Arrows*, London, 1929.
   Hamer, D. A., ed., *Joseph Chamberlain et. al. The Radical Programme*, Brighton, 1971.
   Hey, John D., *Britain in Context*, Oxford, 1979.
   Hobson, John A., *The Crisis of Liberalism: New Issues of Democracy*, London, 1909.

Jane's Fighting Ships, passim.

Liberal Publication Department, *The Government's Record, 1906-1913*, London, 1913.

Liberal Year Book, passim.

Lloyd George, David, *Better Times*, London, n.d. [1910].

——————*The People's Insurance*, London, n.d. [1911].

Lowell, A. Lawrence, *The Government of England*, (New York: 1919), II.

McCalmont's Parliamentary Poll Book of All Elections 1832-1918, reprinted Brighton, 1971.

Morgan, J. Vyrnwy, *A Study in Nationality*, 1911. Reprinted Port Washington, N.Y., 1971.

National Insurance Yearbook, 1913.

Prothero, Rowland E., *The Anti-Tithe Agitation in Wales*, London, 1889.

Stenton, Michael, ed., *Who's Who of British Members of Parliament*, I, 1832-1885 (Hassocks: 1976).

Whitaker's Almanack, passim.

Who's Who, passim.

6. Published letter collections and diaries

Addison, Christopher, *Politics From Within, 1911-1918* (London: 1924), I.

Blunt, Wilfred Scawen, *My Diaries* (London: 1919), II.

Brett, Maurice V., *Journals and Letters of Reginald, Viscount Esher* (London: 1934), I, II.

Brock, Michael and Eleanor, eds., *H. H. Asquith, Letters to Venetia Stanley*, Oxford, 1982.

Callwell, C.E., *Field Marshal Sir Henry Wilson, His Life and Diaries* (London: 1927), I.

Chamberlain, Austen, *Politics From Inside*, London, 1936.

Cross, Colin, ed., *Life With Lloyd George: The Diary of A. J. Sylvester*, London, 1975.

Esher, Oliver, Viscount, ed., *The Captains und the Kings Depart, Journals and Letters of Reginald, Viscount Esher* (New York: 1938), I.

Fitzroy, Almeric, *Memoirs* (London, n.d. [1925]), I.

Gwynn, Stephen, ed., *The Letters and Friendships of Sir Cecil Spring-Rice* (London: 1929), I.

Hamer, F.E., ed., *The Personal Papers of Lord Rendel*, London, 1931.

Hankey, Maurice, Lord, *The Supreme Command, 1914-18* (London: 1961) I.

Masterman, Lucy, *C. F. G. Masterman*, London, 1939.

Morgan, Kenneth, ed., *Lloyd George Family Letters, 1885-1936*, Cardiff, 1973.

Oxford and Asquith, *Memories and Reflections*, Boston, 1928, 2 vols.

Riddell, George, Lord, *More Pages From My Diary, 1908-1914*, London, 1934.

    War Diary, 1914-18, London, 1933.

Roskill, Stephen, *Hankey, Man of Secrets*, (London: 1970), I.

Webb, Beatrice, *Our Partnership*, London, 1948.

Wilson, Trevor, ed., *The Political Diaries of C. P. Scott, 1911-1928*, London, 1970.

Young, Kenneth, ed., *The Diaries of Sir Robert Bruce Lockhart*, London, 1973.

Selected secondary sources

1. Significant Lloyd George biographies and memoirs

Davies, Alfred Thomas, *The Lloyd George I Knew*, London, 1948.

Davies, W. Watkin, *Lloyd George, 1863-1914*, London, 1939.

DuParcq, Herbert, *Life of David Lloyd George* (London: 1913), 4 vols.

Edwards, John Hugh, *From Village Green to Downing Street*, London, 1908.

_____*The Life of David Lloyd George* (London, n.d. [1913]), 4 vols.

Evans, Beriah G., *The Life Romance of Lloyd George*, London, n.d. [1916].

Evans, Olwen Carey, *Lloyd George Was My Father*, Llandysul, 1985.

George, W[illiam] R.P., *Lloyd George, Backbencher*, Llandysul, 1982.

_____*The Making of Lloyd George*, London, 1976.

Grigg, John, *Lloyd George: The People's Champion, 1902-1911*, Berkeley, 1978.

_____*The Young Lloyd George*, London, 1973.

Lloyd George, David, *War Memoirs* (Boston: 1933), I.

Lloyd George, Richard, *My Father Lloyd George*, London, 1960.

Macmillan, Harold, *The Past Masters, Politics and Politicians, 1906-1939*, New York, 1975

McCormick, Donald, *The Mask of Merlin, A Critical Study of David Lloyd George*, London, 1963.

Owen, Frank, *Tempestuous Journey: Lloyd George, His Life and Times*, New York, 1955.

Raymond, E. Thompson, pseud., (Edward Raymond Thompson), *Mr Lloyd George*, New York, 1922.

Rowland, Peter, *David Lloyd George: A Biography*, New York, 1976.

Spender, Harold, *The Prime Minister*, London, 1920.

Sylvester, Albert James, *The Real Lloyd George*, London, 1947.

Taylor, Alan J. P., *Lloyd George, Rise and Fall*, London, 1961.

2. Other useful biographies

Allen, Bernard M., *Sir Robert Morant: A Great Public Servant*, London, 1934.

Amery, Julian, *The Life of Joseph Chamberlain* (London: 1951-69), IV-VI.

Anon., *Albert Spicer, 1847-1934, A Man of His Time*, by 'One of his Family,' London, 1938.

Bell, G.K.A., *Randall Davidson, Archbishop of Canterbury*, London, 1938.

Birkenhead, Earl of, *'F.E.', The Life of F. E. Smith, First Earl of Birkenhead*, London, 1933

Blake, Robert, *The Unknown Prime Minister*, London, 1955.

Bowle, John, *Viscount Samuel, A Biography*, London, 1957.

Briggs, Asa, *Social Thought and Social Action, A Study of the Work of Seebohm Rowntree, 1871-1954*, London, 1961.

Churchill, Randolph Spencer, *Winston S. Churchill* (London: 1969), II.

Collier, Basil, *Brasshat: A Biography of Field Marshall Sir Henry Wilson*, London, 1961.

Crewe, Lord, *Lord Rosebery* (London: 1931), II.

Darlow, T.H., *William Robertson Nicoll, Life and Letters*, London, 1925.

Dugdale, Blanche E., *Arthur James Balfour* (London: 1936), 2 vols.

Eyck, Frank, *G. P. Gooch*, London, 1982.

Fels, Mary, *Joseph Fels, His Life-Work*, New York, 1916.

Gardiner, Alfred G., *The Life of Sir William Harcourt* (New York, n.d. [1923]), II.

Garvin, J.L., *The Life of Joseph Chamberlain*, (London: 1933), II.

Gooch, George Peabody, *The Life of Lord Courtney*, London, 1920.

Gwynn, Denis, *The Life of John Redmond*, London, 1932.

Hamer, D.A., *John Morley*, Oxford, 1968.

Havighurst, Alfred, *Radical Journalist: H. W. Massingham, 1860-1924*, London, 1974.

Holland, Bernard, *The Life of Spencer Compton, Eighth Duke of Devonshire* (London: 1911), II.

Hyde, H. Montgomery, *Lord Reading*, London, 1967.

James, Robert Rhodes, *Rosebery*, New York, 1963.

Jenkins, Roy, *Asquith*, London, 1964.

        Sir Charles Dilke, London, 1958.

Koss, Stephen, *Sir John Brunner, Radical Plutocrat, 1842-1919*, Cambridge, 1970.

        Fleet Street Radical, A.G. Gardiner and the Daily News, London, 1973.

        John Morley at the India Office, 1905-10, New Haven, 1969.

Lee, Sidney, *King Edward VII* (London: 1927), II.

Lerry, George G., *Alfred George Edwards, Archbishop of Wales*, Oswestry, 1940.

Lyons, F.S.L., *John Dillon, A Biography*, London, 1968.

Magnus, Philip, *King Edward the Seventh*, New York, 1964.

Marchant, Sir James, *Dr. John Clifford, C.H., Life, Letters and Reminiscences*, London, 1924.

Marjoribanks, Edward, *For the Defence, The Life of Sir Edward Marshall Hall*, London, 1929.

Masterman, Neville, *The Forerunner, The Dilemmas of Tom Ellis, 1859-1899*, Llandybie, 1972.

Maurice, Sir Frederick, *Haldane, 1856-1915, The Life of Viscount Haldane of Cloan* (London: 1937), I.

McKenna, Stephen, *Reginald McKenna, 1863-1943*, London, 1948.

Morgan, Kenneth, *Keir Hardie, Radical and Socialist*, London, 1975.

Nicolson, Harold, *King George the Fifth*, London, 1952.

O'Brien, Joseph V., *William O'Brien and the Course of Irish Politics*, Berkeley, 1976.

O'Broin, Leon, *The Chief Secretary, Augustine Birrell in Ireland*, London, 1969.

Owen, Eluned E., *The Later Life of Bishop Owen: A Son of Wales* (Llandysul: 1961), II.

Petrie, Charles, *The Life and Letters of the Right Hon. Sir Austen Chamberlain* (London: 1939), I.

Raymond, E. Thompson, pseud. (Edward Raymond Thompson), *Man of Promise, Lord Rosebery, A Critical Study*, London, 1923.

Reading, Marquess of, *Rufus Isaacs, First Marquess of Reading* (London: 1942), I.

Rhondda, Margaret, Viscountess, *D.A. Thomas, Viscount Rhondda*, London, 1921.

Robbins, Keith, *Sir Edward Grey*, London, 1971.

Snead-Cox, John George, *The Life of Cardinal Vaughan* (London: 1910), II.

Sommer, Dudley, *Haldane of Cloan*, London, 1960.

Speaight, Robert, *The Life of Hilaire Belloc*, New York, 1957.

Spender, John Alfred, *The Life of the Right Hon. Sir Henry Campbell- Bannerman* (London: 1924), 2 vols.

Weetman Pearson, First Viscount Cowdrey, 1856-1927, New York, 1977.

and Asquith, Cyril, *Life of Herbert Henry Asquith, Lord Oxford and Asquith* (London: 1932), 2 vols.

Trevelyan, George M., *Grey of Fallodon,* Boston, 1937.

Ward, Maisie, *Gilbert Keith Chesterton,* London, 1958.

Whyte, Frederic, *The Life of W.T. Stead* (London: 1925), II.

Wilson, John, *C.B., A Life of Sir Henry Campbell-Bannerman,* London, 1973.

3. Studies of special political issues, events, or topics

Ayerst, David, *The Manchester Guardian, Biography of a Newspaper,* Ithaca, 1971.

Bagwell, Philip S., *The Railwaymen: The History of the National Union of Railwaymen,* London, 1963.

Bebbington, D. W., *The Nonconformist Conscience, Chapel and Politics, 1870-1914,* London, 1982.

Blowett, Neal, *The Peers, the Parties and the People, The General Elections of 1910,* London, 1972.

Brown, E.H. Phelps, *The Growth of British Industrial Relations,* London, 1965.

Coupland, Sir Reginald, *Welsh and Scottish Nationalism,* London, 1954.

Davey, Arthur, *The British Pro-Boers, 1877-1902,* Capetown, 1978.

Davies, Elwyn and Rees, Alwyn D., eds., *Welsh Rural Communities,* Cardiff, 1962.

Douglas, Roy, *Land, People and Politics,* New York, 1976.

Dunabin, J.P.D., *Rural Discontent in Nineteenth Century Britain,* London, 1974.

Emmett, Isabel, *A North Wales Village, A Social Anthropological Study,* London, 1964.

Emy, H.V., *Liberals, Radicals and Social Politics, 1892-1914,* Cambridge, 1973.

Fair, John D., *British Interparty Conferences: A Study of the Procedure of Conciliation in British Politics, 1867-1971,* Oxford, 1980.

Freeden, Michael, *The New Liberalism, An Ideology of Social Reform,* Oxford, 1978.

Fry, Michael G., *Lloyd George and Foreign Policy,* I, The Education of a Statesmen, 1890-1916, Montreal, 1977.

Gilbert, Bentley B., *The Evolution of National Insurance in Great Britain: The Origins of the Welfare State,* London, 1966.

Gollin, Alfred, *Balfour's Burden, Arthur Balfour and Imperial Preference,* London, 1961.

Hamer, D.A., *Liberal Politics in the Age of Gladstone and Rosebery,* London, 1972.

Harris, José, *Unemployment and Politics,* Oxford, 1972.

Heyck, Thomas William, *The Dimensions of British Radicalism, The Case of Ireland,* Urbana, Illinois, 1978.

Howell, David W., *Land and People in Nineteenth Century Wales,* London, 1977.

Jalland, Patricia, *The Liberals and Ireland, The Ulster Question in British Politics to 1914,* New York, 1980.

Jenkins, Roy, *Mr. Balfour's Poodle,* London, 1954.

Kennedy, Paul, *The Rise of the Anglo-German Antagonism, 1860-1914,* London, 1980.

Koss, Stephen, *Nonconformity in Modern British Politics,* London, 1975.

Lindsay, Jean, *A History of the North Wales Slate Industry,* Newton Abbot, 1974.

Mallet, Bernard, *British Budgets, 1887-88 to 1912-13,* London, 1913.

Marder, Arthur J., *From the Dreadnought to Scapa Flow, The Royal Navy in the Fisher Era,* I, The Road to War (London: 1961).

Matthew, H.C.G., *The Liberal Imperialists,* London, 1973.

Morgan, Kenneth, *Rebirth of a Nation, Wales, 1880-1980,* New York, 1981.

    Wales in British Politics, 1868-1922, Cardiff, 1970.

Morris, A.J.A., ed., *Edwardian Radicalism, 1900-1914,* London, 1974.

    Radicalism Against War, 1906-1914, Totowa, N.J., 1972.

Murray, Bruce K., *The People's Budget, 1909-10: Lloyd George and Liberal Politics,* Oxford, 1980.

Offer, Anver, *Property and Politics, 1870-1914, Landownership, Law, Ideology and Urban Development in England,* Cambridge, 1981.

Pelling, Henry, *Popular Politics and Society in Late Victorian Britain,* London, 1968.

    Social Geography of British Elections, 1885-1910, London, 1967.

Poirier, Philip, *The Advent of the Labour Party,* New York, 1958.

Rempel, Richard A., *Unionist Divided, Arthur Balfour, Joseph Chamberlain and the Unionist Free Traders,* Newton Abbot, 1972.

Rubenstein, W.D., *Men of Property, The Very Wealthy in Britain Since the Industrial Revolution,* London, 1981.

Sacks, Benjamin, *The Religious Issue in the State Schools of England and Wales, 1902-14, A Nation's Quest for Human Dignity,* Albuquerque, N.M., 1961.

Scally, Robert J., *The Origins of the Lloyd George Coalition, The Politics of Social -Imperialism, 1900-1918,* Princeton, 1975.

Sykes, Alan, *Tariff Reform in British Politics, 1903-13,* Oxford, 1979.

Taylor, Alan J.P., ed., *Lloyd George, Twelve Essays,* London, 1971.

Vaughan, Paul, *Doctors' Commons: A Short History of the British Medical Association,* London, 1959.

Williams, David, *A History of Modern Wales,* London, 1950.

Williamson, Samuel R., *The Politics of Grand Strategy: France and Britain Prepare for War, 1904-1914,* Cambridge, Mass., 1969.

4. Memoirs and autobiographies

Amory, Leopold S., *My Political Life* (London: 1953), I.

Askwith, George Rankin, Lord, *Industrial Problems and Disputes,* London, 1920.

Asquith, Herbert, Earl of Oxford and Asquith, *Fifty Years of Parliament,* London, 1926, 2 vols.

Asquith, Margot, *The Autobiography of Margot Asquith* (London: 1922), II.

Beveridge, William H., Lord Beveridge, *Power and Influence,* London, 1953.

Birrell, Augustine, *Things Past Redress,* London, 1937.

Churchill, Winston Spencer, *The World Crisis* (London: 1923), I.

Cox, Alfred, *Among the Doctors,* London, n.d. [1950].

Edwards, Alfred George, Archbishop, *Memories,* London, 1927.

Fisher, John, Baron, *Memories,* London, 1919.

George, William, *My Brother and I,* London, 1958.

Griffith-Boscawen, Arthur S.T., *Fourteen Years in Parliament,* London, 1907.

Haldane, Richard Burdon, *An Autobiography*, London, 1926.

Kearley, Hudson, Viscount Devonport, *The Travelled Road*, privately printed, n.d. [1930].

Kekewich, George W., *The Education Department and After*, London, 1920.

Lloyd George, Frances, Countess, *The Years That Are Past*, London, 1967.

Long, Walter, Viscount, *Memories*, London, 1923.

Lowther, James William, Viscount Ullswater, *A Speaker's Commentaries* (London: 1925), II.

Lucy, Henry W., *The Diary of a Journalist* (London: 1923), III.

Maxwell, Herbert E., *Evening Memories*, London, 1932.

Morley, John, Viscount, *Recollections* (New York: 1917), 2 vols.

Oppenheimer, Francis, *Stranger Within*, London, 1960.

Porritt, Arthur, *The Best I Remember*, New York, 1923.

Richmond, Arthur, *Another Sixty Years*, London, 1965.

Samuel, Herbert, Viscount, *Memoirs*, London, 1945.

Simon, John, Viscount, *Retrospect*, London, 1952.

Spender, Harold, *The Fire of Life, A Book of Memories*, London, n.d. [1926].

Spender, John A., *Life, Journalism and Politics* (New York, n.d. [1927]), I.

Willoughby De Broke, Richard Greville Verney, Lord, *The Passing Years*, London, 1924.

5. Scholarly journals

American Historical Review

British Journal of Educational Studies

Caernarvonshire Historical Society, Transactions

English Historical Review

Historical Journal

Journal of British Studies

Journal of Contemporary History

National Library of Wales, Journal

Scottish Historical Review

Transactions of the Honourable Society of Cymmrodorion

Welsh History Review

6. Unpublished dissertations

Hutcheson, John A., 'Leopold Maxse and the National Review, 1893-1914,' University of North Carolina at Chapel Hill, 1974.

Kaminski, Diane C., 'The Radicalization of a Ministering Angel: A Biography of Emily Hobhouse, 1860-1926,' University of Connecticut, 1977.

Kezirian, Richard, 'David Lloyd George and the origins of the British Welfare State,' University of California at Santa Barbara, 1976.

Wrigley, Christopher John, 'Lloyd George and the Labour Movement,' University of London, 1973.

Index